Ethics: the Big Questions

Philosophy: The Big Questions

Series Editor: James P. Sterba, University of Notre Dame, Indiana

Designed to elicit a philosophical response in the mind of the student, this distinctive series of anthologies provides essential classical and contemporary readings that serve to make the central questions of philosophy come alive for today's students. It presents complete coverage of the Anglo-American tradition of philosophy, as well as the kinds of questions and challenges that it confronts today, both from other cultural traditions and from theoretical movements such as feminism and postmodernism.

Aesthetics: the Big Questions
Edited by Carolyn Korsmeyer

Epistemology: the Big Questions
Edited by Linda Martín Alcoff

Ethics: the Big Questions
Edited by James P. Sterba

Metaphysics: the Big Questions
Edited by Peter van Inwagen and Dean W. Zimmerman

Philosophy of Language: the Big Questions
Edited by Andrea Nye

Philosophy of Religion: the Big Questions
Edited by Eleonore Stump and Michael J. Murray

Race, Class, Gender, and Sexuality: the Big Questions
Edited by Naomi Zack, Laurie Shrage, and Crispin Sartwell

ETHICS:

The Big Questions

EDITED BY JAMES P. STERBA

BLACKWELL
Publishers

First published 1998

2 4 6 8 10 9 7 5 3 1

Blackwell Publishers Inc.
350 Main Street
Malden, Massachusetts 02148
USA

Blackwell Publishers Ltd
108 Cowley Road
Oxford OX4 1JF
UK

Library of Congress Cataloging-in-Publication Data

Ethics : the big questions / edited by James P. Sterba.
      p.   cm. — (Philosophy, the big questions ; 1)
  Includes index.
  ISBN 0-631-20285-4. — ISBN 0-631-20286-2 (pbk.)
  1. Ethics.   I. Sterba, James P. II. Series.
BJ1012.E8957 1998
170—dc21   97-44980
                             CIP

British Library Cataloguing in Publication Data

A CIP catalogue record for this book is available from the British Library.

Typeset in 9½ on 12 pt Galliard
by Ace Filmsetting Ltd, Frome, Somerset
Printed in Great Britain by T.J. International, Padstow, Cornwall

This book is printed on acid-free paper

CONTENTS

INTRODUCTION

Ethics is the philosophical study of morality, and while there are many different ways to take up this study, there are only a few central questions that philosophers have returned to time and time again. These questions are: What is the nature of morality? What is its justification? Its requirements? What important challenges have been raised against it? This anthology seeks to explore answers that have been given by philosophers to these and other related questions.

The Nature of Morality: What is Morality?

In reading 1 from Plato's *Republic*, Glaucon and his brother Adeimantus challenge Socrates to show that morality is good in itself and not simply good as a means. Glaucon tells the story of Gyges of Lydia, a shepherd who found a ring which when turned a certain way made him invisible and who then went on to use the ring for various immoral purposes. Glaucon then asks whether if there were two such rings, one worn by a moral person and the other by an immoral person, there would be any difference in their behavior. He also challenges Socrates to show that it would still be better to be moral than immoral even if all sorts of bad things happened to moral people and all sorts of good things happened to immoral people. Socrates is further challenged by Adeimantus to show that morality is better than immorality even assuming that immoral people were able to sufficiently

appease the gods and so avoid punishment for their bad deeds. Moreover, this challenge of showing that people are always better off acting morally than immorally may be difficult, if not impossible, to meet, if morality at least sometimes requires self-sacrifice.

In reading 2, A. J. Ayer contends that systems of ethics contain a variety of different sorts of claims. First, there are propositions that purport to define ethical terms. According to Ayer, these propositions constitute ethical philosophy, strictly speaking, but they are neutral between all different accounts of what is right and wrong. Second, there are propositions describing the phenomena of moral experience and their causes, but these propositions, Ayer claims, rightly belong to the science of psychology or sociology. Third, there are ethical judgments which, Ayer argues, are rightly classified simply as expressions of feelings or emotion, and, hence, are neither true nor false. Given that the bulk of ethical claims are of this third type, and hence, on Ayer's view, merely the expression of feeling or emotion, this view became known as emotivism.

To many philosophers, however, the disadvantages of the emotivist view far outweigh its advantages. In reading 3, Brand Blanshard raises a number of problems for the emotivist analysis. In general, Blanshard objects to tying "good" or "bad" to our expressions of approval or disapproval. Blanshard contends that things can be good or bad independently of whether we actually express our approval or disapproval of them and independently of the degree to which we express our approval or disapproval of them. For example, Blanshard argues that the suffering of a rabbit in a trap can be bad even when no one actually expresses disapproval of it. But even if Blanshard's objections are telling against the emotivist account as Ayer formulated it, it does seem possible to avoid objections of this sort by providing a more idealized account. Thus, suppose we define "*x* is good" as "An ideal observer with all the relevant information would express approval of *x* because of the (good-making) properties it has." Obviously, it would be necessary to specify in what respects this agent was to be idealized and what counts as relevant information, but it seems that this could be done in such a way as to avoid Blanshard's objections.

Yet while the preceding definition suggests that whenever something is good there is some set of properties that makes it good, it does not tell us specifically how to determine what those properties are. To do so would seem ultimately to involve deriving an evaluative conclusion from descriptive premises, and many philosophers believe that to attempt such a derivation would entail committing the naturalistic fallacy, that is, confusing the intrinsic properties of natural objects with the property of goodness itself.[1] However, John R. Searle argues in reading 4 that such a derivation can be achieved without committing the naturalistic fallacy if we begin with facts about social institutions. He offers the following derivation:

(1) Jones uttered the words "I hereby promise to pay you, Smith, five dollars."
(1a) Under conditions *C* anyone who utters the words "I hereby promise to pay you, Smith, five dollars" promises to pay Smith five dollars.
(1b) Conditions *C* obtain.
(2) Jones promised to pay Smith five dollars.
(2a) All promises are acts of placing oneself under an obligation to do the thing promised.
(3) Jones placed himself under an obligation to pay Smith five dollars.
(3a) All those who place themselves under an obligation are, other things being equal, under an obligation.
(3b) Other things are equal.
(4) Jones is under an obligation to pay Smith five dollars.
(4a) Other things being equal, one ought to do what one is under an obligation to do.
(4b) Others things are equal.
(5) Jones ought to pay Smith five dollars.

In reading 5, Antony Flew contends that the premises of Searle's argument would only be purely descriptive if they are interpreted as part of a detached anthropological report about the institution of promising. Searle admits that his premises could be interpreted in this fashion but contends that it is not the interpretation he intends. As Searle interprets them, his premises are asserted by a participant speaking from within the institution of promising. However, when they are interpreted in this way, as Flew points out, the premises are evaluative as well as descriptive. Searle would not deny this, he would simply add that most of our institutional commitments are like that.

Of course, there is the further question of whether committing ourselves to the institution of promising leads to obligations in just the way Searle claims. Searle holds that performing the speech acts of uttering "I hereby promise" in the absence of any moral constraints still leads to a prima facie obligation to keep the promise. But suppose an underworld figure "promises" to eliminate a non-cooperative, duly elected public official. Surely such a promise would not generate a prima facie *moral* obligation to kill an innocent person. What such a case shows is that there are either moral constraints that determine when we can effectively promise or moral constraints that determine when our promises generate prima facie moral obligations. In subsequent work, Searle seems to endorse this second alternative, claiming that in his argument he was not trying to derive a *moral* "ought" from an "is."[2] Interpreted in this way, however, Searle's argument seems less interesting because many philosophers would grant that obligations that may not be moral can be generated by our involvement in social institutions.

In reading 6, Philippa Foot attempts to establish a stronger conclusion than that defended by Searle against non-naturalists, like Flew and R. M. Hare, who deny that evaluative properties are logically linked to the natural (descriptive) properties of objects. Foot attempts to refute what she takes to be two central claims by such non-naturalists. These claims are:

1. Evaluation can be based on eccentric evidence without a special explanation.
2. Any evidence can be rejected as a basis for evaluation.

To show that claim 1 should be rejected, Foot argues that no one could maintain that someone is good because she clasps and unclasps her hands three times an hour without giving a special explanation of why the person is good. But while Foot's view here seems incontrovertible, non-naturalists need not disagree. For instance, Hare allows that in Foot's example a special explanation *is required* of why a person who clasps and unclasps her hands three times a day is good![3]

With respect to claim 2, Foot rejects the view that one could coherently describe something as injurious yet withhold a negative evaluation, or coherently describe some behavior as courageous yet withhold a positive evaluation. By contrast, non-naturalists think that it is logically possible to use such descriptions without evaluations in such cases. Thus, for example, Hare claims that a person can admit that something is poisonous yet deny that it ought not to be chosen to be eaten.[4] Yet here non-naturalists are only denying that these descriptions entail evaluations that are conclusive; they are not denying that they entail prima facie evaluations. Of course, non-naturalists also claim that it is, *in principle*, possible to provide some pure description of the underlying condition that is injurious or the underlying behavior that is courageous from which not even prima facie evaluations follow.[5] Naturalists, like Foot, would presumably deny that this is possible, but even if non-naturalists were right that such pure descriptions could be provided, there

may be no reason to do so. For all practical purposes, we may be able to begin our moral arguments with at least partially evaluative premises that all parties hold in common. What this would show is that the descriptive–evaluative gap (or the is–ought gap) is, in fact, irrelevant to the task of conducting effective moral arguments in everyday life.

In the final reading of this section (reading 7), Alasdair MacIntyre claims that contemporary moral philosophy is characterized by radical disagreement, interminable arguments, and incommensurable premises, citing a number of examples of current moral disputes whose proposed solutions have various historical origins. According to MacIntyre, since contemporary moral philosophy purports to provide objective solutions to such disputes, it cannot be characterized by an emotivism of meaning, as Ayer attempted. Nevertheless, MacIntyre argues that contemporary moral philosophy can be characterized by an emotivism of use because it fails to effectively resolve these disputes.

One might try to respond to MacIntyre by showing how the particular disputes that he cites can be resolved in ways that should be acceptable to all parties, but since MacIntyre could always cite other disputes, an effective response requires an adequate justification for morality against those who would reject morality altogether, along with an adequate defense of some particular normative perspective against those who favor other moral perspectives. The next two sections of the anthology treat each of these topics in turn.

The Justification of Morality: Why be Moral?

In reading 8, David Hume argues against the view that morality can be justified by reason. According to Hume, "Reason is, and ought only to be the slave of the passions." Reason, according to Hume, has only two functions – to discover relations among abstract ideas (as in mathematics) and to discover truths about matters of fact (as in science and everyday affairs).

According to Hume, reason gives us knowledge about things we want and how best to attain them, but it cannot cause us to want anything and therefore, it cannot by itself move us to act. Only in conjunction with our passions can it do that. In addition, Hume claims that there are only two senses in which any passion can be called unreasonable: first, when it is founded on a false supposition, second, when we choose means insufficient to our end. Thus, according to Hume, it is "not contrary to reason to prefer the destruction of the whole world to the scratching of my finger." But as subsequent readings in this section attempt to show, there may be additional ways to reject certain passions as unreasonable, for example, if the views they support are question-begging.

Hume also maintains that it is impossible to move from "is" to "ought" or from factual claims to normative claims, a view that is contested by Searle and Foot in the previous section. Moreover, it seems that Hume's argument here is based on the mistaken assumption that is-statements could only support ought-statements by entailing them. But there is no general requirement that is-statements could only support ought-statements by entailing them.[6] For example, that Jones's fingerprints are on the murder weapon can support the conclusion that we ought to arrest Jones for the murder without entailing that conclusion.

Moreover, even if Hume were right about there being an is–ought gap, we may still be able to begin our moral arguments, as was noted above, with at least partially evaluative premises that all parties hold in common. This is in fact what Kurt Baier purports to do in reading 9.

In this reading, Baier attempts to justify morality by overcoming the gap between egoism and morality. He begins by distinguishing between self-anchored and society-anchored reasons. Self-anchored reasons are reasons that take into account how options affect oneself or those for whom one cares. Society-anchored reasons are reasons which require the coordination and cooperation of others and which override self-anchored reasons in cases of conflict. Baier then goes on to interpret morality as a system of soci-

ety-anchored reasons of mutual benefit that are appropriate for contexts in which everyone's following self-anchored reasons would have suboptimal results for everyone. So interpreted, moral reasons apply only when there exists an adequate enforcement system that makes acting against those reasons unprofitable.

Morality so construed never requires any degree of altruism or self-sacrifice; it only requires that people act upon reasons of mutual benefit. According to Baier,

> [The] Limited Good Will [of morality] is not a straightforward other-regarding or benevolent, let alone an altruistic . . . pattern. . . . Persons of limited conditional goodwill may thus be motivated primarily by concern for their own good life and their conforming with [moral] guidelines is a contribution to the concerns of others, which (since they may not care about these others) is made mainly or only because the realization of their own ends is seen to depend on the contributions made by others, and because they are prepared to recognize the reasonableness of reciprocity in this matter.[7]

Given this interpretation of morality, it is not possible for the egoist to do better by acting against morality. So construed, morality and egoism do not conflict.

Once morality is conceived in this way as a system of society-anchored reasons of mutual benefit, the apparent conflict between reason and morality is removed. That conflict only existed because morality and people's self-interest at times seemed to pull in different directions. But once morality is conceived as a system of society-anchored reasons of mutual benefit, the possibility of such conflicts is eliminated. Reason and morality are rendered fully compatible, and morality is clearly seen to be required by reason.

One problem with this defense of morality is that it only seems to succeed by redefining morality sothat it no longer demands any degree of altruism or self-sacrifice, e.g. for those who are poor misfortunates, and in that way is rendered compatible with egoism. But redefining morality so that it no longer demands any degree of altruism or self-sacrifice is problematic. That morality requires from us at least a certain degree of altruism or self-sacrifice almost seems constitutive of its very nature. Yet it is one thing to favor a definition of morality that includes a demand for altruism and self-sacrifice, it is another to show that morality so defined is required by reason. Accordingly, it may be that only when morality is understood in the way that Baier proposes as a system of society-anchored reasons of mutual benefit would it be possible to show that morality is required by reason.

In reading 10, Bernard Gert contends that a justified moral system is a moral system that all impartial rational persons could accept as a public system that applies to all rational persons. The goal of a justified system is to lessen the amount of harm suffered by those protected by it. It includes rules prohibiting causing the harms of death, pain, disability, loss of freedom, or loss of pleasure, that all rational persons want to avoid, as well as ideals encouraging the prevention of each of these harms.

Unfortunately, while it is rational for everyone to accept Gert's justified moral system as a public system that applies to all rational persons, it is also rational for everyone to depart from that moral system when it serves his or her interest. So, according to Gert's account, morality is rationally permissible but it is not rationally required. Surprisingly, it is also the case that according to Gert's account of morality, we are not required to help others who are in need, even when we can easily do so.

In reading 11, Alan Gewirth proposes yet another justification for morality. The central premises of Gewirth's argument can be summarized as follows:

(1) All agents regard their purposes as good according to whatever criteria are involved in their actions to fulfill them.
(2) Therefore, all agents must affirm a right to the freedom and well-being necessary to achieve their purposes.
(3) All agents must affirm such a right on the basis simply of being prospective, purposive agents.

(4) Hence, all agents must affirm that every prospective, purposive agent has a right to freedom and well-being.

Gewirth claims that the universalized right affirmed in the conclusion of his argument is a *moral* right and that every agent has to endorse that right under pain of self-contradiction.

There appears to be an interpretation of Gewirth's conclusion that does follow from his premises; unfortunately, it is not the interpretation Gewirth intends. For from the generally acceptable premises of his argument, it does follow that all agents must affirm that every prospective, purposive agent has a right to freedom and well-being, but the universalized right so deduced is still a prudential and not a moral right.

What a prudential right to freedom and well-being implies is an asymmetrically action-guiding "ought." This means that when an agent says that every prospective, purposive agent has a prudential right to freedom and well-being, the action-guiding implications are that the agent ought to take the steps necessary to secure or to retain the agent's own freedom and well-being, but not that the agent ought to take steps to secure or even steps not to interfere with the freedom and well-being of any other agent, except in so far as it is necessary for securing or retaining the agent's own freedom and well-being. And similarly for every other agent. This asymmetrically action-guiding ought is often said to be analogous to the oughts found in the most ordinary cases of competitive games – cases that we otherwise would have thought conform to the requirements of practical reason. For example, in football, a defensive player might think that the opposing team's quarterback ought to pass on third down with five yards to go, while not wanting the quarterback to do so, and hoping to foil any such attempt the quarterback makes.

Unfortunately, the success of Gewirth's argument for the justification of morality depends on the impossibility of interpreting the universalized right to freedom and well-being in his conclusion as anything other than a moral right, that is, a right that is symmetrically action-guiding and entails that others at least ought not to interfere with the right-holder's exercising his or her right. Since, as we have seen, it is possible to interpret this universalized right as a prudential right, Gewirth's argument for the justification of morality in terms of the demands of practical reason cannot succeed as formulated.

In reading 12, Philippa Foot rejects all attempts, like those of Baier and Gewirth, to justify morality as a requirement of practical reason. Foot argues that morality has been mistakenly thought to have some inescapable categorical force when, in fact, it is a system of hypothetical imperatives dependent for its justification on the reasons, wants, and interests people just happen to have. According to Foot, it is possible for people not to have any reason to be moral, and thus to act immorally, without acting contrary to reason. Of course, Foot grants that moral rules are generally thought to have force independent of the reasons people happen to have, and, on this account, are thought to be categorical imperatives. However, to show that this view is mistaken, Foot simply points out that the rules of etiquette are also thought to have the same independent force although we do not classify them as categorical imperatives.

Obviously, the only way to respond fully to Foot's critique is to provide just the sort of justification for morality that she claims can't be done, and this is what most of the selections included in this section attempt to do. Nevertheless, it should be noted that the contrast between morality and etiquette only works with respect to that part of etiquette that is not grounded upon moral rules. For the rest of etiquette, its non-hypothetical character is explainable by the non-hypothetical character of morality itself.

In the final reading of this section (reading 13) I argue that in trying to determine how we should act, we would like to be able to construct a *good* argument favoring morality over egoism, and given that good arguments are non-question-begging, we would like to construct an argument that does not beg the question against egoism. I then go on to argue that morality can be defended in this non-question-begging way as a non-arbitrary compromise between self-interested and altruistic reasons. In this compromise, high-ranking self-interested reasons have priority over low-ranking altruistic reasons and high-ranking altruistic reasons have priority over low-ranking self-interested reasons. Of course, exactly how this compromise is to be worked out is a matter of considerable debate. Utilitarians favor one sort of a resolution, deontologists another, and virtue theorists yet another. Yet however this debate is resolved, it is clear that some sort of a compromise moral solution is rationally preferable to either egoism or pure altruism when judged from a non-question-begging standpoint.

Alternative Moral Perspectives: What does Morality Require?

In the previous Part, the readings explored the question of the justification of morality, and a number of the readings attempted to show just how morality can be justified. But whether such attempts to justify morality succeed or fail, most people do, in fact, want to be moral. So even in the absence of an adequate justification for morality, given people's actual commitments, we can still raise the question of which particular moral perspective they should endorse. Accordingly, in this Part, we shall consider a range of alternative moral perspectives each of which appeals to a different central concept. For utilitarians that central concept is utility, for deontologists it is duty, and for virtue theorists it is virtue. The following sections take up each of these perspectives in turn.

Utility

In reading 14 from *Utilitarianism*, Mill argues that actions are right in proportion as they tend to promote happiness; wrong as they tend to produce the reverse of happiness. By happiness, Mill means pleasure and the absence of pain; by unhappiness, pain and the privation of pleasure. Mill differs from Bentham in maintaining that pleasures can be evaluated in terms of quality as well as quantity. According to Mill, the more desirable pleasures are those that would be preferred by competent judges who have experienced the alternatives. Mill concludes with an argument that everything that people desire is either a part of happiness or a means to it.

In reading 15, Bernard Williams argues against utilitarianism, claiming that it violates personal integrity by requiring us to sacrifice principles and projects that are central and deepest in our lives. He illustrates this with two examples. In one, an unemployed chemist, George, is offered a job doing research in chemical and biological warfare to which he is opposed. Yet it turns out that on utilitarian grounds he should take this job because if he doesn't another scientist without his scruples would take it and do more harm. In the second example, Jim, who is on a botanical expedition, happens upon a group of soldiers who are about to shoot twenty innocent Indians. Pedro, the captain of the soldiers, offers Jim the chance to save nineteen of the Indians by killing one of them himself. According to Williams, utilitarianism requires Jim to accept this offer even in the face of his principled opposition to taking innocent life. In both of these cases, Williams contends, utilitarianism fails to appreciate the importance of principles and projects to people's lives.

In reading 16, Kai Nielsen considers two imaginary cases that are often used as counter-examples to utilitarianism. In the first case (which is essentially the same as Williams's case of Jim and the Indians), an innocent fat person, who was leading a group of people out of a cave, gets stuck in the cave mouth, to which tide waters are returning. It turns out that the only way to save the group from drowning is by blowing up the fat person thereby unblocking the mouth of the cave. In the second case, the authorities could frame an innocent person in order to prevent a mob from doing even greater harm by taking vengeance into their own hands. Nielsen argues that with respect to the second case, utilitarians have very good grounds to generally oppose framing an innocent person even if they cannot oppose it under all possible circumstances. Nielsen further argues that the first case presents a very strong argument against those who think that intentionally killing an innocent person is always wrong. Interestingly, with respect to the

parallel case of Jim and the Indians, Williams himself concedes that "the utilitarian is probably right in this case." Possibly, Nielsen could return the favor by conceding that with respect to Williams's case of George, the chemist, utilitarianism need not require George to take the job of doing research on chemical and biological warfare.

In reading 17, Michael Stocker raises an additional problem for utilitarianism. He argues that in utilitarianism, our motives for acting, such as to do something for a friend, a lover, our family, our community, or our country do not embody our reason or justification for acting, which is to maximize utility overall. It follows, Stocker argues, that under utilitarianism we would have to live a bifurcated or schizophrenic life, which he takes to be a serious objection to the view.

Yet what Stocker finds objectionable in utilitarianism, Peter Railton, in reading 18, only finds paradoxical. Drawing on the paradox of hedonism, which is that one can objectively achieve certain pleasures only by not subjectively aiming at them, Railton argues that we may only be able to objectively maximize utility or overall good consequences by subjectively not aiming at these results. Against Williams, Railton also argues that sometimes the demands of morality require us to alienate ourselves from our projects and principles, and so for that reason such alienation is not objectionable.

Duty

In reading 19 from *Fundamental Principles of a Metaphysics of Morals*, Immanuel Kant argues for the importance of acting from duty. According to Kant, the only thing good without qualification is a good will, and a person acquires both a good will and moral worth by acting from duty. In addition, a person acts from duty by acting with the motive of doing one's duty. By contrast a person acts according to duty by simply doing one's duty with whatever motive one happens to have. Kant further contends that one's duty is to act in accord with objective moral laws. For Kant, such laws are categorical rather than hypothetical imperatives. Hypothetical imperatives either have the form "If one wants x one ought to do *y*," or "Since one wants *x* one ought to do *y*," whereas categorical imperatives have the form "One ought to do *y*, irrespective of what one wants."

According to Kant, we can determine which moral imperatives are valid, i.e. objective moral laws, by applying the test of the Categorical Imperative. This test requires:

> Act only on that maxim which you can at the same time will to be a universal law.

Kant thinks there are alternative formulations of this test which are all equivalent. They are:

> *The Formula of Universal Law:* Act only on that maxim that could become by your will a universal law of nature.

> *The Formula of Humanity:* Act so that you treat humanity, whether in your own person or in that of another, always as an end and never as a means only.

> *Formula of the Kingdom of Ends:* Act as if you were by your maxims in every case a legislating member in the universal Kingdom of Ends.

In reading 20, Fred Feldman analyzes Kant's application of his first formulation of his Categorical Imperatives to the cases of suicide, lying promises, developing one's talents, and helping others in need. Feldman argues that not only does Kant fail to show what he intends to show in these cases, but that it is also not clear how to construct any plausible application of his Categorical Imperative.

Christine Korsgaard in reading 21 discusses two problems of Kantian ethics. The first is that unwavering obedience to moral law can put us at a severe disadvantage when we are dealing with evil people. For example, if you must tell the truth to a would-be murderer inquiring about the whereabouts of your friend, this might well lead to the death of your friend. However, it is often thought that Kant's view absolutely prohibits lying. The second problem is that different formulations of Kant's Categorical Imperative seem

to have different implications for how to deal with would-be murderers. According to Korsgaard, the Formula of Universal Law permits lying to them whereas the Formulas of Humanity and the Kingdom of Ends do not.

Korsgaard offers a single solution to both of these problems. She contends that a defensible moral theory needs two components. One component (ideal theory) tells us what to do in a morally ideal world. The other component (non-ideal theory) tells us how to deal with evil in light of ideal theory. With respect to Kant's theory, Korsgaard contends that the Formulas of Humanity and the Kingdom of Ends can be viewed as the ideal component, the Formula of Universal Law as the non-ideal component. According to Korsgaard, interpreting Kant's theory this way shows how the theory can deal with evil and how the different formulations of the Categorical Imperative can fit together. In passing, Korsgaard also suggests a way to interpret the Formula of Universal Law that avoids Feldman's main criticism of it. Feldman argued that a universal practice of making lying promises to borrow money would not lead to a breakdown of promising altogether. Korsgaard agrees but then contends that all Kant's test requires is the impossibility of a universal practice of making lying promises to borrow money.

In her defense of Kant, Korsgaard shows how important liberty or free assent is to his ideal moral theory. This aspect of Kant's view is further developed by contemporary libertarians like John Hospers (reading 22) who take liberty to be the ultimate moral and political ideal, where "liberty" is typically defined as "the state of being unconstrained by other persons from doing what one wants." This definition limits the scope of liberty in two ways. First, not all constraints, whatever the source, count as a restriction on liberty; the constraints must come from other persons. For example, people who are constrained by natural forces from getting to the top of Mount Everest do not lack liberty in this regard. Second, the constraints must run counter to people's wants. Thus, people who do not want to hear Beethoven's Fifth Symphony do not feel their liberty is restricted when other people forbid its performance, even though the proscription does in fact constrain what they are able to do.

Of course, libertarians may argue that these constraints do restrict a person's liberty because people normally want to be unconstrained by others. But other philosophers have claimed that such constraints point to a serious defect in the libertarian's definition of liberty, which can only be remedied by defining "liberty" more broadly as "the state of being unconstrained by other persons from doing what one is able to do." If we apply this revised definition to the previous example, we find that people's liberty to hear Beethoven's Fifth Symphony would be restricted even if they did not want to hear it (and even if, perchance, they did not want to be unconstrained by others) because other people would still be constraining them from doing what they are able to do.

Confident that problems of defining liberty can be overcome in some satisfactory manner, libertarians go on to characterize their moral and political ideal as requiring that each person should have the greatest amount of liberty commensurate with the same liberty for all. From this ideal, libertarians claim that a number of more specific requirements, in particular a right to life, a right to freedom of speech, press, and assembly, and a right to property can be derived.

It is important to note that the libertarian's right to life is not a right to receive from others the goods and resources necessary for preserving one's life; it is simply a right not to be killed. So understood, the right to life is not a right to receive welfare. In fact, there are no welfare rights in the libertarian view. Accordingly, the libertarian's understanding of the right to property is not a right to receive from others the goods and resources necessary for one's welfare, but rather a right to acquire goods and resources either by initial acquisition or by voluntary agreement.

Obviously, by defending rights such as these, libertarians can only support a limited role for government. That role is simply to prevent and punish initial acts of coercion – the only wrongful actions for libertarians.

Libertarians do not deny that it is a good thing for people to have sufficient goods and resources to meet at least their basic nutritional needs, but libertarians do deny that government has a duty to provide for such needs. Some good things, such as the provision of welfare to the needy, are requirements of charity rather than justice, libertarians claim. Accordingly, failure to make such provision is neither blameworthy nor punishable.

In contrast with libertarians, welfare liberals, like John Rawls (reading 23), take Kant's ethical theory in another direction, taking contractual fairness to be the ultimate moral and political ideal, and contend that the fundamental rights and duties in a society are those that people would agree to under fair conditions.

Note that welfare liberals do not say that the fundamental rights and duties in a society are those to which people actually do agree because these might not be fair at all. For example, people might agree to a certain system of fundamental rights and duties only because they have been forced to do so or because their only alternative is starving to death. Thus, actual agreement is not sufficient, nor is it even necessary, for determining an adequate conception of justice. According to welfare liberals, what is necessary and sufficient is that people would agree to such rights and duties under fair conditions.

But what are fair conditions? According to John Rawls, fair conditions can be expressed by an "original position" in which people are concerned to advance their own interests behind a "veil of ignorance." The effect of the veil of ignorance is to deprive people in the original position of the knowledge they would need to advance their own interests in ways that are morally arbitrary.

Rawls presents the principles of justice he believes would be derived in the original position in two successive formulations. The first formulation is as follows:

I. *Special conception of justice*
   1. Each person is to have an equal right to the most extensive basic liberty compatible with a similar liberty for others.
   2. Social and economic inequalities are

to be arranged so that they are

  (a) reasonably expected to be to everyone's advantage, and

  (b) attached to positions and offices open to all.

II. *General conception of justice*

All social value – liberty and opportunity, income and wealth, and the bases of self-respect – are to be distributed equally unless an unequal distribution or any or all of these values is to everyone's advantage.

Later these principles are more accurately formulated as:

I. *Special conception of justice*

  1. Each person is to have an equal right to the most extensive total system of equal basic liberties compatible with a similar system of liberty for all.

  2. Social and economic inequalities are to be arranged so that they are

     (a) to the greatest benefit of the least advantaged, consistent with the just savings principle, and

     (b) attached to offices and positions open to all under conditions of fair equality of opportunity.

II. *General conception of justice*

All social goods – liberty and opportunity, income and wealth, and the bases of self-respect – are to be distributed equally unless an unequal distribution of any or all of these goods is to the advantage of the least favored.

Under both formulations, the general conception of justice differs from the special conception of justice by allowing trade-offs between liberty and other social goods. According to Rawls, persons in the original position would want the special conception of justice to be applied in place of the general conception of justice whenever social conditions allowed all representative persons to exercise their basic liberties.

Rawls holds that these principles of justice

would be chosen in the original position because persons so situated would find it reasonable to follow the conservative dictates of a "maximin strategy" and thereby secure for themselves the highest minimum payoff.

Rawls's defense of a welfare liberal conception of justice has been challenged in a variety of ways. Some critics have endorsed Rawls's contractual approach while disagreeing with Rawls over what principles of justice would be derived thereby. These critics usually attempt to undermine the use of a maximin strategy in the original position.[8] Other critics, however, have found fault with the contractual approach itself. Libertarians, for example, have challenged the moral adequacy of the very ideal of contractual fairness.

This second challenge to the ideal of contractual fairness is potentially the more damaging because, if valid, it would force supporters to embrace some other political ideal. This challenge, however, fails if it can be shown that the libertarian's own ideal of liberty, when correctly interpreted, leads to much the same practical requirements as are usually associated with the welfare liberal's ideal of contractual fairness, as I attempt to do in reading 24. There I argue that a libertarian ideal of liberty, when correctly interpreted, leads to a universal right to welfare usually associated with the welfare liberal's ideal of contractual fairness. But my argument goes further and shows that recognition of this universal right to welfare also leads to the equalization of resources that is characteristic of a socialist state.

Virtue

In reading 25, from the *Nicomachean Ethics*, Aristotle tries to provide a firm foundation for his ethics of virtue. Aristotle begins by noting that all human activity aims at some good. He then argues that for humans happiness is the ultimate good, but that happiness is wrongly thought to consist simply in pleasure, wealth, and honor. Rightly understood, Aristotle argues, happiness is the activity of the soul exhibiting the best and most complete excellence of virtue. He further argues that happiness also requires certain external goods like friends, wealth, political power, good birth, children, and beauty. Aristotle goes on to define virtue as a state of character which is a mean between two vices, one of defect, the other of excess. For example, liberality is a virtue which is a mean between meanness, a vice of defect, and extravagance, a vice of excess; and courage is mean between cowardice, a vice of defect, and rashness, a vice of excess. However, Aristotle allows that not every action or passion admits of a mean. For example, he thinks that the actions of adultery, theft, and murder are always wrong whatever their consequences. In this respect, Aristotle's view is clearly opposed to utilitarianism for which right and wrong actions are solely determined by their consequences.

While Aristotle identifies happiness with virtuous activity, it is not clear how these two things can or should be identified. Thus, imagine that you are engaged in the following dialogue with Aristotle:

You: Why should I be virtuous?

A: Well, we agree, don't we, that it is a good thing to be happy?

You: Suppose we do.

A: It turns out that being virtuous will make you happy. So that is why you should be virtuous.

You: But according to the ordinary notion of happiness, it seems possible to be happy without always being virtuous.

A: But as I define happiness, being happy is the same as being virtuous.

You: But then doesn't my original question return in a different form? Why should I seek happiness in your sense and thereby always be virtuous rather than seek happiness in the ordinary sense and only sometimes be virtuous?

A: That is an interesting objection.

You: Things are even more complicated than I have indicated so far. With respect to the ordinary notion of happiness, what makes you happy can make other people happy, and so the question arises: Whose happiness should you pursue, yours or theirs?

A: But as I define happiness this can never happen. When happiness and virtue are interdefined, there are no conflicts between one person's happiness and the happiness of others.

You: But given your definition of happiness, we can still ask the question: Why should I strive to be happy/virtuous in your sense of the term, when it may not make me happy or may not make others happy in the ordinary sense of the term?

A: That is another interesting objection.

Obviously, it is important to determine whether Aristotle or Aristotelians have adequate responses to these objections.

In reading 26, Martha Nussbaum defines Aristotelian virtue as being disposed to choose and respond well in the important spheres of shared human experience. She suggests that these spheres are those of mortality, the body, pleasure and pain, cognitive ability, practical reason, early infant development, affiliation, and humor. With respect to each of these spheres, she claims that there are relevant virtues that can be specified in an objective, non-relativist way.

She then considers three challenges to the possibility of providing such an objective, non-relativist account. To the challenge as to whether a single practical solution is sought or desirable in each sphere, Nussbaum responds that in many cases, the best we will be able to achieve is a disjunction of solutions, possibly different ones for different contexts, e.g. friendship will be expressed through different customs in different times and places. To the challenge of whether there is a non-relative, culturally-independent way of understanding what are the appropriate spheres of human experience, Nussbaum responds that while there is no completely non-relative, culturally-independent way of understanding these spheres, it is still possible to show that some understandings are better than others. To the challenge of whether there can be forms of life that do not have all of these spheres, Nussbaum responds that there could be forms of life that do not have private property, and, hence, the virtues that are connected with it, but she is quite skeptical about the possibility of eliminating other spheres of human experience such as those requiring the virtues of courage or justice.

In opposition to Nussbaum, Alasdair MacIntyre in reading 27 provides a more relativistic conception of virtue. MacIntyre begins by distinguishing three different conceptions of virtue. According to one conception found in Homer, a virtue is a quality which enables an individual to discharge his or her social role. According to another conception found in Aristotle and the New Testament, a virtue is a quality which enables an individual to move toward the achievement of the specifically human *telos*, whether natural or supernatural. And according to a third conception found in the writings of Benjamin Franklin among others, a virtue is a quality which has utility in achieving earthly or heavenly success.

After discussing these definitions of virtue, MacIntyre then proposes to define a core concept of virtue in terms of practices. A practice, for MacIntyre, is any coherent and complex form of socially established cooperative human activity through which goods internal to that form of activity are realized in the course of trying to achieve those standards of excellence which are appropriate to and partially definitive of that form of activity, with the result that human powers to achieve excellence, and human conceptions of the ends and goods involved are systematically extended. As examples of practices, MacIntyre cites arts, sciences, games, and the making and sustaining of family life. MacIntyre then goes on to define virtues in terms of practices: a virtue, such as courage, justice or honesty, is an acquired human quality the possession and exercise of which tends to enable us to achieve those goods which are internal to practices, and the lack of which prevents us from achieving any such goods. MacIntyre contends that his conception of virtue is compatible with the first and second conceptions of virtue that he earlier distinguished but not with the third conception found in Franklin's works, because Franklin's conception is utilitarian and does not favor internal goods over external goods in the way required by his own conception of virtue. According to MacIntyre, if virtue is to be effective in producing internal goods, it needs to be exercised without regard to (external) consequences, which is something that MacIntyre thinks a utilitarian account can never do.

In reading 28, William Frankena defends the view that an ethics of virtue and an ethics of duty or principles are complementary aspects of the same morality. According to Frankena, for every moral principle, there will be a morally good trait consisting of a disposition or tendency to act according to that principle, and for every morally good trait, there will be a principle defining the kind of action in which the principle is to express itself. Parodying Kant, Frankena maintains that principles without traits are impotent and traits without principles are blind.

In reading 29, Walter Schaller challenges Frankena's view, maintaining that at least with respect to benevolence, gratitude, and self-respect, an ethics of virtue is more appropriate than an ethics of duty or principles. This is because, according to Schaller, it is not possible to provide an informative rule of what is morally required of us with respect to benevolence, gratitude, and self-respect. At least in these contexts, he claims, an ethics of virtue has primacy. Of course, Schaller would have to allow that in other contexts, especially where certain actions like murder, stealing, and lying are morally prohibited, an ethics of duty or principles does seem to have a comparable primacy over an ethics of virtue.

In reading 30, Julia Annas argues that many of the supposed contrasts between ancient ethical views and modern ethical views do not actually hold, or at least not in the way that they are usually thought. She considers five supposed contrasts:

1. that ancient ethical theories unlike modern ones fail to distinguish between moral and non-moral reasons;
2. that ancient ethical theories are less concerned than modern ones with moral responsibility;
3. that ancient ethical theories range over ar-

eas of life that modern ethical theories do not take to be within the domain of morality;

4. that ancient ethical theories are more agent-centered and modern ones more act-centered;

5. that the concern of ancient ethical theories with the agent's final end renders them in some way more egoistic than modern ethical theories.

Annas argues, in large part by noting the diversity among ancient ethical theories, that none of these contrasts holds, or at least not in the ways they are usually understood to hold. Yet even if Annas is right that none of these contrasts hold between ancient ethical theories and modern ones, there may be one that does hold. It is that ancient ethical theories are non-utilitarian in holding that certain actions like murder are always wrong irrespective of the consequences, and in this respect they contrast with at least modern utilitarian theories which clearly reject the principle that one can never do evil that good may come of it. In this regard Kant's ethics, or at least a Kantian-inspired ethical theory like Rawls's, occupies an interesting middle position between ancient ethics and utilitarian ethics by allowing that one can sometimes do evil that good may come of it (as Korsgaard interprets Kant's theory for non-ideal conditions and as choice behind Rawls's veil of ignorance appears to permit) without going all the way to utilitarianism and requiring the maximization of good consequences or utility. Obviously, the crucial question that remains is which of these three views is most morally defensible: ancient ethics, utilitarian ethics, or Kantian ethics which occupies a mean between the other two views.

Challenges to Morality

Feminism: how is gender relevant to morality?

Feminism is one of the most important contemporary challenges to morality, but the equality of women and men has always had its ancient as well as its modern defenders. One such ancient defender is Musonius Rufus (reading 31) who was born of an Etruscan family in the town of Volsinii probably sometime before AD 30. He is considered to be one of the founders of Stoic philosophy. In his time, he was compared to Socrates, both in his life and work, so that modern scholars sometimes refer to him as "the Roman Socrates."[9] As a prominent Stoic philosopher, he fell out of favor with Nero and was executed sometime before AD 101. One of the stories that has come down to us is that when Musonius was lying chained in the prison of Nero, a friend communicated with him, inquiring what he might do to secure his release. Musonius acknowledged his friend's thoughtfulness, yet politely but firmly refused assistance. When his friend replied, "Socrates the Athenian refused to be released by his friends, and consequently went to trial and was put to death," Musonius answered, "Socrates was put to death because he did not take the trouble to defend himself, but I intend to make my defence. Farewell."[10] Like Socrates, Musonius left no writings of his own. His views, as we have them, come from reports of his discussions written down many years later by his students. A distinctive feature of Musonius's views is his argument for equality between women and men found in the selection excerpted here. Obviously, from a feminist perspective, there is much to appreciate in Musonius Rufus's views.

In reading 32, Annette C. Baier draws on the work of Carol Gilligan to suggest that women favor an ethic of love and caring in contrast to the ethic of obligation favored by men.[11] In Gilligan's own work, the contrast that is drawn is between a caring perspective and a justice perspective. According to Gilligan, these two perspectives are analogous to the alternative ways we tend to organize ambiguous perceptual patterns, for example, seeing a figure first as a square and then as a diamond depending upon its relationship to the surrounding frame. More specifically, Gilligan claims:

> From a justice perspective, the self as moral agent stands as the figure against a ground of social relationships, judging the conflicting claims of

self and others against a standard of equality or equal respect (the Categorical Imperative, the Golden Rule). From a care perspective, the relationship becomes the figure, defining self and others. Within the context of relationship, the self as a moral agent perceives and responds to the perception of need. The shift in moral perspective is manifest by a change in the moral question from "What is just?" to "How to respond?"[12]

Using these perspectives as classificatory tools, Gilligan reports that 69 percent of her sample raised considerations of both justice and care while 67 percent focused their attention on one set of concerns (with focus defined as 75 percent or more of the considerations raised pertaining either to justice or to care).[13] Significantly, with one exception, all of the men who focused, focused on justice. The women were divided, with roughly one-third focusing on care and one-third on justice.

The conclusion that Gilligan wants to draw from this research is that the care perspective is an equally valid moral perspective that has tended to be disregarded in moral theory and psychological research alike because of male bias. To determine whether this conclusion is justified, however, we would need to get clearer about the contrast between the two perspectives. If women and men differ with regard to the perspectives on which they tend to focus, it must be possible to clearly distinguish between the two perspectives. Otherwise bias could enter into the researcher's classification of people's reasons as belonging to one or the other perspective.[14]

Yet rather than try to further distinguish the perspectives, Baier attempts to integrate them under the notion of "appropriate trust." Baier sketches how a theory that employs the notion of appropriate trust might deal with various topics in a way that brings together the concerns of both perspectives. In a subsequent article, Baier goes on to define a relationship of appropriate trust as one that is based upon neither threats nor the successful cover-up of breaches of trust.[15]

One advantage of Baier's approach is that it fits nicely into a general reconciliationist strategy with respect to alternative ethical perspectives. Such a strategy attempts to show that the practical differences between alternative ethical perspectives are not as great as might initially seem to be the case. In reading 24, I pursued this strategy with respect to the libertarian and welfare liberal perspectives, and it may be possible to do the same with respect to other ethical perspectives as well.[16]

In reading 33, Virginia Held attempts to discern some focal points in current feminist attempts to transform ethics into an acceptable theoretical and practical activity. Specifically, she focuses on:

1. the split between reason and emotion where men are associated with reason and women with emotion, and where emotion is devalued, in part, because it is claimed to offer inappropriate guidance for moral theory;

2. the public/private distinction where men are associated with the public world and women with the private world of the home, and where the private world of the home is devalued as being merely natural and biological;

3. the concept of the self where an egoistic or universalistic self is associated with men and a relational self, i.e. a self that defines itself in terms of its existing relationships, is associated with women and where the relational self is devalued as an inappropriate standpoint from which to construct a moral theory.

Held argues that in order for ethics to be transformed into an acceptable theoretical and practical activity, it must take into account the emotions, the private world of the home, and the relational self, all of which draw upon the experience of women.

In reading 34, Joan Tronto attempts to build on the work of Carol Gilligan and Nel Noddings and advance toward an ethic of caring. She begins with the following analysis of caring. According to Tronto, caring implies some on-going responsibility and commitment. "Caring about" refers to less concrete objects, whereas "caring for" implies a specific, particular concrete object that is the focus of the caring. From the perspective of the one caring for a particular other, what is important is attentiveness to the needs of that other and preserving the relationship of care that exists. It essentially involves a displacement from one's own interests to the interests of the cared-for.

However, to come up with an ethics of caring, Tronto contends, we need to go beyond an analysis of caring to describe what constitutes good caring, and this can be difficult to do given that caring is so much tied to particular circumstances. Moreover, the moral judgments made in offering and providing care are more complex than any set of rules can take into account. Accordingly, Tronto claims that we need to rethink what are the appropriate forms of caring and raise the broadest questions concerning the shape of the social and political institutions in our society.

In reading 35, Alison Jaggar takes on the task of characterizing a particular type of moral discourse which she calls Feminist Practical Discourse (FPD). According to Jaggar:

1. FPD typically does not begin with the articulation of general moral principles but instead begins with the creation of opportunities for participants to talk about their own lives.
2. FPD requires that socially disempowered women be heard with special respect.
3. FPD emphasizes the need to provide a supportive environment in which participants will feel safe enough to speak openly about their own lives.
4. FPD's most striking feature is that it is nurturant rather than adversarial.

So characterized, Jaggar's FPD contrasts with the war-making or adversarial way of doing philosophy that dominates much of philosophy these days and maybe has always dominated philosophy. Could it be that Jaggar's feminist and peace-making way of doing philosophy is actually more likely to arrive at justified views than the dominant war-making way that seeks to defeat opponents by whatever means possible?

Environmentalism: who is to count in morality?

Another important challenge to contemporary ethics is environmentalism. Environmentalism challenges contemporary ethics by raising the question of who is to count morally. The standard assumption of traditional ethics is that only humans are to count morally. One of the reasons given for thinking this is the belief that only humans are capable of morality. In reading 36, however, Frans De Waal challenges this belief by showing how chimpanzees practice social reciprocity. This raises the question of whether social reciprocity as practiced by chimpanzees is all that different from the practice of mutual benefit that Kurt Baier claims constitutes justified (human) moralities.

In reading 37, Peter Singer further argues for the liberation of animals by comparing the bias against animals, which he calls "speciesism," with biases against blacks and women. According to Singer, the grounds we have for opposing racism and sexism are also grounds for opposing speciesism, because all forms of discrimination run counter to the principle of equal consideration. Racists violate this principle by giving greater weight to the interests of members of their own race in cases of conflict; sexists violate it by giving greater weight to the interests of members of their own sex in cases of conflict; and speciesists violate it by giving greater weight to the interests of members of their own species in cases of conflict.

Animals have interests, Singer maintains, because they have a capacity for suffering and enjoyment. According to the principle of equal consideration, there is no justification for regarding the pain animals feel as less important than the same amount of pain (or pleasure) humans feel. As for the practical requirements of this view, Singer contends that we cannot go astray if we give the same respect to the lives of animals that we give to the lives of humans at a similar mental level. In the end, Singer thinks, this will require us to make radical changes in our diet, the farming methods we use, experimental procedures in many fields of science, our approach to wildlife and to hunting, trapping and the wearing of furs, and areas of entertainment like circuses, rodeos, and zoos.

In reading 38, Paul W. Taylor presents the following argument:

(1) Humans are members of the earth's community of life.
(2) All living things are related to one another in an order of interdependence.
(3) Each organism is a teleological center of life.
(4) The assertion of human superiority is groundless.
(5) Therefore we should recognize the equal inherent worth of every living being.

Given the general acceptability of the premises (1–3), Taylor devotes most of his time to arguing for (4) on the grounds that we have no non-question-begging reason for maintaining human superiority in the sense that it would justify our domination of other living beings.

The main difficulty with Taylor's argument concerns how we are to weigh human welfare against the welfare of other living beings once we grant that human beings are not superior to other species. In a later book that develops the argument of this essay, Taylor distinguishes between basic and non-basic interests of living beings, but because he doesn't hold that the basic interests always have priority over non-basic interests, it is difficult to know how decisions are to be made when there is conflict between human and non-human interests.

In reading 39, I seek to resolve the debate within environmental ethics between those who defend an anthropocentric ethics and those who defend a non-anthropocentric ethics by showing that when the most morally defensible versions of each of these perspectives are laid out, they do not lead to different practical recommendations. I develop a set of principles for weighing human against non-human welfare, contending that they should be acceptable to defenders of both anthropocentric and non-anthropocentric environmental ethics. Obviously, the crucial questions for evaluating my view are whether my princi-

ples represent common ground between the opposing perspectives, and whether they can be effectively applied.

In reading 40, Karen Warren argues that the domination of nature is connected to the domination of women and that at least within Western culture, the following argument is sanctioned:

(1) Women are identified with nature and the realm of the physical; men are identified with the "human" and the realm of the mental. (For example, naturist language describes women as cows, foxes, chicks, serpents, bitches, beavers, old bats, pussycats, cats, bird-brains, hare-brains. Sexist language feminizes and sexualizes Nature: Nature is raped, mastered, conquered, controlled, mined. Her "secrets" are "penetrated" and her "womb" is put into the services of the "man of science." "Virgin timber" is felled, cut down. "Fertile soil" is tilled and land that lies "fallow" is "barren," useless.)
(2) Whatever is identified with nature and the realm of the physical is inferior to whatever is identified with the "human" and the realm of the mental; or, conversely, the latter is superior to the former.
(3) Thus, women are inferior to men; or, conversely, men are superior to women.
(4) For any x and y, if x is superior to y, then x is justified in subordinating y.
(5) Thus, men are justified in subordinating women.

Warren points out that there is a "logic of domination" to this argument. It begins with a *claim of difference*. It then moves from a claim of difference to a *claim of superiority* and then from a claim of superiority to a *claim of subordination or domination*. Warren contends that this same logic of domination is common to all forms of domination and so is used to support, for example, racism, classism, ageism, as well as sexism and naturism (Warren's term for the domination of nature). If Warren is correct, it follows that if one is against any one of these forms of domination, one should be against them all.

Postmodernism: morality from whose cultural perspective?

Another important challenge to contemporary ethics is postmodernism. Postmodernism challenges morality to take into account all the different perspectives that are relevant to fashioning an acceptable morality. In addition, as Susan Okin points out in reading 41, postmodernism is skeptical of all universal or generalizable claims, including those of feminism, and so it is reluctant to speak of the problems of women as such. However, Okin argues that despite the multitude of differences that exist between women in different cultures, it is possible to find some common ground. Specifically, Okin argues that some of the solutions that Western feminists have proposed for problems facing women in their own societies also seem useful for problems facing women in poor countries, for example, challenging the public/private distinction. She notes that in poor, developing countries, women are being beaten by their husbands and dying needlessly from botched illegal abortions, and that girls go undernourished and undereducated, and contends that the problem of women in such countries are similar but worse than the problems facing women in Western countries.

Responding to Okin, Jane Flax (reading 42) contends that Okin's focus on shared oppression obscures the equally important relations of domination between women. Specifically, she argues that white women tend to ignore their complicity in, and privileges obtained from, their situatedness within relations of race, sexuality (if straight), and geographic location. Moreover, while Okin favors determining social justice from behind a Rawlsian veil of ignorance, Flax contends that just practices depend on "fuller recognition of our differences and their often tangled and bloody histories."

In her response to Flax, Okin (reading 43) questions whether a full recognition of our differences must precede the emergence of just practices. According to Okin, the two processes are more likely to go hand in hand. However, it is not clear that Okin and Flax are actually disagreeing with each other as much as they seem to be. Especially, with respect to specific problems, it seems likely that Okin and Flax would agree about the similarities and differences that are relevant to achieving justice. If ethics is to be defensible, it must face up to these challenges that come from feminism, environmentalism and postmodernism. To do this, ethics will have to take into account the experience of women as well as that of men, it will have to take into account non-humans as well as humans, and the differences as well as the similarities between individuals and groups, especially those that hold between people of different cultures. The result should be a far more comprehensive and, hence, more adequate ethics than anything we have to date.

Notes

1 The idea of a naturalistic fallacy was made famous by G. E. Moore. See his *Principia Ethica*.

2 J. R. Searle, "Reply to 'The Promising Game,' " in *Readings in Contemporary Ethical Theory*, ed. Kenneth Pahed and Marvin Schiller (Englewood Cliffs: Prentice-Hall, 1970), p. 182.

3 R. M. Hare, "Descriptivism," *Proceedings of the British Academy*, 49 (1963), pp. 117–34.

4 Ibid.

5 Ibid. See also reading 5.

6 See Kurt Baier, *The Rational and the Moral Order* (La Salle, Ill.: Open Court, 1995), pp. 31–4.

7 Ibid.

8 See for example, James P. Sterba, "Distributive Justice," *American Journal of Jurisprudence* (1977), pp. 55–79, and John C. Harsanyi,

(Boston: Reidel, 1976) pp. 37–85.

9 Cora E. Lutz, "Musonius Rufus: 'The Roman Socrates,' " *Yale Classical Studies* (1947), pp. 3–117; R. Hirzel, *Der Dialog* (Leipzig, 1985), II, p. 239.

10 Lutz, op. cit., p. 3.

11 Carol Gilligan, *In a Different Voice* (Cambridge: Harvard University Press, 1982); "Moral Orientation and Moral Development," in *Women and Moral Theory*, ed. Evan Kittay and Diana Meyers (Totowa: Rowman and Littlefield, 1987), pp. 19–36.

12 Gilligan, "Moral Orientation and Moral Development," p. 23.

13 Ibid., p. 5.

14 For more discussion of this point, see James P. Sterba, *How to Make People Just* (Totowa, NJ: Rowman and Littlefield, 1988), ch. 12.

15 Annette Baier, "Trust and Antitrust," *Ethics* (1986), p. 255.

16 Sterba, *How to Make People Just*, Part II; and *Justice for Here and Now* (Cambridge University Press, 1998).

PART ONE

THE NATURE OF MORALITY:
WHAT IS MORALITY?

1 Morality as Good in Itself

Plato

With these words I was thinking that I had made an end of the discussion; but the end, in truth, proved to be only a beginning. For Glaucon, who is always the most pugnacious of men, was dissatisfied at Thrasymachus' retirement; he wanted to have the battle out. So he said to me: Socrates, do you wish really to persuade us, or only to seem to have persuaded us, that to be moral is always better than to be immoral?

I should wish really to persuade you, I replied, if I could.

Then you certainly have not succeeded. Let me ask you now: how would you arrange goods – are there not some which we welcome for their own sakes, and independently of their consequences, as, for example, harmless pleasures and enjoyments, which delight us at the time, although nothing follows from them?

I agree in thinking that there is such a class, I replied.

Is there not also a second class of goods, such as knowledge, sight, health, which are desirable not only in themselves, but also for their results?

Certainly, I said.

And would you not recognize a third class, such as gymnastics, and the care of the sick, and the physician's art; also the various ways of money-making – these do us good but we regard them as disagreeable; and no one would choose them for their own sakes, but only for the sake of some reward or result which flows from them?

There is, I said, this third class also. But why do you ask?

Because I want to know in which of the three classes you would place morality?

In the highest class, I reply – among those

From Plato, *The Republic* (London: Macmillan, 1892). Reprinted with permission.

goods which he who would be happy desires both for their own sake and for the sake of their results.

Then the many are of another mind; they think that morality is to be reckoned in the troublesome class, among goods which are to be pursued for the sake of rewards and of reputation, but in themselves are disagreeable and rather to be avoided.

I know, I said, that this is their manner of thinking, and that this was the thesis which Thrasymachus was maintaining just now, when he censured morality and praised immorality. But I am too stupid to be convinced by him.

I wish, he said, that you would hear me as well as him, and then I shall see whether you and I agree. For Thrasymachus seems to me, like a snake, to have been charmed by your voice sooner than he ought to have been; but to my mind the natures of morality and immorality have not yet been made clear. Setting aside their rewards and results, I want to know what they are in themselves, and how they inwardly work in the soul. If you please, then, I will revive the argument of Thrasymachus. And first I will speak of the nature and origin of morality according to the common view of them. Secondly, I will show that all men who practise morality do so against their will, of necessity, but not as a good. And thirdly, I will argue that there is reason in this view, for the life of the immoral is after all better by far than the life of moral – if what they say is true, Socrates, since I myself am not of their opinion. But still I acknowledge that I am perplexed when I hear the voices of Thrasymachus and myriads of others dinning in my ears; and, on the other hand, I have never yet heard the superiority of morality to injustice maintained by anyone in a satisfactory way. I want to hear morality praised in respect of itself; then I shall be satisfied, and you are the person from whom I think that I am most likely to hear this; and therefore I will praise the immoral life to the utmost of my power, and my manner of speaking will indicate the manner in which I desire to hear you too praising morality and censuring immorality. Will you say whether you approve of my proposal?

Indeed I do; nor can I imagine any theme about which a man of sense would oftener wish to converse.

I am delighted, he replied, to hear you say so, and shall begin by speaking, as I proposed, of the nature and origin of morality.

They say that to do wrong is, by nature, good; to have wrong done to you, evil; but that the evil is greater than the good. And so when men have both done and suffered wrong and have had experience of both, not being able to avoid the one and obtain the other, they think that they had better agree among themselves to have neither; hence there arise laws and mutual covenants; and that which is ordained by law is termed by them lawful and right. This they affirm to be the origin and nature of morality; it is a mean or compromise, between the best of all, which is to do wrong and not be punished, and the worst of all, which is to have wrong done to you without the power of retaliation; and justice, being at a middle point between the two, is tolerated not as a good, but as the lesser evil, and honoured by reason of the inability of men to do wrong. For no man who is worthy to be called a man would ever submit to such an agreement if he were able to resist; he would be mad if he did. Such is the received account, Socrates, of the nature and origin of morality.

Now that those who practise morality do so involuntarily and because they have not the power to do what is wrong will best appear if we imagine something of this kind: having given both to the moral and the immoral power to do what they will, let us watch and see whither desire will lead them; then we shall discover in the very act the moral and the immoral man to be proceeding along the same road, following their interest, which all natures deem to be their food, and are only diverted into the path of morality by the force of law. The liberty which we are supposing may be most completely given to them in the form of such a power as is said to have been possessed by Gyges, the ancestor of Croesus the Lydian. According to the tradition, Gyges was a shepherd in the service of the king of Lydia; there was a great storm, and an earthquake made an opening in the earth at the place where he was feeding his flock. Amazed at the sight, he descended into the opening, where, among other marvels, he beheld a hollow brazen horse, having doors, at which he stooping and looking in saw a dead body of stature, as appeared to him, more than human, and having nothing on but a gold ring; this he took from the finger of the dead and reascended. Now the shepherds met together, according to custom, that they might send their monthly report about the flocks to the king; into their assembly he came having the ring on his finger, and as he was sitting among them he chanced to turn the collet of the ring inside his hand, when instantly he became invisible to the rest of the company and they began to speak of him as if he were no longer present. He was astonished at this, and again touching the ring he turned the collet outwards and reappeared; he made several trials of the ring, and always with the same result – when he turned the collet inwards he became invisible, when outwards he reappeared. Whereupon he contrived to be chosen one of the messengers who were sent to the court; where as soon as he arrived he seduced the queen, and with her help conspired against the king and slew him, and took the kingdom. Suppose now that there were two such magic rings, and the moral put on one of them and the immoral the other, no man can be imagined to be of such an iron nature that he would stand fast in morality. No man would keep his hands off what was not his own when he could safely take what he liked out of the market, or go into houses and lie with anyone of his pleasure, or kill or release from prison whom he would, and in all respects be like a God among men. Then the actions of the moral would be as the actions of the immoral; they would both come at last to the same point. And this we may truly affirm to be a great proof that a man is moral, not willingly or because he thinks that morality is any good to him individually, but of necessity, for wherever anyone thinks that he can safely be immoral, there he is immoral. For all men believe in their hearts that immorality is far more profitable to the individual than morality, and he who argues as I have been supposing, will say that they are right. If you could imagine anyone obtaining this power of becoming invisible, and never doing any wrong or touching what was another's, he would be thought by the lookers-on to be a most wretched idiot, although they would praise him to one another's faces, and keep up appearances with one another from a fear that they too might be wronged. Enough of this.

Now, if we are to form a real judgment of the life of the moral and the immoral, we must isolate them; there is no other way; and how is the isolation to be effected? I answer: Let the immoral man be entirely immoral, and the moral man entirely moral, nothing is to be taken away from either of them, and both are to be perfectly furnished for the work of the respective lives. First, let the immoral be like other distinguished masters of craft; like the skilful pilot or physician, who knows intuitively his own powers and keeps within their limits, and who, if he fails at any point, is able to recover himself. So let the immoral make his immoral attempts in the right way, and lie hidden if he means to be great in his immorality (he who is found out is nobody): for the highest reach of immorality is, to be deemed moral when you are not. Therefore I say that in the perfectly immoral man we must assume the most perfect immorality; there is to be no deduction, but we must allow him, while doing the most immoral acts, to have acquired the greatest reputation for morality. If he has taken a false step he must be able to recover himself; he must be one who can speak with effect, if any of his deeds come to light, and who can force his way where force is required by his courage and strength, and command of money and friends. And at his side let us place the moral man in his nobleness and simplicity, wishing, as Aeschylus says, to be and not to seem good. There must be no seeming, for if he seem to be moral he will be honoured and rewarded, and then we shall not know whether he is moral for the sake of moral-

ity or for the sake of honours and rewards; therefore, let him be clothed in morality only, and have no other covering; and he must be imagined in a state of life the opposite of the former. Let him be the best of men, and let him be thought the worst; then he will have been put to the proof; and we shall see whether he will be affected by the fear of infamy and its consequences. And let him continue thus to the hour of death; being just and seeming to one unjust. When both have reached the uttermost extreme, the one of morality and the other of immorality, let judgment be given which of them is the happier of the two.

Heavens! my dear Glaucon, I said, how energetically you polish them up for the decision, first one and then the other, as if they were two statues.

I do my best, he said. And now that we know what they are like there is no difficulty in tracing out the sort of life which awaits either of them. This I will proceed to describe; but as you may think the description a little too coarse, I ask you to suppose, Socrates, that the words which follow are not mine. Let me put them into the mouths of the eulogists of immorality: they will tell you that the moral man who is thought immoral will be scourged, racked, bound – will have his eyes burnt out; and, at last, after suffering every kind of evil, he will be impaled: Then he will understand that he ought to seem only, and not to be, moral; the words of Aeschylus may be more truly spoken of the immoral than of the moral. For the immoral is pursuing a reality; he does not live with a view to appearances – he wants to be really immoral and not to seem only:

His mind has a soil deep and fertile,
Out of which spring his prudent counsels.

In the first place, he is thought moral, and therefore bears rule in the city; he can marry whom he will, and give in marriage to whom he will; also he can trade and deal where he likes, and always to his own advantage, because he has no misgivings about immorality, and at every contest, whether in public or private, he gets the better of his antagonists, and gains at their expense, and is rich, and out of his gains he can benefit his friends, and harm his enemies; moreover, he can offer sacrifices, and delicate gifts to the gods abundantly and magnificently, and can honour the gods or any man whom he wants to honour in a far better style than the just, and therefore he is likely to be dearer than they are to the gods. And thus, Socrates, gods and men are said to unite in making the life of the immoral better than the life of the moral.

I was going to say something in answer to Glaucon, when Adeimantus, his brother, interposed: Socrates, he said, you do not suppose that there is nothing more to be urged?

Why, what else is there? I answered.

The strongest point of all has not been even mentioned, he replied.

Well, then, according to the proverb, 'Let brother help brother' – if he fails in any part do you assist him; although I must confess that Glaucon has already said quite enough to lay me in the dust, and take from me the power of helping morality.

Nonsense, he replied. But let me add something more: There is another side to Glaucon's argument about the praise and censure of morality and immorality, which is equally required in order to bring out what I believe to be his meaning. Parents and tutors are always telling their sons and their wards that they are to be moral; but why? Not for the sake of morality, but for the sake of character and reputation; in the hope of obtaining for him who is reputed just some of those offices, marriages and the like which Glaucon has enumerated among the advantages accruing to the immoral from the reputation of being moral. More, however, is made of appearances by this class of persons than by the others; for they throw in the good opinion of the gods, and will tell you of a shower of benefits which the heavens, as they say, rain upon the pious; and this accords with the testimony of the noble Hesiod and Homer, the first of whom says that the gods make the oaks of the just:

> To bear acorns at their summit, and bees in the
>   middle;
> And the sheep are bowed down with the weight
>   of their fleeces,

and many other blessings of a like kind are provided for them. And Homer has a very similar strain; for he speaks of one whose fame is

> As the fame of some blameless king who, like a
>   god,
> Maintains justice; to whom the black earth
>   brings forth
> Wheat and barley, whose trees are bowed with
>   fruit,
> And his sheep never fail to bear, and the sea
>   gives him fish.

Still grander are the gifts of heaven which Musaeus and his son vouchsafe to the moral; they take them down into the world below, where they have the saints lying on couches at a feast, everlastingly drunk, crowned with garlands; their idea seems to be that an immortality of drunkenness is the [finest wage] of virtue. Some extend their rewards yet further; the posterity, as they say, of the faithful shall survive to the third and fourth generation. This is the style in which they praise morality. But about the wicked there is another strain; they bury them in a slough in Hades, and make them carry water in a sieve; also while they are yet living they bring them to infamy, and inflict upon them the punishments which Glaucon described as the portion of the moral who are reputed to be immoral; nothing else does their invention supply. Such is their manner of praising the one and censuring the other.

Once more, Socrates, I will ask you to consider another way of speaking about morality and immorality, which is not confined to the poets, but is found in prose writers. The universal voice of mankind is always declaring that morality and virtue are honourable, but grievous and toilsome; and that the pleasures of vice . . . are easy of attainment, and are only censured by law and opinion. They say also that honesty is for the most part less profitable than dishonesty; and they are quite ready to call wicked men happy, and to honour them both in public and private when they are rich or in any other way influential, while they despise and overlook those who may be weak and poor, even though acknowledging them to be better than the others. But most extraordinary of all is their mode of speaking about virtue and the gods: they say that the gods apportion calamity and misery to many good men, and good and happiness to the wicked. And mendicant prophets go to rich men's doors and persuade them that they have a power committed to them by the gods of making an atonement for a man's own or his ancestor's sins by sacrifices or charms, with rejoicings and feasts; and they promise to harm an enemy, whether moral or immoral, at a small cost; with magic arts and incantations binding heaven, as they say, to execute their will. And the poets are the authorities to whom they appeal, now smoothing the path of vice with the words of Hesiod:

> Vice may be had in abundance without trouble; the way is smooth and her dwelling-place is near. But before virtue the gods have set toil,

and a tedious and uphill road: then citing Homer as a witness that the gods may be influenced by men; for he also says:

> The gods, too, may be turned from their purpose; and men pray to them and avert their wrath by sacrifices and soothing entreaties, and by libations and the odour of fat, when they have sinned and transgressed.

And they produce a host of books written by Musaeus and Orpheus, who were children of the Moon and the Muses – that is what they say – according to which they perform their ritual, and persuade not only individuals, but whole cities, that expiations and atonements for sin may be made by sacrifices and amusements which fill a vacant hour, and are equally at the service of the living and the dead; the latter sort they call mysteries, and they redeem us from the pains of hell, but if we neglect them no one knows what awaits us.

He proceeded: And now when the young hear all this said about virtue and vice, and the way in which gods and men regard them, how are their minds likely to be affected, my dear Socrates – those of them, I mean, who are quickwitted and, like bees on the wing, light on every flower, and from all that they hear are prone to draw conclu-

sions as to what manner of persons they should be and in what way they should walk if they would make the best of life? Probably the youth will say to himself in the words of Pindar:

> Can I by honesty or by crooked ways of deceit ascend a loftier tower which may be a fortress to me all my days?

For what men say is that, if I am really moral and am not also thought to be moral, profit there is none, but the pain and loss on the other hand are unmistakable. But if, though immoral, I acquire the reputation of being moral, a heavenly life is promised to me. Since then, as philosophers prove, appearance tyrannizes over truth and is lord of happiness, to appearance I must devote myself. I will describe around me a picture and shadow of virtue to be the vestibule and exterior of my house; behind I will trail the subtle and crafty fox, as Archilochus, greatest of sages, recommends. But I hear someone exclaiming that the concealment of wickedness is often difficult; to which I answer, Nothing great is easy. Nevertheless, the argument indicates this, if we would be happy, to be the path along which we should proceed. With a view to concealment we will establish secret brotherhoods and political clubs. And there are professors of rhetoric who teach the art of persuading courts and assemblies; and so, partly by persuasion and partly by force, I shall make unlawful gains and not be punished. Still I hear a voice saying that the gods cannot be deceived, neither can they be compelled. But what if there are no gods? or, suppose them to have no care of human things – why in either case should we mind about concealment? And even if there are gods, and they do care about us, yet we know of them only from tradition and the genealogies of the poets; and these are the very persons who say that they may be influenced and turned by 'sacrifices and soothing entreaties and by offerings'. Let us be consistent then, and believe both or neither. If the poets speak truly, why then we had better do wrong, and offer of the fruits of our crimes; for if we are moral, although we may escape the vengeance of heaven, we shall lose the gains of doing wrong; but, if we are immoral we shall keep the gains, and by our sinning and praying, and praying and sinning, the gods will be propitiated, and we shall not be punished. 'But there is a world below in which either we or our posterity will suffer for our immoral deeds.' Yes, my friend, will be the [reply], but there are mysteries and atoning deities, and these have great power. That is what mighty cities declare; and the children of the gods, who were their poets and prophets, bear a like testimony. On what principle, then, shall we any longer choose morality rather than the worst immorality? When, if we only unite the latter with a deceitful regard to appearance, we shall fare well to our mind both with gods and men, in life and after death, as the most numerous and the highest authorities tell us. Knowing all this, Socrates, how can a man who has any superiority of mind or person or rank or wealth, be willing to honour morality; or indeed to refrain from laughing when he hears morality praised? And even if there should be someone who is able to disprove the truth of my words, and who is satisfied that morality is best, still he is not angry with the immoral, but is very ready to forgive them, because he also knows that men are not moral of their own free will; unless, peradventure, there be someone whom the divinity within him may have inspired with a hatred of immorality, or who has attained knowledge of the truth – but no other man. He only blames immorality who, owing to cowardice or age or some weakness, has not the power of doing wrong. And this is proved by the fact that when he obtains the power, he immediately does what is immoral as far as he can.

The cause of all this, Socrates, was indicated by us at the beginning of the argument, when my brother and I told you how astonished we were to find that of all the professing panegyrists of morality – beginning with the ancient heroes of whom any memorial has been preserved to us, and ending with the men of our own time – no one has ever blamed immorality or praised morality except with a view to the glories, honours and benefits which flow from them. No one has ever adequately described either in verse or prose the true essential nature of either of them abiding in the soul, and invisible to any human or divine eye; or shown that of all the things of a man's soul which he has within him, morality is the greatest good, and immorality the greatest evil. Had this been the universal strain, had you sought to persuade us of this from our youth upwards, we should not have been on the watch to keep one another from doing wrong, but everyone would have been his own watchman, because afraid, if he did wrong, of harbouring in himself the greatest of evils. I dare say that Thrasymachus and others would seriously hold the language which I have been merely repeating, and words even stronger than these about morality and immorality, grossly, as I conceive, perverting their true nature. But I speak in this vehement manner, as I must frankly confess to you, because I want to hear from you the opposite side; and I would ask you to show not only the superiority which morality has over immorality, but what effect they have on the possessor of them which makes the one to be a good and the other an evil to him. And please, as Glaucon requested of you, to exclude reputations; for unless you take away from each of them his true reputation and add on the false, we shall say that you do not praise morality, but the appearance of it; we shall think that you are only exhorting us to keep immorality dark, and that you really agree with Thrasymachus in thinking that morality is another's good and the interest of the stronger, and that immorality is a man's own profit and interest, though injurious to the weaker. Now as you have admitted that morality is one of that highest class of goods which are desired indeed for their results, but in a far greater degree for their own sakes – like sight or hearing or knowledge or health, or any other real and natural and not merely conventional good – I would ask you in your praise of morality to regard one point only: I mean the essential good and evil which morality and immorality work in the possessors of them. Let others praise morality and censure immorality, magnifying the rewards and honours of the one and abusing the other; that is a manner of arguing which, coming from them, I am ready to tolerate, but from you who have spent your whole life in the consideration of this question, unless I hear the contrary from your own lips, I expect something better. And therefore, I say, not only prove to us that morality is better than immorality, but show

what either of them does to the possessor of them, which makes the one to be a good and the other an evil, whether seen or unseen by gods and men.

2   The Emotive Theory of Morality

A. J. Ayer

There is still one objection to be met before we can claim to have justified our view that all synthetic propositions are empirical hypotheses. This objection is based on the common supposition that our speculative knowledge is of two distinct kinds – that which relates to questions of empirical fact, and that which relates to questions of value. It will be said that "statements of value" are genuine synthetic propositions, but that they cannot with any show of justice be represented as hypotheses, which are used to predict the course of our sensations; and, accordingly, that the existence of ethics and aesthetics as branches of speculative knowledge presents an insuperable objection to our radical empiricist thesis.

In face of this objection, it is our business to give an account of "judgments of value" which is both satisfactory in itself and consistent with our general empiricist principles. We shall set ourselves to show that in so far as statements of value are significant, they are ordinary "scientific" statements; and that in so far as they are not scientific, they are not in the literal sense significant, but are simply expressions of emotion which can be neither true nor false. In maintaining this view, we may confine ourselves for the present to the case of ethical statements. What is said about them will be found to apply, *mutatis mutandis*, to the case of aesthetic statements also.

The ordinary system of ethics, as elaborated in the works of ethical philosophers, is very far from

From *Language, Truth and Logic* (New York: Dover, 1952). Reprinted with permission.

being a homogeneous whole. Not only is it apt to contain pieces of metaphysics, and analyses of non-ethical concepts: its actual ethical contents are themselves of very different kinds. We may divide them, indeed, into four main classes. There are, first of all, propositions which express definitions of ethical terms, or judgments about the legitimacy or possibility of certain definitions. Secondly, there are propositions describing the phenomena of moral experience, and their causes. Thirdly, there are exhortations to moral virtue. And, lastly, there are actual ethical judgments. It is unfortunately the case that the distinction between these four classes, plain as it is, is commonly ignored by ethical philosophers; with the result that it is often very difficult to tell from their works what it is that they are seeking to discover or prove.

In fact, it is easy to see that only the first of our four classes, namely that which comprises the propositions relating to the definitions of ethical terms, can be said to constitute ethical philosophy. The propositions which describe the phenomena of moral experience, and their causes, must be assigned to the science of psychology, or sociology. The exhortations to moral virtue are not propositions at all, but ejaculations or commands which are designed to provoke the reader to action of a certain sort. Accordingly, they do not belong to any branch of philosophy or science. As for the expressions of ethical judgments, we have not yet determined how they should be classified. But inasmuch as they are certainly neither definitions nor comments upon definitions, nor quotations, we may say decisively that they do not belong to ethical philosophy. A strictly philosophical treatise on ethics should therefore make no ethical pronouncements. But it should, by giving an analysis of ethical terms, show what is the category to which all such pronouncements belong. And this is what we are now about to do.

A question which is often discussed by ethical philosophers is whether it is possible to find definitions which would reduce all ethical terms to one or two fundamental terms. But this question, though it undeniably belongs to ethical philosophy, is not relevant to our present enquiry. We are not now concerned to discover which term, within the sphere of ethical terms, is to be taken as fundamental; whether, for example, "good" can be defined in terms of "right" or "right" in terms of "good," or both in terms of "value." What we are interested in is the possibility of reducing the whole sphere of ethical terms to non-ethical terms. We are enquiring whether statements of ethical value can be translated into statements of empirical fact.

That they can be so translated is the contention of those ethical philosophers who are commonly called subjectivists, and of those who are known as utilitarians. For the utilitarian defines the rightness of actions, and the goodness of ends, in terms of the pleasure, or happiness, or satisfaction, to which they give rise; the subjectivist, in terms of the feelings of approval which a certain person, or group of people, has towards them. Each of these types of definition makes moral judgments into a sub-class of psychological or sociological judgments; and for this reason they are very attractive to us. For, if either was correct, it would follow that ethical assertions were not generically different from the factual assertions which are ordinarily contrasted with them; and the account which we have already given of empirical hypotheses would apply to them also.

Nevertheless we shall not adopt either a subjectivist or a utilitarian analysis of ethical terms. We reject the subjectivist view that to call an action right, or a thing good, is to say that it is generally approved of, because it is not self-contradictory to assert that some actions which are generally approved of are not right, or that some

things which are generally approved of are not good. And we reject the alternative subjectivist view that a man who asserts that a certain action is right, or that a certain thing is good, is saying that he himself approves of it, on the ground that a man who confessed that he sometimes approved of what was bad or wrong would not be contradicting himself. And a similar argument is fatal to utilitarianism. We cannot agree that to call an action right is to say that of all the actions possible in the circumstances it would cause, or be likely to cause, the greatest happiness, or the greatest balance of pleasure over pain, or the greatest balance of satisfied over unsatisfied desire, because we find that it is not self-contradictory to say that it is sometimes wrong to perform the action which would actually or probably cause the greatest happiness, or the greatest balance of pleasure over pain, or of satisfied over unsatisfied desire. And since it is not self-contradictory to say that some pleasant things are not good, or that some bad things are desired, it cannot be the case that the sentence "x is good" is equivalent to "x is pleasant," or to "x is desired." And to every other variant of utilitarianism with which I am acquainted the same objection can be made. And therefore we should, I think, conclude that the validity of ethical judgments is not determined by the felicific tendencies of actions, any more than by the nature of people's feelings; but that it must be regarded as "absolute" or "intrinsic," and not empirically calculable.

If we say this, we are not, of course, denying that it is possible to invent a language in which all ethical symbols are definable in non-ethical terms, or even that it is desirable to invent such a language and adopt it in place of our own; what we are denying is that the suggested reduction of ethical to non-ethical statements is consistent with the conventions of our actual language. That is, we reject utilitarianism and subjectivism, not as proposals to replace our existing ethical notions by new ones, but as analyses of our existing ethical notions. Our contention is simply that, in our language, sentences which contain normative ethical symbols are not equivalent to sentences which express psychological propositions, or indeed empirical propositions of any kind.

It is advisable here to make it plain that it is only normative ethical symbols, and not descriptive ethical symbols, that are held by us to be indefinable in factual terms. There is a danger of confusing these two types of symbols, because they are commonly constituted by signs of the same sensible form. Thus a complex sign of the form "*x* is wrong" may constitute a sentence which expresses a moral judgment concerning a certain type of conduct, or it may constitute a sentence which states that a certain type of conduct is repugnant to the moral sense of a particular society. In the latter case, the symbol "wrong" is a descriptive ethical symbol, and the sentence in which it occurs expresses an ordinary sociological proposition; in the former case, the symbol "wrong" is a normative ethical symbol, and the sentence in which it occurs does not, we maintain, express an empirical proposition at all. It is only with normative ethics that we are at present concerned; so that whenever ethical symbols are used in the course of this argument without qualification, they are always to be interpreted as symbols of the normative type.

In admitting that normative ethical concepts are irreducible to empirical concepts, we seem to be leaving the way clear for the "absolutist" view of ethics – that is, the view that statements of value are not controlled by observation, as ordinary empirical propositions are, but only by a mysterious "intellectual intuition." A feature of this theory, which is seldom recognized by its advocates, is that it makes statements of value unverifiable. For it is notorious that what seems intuitively certain to one person may seem doubtful, or even false, to another. So that unless it is possible to provide some criterion by which one may decide between conflicting intuitions, a mere appeal to intuition is worthless as a test of a proposition's validity. But in the case of moral judgments, no such criterion can be given. Some moralists claim to settle the matter by saying that they "know" that their own moral judgments are correct. But such an assertion is of purely psychological interest, and has not the slightest tendency to prove the validity of any moral judgment. For dissentient moralists may equally well "know" that their ethical views are correct. And,

as far as subjective certainty goes, there will be nothing to choose between them. When such differences of opinion arise in connection with an ordinary empirical proposition, one may attempt to resolve them by referring to, or actually carrying out, some relevant empirical test. But with regard to ethical statements, there is, on the "absolutist" or "intuitionist" theory, no relevant empirical test. We are therefore justified in saying that on this theory ethical statements are held to be unverifiable. They are, of course, also held to be genuine synthetic propositions.

Considering the use which we have made of the principle that a synthetic proposition is significant only if it is empirically verifiable, it is clear that the acceptance of an "absolutist" theory of ethics would undermine the whole of our main argument. And as we have already rejected the "naturalistic" theories which are commonly supposed to provide the only alternative to "absolutism" in ethics, we seem to have reached a difficult position. We shall meet the difficulty by showing that the correct treatment of ethical statements is afforded by a third theory, which is wholly compatible with our radical empiricism.

We begin by admitting that the fundamental ethical concepts are unanalyzable, inasmuch as there is no criterion by which one can test the validity of the judgments in which they occur. So far we are in agreement with the absolutists. But, unlike the absolutists, we are able to give an explanation of this fact about ethical concepts. We say that the reason why they are unanalyzable is that they are mere pseudo-concepts. The presence of an ethical symbol in a proposition adds nothing to its factual content. Thus if I say to someone, "You acted wrongly in stealing that money," I am not stating anything more than if I had simply said, "You stole that money." In adding that this action is wrong I am not making any further statement about it. I am simply evincing my moral disapproval of it. It is as if I had said, "You stole that money," in a peculiar tone of horror, or written it with the addition of some special exclamation marks. The tone, or the exclamation marks, adds nothing to the literal meaning of the sentence. It merely serves to show that the expression of it is attended by certain feelings in the speaker.

If now I generalize my previous statement and say, "Stealing money is wrong," I produce a sentence which has no factual meaning – that is, expresses no proposition which can be either true or false. It is as if I had written "Stealing money!" – where the shape and thickness of the exclamation marks show, by a suitable convention, that a special sort of moral disapproval is the feeling which is being expressed. It is clear that there is nothing said here which can be true or false. Another man may disagree with me about the wrongness of stealing, in the sense that he may not have the same feelings about stealing as I have, and he may quarrel with me on account of my moral sentiments. But he cannot, strictly speaking, contradict me. For in saying that a certain type of action is right or wrong, I am not making any factual statement, not even a statement about my own state of mind. I am merely expressing certain moral sentiments. And the man who is ostensibly contradicting me is merely expressing his moral sentiments. So that there is plainly no sense in asking which of us is in the right. For neither of us is asserting a genuine proposition.

What we have just been saying about the symbol "wrong" applies to all normative ethical symbols. Sometimes they occur in sentences which record ordinary empirical facts besides expressing ethical feeling about those facts; sometimes they occur in sentences which simply express ethical feeling about a certain type of action, or situation, without making any statement of fact. But in every case in which one would commonly be said to be making an ethical judgment, the function of the relevant ethical word is purely "emotive." It is used to express feeling about certain objects, but not to make any assertion about them.

It is worth mentioning that ethical terms do not serve only to express feeling. They are calculated also to arouse feeling, and so to stimulate action. Indeed some of them are used in such a way as to give the sentences in which they occur the effect of commands. Thus the sentence "It is your duty to tell the truth" may be regarded both as the expression of a certain sort of ethical feeling about truthfulness and as the expression of

the command "Tell the truth." The sentence "You ought to tell the truth" also involves the command "Tell the truth," but here the tone of the command is less emphatic. In the sentence "It is good to tell the truth" the command has become little more than a suggestion. And thus the "meaning" of the word "good," in its ethical usage, is differentiated from that of the word "duty" or the word "ought." In fact we may define the meaning of the various ethical words in terms both of the different feelings they are ordinarily taken to express, and also the different responses which they are calculated to provoke.

We can now see why it is impossible to find a criterion for determining the validity of ethical judgments. It is not because they have an "absolute" validity which is mysteriously independent of ordinary sense-experience, but because they have no objective validity whatsoever. If a sentence makes no statement at all, there is obviously no sense in asking whether what it says is true or false. And we have seen that sentences which simply express moral judgments do not say anything. They are pure expressions of feeling and as such do not come under the category of truth and falsehood. They are unverifiable for the same reason as a cry of pain or a word of command is unverifiable – because they do not express genuine propositions.

Thus, although our theory of ethics might fairly be said to be radically subjectivist, it differs in a very important respect from the orthodox subjectivist theory. For the orthodox subjectivist does not deny, as we do, that the sentences of a moralizer express genuine propositions. All he denies is that they express propositions of a unique non-empirical character. His own view is that they express propositions about the speaker's feelings. If this were so, ethical judgments clearly would be capable of being true or false. They would be true if the speaker had the relevant feelings, and false if he had not. And this is a matter which is, in principle, empirically verifiable. Furthermore they could be significantly contradicted. For if I say, "Tolerance is a virtue," and someone answers, "You don't approve of it," he would, on the ordinary subjectivist theory, be contradicting me. On our theory, he would not be contradicting me, because, in saying that tolerance was a virtue, I should not be making any statement about my own feelings or about anything else. I should simply be evincing my feelings, which is not at all the same thing as saying that I have them.

The distinction between the expression of feeling and the assertion of feeling is complicated by the fact that the assertion that one has a certain feeling often accompanies the expression of that feeling, and is then, indeed, a factor in the expression of that feeling. Thus I may simultaneously express boredom and say that I am bored, and in that case my utterance of the words, "I am bored," is one of the circumstances which make it true to say that I am expressing or evincing boredom. But I can express boredom without actually saying that I am bored. I can express it by my tone and gestures, while making a statement about something wholly unconnected with it, or by an ejaculation, or without uttering any words at all. So that even if the assertion that one has a certain feeling always involves the expression of that feeling, the expression of a feeling assuredly does not always involve the assertion that one has it. And this is the important point to grasp in considering the distinction between our theory and the ordinary subjectivist theory. For whereas the subjectivist holds that ethical statements actually assert the existence of certain feelings, we hold that ethical statements are expressions and excitants of feeling which do not necessarily involve any assertions.

We have already remarked that the main objection to the ordinary subjectivist theory is that the validity of ethical judgments is not determined by the nature of their author's feelings. And this is an objection which our theory escapes. For it does not imply that the existence of any feelings is a necessary and sufficient condition of the validity of an ethical judgment. It implies, on the contrary, that ethical judgments have no validity.

There is, however, a celebrated argument against subjectivist theories which our theory does not escape. It has been pointed out by Moore that if ethical statements were simply statements about the speaker's feelings, it would be impossible to argue about questions of value.[1] To take a typical example: if a man said that thrift was a virtue, and another replied that it was a vice, they would not, on this theory, be disputing with one another. One would be saying that he approved of thrift, and the other that *he* didn't; and there is no reason why both these statements should not be true. Now Moore held it to be obvious that we do dispute about questions of value, and accordingly concluded that the particular form of subjectivism which he was discussing was false.

It is plain that the conclusion that it is impossible to dispute about questions of value follows from our theory also. For as we hold that such sentences as "Thrift is a virtue" and "Thrift is a vice" do not express propositions at all, we clearly cannot hold that they express incompatible propositions. We must therefore admit that if Moore's argument really refutes the ordinary subjectivist theory, it also refutes ours. But, in fact, we deny that it does refute even the ordinary subjectivist theory. For we hold that one really never does dispute about questions of value.

This may seem, at first sight, to be a very paradoxical assertion. For we certainly do engage in disputes which are ordinarily regarded as disputes about questions of value. But, in all such cases, we find, if we consider the matter closely, that the dispute is not really about a question of value, but about a question of fact. When someone disagrees with us about the moral value of a certain action or type of action, we do admittedly resort to argument in order to win him over to our way of thinking. But we do not attempt to show by our arguments that he has the "wrong" ethical feeling towards a situation whose nature he has correctly apprehended. What we attempt to show is that he is mistaken about the facts of the case. We argue that he has misconceived the agent's motive; or that he has misjudged the effects of the action, or its probable effects in view of the agent's knowledge; or that he has failed to take into account the special circumstances in which the agent was placed. Or else we employ more general arguments about the effects which actions of a certain type tend to produce, or the qualities which are usually manifested in their performance. We do this in the hope that we have only to get our opponent to agree with us about the nature of the empirical facts for him to adopt the same moral attitude towards them as we do. And as the people with whom we argue have generally received the same moral education as ourselves, and live in the same social order, our expectation is usually justified. But if our opponent happens to have undergone a different process of moral "conditioning" from ourselves, so that, even when he acknowledges all the facts, he still disagrees with us about the moral value of the actions under discussion, then we abandon the attempt to convince him by argument. We say that it is impossible to argue with him because he has a distorted or undeveloped moral sense; which signifies merely that he employs a different set of values from our own. We feel that our own system of values is superior, and therefore speak in such derogatory terms of his. But we cannot bring forward any arguments to show that our system is superior. For our judgment that it is so is itself a judgment of value, and accordingly outside the scope of argument. It is because argument fails us when we come to deal with pure questions of value, as distinct from questions of fact, that we finally resort to mere abuse.

In short, we find that argument is possible on moral questions only if some system of values is presupposed. If our opponent concurs with us in expressing moral disapproval of all actions of a given type t, then we may get him to condemn a particular action A, by bringing forward arguments to show that A is of type t. For the question whether A does or does not belong to that type is a plain question of fact. Given that a man has certain moral principles, we argue that he must, in order to be consistent, react morally to certain things in a certain way. What we do not and cannot argue about is the validity of these moral principles. We merely praise or condemn them in the light of our own feelings.

If anyone doubts the accuracy of this account of moral disputes, let him try to construct even an imaginary argument on a question of value which does not reduce itself to an argument about a question of logic or about an empirical matter of fact. I am confident that he will not succeed in producing a single example. And if that is the

case, he must allow that its involving the impossibility of purely ethical arguments is not, as Moore thought, a ground of objection to our theory, but rather a point in favor of it.

Having upheld our theory against the only criticism which appeared to threaten it, we may now use it to define the nature of all ethical enquiries. We find that ethical philosophy consists simply in saying that ethical concepts are pseudo-concepts and therefore unanalyzable. The further task of describing the different feelings that the different ethical terms are used to express, and the different reactions that they customarily provoke, is a task for the psychologist. There cannot be such a thing as ethical science, if by ethical science one means the elaboration of a "true" system of morals. For we have seen that, as ethical judgments are mere expressions of feeling, there can be no way of determining the validity of any ethical system, and, indeed, no sense in asking whether any such system is true. All that one may legitimately enquire in this connection is, What are the moral habits of a given person or group of people, and what causes them to have precisely those habits and feelings? And this enquiry falls wholly within the scope of the existing social sciences.

It appears, then, that ethics, as a branch of knowledge, is nothing more than a department of psychology and sociology. And in case anyone thinks that we are overlooking the existence of casuistry, we may remark that casuistry is not a science, but is a purely analytical investigation of the structure of a given moral system. In other words, it is an exercise in formal logic.

When one comes to pursue the psychological enquiries which constitute ethical science, one is immediately enabled to account for the Kantian and hedonistic theories of morals. For one finds that one of the chief causes of moral behavior is fear, both conscious and unconscious, of a god's displeasure, and fear of the enmity of society. And this, indeed, is the reason why moral precepts present themselves to some people as "categorical" commands. And one finds, also, that the moral code of a society is partly determined by the beliefs of that society concerning the conditions of its own happiness – or, in other words, that a society tends to encourage or discourage a given type of conduct by the use of moral sanctions according as it appears to promote or detract from the contentment of the society as a whole. And this is the reason why altruism is recommended in most moral codes and egotism condemned. It is from the observation of this connection between morality and happiness that hedonistic or eudaemonistic theories of morals ultimately spring, just as the moral theory of Kant is based on the fact, previously explained, that moral precepts have for some people the force of inexorable commands. As each of these theories ignores the fact which lies at the root of the other,

both may be criticized as being one-sided; but this is not the main objection to either of them. Their essential defect is that they treat propositions which refer to the causes and attributes of our ethical feelings as if they were definitions of ethical concepts. And thus they fail to recognize that ethical concepts are pseudo-concepts and consequently indefinable. . . .

Note

1 Cf. *Philosophical Studies*, "The Nature of Moral Philosophy."

3 The New Subjectivism in Morality

Brand Blanshard

By the new subjectivism in ethics I mean the view that when anyone says "this is right" or "this is good," he is only expressing his own feeling; he is not asserting anything true or false, because he is not asserting or judging at all; he is really making an exclamation that expresses a favorable feeling.

This view has recently come into much favor. With variations of detail, it is being advocated by Russell, Wittgenstein, and Ayer in England, and by Carnap, Stevenson, Feigl, and others in this country [in the USA]. Why is it that the theory has come into so rapid a popularity? Is it because moralists of insight have been making a fresh and searching examination of moral experience and its expression? No, I think not. A consideration of the names just mentioned suggests a truer reason. All these names belong, roughly speaking, to a single school of thought in the theory of knowledge. If the new view has become popular

From *Philosophy and Phenomenological Research*, vol. 9, no. 3 (1949), pp. 504–11. Reprinted with permission.

in ethics, it is because certain persons who were at work in the theory of knowledge arrived at a new view *there*, and found, on thinking it out, that it required the new view in ethics; the new view comes less from ethical analysis than from logical positivism.

These writers, as positivists or near-positivists, held that every judgment belongs to one or other of two types. On the one hand, it may be a priori or necessary. But then it is always analytic, i.e. it unpacks in its predicate part or all of its subject. Can we safely say that 7 + 5 make 12? Yes, because 12 is what we mean by "7 + 5." On the other hand, the judgment may be too empirical, and then, if we are to verify it, we can no longer look to our meanings only; it refers to sense experience and there we must look for its warrant. Having arrived at this division of judgments, the positivists raised the question of where value judgments fall. The judgment that knowledge is good, for example, did not seem to be analytic; the value that knowledge might have did not seem to be part of our concept of knowledge. But neither was the statement empirical, for goodness was not a quality like red or squeaky that could be seen or heard. What were they to do, then, with these awkward judgments of value? To find a place for them in their theory of knowledge would require them to revise the theory radically, and yet that theory was what they regarded as their most important discovery. It appeared that the theory could be saved in one way only. If it could be shown that judgments of good and bad were not judgments at all, that they asserted nothing true or false, but merely expressed emotions like "Hurrah" or "Fiddlesticks," then these wayward judgments would cease from troubling and weary heads could be at rest. This is the course the positivists took. They explained value judgments by explaining them away.

Now I do not think their view will do. But before discussing it, I should like to record one vote of thanks to them for the clarity with which they have stated their case. It has been said of John Stuart Mill that he wrote so clearly that he could be found out. This theory has been put so clearly and precisely that it deserves criticism of the same kind, and this I will do my best to supply. The theory claims to show by analysis that when we say "That is good," we do not mean to assert a character of the subject of which we are thinking. I shall argue that we do mean to do just that.

Let us work through an example, and the simpler and commoner the better. There is perhaps no value statement on which people would more universally agree than the statement that intense pain is bad. Let us take a set of circumstances in which I happen to be interested on the legislative side and in which I think every one of us might naturally make such a statement. We come upon a rabbit that has been caught in one of the brutal traps in common use. There are signs that it has struggled for days to escape and that in a frenzy of hunger, pain, and fear, it has all but eaten off its own leg. The attempt failed: the animal is now dead. As we think of the long and excruciating pain it must have suffered, we are very likely to say: "It was a bad thing that the little animal should suffer so." The positivist tells us when we say this we are only expressing our

present emotion. I hold, on the contrary, that we mean to assert something of the pain itself, namely that it was bad – bad when and as it occurred.

Consider what follows from the positivist view. On that view, nothing good or bad happened in the case until I came on the scene and made my remark. For what I express in my remark is something going on in me at the time, and that of course did not exist until I did come on the scene. The pain of the rabbit was not itself bad; nothing evil was happening when the pain was being endured; badness, in the only sense in which it is involved at all, waited for its appearance till I came and looked and felt. Now that this is at odds with our meaning may be shown as follows. Let us put to ourselves the hypothesis that we had not come on the scene and that the rabbit never was discovered. Are we prepared to say that in that case nothing bad had occurred in the sense in which we said it did? Clearly not. Indeed we should say, on the contrary, that the accident of our later discovery made no difference whatever to the badness of the animal's pain, that it would have been every whit as bad whether a chance passer-by happened later to discover the body and feel repugnance or not. If so, then it is clear that in saying the suffering was bad we are not expressing our feelings only. We are saying that the pain was bad when and as it occurred and before anyone took an attitude toward it.

The first argument is thus an ideal experiment in which we use the method of difference. It removes our present expression and shows that the badness we meant would not be affected by this, whereas on positivist grounds it should be. The second argument applies the method in the reverse way. It ideally removes the past event, and shows that this would render false what we mean to say, whereas on positivist grounds it should not. Let us suppose that the animal did not in fact fall into the trap and did not suffer at all, but that we mistakenly believe it did, and say as before that its suffering was an evil thing. On the positivist theory, everything I sought to express by calling it evil in the first case is still present in the second. In the only sense in which badness is involved at all, whatever was bad in the first case is still present in its entirety, since all that is expressed in either case is a state of feeling, and that feeling is still there. And our question is, is such an implication consistent with what we meant? Clearly it is not. If anyone asked us, after we made the remark that the suffering was a bad thing, whether we should think it relevant to what we said to learn that the incident had never occurred and no pain had been suffered at all, we should say that it made all the difference in the world, that what we were asserting to be bad was precisely the suffering we thought had occurred back there, that if this had not occurred, there was nothing left to be bad, and that our assertion was in that case mistaken. The suggestion that in saying something evil had occurred we were after all making no mistake, because we had never meant anyhow to say anything about the past suffering, seems to me merely frivolous. If we did not mean to say this, why should we be so relieved on finding that the suffering had not occurred? On the theory before us, such relief would be groundless, for in that suffering itself there would be nothing to be relieved about. The positivist theory would here distort our meaning beyond recognition.

So far as I can see, there is only one way out for the positivist: he holds that goodness and badness lie in feelings of approval or disapproval. And there is a way in which he might hold that badness did in this case precede our own feeling of disapproval without belonging to the pain itself. The pain itself was neutral; but unfortunately the rabbit, on no grounds at all, took up toward this neutral object an attitude of disapproval, and that made it for the first time, and in the only intelligible sense, bad. This way of escape is theoretically possible, but since it has grave difficulties of its own and has not, so far as I know, been urged by positivists, it is perhaps best not to spend time over it.

I come now to a third argument, which again is very simple. When we come upon the rabbit and make our remark about its suffering being a bad thing, we presumably make it with some feeling; the positivists are plainly right in saying that such remarks do usually express feeling. But suppose that a week later we revert to the incident in thought and make our statement again. And suppose that the circumstances have now so changed that the feeling with which we made the remark in the first place has faded. The pathetic evidence is no longer before us; and we are now so fatigued in body and mind that the feeling is, as we say, quite dead. In these circumstances, since what was expressed by the remark when first made is, on the theory before us, simply absent, the remark now expresses nothing. It is as empty as the word "Hurrah" would be when there was no enthusiasm behind it. And this seems to me untrue. When we repeat the remark that such suffering was a bad thing, the feeling with which we made it last week may be at or near the vanishing point, but if we were asked whether we meant to say what we did before, we should certainly answer Yes. We should say that we made our point with feeling the first time and little or no feeling the second time, but that it was the same point we were making. And if we can see that what we meant to say remains the same, while the feeling varies from intensity to near zero, it is not the feeling that we primarily meant to express.

I come now to a fourth consideration. We all believe that toward acts or effects of a certain kind one attitude is fitting and another not; but on the theory before us such a belief would not make sense. Broad and Ross have lately contended that this fitness is one of the main facts of ethics, and I suspect they are right. But this is not exactly my point. My point is this: whether there is such fitness or not, we all assume that there is, and if we do, we express in moral judgments more than the subjectivists say we do. Let me illustrate.

In his novel *The House of the Dead*, Dostoevsky tells of his experiences in a Siberian prison camp. Whatever the unhappy inmates of such camps are like today, Dostoevsky's companions were about as grim a lot as can be imagined. "I have heard stories," he writes, "of the most terrible, the most unnatural actions, of the most monstrous murders, told with the most spontaneous, childishly merry laughter." Most of us would say that in this delight at the killing of others or the causing of suffering there is something very unfitting. If we were asked why we thought so, we should say that these things involve great evil and are wrong, and that to take delight in what is evil or wrong is plainly unfitting. Now on the subjectivist view, this answer is ruled out. For before someone takes up an attitude toward death, suffering, or their infliction, they have no moral quality at all. There is therefore nothing about them to which an attitude of approval or condemnation could be fitting. They are in themselves neutral, and, so far as they get a moral quality, they get it only through being invested with it by the attitude of the onlooker. But if that is true, why is any attitude more fitting than any other? Would applause, for example, be fitting if, apart from the applause, there was nothing good to applaud? Would condemnation be fitting if, independently of the condemnation, there were nothing bad to condemn? In such a case, any attitude would be as fitting or unfitting as any other, which means that the notion of fitness has lost all point.

Indeed we are forced to go much farther. If goodness and badness lie in attitudes only and are brought into being by them, those men who greeted death and misery with childishly merry laughter are taking the only sensible line. If there is nothing evil in these things, if they get their moral complexion only from our feeling about them, why shouldn't they be greeted with a cheer? To greet them with repulsion would turn what before was neutral into something bad; it would needlessly bring badness into the world; and even on subjectivist assumptions that does not seem very bright. On the other hand, to greet them with delight would convert what before was neutral into something good; it would bring goodness into the world. If I have murdered a man and wish to remove the stain, the way is clear. It is to cry, "Hurrah for murder."

What is the subjectivist to reply? I can only guess. He may point out that the inflicting of death is *not* really neutral before the onlooker takes his attitude, for the man who inflicted the death no doubt himself took an attitude, and thus the act had a moral quality derived from this. But that makes the case more incredible still, for the man who did the act presumably approved

it, and if so it was good in the only sense in which anything is good, and then our conviction that the laughter is unfit is more unaccountable still. It may be replied that the victim, too, had his attitude and that since this was unfavorable, the act was not unqualifiedly good. But the answer is plain. Let the killer be expert at his job; let him dispatch his victim instantly before he has time to take an attitude, and then gloat about his perfect crime without ever telling anyone. Then, so far as I can see, his act will be good without any qualification. It would become bad only if someone found out about it and disliked it. And that would be a curiously irrational procedure, since the man's approving of his own killing is in itself just as neutral as the killing that it approves. Why then should anyone dislike it?

It may be replied that we can defend our dislike on this ground that, if the approval of killing were to go unchecked and spread, most men would have to live in insecurity and fear, and these things are undesirable. But surely this reply is not open; these things are not, on the theory, undesirable, for nothing is; in themselves they are neutral. Why then should I disapprove men's living in this state? The answer may come that if other men live in insecurity and fear, I shall in time be infected myself. But even in my own insecurity and fear there is, on the theory before us, nothing bad whatever, and therefore, if I disapprove them, it is without a shadow of ground and with no more fitness in my attitude than if I cordially cheered them. The theory thus conflicts with our judgments of fitness all along the line.

I come now to a fifth and final difficulty with the theory. It makes mistakes about values impossible. There is a whole nest of interconnected criticisms here, some of which have been made so often that I shall not develop them again, such as that I can never agree or disagree in opinion with anyone else about an ethical matter, and that in these matters I can never be inconsistent with others or with myself. I am not at all content with the sort of analysis which says that the only contradictions in such cases have regard to facts and that contradictions about value are only differences of feeling. I think that if anyone tells me that having a bicuspid out without an anaesthetic is not a bad experience and I say it is a very nasty experience indeed, I am differing with him in opinion, and differing about the degree of badness of the experience. But without pressing this further, let me apply the argument in what is perhaps a fresh direction.

There is an old and merciful distinction that moralists have made for many centuries about conduct – the distinction between what is subjectively and what is objectively right. They have said that in any given situation there is some act which, in view of all the circumstances, would be the best act to do; and this is what would be objectively right. The notion of an objectively right act is the ground of our notion of duty; our duty is always to find and do this act if we can. But of course we often don't find it. We often hit upon and do acts that we think are the right ones, but we are mistaken; and then our act is only subjectively right. Between these two acts the disparity may be continual; Professor Prichard suggested that probably few of us in the course of our lives ever succeed in doing *the* right act.

Now so far as I can see, the new subjectivism would abolish this difference at a stroke. Let us take a case. A boy abuses his small brother. We should commonly say, "That is wrong, but perhaps he doesn't know any better. By reason of bad teaching and a feeble imagination, he may see nothing wrong in what he is doing, and may even be proud of it. If so, his act may be subjectively right, though it is miles away from what is objectively right." What concerns me about the new subjectivism is that it prohibits this distinction. If the boy feels this way about his act, then it is right in the only sense in which anything is right. The notion of an objective right lying beyond what he has discovered, and which he ought to seek and do is meaningless. There might, to be sure, be an act that would more generally arouse favorable feelings in others, but that would not make it right for him unless he thought of it and approved it, which he doesn't. Even if he did think of it, it would not be obligatory for him to feel about it in any particular way, since there is nothing in any act, as we have seen, which would make any feeling more suitable than any other.

Now if there is no such thing as an objectively right act, what becomes of the idea of duty? I have suggested that the idea of duty rests on the idea of such an act, since it is always our duty to find that act and do it if we can. But if whatever we feel approval for at the time is right, what is the point of doubting and searching further? Like the little girl in Boston who was asked if she would like to travel, we can answer, "Why should I travel when I'm already there?" If I am reconciled in feeling to my present act, no act I could discover by reflection could be better, and therefore why reflect or seek at all? Such a view seems to me to break the mainspring of duty, to destroy the motive for self-improvement, and to remove the ground for self-criticism. It may be replied that by further reflection I can find an act that would satisfy my feelings more widely than the present one, and that this is the act I should seek. But this reply means either that such general satisfaction is objectively better, which would contradict the theory, or else that, if at the time I don't feel it better, it isn't better, in which case I have no motive for seeking it. When certain self-righteous persons took an inflexible line with Oliver Cromwell, his very Cromwellian reply was, "Bethink ye, gentlemen, by the bowels of Christ, that ye may be mistaken." It was good advice. I hope nobody will take from me the privilege of finding myself mistaken. I should be sorry to think that the self of thirty years ago was as far along the path as the self of today, merely because he was a smug young jackanapes, or even that the paragon of today has as little room for improvement as would be allowed by his myopic complacency.

One final remark. The great problems of the day are international problems. Has the new subjectivism any bearing upon these problems? I think it has, and a somewhat sinister bearing. I would not suggest, of course, that those who hold the theory are one whit less public-spirited than others; surely there are few who could call themselves citizens of the world with more right (if "rights" have meaning any longer) than Lord [Bertrand] Russell. But Lord Russell has confessed himself discontented with his ethical theory, and in view of his breadth of concern, one cannot wonder. For its general acceptance would, so far as one can see, be an international disaster. The assumption behind the old League and the new United Nations was that there is such a thing as right and wrong in the conduct of a nation, a right and wrong that do not depend on how it happens to feel at the time. It is implied, for example, that when Japan invaded Manchuria in 1931 she might be wrong, and that by discussion and argument she might be shown to be wrong. It was implied that when the Nazis invaded Poland they might be wrong, even though German public sentiment overwhelmingly approved it. On the theory before us, it would be meaningless to call these nations mistaken; if they felt approval for what they did, then it was right with as complete a justification as could be supplied for the disapproval felt by the rest of the world. In the present tension between Russia and ourselves [the USA] over eastern Europe, it is nonsense to speak of the right or rational course for either of us to take; if with all the facts before the two parties, each feels approval for its own course, both attitudes are equally justified or unjustified; neither is mistaken; there is no common reason to which they can take an appeal; there are no principles by which an international court could pronounce on the matter, nor would there be any obligation to obey the pronouncement if it were made. This cuts the ground from under any attempt to establish one's case as right or anyone else's case as wrong. So if our friends the subjectivists still hold their theory after I have applied my little ruler to their knuckles, which of course they will, I have but one request to make of them: Don't advertise it to the people in the Kremlin.

4   How to Derive "Ought" from "Is"

John R. Searle

I

It is often said that one cannot derive an 'ought' from an 'is'. This thesis, which comes from a famous passage in Hume's *Treatise*, while not as clear as it might be, is at least clear in broad outline: there is a class of statements of fact which is logically distinct from a class of statements of value. No set of statements of fact by themselves entails any statement of value. Put in more contemporary terminology, no set of *descriptive* statements can entail an *evaluative* statement without the addition of at least one evaluative premise. To believe otherwise is to commit what has been called the naturalistic fallacy.

From *Philosophical Review*, vol. 73 (1964), pp. 43–58. Reprinted with permission.

I shall attempt to demonstrate a counter-example to this thesis.[1] It is not of course to be supposed that a single counter-example can refute a philosophical thesis, but in the present instance if we can present a plausible counter-example and can in addition give some account or explanation of how and why it is a counter-example, and if we can further offer a theory to back up our counter-example – a theory which will generate an indefinite number of counter-examples – we may at the very least cast considerable light on the original thesis; and possibly, if we can do all these things, we may even incline ourselves to the view that the scope of that thesis was more restricted than we had originally supposed. A counter-example must proceed by taking a statement or statements which any proponent of the thesis would grant were purely factual or 'descriptive' (they need not actually contain the word 'is') and show how they are logically related to a statement which a proponent of the thesis would regard as clearly 'evaluative'. (In the present instance it will contain an 'ought'.)[2]

Consider the following series of statements:

1. Jones uttered the words 'I hereby promise to pay you, Smith, five dollars.'
2. Jones promised to pay Smith five dollars.
3. Jones placed himself under (undertook) an obligation to pay Smith five dollars.
4. Jones is under an obligation to pay Smith five dollars.
5. Jones ought to pay Smith five dollars.

I shall argue concerning this list that the relation between any statement and its successor, while not in every case one of 'entailment', is none the less not just a contingent relation; and the additional statements necessary to make the relationship one of entailment do not need to involve any evaluative statements, moral principles, or anything of the sort.

Let us begin. How is (1) related to (2)? In certain circumstances, uttering the words in quotation marks in (1) is the act of making a promise. And it is a part of or a consequence of the meaning of the words in (1) that in those circumstances uttering them is promising. 'I hereby promise' is a paradigm device in English for performing the act described in (2), promising.

Let us state this fact about English usage in the form of an extra premise:

(1a)   Under certain conditions C anyone who utters the words (sentence) 'I hereby promise to pay you, Smith, five dollars' promises to pay Smith five dollars.

What sorts of things are involved under the rubric 'conditions C'? What is involved will be all those conditions, those states of affairs, which are necessary and sufficient conditions for the utterance of the words (sentence) to constitute the successful performance of the act of promising. The conditions will include such things as that the speaker is in the presence of the hearer Smith,

they are both conscious, both speakers of English, speaking seriously. The speaker knows what he is doing, is not under the influence of drugs, not hypnotized or acting in a play, not telling a joke or reporting an event, and so forth. This list will no doubt be somewhat indefinite because the boundaries of the concept of a promise, like the boundaries of most concepts in a natural language, are a bit loose.[3] But one thing is clear; however loose the boundaries may be, and however difficult it may be to decide marginal cases, the conditions under which a man who utters 'I hereby promise' can correctly be said to have made a promise are straightforwardly empirical conditions.

So let us add as an extra premise the empirical assumption that these conditions obtain.

(1b)   Conditions C obtain.

From (1), (1a) and (1b) we derive (2). The argument is of the form: If C then (if U then P): C for conditions, U for utterance, P for promise. Adding the premises U and C to this hypothetical we derive (2). And as far as I can see, no moral premises are lurking in the logical woodpile. More needs to be said about the relation of (1) to (2), but I reserve that for later.

What is the relation between (2) and (3)? I take it that promising is, by definition, an act of placing oneself under an obligation. No analysis of the concept of promising will be complete which does not include the feature of the promiser placing himself under or undertaking or accepting or recognizing an obligation to the promisee, to perform some future course of action, normally for the benefit of the promisee. One may be tempted to think that promising can be analysed in terms of creating expectations in one's hearers, or some such, but a little reflection will show that the crucial distinction between statements of intention on the one hand and promises on the other lies in the nature and degree of commitment or obligation undertaken in promising.

I am therefore inclined to say that (2) entails (3) straight off, but I can have no objection if anyone wishes to add – for the purpose of formal neatness – the tautological premise:

(2a) All promises are acts of placing oneself under (undertaking) an obligation to do the thing promised.

How is (3) related to (4)? If one has placed oneself under an obligation, then, other things being equal, one is under an obligation. That I take it also is a tautology. Of course it is possible for all sorts of things to happen which will release one from obligations one has undertaken and hence the need for the *ceteris paribus* rider. To get an entailment between (3) and (4) we therefore need a qualifying statement to the effect that:

(3a) Other things are equal.

Formalists, as in the move from (2) to (3), may wish to add the tautological premise:

(3b) All those who place themselves under an obligation are, other things being equal, under an obligation.

The move from (3) to (4) is thus of the same form as the move from (1) to (2): If E then (if PUO then UO): E for other things are equal, PUO for place under obligation and UO for under obligation. Adding the two premises E and PUO we derive UO.

Is (3a), the *ceteris paribus* clause, a concealed evaluative premise? It certainly looks as if it might be, especially in the formulation I have given it, but I think we can show that, though questions about whether other things are equal frequently involve evaluative considerations, it is not logically necessary that they should in every case. I shall postpone discussion of this until after the next step.

What is the relation between (4) and (5)? Analogous to the tautology which explicates the relation of (3) and (4) there is here the tautology that, other things being equal, one ought to do what one is under an obligation to do. And here, just as in the previous case, we need some premise of the form:

(4a) Other things are equal.

We need the *ceteris paribus* clause to eliminate the possibility that something extraneous to the relation of 'obligation' to 'ought' might interfere.[4] Here, as in the previous two steps, we eliminate the appearance of enthymeme by pointing out that the apparently suppressed premise is tautological and hence, though formally neat, it is redundant. If, however, we wish to state it formally, this argument is of the same form as the move from (3) to (4): If E then (if UO then O); E for other things are equal, UO for under obligation, O for ought. Adding the premises E and UO we derive O.

Now a word about the phrase 'other things being equal' and how it functions in my attempted derivation. This topic and the closely related topic of defeasibility are extremely difficult and I shall not try to do more than justify my claim that the satisfaction of the condition does not necessarily involve anything evaluative. The force of the expression 'other things being equal' in the present instance is roughly this. Unless we have some reason (that is, unless we are actually prepared to give some reason) for supposing the obligation is void (step 4) or the agent ought not to keep the promise (step 5), then the obligation holds and he ought to keep the promise. It is not part of the force of the phrase 'other things being equal' that in order to satisfy it we need to establish a universal negative proposition to the effect that no reason could ever be given by anyone for supposing the agent is not under an obligation or ought not to keep the promise. That would be impossible and would render the phrase useless. It is sufficient to satisfy the condition that no reason to the contrary can in fact be given.

If a reason is given for supposing the obligation is void or that the promiser ought not to keep the promise, then characteristically a situation calling for evaluation arises. Suppose, for example, we consider a promised act wrong, but we grant that the promiser did undertake an obligation. Ought he to keep the promise? There is no established procedure for objectively deciding such cases in advance, and an evaluation (if that is really the right word) is in order. But unless we have some reason to the contrary, the *ceteris paribus* condition is satisfied, no evaluation is necessary, and the question whether he ought to do it is settled by saying 'he promised.' It is always an open possibility that we may have to make an evaluation in order to derive 'he ought' from 'he promised', for we may have to evaluate a counter-argument. But an evaluation is not logically necessary in every case, for there may as a matter of fact be no counter-arguments. I am therefore inclined to think that there is nothing necessarily evaluative about the *ceteris paribus* condition, even though deciding whether it is satisfied will frequently involve evaluations.

But suppose I am wrong about this: would that salvage the belief in an unbridgeable logical gulf between 'is' and 'ought'? I think not, for we can always rewrite my steps (4) and (5) so that they include the *ceteris paribus* clause as part of the conclusion. Thus from our premises we would then have derived 'Other things being equal Jones ought to pay Smith five dollars', and that would still be sufficient to refute the tradition, for we would still have shown a relation of entailment between descriptive and evaluative statements. It was not the fact that extenuating circumstances can void obligations that drove philosophers to the naturalistic fallacy; it was rather a theory of language, as we shall see later on.

We have thus derived (in as strict a sense of 'derive' as natural languages admit of) an 'ought' from an 'is'. And the extra premises which were needed to make the derivation work were in no case moral or evaluative in nature. They consisted of empirical assumptions, tautologies and descriptions of word usage. It must be pointed out also that the 'ought' is a 'categorical' not a 'hypothetical' ought. (5) does not say that Jones ought to pay up if he wants such and such. It says he ought to pay up, period. Note also that the steps of the derivation are carried on in the third person. We are not concluding 'I ought' from 'I said "I promise"', but 'he ought' from 'he said "I promise"'.

The proof unfolds the connection between the utterance of certain words and the speech act of promising and then in turn unfolds promising into obligation and moves from obligation to

'ought'. The step from (1) to (2) is radically different from the others and requires special comment. In (1) we construe 'I hereby promise . . .' as an English phrase having a certain meaning. It is a consequence of that meaning that the utterance of that phrase under certain conditions is the act of promising. Thus by presenting the quoted expressions in (1) and by describing their use in (1a) we have as it were already invoked the institution of promising. We might have started with an even more ground-floor premise than (1) by saying:

(1b)   Jones uttered the phonetic sequence:/
        aiˈhirbaiˈpramisˈtəpeiˈyuˈsmiθˈfaivˈdal
        ərz/

We would then have needed extra empirical premises stating that this phonetic sequence was associated in certain ways with certain meaningful units relative to certain dialects.

The moves from (2) to (5) are relatively easy. We rely on definitional connections between 'promise', 'obligate', and 'ought', and the only problem which arises is that obligations can be overridden or removed in a variety of ways and we need to take account of that fact. We solve our difficulty by adding further premises to the effect that there are no contrary considerations, that other things are equal.

II

In this section I intend to discuss three possible objections to the derivation.

First objection

Since the first premise is descriptive and the conclusion evaluative, there must be a concealed evaluative premise in the description of the conditions in (2b).

So far, this argument merely begs the question by assuming the logical gulf between descriptive and evaluative which the derivation is designed to challenge. To make the objection stick, the defender of the distinction would have to show how exactly (2b) must contain an evaluative premise and what sort of premise it might be. Uttering certain words in certain conditions just *is* promising and the description of these conditions needs no evaluative element. The essential thing is that in the transition from (1) to (2) we move from the specification of a certain utterance of words to the specification of a certain speech act. The move is achieved because the speech act is a conventional act; and the utterance of words, according to the conventions, constitutes the performance of just that speech act.

A variant of this first objection is to say: all you have shown is that 'promise' is an evaluative, not a descriptive, concept. But this objection again begs the question and in the end will prove disastrous to the original distinction between descriptive and evaluative. For that a man uttered certain words and that these words have the meaning they do are surely objective facts. And if the statement of these two objective facts plus a description of the conditions of the utterance is sufficient to entail the statement (2) which the objector alleges to be an evaluative statement (Jones promised to pay Smith five dollars), then an evaluative conclusion is derived from descriptive premises without even going through steps (3), (4) and (5).

Second objection

Ultimately the derivation rests on the principle that one ought to keep one's promises and that is a moral principle, hence evaluative.

I don't know whether 'one ought to keep one's promises' is a 'moral' principle, but whether or not it is, it is also tautological; for it is nothing more than a derivation from the two tautologies:

All promises are (create, are undertakings of, are acceptances of) obligations,

and

One ought to keep (fulfil) one's obligations.

What needs to be explained is why so many philosophers have failed to see the tautological character of this principle. Three things I think have concealed its character from them.

The first is a failure to distinguish external questions about the institution of promising from internal questions asked within the framework of an institution. The questions 'Why do we have such an institution as promising?' and 'Ought we to have such institutionalized forms of obligation as promising?' are external questions asked about and not within the institution of promising. And the question 'Ought one to keep one's promises?' can be confused with or can be taken as (and I think has often been taken as) an external question roughly expressible as 'Ought one to accept the institution of promising?' But taken literally, as an internal question, as a question about promises and not about the institution of promising, the question 'Ought one to keep one's promises?' is as empty as the question 'Are triangles three-sided?' To recognize something as a promise is to grant that, other things being equal, it ought to be kept.

A second fact which has clouded the issue is this. There are many situations, both real and imaginable, where one ought not to keep a promise, where the obligation to keep a promise is overridden by some further considerations, and it was for this reason that we needed those clumsy *ceteris paribus* clauses in our derivation. But the fact that obligations can be overridden does not show that there were no obligations in the first place. On the contrary. And these original obligations are all that is needed to make the proof work.

Yet a third factor is the following. Many philosophers still fail to realize the full force of saying that 'I hereby promise' is a performative expression. In uttering it one performs but does not describe the act of promising. Once promising is seen as a speech act of a kind different from describing, then it is easier to see that one of the features of the act is the undertaking of an obligation. But if one thinks the utterance of 'I promise' or 'I hereby promise' is a peculiar kind of description – for example, of one's mental state – then the relation between promising and obligation is going to seem very mysterious.

Third objection

The derivation uses only a factual or inverted-commas sense of the evaluative terms employed. For example, an anthropologist observing the behaviour and attitudes of the Anglo-Saxons might well go through these derivations, but nothing evaluative would be included. Thus step (2) is equivalent to 'He did what they call promising' and step (5) to 'According to them he ought to pay Smith five dollars.' But since all of the steps (2) to (5) are in *oratio obliqua,* and hence disguised statements of fact, the fact-value distinction remains unaffected.

This objection fails to damage the derivation, for what it says is only that the steps *can* be reconstrued as in *oratio obliqua,* that we can construe them as a series of external statements, that we can construct a parallel (or at any rate related) proof about reported speech. But what I am arguing is that, taken quite literally, without any *oratio obliqua* additions or interpretations, the derivation is valid. That one can construct a similar argument which would fail to refute the fact-value distinction does not show that this proof fails to refute it. Indeed it is irrelevant.

Notes

Earlier versions of this paper were read before the Stanford Philosophy Colloquium and the Pacific Division of the American Philosophical Association. I am indebted to many people for helpful comments and criticisms, especially Hans Herzberger, Arnold Kaufmann, Benson Mates, A. I. Melden and Dagmar Searle.

1 In its modern version. I shall not be concerned with Hume's treatment of the problem.
2 If this enterprise succeeds, we shall have bridged the gap between 'evaluative' and 'descriptive' and consequently have demonstrated a weakness in this very terminology. At present, however, my strategy is to play along with the terminology, pretending that the notions of evaluative and descriptive are fairly clear. At the end of the paper I shall state in what respects I think they embody a muddle.
3 In addition the concept of a promise is a member of a class of concepts which suffer from looseness of a peculiar kind, viz. defeasibility. Cf. H. L. A. Hart, 'The Ascription of Responsibility and Rights', *Logic and Language*, first series, ed. A. Flew (Oxford, 1951).
4 The *ceteris paribus* clause in this step excludes somewhat different sorts of cases from those excluded in the previous step. In general we say, 'He undertook an obligation, but none the less he is not (now) under an obligation when the obligation has been *removed*, e.g. if the promisee says, 'I release you from your obligation.' But we say, 'He is under an obligation, but none the less ought not to fulfil it' in cases where the obligation is *overridden* by some other consideration, e.g. a prior obligation.

---

5   On Not Deriving "Ought" from "Is"

Antony Flew

. . .

The word nevertheless seems to have gone round that the idea that there is a radical difference between *ought* and *is* is old hat, something which

From *Analysis*, vol. 25 (1964), pp. 25–32. Reprinted with permission.

though still perhaps cherished by out-group backwoodsmen has long since been seen through and discarded by all with-it mainstream philosophers. For instance, in a penetrating article on 'Do illocutionary forces exist?'[1] Mr L. Jonathan Cohen offers some provocative asides: 'the statement-evaluation dichotomy, whatever it may be, is as erroneous on my view as on Austin's'; and 'Indeed there is a case for saying that Austin's recommendation about the word "good" is itself a hangover from the fact-value dichotomy.' Cohen gives no hint as to where and how this dichotomy was so decisively liquidated. But a recent paper by Mr John R. Searle, on 'How to derive "ought" from "is"' can perhaps be seen as an attempt to plug the gap. Searle's stated aim is to show that the Naturalistic Fallacy is not a fallacy, and he gives many signs of thinking of his aspirations in Austinian terms. My object is to show that Searle is entirely unsuccessful, and to suggest that anyone who hopes to succeed where he has failed will have to find other and more powerful arguments.

2. The first point to remark about Searle's article is that he chooses to start from his own characterization of what the Naturalistic Fallacy is supposed to consist in; and that he neither quotes nor gives precise references to any statements by the philosophers with whom he wishes to disagree. His characterization runs:

> It is often said that one cannot derive an 'ought' from an 'is'. This thesis, which comes from a famous passage in Hume's *Treatise*, while not as clear as it might be, is at least clear in broad outline: there is a class of statements of fact which is logically distinct from a class of statements of value. No set of statements of fact by themselves entails any statement of value. Put in more contemporary terminology, no set of *descriptive* statements can entail an *evaluative* statement without the addition of at least one evaluative premise. To believe otherwise is to commit . . . the naturalistic fallacy.   (italics here and always as in original)

Let us consider alongside this paragraph from Searle some sentences written by a contemporary protagonist of the view which Searle is supposed to be challenging. These quotations come from K. R. Popper and – significantly – they come from *The Open Society* (1945):

> The breakdown of magic tribalism is closely connected with the realization that taboos are different in various tribes, that they are imposed and enforced by man, and that they may be broken without unpleasant repercussions if one can only escape the sanctions imposed by one's fellow-men. . . . These experiences may lead to a conscious differentiation between the man-enforced normative laws or conventions, and the natural regularities which are beyond his power. . . . In spite of the fact that this position was reached a long time ago by the Sophist Protagoras . . . it is still so little understood that it seems necessary to explain it in some detail. . . . It is we who impose our standards upon nature, and who introduce in this way morals into the natural world, in spite of the fact that we are part of this world. . . . It is important for the understanding of this attitude to realize that decisions can never be derived from facts (or statements of facts), although they pertain to facts. The decision, for instance to oppose slavery does not depend upon the fact that all men are born free and equal, and no man is born in chains . . . even if they were born in chains, many of us might demand the removal of these chains. . . . The making of a decision, the adoption of a standard, is a fact. But the norm which has been adopted, is not. That most people agree with the norm 'Thou shalt not steal' is a sociological fact. But the norm 'Thou shalt not steal' is not a fact; and it can never be inferred from sentences describing facts. . . . *It is impossible to derive a sentence stating a norm or a decision from a sentence stating a fact;* this is only another way of saying that it is impossible to derive norms or decisions from facts.   (vol. I, pp. 50–3)

Popper's account, even in this abbreviated form, is of course much fuller than that given by Searle; and, partly for that reason, it says or suggests many things which are not comprised in Searle's short paragraph. It presents the idea of the Naturalistic Fallacy as involved in the clash of world-outlooks and personal commitments; and it is governed throughout by the notion that 'we are free to form our own moral opinions in a much stronger sense than we are free to form our own opinions as to what the facts are'.[2] But the most relevant and important difference is that Popper at least suggests, what is true, that the fundamental discrimination in terms of which the Naturalistic Fallacy is being characterized is not, and does not have to be thought to be, a clearcut feature of all actual discourse. It is not something which you cannot fail to observe everywhere as already there and given, if once you have learnt what to look for. There is, rather, a differentiation which has to be made and insisted upon; and the distinction is one the development of which may go against the grain of set habits and powerful inclinations. Our situation in this case is not at all like that represented in the second chapter of the book of *Genesis*, where God presents to Adam the beasts of the field and the fowl of the air, leaving it to him merely to supply names for each natural kind.

Searle's account of the opposing position seems to suggest, what his later criticism appears to be assuming, that its misguided spokesmen must be committed to the notion: that an *is/ought* dichotomy is something which the alert natural historian of utterances could not fail to notice, as somehow already given; and that no utterances can either combine, or be ambiguous as between, these two sorts of claim. Yet when we turn to Popper, and allow him to speak for himself, we find in his account nothing at all to suggest any commitment to the erroneous ideas: that all the utterances which are actually made must already be clearly and unambiguously either statements of fact or expressions of value; or that every actual utterance is either purely a statement of fact or purely normative. What Popper emphasizes is, rather, the epoch-marking importance of the development of this sort of distinction, the great need to insist upon it, and the difficulty of appreciating fully what it does and what it does not imply.

It is perhaps possible that Searle here, like so many others elsewhere, has been misled by Hume's irony; notwithstanding that Searle himself disclaims concern with 'Hume's treatment of the problem'. For Hume does indeed write as if he was quite modestly claiming only to have noticed, and to have become seized by the vast importance of, a distinction which, however unwittingly, everyone was always and systematically making already:[3]

I cannot forbear adding to these reasonings an observation, which may, perhaps, be found of some importance. In every system of morality, which I have hitherto met with, I have always remarked, that the author proceeds for some time in the ordinary way of reasoning, and establishes the being of a God, or makes observations concerning human affairs; when of a sudden I am surprised to find, that instead of the usual copulations of propositions *is*, and *is not*, I meet with no proposition that is not connected with an *ought*, or an *ought not*.

3.   After this somewhat protracted introduction, designed to refresh memories about what is and is not involved in the position which Searle is supposed to be attacking, we can now at last turn to his arguments. He works with the example of promising: 'The proof unfolds the connection between the utterance of certain words and the speech act of promising and then in turn unfolds promising into obligation and moves from obligation to "ought".' The idea is to start with a purely descriptive premise such as 'Jones uttered the words "I hereby promise to pay you, Smith, five dollars"', or that Jones uttered the corresponding phonetic sequence, and to proceed by a series of deductive moves to the purely normative conclusion 'Jones ought to pay Smith five dollars'. Considerable elaboration is necessary, and is provided, in the attempt to deal with the complications arising: because the utterance of such words or sounds will not always rate as a making of the promise; and because the prima facie obligation to keep a promise can be nullified or overridden.

It will, in the light of what has been said in section 2, be sufficiently obvious what sort of moves the critic must make if he hopes to drive a wedge into such a proposed proof. He has to distinguish normative and descriptive elements in the meaning of words like *promise*; and to insist that, however willing we may be to accept the package deal in this particular uncontentious case of promising, it is nevertheless still not possible to deduce the normative from the descriptive part of the combination. The best place to insert the wedge in Searle's argument seems to be where he maintains: 'one thing is clear; however loose the boundaries may be, and however difficult it may be to decide marginal cases, the conditions under which a man who utters 'I hereby promise' can correctly be said to have made a promise are straightforwardly empirical conditions'. The weakness becomes glaring if we summon for comparison some obnoxious contentions of the same form. Terms such as *nigger* or *Jew-boy*, *apostate* or *infidel*, *colonialist* or *kulak* no doubt carry, at least when employed in certain circles, both normative and descriptive meanings; and, presumably, the descriptive element of that meaning can correctly be said to apply whenever the appropriate 'straightforwardly empirical conditions' are satisfied. But in these parallel cases most of us, I imagine, would be careful to use one of the several linguistic devices for indicating that we do not commit ourselves to the norms involved, or that we positively repudiate them. Thus, to revert to Searle's example, one could, without any logical impropriety, say of the man who had in suitable circumstances uttered the words 'I hereby promise . . .' that he had done what is called (by those who accept the social institution of promising) promising. The oddity of this non-committal piece of pure description would lie simply in the perversity of suggesting a policy of non-involvement in an institution which is surely essential to any tolerable human social life.

4. It remains to ask either why these moves do not impinge on Searle as considerable objections or how he thinks to dispose of them. We have already in section 2 offered suggestions bearing on these questions. But more light is to be found by considering in the second part of his article his discussion of 'three possible objections to the derivation'.

(a) The first of these objections consists in simply asserting that 'Since the first premise is descriptive and the conclusion evaluative, there must be a concealed evaluative premise in the description of the conditions. . . .' To which Searle replies that as it stands this objection just begs the question: it requires to be supplemented with some account of the precise location and nature of the concealed evaluative premise. So far, so unexceptionable. The crunch comes when he continues: 'Uttering certain words in certain conditions just *is* promising and the description

of these conditions needs no evaluative element.' For, as we have been urging in section 3, the normative element enters: not with the neutral description of the conditions in which those who accept the social institution of promise-making and promise-keeping would say that someone had made what they call a promise; but at the moment when, by using the word *promise* without reservation, we commit ourselves to that institution.

(b) The second objection considered runs: 'Ultimately the derivation rests on the principle that one ought to keep one's promises and that is a moral principle, hence evaluative.' To this Searle responds that, whether or not this is a moral principle, 'it is also tautological'. He then proceeds to offer three suggestions to explain 'why so many philosophers have failed to see the tautological character of this principle'. This is, perhaps, to go rather too fast. For the sentence 'One ought to keep one's promises' is not in itself and unequivocally either tautological or not. It could without too much strain be given either tautological or substantial or even equivocal employments. If the user is prepared to accept that the absence of obligation is a sufficient reason for withdrawing the word *promise*, then the employment is clearly tautological. But if he is to be taken to be referring to certain specific descriptive conditions, and maintaining that, granted those, certain specific things ought to be done, then, surely, the employment is substantial. And if he is insisting that, granted these specific descriptive conditions, then necessarily those things ought to be done; then he would seem to be equivocating between a substantial and a tautological employment.

The first of Searle's suggestions is that some of his opponents have failed 'to distinguish external questions about the institution of promising from internal questions asked within the framework of the institution'. No doubt some have: though it would be slightly surprising and wholly deplorable to find that many philosophers in an Humean tradition had neglected a distinction of a kind for which one of the classical sources is to be found in the third appendix of the second *Inquiry*. Even so this particular charge rings very badly in the present context. For, as we were urging in section 3, the weakness of Searle's attempted derivation lies precisely in the refusal to allow that the acceptance of a social institution must come between any statement of the purely descriptive conditions for saying that a promise was made, and the drawing of the normative conclusion that something ought to be done.

A more subtle version of the same fault can be seen in Searle's reply to a variant of his first proposed objection, which would protest: 'all you have shown is that "promise" is an evaluative, not a descriptive, concept.' This variant, he claims, 'in the end will prove disastrous to the original distinction between descriptive and evaluative. For that a man uttered certain words and that these words have the meaning that they do are surely objective facts. And if the statement of these two objective facts plus a description of the conditions of the utterance is sufficient to entail the statement . . . which the objector alleges to be an evaluative statement . . . then an evaluative conclusion is derived from descriptive premises . . .'. But here again it is both necessary and decisive to insist on distinguishing: between a detached report on the meanings which some social group gives to certain value words; and the unreserved employment of those words by an engaged participant. For it is between the former and the latter that there comes exactly that commitment to the incapsulated values which alone warrants us to draw the normative conclusions.

Searle's other two suggestions both refer to peculiarities which make his chosen example especially tricky to handle: the second notices the difficulties which arise because the prima facie obligation to keep a promise made may sometimes properly be overridden by other claims: and the third takes cognizance of the fact that the first person present tense 'I promise' is performative. It is not perhaps altogether clear why failure to take the measure of this insight – for which again a classical source can be found in Hume[4] – is supposed to encourage the idea that 'One ought to keep one's promises' is not tautological. What Searle says is: 'If one thinks the utterance of "I promise" or "I hereby promise" is a peculiar kind of description . . . then the relation between promising and obligation is going to seem very mysterious.' Certainly if one thinks that, then there will be a mystery as to why the utterance of these words is construed, by anyone who accepts the institution of promising, as involving the incurring of an obligation. But this is no reason at all for saying that the same misguided person must also by the same token find something mysterious about the notion that, supposing that someone has promised, it follows necessarily that he is obliged.

This is a good occasion to say that where we have spoken of a descriptive element in the meaning of *promise*, we were, of course, intending to include only uses other than the first person present performative. Fortunately the complications connected with that use can for present purposes be largely ignored. For in Searle's candidate proof 'I promise' is mentioned, not used; and so our criticism insists that the normative premise is to be found at the point where the performance is characterized, unreservedly, as a promise.

(c) The third objection considered is that: 'The derivation uses only a factual or inverted-commas sense of the evaluative terms employed.' This discussion is the most interesting for us. It is here that Searle comes nearest to recognizing, and to trying to deal with, the rather obvious sort of criticism which we have been deploying. In formulating this objection Searle recognizes the distinction: between the employment of a term like *promise* in a detached anthropological description of a social practice; and the use of the same term, without reservation, by a committed participant. His reply is: 'This objection fails to damage the derivation, for what it says is only that the steps *can* be reconstrued as in *oratio obliqua*. . . . That one can construct a similar argument which would fail to refute the fact-value distinction does not show that this proof fails to refute it. Indeed it is irrelevant.'

This, of course, is true. And if all spokesmen for the opposition were such men of straw it would be a very easy matter to consign them to the garbage dump. What is so extraordinary is that, having apparently allowed the crucial distinction, Searle fails to notice the decisive objection: that his step from (1), 'Jones uttered the words "I hereby promise to pay you, Smith, five dollars"' to (2), 'Jones promised to pay Smith five dollars' is fallacious; unless, that is, we are supposed, as we are not, to construe (2) as being purely descriptive, as being, as it were, in *oratio obliqua*.

To explain Searle's oversight the only philosophically relevant suggestions we can offer are those indicated in section 2. Yet it really is extremely hard to believe that he is attributing to his opponents the assumptions: that all our discourse is already divided into elements which are either purely normative or exclusively descriptive; and that no legitimate expression could combine in its meaning both normative and descriptive components. For, though such misconceptions could conceivably be derived from a wooden and unsophisticated reading of some of those sentences in the *Treatise*, such a construction must at once make a mystery of any claim that attention to this distinction 'would subvert all the vulgar systems of morality'. This sort of thing

could scarcely even be thought – as quite clearly it has been thought by many of the most distinguished protagonists of the idea of the Naturalistic Fallacy – if what was at stake really was just a matter of noticing a division already clearly and universally obtaining; rather than, as of course it is, a matter of insisting on making discriminations where often there is every sort of combination and confusion. . . .

Notes

1 *Philosophical Quarterly*, 14 (1964).
2 R. M. Hare, *Freedom and Reason* (Oxford, 1963), p. 2. The same author's *The Language of Morals* (Oxford, 1952) is another excellent source for the sophisticated and flexible handling of the idea of the Naturalistic Fallacy; and Hare is, of course, perfectly well aware that the same terms and expressions may combine both descriptive and normative meanings – and hence that normative standards are incapsulated in certain uses of such terms.
3 D. Hume, *Treatise*, III. i. I.
4 *Treatise*, III. ii. 5, 'Of the obligation of promises'.

---

6   Moral Beliefs

Philippa Foot

I

To many people it seems that the most notable advance in moral philosophy during the past fifty years or so has been the refutation of naturalism; and they are a little shocked that at this late date such an issue should be reopened. It is easy to understand their attitude: given certain apparently unquestionable assumptions, it would be about as sensible to try to reintroduce naturalism as to try to square the circle. Those who see it like this have satisfied themselves that they know in advance that any naturalistic theory must have a catch in it somewhere, and are put out at having to waste more time exposing an old fallacy. This paper is an attempt to persuade them to look critically at the premises on which their arguments are based.

It would not be an exaggeration to say that the whole of moral philosophy, as it is now widely

From *Proceedings of the Aristotelian Society*, 59 (1958–9). Reprinted with permission. © The Aristotelian Society 1959.

taught, rests on a contrast between statements of fact and evaluations, which runs something like this: 'The truth or falsity of statements of fact is shown by means of evidence; and what counts as evidence is laid down in the meaning of the expressions occurring in the statement of fact. (For instance, the meaning of "round" and "flat" made Magellan's voyages evidence for the roundness rather than the flatness of the Earth; someone who went on questioning whether the evidence was evidence could eventually be shown to have made some linguistic mistake.) It follows that no two people can make the same statement and count completely different things as evidence; in the end one at least of them could be convicted of linguistic ignorance. It also follows that if a man is given good evidence for a factual conclusion he cannot just refuse to accept the conclusion on the ground that in his scheme of things this evidence is not evidence at all. With evaluations, however, it is different. An evaluation is not connected logically with the factual statements on which it is based. One man may say that a thing is good because of some fact about it; and another may refuse to take that fact as any evidence at all, for nothing is laid down in the meaning of "good" which connects it with one piece of "evidence" rather than another. It follows that a moral eccentric could argue to moral conclusions from quite idiosyncratic premises; he could say, for instance, that a man was a good man because he clasped and unclasped his hands, and never turned NNE after turning SSW. He could also reject someone else's evaluation simply by denying that his evidence was evidence at all.

'The fact about "good" which allows the eccentric still to use this term without falling into a morass of meaninglessness, is its "action-guiding" or "practical" function. This it retains; for like everyone else he considers himself bound to choose the things he calls "good" rather than those he calls "bad". Like the rest of the world he uses "good" in connection only with a "pro-attitude"; it is only that he has pro-attitudes to quite different things, and therefore calls them good.'

There are here two assumptions about 'evalu-

ations', which I will call assumption (1) and assumption (2).

Assumption (1) is that some individual may, without logical error, base his beliefs about matters of value entirely on premises which no one else would recognize as giving any evidence at all. Assumption (2) is that, given the kind of statement which other people regard as evidence for an evaluative conclusion, he may refuse to draw the conclusion because *this* does not count as evidence for *him*.

Let us consider assumption (1). We might say that this depends on the possibility of keeping the meaning of 'good' steady through all changes in the facts about anything which are to count in favour of its goodness. (I do not mean, of course, that a man can make changes as fast as he chooses; only that, whatever he has chosen, it will not be possible to rule him out of order.) But there is a better formulation, which cuts out trivial disputes about the meaning which 'good' happens to have in some section of the community. Let us say that the assumption is that the evaluative function of 'good' can remain constant through changes in the evaluative principle; on this ground it could be said that even if no one can call a man *good* because he clasps and unclasps his hand, he can commend him or express his *pro-attitude*, towards him, and if necessary can invent a new moral vocabulary to express his unusual moral code.

Those who hold such a theory will naturally add several qualifications. In the first place, most people now agree with Hare, against Stevenson, that such words as 'good' only apply to individual cases through the application of general principles, so that even the extreme moral eccentric must accept principles of commendation. In the second place 'commending', 'having a pro-attitude', and so on, are supposed to be connected with doing and choosing, so that it would be impossible to say, e.g. that a man was a good man only if he lived for a thousand years. The range of evaluation is supposed to be restricted to the range of possible action and choice. I am not here concerned to question these supposed restrictions on the use of evaluative terms, but only to argue that they are not enough.

The crucial question is this. Is it possible to extract from the meaning of words such as 'good' some element called 'evaluative meaning' which we can think of as externally related to its objects? Such an element would be represented, for instance, in the rule that when any action was 'commended' the speaker must hold himself bound to accept an imperative 'let me do these things'. This is externally related to its object because, within the limitation which we noticed earlier, to possible actions, it would make sense to think of anything as the subject of such 'commendation'. On this hypothesis a moral eccentric could be described as commending the clasping of hands as the action of a good man, and we should not have to look for some background to give this supposition sense. That is to say, on this hypothesis the clasping of hands could be commended without any explanation; it could be what those who hold such theories call 'an ultimate moral principle'.

I wish to say that this hypothesis is untenable, and that there is no describing the evaluative meaning of 'good', evaluation, commending, or anything of the sort, without fixing the object to which they are supposed to be attached. Without first laying hands on the proper object of such things as evaluation, we shall catch in our net either something quite different, such as accepting an order or making a resolution, or else nothing at all.

Before I consider this question, I shall first discuss some other mental attitudes and beliefs which have this internal relation to their object. By this I hope to clarify the concept of internal relation to an object, and incidentally, if my examples arouse resistance, but are eventually accepted, to show how easy it is to overlook an internal relation where it exists.

Consider, for instance, pride.

People are often surprised at the suggestion that there are limits to the things a man can be proud of, about which indeed he can feel pride. I do not know quite what account they want to give of pride; perhaps something to do with smiling and walking with a jaunty air, and holding an object up where other people can see it; or perhaps they think that pride is a kind of internal sensation, so that one might naturally beat one's breast and say 'pride is something I feel *here*'. The difficulties of the second view are well known; the logically private object cannot be what a name in the public language is the name of.[1] The first view is the more plausible, and it may seem reasonable to say that given certain behaviour a man can be described as showing that he is proud of something, whatever that something may be. In one sense this is true, and in another sense not. Given any description of an object, action, personal characteristic, etc., it is not possible to rule it out as an object of pride. Before we can do so we need to know what would be said about it by the man who is to be proud of it, or feels proud of it; but if he does not hold the right beliefs about it then whatever his attitude is it is not pride. Consider, for instance, the suggestion that someone might be proud of the sky or the sea: he looks at them and what he feels is *pride*, or he puffs out his chest and gestures with *pride* in their direction. This makes sense only if a special assumption is made about his beliefs, for instance, that he is under some crazy delusion and believes that he has saved the sky from falling, or the sea from drying up. The characteristic object of pride is something seen (a) as in some way a man's own, and (b) as some sort of achievement or advantage; without this object pride cannot be described. To see that the second condition is necessary, one should try supposing that a man happens to feel proud because he has laid one of his hands on the other, three times in an hour. Here again the supposition that it is pride that he feels will make perfectly good sense if a special background is filled in. Perhaps he is ill, and it is an achievement even to do this; perhaps this gesture has some religious or political significance, and he is a brave man who will so defy the gods or the rulers. But with no special background there can be no pride, not because no one could psychologically speaking feel pride in such a case, but because whatever he did feel could not logically be pride. Of course, people can see strange things as achievements, though not just anything, and they can identify themselves with remote ancestors, and relations, and neighbours, and even on occasions with Mankind. I do not wish to deny there are many far-fetched and comic examples of pride.

We could have chosen many other examples of mental attitudes which are internally related to their object in a similar way. For instance, fear is not just trembling, and running, and turning pale; without the thought of some menacing evil no amount of this will add up to fear. Nor could anyone be said to feel dismay about something he did not see as bad; if his thoughts about it were that it was altogether a good thing, he could not say that (oddly enough) what he felt about it was dismay. 'How odd, I feel dismayed when I ought to be pleased' is the prelude to a hunt for the adverse aspect of the thing, thought of as lurking behind the pleasant façade. But someone may object that pride and fear and dismay are feelings or emotions and therefore not a proper analogy for 'commendation', and there will be an advantage in considering a different kind of example. We could discuss, for instance, the belief that a certain thing is dangerous, and ask whether this could logically be held about anything whatsoever. Like 'this is good', 'this is dangerous' is an assertion, which we should naturally accept or reject by speaking of its truth or falsity; we seem to support such statements with evidence, and moreover there may seem to be a 'warning function' connected with the word 'dangerous' as there is supposed to be a 'commending function' connected with the word 'good'. For suppose that philosophers, puzzled about the property of dangerousness, decided that the word did not stand for a property at all, but was essentially a practical or action-guiding term, used for *warning*. Unless used in an 'inverted comma sense' the word 'dangerous' was used to warn, and this meant that anyone using it in such a sense committed himself to avoiding the things he called dangerous, to preventing other people from going near them, and perhaps to running in the opposite direction. If the conclusion were not obviously ridiculous, it would be easy to infer that a man whose application of the term was different from ours throughout might say that the oddest things were dangerous without fear of disproof; the idea would be that he could still be described as 'thinking them dan-

gerous', or at least as 'warning', because by his attitude and actions he would have fulfilled the conditions for these things. This is nonsense because without its proper object *warning* like *believing dangerous*, will not be there. It is logically impossible to warn about anything not thought of as threatening evil, and for danger we need a particular kind of serious evil such as injury or death.

There are, however, some differences between thinking a thing dangerous and feeling proud, frightened or dismayed. When a man says that something is dangerous he must support his statement with a special kind of evidence; but when he says that he feels proud or frightened or dismayed the description of the object of his pride or fright or dismay does not have quite this relation to his original statement. If he is shown that the thing he was proud of was not his after all, or was not after all anything very grand, he may have to say that his pride was not justified, but he will not have to take back the statement that he was proud. On the other hand, someone who says that a thing is dangerous, and later sees that he made a mistake in thinking that an injury might result from it, has to go back on his original statement and admit that he was wrong. In neither case, however, is the speaker able to go on as before. A man who discovered that it was not his pumpkin but someone else's which had won the prize could only say that he still felt proud, if he could produce some other ground for pride. It is in this way that even feelings are logically vulnerable to facts.

It will probably be objected against these examples that for part of the way at least they beg the question. It will be said that indeed a man can only be proud of something he thinks a good action, or an achievement, or a sign of noble birth; as he can only feel dismay about something which he sees as bad, frightened at some threatened evil; similarly he can only warn if he is also prepared to speak, for instance, of injury. But this will only limit the range of possible objects of those attitudes and beliefs if the range of these terms is limited in its turn. To meet this objection I shall discuss the meaning of 'injury' because this is the simplest case. Anyone who feels inclined to say that anything could be counted as an achievement, or as the evil of which people were afraid, or about which they felt dismayed, should just try this out. I wish to consider the proposition that anything could be thought of as dangerous, because if it causes injury it is dangerous, and anything could be counted as an injury. I shall consider bodily injury because this is the injury connected with danger; it is not correct to put up a notice by the roadside reading 'Danger!' on account of bushes which might scratch a car. Nor can a substance be labelled 'dangerous' on the ground that it can injure delicate fabrics; although we can speak of the danger that it may do so, that is not the use of the word which I am considering here.

When a body is injured it is changed for the worse in a special way, and we want to know which changes count as injuries. First of all, it matters how an injury comes about; e.g. it cannot be caused by natural decay. Then it seems clear that not just any kind of thing will do, for instance, any unusual mark on the body, however much trouble a man might take to have it removed. By far the most important class of injuries are injuries to a part of the body, counting as injuries because there is interference with the function of that part; injury to a leg, an eye, an ear, a hand, a muscle, the heart, the brain, the spinal cord. An injury to an eye is one that affects, or is likely to affect, its sight; an injury to a hand one which makes it less well able to reach out and grasp, and perform other operations of this kind. A leg can be injured because its movements and supporting power can be affected; a lung because it can become too weak to draw in the proper amount of air. We are most ready to speak of an injury where the function of a part of the body is to perform a characteristic operation, as in these examples. We might hesitate to say that a skull can be injured, and might prefer to speak of damage to it, since although there is indeed a function (a protective function) there is no operation. But thinking of the protective function of the skull we may want to speak of injury here. In so far as the concept of *injury* depends on that of *function* it is narrowly limited, since not even every use to which a part of the body is

put will count as its function. Why is it that, even if it is the means by which they earn their living, we would never consider the removal of the dwarf's hump or the bearded lady's beard as a bodily injury? It will be tempting to say that these things are disfigurements, but this is not the point; if we suppose that a man who had some invisible extra muscle made his living as a court jester by waggling his ears, the ear would not have been injured if this were made to disappear. If it were natural to men to communicate by movements of the ear, then ears would have the function of signalling (we have no word for this kind of 'speaking') and an impairment of this function would be an injury; but things are not like this. This court jester would use his ears to make people laugh, but this is not the function of ears.

No doubt many people will feel impatient when such facts are mentioned, because they think that it is quite unimportant that this or that *happens* to be the case, and it seems to them arbitrary that the loss of the beard, the hump, or the ear muscle would not be called an injury. Isn't the loss of that by which one makes one's living a pretty catastrophic loss? Yet it seems quite natural that these are not counted as injuries if one thinks about the conditions of human life, and contrasts the loss of a special ability to make people gape or laugh with the ability to see, hear, walk, or pick things up. The first is only needed for one very special way of living; the other in any foreseeable future for any man. This restriction seems all the more natural when we observe what other threats besides that of injury can constitute danger: of death, for instance, or mental derangement. A shock which could cause mental instability or impairment of memory would be called dangerous, because a man needs such things as intelligence, memory, and concentration as he needs sight or hearing or the use of hands. Here we do not speak of injury unless it is possible to connect the impairment with some physical change, but we speak of danger because there is the same loss of a capacity which any man needs.

There can be injury outside the range we have been considering; for a man may sometimes be said to have received injuries where no part of his body has had its function interfered with. In general, I think that any blow which disarranged the body in such a way that there was lasting pain would inflict an injury, even if no other ill resulted, but I do not know of any other important extension of the concept.

It seems therefore that since the range of things which can be called injuries is quite narrowly restricted, the word 'dangerous' is restricted in so far as it is connected with injury. We have the right to say that a man cannot decide to call just anything dangerous, however much he puts up fences and shakes his head.

So far I have been arguing that such things as pride, fear, dismay, and the thought that something is dangerous have an internal relation to their object, and hope that what I mean is becoming clear. Now we must consider whether those attitudes or beliefs which are the moral philosopher's study are similar, or whether such things as 'evaluation' and 'thinking something good' and 'commendation' could logically be found in combination with any object whatsoever. All I can do here is to give an example which may make this suggestion seem implausible, and to knock away a few of its supports. The example will come from the range of trivial and pointless actions such as we were considering in speaking of the man who clasped his hands three times an hour, and we can point to the oddity of the suggestion that this can be called a good action. We are bound by the terms of our question to refrain from adding any special background, and it should be stated once more that the question is about what can count in favour of the goodness or badness of a man or an action, and not what could be, or be thought, good or bad with a special background. I believe that the view I am attacking often seems plausible only because the special background is surreptitiously introduced.

Someone who said that clasping the hands three times in an hour was a good action would first have to answer the question 'How do you mean?' For the sentence 'this is a good action' is not one which has a clear meaning. Presumably, since our subject is moral philosophy, it does not

here mean 'that was a good thing to do' as this might be said of a man who had done something sensible in the course of any enterprise whatever; we are to confine our attention to 'the moral use of "good"'. I am not clear that it makes sense to speak of a 'moral use of "good"', but we can pick out a number of cases which raise moral issues. It is because these are so diverse and because 'this is a good action' does not pick out any one of them, that we must ask 'How do you mean?' For instance, some things that are done fulfil a duty, such as the duty of parents to children or children to parents. I suppose that when philosophers speak of good actions they would include these. Some come under the heading of a virtue such as charity, and they will be included too. Others again are actions which require the virtues of courage or temperance, and here the moral aspect is due to the fact that they are done in spite of fear or the temptation of pleasure; they must indeed be done for the sake of some real or fancied good, but not necessarily what philosophers would want to call a moral good. Courage is not *particularly* concerned with saving other people's lives, or temperance with leaving them their share of the food and drink, and the goodness of *what is done* may here be all kinds of usefulness. It is because there are these very diverse cases included (I suppose) under the expression 'a good action' that we should refuse to consider applying it without asking what is meant, and we should now ask what is intended when someone is supposed to say that 'clasping the hands three times in an hour is a good action'. Is it supposed that this action fulfils a duty? Then in virtue of what does a man have this duty, and to whom does he owe it? We have promised not to slip in a special background, but he cannot possibly have a *duty* to clasp his hands unless such a background exists. Nor could it be an act of charity, for it is not thought to do anyone any good, nor again a gesture of humility unless a special assumption turns it into this. The action could be courageous, but only if it were done both in the face of fear and for the sake of a good; and we are not allowed to put in special circumstances which could make this the case.

I am sure that the following objection will now

be raised. 'Of course clasping one's hands three times in an hour cannot be brought under one of the virtues which we recognize, but that is only to say that it is not a good action by our current moral code. It is logically possible that in a quite different moral code quite different virtues should be recognized, for which we have not even got a name.' I cannot answer this objection properly, for that would need a satisfactory account of the concept of a virtue. But anyone who thinks it would be easy to describe a new virtue connected with clasping the hands three times in an hour should just try. I think he will find that he has to cheat, and suppose that in the community concerned the clasping of hands has been given some special significance, or is thought to have some special effect. The difficulty is obviously connected with the fact that without a special background there is no possibility of answering the question 'What's the point?' It is no good saying that there would be a point in doing the action because the action was a morally good action: the question is how it can be given any such description if we cannot first speak about the point. And it is just as crazy to suppose that we can call *anything* the point of doing something without having to say what the point of *that* is. In clasping one's hands one may make a slight sucking noise, but what is the point of that? It is surely clear that moral virtues must be connected with human good and harm, and that it is quite impossible to call anything you like good or harm. Consider, for instance, the suggestion that a man might say he had been harmed because a bucket of water had been taken out of the sea. As usual it would be possible to think up circumstances in which this remark would make sense; for instance, when coupled with a belief in magical influences; but then the harm would consist in what was done by the evil spirits, not in the taking of the water from the sea. It would be just as odd if someone were supposed to say that harm had been done to him because the hairs of his head had been reduced to an even number.[2]

I conclude that assumption (1) is very dubious indeed, and that no one should be allowed to speak as if we can understand 'evaluation', 'commendation' or 'pro-attitude', whatever the actions concerned.

II

I propose now to consider what was called assumption (2), which said that a man might always refuse to accept the conclusion of an argument about values, because what counted as evidence for other people did not count for him. Assumption (2) could be true even if assumption (1) were false, for it might be that once a particular question of values – say a moral question – had been accepted, any disputant was bound to accept particular pieces of evidence as relevant, the same pieces as everyone else, but that he could always refuse to draw any moral conclusions whatsoever or to discuss any questions which introduced moral terms. Nor do we mean 'he might refuse to draw the conclusion' in the trivial sense in which anyone can perhaps refuse to draw *any* conclusion; the point is that any statement of value always seems to go beyond any statement of fact, so that he might have a reason for accepting the factual premises but refusing to accept the evaluative conclusion. That this is so seems to those who argue in this way to follow from the practical implications of evaluation. When a man uses a word such as 'good' in an 'evaluative' and not an 'inverted comma' sense, he is supposed to commit his will. From this it has seemed to follow inevitably that there is a logical gap between fact and value; for is it not one thing to say that a thing is so, and another to have a particular attitude towards its being so; one thing to see that certain effects will follow from a given action, and another to care? Whatever account was offered of the essential feature of evaluation – whether in terms of feelings, attitudes, the acceptance of imperatives or what not – the fact remained that with an evaluation there was a committal in a new dimension, and that this was not guaranteed by any acceptance of facts.

I shall argue that this view is mistaken; that the practical implication of the use of moral terms has been put in the wrong place, and that if it is described correctly the logical gap between factual premises and moral conclusion disappears.

In this argument it will be useful to have as a pattern the practical or 'action-guiding' force of the word 'injury', which is in some, though not all, ways similar to that of moral terms. It is clear, I think, that an injury is necessarily something bad and therefore something which as such anyone always has a reason to avoid, and philosophers will therefore be tempted to say that anyone who uses 'injury' in its full 'action-guiding' sense commits himself to avoiding the things he calls injuries. They will then be in the usual difficulties about the man who says he knows he ought to do something but does not intend to do it; perhaps also about weakness of the will. Suppose that instead we look again at the kinds of things which count as injuries, to see if the connection with the will does not start here. As has been shown, a man is injured whenever some part of his body, in being damaged, has become less well able to fulfil its ordinary function. It follows that he suffers a disability, or is liable to do so; with any injured hand he will be less well able to pick things up, hold on to them, tie them together or chop them up, and so on. With defective eyes there will be a thousand other things he is unable to do, and in both cases we should naturally say that he will often be unable to get what he wants to get or avoid what he wants to avoid.

Philosophers will no doubt seize on the word 'want', and say that if we suppose that a man happens to want the things which an injury to his body prevents him from getting, we have slipped in a supposition about a 'pro-attitude' already; and that anyone who does not happen to have these wants can still refuse to use 'injury' in its prescriptive, or 'action-guiding' sense. And so it may seem that the only way to make a *necessary* connection between 'injury' and the things that are to be avoided, is to say that it is only used in an 'action-guiding' sense when applied to something the speaker intends to avoid. But we should look carefully at the crucial move in that argument, and query the suggestion that someone might happen not to want anything for which he would need the use of hands or eyes. Hands and eyes, like ears and legs, play a part in

so many operations that a man could only be said not to need them if he had no wants at all. That such people exist, in asylums, is not to the present purpose at all; the proper use of his limbs is something a man has reason to want if he wants anything.

I do not know just what someone who denies this proposition could have in mind. Perhaps he is thinking of changing the facts of human existence, so that merely wishing, or the sound of the voice, will bring the world to heel? More likely he is proposing to rig the circumstances of some individual's existence within the framework of the ordinary world, by supposing for instance that he is a prince whose servants will sow and reap and fetch and carry for him, and so use their hands and eyes in his service that he will not need the use of his. Let us suppose that such a story could be told about a man's life; it is wildly implausible, but let us pretend that it is not. It is clear that in spite of this we could say that any man had a reason to shun injury; for even if at the end of his life it could be said that by a strange set of circumstances he had never needed the use of his eyes, or his hands, this could not possibly be foreseen. Only by once more changing the facts of human existence, and supposing every vicissitude foreseeable, could such a supposition be made.

This is not to say that an injury might not bring more incidental gain than necessary harm: one has only to think of times when the order has gone out that able-bodied men are to be put to the sword. Such a gain might even, in some peculiar circumstances, be reliably foreseen, so that a man would have even better reason for seeking than for avoiding injury. In this respect the word 'injury' differs from terms such as 'injustice'; the practical force of 'injury' means only that anyone has *a* reason to avoid injuries, not that he has an overriding reason to do so.

It will be noticed that this account of the 'action-guiding' force of 'injury' links it with reasons for acting rather than with actually doing something. I do not think, however, that this makes it a less good pattern for the 'action-guiding' force of moral terms. Philosophers who have supposed that actual action was required if 'good' were to be used in a sincere evaluation have got into difficulties over weakness of will, and they should surely agree that enough has been done if we can show that any man has reason to aim at virtue and avoid vice. But is this impossibly difficult if we consider the kinds of things that count as virtue and vice? Consider, for instance, the cardinal virtues, prudence, temperance, courage and justice. Obviously any man needs prudence, but does he not also need to resist the temptation of pleasure when there is harm involved? And how could it be argued that he would never need to face what was fearful for the sake of some good? It is not obvious what someone would mean if he said that temperance or courage were not good qualities, and this not because of the 'praising' sense of these *words*, but because of the things that courage and temperance are.

I should like to use these examples to show the artificiality of the notions of 'commendation' and of 'pro-attitudes' as these are commonly employed. Philosophers who talk about these things will say that after the facts have been accepted – say that X is the kind of man who will climb a dangerous mountain, beard an irascible employer for a rise in pay, and in general face the fearful for the sake of something he thinks worth while – there remains the question of 'commendation' or 'evaluation'. If the word 'courage' is used they will ask whether or not the man who speaks of another as having courage is supposed to have commended him. If we say 'yes' they will insist that the judgement about courage *goes beyond the facts*, and might therefore be rejected by someone who refused to do so; if we say 'no' they will argue that 'courage' is being used in a purely descriptive or 'inverted commas sense', and that we have not got an example of the evaluative use of language which is the moral philosopher's special study. What sense can be made, however, of the question 'does he commend?' What is this extra element which is supposed to be present or absent after the facts have been settled? It is not a matter of liking the man who has courage, or of

thinking him altogether good, but of 'commending him for his courage'. How are we supposed to do that? The answer that will be given is that we only commend someone else in speaking of him as courageous if we accept the imperative 'let me be courageous' for ourselves. But this is quite unnecessary. I can speak of someone else as having the virtue of courage, and of course recognize it as a virtue in the proper sense while knowing that I am a complete coward, and making no resolution to reform. I know that I should be better off if I were courageous, and so have a reason to cultivate courage, but I may also know that I will do nothing of the kind.

If someone were to say that courage was not a virtue he would have to say that it was not a quality by which a man came to act well. Perhaps he would be thinking that someone might be worse off for his courage, which is true, but only because an incidental harm might arise. For instance, the courageous man might have underestimated a risk, and run into some disaster which a cowardly man would have avoided because he was not prepared to take any risk at all. And his courage, like any other virtue, could be the cause of harm to him because possessing it he fell into some disastrous state of pride.[3] Similarly, those who question the virtue of temperance are probably thinking not of the virtue itself but of men whose temperance has consisted in resisting pleasure for the sake of some illusory good, or those who have made this virtue their pride. . . .

Notes

1 See L. Wittgenstein, *Philosophical Investigations* (1967), especially sections 243–315.
2 In face of this sort of example many philosophers take refuge in the thicket of aesthetics. It would be interesting to know if they are willing to let their whole case rest on the possibility that there might be aesthetic objections to what was done.
3 Cf. Aquinas, *Summa Theologica*, I–II, q. 55, Art. 4.

7 Moral Disagreement Today and the Claims of Emotivism

Alasdair MacIntyre

The most striking feature of contemporary moral utterance is that so much of it is used to express disagreements; and the most striking feature of the debates in which these disagreements are expressed is their interminable character. I do not mean by this just that such debates go on and on and on – although they do – but also that they apparently can find no terminus. There seems to be no emotional way of securing moral agreement in our culture. Consider three examples of just such contemporary moral debate framed in terms of characteristic and well-known rival moral arguments:

1 (a) A just war is one in which the good to be achieved outweighs the evils involved in waging the war and in which a clear distinction can be made between combatants – whose lives are at stake – and innocent noncombatants. But in a modern war calculation of future escalation is never reliable and no practically applicable distinction between combatants and noncombatants can be made. Therefore no modern war can be a just war and we all now ought to be pacifists.

(b) If you wish for peace, prepare for war. The only way to achieve peace is to deter potential aggressors. Therefore you must build up your armaments and make it clear that going to war on any particular scale is not necessarily ruled out by your policies. An inescapable part of making *this* clear is being prepared both to fight limited wars and to go not only to, but beyond, the nuclear brink on certain types of occasion. Otherwise you will not avoid war *and* you will be defeated.

(c) Wars between the Great Powers are purely destructive; but wars waged to liberate oppressed groups, especially in the Third World, are a necessary and therefore justified means for destroying the exploitative domination which stands between mankind and happiness.

2 (a) Everybody has certain rights over his or her own person, including his or her own body. It follows from the nature of these rights that at the stage when the embryo is essentially part of the mother's body, the mother has a right to make her own uncoerced decision on whether she will have an abortion or not. Therefore abortion is morally permissible and ought to be allowed by law.

(b) I cannot will that my mother should have had an abortion when she was pregnant with me, except perhaps if it had been certain that the embryo was dead or gravely damaged. But if I cannot will this in my own case, how can I consistently deny to others the right to life that I claim for myself? I would break the so-called Golden Rule unless I denied that a mother has in general a right to an abortion. I am not of course thereby committed to the view that abortion ought to be legally prohibited.

(c) Murder is wrong. Murder is the taking of innocent life. An embryo is an identifiable individual, differing from a newborn infant only in being at an earlier

From *After Virtue: A Study in Moral Philosophy* (Notre Dame, IN: University of Notre Dame Press, 1984), pp. 6–18. Reprinted with permission.

stage on the long road to adult capacities and, if any life is innocent, that of an embryo is. If infanticide is murder, as it is, abortion is murder. So abortion is not only morally wrong, but ought to be legally prohibited.

3   (a)   Justice demands that every citizen should enjoy, so far as is possible, an equal opportunity to develop his or her talents and his or her other potentialities. But prerequisites for the provision of such equal opportunity include the provision of equal access to health care and to education. Therefore justice requires the governmental provision of health and educational services, financed out of taxation, and it also requires that no citizen should be able to buy an unfair share of such services. This in turn requires the abolition of private schools and private medical practice.

(b)   Everybody has a right to incur such and only such obligations as he or she wishes, to be free to make such and only such contracts as he or she desires and to determine his or her own free choices. Physicians must therefore be free to practice on such terms as they desire and patients must be free to choose among physicians; teachers must be free to teach on such terms as they choose and pupils and parents to go where they wish for education. Freedom thus requires not only the existence of private practice in medicine and private schools in education, but also the abolition of those restraints on private practice which are imposed by licensing and regulation by such bodies as universities, medical schools, the AMA and the state.

These arguments have only to be stated to be recognized as being widely influential in our society. They have of course their articulate expert spokesmen: Herman Kahn and the Pope, Che Guevara and Milton Friedman are among the authors who have produced variant versions of them. But it is their appearance in newspaper editorials and high-school debates, on radio talk shows and letters to congressmen, in bars, barracks, and boardrooms, it is their typicality that makes them important examples here. What salient characteristics do these debates and disagreements share?

They are of three kinds. The first is what I shall call, adapting an expression from the philosophy of science, the conceptual incommensurability of the rival arguments in each of the three debates. Every one of the arguments is logically valid or can be easily expanded so as to be made so; the conclusions do indeed follow from the premises. But the rival premises are such that we possess no rational way of weighing the claims of one as against another. For each premise employs some quite different normative or evaluative concept from the others, so that the claims made upon us are of quite different kinds. In the first argument, for example, premises which invoke justice and innocence are at odds with premises which invoke success and survival; in the second, premises which invoke rights are at odds with those which invoke universalizability; in the third it is the claim of equality that is matched against that of liberty. It is precisely because there is in our society no established way of deciding between these claims that moral argument appears to be necessarily interminable. From our rival conclusions we can argue back to our rival premises; but when we do arrive at our premises argument ceases and the invocation of one premise against another becomes a matter of pure assertion and counter-assertion. Hence perhaps the slightly shrill tone of so much moral debate.

But that shrillness may have an additional source. For it is not only in arguments with others that we are reduced so quickly to assertion and counter-assertion; it is also in the arguments that we have within ourselves. For whenever an agent enters the forum of public debate he has already presumably, explicitly or implicitly, settled the matter in question in his own mind. Yet if we possess no unassailable criteria, no set of compelling reasons by means of which we may convince our opponents, it follows that in the process of making up our own minds we can have made no appeal to such criteria or such reasons.

If I lack any good reasons to invoke against you, it must seem that I lack any good reasons. Hence it seems that underlying my own position there must be some non-rational decision to adopt that position. Corresponding to the interminability of public argument there is at least the appearance of a disquieting private arbitrariness. It is small wonder we become defensive and therefore shrill.

A second, equally important, but contrasting characteristic of these arguments is that they do none the less purport to be *impersonal* rational arguments and as such are usually presented in a mode appropriate to that impersonality. What is that mode? Consider two different ways in which I may provide backing for an injunction to someone else to perform some specific action. In the first type of case I say, "Do so-and-so." The person addressed replies, "Why should I do so-and-so?" I reply, "Because I wish it." Here I have given the person addressed no reason to do what I command or request unless he or she independently possesses some particular reason for paying regard to my wishes. If I am your superior officer – in the police, say, or the army – or otherwise have power or authority over you, or if you love me or fear me or want something from me, then by saying "Because I wish it" I have indeed given *you* a reason, although not perhaps a sufficient reason, for doing what it is that I enjoin. Notice that in this type of case whether my utterance gives you a reason or not depends on certain characteristics possessed at the time of hearing or otherwise learning of the utterance by you. What reason-giving force the injunction has depends in this way on the personal context of the utterance.

Contrast with this the type of case in which the answer to the question "Why should I do so-and-so?" (after someone has said "Do so-and-so") is not "Because I wish it," but some such utterance as "Because it would give pleasure to a number of people" or "Because it is your duty." In this type of case the reason given for action either is or is not a good reason for performing the action in question independently of who utters it or even of whether it is uttered at all. Moreover the appeal is to a type of considera-

tion which is independent of the relationship between speaker and hearer. Its use presupposes the existence of *impersonal* criteria – the existence, independently of the preferences or attitudes of speaker and hearer, of standards of justice or generosity or duty. The particular link between the context of utterance and the force of the reason-giving which always holds in the case of expressions of personal preferences or desire is severed in the case of moral and other evaluative utterances.

This second characteristic of contemporary moral utterance and argument, when combined with the first, imparts a paradoxical air to contemporary moral disagreement. For if we attended solely to the first characteristic, to the way in which what at first appears to be argument relapses so quickly into unargued disagreement, we might conclude that there is nothing to such contemporary disagreements but a clash of antagonistic wills, each will determined by some set of arbitrary choices of its own. But this second characteristic, the use of expressions whose distinctive function in our language is to embody what purports to be an appeal to objective standards, suggests otherwise. For even if the surface appearance of argument is only a masquerade, the question remains "Why *this* masquerade?" What is it about rational argument which is so important that it is the nearly universal appearance assumed by those who engage in moral conflict? Does not this suggest that the practice of moral argument in our culture expresses at least an aspiration to be or to become rational in this area of our lives?

A third salient characteristic of contemporary moral debate is intimately related to the first two. It is easy to see that the different conceptually incommensurable premises of the rival arguments deployed in these debates have a wide variety of historical origins. The concept of justice in the first argument has its roots in Aristotle's account of the virtues; the second argument's genealogy runs through Bismarck and Clausewitz to Machiavelli; the concept of liberation in the third argument has shallow roots in Marx, deeper roots in Fichte. In the second debate a concept of rights which has Lockean antecedents is matched against a view of universalizability which is recognizably Kantian and an appeal to the moral law which is Thomist. In the third debate an argument which owes debts to T. H. Green and to Rousseau competes with one which has Adam Smith as a grandfather. This catalogue of great names is suggestive; but it may be misleading in two ways. The citing of individual names may lead us to underestimate the complexity of the history and the ancestry of such arguments; and it may lead us to look for that history and that ancestry only in the writings of philosophers and theorists instead of in those intricate bodies of theory and practice which constitute human culture, the beliefs of which are articulated by philosophers and theorists only in a partial and selective manner. But the catalogue of names does suggest how wide and heterogeneous the variety of moral sources is from which we have inherited. The surface rhetoric of our culture is apt to speak complacently of moral pluralism in this connection, but the notion of pluralism is too imprecise. For it may equally well apply to an ordered dialogue of intersecting viewpoints and to an unharmonious melange of ill-assorted fragments. The suspicion – and for the moment it can only be a suspicion – that it is the latter with which we have to deal is heightened when we recognize that all those various concepts which inform our moral discourse were originally at home in larger totalities of theory and practice in which they enjoyed a role and function supplied by contexts of which they have now been deprived. Moreover the concepts we employ have in at least some cases changed their character in the past three hundred years; the evaluative expressions we use have changed their meaning. In the transition from the variety of contexts in which they were originally at home to our own contemporary culture "virtue" and "justice" and "piety" and "duty" and even "ought" have become other than they once were. How ought we to write the history of such changes?

It is in trying to answer this question that the connection between these features of contemporary moral debate and my initial hypothesis becomes clear. For if I am right in supposing that the language of morality passed from a state of order to a state of disorder, this passage will surely be reflected in – in part indeed will actually consist in – just such changes of meaning. Moreover, if the characteristics of our own moral arguments which I have identified – most notably the fact that we simultaneously and inconsistently treat moral argument as an exercise of our rational powers and as mere expressive assertion – are symptoms of moral disorder, we ought to be able to construct a true historical narrative in which at an earlier stage moral argument is very different in kind. Can we?

One obstacle to our so doing has been the persistently unhistorical treatment of moral philosophy by contemporary philosophers in both the writing about and the teaching of the subject. We all too often still treat the moral philosophers of the past as contributors to a single debate with a relatively unvarying subject-matter, treating Plato and Hume and Mill as contemporaries both of ourselves and of each other. This leads to an abstraction of these writers from the cultural and social milieus in which they lived and thought and so the history of their thought acquires a false independence from the rest of the culture. Kant ceases to be part of the history of Prussia, Hume is no longer a Scotsman. For from the standpoint of moral philosophy as *we* conceive it these characteristics have become irrelevances. Empirical history is one thing, philosophy quite another. But are we right in understanding the division between academic disciplines in the way that we conventionally do? Once again there seems to be a possible relationship between the history of moral discourse and the history of the academic curriculum.

Yet at this point it may rightly be retorted: You keep speaking of possibilities, of suspicions, of hypotheses. You allow that what you are suggesting will initially seem implausible. You are in this at least right. For all this resort to conjectures about history is unnecessary. The way in which you have stated the problem is misleading. Contemporary moral argument is rationally interminable, because *all* moral, indeed all evaluative argument is and always must be rationally interminable. Contemporary moral disagreements of a certain kind cannot be resolved, because *no* moral disagreements of that kind in any age, past, present, or future, can be resolved. What you present as a contingent feature of our culture, standing in need of some special, perhaps historical explanation, is a necessary feature of all cultures which possess evaluative discourse. This is a challenge which cannot be avoided at an early stage in this argument. Can it be defeated?

One philosophical theory which this challenge specifically invites us to confront is emotivism. Emotivism is the doctrine that all evaluative judgments and more specifically all moral judgments are *nothing* but expressions of preference, expressions of attitude or feeling, in so far as they are moral or evaluative in character. Particular judgments may of course unite moral and factual elements. "Arson, being destructive of property, is wrong" unites the factual judgment that arson destroys property with the moral judgment that arson is wrong. But the moral element in such a judgment is always to be sharply distinguished from the factual. Factual judgments are true or false; and in the realm of fact there are rational criteria by means of which we may secure agreement as to what is true and what is false. But moral judgments, being expressions of attitude or feeling, are neither true nor false; and agreement in moral judgment is not to be secured by any rational method, for there are none. It is to be secured, if at all, by producing certain non-rational effects on the emotions or attitudes of those who disagree with one. We use moral judgments not only to express our own feelings and attitudes, but also precisely to produce such effects in others. . . .

The emotive theory, . . . purports to be a theory about the meaning of sentences; but the expression of feeling or attitude is characteristically a function not of the meaning of sentences, but of their use on particular occasions. The angry schoolmaster, to use one of Gilbert Ryle's examples, may vent his feelings by shouting at the small boy who has just made an arithmetical mistake, "Seven times seven equals forty-nine!" But the use of this sentence to express feelings or attitudes has nothing whatsoever to do with its meaning. This suggests that we should not sim-

ply rely on these objections to reject the emotive theory, but that we should rather consider whether it ought not to have been proposed as a theory about the *use* – understood as purpose or function – of members of a certain class of expressions rather than about their *meaning* – understood as including all that Frege intended by "sense" and "reference."

Clearly the argument so far shows that when someone utters a moral judgment, such as "This is right" or "This is good," it does not mean the same as "I approve of this, do so as well" or "Hurrah for this!" or any of the other attempts at equivalence suggested by emotive theorists; but even if the meaning of such sentences were quite other than emotive theorists supposed, it might be plausibly claimed, if the evidence was adequate, that in using such sentences to *say* whatever they mean, the agent was in fact *doing* nothing other than expressing his feelings or attitudes and attempting to influence the feelings and attitudes of others. If the emotive theory thus interpreted were correct it would follow that the meaning and the use of moral expressions were, or at the very least had become, radically discrepant with each other. Meaning and use would be at odds in such a way that meaning would tend to conceal use. We could not safely infer what someone who uttered a moral judgment was doing merely by listening to what he said. Moreover the agent himself might well be among those for whom use was concealed by meaning. He might well, precisely because he was self-conscious about the meaning of the words that he used, be assured that he was appealing to independent impersonal criteria, when all that he was in fact doing was expressing his feelings to others in a manipulative way. . . .

. . . Emotivism on this account turns out to be an empirical thesis or rather a preliminary sketch of an empirical thesis, presumably to be filled out later by psychological and sociological and historical observations, about those who continue to use moral and other evaluative expressions, as if they were governed by objective and impersonal criteria, when all grasp of any such criterion has been lost. We should therefore expect emotivist types of theory to arise in a specific local circumstance as a response to types of theory and practice which share certain key features of Moore's intuitionism. Emotivism thus understood turns out to be, as a cogent theory of use rather than a false theory of meaning, connected with one specific stage in moral development or decline, a stage which our own culture entered early in the present century.

PART TWO

THE JUSTIFICATION OF MORALITY:

WHY BE MORAL?

8 On Reason and the Emotions

David Hume

Of the Influencing Motives of the Will

Nothing is more usual in philosophy, and even in common life, than to talk of the combat of passion and reason, to give the preference to reason, and to assert that men are only so far virtuous as they conform themselves to its dictates. Every rational creature, 'tis said, is oblig'd to regulate his actions by reason; and if any other motive or principle challenge the direction of his conduct, he ought to oppose it, 'till it be entirely subdu'd, or at least brought to a conformity with that superior principle. On this method of thinking the greatest part of moral philosophy, ancient and modern, seems to be founded; nor is there an ampler field, as well for metaphysical arguments, as popular declamations, than this suppos'd pre-eminence of reason above passion. The eternity, invariableness, and divine origin of the former have been display'd to the best advantage: the blindness, unconstancy and deceitfulness of the latter have been as strongly insisted on. In order to shew the fallacy of all this philosophy, I shall endeavour to prove *first*, that reason alone can never be a motive to any action of the will; and *secondly*, that it can never oppose passion in the direction of the will.

The understanding exerts itself after two different ways, as it judges from demonstration or probability; as it regards the abstract relations of our ideas, or those relations of objects, of which experience only gives us information. I believe it scarce will be asserted, that the first species of reasoning alone is ever the cause of any action. As its proper province is the world of ideas, and

From *A Treatise on Human Nature*, ed. L. A. Selby-Bigge (Oxford: Clarendon Press, 1888), pp. 413–18, 462–3, 468–70. First published in 1739–40.

as the will always places us in that of realities, demonstration and volition seem, upon that account, to be totally remov'd from each other. Mathematics, indeed, are useful in all mechanical operations, and arithmetic in almost every art and profession: But 'tis not of themselves they have any influence. Mechanics are the art of regulating the motions of bodies *to some design'd end or purpose*; and the reason why we employ arithmetic in fixing the proportions of numbers, is only that we may discover the proportions of their influence and operation. A merchant is desirous of knowing the sum total of his accounts with any person: Why? but that he may learn what sum will have the same *effects* in paying his debt, and going to market, as all the particular articles taken together. Abstract or demonstrative reasoning, therefore, never influences any of our actions, but only as it directs our judgement concerning causes and effects; which leads us to the second operation of the understanding.

'Tis obvious that when we have the prospect of pain or pleasure from any object, we feel a consequent emotion of aversion or propensity, and are carry'd to avoid or embrace what will give us this uneasiness or satisfaction. 'Tis also obvious that this emotion rests not here, but making us cast our view on every side, comprehends whatever objects are connected with its original one by the relation of cause and effect. Here then reasoning takes place to discover this relation; and according as our reasoning varies, our actions receive a subsequent variation. But 'tis evident in this case, that the impulse arises not from reason, but is only directed by it. 'Tis from the prospect of pain or pleasure that the aversion or propensity arises towards any object: and these emotions extend themselves to the causes and effects of that object, as they are pointed out to us by reason and experience. It can never in the least concern us to know that such objects are causes, and such others effects, if both the causes and effects be indifferent to us. Where the objects themselves do not affect us, their connexion can never give them any influence; and 'tis plain, that as reason is nothing but the discovery of this connexion, it cannot be by its means that the objects are able to affect us.

Since reason alone can never produce any action, or give rise to volition, I infer that the same faculty is as incapable of preventing volition, or of disputing the preference with any passion or emotion. This consequence is necessary. 'Tis impossible reason cou'd have the latter effect of preventing volition, but by giving an impulse in a contrary direction to our passion; and that impulse, had it operated alone, would have been able to produce volition. Nothing can oppose or retard the impulse of passion, but a contrary impulse; and if this contrary impulse ever arises from reason, that latter faculty must have an original influence on the will, and must be able to cause, as well as hinder any act of volition. But if reason has no original influence, 'tis impossible it can withstand any principle, which has such an efficacy, or ever keep the mind in suspense a moment. Thus it appears that the principle, which opposes our passion, cannot be the same with reason, and is only call'd so in an improper sense. We speak not strictly and philosophically when we talk of the combat of passion and of reason. Reason is, and ought only to be the slave of the passions, and can never pretend to any other office than to serve and obey them. As this opinion may appear somewhat extraordinary, it may not be improper to confirm it by some other considerations.

A passion is an original existence, or, if you will, modification of existence, and contains not any representative quality, which renders it a copy of any other existence or modification. When I am angry, I am actually possest with the passion, and in that emotion have no more a reference to any other object, than when I am thirsty, or sick, or more than five foot high. 'Tis impossible, therefore, that this passion can be oppos'd by, or be contradictory to truth and reason; since this contradiction consists in the disagreement of ideas, consider'd as copies, with those objects, which they represent.

What may at first occur on this head, is, that as nothing can be contrary to truth or reason, except what has a reference to it, and as the judgements of our understanding only have this reference, it must follow that passions can be contrary to reason only so far as they are *accompany'd* with some judgement or opinion. According to this principle, which is so obvious and natural, 'tis only in two senses that any affection can be call'd unreasonable. First, when a passion, such as hope or fear, grief or joy, despair or security, is founded on the supposition of the existence of objects, which really do not exist. Secondly, when in exerting any passion in action, we chuse means insufficient for the design'd end, and deceive ourselves in our judgement of causes and effects. Where a passion is neither founded on false suppositions, nor chuses means insufficient for the end, the understanding can neither justify nor condemn it. 'Tis not contrary to reason to prefer the destruction of the whole world to the scratching of my finger. 'Tis not contrary to reason for me to *chuse* my total ruin, to prevent the least uneasiness of an *Indian* or person wholly unknown to me. 'Tis as little contrary to reason to prefer even my own acknowledg'd lesser good to my greater, and have a more ardent affection for the former than the latter. A trivial good may, from certain circumstances, produce a desire superior to what arises from the greatest and most valuable enjoyment; nor is there any thing more extraordinary in this, than in mechanics to see one pound weight raise up a hundred by the advantage of its situation. In short, a passion must be accompany'd with some false judgement, in order to its being unreasonable; and even then 'tis not the passion, properly speaking, which is unreasonable, but the judgement.

The consequences are evident. Since a passion can never, in any sense, be call'd unreasonable, but when founded on a false supposition, or when it chuses means insufficient for the design'd end, 'tis impossible that reason and passion can ever oppose each other, or dispute for the government of the will and actions. The moment we perceive the falsehood of any supposition, or the insufficiency of any means our passions yield to our reason without any opposition. I may desire any fruit as of an excellent relish; but whenever you convince me of my mistake, my longing ceases. I may will the performance of certain actions as means of obtaining any desir'd good; but as my willing of these actions is only secondary, and founded on the supposition, that they are causes of the propos'd effect; as soon as I discover the falsehood of that supposition, they must become indifferent to me.

'Tis natural for one, that does not examine objects with a strict philosophic eye, to imagine that those actions of the mind are entirely the same, which produce not a different sensation, and are not immediately distinguishable to the feeling and perception. Reason, for instance, exerts itself without producing any sensible emotion; and except in the more sublime disquisitions of philosophy, or in the frivolous subtilties of the schools, scarce ever conveys any pleasure or uneasiness. Hence it proceeds, that every action of the mind, which operates with the same calmness and tranquillity, is confounded with reason by all those, who judge of things from the first view and appearance. Now 'tis certain, there are certain calm desires and tendencies, which, tho' they be real passions, produce little emotion in the mind, and are more known by their effects than by the immediate feeling or sensation. These desires are of two kinds; either certain instincts originally implanted in our natures, such as benevolence and resentment, the love of life, and kindness to children; or the general appetite to good, and aversion to evil, consider'd merely as such. When any of these passions are calm, and cause no disorder in the soul, they are very readily taken for the determinations of reason, and are suppos'd to proceed from the same faculty, with that, which judges of truth and falsehood. Their nature and principles have been suppos'd the same, because their sensations are not evidently different.

Beside these calm passions, which often determine the will, there are certain violent emotions of the same kind, which have likewise a great influence on that faculty. When I receive any injury from another, I often feel a violent passion of resentment, which makes me desire his evil and punishment, independent of all considerations of pleasure and advantage to myself. When I am immediately threaten'd with any grievous ill, my fears, apprehensions and aversions rise to a great height, and produce a sensible emotion.

The common error of metaphysicians has lain in ascribing the direction of the will entirely to one of these principles, and supposing the other to have no influence. Men often act knowingly against their interest: for which reason the view of the greatest possible good does not always influence them. Men often counteract a violent passion in prosecution of their interests and designs: 'tis not therefore the present uneasiness alone, which determines them. In general we may observe that both these principles operate on the will; and where they are contrary, that either of them prevails, according to the *general* character or *present* disposition of the person. What we call strength of mind, implies the prevalence of the calm passions above the violent; tho' we may easily observe, there is no man so constantly possess'd of this virtue, as never on any occasion to yield to the sollicitations of passion and desire. From these variations of temper proceeds the great difficulty of deciding concerning the actions and resolutions of men, where there is any contrariety of motives and passions. . . .

Moral Distinctions Not Deriv'd from Reason

[U]pon the whole, 'tis impossible that the distinction betwixt moral good and evil can be made by reason; since that distinction has an influence upon our actions, of which reason alone is incapable. Reason and judgement may, indeed, be the mediate cause of an action, by prompting, or by directing a passion: but it is not pretended, that a judgement of this kind, either in its truth or falsehood, is attended with virtue or vice. And as to the judgements, which are caused by our judgements, they can still less bestow those moral qualities on the actions, which are their cause. . . .

But can there be any difficulty in proving, that vice and virtue are not matters of fact, whose existence we can infer by reason? Take any action allow'd to be vicious: wilful murder, for instance. Examine it in all lights, and see if you can find that matter of fact, or real existence, which you call *vice*. In whichever way you take it, you find only certain passions, motives, volitions and thoughts. There is no other matter of fact in the case. The vice entirely escapes you, as long as you consider the object. You never can find it, till you turn your reflexion into your own breast, and find a sentiment of disapprobation, which arises in you, towards this action. Here is a matter of fact; but 'tis the object of feeling, not of reason. It lies in yourself, not in the object. So that when you pronounce any action or character to be vicious, you mean nothing, but that from the constitution of your nature you have a feeling or sentiment of blame from the contemplation of it. Vice and virtue, therefore, may be compar'd to sounds, colours, heat and cold, which, according to modern philosophy, are not qualities in objects, but perceptions in the mind: and this discovery in morals, like that other in physics, is to be regarded as a considerable advancement of the speculative sciences; tho', like that too, it has little or no influence on practice. Nothing can be more real, or concern us more, than our own sentiments of pleasure and uneasiness; and if these be favourable to virtue and unfavourable to vice, no more can be requisite to the regulation of our conduct and behaviour.

I cannot forbear adding to these reasonings an observation, which may, perhaps, be found of some importance. In every system of morality, which I have hitherto met with, I have always remark'd that the author proceeds for some time in the ordinary way of reasoning, and establishes the being of a God, or makes observations concerning human affairs; when of a sudden I am surpriz'd to find, that instead of the usual copulations of propositions, *is*, and *is not*, I meet with no proposition that is not connected with an *ought*, or an *ought not*. This change is imperceptible; but is, however, of the last consequence. For as this *ought* or *ought not* expresses some new relation or affirmation, 'tis necessary that it shou'd be observ'd and explain'd; and at the same time that a reason should be given, for what seems altogether inconceivable, how this new relation can be a deduction from others, which are entirely different from it. But as authors do not commonly use this precaution, I shall presume to recommend it to the readers; and am persuaded that this small attention would subvert all the vulgar systems of morality, and let us see that the distinction of vice and virtue is not founded merely on the relations of objects, nor is perceiv'd by reason.

Moral Distinctions Deriv'd from a Moral Sense

Thus the course of the argument leads us to conclude, that since vice and virtue are not discoverable merely by reason, or the comparison of ideas, it must be by means of some impression or sentiment they occasion, that we are able to mark the difference betwixt them. Our decisions concerning moral rectitude and depravity are evidently perceptions; and as all perceptions are either impressions or ideas, the exclusion of the one is a convincing argument for the other. Morality, therefore, is more properly felt than judg'd of; tho' this feeling or sentiment is commonly so soft and gentle, that we are apt to confound it with an idea, according to our common custom of taking all things for the same, which have any near resemblance to each other.

9   The Rational and the Moral Order

Kurt Baier

. . .

We must ask whether societies could exist without more or less severely sanctioned rules, such as are embodied in the law, in custom, and in social morality, and if so, whether it would be desirable to do away with at least the most intrusively coercive ones, as anarchists believe. Would everyone or indeed anyone be rationally justified in trying to keep them in existence or in resuscitating them once we have gotten rid of them? Would such a rational justification be available for every member of society irrespective of social position, or only for those in favored positions (for the slave as well as the master, or only for the master); can everyone have adequate permissive or even requiring reason to support the existence of a social system with suitably sanctioned rules? Can everyone also have such reason *always* to act as these rules require? If everyone can or does have such reason, can or must these reasons be self-anchored ones or must they be reasons of a *new kind*, and if so, what kind, and how is this kind related to self-anchored ones? I shall address these and a few related questions in the remainder of this chapter.

2   The Rational Limitations of Good Will

Can sanctioned rules be rationally justified? On the face of it, they seem undesirable, for their point is to weight our choices extraneously; they turn some things which it would otherwise be in accordance with (self-anchored) reason for us to choose and which we then could and would

From *The Rational and the Moral* (Peru, IL.: Open Court, 1995), pp. 157–73, 186–93. Reproduced with permission.

choose freely, into things it is now either contrary to reason to choose or else into things we are no longer free to choose or able to choose freely or both. If we still choose to do them, we must now expect to pay a price for doing so, which in a society without such rules would not have been exacted from us by it, perhaps by anybody. (Though this last point is questionable. The vendetta or individual retribution might well take the place of custom or law.)

It may be thought that this need not be so, that such rules push us to choose only those things that are in any case according to self-anchored reason to do. But this is implausible. For sanctioned rules are rigid and uniform in a way in which self-anchored reasons are not. Although, of course, such rules do not hold literally for everyone, they do hold for everyone of a class of people, such as men or children or homeowners, and are, therefore, in some respects like Moore's objective reasons or Nagel's agent-neutral ones. Thus, they abstract from things such as the various class members' conceptions of the good life, their tastes, their ages, and so on, from which their self-anchored dispositive reasons cannot abstract. Indeed, it would be virtually impossible to administer sanctions attached to what people have adequate self-anchored dispositive requiring reason to do. It seems highly plausible, in other words, that a person's self-anchored reasons will tend to come into occasional conflict with the sanctioned rules of his society and that these rules are therefore on the face of it undesirable because they may occasionally or often require behavior that is contrary to self-anchored reason.

It may, of course, be possible to give a rational justification of them, even one in terms of self-anchored reasons. Indeed, that is the position I hope to establish eventually. However, for the moment, I shall suppose the opposite. I shall suppose that, other things equal, it would be better from the points of view of all or most of those living in a given society if that society did not have any sanctioned rules, especially any coercive ones. It is an important implication of this, that fully rational members of a society without such sanctioned rules must, when interacting with others, choose what to do on the basis of "strategic reasoning" along game-theoretic lines but based on their own self-anchored reasons.[1] In such strategic reasoning they must, of course, take into account what other people could or probably will do. If they have reason to think, furthermore, that others are always not only fully but also evaluatively rational, they will also have to take into account what these others have self-anchored reasons to do and what they have reason to expect their fellow "interagents" to do.

Accordingly, the following questions arise. In the absence of sanctioned rules, what weight would it be rational to attach to the concerns of others? What conception of a good life for themselves would it be rational to expect those to have about whom one knows little or nothing? In trying to answer these two questions, we discover what I call the Rational Limitations of Good Will and with it the inescapability of what I call the Problem of General Egoism. Let me now elaborate this.

I do not here mean "egoism" as typically used in everyday conversation where it has a pejorative sense, meaning much the same as selfishness. In that ordinary sense, I suggested, it refers to an attitude leading to the promotion of one's own best interest or good, *beyond the morally permissible*. It is widely held to be one of the most common moral faults. Indeed, the behavior is thought by many to be so common that they find considerable plausibility, at least initially, in an explanatory psychological theory, often called Psychological Egoism, which holds that all human behavior at a certain level of sophistication (say, all chosen, deliberate or intentional, but not involuntary or reflex behavior) is what the agent takes to be promotive of his own best interest or greatest good.

As every philosopher knows, many textbooks on ethics expound a theory entitled "Ethical Egoism" which holds that the morally right thing to do is *always* to promote one's best interest or greatest good (this often baffles students because they feel the name to be an oxymoron). This theory thus denies by implication what I believe is one of our most widely held moral convictions, namely, that in certain circumstances it is morally wrong to promote one's own best interest or greatest good. This is no doubt one of the reasons why Ethical Egoism is not very widely espoused even by philosophers, although many think they can detect highly sophisticated versions of it in Spinoza and Hobbes.

What I here mean by "Egoism" is neither Psychological nor Ethical, but what I have earlier called "Rational Egoism." At this point, we need to distinguish three different versions of it. One is what I shall call (1) "Egoism," which can be ascribed to someone if and only if he always acts *in accordance with* the Principle of Egoism, that is, the principle of always doing whatever there is adequate (cognitive) reason for one to think will be in one's own best interest, irrespective of whether or not he actually *subscribes to* and *acts on* that principle. The second might be called (2) "Principled Egoism," which can be ascribed to a person if and only if he actually subscribes to, and acts on, the Principle of Egoism. A person is a Principled Egoist quite irrespective of the reason(s) for which he has come to hold this principle, even if he has no reason at all to hold it, although of course we may suppose that there always is a reason (explanation) *why* he holds it, even if neither he nor anyone else knows what it is. The third is what might be called (3) "Principled Rational Egoism" (PRE). This can be attributed to someone if and only if he subscribes both to (a) the Principle of Rationality (PR), *always to do* what he has adequate (cognitive) reason to think has the weight of (practical) reason behind it, and to (b) the Theory of Rational Egoism (TRE), that the fact that S's doing A would be in his best interest is *the only*, or is *an indefeasible*, reason for him to do A.

The Problem of General Egoism seems inescapable not because we are *all* egoists in the ordinary sense (though no doubt some of us are), nor because we are *all* Egoists, Principled Egoists, or Principled Rational Egoists, or because Psychological Egoism is true, for there is no good reason to believe that any of this is so, and good reason to believe that none of it is.

The Problem of General Egoism seems inescapable if it is plausible to hold, as I do, that many, perhaps most of us, are what might be called "Limited Egoists,"[2] that is, people with the following differential attitudes to others. They love or are friendly with or have sympathies for or are concerned about the well-being of *some* others, for example, lovers, parents, children, friends, family, fellow citizens, and therefore would set aside their own good *to some extent* if they would thereby prevent harm from coming to those people or even merely to make them better off than they now are. . . . They may even love some others more than they love themselves and would therefore be prepared to sacrifice their own greater good for the lesser good of these loved ones. They might even give their life for them. At the same time, as far as quite large numbers of people are concerned (say, people of other races or living in other distant lands), such Limited Egoists, though perhaps not entirely indifferent, still care a lot less about those strangers than about themselves and about their loved ones, so that their concern for these others will not show itself much or at all in their interactions with them. This probably large number of people is (in the absence of suitably sanctioned rules with suitable content) disposed to behave in relation to the bulk of humankind in much the same way as if they were Egoists, Principled Egoists, or Principled Rational Egoists.

Mutatis mutandis, much the same would seem to be true for people's negative attitudes toward others. In some conceptions of the good life, hatred of and struggle against some people will be an important valued element. For such people, fulfillment requires battles and crusades against some "infidels," or "barbarians," or "subhumans," perhaps their extermination. However, even most such crusaders' conception of the good life for themselves identifies only a relatively small number of villains. Concerning the rest, their attitude is usually concern and affection for some and indifference for the bulk of people. I should perhaps add that it seems there are not many if indeed any genuine misanthropes. For most people the fact that some *stranger* (hence not known to be a villain) is in peril is an (admittedly rather weak) *pro tanto* reason to throw the (cost-free) rope rather than to administer the (cost-free) kick. When neither costs much, I believe, and I think most of us believe, that most of us tend to come to the aid of strangers in peril rather than to finish them off.[3]

It also seems plausible to think that where this is what such Limited Egoists are inclined to do on impulse without prior reflection, most would also do it on reflection. They might well be prepared to adopt a principle to that effect and they would probably think that to act in this way would be rational. They would then be "Limited Principled Egoists," and "Limited Principled Rational Egoists." The last would hold that, perhaps because of one's limited resources, reason requires one to allocate them in ways which reflect the differences in one's actual concern for different people.

But then it seems that, in the absence of sanctioned rules, this sort of Limited Egoism is bound to become general in our relation to strangers. For our reflections suggest that a lot of people, whether or not themselves Egoists or Limited Egoists, will have (cognitive) reason to expect that they often will be, and on any particular occasion may well be, interacting with a stranger who is such a (Limited) Egoist. If rational, they will be interacting with one another in accordance with strategic reasoning, as taught by game theory. But if a person's attitude toward another is the one he would adopt toward a stranger if he thought the stranger might well be an Egoist or a Limited Egoist, then on very many occasions his response will be indistinguishable from that of (Unlimited) Egoists or one of the other varieties of Egoism. This is what I mean by the Problem of General Egoism.

The crucial question, then, is whether for these cases, people fare better with or without sanctioned rules designed suitably to modify strategic egoistic interaction. If my reflections in the last few paragraphs are sound, then many people interacting with one another are likely on many occasions to act as Limited Egoists would. It will therefore be important to examine the behavior of people in a world in which they find it plausible to regard one another (other things equal) as one or other of the three kinds of Egoists I distinguished, and in which they interact with one another in accordance with strategic reasoning, whether this means in accordance with the principle of maximizing their preference satisfaction or on the basis of self-interested or self-anchored reason.[4]

3   Prisoner's Dilemma

In recent years, many philosophers[5] have been influenced by this sort of reflection which goes back at least as far as Hobbes. I want to stress, what should already be clear by implication, that the Problem of General Egoism does not depend on everyone's actually being an Egoist of one or the other kind described. Rather, it arises out of the plausibility of the belief that persons one does not know may well be or may well (at best) behave like Principled Limited Egoists. Nor is the problem avoided if everyone always acts on self-anchored reasons, since it is plausible to think that, in the absence of suitable socialization and suitably sanctioned social rules, many or most people will adopt conceptions of the good life for themselves in which their prudential reasons are outweighed only by the strong positive or negative attitudes which they develop, in the course of their lives, toward relatively few people with whom they stand in a special relation of love, friendship, and affection, or hate, enmity, and dislike; and, of course, the latter is no help anyway.

The Problem of General Egoism (as I call it) has been explored most fully in game theory, which officially operates with the theory of the rationality of agent-utility maximization, but then usually proceeds as if everyone's preferences were "nontuistic" (that is, self-regarding) and as if, in the absence of contrary evidence, people with whom we interact had acted on the principle of always doing what accords with reason. Together,

these two assumptions come to the same thing as that which I have called "Principled Rational Egoism." However, if my reflections on the previous section are sound, then the Problem of General Egoism arises not only out of these strong, and, I think, psychologically unrealistic, assumptions of game theory. As Hobbes saw, in the absence of suitably sanctioned social rules with suitable remotivating content (as in his state of nature), the problem may arise, even if people interacting with one another are not themselves Principled Limited (let alone Unlimited) Rational Egoists. It does arise if, in such a "state of nature,"[6] it is plausible for people to suppose, when interacting with strangers, that these may well be (Unlimited) Egoists and also be rational and that they will in turn suppose that those strangers with whom they interact may well be (Unlimited) Egoists and rational. Under these conditions, it seems, they would interact with one another in the same way as they would if they were Principled Rational Egoists. We can therefore rely for our investigation on game theoretic discussions of the topic most relevant here, namely, whether in view of certain types of interaction – of which so-called Prisoner's Dilemma is the best known – Rational Egoism is a tenable theory of rationality.

The story of Prisoner's Dilemma (PD) (attributed to A. W. Tucker) is by now so well known that I can be very brief. It concerns two prisoners, say, Ann (A) and Bill (B), accused of jointly committing crimes, who have been told that, if both confess, both will be sentenced to two years in prison; if neither confesses, both to one year; and if one confesses while the other does not, the former will get off free, while the latter will get three years.[7]

		B	
		Confess	Not Confess
A	Confess	3rd Preference for B 3rd Preference for A	4th Preference for B 1st Preference for A
	Not Confess	1st Preference for B 4th Preference for A	2nd Preference for B 2nd Preference for A

What make this a PD situation are three things: (1) that the outcome for each depends on what both do, but what one does is independent of what the other does: each must choose in ignorance of which of the alternatives the other will choose, though each knows what are the choices before both of them; (2) that it has the following "payoff" pattern when ranked in terms of each prisoner's first-order preference ordering; in this case, each has a preference for shorter over longer prison terms for himself; and (3) that each knows that the other is (what I have called) "evaluatively rational," and knows also what the other's preference ordering is. This shows that by not confessing, A either gets her fourth preference (if B confesses) or her second preference (if B does not confess); whereas by confessing, she either gets her third preference (if he also confesses) or her first preference (if he does not confess). Thus whatever B does, A does better by confessing than by not confessing (third rather than fourth or first rather than second preference). And since the payoff pattern is symmetrical for A and B, each does better by confessing than by not confessing, whatever the other does. Hence confessing is A's *best reply* to whatever B does. Hence if people have adopted and act on the Principle of Rationality, if the only reasons in which they believe are self-anchored ones, if they subscribe to the theory of Rational Egoism (rather than, as I do, in the theory that bases self-anchored reasons on the agent's own point of view which does not imply Egoism), and if that theory requires them always to make their best reply (where there is one), then each will confess. At the same time, *both* will *fare better*, in terms of their preference satisfaction, if both do not confess. Thus, we have the seemingly paradoxical result that *each does better* for himself or herself by confessing than by not confessing, but *both fare better* if they do not confess than if they do;[8] and not only that, but *each* fares better if *both* do not confess than if both confess. But bear in mind that, as things are set up, A's and B's choices are made independently of each other: neither knows what the other is or will be doing. Indeed, in the absence of suitably sanctioned rules, neither would seem able to acquire reliable evidence of what the other will be doing, since, as I argued, it is plausible to think it not unlikely that the stranger with whom one interacts is an Unlimited Egoist and is only pretending to be a Limited, or no sort of Egoist at all.

Does this show that the Theory of Rational Egoism is unsound, that no society should teach it, and that people who want to be rational should not accept it? To clarify this, let us borrow a few further distinctions from game theory. The first is between "zero-sum" and "cooperative" interactions. In the first type, what one party gains, the other loses. If you win our game of chess, I lose it. In a cooperative game, all parties may do better if they act "in a cooperative way" than if they do not. PD is a cooperative type of game (interaction). Both fare better if both follow "the coordinative guideline," that is, if neither confesses, than *either or both* would if each made his "best reply" to the other. Let us use "cooperating" as short for "following a joint coordinative guideline in a cooperative type of interaction."

A second distinction is between "independent" and "interdependent" interaction. Suppose that I like my job but am dissatisfied with my present salary, but would be satisfied with a modest raise. I also know that my own company would at least match any offer I may receive from some other prestigious firm, but will not give me a raise unless I receive such an offer. Lastly, I know that my firm believes I shall not get such an offer unless I seriously look for one, an activity they know I hate. I also know that my company is convinced that if I make a serious effort to get such a job, I will succeed and that for this reason, the moment I start seriously looking, they will offer me a modest raise. If I receive such a modest offer from my firm before I receive a good offer from another, I stop looking because I hate spending my time on doing it and the moderate raise will satisfy me. But, if I have received an outside offer before my firm offers the moderate raise, then I shall expect a matching offer from them or else leave. If all this is known both to me and the firm, then my interaction with my firm is interdependent since what I do depends on my knowledge of how they would react to my behavior, and vice versa. I begin to look for a job because I know that though they would match an offer, they will not give me even a moderate raise if I don't make efforts to find another job because they know I would not get such an offer without such an effort. The firm risks losing me because they think I may well never start looking for another job or that they can keep me if they give me a moderate raise the moment I start looking. By contrast, in PD, the interaction is independent. Each interacting agent knows only what his and the other's options are and what his relevant preferences are, *but not which of them the other will choose*, so they cannot make their own action dependent on what they know the other will do. In such a situation, it is natural for them to make their best reply, *whatever the other may do*, that is, to do whatever is the best thing for them to do from what, as they believe, is the point of view of practical reason.

A third distinction is between "coordinated" and "uncoordinated" interaction. Eight men rowing a boat will do better if they coordinate their rowing than if they do not.[9] They may do better still if they have a cox coordinating their strokes. Coordinated differs from interdependent interaction. The latter is interaction on the basis of each agent's knowledge of how the other will react to his actions. In the former, each agent follows the coordinating guideline in the hope, belief, or knowledge that the others are also following it. Where all would gain equally, as in the rowing example, it is in accordance with reason to assume that, if all are rational, all will cooperate and that all are sufficiently rational to know that the coordinated behavior is in accordance with reason, the uncoordinated contrary to it.

PD is different in that the fact that both would gain equally if both behaved cooperatively does not enable either to infer that it would be in accordance with reason for either to act cooperatively, since neither can infer that his "partner" is rational, that his partner knows he is rational, and that his partner knows that he knows his partner is. Unless both know at least this much, neither can infer that the other will act cooperatively. For if either of them, say A, is unsure of some of these matters, she may think one or both of two things: she may think that the other (B)

will hope that he (B) can, one-sidedly, act uncooperatively (i.e. confess) and so obtain his most preferred outcome; and/or she may think that (B), though he would be disposed to act cooperatively if he knew she, too, was so disposed, would not risk doing so unless *he knew* that she was so disposed and that *she knew* that he too was so disposed. The possible unwillingness of either to renounce her or his most preferred outcome by acting cooperatively (that is, their possible Unlimited Egoism), and/or the possible unwillingness of either to risk the other's possible unwillingness to renounce his best outcome make it contrary to reason for them to act cooperatively.

It is not even crystal clear that this additional knowledge about one another's rationality would help to resolve the problem. For how could anyone acquire such knowledge? Suppose both my partner and I have that knowledge. Am I *locked into* doing what is rational? Could I not, assuming that the other is rational and so "locked into" the cooperative strategy, act uncooperatively myself? But if, when he knows that I am rational, I am not locked into the cooperative strategy, why should he be so locked? But since, it would seem, nothing could literally lock us into that strategy, the hope that we could acquire this sort of knowledge would seem to be naive. For if the "knowledge" that the other is rational implies that he is locked into cooperative behavior, then the fact that no one ever is locked into this or any sort of such behavior would seem to make that knowledge hard or impossible to acquire.

In any case, even if we could in principle acquire that sort of knowledge, it is unlikely to be available to most or indeed any of us in the circumstances typical of interaction with strangers.[10] It seems to me that, therefore, in many or most such cases, going for the best worst outcome (two years in prison) thereby avoiding the worst worst (three years in prison) and still having a chance of the best best outcome (getting off free), though precluding the worst best outcome (one year in prison) would seem the only course in accordance with reason.[11]

It seems plain, then, that what TRE (the Theory of Rational Egoism) tells individual agents to do depends on the circumstances in which they find themselves. If they face one another as strangers, neither having any special reason (such as love, friendship, hatred, or revenge) to take into account (one way or the other) the interests of the other, neither to be concerned to harm or to benefit the other, but merely to promote their own good, and if neither has any *assurance* that the other will or will not follow the coordinative guideline, even though both know what it requires, then depending to some extent on how bad the worst and how good the best outcome, and on how risk prone or averse it is in accordance with reason to be, the TRE sometimes tells them to play it safe, to go for "the best worst" outcome, in this case for the third preference. In the absence of any assurance of cooperation, that theory may often require them to make their best reply despite its relatively poor payoff to both of them.

And this advice by that theory seems right. In such circumstances, the best thing one can do is to make the best reply, as one sees it. No guideline of practical reason can in this sort of situation *ensure* a better outcome for an individual. At the same time, it is plain (as Hobbes clearly saw) that from the point of view of an optimizer, this is unsatisfactory, since both *could* fare better if both followed the coordinative guideline. What follows from this, however, is not that, according to TRE, it would in this situation be in accordance with reason for each to follow that coordinative guideline, but rather for each *to try to change the situation* so that each can in reason do so.

The first thing to be done, according to TRE, therefore is to solve the so-called assurance problem,[12] that is, the problem of obtaining assurance that others will follow the coordinative guideline. For in the absence of that assurance, following it risks being saddled with one's worst outcome. How can the assurance problem be solved? We have already cast doubt on a solution based on acquiring certain complex knowledge.

Could we perhaps solve this problem simply by getting the agents in such situations to agree to follow the coordinative guidelines? This idea, at the heart of the social contract tradition, raises

at least three very difficult problems. The first is a purely practical one, though it is sufficient, I think, to dispose of the idea that the assurance we seek has actually been brought about by such an original social contract.[13] One thing that prevents this ball from ever starting to roll is simply that it would be impossible in the circumstances envisaged to get all the people together and to agree on a given set of guidelines sufficiently detailed to provide guidance for the major practical problems arising even in a small group of interacting people.

The second difficulty, usually called the coordination problem,[14] is of considerable theoretical importance. It concerns the question of what would be a rational set of coordinative guidelines and how those to be guided by them would come to know the particular one from among the various possible ones which *actually is to co-ordinate* their behavior. It is easy to forget the magnitude of this problem when one thinks only of PD. For its structure is so simple that there can be only one coordinative guideline: not to confess; and it is completely symmetrical, hence the question of its justice or fairness does not arise: both prisoners gain and lose the same amount by the only two options open to them. But in the enormous numbers of PD situations which arise in real life, there will be many alternative sets of coordinative guidelines which, while benefiting some or all, would not benefit them equally or equitably. . . .

The third problem is this. It may well appear to be required by the Theory of Rational Egoism that people in PD situations draw up coordinating guidelines and make agreements to follow them rather than make their best reply to whatever others can do. But since it is in accordance with that theory to do this only if one's cooperation is both a necessary and sufficient condition of other people's cooperation, it cannot be in accordance with it to keep the agreement one has made. For even though one's making the agreement may be a sufficient condition of *other* people's cooperation, one's own actual cooperation is not a necessary condition of it. One can sometimes profitably break such agreements. But if one's own cooperation is not a necessary condition, then it may not be in accordance with this theory to adhere to the agreement, since one may be able to do better for oneself by breaking it as long as the others keep it. And conversely, since one's own cooperation may not be a necessary condition of others cooperating, no particular other person's cooperation is either. But that shows that the agreement itself is not a sufficient condition of other people's cooperation. Therefore it is not in accordance with TRE for oneself or anyone else to cooperate, since the existence of an agreement alone does not solve the assurance problem. As Hobbes pointed out, contracts alone are empty words[15] (for a subscriber of TRE, as he appears to have been).

The coordination problem does raise doubts about the soundness of TRE, however, for it would seem that its adherents are committed, by their conception of what is in accordance with reason, to a choice that produces a suboptimal state of affairs, since different choices could produce a better one for at least some of them without it being less good for anyone, and perhaps better for all, perhaps even better for all alike. I shall return to this point shortly.

The upshot of these reflections is to confirm that TRE is plausible only if it is interpreted as requiring the pursuit of one's own good in whatever *happens to be the best possible way* in the particular circumstances in which one finds oneself. If it were interpreted as specifying or implying a certain specific method or policy or strategy, namely, the strategy of making the best possible uncoordinated reply in interaction, then it could not be acceptable. For if it turns out, as it seems to, that one's good depends at least as much on what others are doing as on what one is doing oneself, such an uncoordinated, individualistic approach to the promotion of one's own good is clearly not always the best possible. It would surely be preferable, from a rational point of view, to work for a state of affairs in which one's own promotion of one's own good is reliably coordinated with other people's promotion of their own good, so as to avoid the suboptimal outcomes necessarily produced by uncooperative strategies in PD and similar situations.

Let us then look at the oldest solution to the assurance problem: a suitable change in the PD situation making the uncoordinated best reply either impossible or undesirable. Hobbes thought of the condition in which PD arises as a State of Nature, that is, one in which, although (implausibly) all can work out for themselves roughly what the "best" coordinating guidelines would have to be, there is no way of agreeing on the necessary details and there is no assurance of reciprocity. Such a state, Hobbes argued, is governed by what he called the Right of Nature, for in that state it is rational, that is, prudent, for anyone and everyone to do whatever in his judgment is necessary for the promotion of his good (which Hobbes appears to have located above all in the preservation of his life and secondarily in "commodious living"). But although in his view a rational person would be willing, *on a basis of reciprocity*, to lay down whatever part of his Right of Nature necessary to avoid the mutual harm caused by each person's untrammeled exercise of the Right of Nature in his pursuit of his own good, no one can have assurance of reciprocity as long as he lives in a State of Nature. But since only reciprocity makes it beneficial for anyone to lay down any part of his Right of Nature, so in the absence of assurance of reciprocity, it is not prudent and so, in Hobbes' view, not rational for anyone to do so.[16]

Hobbes thought that the existence of an effective social order with adequate sanctions guaranteed the prevalence of the conditions which assured its members of reciprocity. For promulgation of the guidelines ensures that those willing to cooperate *know how* to do so, thus solving the coordination problem. And their enforcement ensures the prudence of cooperation, thus making it prudent for anyone and everyone to follow, and imprudent to break, whatever (with minimal exceptions, such as the requirement to commit suicide) are the coordinative guidelines promulgated and enforced by one's society. This solves the assurance problem.

Hobbes thought it right to identify rationality with prudence, for although he admitted that it might in some cases turn out to have been in one's best interest to break [the law], he argued that it could never be prudent to break it, taking into account the probability and the seriousness of being caught.[17] However, this argument depends on two claims, only one of which is sound, namely, that under the conditions Hobbes envisages, anyone who violates the law can gain from his violation only by "the errors of other men." The second, namely, that one "could not foresee nor reckon upon such errors" and that therefore one always necessarily acts contrary to reason in breaking the law, is open to two serious objections.

The first objection, for argument's sake, grants Hobbes the possibility of a flawlessly efficient state, one capable of catching and convicting all (or very nearly all) lawbreakers and of inflicting such heavy punishment on them that in such a state it is indeed always necessarily contrary to (Hobbesian) reason for anyone to break the law. The problem with this is that, if such a state is indeed possible, the cost of maintaining it would be staggering. It is more than doubtful whether, under such a monstrous police state, the loss in freedom and the risk of false conviction by a court could possibly be outweighed by the gain in having rationality and prudence coincide, as Hobbes's theory of practical reason would seem to require.

The second objection looks more closely into the possibility of such an absolute state composed of Hobbesian individuals. All the members of a community (if that is not here an oxymoron), or most of whom are, and suspect one another of being, Principled Rational Egoists, have reason to want to be in a position to break the law and get away with impunity, but at the same time want also to ensure that others will never be in that position. Every one in such a community thus has reason to ensure, through supporting stringent policies of "law and order," that crime never pays *other* people, while at the same time ensuring that it pays *him*. He therefore has reason to attempt, perhaps by bribes, threats, and other methods, to induce officials to bend the law in his favor or simply to close their eyes when he breaks it. Conversely, its officials whose task it is to ensure that the laws are enforced, have reason to bend the law in favor of those who are able and willing to make it worth their while.

Given the unequal ability of people to promote their own interest in these various ways, a society of consistent adherents of this theory will tend to depart from stringent uniform enforcement of the laws. What is worse, every such person will want, by lobbying and similar methods, to ensure that the laws are written so as to favor him more than others. As officials find it in their best interest and so rational to exempt some from punishment and to pass inequitable laws favoring some more than others, it will become more and more in the interest of more and more of the socially disfavored to try and break the law, even as the risk to themselves of being caught increases, because for them the advantage of obeying the laws tends to diminish, whereas that of breaking them to grow. Such egoistic societies will, therefore, tend to be unstable, with periodic upheavals and revolutions and many of the drawbacks of Hobbes's State of Nature, which they were supposed to remedy.

It is sometimes argued that Hobbes's mistake lies in his account of human psychology: we are not as egoistic as he makes us out to be. This may well be true, but it does not solve the problem Hobbes faces. If TRE (the Theory of Rational Egoism), to which Principled Rational Egoists subscribe, is sound, then in certain situations such as Prisoner's Dilemma, setting aside one's own interest to promote that of others is irrational unless one has very good reason to think that others will do likewise. All that is needed, then, for optimal outcomes of our interactions might seem to be two things. One is a slight change in our theory of rationality: the point of view of practical reason is not that of the agent's own greatest good or best interest or maximization of revealed preference-satisfaction, but what I have called his own point of view, that is, that of his own sound conception of a good life for himself. The other is a more altruistic attitude of people toward one another, a greater concern for the good or interests of a greater number of one's fellow members.

[. . .]

5 Conditional Good Will

What then, would be the ideally rational SD preference pattern?* We first consider what we may regard as the "standard" case. Its conditions are as follows: there is interaction; people's actions are independent of one another; many people are indifferent about one another's well-being and/or are ignorant of one another's SD preferences; there are no socially recognized and adequately sanctioned uniform coordinating guidelines; and/or, even where people can easily determine such guidelines for themselves (as in PD), they lack the assurance that others will follow them. In such a situation, any SD-preference pattern other than SF [self-favoring] would be contrary to reason since in this standard situation – where "other things are equal" e.g. the other is not one of the comparatively few whom one loves – it would be contrary to (self-anchored) reason to put anyone else's concerns as high as, let alone higher than, one's own.

However, since, when generalized, interaction on an SF-preference pattern leads to suboptimal results in PD situations, there is then reason for everyone to try to change this standard situation so as to make it according to reason to act in ways that would generate both individually and collectively optimal results, as would be achieved in PD by all cooperating. If, as I have argued, changes in one's second-order preferences will not suffice to achieve this, then three other changes would seem to be needed or at any rate helpful: the promulgation by a rational order of uniform coordinative guidelines generally recognized as defeating what are reasons in the standard situation, the creation of the assurance that people, whether ideally rational or not, will follow these guidelines by attaching suitable sanctions to them, and a suitable modification of SF preferences to make the effectiveness of the sanctions less crucial. For if we all retain our SF preferences and know that we all do, then we

ourselves are not trustworthy, and we know others not to be either. But then it would be contrary to reason for others who are trustworthy to include *us* in a cooperative scheme capable of ensuring optimal results, since these results depend on all their members being sufficiently trustworthy, even without perfectly effective sanctions. Similarly, if some people with whom we interact are not trustworthy, then it would be contrary to reason to include *them* in our cooperative scheme. If a group consisting entirely of untrustworthy people nevertheless set up such a cooperative scheme, then the best they can hope for is the sort of Hobbesian order (or disorder) I described earlier. If a mixed group, some trustworthy, some untrustworthy, forms such a cooperative scheme, then the trustworthy ones will tend to be exploited by the untrustworthy ones.

Grant, then, that reason requires not only a change of external conditions but also a modification, on a basis of reciprocity, of interagents' SF preferences. But exactly what is the ideally rational change? Hobbes appears to have hit upon the minimal change necessary: the mutual laying down, on a basis of reciprocity, of those parts of what he called the Right of Nature that stand in the way of the optimal working of a cooperative scheme. But, of course, Hobbes's second Law of Nature tells us what reason requires us to do in "ideal" circumstances and what it requires in others. In conditions of imperfect assurance of reciprocity and of imperfect rationality of our own and other people's preference structure, it tells us to do things that have suboptimal outcomes. Applying the preceding reflections to Hobbes's point, we can say that in these "ideal" circumstances reason requires that wherever the coordinating guidelines, whose universal adoption would ensure optimality, require us to set aside or modify our own actual SD preferences, we do so even if we cannot also suitably change our conflicting first-order ones. We must, if necessary, change or curb our SF preferences so that we are prepared always to follow the coordinative guidelines – of course, provided others do likewise – even when our current SF preferences would require us to ignore them and especially when we know

---

* SD preferences or self-involving distributive preferences are the weight one gives to the satisfaction of one's own preferences relative to those of one's partner (or opponent) in interactions – Ed.

or have reason to believe that others are following them.

I call this modification of SF preferences an attitude of "Limited Conditional Good Will." It is limited in that it is not a disposition to promote or protect other people's good on all occasions, but only when it is required by certain coordinative rules that apply to one. And it is conditional in that one's willingness to do so is dependent on a certain contingency, namely, that all others to whom the rules apply do likewise, or, if not all do so, that those who don't do not profit from their nonconformity and preferably are treated in a way intended to remotivate them (e.g. punished). This attitude need not, of course, be based on a concern for others, though the practical effects will be the same as if it were. It need only be an attitude based on the recognition that oneself and others alike are dependent on one another for our attainment of the good life, and that each of us should therefore be prepared, on the basis of reciprocity, to contribute his or her share to the good life of others by making the necessary modification in the untrammeled pursuit of his or her own good life. The main modification of SF preferences required by reason is thus only the willingness to recognize the fact that in PD and similar situations all will fare better by everyone following certain coordinative guidelines, than by each making his (uncoordinated) best reply.

Thus Limited Conditional Good Will is not a straightforward other-regarding or benevolent, let alone an altruistic, SD pattern. . . . Nor is it a utilitarian willingness to generate the greatest total of preference-satisfaction with no concern about whose preferences thereby get satisfied or are left unsatisfied. It is, rather, a willingness not to seek to achieve the good life by making what one thinks the best reply, in those types of situation in which everyone's doing so has suboptimal effects, but instead to follow uniform publicly recognized guidelines, designed to achieve optimal outcomes (or at any rate better ones than would result from independent reasoning by all) and where there is adequate assurance that all concerned, or a sufficient number of them, will follow these guidelines. Persons of limited con-

ditional goodwill may thus be motivated primarily by concern for their own good life, and their conforming with the guidelines is a contribution to the concerns of others, which (since they may not care about these others) is made mainly or only because the realization of their own ends is seen to depend on the contributions made by others, and because they are prepared to recognize the reasonableness of reciprocity in this matter.

At the same time, behavior so motivated is not a case of treating others merely as means to our ends, for one asks for and accepts their contribution to the promotion of one's own good on a basis of reciprocity. Such interagents are not using or exploiting one another, but participating in a mutually beneficial scheme, even when they don't do so from love, affection, kindness, benevolence, or pity. It is a paler substitute for these in those cases when all they feel for one another is the respect they have come to recognize as reasonable if and to the extent that they all play their part in such a mutually beneficial cooperative scheme. They have come to recognize this respect as reasonable because they recognize one another as fully rational beings who conform their behavior to self-anchored reasons except in those cases in which everyone's doing so has suboptimal consequences, when they think it contrary to reason not to conform to known coordinative guidelines which eliminate the suboptimality of consequences, provided only they have adequate assurance that others do likewise.

If we suppose, as seems plausible, that the guidelines that overrule self-anchored reasons would sometimes be followed only very grudgingly and sometimes not followed at all, then an additional change may be necessary. For, given their function, these coordinative guidelines really will at times, perhaps often, conflict with people's self-anchored reasons. That additional change could be brought about by a suitable method of socialization and/or the imposition of appropriate sanctions. But if we are not to have an incoherent system of practical reasons, the coordinative guidelines must be recognized not merely as self-anchored reasons that defeat others in virtue of the sanctions attached to them, as Hobbes may sometimes seem to imply, but as practical reasons that from their nature, independently of the sanctions, defeat self-anchored ones when they conflict. Since, as we supposed, these guidelines are developed, promulgated, and sanctioned by a society, we can think of the reasons based on them as society-anchored.

Conflicts between society- and self-anchored reasons differ in certain respects from conflicts between two or more self-anchored reasons. One is that people may occasionally hope, sometimes with good reason, that they can ignore the society-anchored reasons without suffering the consequences of not following them that one inevitably suffers if one follows the less weighty *rather than* the weightier self-anchored reason, and even when one follows the weightier, *thereby* ignoring the less weighty one. The usual reason for this hope is, of course, that the sanctions may not be effective.[18]

The second difference is that such society-anchored reasons are dependent in a sense in which self-anchored reasons are independent. One has an independent reason to do a certain thing if one has it independently of whether other people have and follow the same reason on the same or on other occasions. The reason I have cut down on carbohydrates is an independent one because I have it and benefit from acting on it even if no one else has it or acts on it. By contrast, a society-anchored reason is more or less dependent on others also having it, *and* following it when they have it.

The third difference resulting from the other two is that the question of whether or not we conform is always also other people's business and so our compliance is inevitably of some (greater or lesser) importance to others, and theirs to us, so that compliance is of importance to all parties in a cooperative scheme whereas this is not so in a system of merely self-anchored practical reasons.

Note that such reasons though society-anchored may (and perhaps must) also be indirectly self-anchored, and this in two respects. The first is that their primary appeal may be of the same kind: that following them promises a better chance of leading a good life for those governed by them. The second is that *what* they recommend us to do is determined by the contribution which the doing of it by all who have the reason, makes to each agent's chances of leading a good life as he conceives of it. However, they are not "directly" self-anchored, because the direct contribution of action in accordance with them is to *other* people's lives, whether or not the agent cares about them. Nevertheless, if sound, they are indirectly self-anchored because each person with limited conditional good-will follows them mainly or only because he assumes that (by and large) each person governed by them is willing to follow them and so to contribute to others, on condition that others do likewise. All are willing to contribute on a basis of reciprocity or mutuality, and those (necessarily few, if the system is to work) who do not, will (by and large) be dealt with in a way designed not to make their failure to comply profitable for them or harmful to their victims.

The question then arises whether society-anchored reasons can be thus indirectly self-anchored and if so, exactly how. How could they be, one may ask, when they are in conflict with self-anchored ones? Well, is it not enough that everyone will fare better if such society-anchored reasons are recognized in and by the society that creates (that is, formulates, promulgates, and sanctions) them? Can we not say that what makes such reasons superior to self-anchored ones is that everyone fares better if everyone acts in accordance with them rather than in accordance with the self-anchored reasons with which they conflict?

I think this Hobbes-like argument is on the right track, but it has at least one very serious flaw. Surely, a slave in a slave society or an untouchable in a rigid caste society would not rightly regard all the coercive rules of her society, at least not all those concerning slavery or the subordination of untouchables, as adequate reasons to do what they require of her. Would it not be a mistake to regard such a society's customary or legal requirements as reasons defeating their self-anchored ones, even if life really were better even for slaves or untouchables, relative to some plausible benchmark, than if they were not so regarded? Why would it be a mistake to hold that the requirements of any such coercive social order are *rightly* regarded and so *really constitute* adequate reasons for members of such an order to act accordingly?

The mistake, I think, is this. If these requirements are really to defeat self-anchored reasons when they conflict, then *everyone* must have *adequate* self-anchored reasons to want them generally so regarded. Now if my earlier argument was sound, then it may well be the case that, whatever (within certain limits) the nature of the social order, everyone is better off under it than in a Hobbesian state of nature or at any rate in a society that recognized only self-anchored practical reasons, and still better off if the social requirements are regarded as defeating reasons than if they are regarded as necessary but irksome obstacles to promoting one's own good or the good life as one conceives it. Nevertheless, this shows only that everyone has *some*, but not that he has *adequate*, reason to want these requirements regarded as reasons that defeat conflicting self-anchored ones.

What, then, would make them adequate? It seems that the society and its sanctioned rules would have to meet certain standards of excellence. The following is a very high standard which, if reached, would yield adequate reasons so to regard them: that the society be so organized that everyone has *the best possible self-anchored* reason *anyone* could in reason *demand* for wanting the social requirements regarded as paramount reasons, namely, the best possible reasons *everyone* could *have*. A person's self-anchored reason for wanting the social requirements so regarded would be the better, the more favorable the social rules are to him and those he cares about. Of course, a person could always ask for better self-anchored reasons than he already has, for there seems to be virtually no limit to the advantages and privileges a society may grant him. It does seem, however, that there is a rational limit to the improvement of a self-anchored reason anyone can in such a context demand: he cannot *in reason* demand a better reason than *everyone* can have. It would seem, therefore, that the best self-anchored reason *anyone* can in reason *demand* for wanting the social requirements

generally regarded as paramount reasons (that is, the best self-anchored reason *everyone* can *have*) is that the social order be not simply for the good of everyone (almost any social order might achieve that) but for the good of everyone *alike* – that, in other words, it be *equitable*. The main reason for this is that socially recognized and suitably sanctioned coordinative guidelines for PD and similar situations are intended to guide people to promote the best possible life for themselves but burdened by a contribution by all participants in such a cooperative scheme to one another's good life. The reason why they must make that contribution to other people's lives is that everyone would fare worse if they did not make it. For this reason, everyone must admit that the guidelines based on such social rules must override self-anchored reasons whenever they conflict but (unless there is another way of showing that they constitute overruling practical reasons) they must indirectly be grounded in adequate self-anchored reasons. Everyone who is to have adequate reason to regard these social rules as society-based reasons must have adequate self-anchored reasons to want these rules recognized as paramount over self-anchored ones with which they conflict. But no one has reason to accept any such reason as adequate unless it is as good as anyone can have without thereby making someone else's reason less good than his. For why should any fully rational person welcome a transition from a system of merely self-anchored reasons to one in which self-anchored ones are defeated by society-anchored ones or resist a transition in the opposite direction, unless the contribution to other people's lives they require of him is no greater than that which they require of others, and that general conformity to them equally improves other people's lives? It seems that if a social order comes up to this standard, then everyone has adequate self-anchored reason to want its requirements generally recognized as reasons defeating self-anchored ones. And in that case they are rightly so regarded, and therefore really are such paramount reasons.

However, it seems plain that this is an unjustifiably high standard of adequacy for recognizing social requirements as such paramount reasons.

For one thing, it is not clear that a society's requirements could be so formulated that the "sacrifices" (frustrations of self-anchored reasons) each is asked to shoulder are the same and that the improvements thereby made to each life also are the same. Even if such an arrangement is possible, no one may know what it would be like, or how one could get to it from the current social structure, or whether one had reached it as far as this is possible. Again, it will often be very difficult to tell how close to one's conception of the good life one would get by strategic reasoning based on self-anchored reasons in a social order that recognized only self-anchored reasons but also had sanctioned social rules not recognized as society-anchored reasons, and then it would be difficult to tell just how much better or worse one's life is made when these social requirements come to be recognized as society-based reasons, or how great a further improvement or deterioration would be brought about if the rules were changed so as to be equitable.

All the same, the advantages of having the requirements so recognized would seem to be great and should, it seems to me, be allowed to outweigh some of the disadvantages to those whom the social order appears to treat less favorably. So perhaps we should be satisfied with the following lower standard. Since equity is hard to attain and since it is also hard to know when it is and when it is not attained, there should be institutions (such as a supreme court) set up to keep check on the equity of the guidelines and empowered to set in motion recognized processes of correction. Clearly, this would seem to be a minimum condition of regarding inequitable guidelines as practical reasons defeating self-anchored ones. But if the machinery for detecting and correcting them is well designed and reasonably effective, and if the society encourages critical discussion of both the social requirements and the institution of correction, then this may well be the best we can do to get as close as possible to a truly equitable society, especially in view of the vagueness and unavoidable contentiousness of the idea of equity. But in that case, even the requirements of such an inequitable society which, however, is trying as hard as possible to become equitable may constitute paramount society-based reasons. If so, then there would also be justification for the imposition of appropriately sanctioning the social rules that impose these requirements. If this is right, then it solves the problem I raised in section 2 of this chapter.

This concludes my account of the order of reason. It also concludes, for the time being, my discussion of society-anchored reasons and their relation to self-anchored ones.

Notes

1 For an account of strategic reasoning, see Jon Elster, *Ulysses and the Sirens: Studies in Rationality and Irrationality* (Cambridge: Cambridge University Press, 1979). There is some similarity between one's acting for self-anchored reasons and maximizing one's utility (as understood by Elster and many others), but I believe there are serious difficulties with their conception of preferences on which their concept of utility is based. See my "Rationality, Value and Preference."

2 Here my views are close to those of David Hume, *Treatise*, pp. 486–7.

3 But see Colin Turnbull's depressing account of the Ik, in his *The Mountain People* (New York: Simon & Schuster, 1972), which gives plausibility to the view that whether, in the absence of a reason to the contrary, we are benevolent or malevolent, depends on the climate of life in which we grew up and now find ourselves.

4 As should by now be clear, the main difference between the principle of maximizing one's preference satisfaction and the principle of acting on the balance of self-anchored reasons is that the former imposes only very few if any constraints on what are admissible preferences whereas the latter restricts relevant preferences in various major ways. We already noted that they are those based on what is a good thing from one's own point of view. And we shall shortly note another restriction. For a discussion of the relevant limitations on preferences, see my "Rationality, Value and Preference"; Amartya Sen, "Behaviour and the Concept of Preferences," *Economica*, 11 (1973), pp. 241–59; and Gauthier, *Morals by Agreement*, pp. 26–38.

5 Including myself (see my paper "Rationality and Morality," with a reply by Sen, *Erkenntnis*, 11

(1977), pp. 197–223; also notably Gauthier, e.g. *Morals by Agreement*, especially pp. 79–82; Sen, e.g. "Choice, Orderings, and Morality," along with J. W. N. Watkins's reply "Self-Interest and Morality" and Sen's rejoinder, *Practical Reason*, ed. Stephan Körner (New Haven, CT: Yale University Press, 1974), pp. 54–82; and Derek Parfit, "Prudence, Morality, and the Prisoner's Dilemma," *Proceedings of the British Academy*, 65 (London: Oxford University Press, 1979), pp. 539–64.

6 Of course, if my account of reason is sound, people cannot be rational (in my sense) in a Hobbesian State of Nature (if indeed such a state is conceivable), but they can be rational in the sort of society which provides guidelines only of practical reasons that are self-anchored (if that sort of society is conceivable).

7 For those if any not yet familiar with PD, here is the payoff matrix in terms of years in prison:

		B	
		Confess	Not Confess
A	Confess	2 / 2	3 / 0
	Not Confess	0 / 3	1 / 1

8 In this formulation, I have followed Derek Parfit, "Prudence, Morality, and the Prisoner's Dilemma," p. 550.

9 But see the qualifications J. L. Mackie makes to this Humean claim in his book, *Hume's Moral Theory* (London: Routledge and Kegan Paul, 1980), pp. 88–90.

10 For a different view, see Gauthier's claim that we are, all or most of us, sufficiently "translucent" for others to know whether we are "straightforward" or "constrained maximizers," that is, whether in PD we will always make our best reply, or whether we will cooperate provided others also do so. *Morals by Agreement*, p. 174.

11 I am not denying that in stable conditions, where so-called "iterated PDs" occur, mutual confidence can be built up by certain strategies, such as "tit for tat," but not all circumstances are like that and in the absence of a social order with its trust-building institutions, such situations are likely to be rare and short-lived. Of course, once there are these institutions, the matter is very different. Indeed, it seems to me that the assumption that these transactions would occur in a genuine "state of nature" is incoherent.

12 Cf. Rawls, *A Theory of Justice*, p. 269.

13 See David Braybrooke, "The Insoluble Problem of the Social Contract," *Dialogue*, 15 (March 1976), pp. 3–37.

14 Cf. Rawls, *A Theory of Justice*, p. 269.

15 Hobbes, *Leviathan*, p. 201.

16 Hobbes's exception: *Leviathan*, pp. 203–5.

17 Hobbes, *Leviathan*, pp. 203–5.

18 A less usual reason is that someone may be perfectly willing to endure the sanction, as when someone hates another so much that he will choose certain death rather than refrain from murdering his enemy.

10   Moral Theory and Rationality

Bernard Gert

A Moral Theory

A moral theory is an attempt to make explicit, explain, and, if possible, justify morality – that is, the moral system that people use in making their moral judgments and in deciding how to act when confronting moral problems. It attempts to provide a usable account of our common morality; an account of the moral system that can actually be used by people when they are confronted with new or difficult moral decisions.[1] It must include an accurate account of the concepts of rationality, impartiality, and a public system, not only because they are necessary for providing a justification of morality, but also because they are essential to providing an adequate account of it. Indeed, a moral theory can be thought of as an analysis of the concepts of rationality, impartiality, a public system, and morality itself, showing how these concepts are related to each other. . . .

Rationality is the fundamental normative concept. A person seeking to convince people to act in a certain way must try to show that this way of acting is rational – that is, either rationally required or rationally allowed. We use the term "irrational" in such a way that everyone would admit that if a certain way of acting has been shown to be irrational – that is, not even rationally allowed – no one ought to act in that way.[2] But that a way of acting is rationally allowed does not mean that everyone agrees that one ought to act in that way. On the contrary, given that it is often not irrational (i.e. rationally allowed) to act immorally, it is clear that many hold that one should not act in some ways that are rationally allowed. However, there is universal agreement

From *Morality and the New Genetics* (Sudburg, MA: Jones and Bartlett, 1996). Reprinted with permission.

that any action that is not rationally allowed ought not be done; that is, no one ever ought to act irrationally. If rationality is to have this kind of force, the account of rationality must make it clear why everyone immediately agrees that no one ever ought to act irrationally.

To say that everyone agrees that they ought never act irrationally is not to say that people never do act irrationally. People sometimes act without considering the harmful consequences of their actions on themselves; and, although they do not generally do so, strong emotions sometimes lead people to act irrationally. But regardless of how they actually act, people acknowledge that they should not act irrationally. A moral theory must provide an account of rationality such that, even though people do sometimes act irrationally, no one thinks that he ought to act irrationally. It must also relate this account of rationality to morality.

Impartiality is universally recognized as an essential feature of morality. A moral theory must make clear why morality requires impartiality only when one acts in a kind of way that harms people or increases their probability of suffering harm and does not require impartiality when deciding which people to help – for example, which charity to give to. Most philosophical accounts of morality are correctly regarded as having so little practical value because of their failure to consider the limits on the moral requirement of impartiality. That an adequate account of impartiality requires relating impartiality to some group (e.g. as a father is impartial with regard to his children) explains why abortion and the treatment of animals are such difficult problems. People may differ concerning the size of the group with regard to which morality requires impartiality: some holding that this group is limited to actual moral agents; some holding that it should include potential moral agents – for example, fetuses; and still others claiming that it includes all sentient beings – for example, most mammals. We do not think there are conclusive arguments for any of these views. . . .

Rationality as Avoiding Harms

Rationality is very intimately related to harms and benefits. Everyone agrees that, unless one has an adequate reason for doing so, it would be irrational to avoid any benefit or not to avoid any harm. The present account of rationality, although it accurately describes the way in which the concept of rationality is ordinarily used, differs radically from the accounts normally provided by philosophers in two important ways. First, it starts with irrationality rather than rationality, and second, it defines irrationality by means of a list rather than a formula. The basic definition is as follows: *A person acts irrationally when (s)he acts in a way that (s)he knows (justifiably believes), or should know, will significantly increase the probability that (s)he, or those (s)he cares for, will suffer death, pain, disability, loss of freedom, or loss of pleasure: and (s)he does not have an adequate reason for so acting.*

The close relation between irrationality and harm is made explicit by this definition, because this list also defines what counts as a harm or an evil. Everything that anyone counts as a harm or an evil – for example, thwarted desires, diseases or maladies, and punishment – is related to at least one of the items on this list. All of these items are broad categories; so nothing is ruled out as a harm or evil that is normally regarded as a harm. That everyone agrees on what the harms are does not mean that they all agree on the ranking of these harms. Further, pain and disability have degrees, and death occurs at very different ages; so there is no universal agreement that one of these harms is always worse than the others. Some people rank dying several months earlier as worse than a specified amount of pain and suffering, whereas other people rank that same amount of pain and suffering as worse. Thus, for most terminally ill patients, it is rationally allowed

either to refuse death-delaying treatments or to consent to them. . . .

If a person knowingly makes a decision that involves an increase in the probability of herself suffering some harm, her decision will be irrational unless she has an adequate reason for that decision. Thus, not only what counts as a reason, but also what makes a reason adequate must be clarified. *A reason is a conscious belief that one's action will help anyone, not merely oneself or those one cares about, avoid one of the harms, or gain some, good – namely, ability, freedom, or pleasure – and this belief is not seen to be inconsistent with one's other beliefs by almost everyone with similar knowledge and intelligence.* What was said about evils or harms in the preceding paragraph also holds for the goods or benefits mentioned in this definition of a reason. Everything that people count as a benefit or a good (e.g. health, love, and friends) is related to one or more of the items on this list or to the absence of one or more of the items on the list of harms. Complete agreement on what counts as a good is compatible with considerable disagreement on whether one good is better than another or whether gaining a given good or benefit adequately compensates for suffering a given harm or evil.

A reason is adequate if any significant group of otherwise rational people regard the harm avoided or benefit gained as at least as important as the harm suffered. People are otherwise rational if they do not knowingly suffer any avoidable harm without some reason. No rankings that are held by any significant religious, national, or cultural group count as irrational – for example, the ranking by Jehovah's Witnesses of the harms that would be suffered in an afterlife as worse than dying decades earlier than one would if one accepted a transfusion is not an irrational ranking. Similarly, psychiatrists do not regard any beliefs held by any significant religious, national, or cultural group as delusions or irrational beliefs; for example, the belief by Jehovah's Witnesses that accepting blood transfusions will have bad consequences for one's afterlife is not regarded as an irrational belief or delusion. The intent is to not rule out as an adequate reason any relevant belief that has any plausibility; the goal is to count as irrational actions only those actions on which there is close to universal agreement that they should not be done.

Any action that is not irrational is rational. This results in two categories of rational actions, those that are rationally required and those that are merely rationally allowed. Because no action will be irrational if one has a relevant religious or cultural reason for doing it, and that reason is taken as adequate by a significant group of people, in what follows we shall ignore particular religious or cultural beliefs by assuming that the persons involved have no beliefs that are not commonly held. Given this assumption, an example of a rationally required action – that is, an action that it would be irrational not to do – would be taking a proven and safe antibiotic for a life-threatening infection. On the same assumption, refusing a death-delaying treatment for a painful terminal disease will be a rationally allowed action – that is, an action that it is irrational neither to do nor not to do. These two categories share no common feature except that they are both not irrational. This account of rationality has the desired result that everyone who is regarded as rational always wants himself and his friends to act rationally. Certainly, on this account of rationality, no one would ever want himself or anyone for whom he is concerned to act irrationally.

Although this account of rationality may sound obvious, it is in conflict with the most common account of rationality, where rationality is limited to an instrumental role. A rational action is often defined as one that maximizes the satisfaction of all of one's desires, but without putting any limit on the content of those desires. This results in an irrational action being defined as any action that is inconsistent with such maximization. But unless desires for any of the harms on the list are ruled out, it turns out that people would not always want those for whom they are concerned to act rationally. If a genetic counselor has a young patient who, on finding out that he has the gene for Huntington's disease, becomes extremely depressed and desires to kill himself now, more than twenty years before he will become symptomatic, no one will encourage him to satisfy that desire even if doing so will maximize the satisfaction of his present desires. Rather, everyone concerned with him will encourage him to seek counseling. They will all hope that he will be cured of his depression and then come to see that he has no adequate reason to deprive himself of twenty good years of life.[3] That rationality has a definite content and is not limited to a purely instrumental role (for example, acting so as to maximize the satisfaction of all one's desires) conflicts with most accounts of rational actions, both philosophical and non-philosophical.[4]

Scientists may claim that both of these accounts of rationality are misconceived. They may claim that, on the basic account of rationality, it is not primarily related to actions at all, but rather rationality is reasoning correctly. Scientific rationality consists of using those scientific methods best suited for discovering truth. Although I do not object to this account of rationality, I think that it cannot be taken as the fundamental sense of rationality. The account of rationality as avoiding harms is more basic than that of reasoning correctly, or scientific rationality. Scientific rationality cannot explain why it is irrational not to avoid suffering avoidable harms when no one benefits in any way. The avoiding-harm account of rationality does explain why it is rational to reason correctly and to discover new truth – namely, because doing so helps people to avoid harms and to gain benefits.

Rationality, Morality, and Self-interest

Although morality and self-interest do not usually conflict, the preceding account of rationality makes clear that, when they do conflict, it is not irrational to act in either way. Although this means that it is never irrational to act contrary to one's own best interests in order to act morally, it also means that it is never irrational to act in one's own best interest even though this is immoral. Further, it may even be rationally allowed to act contrary to both self-interest and morality if, for example, friends, family, or colleagues benefit. This is often not realized, and some physicians and scientists believe that they cannot be acting immorally if they act to benefit others and contrary to their own self-interest. This leads some to immorally cover up the mistakes of their colleagues, believing that they are acting morally, because they, themselves, have nothing to gain and are even putting themselves at risk.

Although some philosophers have tried to show that it is irrational to act immorally, this conflicts with the ordinary understanding of the matter. There is general agreement, for example, that it may be rational for someone to deceive a client about a mistake that one's genetic counseling facility has made, even if this is acting immorally. The motivation for one to act morally . . . primarily comes from one's concern for others, together with a realization that it would be arrogant to think that morality does not apply to oneself and one's colleagues in the same way that it applies to everyone else. Our attempt to provide a useful guide for determining what ways of behaving are morally acceptable presupposes that the readers of this chapter want to act morally.

Impartiality

Impartiality, like simultaneity, is usually taken to be a simpler concept than it really is. Einstein showed that one cannot simply ask whether A and B occurred simultaneously, one must ask whether A and B occurred simultaneously with regard to some particular observer, C. Similarly, one cannot simply ask if A is impartial, one must ask whether A is impartial with regard to some group in a certain respect. The following analysis of the basic concept of impartiality shows that to fully understand what it means to say that a person is impartial involves knowing both the group with regard to which her impartiality is being judged and the respect in which her actions are supposed to be impartial with regard to that group. *A is impartial in respect R with regard to group G if and only if A's actions in respect R are not influenced at all by which members of G benefit or are harmed by these actions.*

The minimal group toward which morality requires impartiality consists of all moral agents (those who are held morally responsible for their actions), including oneself, and former moral agents who are still persons (incompetent but not permanently unconscious patients). This group is the minimal group because everyone agrees that the moral rules – for example, "Do not kill" and "Do not deceive" – require acting impartially with regard to a group including at least all of these people. Further, in the United States and the rest of the industrialized world, almost everyone would include in the group toward whom the moral rules require impartiality infants and older children who are not yet moral agents. However, the claim that moral rules require impartiality with regard to any more-inclusive group is more controversial. Many hold that this group should not be any more inclusive, whereas many others hold that this group should include all potential moral agents, whether sentient or not – for example, a fetus from the time of conception. . . . Still others hold that this group should include all sentient beings – that is, all beings who can feel pleasure or pain, whether potential moral agents or not – for example, all mammals.

The debates about abortion and animal rights are best understood as debates about who should be included in the group toward which the moral rules require impartiality. Because fully informed rational persons can disagree about who is included in the group toward which morality requires impartiality, there is no way to resolve the issue philosophically. This is why discussions of abortion and animal rights are so emotionally charged and often involve violence. Morality, however, does set limits to the morally allowable ways of settling unresolvable moral disagreements. These ways cannot involve violence or other unjustified violations of the moral rules but must be settled peacefully. Indeed, one of the proper functions of a democratic government is to settle unresolvable moral disagreements by peaceful means.

The respect in which morality requires impartiality toward the minimal group (or some larger group) is when considering violating a moral rule – say, killing or deceiving. Persons are not required to be impartial in following the moral ideals – for example, relieving pain and suffering. The failure to distinguish between moral rules, which can and should be obeyed impartially with respect to the minimal group, and moral ideals, which cannot be obeyed impartially even with regard to this group, is the cause of much confusion in discussing the relation of impartiality to morality. The kind of impartiality required by the moral rules involves allowing a violation of a moral rule with regard to one member of the group (for example, a stranger) only when such a violation would be allowed with regard to everyone else in the group (e.g. friends or relatives). It also involves allowing a violation of a moral rule by one member of the group (say, oneself) only when everyone else in the group (say, strangers) would be allowed such a violation.

Acting in an impartial manner with regard to the moral rules is analogous to a referee impartially officiating a basketball game, except that the referee is not part of the group toward which he is supposed to be impartial. The referee judges all participants impartially if he makes the same decision regardless of which player or team is benefited or harmed by that decision. All impartial referees need not prefer the same style of basketball; one referee might prefer a game with less bodily contact, hence calling more fouls, whereas another may prefer a more physical game, hence calling fewer fouls. Impartiality allows these differences as long as the referee does not favor any particular team or player over any other. In the same way, moral impartiality allows for differences in the ranking of various harms and benefits as long as one would be willing to make these rankings part of the moral system and one does not favor any particular person in the group, including oneself or a friend, over any others when one decides to violate a moral rule or judges whether a violation is justified.

A Public System

A *public system* is a system that, in normal circumstances, has the following two characteristics. First, all persons to whom it applies – that is, those whose behavior is to be guided and judged by that system – understand it – that is, know what behavior the system prohibits, requires, encourages, and allows. Second, it is not irrational for any of these persons to accept being guided and judged by that system. The clearest example of a public system is a game. A game has an inherent goal and a set of rules that form a system that is understood by all of the players – that is, they all know what kind of behavior is prohibited, required, encouraged, and allowed by the game; and it is not irrational for all players to use the goal and the rules of the game to guide their own behavior and to judge the behavior of other players by them. Although a game is a public system, it applies only to those playing the game. Morality is a public system that applies to all moral agents; all people are subject to morality simply by virtue of being rational persons who are responsible for their actions.

In order for morality to be known by all rational persons, it cannot be based on any beliefs that are not shared by all rational persons. Those beliefs that are held by all rational persons (rationally required beliefs) include general factual beliefs such as: people are mortal, can suffer pain, can be disabled, and can be deprived of freedom or pleasure; also people have limited knowledge – that is, people know some things about the world, but no one knows everything. On the other hand, not all rational people share the same scientific and religious beliefs; so no scientific or religious beliefs can form part of the basis of morality itself, although, of course, such beliefs are often relevant to making particular moral judgments. Parallel to the rationally required general beliefs, only personal beliefs that all rational persons have about themselves (e.g. beliefs that they themselves can be killed and suffer pain and so forth) can be included as part of the foundation for morality. Excluded as part of a foundation for morality are all personal beliefs about one's race, sex, religion, and so forth, because not all rational persons share these same beliefs about themselves.

Although morality itself can be based only on those factual beliefs that are shared by all rational persons, particular moral decisions and judgments obviously depend not only on the moral system, but also on factual beliefs about the situation. Most actual moral disagreements are based on a disagreement on the facts of the case, but particular moral decisions and judgments may also depend on the rankings of the harms and benefits. A decision about whether to withhold a proband's genetic information from him involves a belief about the magnitude of the risk – for example, what the probability is of the information leading him to kill himself – and the ranking of that degree of risk of death against the certain loss of freedom to act on the information that would result from withholding that information. Equally informed impartial rational persons may differ not only in their beliefs about the degree of risk, but also in their rankings of the harms involved, and either of these differences may result in their disagreeing on what morally ought to be done.

Morality

Although morality is a public system that is known by all those who are held responsible for their actions (all moral agents), it is not a simple system. A useful analogy is the grammatical system used by all competent speakers of a language. Almost no competent speaker can explicitly describe this system, yet they all know it in the sense that they use it when speaking and in interpreting the speech of others. If presented with an explicit account of the grammatical system, competent speakers have the final word on its accuracy. They should not accept any description of the grammatical system if it rules out speaking in a way that they regard as acceptable or allows speaking in a way that they regard as completely unacceptable.

In a similar fashion, a description of morality or the moral system that conflicts with one's own considered moral judgments normally should not be accepted. However, an explicit account of the systematic character of morality may make apparent some inconsistencies in one's own moral judgments. Moral problems cannot be adequately discussed as if they were isolated problems whose

solution did not have implications for all other moral problems. Fortunately, everyone has a sufficient number of moral judgments that they know to be both correct and consistent so that they are able to judge whether a proposed moral theory provides an accurate account of morality. Although few, if any, people consciously hold the moral system described here, we believe that this moral system is used by most people when they think seriously about how to act when confronting a moral problem themselves or in making moral judgment on others.

Providing an explicit account of morality may reveal that some of one's moral judgments are inconsistent with the vast majority of one's other judgments. Thus one may come to see that what was accepted by oneself as a correct moral judgment is in fact mistaken. Even without challenging the main body of accepted moral judgments, particular moral judgments, even of competent people, may sometimes be shown to be mistaken, especially when long accepted ways of thinking are being challenged. In these situations, one may come to see that one was misled by superficial similarities and differences and so was led into acting or making judgments that are inconsistent with the vast majority of one's other moral judgments. For example, today most doctors in the United States regard the moral judgments that were made by most doctors in the United States in the 1950s about the moral acceptability of withholding information from their patients as inconsistent with the vast majority of their other moral judgments. However, before concluding that some particular moral judgment is mistaken, one must show how this particular judgment is inconsistent with most of one's more basic moral judgments. These basic moral judgments are not personal idiosyncratic judgments but are shared by all who accept any of the variations of our common moral system – for example, that it is wrong to kill and cause pain to others simply because one feels like doing so.

Morality has the inherent goal of lessening the amount of harm suffered by those included in the protected group, either the minimal group or some larger group; it has rules that prohibit some kinds of actions (for example, killing) and require others (for example, keeping promises) and moral ideals that encourage certain kinds of actions (for example, relieving pain). It also contains a procedure for determining when it is justified to violate a moral rule – for example, when a moral rule and a moral ideal conflict. Morality does not provide unique answers to every question; rather it sets the limits to genuine moral disagreement. One of the tasks of a moral theory is to explain why, even when there is complete agreement on the facts, genuine moral disagreement cannot be eliminated, but it must also explain why this disagreement has legitimate limits. It is very important to realize that unresolvable moral disagreement on some important issues (for example, abortion) is compatible with total agreement in the overwhelming number of cases on which moral judgments are made. . . .

Moral disagreement not only results from factual disagreement and different rankings of the harms and benefits, but also from disagreement about the scope of morality – that is, who is protected by morality. This disagreement is closely related to the disagreement about who should be included in the group toward which morality requires impartiality. Some maintain that morality is only, or primarily, concerned with the suffering of harm by moral agents, whereas others maintain that the death and pain of those who are not moral agents is as important, or almost so, as the harms suffered by moral agents. Abortion and the treatment of animals are currently among the most controversial topics that result from this unresolvable disagreement concerning the scope of morality. Some interpret the moral rule "Do not kill" as prohibiting killing fetuses and some do not. Some interpret the moral rule "Do not kill" as prohibiting killing animals and some do not. But, even if one regards fetuses and animals as not included in the group impartially protected by morality, this does not mean that one need hold they should receive no protection. There is a wide range of morally acceptable options concerning the amount of protection that should be provided to those who are not included in the group toward which morality requires impartiality.

Disagreement about the scope of morality is only one of the factors that affect the interpretation of the rules. Another factor is disagreement on what counts as breaking the rule – for example, what counts as killing or deceiving, even when it is clear that the person killed or deceived is included in the group impartially protected by morality. People sometimes disagree on when not feeding counts as killing or when not telling counts as deceiving. But, though there is some disagreement in interpretation, most cases are clear and there is complete agreement on the moral rules and ideals to be interpreted. All impartial rational persons agree on the kinds of actions that need justification (e.g. killing and deceiving) and the kinds that are praiseworthy (e.g. relieving pain and suffering). Thus all agree on what moral rules and ideals they would include in a public system that applies to all moral agents. These rules and ideals are part of our common conception of morality, because it is our view that a moral theory must explain and, if possible, justify our common conception of morality; it should not, as most moral theories do, put forward some substitute for it.

With regard to (at least) the minimal group, there are certain kinds of actions that everyone considers to be immoral unless one has an adequate justification for doing them. Among these kinds of actions are killing, causing pain, deceiving, and breaking promises. Anyone who kills people, causes them pain, deceives them, or breaks a promise, and does so without an adequate justification, is universally regarded as acting immorally. Saying that there is a moral rule prohibiting a kind of act is simply another way of saying that a certain kind of act is immoral unless it is justified. Saying that breaking a moral rule is justified in a particular situation – for example, breaking a promise in order to save a life – is another way of saying that a kind of act that would be immoral if not justified is justified in this kind of situation. When no moral rule is being violated, saying that someone is following a moral ideal – for example, relieving pain – is another way of saying that he is doing a kind of action regarded as morally good. Using the terminology of moral rules and moral ideals, and justified and unjustified violations, allows us to formulate a precise account of morality, showing how its various component parts are related. We believe such an account may be helpful to those who must confront the problems raised by the information that has been and will be gained from the new genetics.

A Justified Moral System

A moral system that all impartial rational persons could accept as a public system that applies to all rational persons is a *justified moral system*. Like all justified moral systems, the goal of our common morality is to lessen the amount of harm suffered by those protected by it; it is constrained by the limited knowledge of people and by the need for the system to be understood by everyone to whom it applies. It includes rules prohibiting causing each of the five harms that all rational persons want to avoid and ideals encouraging the prevention of each of these harms.

The Moral Rules

Each of the first five rules prohibits directly causing one of the five harms or evils:

- do not kill (equivalent to causing permanent loss of consciousness);
- do not cause pain (includes mental suffering – for example, sadness and anxiety);
- do not disable (includes loss of physical, mental, and volitional abilities);
- do not deprive of freedom (includes freedom to act and from being acted on);
- do not deprive of pleasure (includes future as well as present pleasure).

The second five rules include those rules that, when not followed in particular cases, usually cause harm, and general disobedience always results in more harm being suffered:

- do not deceive (includes more than lying);
- keep your promise (equivalent to do not break your promise);
- do not cheat (primarily violating rules of a voluntary activity);
- obey the law (equivalent to do not break the law);
- do your duty (equivalent to do not neglect your duty). The term "duty" is being used in its everyday sense to refer to what is required by one's role in society, primarily one's job, not as philosophers customarily use it, which is to say, simply as a synonym for "what one morally ought to do."

The Moral Ideals

In contrast with the moral rules, which prohibit doing those kinds of actions that cause people to suffer some harm or increase the risk of their suffering some harm, the moral ideals encourage one to do those kinds of actions that lessen the amount of harm suffered (including providing goods for those who are deprived) or decrease the risk of people suffering harm. As long as one avoids violating a moral rule, following any moral ideal is encouraged. In particular circumstances, it may be worthwhile to talk of specific moral ideals: for example, one can claim that there are five specific moral ideals involved in preventing harm, one for each of the five kinds of harms. Physicians seem primarily devoted to the ideals of preventing death, pain, and disability. Genetic counselors may have as their primary ideal preventing the loss of freedom of their clients. . . . One can also specify particular moral ideals that involve preventing unjustified violations of each of the moral rules. In so far as a misunderstanding of morality may lead to unjustified violations of the moral rules, providing a proper understanding of morality may also be following a moral ideal.

Although it is not important to decide how specific to make the moral ideals, it is important to distinguish moral ideals from other ideals. Utilitarian ideals involve promoting goods (for example, abilities and pleasure) for those who are not deprived. Such ideals are followed by those who train athletes or who create delicious new recipes. Religious ideals involve promoting activities, traits of character, and so forth, that are idiosyncratic to a particular religion or group of religions. Personal ideals involve promoting some activities, traits of character, etc., which are idiosyncratic to particular persons (for example, ambition) about which there is not universal agreement. Except in very special circumstances, only moral ideals can justify violating a moral rule with regard to someone without her consent.

It is the possibility of being impartially obeyed all of the time that distinguishes the moral rules from the moral ideals. Impartial rational persons favor people following both the moral rules and the moral ideals, but it is only failure to obey a moral rule that requires an excuse or a justification. This account of moral rules and ideals should not be at all surprising. All that is being claimed is that everyone counts certain kinds of actions as immoral – for example, killing, causing pain, deceiving, and breaking promises – unless one can justify doing that kind of act and that no one doubts that acting to relieve pain and suffering is encouraged by morality. That two moral rules can conflict – for example, doing one's duty may require causing pain – makes it clear that it would be a mistake to conclude that one should always avoid breaking a moral rule. Sometimes breaking one of these rules is so strongly justified that not only is there nothing immoral about breaking it, it would be immoral not to break the rule. A physician who, with the rational informed consent of a competent patient, performs some painful procedure in order to prevent much more serious pain or death breaks the moral rule against causing pain but is not doing anything that is immoral in the slightest. In fact, refusing to do the necessary painful procedure, given the conditions specified, would itself be a violation of one's duty as a doctor and thus would need justification in order not to be immoral. It is clear, therefore, that to say that someone has broken a moral rule is not, by itself, to say that anything wrong has been done; it is only to say that some justification is needed.

[. . .]

Justifying Violations of the Moral Rules

Almost everyone agrees that the moral rules are not absolute, that they have justified exceptions; most agree that even killing is justified in self-defense. Further, there is widespread agreement on several features that all justified exceptions have. The first of these involves impartiality. There is general agreement that all justified violations of the rules are such that, if they are justified for any person, they are justified for every person when all of the morally relevant features are the same. The major, and probably only, value of simple slogans like the Golden Rule, "Do unto others as you would have them do unto you," and Kant's Categorical Imperative, "Act only on that maxim that you could will to be a universal law," is as devices to persuade people to act impartially when they are contemplating violating a moral rule. However, given that these slogans are often misleading, it would be better to consider whether an impartial rational person could publicly allow that kind of violation when trying to decide what to do in difficult cases.

There is almost complete agreement that it has to be rational to favor everyone being allowed to violate the rule in these circumstances. Suppose that someone suffering from a mental disorder both wants to inflict pain on others and wants pain inflicted on himself. He favors allowing any person who wants others to cause him pain to cause pain to others, whether or not they want pain inflicted on them. Whether or not this person is acting in accord with the Golden Rule or the Categorical Imperative, it is not sufficient to justify that kind of violation. No impartial rational person would favor allowing those who want pain caused to them to cause pain to everyone else, whether or not they want pain caused to them. The result of allowing that kind of violation would be an increase in the amount of pain suffered with almost no compensating benefit, which is clearly irrational.

Finally, there is general agreement that a violation is justified only if it is rational to favor that violation even if everyone knows that this kind of violation is allowed – that is, the violation must be publicly allowed. A violation is not justified simply if it would be rational to favor allowing everyone to violate the rule in the same circumstances, but only if almost no one knows that it is allowable to violate the rule in those circumstances. For example, it might be rational for one to favor allowing a physician to deceive a patient about his diagnosis if that patient were likely to be upset by knowing the truth, when almost no one knows that such deception is allowed. But that would not make deception in these circumstances justified. It has to be rational to favor allowing this kind of deception when everyone knows that one is allowed to deceive in these circumstances. One must be prepared to publicly defend this kind of deception, if it were discovered. Only the requirement that the violation be publicly allowed guarantees the kind of impartiality required by morality.

Not everyone agrees on which violations satisfy these three conditions, but there is general agreement that no violation is justified unless it satisfies all three of these conditions. Allowing for some disagreement while acknowledging the significant agreement concerning justified violations of the moral rules results in the following formulation of the appropriate moral attitude toward violations of the moral rules: *Everyone is always to obey the rule unless an impartial rational person can advocate that violating it be publicly allowed. Anyone who violates the rule when no*

impartial rational person can advocate that such a violation be publicly allowed may be punished. (The "unless" clause only means that, when an impartial rational person can advocate that such a violation be publicly allowed, impartial rational persons may disagree on whether or not one should obey the rule. It does not mean that they agree that one should not obey the rule.)

[. . .]

Notes

1 A more extended account of morality, and of the moral theory that justifies it, is contained in *Morality: A New Justification of the Moral Rules*, by Bernard Gert (Oxford University Press, 1988), 317pp. (paperback), 1989.

2 We are aware that the terms "rational" and "irrational" are used in many different ways – for example, "irrational" means spontaneous. However, we think that there is a basic concept of rationality and that is the one that we are attempting to describe.

3 See "Irrationality and the DSM-III-R Definition of Mental Disorder," *Analyze & Kritik*, vol. 12, no. 1 (July 1990), pp. 34–46, by Bernard Gert.

4 See "Rationality, Human Nature, and Lists," *Ethics*, vol. 100, no. 2 (1990), pp. 279–300, and "Defending Irrationality and Lists," *Ethics*, vol. 103, no. 2 (1993), pp. 329–36, by Bernard Gert.

---

11   The Justificatory Argument for Human Rights

Alan Gewirth

I now wish to present my own answer to the justificatory or epistemological question of human rights. It will be recalled that the Justifying Ba-

From *Social Philosophy & Policy*, vol. 1, no. 2 (1984), pp. 1–24. Reprinted with permission.

sis or Ground of human rights must be a normative moral principle that serves to prove or establish that every person morally ought to have the necessary goods of action as something to which he or she is entitled. The epistemological question, hence, comes down to whether such a moral principle can be rationally justified.

It is important to note that not all moral principles will serve for this purpose. Utilitarian, organicist, and elitist moral principles either do not justify any moral rights at all, or justify them only as ancillary to and contingent upon various collective goals,[1] or do make rights primary but not as equally distributed among all humans. Hence, it will be necessary to show how the moral principle that justifies equal human rights is superior, in point of rational cogency, to these other kinds of moral principles.

Now, there are well-known difficulties in the attempt to provide a rational justification of any moral principle. Obviously, given some high-level moral principle, we can morally justify some specific moral rule or particular moral judgment or action by showing how its rightness follows from the principle. But how can we justify the basic principle itself? Here, by definition, there is no higher or more general moral principle to be appealed to as an independent variable. Is it the case, then, that justification comes to a stop here? This would mean that we cannot rationally adjudicate between *conflicting* moral principles and ways of life and society, such as those epitomized, for example, by Kant's categorical imperative, Bentham's utilitarianism, Kierkegaard's theological primacy, Stirner's egoism, Nietzsche's exaltation of the superman, Spencer's doctrine of the survival of the fittest, and so on.

The Problem of the Independent Variable

One of the central problems here is that of the independent variable. Principles serve as independent variables for justifying lower-level rules and judgments; but what is the independent variable for justifying principles themselves? Another way to bring out this problem in relation to morality is to contrast particular empirical statements and particular moral judgments. Consider, on the one hand, such a statement as "Mrs Jones *is* having an abortion," and, on the other hand, "Mrs Jones *ought* to have an abortion." We know, at least in principle, how to go about checking

the truth of the first statement, namely, by referring to certain empirical facts that serve as the independent variables for the statement to be checked against. But how do we go about checking the truth of the second statement, that Mrs Jones *ought* to have an abortion? Indeed, what would it *mean* for the second statement to be true? What is the independent variable for *it* to be checked against? For the first statement to be true means that it corresponds to certain empirical facts. But with regard to a judgment like "Mrs Jones *ought* to have an abortion," what facts would *it* have to correspond to in order to be true? Is there any moral '*ought*' in the world, in the way in which the factual '*is*' is in the world, serving as the independent variable for testing or confirming the relevent statements? If not, then is the moral judgment in no sense either true or false?

The problem we have reached, then, is whether there is any non-question-begging answer to the problem of the independent variable in morality. I now want to suggest that there is. To see this, we must recall that all moral precepts, regardless of their greatly varying contents, are concerned with how persons ought to *act* toward one another. Think, for example, of the Golden Rule: "Do unto others as you would have them do unto you." Think also of Kant's categorical imperative: "*Act* in such a way that the maxim of your action can be a universal law." Similarly, Bentham tells us to *act* so as to maximize utility; Nietzsche tells us to *act* in accord with the ideals of the superman; Marx tells us to *act* in accord with the interests of the proletariat; Kierkegaard tells us to *act* as God commands, and so forth.

The independent variable of all morality, then, is human *action*. This independent variable cuts across the distinctions between secular and religious moralities, between egalitarian and elitist moralities, between deontological and teleological moralities, and so forth.

But how does this independent variable of action help us to resolve the difficulties of moral justification? Surely we can't take the various rival moral principles and justify one of them as against the others simply by checking it against the fact of human action. Moreover, since if action is to be genuinely the non-question-begging independent variable of morality, it must fit *all* moral principles, how does action enable us to justify *one* moral principle *as against* its rivals?

The answer to these questions is given by the fact that action has what I have called a *normative structure*, in that, logically implicit in action, there are certain evaluative and deontic judgments, certain judgments about goods and rights made by agents; and when these judgments are subjected to certain morally neutral rational requirements, they entail a certain supreme moral principle. Hence, if any agent denies the principle, he can be shown to have contradicted himself, so that his denial, and the actions stemming from it, cannot be rationally justifiable. Thus, together with action, the most basic kind of reason, deductive rationality, also serves as an independent variable for the justification of the supreme principle of morality.

Why Action Gives the Principle a Rationally Necessary Acceptability

It is important to note that because the principle is grounded in the generic features of action, it has a certain kind of *material necessity*. It will be recalled that some of the justificatory arguments for rights examined above failed because they did not satisfy the condition that they be acceptable to all rational persons as a matter of rational necessity. For example, why must any rational person accept Rawls's starting point in the "veil of ignorance"? Why, for that matter, is it rationally necessary for any rational person to accept the Golden Rule or any other moral principle that has hitherto been propounded?

The condition of rationally necessary acceptability is fulfilled, however, when the independent variable of the argument is placed in the generic features of action. For this involves that, simply by virtue of being an agent, one logically must accept the argument and its conclusion that all persons equally have certain moral rights. Now, being an actual or prospective agent is not an optional or variable condition for any person, except in the sense that he may choose to commit suicide or, perhaps, to sell himself into slavery; and even then the steps he intentionally takes toward these goals involve agency on his part. Hence, if there are moral rights and duties that logically accrue to every person simply by virtue of being an actual or prospective agent, the argument that traces this logical sequence will necessarily be rationally acceptable to every agent: he will have to accept the argument on pain of self-contradiction.

There is a sense in which this grounding of the moral principle in action involves a foundationalist conception of justification. For, as we shall see, the argument begins with a statement attributable to any agent, that he performs some purposive action. This statement is based on the agent's direct awareness of what he is doing, and it leads, in a unilinear sequence, to his statement that he and all other agents have certain rights and correlative duties. I need not be concerned, in the present context, with further epistemological issues about the certainty or trustworthiness of the rational agent's direct awareness or about any presumed "data" on which this awareness might be based. . . .

My argument, in contrast, begins not from variable moral judgments but from statements that must be accepted by every agent because they derive from the generic features of purposive action. Hence, my argument is not "foundationalist" in the sense that it begins from *moral* or *evaluative* statements that are taken to be self-justifying or self-evident. The present argument is one in which statements about actions, and not statements about values or duties, are taken as the basic starting point. And these statements entail, in a non-circular sense, certain judgments about the existence of human rights.

The Argument for Equal Human Rights

I shall, now, give a brief outline of the rational line of argument that goes from action, through its normative structure, to the supreme principle of morality, and thence to equal human rights.

In my book, *Reason and Morality*,[2] I have presented a full statement of the argument, so that for present purposes I shall stress only certain main points.

To begin with, we must note certain salient characteristics of action. In ordinary as well as scientific language, the word "action" is used in many different senses: we talk, for example, about physical action at a distance, about the action of the liver, and so forth. But the meaning of "action" that is relevant here is that which is the common object of all moral and other practical precepts, such as the examples I gave before. Moral and other practical precepts, as we have seen, tell persons to *act* in many different ways. But amid these differences, the precepts all assume that the persons addressed by them can control their behavior by their unforced choice with a view to achieving whatever the precepts require. All actions as envisaged by moral and other practical precepts, then, have two *generic features*. One is *voluntariness* or *freedom*, in that the agents control or can control their behavior by their unforced choice while having knowledge of relevant circumstances. The other generic feature is *purposiveness* or *intentionality*, in that the agents aim to attain some end or goal which constitutes their reason for acting; this goal may consist either in the action itself or in something to be achieved by the action.

Now, let us take any agent *A*, defined as an actual or prospective performer of actions in the sense just indicated. When he performs an action, he can be described as saying or thinking:

(1)   I do *X* for end or purpose *E*.

Since *E* is something he unforcedly chooses to attain, he thinks *E* has sufficient value to merit his moving from quiescence to action in order to attain it. Hence, from his standpoint, (1) entails

(2)   "*E* is good."

Note that (2) is here presented in quotation marks, as something said or thought by the agent *A*. The kind of goodness he here attributes to *E*

need not be moral goodness; its criterion varies with whatever purpose the agent may have in doing *X*. But what it shows already is that, in the context of action, the "Fact–Value gap" is already bridged, for by the very *fact* of engaging in action, every agent must implicitly accept for himself a certain *value*-judgment about the value or goodness of the purposes for which he acts.

Now, in order to act for *E*, which he regards as good, the agent *A* must have the proximate necessary conditions of action. These conditions are closely related to the generic features of action that I mentioned before. You will recall that these generic features are voluntariness or freedom and purposiveness or intentionality. But when purposiveness is extended to the general conditions required for success in achieving one's purposes, it becomes a more extensive condition which I shall call *well-being*. Viewed from the standpoint of action, then, well-being consists in having the various substantive conditions and abilities, ranging from life and physical integrity to self-esteem and education, that are required if a person is to act either at all or with general chances of success in achieving the purposes for which he acts. So freedom and well-being are the necessary conditions of action and of successful action in general. Hence, from the agent's standpoint, from (2) "*E* is good" there follows

(3)   My freedom and well-being are necessary goods.

This may also be put as

(4)   I must have freedom and well-being,

where this "must" is a practical-prescriptive requirement, expressed by the agent, as to his having the necessary conditions of his action.

Now from (4) there follows

(5)   I have rights to freedom and well-being.

To show that (5) follows from (4), let us suppose that the agent were to deny (5). In that case, because of the correlativity of rights and strict "oughts," he would also have to deny

(6)   All other persons ought at least to refrain from removing or interfering with
my freedom and well-being.

By denying (6), he must accept

(7)   It is not the case that all other persons
ought at least to refrain from removing
or interfering with my freedom and well-
being.

By accepting (7), he must also accept

(8)   Other persons may (i.e. It is permissible
that other persons) remove or interfere
with my freedom and well-being.

And by accepting (8), he must accept

(9)   I may not (i.e. It is permissible that I
not) have freedom and well-being.

But (9) contradicts (4), which said "I must
have freedom and well-being." Since every agent
must accept (4), he must reject (9). And since
(9) follows from the denial of (5), "I have rights
to freedom and well-being," every agent must
also reject that denial. Hence, every agent logically must accept (5) "I have rights to freedom
and well-being."

What I have shown so far, then, is that the
concept of a right, as a justified claim or entitlement, is logically involved in all action as a concept that signifies for every agent his claim and
requirement that he have, and at least not be
prevented from having, the necessary conditions
that enable him to act in pursuit of his purposes.
I shall sometimes refer to these rights as *generic
rights*, since they are rights that the generic features of action and of successful action characterize one's behavior.

It must be noted, however, that, so far, the
criterion of these rights that every agent must
claim for himself is only prudential, not moral,
in that the criterion consists for each agent in his
own needs of agency in pursuit of his own pur-

poses. Even though the right-claim is addressed
to all other persons as a correlative "ought"-judg-
ment, still its justifying criterion for each agent
consists in the necessary conditions of his own
action.

To see how this prudential right-claim also
becomes a moral right, we must go through some
further steps. Now, the sufficient as well as the
necessary reason or justifying condition for which
every agent must hold that he has rights to freedom and well-being is that he is a prospective
purposive agent. Hence, he must accept

(10)   I have rights to freedom and well-
being because I am a prospective purposive agent,

where this "because" signifies a sufficient as well
as a necessary justifying condition.

Suppose some agent were to reject (10), and
were to insist, instead, that the only reason he
has the generic rights is that he has some more
restrictive characteristic R. Examples of R would
include: being an American, being a professor,
being an *Übermensch*, being male, being a capitalist or a proletarian, being white, being named
"Wordsworth Donisthorpe," and so forth. Thus,
the agent would be saying

(11)   I have rights to freedom and well-
being *only* because I am R,

where "R" is something more restrictive than
being a prospective purposive agent.

Such an agent, however, would contradict himself. For he would then be in the position of saying that if he did *not* have R, he would *not* have
the generic rights, so that he would have to accept

(12)   I do not have rights to freedom and
well-being.

But we saw before that, as an agent, he *must*
hold that he has rights to freedom and well-being. Hence, he must drop his view that R alone
is the sufficient justifying condition of his having
the generic rights, so that he must accept that

simply being a prospective purposive agent is a sufficient as well as a necessary justifying condition of his having rights to freedom and well-being. Hence, he must accept (10).

Now by virtue of accepting (10), the agent must also accept

(13) All prospective purposive agents have rights to freedom and well-being.

(13) follows from (10) because of the principle of universalization. If some predicate P belongs to some subject S because that subject has some general quality Q (where this "because" signifies a sufficient reason), then that predicate logically must belong to every subject that has Q. Hence, since the predicate of having the generic rights belongs to the original agent because he is a prospective purposive agent, he logically must admit that every purposive agent has the generic rights.

At this point the rights become moral ones, and not only prudential, on that meaning of "moral" where it has both the formal component of setting forth practical requirements that are categorically obligatory, and the material component that those requirements involve taking favorable account of the interests of persons other than or in addition to the agent or the speaker. When the original agent now says that *all* prospective purposive agents have rights to freedom and well-being, he is logically committed to respecting and hence taking favorable account of the interests of all other persons with regard to their also having the necessary goods or conditions of action.

Since all other persons are actual or potential recipients of his action, every agent is logically committed to accepting

(14) I ought to act in accord with the generic rights of my recipients as well as of myself.

This requirement can also be expressed as the general moral principle:

(15) Act in accord with the generic rights

of your recipients as well as of yourself.

I shall call this the Principle of Generic Consistency (*PGC*), since it combines the formal consideration of consistency with the material consideration of the generic features and rights of action. As we have seen, every agent, on pain of contradiction and hence of irrationality, must accept this principle as governing all his interpersonal actions.

This, then, completes my argument for equal human rights. Its central point can be summarized in two main parts. In the first part (steps 1 to 9), I have argued that every agent logically must hold or accept that he has rights to freedom and well-being as the necessary conditions of his action, as conditions that he *must* have; for if he denies that he has these rights, then he must accept that other persons may remove or interfere with his freedom and well-being, so that he *may not* have them; but this would contradict his belief that he *must* have them. In the second part (steps 10 to 14), I have argued that the agent logically must accept that all other prospective purposive agents have the same rights to freedom and well-being as he claims for himself.

Since all humans are actual, prospective, or potential agents, the rights in question belong equally to all humans. Thus, the argument fulfills the specifications for human rights that I mentioned at the outset: that both the Subjects and the Respondents of the rights are all humans equally, that the Objects of the rights are the necessary goods of human action, and that the Justifying Basis of the rights is a valid moral principle.

Notes

1 I have tried to show this elsewhere with regard to utilitarianism. See Alan Gewirth, "Can Utilitarianism Justify Any Moral Rights?" in *Nomos XXIV: Ethics, Economics, and the Law*, ed. J. Roland Pennock and John W. Chapman (New York: New York University Press, 1982), pp. 158–78.
2 Alan Gewirth, *Reason and Morality* (Chicago: University of Chicago Press, 1978), chs 1–3.

12   Morality as a System of Hypothetical Imperatives

Philippa Foot

There are many difficulties and obscurities in Kant's moral philosophy, and few contemporary moralists will try to defend it all; many, for instance, agree in rejecting Kant's derivation of duties from the mere form of law expressed in terms of a universally legislative will. Nevertheless, it is generally supposed, even by those who would not dream of calling themselves his followers, that Kant established one thing beyond doubt – namely, the necessity of distinguishing moral judgments from hypothetical imperatives. That moral judgments cannot be hypothetical imperatives has come to seem an unquestionable truth. It will be argued here that it is not.

In discussing so thoroughly Kantian a notion as that of the hypothetical imperative, one naturally begins by asking what Kant himself meant by a hypothetical imperative, and it may be useful to say a little about the idea of an imperative as this appears in Kant's works. In writing about imperatives Kant seems to be thinking at least as much of statements about what ought to be or should be done, as of injunctions expressed in the imperative mood. He even describes as an imperative the assertion that it would be "good to do or refrain from doing something"[1] and explains that for a will that "does not always do something simply because it is presented to it as a good thing to do" this has the force of a command of reason. We may therefore think of Kant's imperatives as statements to the effect that something ought to be done or that it would be good to do it.

The distinction between hypothetical imperatives and categorical imperatives, which plays so important a part in Kant's ethics, appears in char-

acteristic form in the following passages from the *Foundations of the Metaphysics of Morals*:

> All imperatives command either hypothetically or categorically. The former present the practical necessity of a possible action as a means to achieving something else which one desires (or which one may possibly desire). The categorical imperative would be one which presented an action as of itself objectively necessary, without regard to any other end.[2]

> If the action is good only as a means to something else, the imperative is hypothetical; but if it is thought of as good in itself, and hence as necessary in a will which of itself conforms to reason as the principle of this will, the imperative is categorical.[3]

The hypothetical imperative, as Kant defines it, "says only that the action is good to some purpose" and the purpose, he explains, may be possible or actual. Among imperatives related to actual purposes Kant mentions rules of prudence, since he believes that all men necessarily desire their own happiness. Without committing ourselves to this view it will be useful to follow Kant in classing together as "hypothetical imperatives" those telling a man what he ought to do because (or if) he wants something and those telling him what he ought to do on grounds of self-interest. Common opinion agrees with Kant in insisting that a moral man must accept a rule of duty whatever his interests or desires.[4]

Having given a rough description of the class of Kantian hypothetical imperatives it may be useful to point to the heterogeneity within it. Sometimes what a man should do depends on his passing inclination, as when he wants his coffee hot and should warm the jug. Sometimes it depends on some long-term project, when the

From *Philosophical Review*, vol. 8, no. 3 (1972), pp. 305–16. Reprinted with permission. For Foot's present views, see "Does Moral Subjectivism Rest on a Mistake?" *Oxford Journal of Legal Studies*, 15 (1995), pp. 100–20.

feelings and inclinations of the moment are ir-relevant. If one wants to be a respectable phi-losopher one should get up in the mornings and do some work, though just at that moment when one should do it the thought of being a respect-able philosopher leaves one cold. It is true nev-ertheless to say of one, at that moment, that one wants to be a respectable philosopher,[5] and this can be the foundation of a desire-dependent hy-pothetical imperative. The term "desire" as used in the original account of the hypothetical im-perative was meant as a grammatically conven-ient substitute for "want," and was not meant to carry any implication of inclination rather than long-term aim or project. Even the word "project," taken strictly, introduces undesirable restrictions. If someone is devoted to his family or his country or to any cause, there are certain things he wants, which may then be the basis of hypothetical imperatives, without either inclina-tions or projects being quite what is in question. Hypothetical imperatives should already be ap-pearing as extremely diverse; a further important distinction is between those that concern an in-dividual and those that concern a group. The desires on which a hypothetical imperative is de-pendent may be those of one man, or may be taken for granted as belonging to a number of people, engaged in some common project or sharing common aims.

Is Kant right to say that moral judgments are categorical, not hypothetical, imperatives? It may seem that he is, for we find in our language two different uses of words such as "should" and "ought," apparently corresponding to Kant's hypothetical and categorical imperatives, and we find moral judgments on the "categorical" side. Suppose, for instance, we have advised a traveler that he should take a certain train, believing him to be journeying to his home. If we find that he has decided to go elsewhere, we will most likely have to take back what we said: the "should" will now be unsupported and in need of sup-port. Similarly, we must be prepared to withdraw our statement about what he should do if we find that the right relation does not hold between the action and the end – that it is either no way of getting what he wants (or doing what he wants

to do) or not the most eligible among possible means. The use of "should" and "ought" in moral contexts is, however, quite different. When we say that a man should do something and in-tend a moral judgment we do not have to back up what we say by considerations about his in-terests or his desires; if no such connection can be found the "should" need not be withdrawn. It follows that the agent cannot rebut an asser-tion about what, morally speaking, he should do by showing that the action is not ancillary to his interests or desires. Without such a connection the "should" does not stand unsupported and in need of support; the support that *it* requires is of another kind.[6]

There is, then, one clear difference between moral judgments and the class of "hypothetical imperatives" so far discussed. In the latter "should" is used "hypothetically," in the sense defined, and if Kant were merely drawing atten-tion to this piece of linguistic usage his point would be easily proved. But obviously Kant meant more than this; in describing moral judg-ments as non-hypothetical – that is, categorical imperatives – he is ascribing to them a special dignity and necessity which this usage cannot give. Modern philosophers follow Kant in talk-ing, for example, about the "unconditional re-quirement" expressed in moral judgments. These tell us what we have to do whatever our interests or desires, and by their inescapability they are distinguished from hypothetical imperatives.

The problem is to find proof for this further feature of moral judgments. If anyone fails to see the gap that has to be filled it will be useful to point out to him that we find "should" used non-hypothetically in some non-moral statements to which no one attributes the special dignity and necessity conveyed by the description "categori-cal imperative." For instance, we find this non-hypothetical use of "should" in sentences enunciating rules of etiquette, as, for example, that an invitation in the third person should be answered in the third person, where the rule does not *fail to apply* to someone who has his own good reasons for ignoring this piece of nonsense, or who simply does not care about what, from the point of view of etiquette, he should do. Similarly, there is a non-hypothetical use of "should" in contexts where something like a club rule is in question. The club secretary who has told a member that he should not bring ladies into the smoking room does not say, "Sorry, I was mistaken" when informed that this member is resigning tomorrow and cares nothing about his reputation in the club. Lacking a connection with the agent's desires or interests, this "should" does not stand "unsupported and in need of support"; it requires only the backing of the rule. The use of "should" is therefore "non-hypothetical" in the sense defined.

It follows that if a hypothetical use of "should" gives a hypothetical imperative, and a non-hypothetical use of "should" a categorical imperative, then "should" statements based on rules of etiquette, or rules of a club, are categorical imperatives. Since this would not be accepted by defenders of the categorical imperative in ethics, who would insist that these other "should" statements give hypothetical imperatives, they must be using this expression in some other sense. We must therefore ask what they mean when they say that "You should answer . . . in the third person" is a hypothetical imperative. Very roughly the idea seems to be that one may reasonably ask why anyone should bother about what should (should from the point of view of etiquette) be done, and that such considerations deserve no notice unless reason is shown. So although people give as their reason for doing something the fact that it is required by etiquette, we do not take this consideration as *in itself giving us reason to act*. Considerations of etiquette do not have any automatic reason-giving force, and a man might be right if he denied that he had reason to do "what's done."

This seems to take us to the heart of the matter, for, by contrast, it is supposed that moral considerations necessarily give reasons for acting to any man. The difficulty is, of course, to defend this proposition which is more often repeated than explained. Unless it is said, implausibly, that all "should" or "ought" statements give reasons for acting, which leaves the old problem of assigning a special categorical status to moral judgment, we must be told what it

is that makes the moral "should" relevantly different from the "shoulds" appearing in normative statements of other kinds.[7] Attempts have sometimes been made to show that some kind of irrationality is involved in ignoring the "should" of morality: in saying "Immoral – so what?" as one says "Not *comme il faut* – so what?" But as far as I can see these have all rested on some illegitimate assumption, as, for instance, of thinking that the amoral man, who agrees that some piece of conduct is immoral but takes no notice of that, is inconsistently disregarding a rule of conduct that he has accepted; or again of thinking it inconsistent to desire that others will not do to one what one proposes to do to them. The fact is that the man who rejects morality because he sees no reason to obey its rules can be convicted of villainy but not of inconsistency. Nor will his actions necessarily be irrational. Irrational actions are those in which a man in some way defeats his own purposes, doing what is calculated to be disadvantageous or to frustrate his ends. Immorality does not *necessarily* involve any such thing.

It is obvious that the normative character of moral judgment does not guarantee its reason-giving force. Moral judgments are normative, but so are judgments of manners, statements of club rules, and many others. Why should the first provide reasons for acting as the others do not? In every case it is because there is a background of teaching that the non-hypothetical "should" can be used. The behavior is required, not simply recommended, but the question remains as to why we should do what we are required to do. It is true that moral rules are often enforced much more strictly than the rules of etiquette, and our reluctance to press the non-hypothetical "should" of etiquette may be one reason why we think of the rules of etiquette as hypothetical imperatives. But are we then to say that there is nothing behind the idea that moral judgments are categorical imperatives but the relative stringency of our moral teaching? I believe that this may have more to do with the matter than the defenders of the categorical imperative would like to admit. For if we look at the kind of thing that is said in its defense we may find ourselves puzzled about what the words can even mean unless we connect them with the feelings that this stringent teaching implants. People talk, for instance, about the "binding force" of morality, but it is not clear what this means if not that we *feel* ourselves unable to escape. Indeed the "inescapability" of moral requirements is often cited when they are being contrasted with hypothetical imperatives. No one, it is said, escapes the requirements of ethics by having or not having particular interests or desires. Taken in one way this only reiterates the contrast between the "should" of morality and the hypothetical "should," and once more places morality alongside of etiquette. Both are inescapable in that behavior does not cease to offend against either morality or etiquette because the agent is indifferent to their purposes and to the disapproval he will incur by flouting them. But morality is supposed to be inescapable in some special way and this may turn out to be merely the reflection of the way morality is taught. Of course, we must try other ways of expressing the fugitive thought. It may be said, for instance, that moral judgments have a kind of necessity since they tell us what we "must do" or "have to do" whatever our interests and desires. The sense of this is, again, obscure. Sometimes when we use such expressions we are referring to physical or mental compulsion. (A man has to go along if he is pulled by strong men, and he has to give in if tortured beyond endurance.) But it is only in the absence of such conditions that moral judgments apply. Another and more common sense of the words is found in sentences such as "I caught a bad cold and had to stay in bed" where a penalty for acting otherwise is in the offing. The necessity of acting morally is not, however, supposed to depend on such penalties. Another range of examples, not necessarily having to do with penalties, is found where there is an unquestioned acceptance of some project or role, as when a nurse tells us that she has to make her rounds at a certain time, or we say that we have to run for a certain train.[8] But these too are irrelevant in the present context, since the acceptance condition can always be revoked.

No doubt it will be suggested that it is in some

other sense of the words "have to" or "must" that one has to or must do what morality demands. But why should one insist that there must be such a sense when it proves so difficult to say what it is? Suppose that what we take for a puzzling thought were really no thought at all but only the reflection of our *feelings* about morality? Perhaps it makes no sense to say that we "have to" submit to the moral law, or that morality is "inescapable" in some special way. For just as one may feel as if one is falling without believing that one is moving downward, so one may feel as if one has to do what is morally required without believing oneself to be under physical or psychological compulsion, or about to incur a penalty if one does not comply. No one thinks that if the word "falling" is used in a statement reporting one's sensations it must be used in a special sense. But this kind of mistake may be involved in looking for the special sense in which one "has to" do what morality demands. There is no difficulty about the idea that we feel we *have to* behave morally, and given the psychological conditions of the learning of moral behavior it is natural that we should have such feelings. What we cannot do is quote them in support of the doctrine of the categorical imperative. It seems, then, that in so far as it is backed up by statements to the effect that the moral *is* inescapable, or that we *do* have to do what is morally required of us, it is uncertain whether the doctrine of the categorical imperative even makes sense.

The conclusion we should draw is that moral judgments have no better claim to be categorical imperatives than do statements about matters of etiquette. People may indeed follow either morality or etiquette without asking why they should do so, but equally well they may not. They may ask for reasons and may reasonably refuse to follow either if reasons are not to be found.

It will be said that this way of viewing moral considerations must be totally destructive of morality, because no one could ever act morally unless he accepted such considerations as in themselves sufficient reason for action. Actions that are truly moral must be done "for their own sake," "because they are right," and not for some ulterior purpose. This argument we must examine with care, for the doctrine of the categorical imperative has owed much to its persuasion.

Is there anything to be said for the thesis that a truly moral man acts "out of respect for the moral law" or that he does what is morally right because it is morally right? That such propositions are not prima facie absurd depends on the fact that moral judgment concerns itself with a man's reasons for acting as well as with what he does. Law and etiquette require only that certain things are done or left undone, but no one is counted as charitable if he gives alms "for the praise of men," and one who is honest only because it pays him to be honest does not have the virtue of honesty. This kind of consideration was crucial in shaping Kant's moral philosophy. He many times contrasts acting out of respect for the moral law with acting from an ulterior motive, and what is more from one that is self-interested. In the early *Lectures on Ethics* he gave the principle of truth-telling under a system of hypothetical imperatives as that of not lying *if it harms one* to lie. In the *Metaphysics of Morals* he says that ethics cannot start from the ends which a man may propose to himself, since these are all "selfish."[9] In the *Critique of Practical Reason* he argues explicitly that when acting not out of respect for the moral law but "on a material maxim" men do what they do for the sake of pleasure or happiness.

> All material practical principles are, as such, of one and the same kind and belong under the general principle of self love or one's own happiness.[10]

Kant, in fact, was a psychological hedonist in respect of all actions except those done for the sake of the moral law, and this faulty theory of human nature was one of the things preventing him from seeing that moral virtue might be compatible with the rejection of the categorical imperative.

If we put this theory of human action aside, and allow as ends the things that seem to be ends, the picture changes. It will surely be allowed that quite apart from thoughts of duty a man may care about the suffering of others, having a sense of identification with them, and wanting to help if he can. Of course, he must want not the reputation of charity, nor even a gratifying role helping others, but, quite simply, their good. If this is what he does care about, then he will be attached to the end proper to the virtue of charity and a comparison with someone acting from an ulterior motive (even a respectable ulterior motive) is out of place. Nor will the conformity of his action to the rule of charity be merely contingent. Honest action may happen to further a man's career; charitable actions do not *happen* to further the good of others.

Can a man accepting only hypothetical imperatives possess other virtues besides that of charity? Could he be just or honest? This problem is more complex because there is no one end related to such virtues as the good of others is related to charity. But what reason could there be for refusing to call a man a just man if he acted justly because he loved truth and liberty, and wanted every man to be treated with a certain minimum respect? And why should the truly honest man not follow honesty for the sake of the good that honest dealing brings to men? Of course, the usual difficulties can be raised about the rare case in which no good is foreseen from an individual act of honesty. But it is not evident that a man's desires could not give him reason to act honestly even here. He wants to live openly and in good faith with his neighbors; it is not all the same to him to lie and conceal.

If one wants to know whether there could be a truly moral man who accepted moral principles as hypothetical rules of conduct, as many people accept rules of etiquette as hypothetical rules of conduct, one must consider the right kind of example. A man who demanded that morality should be brought under the heading of self-interest would not be a good candidate, nor would anyone who was ready to be charitable or honest only so long as he felt inclined. A cause such as justice makes strenuous demands, but this is not peculiar to morality, and men are prepared to toil to achieve many ends not endorsed by morality. That they are prepared to fight so hard for moral ends – for example, for liberty and justice – depends on the fact that these are the kinds of ends that arouse devotion. To sacrifice a great deal for the sake of etiquette one would need to be under the spell of the emphatic "ought." One could hardly be devoted to behaving *comme il faut*.

In spite of all that has been urged in favor of the hypothetical imperative in ethics, I am sure that many people will be unconvinced and will argue that one element essential to moral virtue is still missing. This missing feature is the recognition of a *duty* to adopt those ends which we have attributed to the moral man. We have said that he *does* care about others, and about causes such as liberty and justice; that it is on this account that he will accept a system of morality. But what if he never cared about such things, or what if he ceased to care? Is it not the case that he *ought* to care? This is exactly what Kant would say, for though at times he sounds as if he thought that morality is not concerned with ends, at others he insists that the adoption of ends such as the happiness of others is itself dictated by morality.[11] How is this proposition to be regarded by one who rejects all talk about the binding force of the moral law? He will agree that a moral man has moral ends and cannot be indifferent to matters such as suffering and injustice. Further, he will recognize in the statement that one *ought* to care about these things a correct application of the non-hypothetical moral "ought" by which society is apt to voice its demands. He will not, however, take the fact that he ought to have certain ends as in itself reason to adopt them. If he himself is a moral man then he cares about such things, but not "because he ought." If he is an amoral man he may deny that he has any reason to trouble his head over this or any other moral demand. Of course he may be mistaken, and his life as well as others' lives may be most sadly spoiled by his selfishness. But this is not what is urged by those who think they can close the matter by an emphatic use of "ought." My argument is that they are relying on an illusion, as if trying to give the moral "ought" a magic force.[12]

This conclusion may, as I said, appear dangerous and subversive of morality. We are apt to panic at the thought that we ourselves, or other people, might stop caring about the things we do

care about, and we feel that the categorical imperative gives us some control over the situation. But it is interesting that the people of Leningrad were not similarly struck by the thought that only the *contingent* fact that other citizens shared their loyalty and devotion to the city stood between them and the Germans during the terrible years of the siege. Perhaps we should be less troubled than we are by fear of defection from the moral cause; perhaps we should even have less reason to fear it if people thought of themselves as volunteers banded together to fight for liberty and justice and against inhumanity and oppression. It is often felt, even if obscurely, that there is an element of deception in the official line about morality. And while some have been persuaded by talk about the authority of the moral law, others have turned away with a sense of distrust.

Notes

So many people have made useful comments on drafts of this article that I despair of thanking them all. Derek Parfit's help has been sustained and invaluable, and special thanks are also due to Barry Stroud.

An earlier version of this paper was read at the Center for Philosophical Exchange, Brockport, NY, and published in *Philosophical Exchange* (Summer 1971).

1 *Foundations of the Metaphysics of Morals*, Sec. II, trans. L. W. Beck.

2 Ibid.

3 Ibid.

4 According to the position sketched here we have three forms of the hypothetical imperative: "If you want *x* you should do *y*," "Because you want *x* you should do *y*," and "Because *x* is in your interest you should do *y*." For Kant the third would automatically be covered by the second.

5 To say that at that moment one wants to be a respectable philosopher would be another matter. Such a statement requires a special connection between the desire and the moment.

6 I am here going back on something I said in an earlier article ("Moral Beliefs," *Proceedings of the Aristotelian Society, 1958–1959*) where I thought it necessary to show that virtue must benefit the agent. I believe the rest of the article can stand.

7 To say that moral considerations are *called* reasons is blatantly to ignore the problem.

8 I am grateful to Rogers Albritton for drawing my

attention to this interesting use of expressions such as "have to" or "must."

9 Pt II, Introduction, Sec. II.

10 Immanuel Kant, *Critique of Practical Reason*, trans. L. W. Beck, p. 133.

11 See, e.g. *The Metaphysics of Morals*, Pt II, Sec. 30.

12 See G. E. M. Anscombe, "Modern Moral Philosophy," *Philosophy* (1958). My view is different from Miss Anscombe's, but I have learned from her.

13 From Rationality to Morality

James P. Sterba

To defend morality, it would be helpful to show that morality is grounded in rationality. This requires not simply showing that morality is rationally permissible because that would imply that egoism and immorality were rationally permissible as well. Rather what needs to be shown is that morality is rationally required, thus excluding egoism and immorality as rationally permissible.[1] Unfortunately, the goal of showing that morality is rationally required has been abandoned by most contemporary philosophers, who seem content to show that morality is simply rationally permissible.[2] No doubt most contemporary philosophers would like to have an argument showing that morality is rationally required, but given the history of past failures to provide a convincing argument of this sort, most contemporary philosophers have simply given up hope of defending morality in this way.[3] In this paper, I propose to provide just such a defense of morality, and then consider a number of objections to it.

My own defense of morality employs the same general strategy as those offered by Baier and Gewirth. It primarily differs from theirs in that it introduces the perspective of altruism in constructing a non-question-begging argument to show that egoism is contrary to reason. But I claim that this is just the missing ingredient that is needed to make the argument work.

Reprinted by permission of James P. Sterba.

Let us begin by imagining that each of us is capable of entertaining and acting upon both self-interested and moral reasons and that the question we are seeking to answer is what sort of reasons for action it would be rational for us to accept.[4] This question is not about what sort of reasons we should publicly affirm, since people will sometimes publicly affirm reasons that are quite different from those they are prepared to act upon. Rather it is a question about what reasons it would be rational for us to accept at the deepest level – in our heart of hearts.

Of course, there are people who are incapable of acting upon moral reasons. For such people, there is no question about their being required to act morally or altruistically. Yet the interesting philosophical question is not about such people but about people, like ourselves, who are capable of acting self-interestedly or morally and are seeking a rational justification for following a particular course of action.

In trying to determine how we should act, we would like to be able to construct a *good* argument favoring morality over egoism, and given that good arguments are non-question-begging, we would like to construct an argument that does not beg the question against egoism.[5] The question at issue here is what reasons each of us should take as supreme, and this question would be begged against egoism if we propose to answer it simply by assuming from the start that moral reasons are the reasons that each of us should take as supreme. But the question would be begged against morality as well if we proposed to answer the question simply by assuming from the start that self-interested reasons are the reasons that each of us should take as supreme. This means, of course, that we cannot answer the question of what reasons we should take as supreme simply by assuming the general principle of egoism:

Each person ought to do what best serves his or her overall self-interest.

We can no more argue for egoism simply by denying the relevance of moral reasons to rational choice than we can argue for pure altruism simply by denying the relevance of self-interested reasons to rational choice and assuming the following principle of pure altruism:

Each person ought to do what best serves the overall interest of others.[6]

Consequently, in order not to beg the question against either egoism or altruism, we have no other alternative but to grant the prima facie relevance of both self-interested and moral reasons to rational choice and then try to determine which reasons we would be rationally required to act upon, all things considered.[7]

Here it might be objected that we *do* have non-question-begging grounds for favoring self-interested reasons over moral reasons, if not egoism over altruism. From observing ourselves and others, don't we find that self-interested reasons are better motivators than are moral reasons as evidenced by the fact that there seem to be more egoistically-inclined people in the world than there are altruistically-inclined people? It might be argued that because of this difference in motivational capacity, self-interested and moral reasons should not *both* be regarded as prima facie relevant to rational choice.

But is there really this difference in motivational capacity? Do human beings really have a greater capacity for self-interested behavior than for moral or altruistic behavior? If we focus for a change on the behavior of women, I think we are likely to observe considerably more altruism than egoism among women, particularly with respect to the care of their families.[8] Of course, if we look to men, given the prevailing patriarchal social structures, we may tend to find more egoism than altruism.[9] But most likely any differences that exist between men and women in this regard, irrespective of whether we consider them to be good or bad, are primarily due to the dominant patterns of socialization – nurture rather than nature.[10] In any case, it is beyond dispute that we humans are capable of both self-interested and altruistic behavior, and given that we have these capabilities, it seems reasonable to ask which ones should have priority.[11]

Our situation is that we find ourselves with some capacity to move along a spectrum from egoism to pure altruism with someone like Mother Teresa of Calcutta representing the paradigm of pure altruism and someone like Thrasymachus of Plato's *Republic* representing the paradigm of egoism. Obviously, our ability to move along this spectrum will depend on our starting point, the strength of our habits, and the social circumstances under which we happen to be living. But at the outset, it is reasonable to abstract from these individual variations and simply focus on the general capacity virtually all of us have to act on both self-interested and moral reasons. From this, we should conclude that both sorts of reasons are relevant to rational choice and then ask the question which reasons should have priority. Later, with this question answered, we can take into account individual differences and the effects of socialization to adjust our expectations and requirements for particular individuals and groups. Initially, however, all we need to recognize is the relevance of both self-interested and altruistic reasons to rational choice.

In this regard, there are two kinds of cases that must be considered. First, there are cases in which there is a conflict between the relevant self-interested and moral reasons.[12] Second, there are cases in which there is no such conflict.

Now it seems obvious that where there is no conflict and both reasons are conclusive reasons of their kind, both reasons should be acted upon. In such contexts, we should do what is favored both by morality and by self-interest.

Consider the following example. Suppose you accepted a job marketing a baby formula in underdeveloped countries, where the formula was improperly used, leading to increased infant mortality.[13] Imagine that you could just as well have accepted an equally attractive and rewarding job marketing a similar formula in developed countries, where the misuse does not occur, so that a rational weighing of the relevant self-interested reasons alone would not have favored your acceptance of one of these jobs over the other.[14] At the same time, there were obviously moral reasons that condemned your acceptance of the first job – reasons that you presumably are or were able to acquire. Moreover, by assumption in this case, the moral reasons do not clash with the relevant self-interested reasons; they simply made a recommendation where the relevant self-interested reasons were silent. Consequently, a rational weighing of all the relevant reasons in this case could not but favor acting in accord with the relevant moral reasons.[15]

Yet it might be objected that in cases of this sort there frequently will be other reasons significantly opposed to the relevant moral reasons – other reasons that you are or were able to acquire. Such reasons will be either *malevolent* reasons seeking to bring about the suffering and death of other human beings, *benevolent* reasons concerned to promote non-human welfare even at the expense of human welfare or *aesthetic* reasons concerned to preserve and promote objects of aesthetic value even if those objects will not be appreciated by any living being. But assuming that such malevolent reasons are ultimately rooted in some conception of what is good for oneself or others, these reasons would have already been taken into account, and by assumption outweighed by the other relevant reasons in this case.[16] And although benevolent reasons concerned to promote non-human welfare would have been taken into account, such reasons are not directly relevant to justifying morality over egoism.[17] Finally, although aesthetic reasons concerned to preserve and promote aesthetic objects, even if those objects will not be appreciated by any living being, might theoretically weigh against

human interests, for all practical purposes, the value of such aesthetic objects will tend to correlate with the value of the aesthetic experiences such objects provide to humans.[18] Consequently, even with the presence of these other kinds of reasons, your acceptance of the first job can still be seen to be contrary to the relevant reasons in this case.

Needless to say, defenders of egoism cannot but be disconcerted with this result since it shows that actions that accord with egoism are contrary to reason at least when there are two equally good ways of pursuing one's self-interest, only one of which does not conflict with the basic requirements of morality. Notice also that in cases where there are two equally good ways of fulfilling the basic requirements of morality, only one of which does not conflict with what is in a person's overall self-interest, it is not at all disconcerting for defenders of morality to admit that we are rationally required to choose the way that does not conflict with what is in our overall self-interest. Nevertheless, exposing this defect in egoism for cases where moral reasons and self-interested reasons do not conflict would be but a small victory for defenders of morality if it were not also possible to show that in cases where such reasons do conflict, moral reasons would have priority over self-interested reasons.

Now when we rationally assess the relevant reasons in such conflict cases, it is best to cast the conflict not as a conflict between self-interested reasons and moral reasons but instead as a conflict between self-interested reasons and altruistic reasons.[19] Viewed in this way, three solutions are possible. First, we could say that self-interested reasons always have priority over conflicting altruistic reasons. Second, we could say, just the opposite, that altruistic reasons always have priority over conflicting self-interested reasons. Third, we could say that some kind of compromise is rationally required. In this compromise, sometimes self-interested reasons would have priority over altruistic reasons, and sometimes altruistic reasons would have priority over self-interested reasons.

Once the conflict is described in this manner, the third solution can be seen to be the one that

Table 1

Individual A		Individual B	
Self-interested reasons	Altruistic reasons	Self-interested reasons	Altruistic reasons
1	1	1	1
2	2	2	2
3	3	3	3
.	.	.	.
.	.	.	.
.	.	.	.
N	N	N	N

is rationally required. This is because the first and second solutions give exclusive priority to one class of relevant reasons over the other, and only a completely question-begging justification can be given for such an exclusive priority. Only by employing the third solution, and sometimes giving priority to self-interested reasons, and sometimes giving priority to altruistic reasons, can we avoid a completely question-begging resolution.

Consider the following example. Suppose you are in the waste disposal business and you have decided to dispose of toxic wastes in a manner that is cost-efficient for you but predictably causes significant harm to future generations. Imagine that there are alternative methods available for disposing of the waste that are only slightly less cost-efficient and will not cause any significant harm to future generations.[20] In this case, you are to weigh your self-interested reasons favoring the most cost-efficient disposal of the toxic wastes against the relevant altruistic reasons favoring the avoidance of significant harm to future generations. If we suppose that the projected loss of benefit to yourself was ever so slight and the projected harm to future generations was ever so great, then a non-arbitrary compromise between the relevant self-interested and altruistic reasons would have to favor the altruistic reasons in this case. Hence, as judged by a non-question-begging standard of rationality, your method of waste disposal is contrary to the relevant reasons.

Notice also that this standard of rationality will

not support just any compromise between the relevant self-interested and altruistic reasons. The compromise must be a non-arbitrary one, for otherwise it would beg the question with respect to the opposing egoistic and altruistic views. Such a compromise would have to respect the rankings of self-interested and altruistic reasons imposed by the egoistic and altruistic views, respectively. Since for each individual there is a separate ranking of that individual's relevant self-interested and altruistic reasons, we can represent these rankings from the most important reasons to the least important reasons in table 1.

Accordingly, any non-arbitrary compromise among such reasons in seeking not to beg the question against egoism or altruism will have to give priority to those reasons that rank highest in each category. Failure to give priority to the highest-ranking altruistic or self-interested reasons would, other things being equal, be contrary to reason.

Of course, there will be cases in which the only way to avoid being required to do what is contrary to your highest-ranking reasons is by requiring someone else to do what is contrary to her highest-ranking reasons. Some of these cases will be "lifeboat cases." But although such cases are surely difficult to resolve (maybe only a chance mechanism can offer a reasonable resolution), they surely do not reflect the typical conflict between the relevant self-interested and altruistic reasons that we are or were able to acquire. Typically, one or the other of the conflicting reasons will rank significantly higher on its respective scale, thus permitting a clear resolution.[21]

Now it is important to see how morality can be viewed as just such a non-arbitrary compromise between self-interested and altruistic reasons. First, a certain amount of self-regard is morally required or at least morally acceptable. Where this is the case, high-ranking self-interested reasons have priority over low-ranking altruistic reasons. Second, morality obviously places limits on the extent to which people should pursue their own self-interest. Where this is the case, high-ranking altruistic reasons have priority over low-ranking self-interested reasons. In this way, morality can be seen to be a non-arbitrary compromise between self-interested and altruistic reasons, and the "moral reasons" that constitute that compromise can be seen as having priority over the self-interested or altruistic reasons that conflict with them.[22]

Now it might be objected that although the egoistic and the altruistic views are admittedly question-begging, the compromise view is equally so and, hence, is in no way preferable to the other views. In response, I deny that the compromise view is equally question-begging when compared with the egoistic and altruistic views but I concede that the view is to a lesser degree question-begging none the less. For a completely non-question-begging view starts with assumptions that are acceptable to all sides of a dispute. However, the assumption of the compromise view that high-ranking altruistic reasons have priority over conflicting low-ranking self-interested reasons is not acceptable from an egoistic perspective. Nor is the compromise view's assumption that high-ranking self-interested reasons have priority over conflicting low-ranking altruistic reasons acceptable from an altruistic perspective. Relevantly, what altruism assumes is that:

1. all high-ranking altruistic reasons have priority over conflicting lower-ranking self-interested reasons;
2. all low-ranking altruistic reasons have priority over conflicting higher-ranking self-interested reasons.

By contrast, what egoism assumes is that:

1'. all high-ranking self-interested reasons have priority over conflicting lower-ranking altruisic reasons;
2'. all low-ranking self-interested reasons have priority over conflicting higher-ranking altruistic reasons.

And what the compromise view assumes is (1) and (1'). So part of what the compromise view assumes about the priority of reasons, i.e. (1) is not acceptable from an egoistic perspective, and another part, i.e. (1') is not acceptable from an altruistic perspective; hence, to that extent the compromise view does beg the question against each view. Nevertheless, since the whole of what egoism assumes about the priority of reasons, that is, (1) and (2) are unacceptable from an altruistic perspective and the whole of what altruism assumes about the priority of reasons, that is, (1') and (2') are unacceptable from an egoistic perspective, each of these views begs the question against the other to a far greater extent than the compromise view does against each of them. Of course, it would be preferable to have an alternative that did not beg the question at all, but with respect to specifying the priority of self-interested and altruistic reasons, no such alternative exists. Consequently, on the grounds of making the fewest question-begging assumptions given that it shares important common ground with both the egoistic and altruistic perspectives, the compromise view is the only non-arbitrary resolution of the conflict between egoism and altruism.

Notice, too, that this defense of morality succeeds not only against the view that egoism is rationally preferable to morality but also against the view that egoism is only rationally on a par with morality. The "weaker view" does not claim that we all ought to be egoists. Rather it claims that there is just as good reason for us to be egoists as there is for us to be pure altruists or anything in between. Kai Nielsen summarizes this view:

> We have not been able to show that reason requires the moral point of view or that all really

rational persons not be individual egoists. Reason doesn't decide here.[23]

Yet since the above defense of morality shows morality to be the only non-arbitrary resolution of the conflict between self-interested and altruistic reasons, it is not the case that there is just as good reason for us to endorse morality as there is for us to endorse egoism or altruism. Thus, the above defense of morality succeeds against the weaker as well as against the stronger interpretation of egoism.

It might be objected that this defense of morality could be undercut if in the debate over egoism, altruism, and morality, we simply give up any attempt to show that any one of these views is rationally preferable to the others. But we cannot rationally do this. For we are engaged in this debate as people who can act self-interestedly, can act altruistically, can act morally; and we are trying to discover which of these ways of acting is rationally justified. To rationally resolve this question, we must be committed to finding out whether one of these views is more rationally defensible than the others. So as far as I can tell, there is no escaping the conclusion that morality is more rationally defensible than either egoism and altruism.

Unfortunately, this approach to defending morality has been generally neglected by previous moral theorists. The reason is that such theorists have tended to cast the basic conflict with egoism as a conflict between morality and self-interest. For example, according to Kurt Baier,

The very *raison d'être* of a morality is to yield reasons which overrule the reasons of self-interest in those cases when everyone's following self-interest would be harmful to everyone.[24]

Viewed in this light, it did not seem possible for the defender of morality to be supporting a compromise view, for how could such a defender say that, when morality and self-interest conflict, morality should sometimes be sacrificed for the sake of self-interest? But while previous theorists understood correctly that moral reasons could not be compromised in favor of self-interested reasons, they failed to recognize that this is because moral reasons are already the result of a non-arbitrary compromise between self-interested and altruistic reasons. Thus, unable to see how morality can be represented as a compromise solution, previous theorists have generally failed to recognize this approach to defending morality.

In setting out this defense of morality, I assumed that we humans have the capacity to move along a spectrum from egoism to pure altruism. I granted that our ability to move along this spectrum will depend on our starting point, the strength of our habits and the social circumstances under which we happen to be living. But I argued that, at the outset, it is reasonable to abstract from these individual variations and simply focus on the general capacity virtually all of us have to act on both self-interested and moral reasons. Now, however, that I have argued that both self-interested and altruistic reasons are relevant to rational choice and assigned priorities in cases of conflict, it is appropriate to return to the question of how individual differences and the effects of socialization should adjust our expectations and requirements for particular individuals and groups.

Here two kinds of cases seem particularly relevant. In one case, certain people by nature lack, to some degree, the capacity to act on high-ranking altruistic reasons when they conflict with low-ranking self-interested reasons. In the other case, certain people due to socialization lack, to some degree, the capacity to act on high-ranking altruistic reasons when they conflict with low-ranking self-interested reasons. Obviously, people who have the capacity for altruism will have to try to work around and, if necessary, protect themselves from those who, to varying degrees, lack this capacity. In cases in which those who lack this capacity are themselves at least partially responsible for this lack, blame and censure would also be appropriate.[25] Nevertheless, as long as the great majority of people have by nature and/or by nurture the capacity to act on high-ranking altruistic reasons when they conflict with low-ranking self-interested reasons, it should be possible to set up a social order that corresponds with the requirements of morality.[26] Moreover, once we take into account the capacities of both men and women there is good reason to think that the greater majority of humankind do have this capacity for altruism.[27]

Objections

Let's call my defense of morality "Morality as Compromise." I now want to deal with three specific objections that have been raised to it. These objections come from Jeffrey Reiman and Eric Mack.[28]

In responding to an earlier version of Morality as Compromise, Jeffrey Reiman questions whether my argument suffices to show altruistic reasons should be regarded as prima facie relevant to rational choice. Reiman claims that to regard them as prima facie relevant, it is not enough to show that a person does not have any non-question-begging grounds for *rejecting* altruistic reasons. Before regarding them as relevant, Reiman thinks that a person who already regards self-interested reasons as obviously relevant must be given a non-question-begging reason for *accepting* altruistic reasons as prima facie relevant. Presumably, Reiman also thinks that a person who already regards altruistic reasons as obviously relevant must be given a non-question-begging reason for *accepting* self-interested reasons as well.

But why is it reasonable to demand non-question-begging grounds for accepting reasons to which I am not already committed when I don't require non-question-begging grounds for continuing to accept the reasons to which I am already committed? Why is it reasonable to demand a higher standard of acceptability of reasons that I might come to accept than I demand of reasons I have already accepted?

The situation is even worse because by allowing ourselves to retain our old reasons on lesser grounds than we require of ourselves for accepting new reasons, we may effectively block the acquisition of new reasons which are better grounded than our old reasons simply because these new reasons happen to conflict with our

old reasons. Clearly, a more reasonable strategy would be to evaluate both new and old reasons by the same standard. If we were to proceed in this fashion, then, both self-interested and altruistic reasons would have to be regarded as prima facie relevant since we lack a non-question-begging reason to reject reasons of either kind.

It is also the case that we all find ourselves somewhere on the spectrum between egoism and altruism with some capacity and opportunity to move toward one or the other, and with a strong interest in resolving the question of how we should act in this regard in a reasonable manner.

Reiman goes on to suggest that regarding both self-interested and altruistic reasons as prima facie relevant on these grounds would be analogous to naturalists and supernaturalists splitting the difference between their views and counting supernatural reasons as valid half the time. But as I understand the debate between naturalism and supernaturalism, many naturalists claim to have non-question-begging reasons for rejecting supernaturalism, and some supernaturalists claim to have non-question-begging grounds for rejecting naturalism. So this example does not parallel the case of egoism and altruism as I envision it.

But suppose there were equally good reasons for naturalism as for supernaturalism would we be rationally required to act on naturalism half the time and supernaturalism the other half of the time, as Reiman suggests? In this case, a far more reasonable resolution would be to continue to lead the life of a naturalist or a supernaturalist at the practical level while periodically re-evaluating the relevant reasons with the hope of some day resolving this issue. This interim solution is preferable because there is no way to compromise the issue between naturalism and supernaturalism that would respect the most important elements of each view. That is why the conflict between naturalism and supernaturalism differs from the conflict between egoism and altruism because in the latter case there is a way to compromise the issue between the two views which respects the most important elements of each: Favor high-ranking self-interested reasons over low-ranking altruistic reasons and favor high-ranking altruistic reasons over low-ranking self-interested reasons.

This illustrates how the requirement of non-question-beggingness favors different solutions in different contexts. Thus, in contexts where action can be deferred, it favors deferring action until compelling reasons favoring one course of action can be found, for example, putting off your choice of a vacation spot until you have good reasons for going to a particular spot. However, in contexts where action cannot be deferred, either it is or it is not possible to combine the best parts of the existing alternatives into a single course of action. If it is not possible to combine the best parts of the existing alternatives, as in the case of naturalism and supernaturalism, the requirement of non-question-beggingness favors arbitrarily choosing between them, while periodically re-examining the situation to determine whether compelling reasons can be found favoring one alternative over the others. If it is possible to combine existing alternatives, however, as in the case of egoism and altruism, the requirement of non-question-beggingness favors this course of action. It is on this account that I argue that Morality as Compromise is rationally preferable to either egoism or altruism.[29]

Eric Mack has raised a different objection to Morality as Compromise.[30] He questions whether a non-arbitrary weighing of all the relevant self-interested reasons and altruistic reasons would lead to the kind of resolutions that I favor. He gives the example of a rich woman in severe conflict with a poor man, having the following self-interested and altruistic reasons:

Altruistic reasons
1. not to kill the poor man
2. not to exploit the poor man
3. not to prevent the poor man from appropriating her surplus crucial for meeting basic needs

Self-interested reasons
1. to retain control of her body
2. to retain control of her possessions crucial for meeting basic needs
3. to retain control of her possessions

4. to retain her surplus

Given these rankings, Mack claims that the rich woman's third altruistic reason would triumph over her fourth self-interested reason. But suppose that we alter the list of altruistic reasons to include two other reasons as follows:

Altruistic reasons
1. not to kill the poor man
2. not to exploit the poor man
3. not to maim the poor man
4. not to deceive the poor man
5. not to prevent the poor man from appropriating her surplus

Given these rankings, Mack claims that the rich woman's fifth altruistic reason would no longer triumph over her fourth self-interested reason. Mack contends that this shows that this whole procedure for ranking reasons is arbitrary, and so it cannot be used to support morality over egoism in the way I propose.

Actually, I agree with Mack that *his procedure* for determining the ranking of self-interested and altruistic reasons is arbitrary. The arbitrariness is evident in the fact that Mack's lists of self-interested and altruistic reasons are not of the same sort. His list of self-interested reasons is more generic while his lists of altruistic reasons are more specific. No wonder, then, that Mack derives from these lists results everyone would want to reject. But this does not show that no non-arbitrary ranking is possible.

For example, suppose we make both lists generic as follows:

Altruistic reasons
1. to meet the basic needs of others
2. to meet the non-basic needs of others

Self-interested reasons
1. to meet one's basic needs
2. to meet one's non-basic needs

Here there is no problem determining that a non-arbitrary weighing of these prima facie relevant reasons would require us to rank the first self-interested reason over the second altruistic reason, other things being equal, and rank the first altruistic reason over the second self-interested reason, other things being equal.

Of course, there will be problems determining which particular needs are basic or non-basic. Obviously, some needs are near the borderline. But just as obviously, many needs can be seen to belong to one class or the other, thereby enabling us to non-arbitrarily resolve conflicts between self-interested and altruistic reasons in the way I propose in Morality as Compromise.

The last specific objection that I wish to consider is one raised by Jeffrey Reiman.[31] The objection is that a justification of morality like my own does not even succeed in its own terms, that is, it does not succeed in justifying morality. According to Reiman, avoiding inconsistency (as in Gewirth's justification) or avoiding question-beggingness (as in mine) are only logical requirements, whereas the offense of being immoral is something more than a logical offense. Reiman claims that a justification of morality, like my own, only succeeds in showing that the egoist or immoralist is guilty of a logical mistake, and that is not enough. Reiman asks us to imagine a murderer who says, "Yes, I've been inconsistent (or begged the question) but that is *all* I've done." Reiman claims that morality requires something more, it requires that we recognize the reality of other people, and immorality denies that reality.[32]

But notice that if Reiman's view of morality were sound, egoists and immoralists, by denying the reality of other people, would be solipsists, but clearly they are not.[33] Nevertheless, there is something to Reiman's objection. Putting a defense of morality in terms of a non-question-begging compromise between relevant self-interested and altruistic reasons for action can obscure the fact that what is at stake is the prohibition of the infliction of basic harm on others for the sake of non-basic benefit to oneself, given that the infliction of such harm is what egoism would require. Thus, what needs to be made clear is that the failure to be moral involves both a logical and a material mistake. The logical mistake is

that of begging the question or acting contrary to reason. The material mistake is the infliction of basic harm for the sake of non-basic benefit. Both of these mistakes characterize any failure to be moral, and they entail each other.[34] They are simply two different aspects of the same act.

In this paper, I have argued that a commitment to morality is not only rationally permissible but also rationally required. Morality is rationally required, I claim, as a compromise that favors high-ranking self-interested reasons over low-ranking altruistic reasons and high-ranking altruistic reasons over low-ranking self-interested reasons. Of course, exactly how this compromise is to be worked out is a matter of considerable debate. Utilitarians favor one sort of a resolution, contractarians another, and libertarians yet another. My own view is that this debate can be adequately resolved at the practical level by showing how theoretically different views lead to the same practical requirements. For example, I have argued that libertarian, contractarian, and socialist views, when properly interpreted, all lead to the same practical requirements. Yet however this debate is resolved, what I have argued here is that Morality as Compromise is rationally preferable to either egoism or pure altruism when judged from a non-question-begging standpoint.

Notes

1 While egoism is an ethical perspective because it provides norms about how one should behave, it is not a moral perspective because it never requires a person to sacrifice her overall interest for the sake of others.

2 Again John Rawls is typical here. See his *A Theory of Justice* (Cambridge, MA: Harvard University Press, 1971), p. 136.

3 Ibid.

4 "Ought" presupposes "can" here. So unless people have the capacity to entertain and follow both self-interested and moral reasons for acting, it does not make any sense asking whether they ought or ought not to do so. Moreover, moral reasons here are understood to necessarily include (some) altruistic reasons but not necessarily to exclude (all) self-interested reasons. So the question of whether it would be rational for us to follow self-interested reasons rather than moral reasons

should be understood as the question of whether it would be rational for us to follow self-interested reasons exclusively rather than some appropriate set of self-interested reasons and altruistic reasons which constitutes the class of moral reasons.

5   Of course, we don't need to seek to construct a good argument in support of all of our views, but our view about whether morality or egoism has priority is an important enough question to call for the support of a good argument.

6   I understand the pure altruist to be the mirror image of the pure egoist. Whereas the pure egoist thinks that the interests of others count for them but not for herself except instrumentally, the pure altruist thinks that her own interests count for others but not for herself except instrumentally

7   Self-interested reasons favor both relational and non-relational goods for the self, while altruistic reasons favor both relational and non-relational goods for others.

8   Nel Noddings, *Caring: A Feminine Approach to Ethics and Moral Education* (Berkeley: University of California Press, 1984); Joyce Trebilcot (ed.), *Mothering* (Totowa: Rowman and Littlefield, 1983); Susan Brownmiller, *Femininity* (New York: Ballantine Books, 1984).

9   James Doyle, *The Male Experience* (Dubuque: W. C. Brown, 1983); Marie Richmond-Abbot (ed.), *Masculine and Feminine*, 2nd edn (New York: Random House, 1991).

10 Victor Seidler, *Rediscovering Masculinity* (New York: Routledge, 1989); Larry May and Robert Strikwerda, *Rethinking Masculinity* (Lanham, MD: Rowman and Littlefield, 1992).

11 This is not to deny that we usually have greater knowledge and certainty about what is in our own self-interest than about what is in the interest of others and that this difference in our knowledge and certainty can have a practical effect on what good we should do in particular contexts. It is just that the debate between egoism and morality gets started at the theoretical level where no assumption is made about this difference in our knowledge and certainty, since we can, and frequently do, have adequate knowledge and certainty about both what is in our own self-interest and what is in the interest of others.

12 For an account of what counts as relevant self-interested or moral reasons, see my *How to Make People Just* (Totowa, NJ: Rowman and Littlefield,

1988), pp. 165–6.

13 For a discussion of the causal links involved here, see *Marketing and Promotion of Infant Formula in Developing Countries*. Hearing before the Subcommittee of International Economic Policy and Trade of the Committee on Foreign Affairs, U.S. House of Representatives, 1980. See also Maggie McComas et al., *The Dilemma of Third World Nutrition* (1983).

14 Assume that both jobs have the same beneficial effects on the interests of others.

15 I am assuming that acting contrary to reason is a significant failing with respect to the requirements of reason, and that there are many ways of not acting in (perfect) accord with reason that do not constitute acting contrary to reason.

16 To deal with pure sadists (if any exist) for whom malevolent reasons or the reasons on which such reasons are grounded would not have been outweighed by other self-interested reasons, we might introduce an additional argument to show that pure sadists should team up with pure masochists (if any exist)!

17 Of course, such reasons will have to be taken into account at some point in a conception of justice for here and now, but the method of integrating such reasons will simply parallel the method already used for integrating self-interested and altruistic reasons. In reading 39, I consider how such reasons to promote non-human welfare should be integrated into a conception of justice. It is not clear how there could be any other kind of reasons that would be relevant to rational choice, but if there were such they would have to relate to some other kind of good that we could plausibly be maintained to pursue.

18 In G. E. Moore's thought experiment of whether a beautiful world should be preferred to an ugly world if no one were to have experience of either, Moore's preference for the beautiful world was based on the assumption that humans would not be affected one way or the other by the choice. See G. E. Moore, *Principia Ethica* (Cambridge, England: Cambridge University Press, 1966), pp. 83–5. Moreover, although there are many aesthetic objects that we restrict our experience of in order to better preserve them, even in such cases, it still seems that the value of such objects correlates with the value of the aesthetic experiences that such objects have produced in the past or could produce in the future for beings like ourselves.

19 This is because, as I shall argue, morality itself already represents a compromise between egoism and altruism. So to ask that moral reasons be weighed against self-interested reasons is, in effect, to count self-interested reasons twice – once in the compromise between egoism and altruism and then again when moral reasons are weighed against self-interested reasons. But to count self-interested reasons twice is clearly objectionable.

20 Assume that all these methods of waste disposal have roughly the same amount of beneficial effects on the interests of others.

21 It is important to point out here that this defense of morality presupposes that we can establish a conception of the good, at least to the degree that we can determine high- and low-ranking self-interested and altruistic reasons for each agent.

22 It is worth pointing out here an important difference between these self-interested and altruistic reasons that constitute moral reasons. It is that the self-interested reasons render the pursuit of self-interest permissible whereas the altruistic reasons require the pursuit of altruism. This is because it is always possible to sacrifice oneself more than morality demands and thus act supererogatorily. Yet even here there are limits and one can sacrifice oneself too much, as presumably the pure altruist does, and consequently, be morally blameworthy for doing so.

23 Kai Nielsen, "Why Should I be Moral? Revisited," *American Philosophical Quarterly*, vol. 21 (1984), p. 90.

24 Kurt Baier, *The Moral Point of View*, abridged edn (New York: Random House, 1965), p. 150.

25 The justification for blaming and censuring such persons is not based on any possibility for reforming them, because we were assuming that they were incapable of reform. Rather the justification is based on what the persons in question deserve because of their past behavior and on whatever usefulness blaming and censuring them would have in deterring others.

26 What it is rational for those who lack even the minimal capacity for altruism to do is a question that I will not take up here.

27 Not all the reasons that people are or were able to acquire are relevant to an assessment of the reasonableness of their conduct. First, reasons that are evokable only from some logically possible set of opportunities are simply not relevant; the reasons must be evokable from the opportunities people actually possessed. Second, reasons that radically different people could have acquired are also not relevant. Instead, relevant reasons are those that people could have acquired without radical changes in their developing identities. Third, some reasons are not important enough to be relevant to a reasonable assessment of conduct. For example, a reason that I am able to acquire, which would lead me to promote my own interests or that of a friend just slightly more than I am presently doing, is hardly relevant to an assessment of the reasonableness of my conduct. Surely, I could not be judged as unreasonable for failing to acquire such a reason. Rather, relevant reasons are those that would lead one to avoid a *significant harm* to oneself (or others) or to secure a *significant benefit* to oneself (or others) at an acceptable cost to oneself (or others).

It is also worth noting that a given individual may not actually reflect on all the reasons that are relevant to deciding what she should do. In fact, one could do so only if one had already acquired all the relevant reasons. Nevertheless, reasonable conduct is ideally determined by a rational weighing of all the reasons that are relevant to deciding what one should do so that failing to accord with a rational weighing of all such reasons is to act contrary to reason.

28 Jeffrey Reiman, "What Ought "'Ought' Implies 'Can' " Imply? Comments on James Sterba's *How To Make People Just*," *Journal of Social Philosophy*, Special Issue, vol. 22 (1991), pp. 73–80; Eric Mack, "Libertarianism Untamed," *Journal of Social Philosophy*, Special Issue, vol. 22 (1991), pp. 64–72. See also Jeffrey Reiman, *Justice and Modern Moral Philosophy* (New Haven, CT: Yale University Press, 1990), pp. 92–112.

29 There is also the additional reason discussed earlier that egoism fails to meet its burden of proof.

30 Mack, "Libertarianism Untamed."

31 Reiman, "What Ought " 'Ought' Implies 'Can' " Imply? Comments on James Sterba's *How To Make People Just*," pp. 73–80. This objection was actually directed against Alan Gewirth's defense of morality, but in private correspondence, Reiman has directed it against my own view as well.

32 *Justice and Modern Moral Philosophy*, pp. 112–29.

33 In private correspondence, Reiman claims that, as he understands the denial of the reality of other people, it does not require solipsism but only the failure to "recognize the first-person reality of

other people" (August 2, 1995). But even given this interpretation, it still seems that Reiman is making too strong a claim about the egoist. For example, the egoist does not have to deny that other human beings are in pain, as would seemingly be the case if the egoist failed to "recognize the first-person reality of other people."

34 The logical mistake of begging the question entails, in this context, preferring low-ranking self-interested reasons over high-ranking altruistic reasons or low-ranking altruistic reasons over high-ranking self-interested reasons, which, in turn, entails the material mistake of inflicting basic harm for the sake of non-basic benefit. Likewise, the material mistake of inflicting basic harm for the sake of non-basic benefit entails preferring low-ranking self-interested reasons over high-ranking altruistic reasons which, in turn, entails the logical mistake of begging the question.

PART THREE

ALTERNATIVE MORAL PERSPECTIVES:
WHAT DOES MORALITY REQUIRE?

Virtue

Utility

---

14 Utilitarianism

John Stuart Mill

Chapter I: General Remarks

There are few circumstances among those which make up the present condition of human knowledge more unlike what might have been expected, or more significant of the backward state in which speculation on the most important subjects still lingers, than the little progress which has been made in the decision of the controversy respecting the criterion of right and wrong. From the dawn of philosophy, the question concerning the *summum bonum*, or, what is the same thing, concerning the foundation of morality, has been accounted the main problem in speculative thought, has occupied the most gifted intellects and divided them into sects and schools carrying on a vigorous warfare against one another. And after more than two thousand years the same discussions continue, philosophers are still ranged under the same contending banners, and neither thinkers nor mankind at large seem nearer to being unanimous on the subject than when the youth Socrates listened to the old Protagoras and asserted (if Plato's dialogue be grounded on a real conversation) the theory of utilitarianism against the popular morality of the so-called sophist.

It is true that similar confusion and uncertainty and, in some cases, similar discordance exist respecting the first principles of all the sciences, not excepting that which is deemed the most certain of them – mathematics, without much

From *Utilitarianism* (first published 1863). Reprinted with permission.

impairing, generally indeed without impairing at all, the trustworthiness of the conclusions of those sciences. An apparent anomaly, the explanation of which is that the detailed doctrines of a science are not usually deduced from, nor depend for their evidence upon, what are called its first principles. Were it not so, there would be no science more precarious, or whose conclusions were more insufficiently made out, than algebra, which derives none of its certainty from what are commonly taught to learners as its elements, since these, as laid down by some of its most eminent teachers, are as full of fictions as English law, and of mysteries as theology. The truths which are ultimately accepted as the first principles of a science are really the last results of metaphysical analysis practiced on the elementary notions with which the science is conversant; and their relation to the science is not that of foundations to an edifice, but of roots to a tree, which may perform their office equally well though they be never dug down to and exposed to light. But though in science the particular truths precede the general theory, the contrary might be expected to be the case with a practical art, such as morals or legislation. All action is for the sake of some end, and rules of action, it seems natural to suppose, must take their whole character and color from the end to which they are subservient. When we engage in a pursuit, a clear and precise conception of what we are pursuing would seem to be the first thing we need, instead of the last we are to look forward to. A test of right and wrong must be the means, one would think, of ascertaining what is right or wrong, and not a consequence of having already ascertained it.

The difficulty is not avoided by having recourse to the popular theory of a natural faculty, a sense of instinct, informing us of right and wrong. For – besides that the existence of such a moral instinct is itself one of the matters in dispute – those believers in it who have any pretensions to philosophy have been obliged to abandon the idea that it discerns what is right or wrong in the particular case in hand, as our other senses discern the sight or sound actually present. Our moral faculty, according to all those of its interpreters who are entitled to the name of thinkers, supplies us only with the general principles of moral judgments; it is a branch of our reason, not of our sensitive faculty, and must be looked to for the abstract doctrines of morality, not for perception of it in the concrete. The intuitive, no less than what may be termed the inductive, school of ethics insists on the necessity of general laws. They both agree that the morality of an individual action is not a question of direct perception, but of the application of a law to an individual case. They recognize also, to a great extent, the same moral laws, but differ as to their evidence and the source from which they derive their authority. According to the one opinion, the principles of morals are evident a priori, requiring nothing to command assent except that the meaning of the terms be understood. According to the other doctrine, right and wrong, as well as truth and falsehood, are questions of observation and experience. But both hold equally that morality must be deduced from principles; and the intuitive school affirm as strongly as the inductive that there is a science of morals. Yet they seldom attempt to make out a list of the a priori principles which are to serve as the premises of the science; still more rarely do they make any effort to reduce those various principles to one first principle or common ground of obligation. They either assume the ordinary precepts of morals as of a priori authority, or they lay down as the common groundwork of those maxims some generality much less obviously authoritative than the maxims themselves, and which has never succeeded in gaining popular acceptance. Yet to support their pretensions there ought either to be some one fundamental principle or law at the root of all morality, or, if there be several, there should be a determinate order of precedence among them; and the one principle, or the rule for deciding between the various principles when they conflict, ought to be self-evident.

To inquire how far the bad effects of this deficiency have been mitigated in practice, or to what extent the moral beliefs of mankind have been vitiated or made uncertain by the absence of any distinct recognition of an ultimate standard, would imply a complete survey and criticism of past and present ethical doctrine. It would, however, be easy to show that whatever steadiness or consistency these moral beliefs have attained has been mainly due to the tacit influence of a standard not recognized. Although the non-existence of an acknowledged first principle has made ethics not so much a guide as a consecration of men's actual sentiments, still, as men's sentiments, both of favor and of aversion, are greatly influenced by what they suppose to be the effects of things upon their happiness, the principle of utility, or, as Bentham latterly called it, the greatest happiness principle, has had a large share in forming the moral doctrines even of those who most scornfully reject its authority. Nor is there any school of thought which refuses to admit that the influence of actions on happiness is a most material and even predominant consideration in many of the details of morals, however unwilling to acknowledge it as the fundamental principle of morality and the source of moral obligation. I might go much further and say that to all those a priori moralists who deem it necessary to argue at all, utilitarian arguments are indispensable. It is not my present purpose to criticize these thinkers; but I cannot help referring, for illustration, to a systematic treatise by one of the most illustrious of them, the *Metaphysics of Ethics* by Kant. This remarkable man, whose system of thought will long remain one of the landmarks in the history of philosophical speculation, does, in the treatise in question, lay down a universal first principle as the origin and ground of moral obligation; it is this: "So act that the rule on which thou actest would admit of being adopted as a law by all rational beings." But when he begins to deduce from this precept any of the actual duties of morality, he fails, almost grotesquely, to show that there would be any contradiction, any logical (not to say physical) impossibility, in the adoption by all rational beings of the most outrageously immoral rules of conduct. All he shows is that the *consequences* of their universal adoption would be such as no one would choose to incur.

On the present occasion, I shall, without further discussion of the other theories, attempt to contribute something toward the understanding and appreciation of the "utilitarian" or "happiness" theory, and toward such proof as it is susceptible of. It is evident that this cannot be proof in the ordinary and popular meaning of the term. Questions of ultimate ends are not amenable to direct proof. Whatever can be proved to be good must be so by being shown to be a means to something admitted to be good without proof. The medical art is proved to be good by its conducing to health; but how is it possible to prove that health is good? The art of music is good, for the reason, among others, that it produces pleasure; but what proof is it possible to give that pleasure is good? If, then, it is asserted that there is a comprehensive formula, including all things which are in themselves good, and that whatever else is good is not so as an end but as a means, the formula may be accepted or rejected, but is not a subject of what is commonly understood by proof. We are not, however, to infer that its acceptance or rejection must depend on blind impulse or arbitrary choice. There is a larger meaning of the word "proof," in which this question is as amenable to it as any other of the disputed questions of philosophy. The subject is within the cognizance of the rational faculty; and neither does that faculty deal with it solely in the way of intuition. Considerations may be presented capable of determining the intellect either to give or withhold its assent to the doctrine; and this is equivalent to proof.

We shall examine presently of what nature are these considerations; in what manner they apply to the case, and what rational grounds, therefore, can be given for accepting or rejecting the utilitarian formula. But it is a preliminary condition of rational acceptance or rejection that the formula should be correctly understood. I believe that the very imperfect notion ordinarily formed of its meaning is the chief obstacle which impedes its reception, and that, could it be cleared even from only the grosser misconceptions, the question would be greatly simplified and a large proportion of its difficulties removed. Before, therefore, I attempt to enter into the philosophical grounds which can be given for assenting to the utilitarian standard, I shall offer some illustrations of the doctrine itself, with the view of showing more clearly what it is, distinguishing it from what it is not, and disposing of such of the practical objections to it as either originate in, or are closely connected with, mistaken interpretations of its meaning. Having thus prepared the ground, I shall afterwards endeavor to throw such light as I can call upon the question considered as one of philosophical theory.

Chapter II: What Utilitarianism Is

A passing remark is all that needs be given to the ignorant blunder of supposing that those who stand up for utility as the test of right and wrong use the term in that restricted and merely colloquial sense in which utility is opposed to pleasure. An apology is due to the philosophical opponents of utilitarianism for even the momentary appearance of confounding them with anyone capable of so absurd a misconception; which is the more extraordinary, inasmuch as the contrary accusation, of referring everything to pleasure, and that, too, in its grossest form, is another of the common charges against utilitarianism: and, as has been pointedly remarked by an able writer, the same sort of persons, and often the very same persons, denounce the theory "as impracticably dry when the word 'utility' precedes the word 'pleasure,' and as too practically voluptuous when the word 'pleasure' precedes the word 'utility.'" Those who know anything about the matter are aware that every writer, from Epicurus to Bentham, who maintained the theory of utility meant by it, not something to be contradistinguished from pleasure, but pleasure itself, together with exemption from pain; and instead of opposing the useful to the agreeable or the ornamental, have always declared that the useful means these, among other things. Yet the common herd, including the herd of writers, not only in newspapers and periodicals, but in books of weight and pretension, are perpetually falling into this shallow mistake. Having caught up the word "utilitarian," while knowing nothing whatever about it but its sound, they habitually express by it the rejection or the neglect of pleasure in some of its forms: of beauty, of ornament, or of amusement. Nor is the term thus ignorantly misapplied solely in disparagement, but occasionally in compliment, as though it implied superiority to frivolity and the mere pleasures of the moment. And this perverted use is the only one in which the word is popularly known, and the one from which the new generation are acquiring their sole notion of its meaning. Those who introduced the word, but who had for many years discontinued it as a distinctive appellation, may well feel themselves called upon to resume it if by doing so they can hope to contribute anything toward rescuing it from this utter degradation.[1]

The creed which accepts as the foundation of morals "utility" or the "greatest happiness principle" holds that actions are right in proportion as they tend to promote happiness; wrong as they tend to produce the reverse of happiness. By happiness is intended pleasure and the absence of pain; by unhappiness, pain and the privation of pleasure. To give a clear view of the moral standard set up by the theory, much more requires to be said; in particular, what things it includes in the ideas of pain and pleasure, and to what extent this is left an open question. But these supplementary explanations do not affect the theory of life on which this theory of morality is grounded – namely, that pleasure and freedom from pain are the only things desirable as ends; and that all desirable things (which are as numerous in the utilitarian as in any other scheme) are desirable either for pleasure inherent in themselves or as means to the promotion of pleasure and the prevention of pain.

Now such a theory of life excites in many minds, and among them in some of the most estimable in feeling and purpose, inveterate dislike. To suppose that life has (as they express it) no higher end than pleasure – no better and nobler object of desire and pursuit – they designate as utterly mean and groveling, as a doctrine worthy only of swine, to whom the followers of Epicurus were, at a very early period, contemptuously likened; and modern holders of the doctrine are occasionally made the subject of equally polite comparisons by its German, French, and English assailants.

When thus attacked, the Epicureans have always answered that it is not they, but their accusers, who represent human nature in a degrading light, since the accusation supposes human beings to be capable of no pleasures except those of which swine are capable. If this supposition were true, the charge could not be gainsaid, but would then be no longer an imputation; for if the sources of pleasure were precisely the same to human beings and to swine, the rule of life which is good enough for the one would be good enough for the other. The comparison of the Epicurean life to that of beasts is felt as degrading, precisely because a beast's pleasures do not satisfy a human being's conceptions of happiness. Human beings have faculties more elevated than the animal appetites and, when once made conscious of them, do not regard anything as happiness which does not include their gratification. I do not, indeed, consider the Epicureans to have been by any means faultless in drawing out their scheme of consequences from the utilitarian principle. To do this in any sufficient manner, many Stoic, as well as Christian, elements require to be included. But there is no known Epicurean theory of life which does not assign to the pleasures of the intellect, of the feelings and imagination, and of the moral sentiments a much higher value as pleasures than to those of mere sensation. It must be admitted, however, that utilitarian writers in general have placed the superiority of mental over bodily pleasures chiefly in the greater permanency, safety, uncostliness, etc., of the former – that is, in their circumstantial advantages rather than in their intrinsic nature. And on all these points utilitarians have fully proved their case; but they might have taken the other and, as it may be called, higher ground with entire consistency. It is quite compatible with the principle of utility to recognize the fact that some kinds of pleasure are more desirable and more valuable than others. It would be absurd that, while in estimating all other things quality is considered as well as quantity, the estimation of pleasure should be supposed to depend on quantity alone.

If I am asked what I mean by difference of quality in pleasures, or what makes one pleasure more valuable than another, merely as a pleasure, except its being greater in amount, there is but one possible answer. Of two pleasures, if there be one to which all or almost all who have experience of both give a decided preference, irrespective of any feeling of moral obligation to prefer it, that is the more desirable pleasure. If one of the two is, by those who are competently acquainted with both, placed so far above the other that they prefer it, even though knowing it to be attended with a greater amount of discontent, and would not resign it for any quantity of the other pleasure which their nature is capable of, we are justified in ascribing to the preferred enjoyment a superiority in quality so far outweighing quantity as to render it, in comparison, of small account.

Now it is an unquestionable fact that those who are equally acquainted with and equally capable of appreciating and enjoying both do give a most marked preference to the manner of existence which employs their higher faculties. Few human creatures would consent to be changed into any of the lower animals for a promise of the fullest allowance of a beast's pleasures; no intelligent human being would consent to be a fool, no instructed person would be an ignoramus, no person of feeling and conscience would be selfish and base, even though they should be persuaded that the fool, the dunce, or the rascal is better satisfied with his lot than they are with theirs. They would not resign what they possess more than he for the most complete satisfaction of all the desires which they have in common with him. If they ever fancy they would, it is only in cases of unhappiness so extreme that to escape from it they would exchange their lot for almost any other, however undesirable in their own eyes. A being of higher faculties requires more to make him happy, is capable probably of more acute suffering, and certainly accessible to it at more points, than one of an inferior type; but in spite of these liabilities, he can never really wish to sink into what he feels to be a lower grade of existence. We may give what explanation we please of this unwillingness; we may attribute it to pride, a name which is given indiscriminately to some of the most and to some of the least estimable feelings of which mankind are capable; we may refer it to the love of liberty and personal independence, an appeal to which was with the Stoics one of the most effective means for the inculcation of it; to the love of power or to the love of excitement, both of which do really enter into and contribute to it; but its most appropriate appellation is a sense of dignity, which all human beings possess in one form or other, and in some, though by no means in exact, proportion to their higher faculties, and which is so essential a part of the happiness of those in whom it is strong that nothing which conflicts with it could be otherwise than momentarily an object of desire to them. Whoever supposes that this preference takes place at a sacrifice of happiness – that the superior being, in anything like equal circumstances, is not happier than the inferior – confounds the two very different ideas of happiness and content. It is indisputable that the being whose capacities of enjoyment are low has the greatest chance of having them fully satisfied; and a highly endowed being will always feel that any happiness which he can look for, as the world is constituted, is imperfect. But he can learn to bear its imperfections, if they are at all bearable; and they will not make him envy the being who is indeed unconscious of the imperfections, but only because he feels not at all the good which those imperfections qualify. It is better to be a human being dissatisfied than a pig satisfied; better to be Socrates dissatisfied than a fool satisfied. And if the fool, or the pig, are of a different opinion, it is because they only know their own side of the question. The other party to the comparison knows both sides.

It may be objected that many who are capable of the higher pleasures occasionally, under the influence of temptation, postpone them to the lower. But this is quite compatible with a full appreciation of the intrinsic superiority of the higher. Men often, from infirmity of character, make their election for the nearer good, though they know it to be the less valuable; and this no less when the choice is between two bodily pleasures than when it is between bodily and mental. They pursue sensual indulgences to the injury of health, though perfectly aware that health is the greater good. It may be further objected that many who begin with youthful enthusiasm for everything noble, as they advance in years, sink into indolence and selfishness. But I do not believe that those who undergo this very common change voluntarily choose the lower description of pleasures in preference to the higher. I believe that, before they devote themselves exclusively to the one, they have already become incapable of the other. Capacity for the nobler feelings is in most natures a very tender plant, easily killed, not only by hostile influences, but by mere want of sustenance; and in the majority of young persons it speedily dies away if the occupations to which their position in life has devoted them, and the society into which it has thrown them, are not favorable to keeping that higher capacity in exercise. Men lose their high aspirations as they lose their intellectual tastes, because they have not time or opportunity for indulging them; and they addict themselves to inferior pleasures, not because they deliberately prefer them, but because they are either the only ones to which they have access or the only ones which they are any longer capable of enjoying. It may be questioned whether anyone who has remained equally susceptible to both classes of pleasures ever knowingly and calmly preferred the lower, though many, in all ages, have broken down in an ineffectual attempt to combine both.

From this verdict of the only competent judges, I apprehend there can be no appeal. On a question which is the best worth having of two pleasures, or which of two modes of existence is the most grateful to the feelings, apart from its moral attributes and from its consequences, the judgment of those who are qualified by knowledge of both, or, if they differ, that of the majority among them, must be admitted as final. And there needs be the less hesitation to accept this judgment respecting the quality of pleasures, since there is no other tribunal to be referred to even on the question of quantity. What means are there of determining which is the acutest of two pains, or the intensest of two pleasurable sensations, except the general suffrage of those who are familiar with both? Neither pains nor pleasures are homogeneous, and pain is always heterogeneous with pleasure. What is there to decide whether a particular pleasure is worth purchasing at the cost of a particular pain, except the feelings and judgment of the experienced? When, therefore, those feelings and judgment declare the pleasures derived from the higher faculties to be preferable *in kind*, apart from the question of intensity, to those of which the animal nature, disjoined from the higher faculties, is susceptible, they are entitled on this subject to the same regard.

I have dwelt on this point as being a necessary part of a perfectly just conception of utility or happiness considered as the directive rule of human conduct. But it is by no means an indispensable condition to the acceptance of the utilitarian standard; for that standard is not the agent's own greatest happiness, but the greatest amount of happiness altogether; and if it may possibly be doubted whether a noble character is always the happier for its nobleness, there can be no doubt that it makes other people happier, and that the world in general is immensely a gainer by it. Utilitarianism, therefore, could only attain its end by the general cultivation of nobleness of character, even if each individual were only benefited by the nobleness of others, and his own, so far as happiness is concerned, were a sheer deduction from the benefit. But the bare enunciation of such an absurdity as this last renders refutation superfluous.

According to the greatest happiness principle, as above explained, the ultimate end, with reference to and for the sake of which all other things are desirable – whether we are considering our

own good or that of other people – is an existence exempt as far as possible from pain, and as
rich as possible in enjoyments, both in point of
quantity and quality; the test of quality and the
rule for measuring it against quantity being the
preference felt by those who, in their opportunities of experience, to which must be added their
habits of self-consciousness and self-observation,
are best furnished with the means of comparison. This, being according to the utilitarian opinion the end of human action, is necessarily also
the standard of morality, which may accordingly
be defined "the rules and precepts for human
conduct," by the observance of which an existence such as has been described might be, to the
greatest extent possible, secured to all mankind;
and not to them only, but, so far as the nature of
things admits, to the whole sentient creation. . . .

Unquestionably it is possible to do without
happiness; it is done involuntarily by nineteen-
twentieths of mankind, even in those parts of our
present world which are least deep in barbarism;
and it often has to be done voluntarily by the
hero or the martyr, for the sake of something
which he prizes more than his individual happiness. But this something, what is it, unless the
happiness of others or some of the requisites of
happiness? It is noble to be capable of resigning
entirely one's own portion of happiness, or
chances of it; but, after all, this self-sacrifice must
be for some end; it is not its own end; and if we
are told that its end is not happiness but virtue,
which is better than happiness, I ask, would the
sacrifice be made if the hero or martyr did not
believe that it would earn for others immunity
from similar sacrifices? Would it be made if he
thought that his renunciation of happiness for
himself would produce no fruit for any of his
fellow creatures, but to make their lot like his
and place them also in the condition of persons
who have renounced happiness? All honor to
those who can abnegate for themselves the personal enjoyment of life when by such renunciation they contribute worthily to increase the
amount of happiness in the world; but he who
does it or professes to do it for any other purpose is no more deserving of admiration than
the ascetic mounted on his pillar. He may be an

inspiriting proof of what men *can* do, but assuredly not an example of what they *should*.

Though it is only in a very imperfect state of
the world's arrangements that anyone can best
serve the happiness of others by the absolute sacrifice of his own, yet, so long as the world is in
that imperfect state, I fully acknowledge that the
readiness to make such a sacrifice is the highest
virtue which can be found in man. I will add that
in this condition of the world, paradoxical as the
assertion may be, the conscious ability to do without happiness gives the best prospect of realizing such happiness as is attainable. For nothing
except that consciousness can raise a person above
the chances of life by making him feel that, let
fate and fortune do their worst, they have not
power to subdue him; which, once felt, frees him
from excess of anxiety concerning the evils of life
and enables him, like many a Stoic in the worst
times of the Roman Empire, to cultivate in
tranquility the sources of satisfaction accessible
to him, without concerning himself about the
uncertainty of their duration any more than about
their inevitable end.

Meanwhile, let utilitarians never cease to claim
the morality of self-devotion as a possession which
belongs by as good a right to them as either to
the Stoic or to the Transcendentalist. The utilitarian morality does recognize in human beings
the power of sacrificing their own greatest good
for the good of others. It only refuses to admit
that the sacrifice is itself a good. A sacrifice which
does not increase or tend to increase the sum
total of happiness, it considers as wasted. The
only self-renunciation which it applauds is devotion to the happiness, or to some of the means of
happiness, of others, either of mankind collectively or of individuals within the limits imposed
by the collective interests of mankind.

I must again repeat what the assailants of utilitarianism seldom have the justice to acknowledge,
that the happiness which forms the utilitarian
standard of what is right in conduct is not the
agent's own happiness but that of all concerned.
As between his own happiness and that of others, utilitarianism requires him to be as strictly
impartial as a disinterested and benevolent spectator. In the golden rule of Jesus of Nazareth,

we read the complete spirit of the ethics of utility. "To do as you would be done by," and "to love your neighbor as yourself," constitute the ideal perfection of utilitarian morality. As the means of making the nearest approach to this ideal, utility would enjoin, first, that laws and social arrangements should place the happiness or (as, speaking practically, it may be called) the interest of every individual as nearly as possible in harmony with the interest of the whole; and, secondly, that education and opinion, which have so vast a power over human character, should so use that power as to establish in the mind of every individual an indissoluble association between his own happiness and the good of the whole, especially between his own happiness and the practice of such modes of conduct, negative and positive, as regard for the universal happiness prescribes; so that not only he may be unable to conceive the possibility of happiness to himself, consistently with conduct opposed to the general good, but also that a direct impulse to promote the general good may be in every individual one of the habitual motives of action, and the sentiments connected therewith may fill a large and prominent place in every human being's sentient existence. If the impugners of the utilitarian morality represented it to their own minds in this its true character, I know not what recommendation possessed by any other morality they could possibly affirm to be wanting to it; what more beautiful or more exalted developments of human nature any other ethical system can be supposed to foster, or what springs of action, not accessible to the utilitarian, such systems rely on for giving effect to their mandates.

The objectors to utilitarianism cannot always be charged with representing it in a discreditable light. On the contrary, those among them who entertain anything like a just idea of its disinterested character sometimes find fault with its standard as being too high for humanity. They say it is exacting too much to require that people shall always act from the inducement of promoting the general interests of society. But this is to mistake the very meaning of a standard of morals and confound the rule of action with the motive of it. It is the business of ethics to tell us what are our duties, or by what test we may know them; but no system of ethics requires that the sole motive of all we do shall be a feeling of duty; on the contrary, ninety-nine hundredths of all our actions are done from other motives, and rightly so done if the rule of duty does not condemn them. It is the more unjust to utilitarianism that this particular misapprehension should be made a ground of objection to it, inasmuch as utilitarian moralists have gone beyond almost all others in affirming that the motive has nothing to do with the morality of the action, though much with the worth of the agent. He who saves a fellow creature from drowning does what is morally right, whether his motive be duty or the hope of being paid for his trouble; he who betrays the friend that trusts him is guilty of a crime, even if his object be to serve another friend to whom he is under greater obligations.[2] But to speak only of actions done from the motive of duty, and in direct obedience to principle: it is a misapprehension of the utilitarian mode of thought to conceive it as implying that people should fix their minds upon so wide a generality as the world, or society at large. The great majority of good actions are intended not for the benefit of the world, but for that of individuals, of which the good of the world is made up; and the thoughts of the most virtuous man need not on these occasions travel beyond the particular persons concerned, except so far as is necessary to assure himself that in benefiting them he is not violating the rights, that is, the legitimate and authorized expectations, of anyone else. The multiplication of happiness is, according to the utilitarian ethics, the object of virtue: the occasions on which any person (except one in a thousand) has it in his power to do this on an extended scale – in other words, to be a public benefactor – are but exceptional; and on these occasions alone is he called on to consider public utility; in every other case, private utility, the interest or happiness of some few persons, is all he has to attend to. Those alone the influence of whose actions extends to society in general need concern themselves habitually about so large an object. In the case of abstinences indeed – of things which people forbear to do from moral considerations, though the consequences in the particular case might be beneficial – it would be unworthy of an intelligent agent not to be consciously aware that the action is of a class which, if practiced generally, would be generally injurious, and that this is the ground of the obligation to abstain from it. The amount of regard for the public interest implied in this recognition is no greater than is demanded by every system of morals, for they all enjoin to abstain from whatever is manifestly pernicious to society. . . .

It may not be superfluous to notice a few more of the common misapprehensions of utilitarian ethics, even those which are so obvious and gross that it might appear impossible for any person of candor and intelligence to fall into them; since persons, even of considerable mental endowment, often give themselves so little trouble to understand the bearings of any opinion against which they entertain a prejudice, and men are in general so little conscious of this voluntary ignorance as a defect that the vulgarest misunderstandings of ethical doctrines are continually met with in the deliberate writings of persons of the greatest pretensions both to high principle and to philosophy. We not uncommonly hear the doctrine of utility inveighed against as a *godless* doctrine. If it be necessary to say anything at all against so mere an assumption, we may say that the question depends upon what idea we have formed of the moral character of the Deity. If it be a true belief that God desires, above all things, the happiness of his creatures, and that this was his purpose in their creation, utility is not only not a godless doctrine, but more profoundly religious than any other. If it be meant that utilitarianism does not recognize the revealed will of God as the supreme law of morals, I answer that a utilitarian who believes in the perfect goodness and wisdom of *God* necessarily believes that whatever God has thought fit to reveal on the subject of morals must fulfill the requirements of utility in a supreme degree. But others besides utilitarians have been of opinion that the Christian revelation was intended, and is fitted, to inform the hearts and minds of mankind with a spirit which should enable them to find for themselves what is right, and incline them to do it when found, rather than to tell them, except in a very general way, what it is; and that we need a doctrine of ethics, carefully followed out, to *interpret* to us the will of God. Whether this opinion is correct or not, it is superfluous here to discuss; since whatever aid religion, either natural or revealed, can afford to ethical investigation is as open to the utilitarian moralist as to any other. He can use it as the testimony of God to the usefulness or hurtfulness of any given course of action by as good a right as others can use it for the indication of a transcendental law having no connection with usefulness or with happiness. . . .

Again, defenders of utility often find themselves called upon to reply to such objections as this – that there is not time, previous to action, for calculating and weighing the effects of any line of conduct on the general happiness. This is exactly as if anyone were to say that it is impossible to guide our conduct by Christianity because there is not time, on every occasion on which anything has to be done, to read through the Old and New Testaments. The answer to the objection is that there has been ample time, namely, the whole past duration of the human species. During all that time mankind have been learning by experience the tendencies of actions; on which experience all the prudence as well as all the morality of life are dependent. People talk as if the commencement of this course of experience had hitherto been put off, and as if, at the moment when some man feels tempted to meddle with the property or life of another, he had to begin considering for the first time whether murder and theft are injurious to human happiness. Even then I do not think that he would find the question very puzzling; but, at all events, the matter is now done to his hand. It is truly a whimsical supposition that, if mankind were agreed in considering utility to be the test of morality, they would remain without any agreement as to what *is* useful, and would take no measures for having their notions on the subject taught to the young and enforced by law and opinion. There is no difficulty in proving any ethical standard whatever to work ill if we suppose universal idiocy to be conjoined with it; but on any hypothesis short of that, mankind must by this time have acquired positive beliefs as to the effects of some actions on their happiness; and the beliefs which have thus come down are the rules of morality for the multitude, and for the philosopher until he has succeeded in finding better. That philosophers might easily do this, even now, on many subjects; that the received code of ethics is by no means of divine right; and that mankind have still much to learn as to the effects of actions on the general happiness, I admit or rather earnestly maintain. The corollaries from the principle of utility, like the precepts of every practical art, admit of indefinite improvement, and, in a progressive state of the human mind, their improvement is perpetually going on. But to consider the rules of morality as improvable is one thing; to pass over the intermediate generalization entirely and endeavor to test each individual action directly by the first principle is another. It is a strange notion that the acknowledgment of a first principle is inconsistent with the admission of secondary ones. To inform a traveler respecting the place of his ultimate destination is not to forbid the use of landmarks and direction-posts on the way. The proposition that happiness is the end and aim of morality does not mean that no road ought to be laid down to that goal, or that persons going thither should not be advised to take one direction rather than another. Men really ought to leave off talking a kind of nonsense on this subject, which they would neither talk nor listen to on other matters of practical concernment. Nobody argues that the art of navigation is not founded on astronomy because sailors cannot wait to calculate the Nautical Almanac. Being rational creatures, they go to sea with it ready calculated; and all rational creatures go out upon the sea of life with their minds made up on the common questions of right and wrong, as well as on many of the far more difficult questions of wise and foolish. And this, as long as foresight is a human quality, it is to be presumed they will continue to do. Whatever we adopt as the fundamental principle of morality, we require subordinate principles to apply it by; the impossibility of doing without them, being common to all systems, can afford no argument against any one in particular; but gravely to argue as if

no such secondary principles could be had, and as if mankind had remained till now, and always must remain, without drawing any general conclusions from the experience of human life is as high a pitch, I think, as absurdity has ever reached in philosophical controversy.

The remainder of the stock arguments against utilitarianism mostly consist in laying to its charge the common infirmities of human nature, and the general difficulties which embarrass conscientious persons in shaping their course through life. We are told that a utilitarian will be apt to make his own particular case an exception to moral rules, and, when under temptation, will see a utility in the breach of a rule, greater than he will see in its observance. But is utility the only creed which is able to furnish us with excuses for evil-doing and means of cheating our own conscience? They are afforded in abundance by all doctrines which recognize as a fact in morals the existence of conflicting considerations, which all doctrines do that have been believed by sane persons. It is not the fault of any creed, but of the complicated nature of human affairs, that rules of conduct cannot be so framed as to require no exceptions, and that hardly any kind of action can safely be laid down as either always obligatory or always condemnable. There is no ethical creed which does not temper the rigidity of its laws by giving a certain latitude, under the moral responsibility of the agent, for accommodation to peculiarities of circumstances; and under every creed, at the opening thus made, self-deception and dishonest casuistry get in. There exists no moral system under which there do not arise unequivocal cases of conflicting obligation. These are the real difficulties, the knotty points both in the theory of ethics and in the conscientious guidance of personal conduct. They are overcome practically, with greater or with less success, according to the intellect and virtue of the individual; but it can hardly be pretended that anyone will be the less qualified for dealing with them, from possessing an ultimate standard to which conflicting rights and duties can be referred. If utility is the ultimate source of moral obligations, utility may be invoked to decide between them when their demands are incompatible. Though the application of the standard may be difficult, it is better than none at all; while in other systems, the moral laws all claiming independent authority, there is no common umpire entitled to interfere between them; their claims to precedence one over another rest on little better than sophistry, and, unless determined, as they generally are, by the unacknowledged influence of consideration of utility, afford a free scope for the action of personal desires and partialities. We must remember that only in these cases of conflict between secondary principles is it requisite that first principles should be appealed to. There is no case of moral obligation in which some secondary principle is not involved; and if only one, there can seldom be any real doubt which one it is, in the mind of any person by whom the principle itself is recognized.

Chapter IV: Of What Sort of Proof the Principle of Utility Is Susceptible

It has already been remarked that questions of ultimate ends do not admit of proof, in the ordinary acceptation of the term. To be incapable of proof by reasoning is common to all first principles; to the first premises of our knowledge, as well as to those of our conduct. But the former, being matters of fact, may be the subject of a direct appeal to the faculties which judge of fact – namely, our senses and our internal consciousness. Can an appeal be made, to the same faculties on questions of practical ends? Or by what other faculty is cognizance taken of them?

Questions about ends are, in other words, questions about what things are desirable. The utilitarian doctrine is that happiness is desirable, and the only thing desirable, as an end; all other things being only desirable as means to that end. What ought to be required of this doctrine – what conditions is it requisite that the doctrine should fulfill – to make good its claim to be believed?

The only proof capable of being given that an object is visible, is that people actually see it. The only proof that a sound is audible, is that people hear it: and so of the other sources of our expe-

rience. In like manner, I apprehend, the sole evidence it is possible to produce that anything is desirable, is that people do actually desire it. If the end which the utilitarian doctrine proposes to itself were not, in theory and in practice, acknowledged to be an end, nothing could ever convince any person that it was so. No reason can be given why the general happiness is desirable, except that each person, so far as he believes it to be attainable, desires his own happiness. This, however, being a fact, we have not only all the proof which the case admits of, but all which it is possible to require, that happiness is a good: that each person's happiness is a good to that person, and the general happiness, therefore, a good to the aggregate of all persons. Happiness has made out its title as *one* of the ends of conduct, and consequently one of the criteria of morality.

But it has not, by this alone, proved itself to be the sole criterion. To do that, it would seem, by the same rule, necessary to show, not only that people desire happiness, but that they never desire anything else. Now it is palpable that they do desire things which, in common language, are decidedly distinguished from happiness. They desire, for example, virtue, and the absence of vice, no less really than pleasure and the absence of pain. The desire of virtue is not as universal; but it is as authentic a fact, as the desire of happiness. And hence the opponents of the utilitarian standard deem that they have a right to infer that there are other ends of human action besides happiness, and that happiness is not the standard of approbation and disapprobation.

But does the utilitarian doctrine deny that people desire virtue, or maintain that virtue is not a thing to be desired? The very reverse. It maintains not only that virtue is to be desired, but that it is to be desired disinterestedly, for itself. Whatever may be the opinion of utilitarian moralists as to the original conditions by which virtue is made virtue; however they may believe (as they do) that actions and dispositions are only virtuous because they promote another end than virtue; yet this being granted, and it having been decided, from considerations of this description, what *is* virtuous, they not only place virtue at the very head of the things which are good as means to the ultimate end, but they also recognize as a psychological fact the possibility of its being, to the individual, a good in itself, without looking to any end beyond it; and hold, that the mind is not in a right state, not in a state conformable to utility, not in the state most conducive to the general happiness, unless it does love virtue in this manner – as a thing desirable in itself, even although, in the individual instance, it should not produce those other desirable consequences which it tends to produce and on account of which it is held to be virtue. This opinion is not, in the smallest degree, a departure from the happiness principle. The ingredients of happiness are very various, and each of them is desirable in itself, and not merely when considered as swelling an aggregate. The principle of utility does not mean that any given pleasure, as music for instance, or any given exemption from pain, as for example health, are to be looked upon as a means to a collective something termed happiness, and to be desired on that account. They are desired and desirable in and for themselves; besides being means, they are part of the end. Virtue, according to the utilitarian doctrine, is not naturally and originally part of the end, but it is capable of becoming so; and in those who love it disinterestedly it has become so, and is desired and cherished, not as a means to happiness, but as a part of their happiness.

To illustrate this farther, we may remember that virtue is not the only thing, originally a means, and which if it were not a means to anything else, would be and remain indifferent, but which by association with what it is a means to, comes to be desired for itself, and that too with the utmost intensity. What, for example, shall we say of the love of money? There is nothing originally more desirable about money than about any heap of glittering pebbles. Its worth is solely that of the things which it will buy; the desires for other things than itself, which it is a means of gratifying. Yet the love of money is not only one of the strongest moving forces of human life, but money is, in many cases, desired in and for itself; the desire to possess it is often stronger than the desire to use it, and goes on increasing when all

the desires which point to ends beyond it, to be encompassed by it, are falling off. It may be then said truly, that money is desired not for the sake of an end, but as part of the end. From being a means to happiness, it has come to be itself a principal ingredient of the individual's conception of happiness. The same may be said of the majority of the great objects of human life – power, for example, or fame; except that to each of these there is a certain amount of immediate pleasure annexed, which has at least the semblance of being naturally inherent in them; a thing which cannot be said of money. Still, however, the strongest natural attraction, both of power and of fame, is the immense aid they give to the attainment of our other wishes; and it is the strong association thus generated between them and all our objects of desire, which gives to the direct desire of them the intensity it often assumes, so as in some characters to surpass in strength all other desires. In these cases the means have become a part of the end, and a more important part of it than any of the things which they are means to. What was once desired as an instrument for the attainment of happiness, has come to be desired for its own sake. In being desired for its own sake it is, however, desired as *part* of happiness. The person is made, or thinks he would be made, happy by its mere possession; and is made unhappy by failure to obtain it. The desire of it is not a different thing from the desire of happiness, any more than the love of music or the desire of health. They are included in happiness. They are some of the elements of which the desire of happiness is made up. Happiness is not an abstract idea, but a concrete whole; and these are some of its parts. And the utilitarian standard sanctions and approves there being so. Life would be a poor thing, very ill provided with sources of happiness, if there were not this provision of nature, by which things originally indifferent, but conducive to, or otherwise associated with, the satisfaction of our primitive desires, become in themselves sources of pleasure more valuable than the primitive pleasures, both in permanency, in the space of human existence than they are capable of covering, and even in intensity.

Virtue, according to the utilitarian conception, is a good of this description. There was no original desire of it, or motive to it, save its conduciveness to pleasure, and especially to protection from pain. But through the association thus formed, it may be felt a good in itself, and desired as such with as great intensity as any other good; and with this difference between it and the love of money, of power, or of fame, that all of these may, and often do, render the individual noxious to the other members of the society to which he belongs, whereas there is nothing which makes him so much a blessing to them as the cultivation of the disinterested love of virtue. And consequently, the utilitarian standard, which it tolerates and approves those other acquired desires, up to the point beyond which they would be more injurious to the general happiness than promotive of it, enjoins and requires the cultivation of the love of virtue up to the greatest strength possible, as being above all things important to the general happiness.

It results from the preceding considerations, that there is in reality nothing desired except happiness. Whatever is desired otherwise than as a means to some end beyond itself, and ultimately to happiness, is desired as itself a part of happiness, and is not desired for itself until it has become so. Those who desire virtue for its own sake, desire it either because the consciousness of it is a pleasure, or because the consciousness of being without it is a pain, or for both reasons united; as in truth the pleasure and pain seldom exist separately, but almost always together, the same person feeling pleasure in the degree of virtue attained, and pain in not having attained more. If one of these gave him no pleasure, and the other no pain, he would not love or desire virtue, or would desire it only for the other benefits which it might produce to himself or to persons whom he cared for.

We have now, then, an answer to the question, of what sort of proof the principle of utility is susceptible. If the opinion which I have now stated is psychologically true – if human nature is so constituted as to desire nothing which is not either a part of happiness or a means of happiness, we can have no other proof, and we re-quire no other, that these are the only things desirable. If so, happiness is the sole end of human action, and the promotion of it the test by which to judge of all human conduct; from whence it necessarily follows that it must be the criterion of morality, since a part is included in the whole.

And now to decide whether this is really so; whether mankind do desire nothing for itself but that which is a pleasure to them, or of which the absence is a pain; we have evidently arrived at a question of fact and experience, dependent like all similar questions, upon evidence. It can only be determined by practiced self-consciousness and self-observation, assisted by observation of others. I believe that these sources of evidence, impartially consulted, will declare that desiring a thing and finding it pleasant, aversion to it and thinking of it as painful, are phenomena entirely inseparable, or rather two parts of the same phenomenon; in strictness of language, two different modes of naming the same psychological fact: that to think of an object as desirable (unless for the sake of its consequences), and to think of it as pleasant, are one and the same thing; and that to desire anything, except in proportion as the idea of it is pleasant, is a physical and metaphysical impossibility.

So obvious does this appear to me, that I expect it will hardly be disputed: and the objection made will be, not that desire can possibly be directed to anything ultimately except pleasure and exemption from pain, but that the will is a different thing from desire; that a person of confirmed virtue, or any other person whose purposes are fixed, carries out his purposes without any thought of the pleasure he has in contemplating them, or expects to derive from their fulfillment; and persists in acting on them, even though these pleasures are much diminished, by changes in his character or decay of his passive sensibilities, or are outweighed by the pains which the pursuit of the purposes may bring upon him. All this I fully admit, and have stated it elsewhere, as positively and emphatically as any one. Will, the active phenomenon, is a different thing from desire, the state of passive sensibility, and though originally an offshoot from it, may in time take root and detach itself from the parent stock; so much so that in the case of an habitual purpose, instead of willing the thing because we desire it, we often desire it only because we will it. This, however, is but an instance of that familiar fact, the power of habit, and is nowise confined to the case of virtuous actions. Many indifferent things, which men originally did from a motive of some sort, they continue to do from habit. Sometimes this is done unconsciously, the consciousness coming only after the action: at other times with conscious volition, but volition which has become habitual, and is put into operation by the force of habit, in opposition perhaps to the deliberate preference, as often happens with those who have contracted habits of vicious or hurtful indulgence. Third and last comes the case in which the habitual act of will in the individual instance is not in contradiction to the general intention prevailing at other times, but in fulfillment of it; as in the case of the person of confirmed virtue, and of all who pursue deliberately and consistently any determinate end. The distinction between will and desire thus understood, is an authentic and highly important psychological fact; but the fact consists solely in this – that will, like all other parts of our constitution, is amenable to habit, and that we may will from habit what we no longer desire for itself, or desire only because we will it. It is not the less true that will, in the beginning, is entirely produced by desire; including in that term the repelling influence of pain as well as the attractive one of pleasure. Let us take into consideration, no longer the person who has a firmed will to do right, but him in whom that virtuous will is still feeble, conquerable by temptation, and not to be fully relied on; by what means can it be strengthened? How can the will to be virtuous, where it does not exist in sufficient force, be implanted or awakened? Only by making the person *desire* virtue – by making him think of it in a pleasurable light, or of its absence in a painful one. It is by associating the doing right with pleasure, or the doing wrong with pain, or by eliciting and impressing and bringing home to the person's experience the pleasure naturally involved in the one or the pain in the other, that it is possible to call forth that will to be virtuous,

which, when confirmed, acts without any thought of either pleasure or pain. Will is the child of desire, and passes out of habit. That which is the result of habit affords no presumption of being intrinsically good; and there would be no reason for wishing that the purpose of virtue should become independent of pleasure and pain, were it not that the influence of the pleasurable and painful associations which prompt to virtue is not sufficiently to be depended on for unerring constancy of action until it has acquired the support of habit. Both in feeling and in conduct, habit is the only thing which imparts certainty; and it is because of the importance to others of being able to rely absolutely on one's feelings and conduct, and to oneself of being able to rely on one's own, that the will to do right ought to be cultivated into this habitual independence. In other words, this state of the will is a means to good, not intrinsically a good; and does not contradict the doctrine that nothing is a good to human beings but in so far as it is either itself pleasurable, or a means of attaining pleasure or averting pain.

But if this doctrine be true, the principle of utility is proved. Whether it is so or not, must now be left to the consideration of the thoughtful reader.

Notes

1   The author of this essay has reason for believing himself to be the first person who brought the word "utilitarian" into use. He did not invent it, but adopted it from a passing expression in Mr [John] Galt's *Annals of the Parish*. After using it as a designation for several years, he and others abandoned it from a growing dislike to anything resembling a badge or watchword of sectarian distinction. But as a name for one single opinion, – not a set of opinions – to denote the recognition of utility as a standard, not any particular way of applying it – the term supplies a want in the language, and offers, in many cases, a convenient mode of avoiding tiresome circumlocution.

2   An opponent, whose intellectual and moral fairness it is a pleasure to acknowledge (the Revd. J. Llewellyn Davies), has objected to this passage, saying, "Surely the rightness or wrongness of saving a man from drowning does depend very much upon

the motive with which it is done. Suppose that a tyrant, when his enemy jumped into the sea to escape from him, saved him from drowning simply in order that he might inflict upon him more exquisite tortures, would it tend to clearness to speak of that rescue as 'a morally right action'? Or suppose again, according to one of the stock illustrations of ethical inquiries, that a man betrayed a trust received from a friend, because the discharge of it would fatally injure that friend himself or someone belonging to him, would utilitarianism compel one to call the betrayal 'a crime' as much as if it had been done from the meanest motive?"

I submit that he who saves another from drowning in order to kill him by torture afterwards does not differ only in motive from him who does the same thing from duty or benevolence; the act itself is different. The rescue of the man is, in the case supposed, only the necessary first step of an act far more atrocious than leaving him to drown

would have been. Had Mr Davies said, "The rightness or wrongness of saving a man from drowning does depend very much" – not upon the motive, but – "upon the *intention*," no utilitarian would have differed from him. Mr Davies, by an oversight too common not to be quite venial, has in this case confounded the very different ideas of Motive and Intention. There is no point which utilitarian thinkers (and Bentham pre-eminently) have taken more pains to illustrate than this. The morality of the action depends entirely upon the intention – that is, upon what the agent *wills to do*. But the motive, that is, the feeling which makes him will so to do, if it makes no difference in the act, makes none in the morality: though it makes a great difference in our moral estimation of the agent, especially if it indicates a good or a bad habitual *disposition* – a bent of character from which useful, or from which hurtful actions are likely to arise.

---

15   Against Utilitarianism

Bernard Williams

Negative Responsibility: And Two Examples

Consequentialism is basically indifferent to whether a state of affairs consists in what I do, or is produced by what I do, where that notion is itself wide enough to include, for instance, situations in which other people do things which I have made them do, or allowed them to do, or encouraged them to do, or given them a chance to do. All that consequentialism is interested in is the idea of these doings being *consequences* of what I do, and that is a relation broad enough to include the relations just mentioned, and many others.

From *Utilitarianism: For and Against*, by Bernard Williams and J. J. C. Smart (Cambridge University Press, 1973), pp. 97–9; 101–3; 108–9; 112–18. Reprinted with permission.

Just what the relation is, is a different question, and at least as obscure as the nature of its relative, cause and effect. It is not a question I shall try to pursue; I will rely on cases where I suppose that any consequentialist would be bound to regard the situations in question as consequences of what the agent does. There are cases where the supposed consequences stand in a rather remote relation to the action, which are sometimes difficult to assess from a practical point of view, but which raise no very interesting question for the present enquiry. The more interesting points about consequentialism lie rather elsewhere. There are certain situations in which the causation of the situation, the relation it has to what I do, is in no way remote or problematic in itself, and entirely justifies the claim that the situation is a consequence of what I do: for instance, it is quite clear, or reasonably clear, that if

I do a certain thing, this situation will come about, and if I do not, it will not. So from a consequentialist point of view it goes into the calculation of consequences along with any other state of affairs accessible to me. Yet from some, at least, non-consequentialist points of view, there is a vital difference between some such situations and others: namely, that in some a vital link in the production of the eventual outcome is provided by *someone else's* doing something. But for, consequentialism, all causal connections are on the same level, and it makes no difference, so far as that goes, whether the causation of a given state of affairs lies through another agent, or not.

Correspondingly, there is no relevant difference which consists *just* in one state of affairs being brought about by me, without intervention of other agents, and another being brought about through the intervention of other agents; although some genuinely causal differences involving a difference of value may correspond to that (as when, for instance, the other agents derive pleasure or pain from the transaction), that kind of difference will already be included in the specification of the state of affairs to be produced. Granted that the states of affairs have been adequately described in causally and evaluatively relevant terms, it makes no further comprehensible difference who produces them. It is because consequentialism attaches value ultimately to states of affairs, and its concern is with what states of affairs the world contains, that it essentially involves the notion of *negative responsibility*: that if I am ever responsible for anything, then I must be just as much responsible for things that I allow or fail to prevent, as I am for things that I myself, in the more everyday restricted sense, bring about.[1] Those things also must enter my deliberations, as a responsible moral agent, on the same footing. What matters is what states of affairs the world contains, and so what matters with respect to a given action is what comes about if it is done, and what comes about if it is not done, and those are questions not intrinsically affected by the nature of the causal linkage, in particular by whether the outcome is partly produced by other agents.

The strong doctrine of negative responsibility flows directly from consequentialism's assignment of ultimate value to states of affairs. Looked at from another point of view, it can be seen also as a special application of something that is favoured in man: moral outlooks not themselves consequentialist – something which, indeed, some thinkers have been disposed to regard as the essence of morality itself: a principle of impartiality. Such a principle will claim that there can be no relevant difference from a moral point of view which consists just in the fact, not further explicable in general terms, that benefits or harms accrue to one person rather than to another – 'it's me' can never in itself be a morally comprehensible reason.[2] [By] this principle, familiar with regard to the reception of harms and benefits, we can see consequentialism as extending to their production: from the moral point of view, there is no comprehensible difference which consists just in my bringing about a certain outcome rather than someone else's producing it. That the doctrine of negative responsibility represents in this way the extreme of impartiality, and abstracts from the identity of the agent, leaving just a locus of causal intervention in the world – that fact is not merely a surface paradox. It helps to explain why consequentialism can seem to some to express a more serious attitude than non-consequentialist views, why part of its appeal is to a certain kind of high-mindedness. Indeed, that is part of what is wrong with it.

For a lot of the time so far we have been operating at an exceedingly abstract level. This has been necessary in order to get clearer in general terms about the differences between consequentialist and other outlooks, an aim which is important if we want to know what features of them lead to what results for our thought. Now, however, let us look more concretely at two examples, to see what utilitarianism might say about them, what we might say about utilitarianism and, most importantly of all, what would be implied by certain ways of thinking about the situations. The examples are inevitably schematized, and they are open to the objection that they beg as many questions as they illuminate. There are two ways in particular in which examples in moral philosophy tend to beg important questions. One is that, as presented, they arbitrarily cut off and restrict the range of alternative courses of action – this objection might particularly be made against the first of my two examples. The second is that they inevitably present one with the situation as a going concern, and cut off questions about how the agent got into it, and correspondingly about moral considerations which might flow from that: this objection might perhaps specially arise with regard to the second of my two situations. These difficulties, however, just have to be accepted, and if anyone finds these examples cripplingly defective in this sort of respect, then he must in his own thought rework them in richer and less question-begging form. If he feels that no presentation of any imagined situation can ever be other than misleading in morality, and that there can never be any substitute for the concrete experienced complexity of actual moral situations, then this discussion, with him, must certainly grind to a halt: but then one may legitimately wonder whether every discussion with him about conduct will not grind to a halt, including any discussion about the actual situations, since discussion about how one would think and feel about situations somewhat different from the actual (that is to say, situations to that extent imaginary) plays an important role in discussion of the actual.

(1) George, who has just taken his PhD in chemistry, finds it extremely difficult to get a job. He is not very robust in health, which cuts down the number of jobs he might be able to do satisfactorily. His wife has to go out to work to keep them, which itself causes a great deal of strain, since they have small children and there are severe problems about looking after them. The results of all this, especially on the children, are damaging. An older chemist, who knows about this situation, says that he can get George a decently paid job in a certain laboratory, which pursues research into chemical and biological warfare. George says that he cannot accept this, since he is opposed to chemical and biological warfare. The older man replies that he is not too keen on it himself, come to that, but after all George's refusal is not going to make the job or the laboratory go away; what is more, he happens to know that if George refuses the job, it will certainly go to a contemporary of George's who is not inhibited by any such scruples and is likely if appointed to push along the research with greater zeal than George would. Indeed, it is not merely concern for George and his family, but (to speak frankly and in confidence) some alarm about this other man's excess of zeal, which has led the older man to offer to use his influence to get George the job. . . . George's wife, to whom he is deeply attached, has views (the details of which need not concern us) from which it follows that at least there is nothing particularly wrong with research into CBW. What should he do?

(2) Jim finds himself in the central square of a small South American town. Tied up against the wall are a row of twenty Indians, most terrified, a few defiant, in front of them several armed men in uniform. A heavy man in a sweat-stained khaki shirt turns out to be the captain in charge and, after a good deal of questioning of Jim which establishes that he got there by accident while on a botanical expedition, explains that the Indians are a random group of the inhabitants who, after recent acts of protest against the government, are just about to be killed to remind other possible protestors of the advantages of not protesting. However, since Jim is an honoured visitor from another land, the captain is happy to offer him a guest's privilege of killing one of the Indians himself. If Jim accepts, then as a special mark of the occasion, the other Indians will be let off. Of course, if Jim refuses, then there is no special occasion, and Pedro here will do what he was about to do when Jim arrived, and kill them all. Jim, with some desperate recollection of schoolboy fiction, wonders whether if he got hold of a gun, he could hold the captain, Pedro and the rest of the soldiers to threat, but it is quite clear from the set-up that nothing of that kind is going to work: any attempt at that sort of thing will mean that all the Indians will be killed, and himself. The men against the wall, and the other villagers, understand the situation, and are obviously begging him to accept. What should he do?

To these dilemmas, it seems to me that utilitarianism replies, in the first case, that George should accept the job, and in the second, that Jim should kill the Indian. Not only does utilitarianism give these answers but, if the situations are essentially as described and there are no further special factors, it regards them, it seems to me, as *obviously* the right answers. But many of us would certainly wonder whether, in (1), that could possibly be the right answer at all; and in the case of (2), even one who came to think that perhaps that was the answer, might well wonder whether it was obviously the answer. Nor is it just a question of the rightness or obviousness of these answers. It is also a question of what sort of considerations come into finding the answer. A feature of utilitarianism is that it cuts out a kind of consideration which for some others makes a difference to what they feel about such cases: a consideration involving the idea, as we might first and very simply put it, that each of us is specially responsible for what *he* does, rather than for what other people do. This is an idea closely connected with the value of integrity. It is often suspected that utilitarianism, at least in its direct forms, makes integrity as a value more or less unintelligible. I shall try to show that this suspicion is correct. Of course, even if that is correct, it would not necessarily follow that we should reject utilitarianism; perhaps, as utilitarians sometimes suggest, we should just forget about integrity, in favour of such things as a concern for the general good. However, if I am right, we cannot merely do that, since the reason why utilitarianism cannot understand integrity is that it cannot coherently describe the relations between a man's projects and his actions.

Two Kinds of Remoter Effect

A lot of what we have to say about this question will be about the relations between my projects and other people's projects. But before we get on to that, we should first ask whether we are assuming too hastily what the utilitarian answers to the dilemmas will be. In terms of more direct effects of the possible decisions, there does not

indeed seem much doubt about the answer in either case; but it might be said that in terms of more remote or less evident effects counterweights might be found to enter the utilitarian scales. Thus the effect on George of a decision to take the job might be invoked, or its effect on others who might know of his decision. The possibility of there being more beneficent labours in the future from which he might be barred or disqualified, might be mentioned; and so forth. Such effects – in particular, possible effects on the agent's character, and effects on the public at large – are often invoked by utilitarian writers dealing with problems about lying or promise-breaking, and some similar considerations might be invoked here.

There is one very general remark that is worth making about arguments of this sort. The certainty that attaches to these hypotheses about possible effects is usually pretty low; in some cases, indeed, the hypothesis invoked is so implausible that it would scarcely pass if it were not being used to deliver the respectable moral answer, as in the standard fantasy that one of the effects of one's telling a particular lie is to weaken the disposition of the world at large to tell the truth. The demands on the certainty or probability of these beliefs as beliefs about particular actions are much milder than they would be on beliefs favouring the unconventional course. It may be said that this is as it should be, since the presumption must be in favour of the conventional course: but that scarcely seems a *utilitarian* answer, unless utilitarianism has already taken off in the direction of not applying the consequences to the particular act at all.

Leaving aside that very general point, I want to consider now two types of effect that are often invoked by utilitarians, and which might be invoked in connection with these imaginary cases. The attitude or tone involved in invoking these effects may sometimes seem peculiar; but that sort of peculiarity soon becomes familiar in utilitarian discussions, and indeed it can be something of an achievement to retain a sense of it.

First, there is the psychological effect on the agent. Our descriptions of these situations have not so far taken account of how George or Jim will be after they have taken the one course or the other; and it might be said that if they take the course which seemed at first the utilitarian one, the effects on them will be in fact bad enough and extensive enough to cancel out the initial utilitarian advantages of that course. Now there is one version of this effect in which, for a utilitarian, some confusion must be involved, namely that in which the agent feels bad, his subsequent conduct and relations are crippled and so on, *because he thinks that he has done the wrong thing* – for if the balance of outcomes was as it appeared to be *before* invoking this effect, then he has not (from the utilitarian point of view) done the wrong thing. So that version of the effect, for a rational and utilitarian agent, could not possibly make any difference to the assessment of right and wrong. However, perhaps he is not a thoroughly rational agent, and is disposed to have bad feelings, whichever he decided to do. Now such feelings, which are from a strictly utilitarian point of view irrational – nothing, a utilitarian can point out, is advanced by having them – cannot, consistently, have any great weight in a utilitarian calculation. I shall consider in a moment an argument to suggest that they should have no weight at all in it. But short of that, the utilitarian could reasonably say that such feelings should not be encouraged, even if we accept their existence, and that to give them a lot of weight is to encourage them. Or, at the very best, even if they are straightforwardly and without any discount to be put into the calculation, their weight must be small: they are after all (and at best) one man's feelings.

That consideration might seem to have particular force in Jim's case. In George's case, his feelings represent a larger proportion of what is to be weighed, and are more commensurate in character with other items in the calculation. In Jim's case, however, his feelings might seem to be of very little weight compared with other things that are at stake. There is a powerful and recognizable appeal that can be made on this point: as that a refusal by Jim to do what he has been invited to do would be a kind of self-indulgent squeamishness. That is an appeal which can be made by other than utilitarians – indeed, there

are some uses of it which cannot be consistently made by utilitarians, as when it essentially involves the idea that there is something dishonourable about such self-indulgence. But in some versions it is a familiar, and it must be said a powerful, weapon of utilitarianism. One must be clear, though, about what it can and cannot accomplish. The most it can do, so far as I can see, is to invite one to consider how seriously, and for what reasons, one feels that what one is invited to do is (in these circumstances) wrong, and in particular, to consider that question from the utilitarian point of view. When the agent is not seeing the situation from a utilitarian point of view, the appeal cannot force him to do so; and if he does come round to seeing it from a utilitarian point of view, there is virtually nothing left for the appeal to do. If he does not see it from a utilitarian point of view, he will not see his resistance to the invitation, and the unpleasant feelings he associates with accepting it, *just* as disagreeable experiences of his; they figure rather as emotional expressions of a thought that to accept would be wrong. He may be asked, as by the appeal, to consider whether he is right, and indeed whether he is fully serious, in thinking that. But the assertion of the appeal, that he is being self-indulgently squeamish, will not itself answer that question, or even help to answer it, since it essentially tells him to regard his feelings just as unpleasant experiences of his, and he cannot, by doing that, answer the question they pose when they are precisely not so regarded, but are regarded as indications[3] of what he thinks is right and wrong. If he does come round fully to the utilitarian point of view then of course he will regard these feelings just as unpleasant experiences of his. And once Jim – at least – has come to see them in that light, there is nothing left for the appeal to do, since *of course* his feelings, so regarded, are of virtually no weight at all in relation to the other things at stake. The 'squeamishness' appeal is not an argument which adds in a hitherto neglected consideration. Rather, it is an invitation to consider the situation, and one's own feelings, from a utilitarian point of view.

The reason why the squeamishness appeal can be very unsettling, and one can be unnerved by the suggestion of self-indulgence in going against utilitarian considerations, is not that we are utilitarians who are uncertain what utilitarian value to attach to our moral feelings, but that we are partially at least not utilitarians, and cannot regard our moral feelings merely as objects of utilitarian value. Because our moral relation to the world is partly given by such feelings, and by a sense of what we can or cannot 'live with', to come to regard those feelings from a purely utilitarian point of view, that is to say, as happenings outside one's moral self, is to lose a sense of one's moral identity; to lose, in the most literal way, one's integrity. At this point utilitarianism alienates one from one's moral feelings; we shall see a little later how, more basically, it alienates one from one's actions as well.

If, then, one is really going to regard one's feelings from a strictly utilitarian point of view, Jim should give very little weight at all to his; it seems almost indecent, in fact, once one has taken that point of view, to suppose that he should give any at all. In George's case one might feel that things were slightly different. It is interesting, though, that one reason why one might think that – namely that one person principally affected is his wife – is very dubiously available to a utilitarian. George's wife has some reason to be interested in George's integrity and his sense of it; the Indians, quite properly, have no interest in Jim's. But it is not at all clear how utilitarianism would describe that difference.

There is an argument, and a strong one, that a strict utilitarian should give not merely small extra weight, in calculations of right and wrong, to feelings of this kind, but that he should give absolutely no weight to them at all. This is based on the point, which we have already seen, that if a course of action is, before taking these sorts of feelings into account, utilitarianly preferable, then bad feelings about that kind of action will be from a utilitarian point of view irrational. Now it might be thought that even if that is so, it would not mean that in a utilitarian calculation such feelings should not be taken into account; it is after all a well-known boast of utilitarianism that it is a realistic outlook which seeks the best in the world as it is, and takes any form of happi-

ness or unhappiness into account. While a utilitarian will no doubt seek to diminish the incidence of feelings which are utilitarianly irrational – or at least of disagreeable feelings which are so – he might be expected to take them into account while they exist. This is without doubt classical utilitarian doctrine, but there is good reason to think that utilitarianism cannot stick to it without embracing results which are startlingly unacceptable and perhaps self-defeating.

Suppose that there is in a certain society a racial minority. Considering merely the ordinary interests of the other citizens, as opposed to their sentiments, this minority does no particular harm; we may suppose that it does not confer any very great benefits either. Its presence is in those terms neutral or mildly beneficial. However, the other citizens have such prejudices that they find the sight of this group, even the knowledge of its presence, very disagreeable. Proposals are made for removing in some way this minority. If we assume various quite plausible things (as that programmes to change the majority sentiment are likely to be protracted and ineffective) then even if the removal would be unpleasant for the minority, a utilitarian calculation might well end up favouring this step, especially if the minority were a rather small minority and the majority were very severely prejudiced, that is to say, were made very severely uncomfortable by the presence of the minority.

A utilitarian might find that conclusion embarrassing; and not merely because of its nature, but because of the grounds on which it is reached. While a utilitarian might be expected to take into account certain other sorts of consequences of the prejudice, as that a majority prejudice is likely to be displayed in conduct disagreeable to the minority, and so forth, he might be made to wonder whether the unpleasant experiences of the prejudiced people should be allowed, *merely as such*, to count. If he does count them, merely as such, then he has once more separated himself from a body of ordinary moral thought which he might have hoped to accommodate; he may also have started on the path of defeating his own view of things. For one feature of these sentiments is that they are from the utilitarian point of view itself irrational, and a thoroughly utilitarian person would either not have them, or if he found that he did tend to have them, would himself seek to discount them. Since the sentiments in question are such that a rational utilitarian would discount them in himself, it is reasonable to suppose that he should discount them in his calculations about society; it does seem quite unreasonable for him to give just as much weight to feelings – considered just in themselves, one must recall, as experiences of those that have them – which are essentially based on views which are from a utilitarian point of view irrational, as to those which accord with utilitarian principles. Granted this idea, it seems reasonable for him to rejoin a body of moral thought in other respects congenial to him, and discount those sentiments, just considered in themselves, totally, on the principle that no pains or discomforts are to count in the utilitarian sum which their subjects have just because they hold views which are by utilitarian standards irrational. But if he accepts that, then in the cases we are at present considering no extra weight at all can be put in for bad feelings of George or Jim about their choices, if those choices are, leaving out those feelings, on the first round utilitarianly rational.

Integrity

The [two] situations have in common that if the agent does not do a certain disagreeable thing, someone else will, and in Jim's situation at least the result, the state of affairs after the other man has acted, if he does, will be worse than after Jim has acted, if Jim does. The same, on a smaller scale, is true of George's case. I have already suggested that it is inherent in consequentialism that it offers a strong doctrine of negative responsibility: if I know that if I do x, o_1 will eventuate, and if I refrain from doing x, o_2 will, and that o_2 is worse than o_1, then I am responsible for o_2 if I refrain voluntarily from doing x. 'You could have prevented it', as will be said, and truly, to Jim, if he refuses, by the relatives of the other Indians.

In the present cases, the situation of o_2 includes another agent bringing about results worse than o_1. So far as o_2 has been identified up to this point – merely as the worse outcome which will eventuate if I refrain from doing x – we might equally have said that what that other brings about is o_2; but that would be to underdescribe the situation. For what occurs if Jim refrains from action is not solely twenty Indians dead, but *Pedro's killing twenty Indians*, and that is not a result which Pedro brings about, though the death of the Indians is. We can say: what one does is not included in the outcome of what one does, while what another does can be included in the outcome of what one does. For that to be so, as the terms are now being used, only a very weak condition has to be satisfied: for Pedro's killing the Indians to be the outcome of Jim's refusal, it only has to be casually true that if Jim had not refused, Pedro would not have done it.

That may be enough for us to speak, in some sense, of Jim's responsibility for that outcome, if it occurs; but it is certainly not enough, it is worth noticing, for us to speak of Jim's *making* those things happen. For granted this way of their coming about, he could have made them happen only by making Pedro shoot, and there is no acceptable sense in which his refusal makes Pedro shoot. If the captain had said on Jim's refusal, 'you leave me with no alternative,' he would have been lying, like most who use that phrase. While the deaths, and the killing, may be the outcome of Jim's refusal, it is misleading to think, in such a case, of Jim having an *effect* on the world through the medium (as it happens) of Pedro's acts; for this is to leave Pedro out of the picture in his essential role of one who has intentions and projects, projects for realizing which Jim's refusal would leave an opportunity. Instead of thinking in terms of supposed effects of Jim's projects on Pedro, it is more revealing to think in terms of the effects of Pedro's projects on Jim's decision.

Utilitarianism would do well then to acknowledge the evident fact that among the things that make people happy is not only making other people happy, but being taken up or involved in any of a vast range of projects, or – if we waive the evangelical and moralizing associations of the word – commitments. One can be committed to such things as a person, a cause, an institution, a career, one's own genius, or the pursuit of danger.

Now none of these is itself the *pursuit of happiness*: by an exceedingly ancient platitude, it is not at all clear that there could be anything which was just that, or at least anything that had the slightest chance of being successful. Happiness, rather, requires being involved in, or at least content with, something else. It is not impossible for utilitarianism to accept that point: it does not have to be saddled with a naïve and absurd philosophy of mind about the relation between desire and happiness. What it does have to say is that if such commitments are worthwhile, then pursuing the projects that flow from them, and realizing some of those projects, will make the person for whom they are worthwhile, happy. It may be that to claim that is still wrong: it may well be that a commitment can make sense to a man (can make sense of his life) without his supposing that it will make him *happy*. But that is not the present point; let us grant to utilitarianism that all worthwhile human projects must conduce, one way or another, to happiness. The point is that even if that is true, it does not follow, nor could it possibly be true, that those projects are themselves projects of pursuing happiness. One has to believe in, or at least want, or quite minimally, be content with, other things, for there to be anywhere that happiness can come from.

Utilitarianism, then, should be willing to agree that its general aim of maximizing happiness does not imply that what everyone is doing is just pursuing happiness. On the contrary, people have to be pursuing other things. What those other things may be, utilitarianism, sticking to its professed empirical stance, should be prepared just to find out. No doubt some possible projects it will want to discourage, on the grounds that their being pursued involves a negative balance of happiness to others: though even there, the unblinking accountant's eye of the strict utilitarian will have something to put in the positive column, the satisfactions of the destructive agent. Beyond that, there will be a vast variety of generally beneficent or at least harmless projects; and some no doubt, will take the form not just of tastes or fancies, but of what I have called 'commitments'. It may even be that the utilitarian researcher will find that many of those with commitments, who have really identified themselves with objects outside themselves, who are thoroughly involved with other persons, or institutions, or activities or causes, are actually happier than those whose projects and wants are not like that. If so, that is an important piece of utilitarian empirical love.

When I say 'happier' here, I have in mind the sort of consideration which any utilitarian would be committed to accepting: as for instance that such people are less likely to have a breakdown or commit suicide. Of course that is not all that is actually involved, but the point in this argument is to use to the maximum degree utilitarian notions, in order to locate a breaking point in utilitarian thought. In appealing to this strictly utilitarian notion, I am being more consistent with utilitarianism than Smart is. In his struggles with the problem of the brain-electrode man, Smart commends the idea that 'happy' is a partly evaluative term, in the sense that we call 'happiness' those kinds of satisfaction which, as things are, we approve of. But *by what standard* is this surplus element of approval supposed, from a utilitarian point of view, to be allocated? There is no source for it, on a strictly utilitarian view, except further degrees of satisfaction, but there are none of those available, or the problem would not arise. Nor does it help to appeal to the fact that we dislike in prospect things which we like when we get there, for from a utilitarian point of view it would seem that the original dislike was merely irrational or based on an error. Smart's argument at this point seems to be embarrassed by a well-known utilitarian uneasiness, which comes from a feeling that it is not respectable to ignore the 'deep', while not having anywhere left in human life to locate it.

Let us now go back to the agent as utilitarian, and his higher-order project of maximizing desirable outcomes. At this level, he is committed only to that: what the outcome will actually consist of will depend entirely on the facts, on what persons with what projects and what potential satisfactions there are within calculable reach of the causal levers near which he finds himself. His own substantial projects and commitments come into it, but only as one lot among others – they potentially provide one set of satisfactions among those which he may be able to assist from where he happens to be. He is the agent of the satisfaction system who happens to be at a particular point at a particular time: in Jim's case, our man in South America. His own decisions as a utilitarian agent are a function of all the satisfactions which he can effect from where he is: and this means that the projects of others, to an indeterminately great extent, determine his decision.

This may be so either positively or negatively. It will be so positively if agents within the causal field of his decision have projects which are at any rate harmless, and so should be assisted. It will equally be so, but negatively, if there is an agent within the causal field whose projects are harmful, and have to be frustrated to maximize desirable outcomes. So it is with Jim and the soldier Pedro. On the utilitarian view, the undesirable projects of other people as much determine, in this negative way, one's decisions as the desirable ones do positively: if those people were not there, or had different projects, the causal nexus would be different, and it is the actual state of the causal nexus which determines the decision. The determination to an indefinite degree of my decisions by other people's projects is just another aspect of my unlimited responsibility to act for the best in a causal framework formed to a considerable extent by their projects.

The decision so determined is, for utilitarianism, the right decision. But what if it conflicts with some project of mine? This, the utilitarian will say, has already been dealt with: the satisfaction to you of fulfilling your project, and any satisfactions to others of your so doing, have already been through the calculating device and have been found inadequate. Now in the case of many sorts of projects, that is a perfectly reasonable sort of answer. But in the case of projects of the sort I have called 'commitments', those with which one is more deeply and extensively involved and identified, this cannot just by itself be an adequate answer, and there may be no adequate answer at all. For, to take the extreme sort of case, how can a man, as a utilitarian agent, come

to regard as one satisfaction among others, and a dispensable one, a project or attitude round which he has built his life, just because someone else's projects have so structured the causal scene that that is how the utilitarian sum comes out?

The point here is not, as utilitarians may hasten to say, that if the project or attitude is that central to his life, then to abandon it will be very disagreeable to him and great loss of utility will be involved. I have already argued . . . that it is not like that; on the contrary, once he is prepared to look at it like that, the argument in any serious case is over anyway. The point is that he is identified with his actions as flowing from projects and attitudes which in some cases he takes seriously at the deepest level, as what his life is about (or, in some cases, this section of his life – seriousness is not necessarily the same as persistence). It is absurd to demand of such a man, when the sums come in from the utility network which the projects of others have in part determined, that he should just step aside from his own project and decision and acknowledge the decision which utilitarian calculation requires. It is to alienate him in a real sense from his actions and the source of his action in his own convictions. It is to make him into a channel between the input of everyone's projects, including his own, and an output of optimistic decision; but this is to neglect the extent to which *his* actions and *his* decisions have to be seen as the actions and decisions which flow from the projects and attitudes with which he is most closely identified. It is thus, in the most literal sense, an attack on his integrity.

These sorts of considerations do not in themselves give solutions to practical dilemmas such as those provided by our examples; but I hope they help to provide other ways of thinking about them. In fact, it is not hard to see that in George's case, viewed from this perspective, the utilitarian solution would be wrong. Jim's case is different, and harder. But if (as I suppose) the utilitarian is probably right in this case, that is not to be found out just by asking the utilitarian's questions. Discussions of it – and I am not going to try to carry it further here – will have to take seriously the distinction between my killing someone, and its coming about because of what I do that someone else kills them: a distinction based, not so much on the distinction between action and inaction, as on the distinction between my projects and someone else's projects. At least it will have to start by taking that seriously, as utilitarianism does not; but then it will have to build out from there by asking why that distinction seems to have less, or a different, force in this case than it has in George's. One question here would be how far one's powerful objection to killing people just is, in fact, an application of a powerful objection to their being killed. Another dimension of that is the issue of how much it matters that the people at risk are actual, and there, as opposed to hypothetical, or future, or merely elsewhere.

There are many other considerations that could come into such a question, but the immediate point of all this is to draw one particular contrast with utilitarianism: that to reach a grounded decision in such a case should not be regarded as a matter of just discounting one's reactions, impulses and deeply held projects in the face of the pattern of utilities, nor yet merely adding them in – but in the first instance of trying to understand them.

Of course, time and circumstances are unlikely to make a grounded decision, in Jim's case at least, possible. It might not even be decent. Instead of thinking in a rational and systematic way either about utilities or about the value of hu-

man life, the relevance of the people at risk being present, and so forth, the presence of the people at risk may just have its effect. The significance of the immediate should not be underestimated. Philosophers, not only utilitarian ones, repeatedly urge one to view the world *sub specie aeternitatis*, but for most human purposes that is not a good *species* to view it under. If we are not agents of the universal satisfaction system, we are not primarily janitors of any system of values, even our own: very often, we just act, as a possibly confused result of the situation in which we are engaged. That, I suspect, is very often an exceedingly good thing. . . .

Notes

1   This is a fairly modest sense of 'responsibility' introduced merely by one's ability to reflect on, and decide, what one ought to do. This presumably escapes J. J. C. Smart's ban on the notion of 'the responsibility' as 'a piece of metaphysical nonsense' – his remark seems to be concerned solely with situations of interpersonal blame.

2   There is a tendency in some writers to suggest that it is not a comprehensible reason at all. But this, I suspect, is due to the overwhelming importance those writers ascribe to the moral point of view.

3   On the non-cognitivist metaethic in terms of which Smart presents his utilitarianism, the term 'indications' here would represent an understatement.

---

16   Traditional Morality and Utilitarianism

Kai Nielsen

I

It is sometimes claimed that any consequentialist view of ethics has monstrous implications which

From *Ethics*, vol. 82 (1972), pp. 113–24. Reprinted with permission.

make such a conception of morality untenable. What we must do – so the claim goes – is reject all forms of consequentialism and accept what has been labeled "conservatism" or "moral absolutism." By "conservatism" is meant, here, a normative ethical theory which maintains that there is a privileged moral principle or cluster of moral principles, prescribing determinate actions, with which it would always be wrong not to act in accordance no matter what the consequences. A key example of such a principle is the claim that it is always wrong to kill an innocent human, whatever the consequences of not doing so.

I will argue that such moral conservatism is itself unjustified and, indeed, has morally unacceptable consequences, while consequentialism does not have implications which are morally monstrous and does not contain evident moral mistakes.

A consequentialist maintains that actions, rules, policies, practices, and moral principles are ultimately to be judged by certain consequences: to wit (for a very influential kind of consequentialism), by whether doing them more than or at least as much as doing anything else, or acting in accordance with them more than or at least as much as acting in accordance with alternative policies, practices, rules, or principles, tends, on the whole, and for *everyone* involved, to maximize satisfaction and minimize dissatisfaction. The states of affairs to be sought are those which maximize these things to the greatest extent possible for all mankind. But while this all sounds very humane and humanitarian, when its implications are thought through, it has been forcefully argued, it will be seen actually to have inhumane and morally intolerable implications. Circumstances could arise in which one holding such a view would have to assert that one was justified in punishing, killing, torturing, or deliberately harming the innocent, and such a consequence is, morally speaking, unacceptable.[1] As Anscombe has put it, anyone who "really thinks, *in advance*, that it is open to question whether such an action as procuring the judicial execution of the innocent should be quite excluded from consideration – I do not want to argue with him; he shows a corrupt mind."[2]

At the risk of being thought to exhibit a corrupt mind and a shallow consequentialist morality, I should like to argue that things are not as simple and straightforward as Anscombe seems to believe.

Surely, every moral man must be appalled at the judicial execution of the innocent or at the punishment, torture, and killing of the innocent. Indeed, being appalled by such behavior partially defines what it is to be a moral agent. And a consequentialist has very good utilitarian grounds for being so appalled, namely, that it is always wrong to inflict pain for its own sake. But this does not get to the core considerations which divide a conservative position such as Anscombe's from a consequentialist view. There are a series of tough cases that need to be taken to heart and their implications thought through by any reflective person, be he a conservative or a consequentialist. By doing this, we can get to the heart of the issue between conservatism and consequentialism. Consider this dash between conservatism and consequentialism arising over the problem of a "just war."

> If we deliberately bomb civilian targets, we do not pretend that civilians are combatants in any simple fashion, but argue that this bombing will terminate hostilities more quickly, and will minimize all around suffering. It is hard to see how any brand of utilitarian will escape Miss Anscombe's objections. We are certainly killing the innocent . . . we are not killing them for the sake of killing them, but to save the lives of other innocent persons. Utilitarians, I think, grit their teeth and put up with this as part of the logic of total war; Miss Anscombe and anyone who thinks like her surely has to either redescribe the situation to ascribe guilt to the civilians or else she has to refuse to accept this sort of military tactics as simply wrong.[3]

It is indeed true that we cannot but feel the force of Anscombe's objections here. But is it the case that anyone shows a corrupt mind if he defends such bombing when, horrible as it is, it will quite definitely lessen appreciably the total amount of suffering and death in the long run, and if he is sufficiently non-evasive not to rationalize such a bombing of civilians into a situation in which all the putatively innocent people – children and all – are somehow in some measure judged guilty? Must such a man exhibit a corrupt moral sense if he refuses to hold that such military tactics are never morally justified? Must this be the monstrous view of a fanatical man devoid of any proper moral awareness? It is difficult for me to believe that this must be so.

Consider the quite parallel actions of guerrilla fighters and terrorists in wars of national liberation. In certain almost unavoidable circumstances, they must deliberately kill the innocent. We need to see some cases in detail here to get the necessary contextual background, and for this reason the motion picture *The Battle of Algiers* can be taken as a convenient point of reference. There we saw Algerian women – gentle, kindly women with children of their own and plainly people of moral sensitivity – with evident heaviness of heart, plant bombs which they had every good reason to believe would kill innocent people, including children; and we also saw a French general, also a human being of moral fiber and integrity, order the torture of Arab terrorists and threaten the bombing of houses in which terrorists were concealed but which also contained innocent people, including children. There are indeed many people involved in such activities who are cruel, sadistic beasts, or simply morally indifferent or, in important ways, morally uncomprehending. But the characters I have referred to from *The Battle of Algiers* were not of that stamp. They were plainly moral agents of a high degree of sensitivity, and yet they deliberately killed or were prepared to kill the innocent. And, with inessential variations, this is a recurrent phenomenon of human living in extreme situations. Such cases are by no means desert-island or esoteric cases.

It is indeed arguable whether such actions are always morally wrong – whether anyone should ever act as the Arab women or French general acted. But what could not be reasonably maintained, *pace* Anscombe, by any stretch of the imagination, is that the characters I described from *The Battle of Algiers* exhibited corrupt minds. Possibly morally mistaken, yes; guilty of moral corruption, no.

Dropping the charge of moral corruption but sticking with the moral issue about what actions are right, is it not the case that my consequentialist position logically forces me to conclude that under some circumstances – where

the good to be achieved is great enough – I must not only countenance but actually advocate such violence toward the innocent? But is it not always, no matter what the circumstances or consequences, wrong to countenance, advocate, or engage in such violence? To answer such a question affirmatively is to commit oneself to the kind of moral absolutism or conservatism which Anscombe advocates. But, given the alternatives, should not one be such a conservative or at least hold that certain deontological principles must never be overridden?

I will take, so to speak, the papal bull by the horns and answer that there are circumstances when such violence must be reluctantly assented to or even taken to be something that one, morally speaking, must do. But, *pace* Anscombe, this very much needs arguing, and I shall argue it; but first I would like to set out some further but simpler cases which have a similar bearing. They are, by contrast, artificial cases. I use them because, in their greater simplicity, by contrast with my above examples, there are fewer variables to control and I can more conveniently make the essential conceptual and moral points. But, if my argument is correct for these simpler cases, the line of reasoning employed is intended to be applicable to those more complex cases as well.

II

Consider the following cases embedded in their exemplary tales:

The case of the innocent fat man

Consider the story (well known to philosophers) of the fat man stuck in the mouth of a cave on a coast. He was leading a group of people out of the cave when he got stuck in the mouth of the cave and in a very short time high tide will be upon them, and unless he is promptly unstuck, they all will be drowned except the fat man, whose head is out of the cave. But, fortunately or unfortunately, someone has with him a stick of dynamite. The short of the matter is, either they use the dynamite and blast the poor innocent fat man out of the mouth of the cave or everyone else drowns. Either one life or many lives. Our conservative presumably would take the attitude that it is all in God's hands and say that he ought never to blast the fat man out, for it is always wrong to kill the innocent. Must or should a moral man come to that conclusion? I shall argue that he should not.

My first exemplary tale was designed to show that our normal, immediate, rather absolutistic, moral reactions need to be questioned along with such principles as "The direct intention of the death of an innocent person is never justifiable." I have hinted (and later shall argue) that we should *beware* of our moral outrage here – our naturally conservative and unreflective moral reactions – for here the consequentialist has a strong case for what I shall call "moral radicalism." But, before turning to a defense of that, I want to tell another story taken from Philippa Foot but used for my own purposes.[4] This tale, I shall argue, has a different import than our previous tale. Here our unrehearsed, commonsense moral reactions will stand up under moral scrutiny. But, I shall also argue when I consider them in Section III, that our commonsense moral reactions here, initial expectations to the contrary notwithstanding, can be shown to be justified on consequentialist grounds. The thrust of my argument for this case is that we are not justified in opting for a theistic and/or deontological absolutism or in rejecting consequentialism.

The magistrate and the threatening mob

A magistrate or judge is faced with a very real threat from a large and uncontrollable mob of rioters demanding a culprit for a crime. Unless the criminal is produced, promptly tried, and executed, they will take their own bloody revenge on a much smaller and quite vulnerable section of the community (a kind of frenzied pogrom). The judge knows that the real culprit is unknown and that the authorities do not even have a good clue as to who he may be. But he also knows that there is within easy reach a disreputable, thoroughly disliked, and useless man, who, though innocent, could easily be framed so that the mob would be quite convinced that he was guilty and would be pacified if he were promptly executed. Recognizing that he can prevent the occurrence of extensive carnage only by framing some innocent person, the magistrate has him framed, goes through the mockery of a trial, and has him executed. Most of us regard such a framing and execution of such a man in such circumstances as totally unacceptable.[5] There are some who would say that it is categorically wrong – morally inexcusable – *whatever the circumstances*. Indeed, such a case remains a problem for the consequentialist, but here again, I shall argue, one can consistently remain a consequentialist and continue to accept commonsense moral convictions about such matters.

My storytelling is at an end. The job is to see what the stories imply. We must try to determine whether thinking through their implications should lead a clear-headed and morally sensitive man to abandon consequentialism and to adopt some form of theistic absolutism and/or deontological absolutism. I shall argue that it does not.

III

I shall consider the last case first because there are good reasons why the consequentialist should stick with commonsense moral convictions for such cases. I shall start by giving my rationale for that claim. If the magistrate were a tough-minded but morally conscientious consequentialist, he could still, on straightforward consequentialist grounds, refuse to frame and execute the innocent man, even knowing that this would unleash the mob and cause much suffering and many deaths. The rationale for his particular moral stand would be that, by so framing and then executing such an innocent man, he would, in the long run, cause still more suffering through the resultant corrupting effect on the institution of justice. That is, in a case involving such extensive general interest in the issue – without that, there would be no problem about preventing the carnage or call for such extreme measures – knowledge that the man was framed, that the law had prostituted itself, would, surely, eventually leak out. This would encourage mob action in other circumstances, would lead to an increased skepticism about the incorruptibility or even the reliability of the judicial process, and would set a dangerous precedent for less clearheaded or less scrupulously humane magistrates. Given such a potential for the corruption of justice, a utilitarian or consequentialist judge or magistrate could, on good utilitarian or consequentialist grounds, argue that it was morally wrong to frame an innocent man. If the mob must rampage if such a sacrificial lamb is not provided, then the mob must rampage.

Must a utilitarian or consequentialist come to such a conclusion? The answer is no. It is the conclusion which is, as things stand, the most reasonable conclusion, but that he *must* come to it is far too strong a claim. A consequentialist could *consistently* – I did not say successfully – argue that, in taking the above tough-minded utilitarian position, we have overestimated the corrupting effects of such judicial railroading. His circumstance was an extreme one: a situation not often to be repeated even if, instead of acting as he did, he had set a precedent by such an act of judicial murder. A utilitarian rather more skeptical than most utilitarians about the claims of commonsense morality might reason that the lesser evil here is the judicial murder of an innocent man, vile as it is. He would persist in his moral iconoclasm by standing on the consequentialist rock that the lesser evil is always to be preferred to the greater evil.

The short of it is that utilitarians could disagree, as other consequentialists could disagree, about what is morally required of us in that case. The disagreement here between utilitarians or consequentialists of the same type is not one concerning fundamental moral principles but a disagreement about the empirical facts, about what course of action would in the long run produce the least suffering and the most happiness for *everyone* involved.[6]

However, considering the effect advocating the deliberate judicial killing of an innocent man would have on the reliance people put on commonsense moral beliefs of such a ubiquitous

sort as the belief that the innocent must not be harmed, a utilitarian who defended the centrality of commonsense moral beliefs would indeed have a strong utilitarian case here. But the most crucial thing to recognize is that, to regard such judicial bowing to such a threatening mob as unqualifiedly wrong, as morally intolerable, one need not reject utilitarianism and accept some form of theistic or deontological absolutism.

It has been argued, however, that, in taking such a stance, I still have not squarely faced the moral conservative's central objection to the judicial railroading of the innocent. I allow, as a consequentialist, that there could be circumstances, at least as far as logical possibilities are concerned, in which such a railroading would be justified but that, as things actually go, it is not and probably never in fact will be justified. But the conservative's point is that *in no circumstances, either actual or conceivable, would it be justified*. No matter what the consequences, it is unqualifiedly unjustified. To say, as I do, that the situations in which it might be justified are desert-island, esoteric cases which do not occur in life, is not to the point, for, as Alan Donagan argues, "Moral theory is a priori, as clear-headed utilitarians like Henry Sidgwick recognized. It is, as Leibniz would say, 'true of all possible worlds'."[7] Thus, to argue as I have and as others have that the counter-examples directed against the consequentialist's appeal to conditions which are never in fact fulfilled or are unlikely to be fulfilled is beside the point.[8] Whether "a moral theory is true or false depends on whether its implications for all possible worlds are true. Hence, whether utilitarianism (or consequentialism) is true or false cannot depend on how the actual world is."[9] It is possible to specify logically conceivable situations in which consequentialism would have implications which are monstrous – for example, certain beneficial judicial murders of the innocent (whether they are even remotely likely to obtain is irrelevant) – hence consequentialism must be false.

We should not take such a short way with consequentialists, for what is true in Donagan's claim about moral theory's being a priori will not refute or even render implausible consequentialism, and what would undermine it in such a claim about the a priori nature of moral theory and presumably moral claims is not true.

To say that moral theory is a priori is probably correct if that means that categorical moral claims – fundamental moral statements – cannot be deduced from empirical statements or non-moral theological statements, such that it is a contradiction to assert the empirical and/or non-moral theological statements and deny the categorical moral claims or vice versa.[10] In that fundamental sense, it is reasonable and, I believe, justifiable to maintain that moral theory is autonomous and a priori. It is also a priori in the sense that moral statements are not themselves a kind of empirical statement. That is, if I assert "One ought never to torture any sentient creature" or "One ought never to kill an innocent man," I am not trying to predict or describe what people do or are likely to do but am asserting what they are *to do*. It is also true that, if a moral statement is true, it holds for all possible worlds *in which situations that are exactly the sort characterized in the statement obtain*. If it is true for one, it is true for all. You cannot consistently say that *A* ought to do *B* in situation *Y* and deny that someone exactly like *A* in a situation exactly like *Y* ought to do *B*.

In these ways, moral claims and indeed moral theory are a priori. But it is also evident that none of these ways will touch the consequentialist or utilitarian arguments. After all, the consequentialist need not be, and typically has not been, an ethical naturalist – he need not think moral claims are derivable from factual claims or that moral claims are a subspecies of empirical statement and he could accept – indeed, he must accept – what is an important truism anyway, that you cannot consistently say that *A* ought to do *B* in situation *Y* and deny that someone exactly like *A* in a situation exactly like *Y* ought to do *B*. But he could and should deny that moral claims are a priori in the sense that rational men must or even will make them without regard for the context, the situation, in which they are made. We say people ought not to drive way over the speed limit, or speed on icy roads, or throw knives at each other. But, if human beings had a kind of

metallic exoskeleton and would not be hurt, disfigured, or seriously inconvenienced by knives sticking in them or by automobile crashes, we would not – so evidently at least – have good grounds for saying such speeding or knife throwing is wrong. It would not be so obvious that it was unreasonable and immoral to do these things if these conditions obtained.

In the very way we choose to describe the situation when we make ethical remarks, it is important in making this choice that we know what the world is like and what human beings are like. Our understanding of the situation, our understanding of human nature and motivation cannot but affect our structuring of the moral case. The consequentialist is saying that, as the world goes, there are good grounds for holding that judicial killings are morally intolerable, though he would have to admit that if the world (including human beings) were very different, such killings could be something that ought to be done. But, in holding this, he is not committed to denying the universalizability of moral judgments, for, where he would reverse or qualify the moral judgment, the situation must be different. He is only committed to claiming that, where the situation is the same or relevantly similar and the persons are relevantly similar, they must, if they are to act morally, do the same thing. However, he is claiming both (1) that, as things stand, judicial killing of the innocent is always wrong and (2) that it is an irrational moral judgment to assert of reasonably determinate actions (e.g. killing an innocent man) that they are unjustifiable and morally unacceptable in all possible worlds, whatever the situation and whatever the consequences.

Donagan's claims about the a priori nature of moral theories do not show such a consequentialist claim to be mistaken or even give us the slightest reason for thinking that it is mistaken. What is brutal and vile, for example, throwing a knife at a human being just for the fun of it, would not be so, if human beings were invulnerable to harm from such a direction because they had a metallic exoskeleton. Similarly, what is, as things are, morally intolerable, for example, the judicial killing of the innocent, need not be morally intolerable in all conceivable circumstances.

Such considerations support the utilitarian or consequentialist skeptical of simply taking the claims of our commonsense morality as a rock-bottom ground of appeal for moral theorizing. Yet it may also well be the case – given our extensive cruelty anyway – that, if we ever start sanctioning such behavior, an even greater callousness toward life than the very extensive callousness extant now will, as a matter of fact, develop. Given a normative ethical theory which sanctions, *under certain circumstances*, such judicial murders, there may occur an undermining of our moral disapproval of killing and our absolutely essential moral principle that all human beings, great and small, are deserving of respect. This is surely enough, together with the not unimportant weight of even our unrehearsed moral feelings, to give strong utilitarian weight *here* to the dictates of our commonsense morality. Yet, I think I have also said enough to show that someone who questions their "unquestionableness" in such a context does not thereby exhibit a "corrupt mind" and that it is an open question whether he must be conceptually confused or morally mistaken over this matter.

IV

So far, I have tried to show with reference to the case of the magistrate and the threatening mob how consequentialists can reasonably square their normative ethical theories with an important range of commonsense moral convictions. Now, I wish by reference to the case of the innocent fat man to establish that there is at least a serious question concerning whether such fundamental commonsense moral convictions should always function as "moral facts" or a kind of moral ground to test the adequacy of normative ethical theories or positions. I want to establish that careful attention to such cases shows that we are not justified in taking the principles embodied in our commonsense moral reasoning about such cases as normative for all moral decisions. That a normative ethical theory is incompatible with some

of our "moral intuitions" (moral feelings or convictions) does not refute the normative ethical theory. What I will try to do here is to establish that this case, no more than the case examined in Section III, gives us adequate grounds for abandoning consequentialism and for adopting moral conservativism.

Forget the levity of the example and consider the case of the innocent fat man. If there really is no other way of unsticking our fat man and if plainly, without blasting him out, everyone in the cave will drown, then, innocent or not, he should be blasted out. This indeed overrides the principle that the innocent should never be deliberately killed, but it does not reveal a callousness toward life, for the people involved are caught in a desperate situation in which, if such extreme action is not taken, many lives will be lost and far greater misery will obtain. Moreover, the people who do such a horrible thing or acquiesce in the doing of it are not likely to be rendered more callous about human life and human suffering as a result. Its occurrence will haunt them for the rest of their lives and is as likely as not to make them more rather than less morally sensitive. It is not even correct to say that such a desperate act shows a lack of respect for persons. We are not treating the fat man merely as a means. The fat man's person – his interests and rights – are not ignored. Killing him is something which is undertaken with the greatest reluctance. It is only when it is quite certain that there is no other way to save the lives of the others that such a violent course of action is justifiably undertaken.

Alan Donagan, arguing rather as Anscombe argues, maintains that "to use any innocent man ill for the sake of some public good is directly to degrade him to being a mere means" and to do this is of course to violate a principle essential to morality, that is, that human beings should never merely be treated as means but should be treated as ends in themselves (as persons worthy of respect).[11] But, as my above remarks show, it need not be the case, and in the above situation it is not the case, that in killing such an innocent man we are treating him *merely* as a means. The action is universalizable, all alternative actions which would save his life are duly considered, the blasting out is done only as a last and desperate resort with the minimum of harshness and indifference to his suffering and the like. It indeed sounds ironical to talk this way, given what is done to him. But if such a terrible situation were to arise, there would always be more or less humane ways of going about one's grim task. And in acting in the more humane ways toward the fat man, as we do what we must do and would have done to ourselves were the roles reversed, we show a respect for his person.[12]

In so treating the fat man – not just to further the public good but to prevent the certain death of a whole group of people (that is, to prevent an even greater evil than his being killed in this way) – the claims of justice are not overridden either, for each individual involved, if he is reasoning correctly, should realize that if he were so stuck rather than the fat man, he should in such situations be blasted out. Thus, there is no question of being unfair. Surely we must choose between evils here, but is there anything more reasonable, more morally appropriate, than choosing the lesser evil when doing or allowing some evil that cannot be avoided? That is, where there is no avoiding both and where our actions can determine whether a greater or lesser evil obtains, should we not plainly always opt for the lesser evil? And is it not obviously a greater evil that all those other innocent people should suffer and die than that the fat man should suffer and die? Blowing up the fat man is indeed monstrous. But letting him remain stuck while the whole group drowns is still more monstrous.

The consequentialist is on strong moral ground here, and, if his reflective moral convictions do not square either with certain unrehearsed or with certain reflective particular moral convictions of human beings, so much the worse for such commonsense moral convictions. One could even usefully and relevantly adapt here – though for a quite different purpose – an argument of Donagan's. Consequentialism of the kind I have been arguing for provides so persuasive "a theoretical basis for common morality that when it contradicts some moral intuition, it is natural to suspect that intuition, not theory, is corrupt."[13] Given the comprehensiveness, plausibility, and

overall rationality of consequentialism, it is not unreasonable to override even a deeply felt moral conviction if it does not square with such a theory, though, if it made no sense or overrode the bulk of or even a great many of our considered moral convictions, that would be another matter indeed.

Anticonsequentialists often point to the inhumanity of people who will sanction such killing of the innocent, but cannot the compliment be returned by speaking of the even greater inhumanity, conjoined with evasiveness, of those who will allow even more death and far greater misery and then excuse themselves on the ground that they did not intend the death and misery but merely forbore to prevent it? In such a context, such reasoning and such forbearing to prevent seems to me to constitute a moral evasion. I say it is evasive because rather than steeling himself to do what in normal circumstances would be a horrible and vile act but in this circumstance is a harsh moral necessity, he allows, when he has the power to prevent it, a situation which is still many times worse. He tries to keep his "moral purity" and avoid "dirty hands" at the price of utter moral failure and what Kierkegaard called "doublemindedness." It is understandable that people should act in this morally evasive way but this does not make it right.

My consequentialist reasoning about such cases as the case of the innocent fat man is very often resisted on the grounds that it starts a very dangerous precedent. People rationalize wildly and irrationally in their own favor in such situations. To avoid such rationalization, we must stubbornly stick to our deontological principles and recognize as well that very frequently, if people will put their wits to work or just endure, such admittedly monstrous actions done to prevent still greater evils will turn out to be unnecessary.

The general moral principles surrounding bans on killing the innocent are strong and play such a crucial role in the ever-floundering effort to humanize the savage mind – savage as a primitive and savage again as a contemporary in industrial society – that it is of the utmost social utility, it can be argued, that such bans against killing the innocent not be called into question in any practical manner by consequentialist reasoning.

However, in arguing in this way, the moral conservative has plainly shifted his ground, and he is himself arguing on consequentialist grounds that we must treat certain non-consequentialist moral principles as absolute (as principles which can never *in fact*, from a reasonable moral point of view, be overridden, for it would be just too disastrous to do so).[14] But now he is on my home court, and my reply is that there is no good evidence at all that in the circumstances I characterized, overriding these deontological principles would have this disastrous effect. I am aware that a bad precedent could be set. Such judgments must not be made for more doubtful cases. But my telling my two stories in some detail, and my contrasting them, was done in order to make evident the type of situation, with its attendant rationale, in which the overriding of those deontological principles can be seen clearly to be justified and the situations in which this does obtain and why. My point was to specify the situations in which we ought to override our commonsense moral convictions about those matters, and the contexts in which we are not so justified or at least in which it is not clear which course of action is justified.[15]

If people are able to be sufficiently clearheaded about these matters, they can see that there are relevant differences between the two sorts of cases. But I was also carefully guarding against extending such "moral radicalism" – if such it should be called – to other and more doubtful cases. Unless solid empirical evidence can be given that such a "moral radicalism" would – if it were to gain a toehold in the community – overflow destructively and inhumanely into the other doubtful and positively unjustifiable situations, nothing has been said to undermine the correctness of my consequentialist defense of "moral radicalism" in the contexts in which I defended it.[16]

Notes

1 Alan Donagan, "Is there a Credible Form of Utilitarianism?" and H. J. McCloskey, "A Non-Utilitarian Approach to Punishment," both in Michael D. Bayles (ed.), *Contemporary Utilitarianism* (Garden City, NY: Doubleday, 1968).

2 Elizabeth Anscombe, "Modern Moral Philosophy," *Philosophy*, 23 (January 1957), pp. 16–17.

3 Alan Ryan, "Review of Jan Narveson's *Morality and Utility*," *Philosophical Books*, 9, no. 3 (October 1958), p. 14.

4 Philippa Foot, "The Problem of Abortion and the Doctrine of the Double Effect," *Oxford Review*, no. 5 (1967), pp. 5–15.

5 Later, I shall show that there are desert-island circumstances – i.e. highly improbable situations – in which such judicial railroading might be a moral necessity. But I also show what little force desert-island cases have in the articulation and defense of a normative ethical theory.

6 "Everyone" here is used distributively; i.e. I am talking about the interests of each and every one. In that sense, everyone's interests need to be considered.

7 Donagan, "Is There a Credible Form?" p. 189.

8 T. L. S. Sprigge argues in such a manner in his "A Utilitarian Reply to Dr McCloskey," in Michael D. Bayles (ed), *Contemporary Utilitarianism* (Garden City, NY: Doubleday, 1968).

9 Donagan, "Is There a Credible Form?" p. 194.

10 There is considerable recent literature about whether it is possible to derive moral claims from non-moral claims. See W. D. Hudson (ed.), *The Is–Ought Question: A Collection of Papers on the Central Problem in Moral Philosophy* (New York: St Martin's Press, 1969).

11 Donagan, "Is There a Credible Form?" pp. 199–200.

12 Again, I am not asserting that we would have enough fortitude to assent to it were the roles actually reversed. I am making a conceptual remark about what as moral beings we must try to do and not a psychological observation about what we can do.

13 Donagan, "Is There a Credible Form?" p. 198.

14 Jonathan Bennett, "Whatever the Consequences," *Analysis*, 26 (1966), has shown that this is a very common equivocation for the conservative and makes, when unnoticed, his position seem more plausible than it actually is.

15 I have spoken, conceding this to the Christian absolutist for the sake of the discussion, as if (1) it is fairly evident what our commonsense moral convictions are here and (2) that they are deontological principles taken to hold no matter

what the consequences. But that either (1) or (2) is clearly so seems to me very much open to question.

16 I do not mean to suggest that I am giving a blanket defense to our commonsense morality; that is one of the last things I would want to do. Much of what we or any other tribe take to be commonsense morality is little better than a set of magical charms to deal with our social environment. But I was defending the importance of such cross-culturally ubiquitous moral principles as that one ought not to harm the innocent or that promises ought to be kept. However, against Christian absolutists of the type I have been discussing, I take them to be prima facie obligations. This means that they always hold *ceteris paribus*, but the *ceteris paribus* qualification implies that they can be overridden on occasion. On my account, appeal to consequences and considerations about justice and respect for persons determines when they should on a given occasion be overridden.

---

17 The Schizophrenia of Modern Ethical Theories

Michael Stocker

Modern ethical theories, with perhaps a few honorable exceptions, deal only with reasons, with values, with what justifies. They fail to examine motives and the motivational structures and constraints of ethical life. They not only fail to do this, they fail as ethical theories by not doing this – as I shall argue in this paper. I shall also attempt two correlative tasks: to exhibit some constraints that motivation imposes on ethical theory and life; and to advance our understanding of the relations between reason and motive.

One mark of a good life is a harmony between one's motives and one's reasons, values, justifications. Not to be moved by what one values – what one believes good, nice, right, beautiful, and so on – bespeaks a malady of the spirit. Not to value what moves one also bespeaks a malady of the spirit. Such a malady, or such maladies, can properly be called *moral schizophrenia* – for they are a split between one's motives and one's reasons. (Here and elsewhere, "reasons" will stand also for "values" and "justifications.")

An extreme form of such schizophrenia is characterized, on the one hand, by being moved to do what one believes bad, harmful, ugly, abasing; on the other, by being disgusted, horrified, dismayed by what one wants to do. Perhaps such cases are rare. But a more modest schizophrenia between reason and motive is not, as can be seen in many examples of weakness of the will, indecisiveness, guilt, shame, self-deception, rationalization, and annoyance with oneself. . . .

The sort of disharmony I have in mind can be brought out by considering a problem for egoists, typified by hedonistic egoists. Love, friendship, affection, fellow feeling, and community are important sources of personal pleasure. But can such egoists get these pleasures? I think not – not so long as they adhere to the motive of pleasure-for-self.

The reason for this is not that egoists cannot get together and decide, as it were, to enter into a love relationship. Surely they can (leaving aside the irrelevant problems about deciding to do such a thing). And they can do the various things calculated to bring about such pleasure: have absorbing talks, make love, eat delicious meals, see interesting films, and so on, and so on.

None the less, there is something necessarily lacking in such a life: love. For it is essential to the very concept of love that one care for the

From *Philosophy and Public Affairs*, vol. 13 (1984), pp. 134–63. Reprinted with permission.

beloved, that one be prepared to act for the sake of the beloved. More strongly, one must care for the beloved and act for that person's sake as a final goal; the beloved, or the beloved's welfare or interest, must be a final goal of one's concern and action.

To the extent that my consideration for you – or even my trying to make you happy – comes from my desire to lead an untroubled life, a life that is personally pleasing for me, I do not act for your sake. In short, to the extent that I act in various ways toward you with the final goal of getting pleasure – or, more generally, good – for myself, I do not act for your sake.

When we think about it this way, we may get some idea of why egoism is often claimed to be essentially lonely. For it is essentially concerned with external relations with others, where, except for their effects on us, one person is no different from, nor more important, valuable, or special than any other person or even any other thing. The individuals as such are not important, only their effects on us are; they are essentially replaceable, anything else with the same effects would do as well. And this, I suggest, is intolerable personally. To think of yourself this way, or to believe that a person you love thinks of you this way, is intolerable. And for conceptual, as well as psychological, reasons it is incompatible with love.

It might be suggested that it is rather unimportant to have love of this sort. But this would be a serious error. The love here is not merely modern-romantic or sexual. It is also the love among members of a family, the love we have for our closest friends, and so on. Just what sort of life would people have who never "cared" for anyone else, except as a means to their own interests? And what sort of life would people have who took it that no one loved them for their own sake, but only for the way they served the other's interest?

Just as the notion of doing something for the sake of another, or of caring for the person for that person's sake, is essential for love, so too is it essential for friendship and all affectionate relations. Without this, at best we could have good relations, friendly relations. And similarly, such caring and respect is essential for fellow feeling and community.

Before proceeding, let us contrast this criticism of egoism with a more standard one. My criticism runs as follows: hedonistic egoists take their own pleasure to be the sole justification of acts, activities, ways of life; they should recognize that love, friendship, affection, fellow feeling, and community are among the greatest (sources of) personal pleasures. Thus, they have good reason, on their own grounds, to enter such relations. But they cannot act in the ways required to get those pleasures, those great goods, if they act on their motive of pleasure-for-self. They cannot act for the sake of the intended beloved, friend, and so on; thus, they cannot love, be or have a friend, and so on. To achieve these great personal goods, they have to abandon that egoistical motive. They cannot embody their reason in their motive. Their reasons and motives make their moral lives schizophrenic.

The standard criticism of egoists is that they simply cannot achieve such non-egoistical goods, that their course of action will, as a matter of principle, keep them from involving themselves with others in the relevant ways, and so on. This criticism is not clearly correct. For there may be nothing inconsistent in egoists' adopting a policy that will allow them to forget, as it were, that they are egoists, a policy that will allow and even encourage them to develop such final goals and motives as caring for another for that person's own sake. Indeed, as has often been argued, the wise egoist would do just this.

Several questions should be asked of this response: would the transformed person still be an egoist? Is it important, for the defense of egoism, that the person remain an egoist? Or is it important only that the person live in a way that would be approved of by an egoist? It is, of course, essential to the transformation of the person from egoistical motivation to caring for others that the person-as-egoist lose conscious control of him/herself. This raises the question of whether such people will be able to check up and see how their transformed selves are getting on in achieving egoistically approved goals. Will they have a mental alarm clock which wakes them up from their non-egoistical transforms every once in a while, to allow them to reshape these transforms if they are not getting enough personal pleasure – or, more generally, enough good? I suppose that this would not be impossible. But it hardly seems an ideal, or even a very satisfactory, life. It is bad enough to have a private personality, which you must hide from others; but imagine having a personality that you must hide from (the other parts of) yourself. Still, perhaps this is possible. If it is, then it seems that egoists may be able to meet this second criticism. But this does not touch my criticism: that they will not be able to embody their reason in their motives; that they will have to lead a bifurcated, schizophrenic life to achieve what is good.

This might be thought a defect of only such ethical theories as egoism. But consider those utilitarianisms which hold that an act is right, obligatory, or whatever if and only if it is optimific in regard to pleasure and pain (or weighted expectations of them). Such a view has it that the only good reason for acting is pleasure vs. pain, and thus should highly value love, friendship, affection, fellow feeling, and community. Suppose, now, you embody this utilitarian reason as your motive in your actions and thoughts toward someone. Whatever your relation to that person, it is necessarily not love (nor is it friendship, affection, fellow feeling, or community). The person you supposedly love engages your thought and action not for him/herself, but rather as a source of pleasure.

The problem is not simply that pleasure is taken to be the only good, the only right-making feature. To see this, consider G. E. Moore's formalistic utilitarianism, which tells us to maximize goodness, without claiming to have identified all the goods. If, as I would have it and as Moore agrees, love relations and the like are goods, how could there be any disharmony here? Would it not be possible to embody Moore's justifying reason as a motive and still love? I do not think so.

First, if you try to carry on the relationship for the sake of goodness, there is no essential commitment even to that activity, much less to the persons involved. So far as goodness is involved,

you might as well love as ski or write poetry or eat a nice meal or. . . . Perhaps it would be replied that there is something special about that good, the good of love – treating it now not *qua* good but *qua* what is good or *qua* this good. In such a case, however, there is again an impersonality so far as the individuals are concerned. Any other person who would elicit as much of this good would be as proper an object of love as the beloved. To this it might be replied that it is that good which is to be sought – with emphasis on the personal and individual features, the features that bind these people together. But now it is not clear in what sense goodness is being sought, nor that the theory is still telling us to maximize goodness.[1] True, the theory tells us to bring about this good, but now we cannot separate what is good, the love, from its goodness. And this simply is not Moore's utilitarianism.

Just as egoism and the above sorts of utilitarianisms necessitate a schizophrenia between reason and motive – and just as they cannot allow for love, friendship, affection, fellow feeling, and community – so do current rule utilitarianisms. And so do current deontologies.

What is lacking in these theories is simply – or not so simply – the person. For, love, friendship, affection, fellow feeling, and community all require that the other person be an essential part of what is valued. The person – not merely the person's general values nor even the person-*qua*-producer-or-possessor-of-general-values – must be valued. The defect of these theories in regard to love, to take one case, is not that they do not value love (which, often, they do not) but that they do not value the beloved. Indeed, a person who values and aims at simply love, that is, love-in-general or even love-in-general-exemplified-by-this-person "misses" the intended beloved as surely as does an adherent of the theories I have criticized.

The problem with these theories is not, however, with *other*-people-as-valuable. It is simply – or not so simply – with *people*-as-valuable. Just as they would do *vis-à-vis* other people, modern ethical theories would prevent each of us from loving, caring for, and valuing ourself – as opposed to loving, caring for, and valuing our general values or ourself-*qua*-producer-or-possessor-of-general-values. In these externality-ridden theories, there is as much a disappearance or non-appearance of the self as of other people. Their externality-ridden universes of what is intrinsically valuable are not solipsistic; rather, they are devoid of all people.[2]

It is a truism that it is difficult to deal with people as such. It is difficult really to care for them for their own sake. It is psychically wearing and exhausting. It puts us in too open, too vulnerable a position. But what must also be looked at is what it does to us – taken individually and in groups as small as a couple and as large as society – to view and treat others externally, as essentially replaceable, as mere instruments or repositories of general and non-specific value; and what it does to us to be treated, or believe we are treated, in these ways.

At the very least, these ways are dehumanizing. To say much more than this would require a full-scale philosophical anthropology showing how such personal relations as love and friendship are possible, how they relate to larger ways and structures of human life, and how they – and perhaps only they – allow for the development of those relations which are constitutive of a human life worth living: how, in short, they work together to produce the fullness of a good life, a life of eudaimonia.

Having said this, it must be acknowledged that there are many unclarities and difficulties in the notion of valuing a person, in the notion of a person-as-valuable. When we think about this – e.g. what and why we value – we seem driven either to omitting the person and ending up with a person-*qua*-producer-or-possessor-of-general-values or with a person's general values, or to omitting them and ending up with a bare particular ego.

In all of this, perhaps we could learn from the egoists. Their instincts, at least, must be to admit themselves, each for self, into their values. At the risk of absurdity – indeed, at the risk of complete loss of appeal of their view – what they find attractive and good about good-for-self must be, not only the good, but also and pre-eminently the for-self.

At this point, it might help to restate some of the things I have tried to do and some I have not. Throughout I have been concerned with what sort of motives people can have if they are to be able to realize the great goods of love, friendship, affection, fellow feeling, and community. And I have argued that, if we take as motives, embody in our motives, those various things which recent ethical theories hold to be ultimately good or right, we will, of necessity, be unable to have those motives. Love, friendship, affection, fellow feeling, and community, like many other states and activities, essentially contain certain motives and essentially preclude certain others; among those precluded we find motives comprising the justifications, the goals, the goods of those ethical theories most prominent today. To embody in one's motives the values of current ethical theories is to treat people externally and to preclude love, friendship, affection, fellow feeling, and community – both with others and with oneself. To get these great goods while holding those current ethical theories requires a schizophrenia between reason and motive.

I have not argued that if you have a successful love relationship, friendship, . . . then you will be unable to achieve the justifications, goals, goods posited by those theories. You can achieve them, but not by trying to live the theory directly. Or, more exactly, to the extent that you live the theory directly, to that extent you will fail to achieve its goods. . . .

Notes

I wish to thank all those who have heard or read various versions of this paper and whose comments have greatly encouraged and helped me.

1 Taking love and people-in-certain-relations as intrinsically valuable helps show mistaken various views about acting rationally (or well). First, maximization: i.e. if you value "item" C and if state S has more C than does S', you act rationally only if you choose S – unless S', has more of other items you value than does S, or your cost in getting S, as opposed to S', is too high, or you are not well enough informed. Where C is love (and indeed where C is many, if not most, valuable things), this does not hold – not even if all the values involved

are self-regarding. Second, paying attention to value differences, being alive to them and their significance for acting rationally: just consider a person who (often) checks to see whether a love relation with another person would be "better" than the present love.

2   Moore's taking friendship to be an intrinsic good is an exception to this. But if the previous criticism of Moore holds, his so taking friendship introduces serious strains, verging on inconsistencies, into his theory.

---

18   Alienation, Consequentialism, and the Demands of Morality

Peter Railton

Introduction

Living up to the demands of morality may bring with it alienation – from one's personal commitments, from one's feelings or sentiments, from other people, or even from morality itself. In this article I will discuss several apparent instances of such alienation, and attempt a preliminary assessment of their bearing on questions about the acceptability of certain moral theories. Of special concern will be the question whether problems about alienation show consequentialist moral theories to be self-defeating.

I will not attempt a full or general characterization of alienation. Indeed, at a perfectly general level alienation can be characterized only very roughly as a kind of estrangement, distancing, or separateness (not necessarily consciously attended to) resulting in some sort of loss (not necessarily consciously noticed).[1] Rather than seek a general analysis I will rely upon examples to convey a sense of what is involved in the sorts of alienation with which I am concerned. There is nothing in a word, and the phenomena to be discussed below could all be considered while avoiding the controversial term "alienation." My sense, however, is that there is some point in using this formidable term, if only to draw atten-

From *The Journal of Philosophy*, vol. 73, no. 14 (1976). Reprinted with permission.

tion to commonalities among problems not always noticed. . . .

Let us begin with two examples.

1   John and Anne and Lisa and Helen

To many, John has always seemed a model husband. He almost invariably shows great sensitivity to his wife's needs, and he willingly goes out of his way to meet them. He plainly feels great affection for her. When a friend remarks upon the extraordinary quality of John's concern for his wife, John responds without any self-indulgence or self-congratulation, "I've always thought that people should help each other when they're in a specially good position to do so. I know Anne better than anyone else does, so I know better what she wants and needs. Besides, I have such affection for her that it's no great burden – instead, I get a lot of satisfaction out of it. Just think how awful marriage would be, or life itself, if people didn't take special care of the ones they love." His friend accuses John of being unduly modest, but John's manner convinces him that he is telling the truth: this is really how he feels.

Lisa has gone through a series of disappointments over a short period, and has been profoundly depressed. In the end, however, with the help of others she has emerged from the long night of anxiety and melancholy. Only now is she able to talk openly with friends about her state of mind, and she turns to her oldest friend, Helen, who was a mainstay throughout. She'd like to find a way to thank Helen, since she's only too aware of how much of a burden she's been over these months, how much of a drag and a bore, as she puts it. "You don't have to thank me, Lisa," Helen replies, "you deserved it. It was the least I could do after all you've done for me. We're friends, remember? And we said a long time ago that we'd stick together no matter what. Some day I'll probably ask the same thing of you, and I know you'll come through. What else are friends for?" Lisa wonders whether Helen is saying this simply to avoid creating feelings of guilt, but Helen replies that she means every word – she couldn't bring herself to lie to Lisa if she tried.

2   What's Missing?

What is troubling about the words of John and Helen? Both show stout character and moral awareness. John's remarks have a benevolent, consequentialist cast, while Helen reasons in a deontological language of duties, reciprocity, and respect. They are not self-centered or without feeling. Yet something seems wrong.

The place to look is not so much at what they say as what they don't say. Think, for example, of how John's remarks might sound to his wife. Anne might have hoped that it was, in some ultimate sense, in part for *her* sake and the sake of their love as such that John pays such special attention to her. That he devotes himself to her because of the characteristically good consequences of doing so seems to leave her, and their relationship as such, too far out of the picture – this despite the fact that these characteristically good consequences depend in important ways on his special relation to her. She is being taken into account by John, but it might seem she is justified in being hurt by the way she is being taken into account. It is as if John viewed her, their relationship, and even his own affection for

her from a distant, objective point of view – a moral point of view where reasons must be reasons for any rational agent and so must have an impersonal character even when they deal with personal matters. His wife might think a more personal point of view would also be appropriate, a point of view from which "It's my wife" or "It's Anne" would have direct and special relevance, and play an unmediated role in his answer to the question "*Why* do you attend to her so?"

Something similar is missing from Helen's account of why she stood by Lisa. While we understand that the specific duties she feels toward Lisa depend upon particular features of their relationship, still we would not be surprised if Lisa finds Helen's response to her expression of gratitude quite distant, even chilling. We need not question whether she has strong feeling for Lisa, but we may wonder at how that feeling finds expression in Helen's thinking.[2]

John and Helen both show alienation: there would seem to be an estrangement between their affections and their rational, deliberative selves; an abstract and universalizing point of view mediates their responses to others and to their own sentiments. We should not assume that they have been caught in an uncharacteristic moment of moral reflection or after-the-fact rationalization; it is a settled part of their characters to think and act from a moral point of view. It is as if the world were for them a fabric of obligations and permissions in which personal considerations deserve recognition only to the extent that, and in the way that, such considerations find a place in this fabric.

To call John and Helen alienated from their affections or their intimates is not of itself to condemn them, nor is it to say that they are experiencing any sort of distress. One may be alienated from something without recognizing this as such or suffering in any conscious way from it, much as one may simply be uninterested in something without awareness or conscious suffering. But alienation is not mere lack of interest: John and Helen are not *uninterested* in their affections or in their intimates; rather, their interest takes a certain alienated form. While this alienation may not itself be a psychological affliction, it may be the basis of such afflictions – such as a sense of loneliness or emptiness – or of the loss of certain things of value – such as a sense of belonging or the pleasures of spontaneity. Moreover, their alienation may cause psychological distress in others, and make certain valuable sorts of relationships impossible.

However, we must be on guard lest oversimple categories distort our diagnosis. It seems to me wrong to picture the self as ordinarily divided into cognitive and affective halves, with deliberation and rationality belonging to the first, and sentiments belonging to the second. John's alienation is not a problem on the boundary of naturally given cognitive and affective selves, but a problem partially constituted by the bifurcation of his psyche into these separate spheres. *John*'s deliberative self seems remarkably divorced from his affections, but not all psyches need be so divided. That there is a cognitive element in affection – that affection is not a mere "feeling" that is a given for the deliberative self but rather involves as well certain characteristic modes of thought and perception – is suggested by the difficulty some may have in believing that John really does love Anne if he persistently thinks about her in the way suggested by his remarks. Indeed, his affection for Anne does seem to have been demoted to a mere "feeling". For this reason among others, we should not think of John's alienation from his affections and his alienation from Anne as wholly independent phenomena, the one the cause of the other. Of course, similar remarks apply to Helen.

3   The Moral Point of View

Perhaps the lives of John and Anne or Helen and Lisa would be happier or fuller if none of the alienation mentioned were present. But is this a problem for *morality*? If, as some have contended, to have a morality is to make normative judgments from a moral point of view and be guided by them, and if by its nature a moral point of view must exclude considerations that lack universality, then any genuinely moral way of going about life would seem liable to produce the sorts of alienation mentioned above. Thus it would be a conceptual confusion to ask that we never be required by morality to go beyond a personal point of view, since to fail ever to look at things from an impersonal (or non-personal) point of view would be to fail ever to be distinctively moral – not immoralism, perhaps, but amoralism. This would not be to say that there are not other points of view on life worthy of our attention, or that taking a moral point of view is always appropriate – one could say that John and Helen show no moral defect in thinking so impersonally, although they do moralize to excess. But the fact that a particular morality requires us to take an impersonal point of view could not sensibly be held against it, for that would be what makes it a morality at all.

This sort of position strikes me as entirely too complacent. First, we must somehow give an account of practical reasoning that does not merely multiply points of view and divide the self – a more unified account is needed. Second, we must recognize that loving relationships, friendships, group loyalties, and spontaneous actions are among the most important contributors to whatever it is that makes life worth while; any moral theory deserving serious consideration must itself give them serious consideration. As William K. Frankena has written, "Morality is made for man, not man for morality." Moral considerations are often supposed to be overriding in practical reasoning. If we were to find that adopting a particular morality led to irreconcilable conflict with central types of human well-being – as cases akin to John's and Helen's have led some to suspect – then this surely would give us good reason to doubt its claims.

For example, in the closing sentences of *A Theory of Justice* John Rawls considers the "perspective of eternity," which is impartial across all individuals and times, and writes that this is a "form of *thought and feeling* that rational persons can adopt in the world." "Purity of heart," he concludes, "would be to see clearly and act with grace and self-command from this point of view." This may or may not be purity of heart, but it could not be the standpoint of actual life without radically detaching the individual from a range of personal concerns and commitments. Presumably we should not read Rawls as recommending that we adopt this point of view in the bulk of our actions in daily life, but the fact that so purely abstracted a perspective is portrayed as a kind of moral ideal should at least start us wondering. If to be more perfectly moral is to ascend ever higher toward *sub specie aeternitatis* abstraction, perhaps we made a mistake in boarding the moral escalator in the first place. Some of the very "weaknesses" that prevent us from achieving this moral ideal – strong attachments to persons or projects – seem to be part of a considerably more compelling human ideal.

Should we say at this point that the lesson is that we should give a more prominent role to the value of non-alienation in our moral reasoning? That would be too little too late: the problem seems to be the way in which morality asks us to look at things, not just the things it asks us to look at.

4   The "Paradox of Hedonism"

Rather than enter directly into the question whether being moral is a matter of taking a moral point of view and whether there is thus some sort of necessary connection between being moral and being alienated in a way detrimental to human flourishing, I will consider a related problem the solution to which may suggest a way of steering around obstacles to a more direct approach.

One version of the so-called "paradox of hedonism" is that adopting as one's exclusive ultimate end in life the pursuit of maximum happiness may well prevent one from having certain experiences or engaging in certain sorts of relationships or commitments that are among the greatest sources of happiness. The hedonist, looking around him, may discover that some of those who are less concerned with their own happiness than he is, and who view people and projects less instrumentally than he does, actually manage to live happier lives than he despite his dogged pursuit of happiness. The "paradox" is pragmatic,

not logical, but it looks deep none the less: the hedonist, it would appear, ought not to be a hedonist. It seems, then, as if we have come across a second case in which mediating one's relations to people or projects by a particular point of view – in this case, a hedonistic point of view – may prevent one from attaining the fullest possible realization of sought-after values.

However, it is important to notice that even though adopting a hedonistic life project may tend to interfere with realizing that very project, there is no such natural exclusion between acting for the sake of another or a cause as such and recognizing how important this is to one's happiness. A spouse who acts for the sake of his mate may know full well that this is a source of deep satisfaction for him – in addition to providing him with reasons for acting internal to it, the relationship may also promote the external goal of achieving happiness. Moreover, while the pursuit of happiness may not be the reason he entered or sustains the relationship, he may also recognize that if it had not seemed likely to make him happy he would not have entered it, and that if it proved over time to be inconsistent with his happiness he would consider ending it

It might be objected that one cannot really regard a person or a project as an end as such if one's commitment is in this way contingent or overridable. But were this so, we would be able to have very few commitments to ends as such. For example, one could not be committed to both one's spouse and one's child as ends as such, since at most one of these commitments could be overriding in cases of conflict. It is easy to confuse the notion of a commitment to an end *as such* (or *for its own sake*) with that of an *overriding* commitment, but strength is not the same as structure. To be committed to an end as such is a matter of (among other things) whether it furnishes one with reasons for acting that are not mediated by other concerns. It does not follow that these reasons must always outweigh whatever opposing reasons one may have, or that one may not at the same time have other, mediating reasons that also incline one to act on behalf of that end.

Actual commitments to ends as such, even

when very strong, are subject to various qualifications and contingencies. If a friend grows too predictable or moves off to a different part of the world, or if a planned life project proves less engaging or practical than one had imagined, commitments and affections naturally change. If a relationship were highly vulnerable to the least change, it would be strained to speak of genuine affection rather than, say, infatuation. But if members of a relationship came to believe that they would be better off without it, this ordinarily would be a non-trivial change, and it is not difficult to imagine that their commitment to the relationship might be contingent in this way but none the less real. Of course, a relationship involves a shared history and shared expectations as well as momentary experiences, and it is unusual that affection or concern can be changed overnight, or relationships begun or ended at will. Moreover, the sorts of affections and commitments that can play a decisive role in shaping one's life and in making possible the deeper sorts of satisfactions are not those that are easily overridden or subject to constant reassessment or second-guessing. Thus a sensible hedonist would not forever be subjecting his affections or commitments to egoistic calculation, nor would he attempt to break off a relationship or commitment merely because it might seem to him at a given moment that some other arrangement would make him happier. Commitments to others or to causes as such may be very closely linked to the self, and a hedonist who knows what he's about will not be one who turns on his self at the slightest provocation. Contingency is not expendability, and while some commitments are remarkably non-contingent – such as those of parent to child or patriot to country – it cannot be said that commitments of a more contingent sort are never genuine, or never conduce to the profounder sorts of happiness.

Following these observations, we may reduce the force of the "paradox of hedonism" if we distinguish two forms of hedonism. *Subjective hedonism* is the view that one should adopt the hedonistic point of view in action, that is, that one should whenever possible attempt to determine which act seems most likely to contribute

optimally to one's happiness, and behave accordingly. *Objective hedonism* is the view that one should follow that course of action which would in fact most contribute to one's happiness, even when this would involve *not* adopting the hedonistic point of view in action. An act will be called *subjectively hedonistic* if it is done from a hedonistic point of view; an act is *objectively hedonistic* if it is that act, of those available to the agent, which would most contribute to his happiness.[3] Let us call someone a *sophisticated hedonist* if he aims to lead an objectively hedonistic life (that is, the happiest life available to him in the circumstances) and yet is not committed to subjective hedonism. Thus, within the limits of what is psychologically possible, a sophisticated hedonist is prepared to eschew the hedonistic point of view whenever taking this point of view conflicts with following an objectively hedonistic course of action. The so-called paradox of hedonism shows that there will be such conflicts: certain acts or courses of action may be objectively hedonistic only if not subjectively hedonistic. When things are put this way, it seems that the sophisticated hedonist faces a problem rather than a paradox: how to act in order to achieve maximum possible happiness if this is at times – or even often – *not* a matter of carrying out hedonistic deliberations.

The answer in any particular case will be complex and contextual – it seems unlikely that any one method of decision-making would always promote thought and action most conducive to one's happiness. A sophisticated hedonist might proceed precisely by looking at the complex and contextual: observing the actual modes of thought and action of those people who are in some ways like himself and who seem most happy. If our assumptions are right, he will find that few such individuals are subjective hedonists; instead, they act for the sake of a variety of ends as such. He may then set out to develop in himself the traits of character, ways of thought, types of commitment, and so on, that seem common in happy lives. For example, if he notes that the happiest people often have strong loyalties to friends, he must ask how he can become a more loyal friend – not merely how he can seem to be a loyal friend (since those he has observed are not happy because they merely seem loyal) – but how he can in fact be one.

Could one really make such changes if one had as a goal leading an optimally happy life? The answer seems to me a qualified *yes*, but let us first look at a simpler case. A highly competitive tennis player comes to realize that his obsession with winning is keeping him from playing his best. A pro tells him that if he wants to win he must devote himself more to the game and its play as such and think less about his performance. In the commitment and concentration made possible by this devotion, he is told, lies the secret of successful tennis. So he spends a good deal of time developing an enduring devotion to many aspects of the activity, and finds it peculiarly satisfying to become so absorbed in it. He plays better, and would have given up the program of change if he did not, but he now finds that he plays tennis more for its own sake, enjoying greater internal as well as external rewards from the sport. Such a person would not keep thinking – on or off the court – "No matter how I play, the only thing I really care about is whether I win!" He would recognize such thoughts as self-defeating, as evidence that his old, unhelpful way of looking at things was resuming. Nor would such a person be self-deceiving. He need not hide from himself his goal of winning, for this goal is consistent with his increased devotion to the game. His commitment to the activity is not eclipsed by, but made more vivid by, his desire to succeed at it.

The same sort of story might be told about a sophisticated hedonist and friendship. An individual could realize that his instrumental attitude toward his friends prevents him from achieving the littlest happiness friendship affords. He could then attempt to focus more on his friends as such, doing this somewhat deliberately, perhaps, until it comes more naturally. He might then find his friendships improved and himself happier. If he found instead that his relationships were deteriorating or his happiness declining, he would reconsider the idea. None of this need be hidden from himself: the external goal of happiness reinforces the internal goals of his relationships. The sophisticated hedonist's motivational structure should therefore meet a *counterfactual condition*: he need not always act for the sake of happiness, since he may do various things for their own sake or for the sake of others, but he would not act as he does if it were not compatible with his leading an objectively hedonistic life. Of course, a sophisticated hedonist cannot guarantee that he will meet this counterfactual condition, but only attempt to meet it as fully as possible.

Success at tennis is a relatively circumscribed goal, leaving much else about one's life undefined. Maximizing one's happiness, by contrast, seems all-consuming. Could commitments to other ends survive alongside it? Consider an analogy. Ned needs to make a living. More than that, he needs to make as much money as he can – he has expensive tastes, a second marriage, and children reaching college age, and he does not have extensive means. He sets out to invest his money and his labor in ways he thinks will maximize return. Yet it does not follow that he acts as he does solely for the sake of earning as much as possible. Although it is obviously true that he does what he does because he believes that it will maximize return, this does not preclude his doing it for other reasons as well, for example, for the sake of living well or taking care of his children. This may continue to be the case even if Ned comes to want money for its own sake, that is, if he comes to see the accumulation of wealth as intrinsically as well as extrinsically attractive. Similarly, the stricture that one seek the objectively hedonistic life certainly provides one with considerable guidance, but it does not supply the whole of one's motives and goals in action.

My claim that the sophisticated hedonist can escape the paradox of hedonism was, however, qualified. It still seems possible that the happiest sorts of lives ordinarily attainable are those led by people who would reject even sophisticated hedonism, people whose character is such that if they were presented with a choice between two entire lives one of which contains less total happiness but none the less realizes some other values more fully, they might well knowingly choose against maximal happiness. If this were so, it would show that a sophisticated hedonist might have reason for changing his beliefs so that he no longer accepts hedonism in any form. This still would not refute objective hedonism as an account of the (rational, prudential, or moral) *criterion* one's acts should meet, for it would be precisely in order to meet this criterion that the sophisticated hedonist would change his beliefs.

5 The Place of Non-Alienation Among Human Values

Before discussing the applicability of what has been said about hedonism to morality, we should notice that alienation is not always a bad thing, that we may not want to overcome all forms of alienation, and that other values, which may conflict with non-alienation in particular cases, may at times have a greater claim on us. Let us look at a few such cases.

It has often been argued that a morality of duties and obligations may appropriately come into play in familial or friendly relationships when the relevant sentiments have given out, for instance, when one is exasperated with a friend, when love is tried, and so on. "Ought" implies "can" (or, at least, "could"), and while it may be better in human terms when we do what we ought to do at least in part out of feelings of love, friendship, or sympathy, there are times when we simply cannot muster these sentiments, and the right thing to do is to act as love or friendship or sympathy would have directed rather refuse to perform any act done merely from a sense of duty.

But we should add a further role for unspontaneous, morally motivated action: even when love or concern is strong, it is often desirable that people achieve some distance from their sentiments or one another. A spouse may act toward his mate in a grossly overprotective way; a friend may indulge another's ultimately destructive tendencies; a parent may favor one child inordinately. Strong and immediate affection may overwhelm one's ability to see what another person actually needs or deserves. In such cases a certain distance between people or between an individual and his sentiments, and an intrusion of moral considerations into the gap thus created, may be a good thing, and part of genuine affection or commitment. The opposite view, that no such mediation is desirable as long as affection is strong, seems to me a piece of romanticism. Concern over alienation therefore ought not to take the form of a cult of "authenticity at any price."

Moreover, there will occur regular conflicts between avoiding alienation and achieving other important individual goals. One such goal is autonomy. Bernard Williams has emphasized that many of us have developed certain "ground projects" that give shape and meaning to our lives, and has drawn attention to the damage an individual may suffer if he is alienated from his ground projects by being forced to look at them as potentially overridable by moral considerations. But against this it may be urged that it is crucial for autonomy that one hold one's commitments up for inspection – even one's ground projects. Our ground projects are often formed in our youth, in a particular family, class, or cultural background. It may be alienating and even disorienting to call these into question, but to fail to do so is to lose autonomy. Of course, autonomy could not sensibly require that we question all of our values and commitments at once nor need it require us to be forever detached from what we are doing. It is quite possible to submit basic aspects of one's life to scrutiny and arrive at a set of autonomously chosen commitments that form the basis of an integrated life. Indeed, psychological conflicts and practical obstacles give us occasion for re-examining our basic commitments rather more often than we'd like.

At the same time, the tension between autonomy and non-alienation should not be exaggerated. Part of avoiding exaggeration is giving up the Kantian notion that autonomy is a matter of escaping determination by any contingency whatsoever. Part, too, is refusing to conflate autonomy with sheer independence from others. Both Rousseau and Marx emphasized that achieving control over one's own life requires participation in certain sorts of social relations – in fact, relations in which various kinds of alienation have been minimized.

Autonomy is but one value that may enter into complex trade-offs with non-alienation. Alienation and inauthenticity do have their uses. The alienation of some individuals or groups from their milieu may at times be necessary for fundamental social criticism or cultural innovation. And without some degree of inauthenticity, it is doubtful whether civil relations among people could long be maintained. It would take little ingenuity, but too much of the reader's patience, to construct here examples involving troubling conflicts between non-alienation and virtually any other worthy goal.

6 Reducing Alienation in Morality

Let us now move to morality proper. To do this with any definiteness, we must have a particular morality in mind. For various reasons, I think that the most plausible sort of morality is consequentialist in form, assessing rightness in terms of contribution to the good. In attempting to sketch how we might reduce alienation in moral theory and practice, therefore, I will work within a consequentialist framework (although a number of the arguments I will make could be made, *mutatis mutandis*, by a deontologist).

Of course, one has adopted no morality in particular even in adopting consequentialism unless one says what the good is. Let us, then, dwell briefly on axiology. One mistake of dominant consequentialist theories, I believe, is their failure to see that things other than subjective states can have intrinsic value. Allied to this is a tendency to reduce all intrinsic values to one – happiness. Both of these features of classical utilitarianism reflect forms of alienation. First, in divorcing subjective states from their objective counterparts, and claiming that we seek the latter exclusively for the sake of the former, utilitarianism cuts us off from the world in a way made graphic by examples such as that of the experience machine, a hypothetical device that can be programmed to provide one with whatever subjective states he may desire. The experience machine affords us decisive subjective advantages over actual life: few, if any, in actual life think they have achieved all that they could want, but the machine makes possible for each an existence that he cannot distinguish from such a happy state of affairs. Despite this striking advantage, most rebel at the notion of the experience machine. As Robert Nozick and others have pointed out, it seems to matter to us what we actually *do* and *are* as well as how life *appears* to us. We see the point of our lives as bound up with the world and other people in ways not captured by subjectivism, and our sense of loss in contemplating a life tied to an experience machine, quite literally alienated from the surrounding world, suggests where subjectivism has gone astray. Second, the reduction of all goals to the purely abstract goal of happiness or pleasure, as in hedonistic utilitarianism, treats all other goals instrumentally. Knowledge or friendship may promote happiness, but is it a fair characterization of our commitment to these goals to say that this is the only sense in which they are ultimately valuable? Doesn't the insistence that there is an abstract and uniform goal lying behind all of our ends bespeak an alienation from these particular ends?

Rather than pursue these questions further here, let me suggest an approach to the good that seems to me less hopeless as a way of capturing human value: a pluralistic approach in which several goods are viewed as intrinsically, non-morally valuable – such as happiness, knowledge, purposeful activity, autonomy, solidarity, respect, and beauty.[4] These goods need not be ranked lexically, but may be attributed weights, and the criterion of rightness for an act would be that it must contribute to the weighted sum of these values in the long run. This creates the possibility of trade-offs among values of the kinds discussed in the previous section. However, I will not stop here to develop or defend such an account of the good and the right, since our task is to show how certain problems of alienation that arise in moral contexts might be dealt with if morality is assumed to have such a basis.

Consider, then, Juan, who, like John, has always seemed a model husband. When a friend remarks on the extraordinary concern he shows for his wife, Juan characteristically responds: "I love Linda. I even *like* her. So it means a lot to me to do things for her. After all we've been through, it's almost a part of me to do it." But his friend knows that Juan is a principled individual, and asks Juan how his marriage fits into that larger scheme. After all, he asks, it's fine for Juan and his wife to have such a close relationship, but what about all the other, needier people Juan could help if he broadened his horizon still further? Juan replies, "Look, it's a better world when people can have a relationship like ours – and nobody could if everyone were always asking themselves who's got the most need. It's not easy to make things work in this world, and one of the best things that happens to people is to have a close relationship like ours. You'd make things worse in a hurry if you broke up those close relationships for the sake of some higher goal. Anyhow, I know that you can't always put family first. The world isn't such a wonderful place that it's OK just to retreat into your own little circle. But still, you need that little circle. People get burned out, or lose touch, if they try to save the world by themselves. The ones who can stick with it and do a good job of making things better are usually the ones who can make that fit into a life that does not make them miserable. I haven't met any real saints lately, and I don't trust people who think they *are* saints."

If we contrast Juan with John, we do not find that the one allows moral considerations to enter his personal life while the other does not. Nor do we find that one is less serious in his moral concern. Rather, what Juan recognizes to be morally required is not by its nature incompatible with acting directly for the sake of another. It is important to Juan to subject his life to moral scrutiny – he is not merely stumped when asked for a defense of his acts above a personal level, he does not *just* say "Of course I take care of her, she's my wife!" or "It's Linda" and refuse to listen to the more impersonal considerations raised by his friend. It is consistent with what he says to imagine that his motivational structure has a form akin to that of the sophisticated hedonist, that is, his motivational structure meets a counterfactual condition: while he ordinarily does not

do what he does simply for the sake of doing what's right, he would seek to lead a different sort of life if he did not think his were morally defensible. His love is not a romantic submersion in the other to the exclusion of worldly responsibilities, and to that extent it may be said to involve a degree of alienation from Linda. But this does not seem to drain human value from their relationship. Nor need one imagine that Linda would be saddened to hear Juan's words the way Anne might have been saddened to overhear the remarks of John.

Moreover, because of his very willingness to question his life morally, Juan avoids a sort of alienation not sufficiently discussed – alienation from others, beyond one's intimate ties. Individuals who will not or cannot allow questions to arise about what they are doing from a broader perspective are in an important way cut off from their society and the larger world. They may not be troubled by this in any very direct way, but even so they may fail to experience that powerful sense of purpose and meaning that comes from seeing oneself as part of something larger and more enduring than oneself or one's intimate circle. The search for such a sense of purpose and meaning seems to be ubiquitous – surely much of the impulse to religion, to ethnic or regional identification (most strikingly, in the "rediscovery" of such identities), or to institutional loyalty stems from this desire to see ourselves as part of a more general, lasting, and worthwhile scheme of things. This presumably is part of what is meant by saying that secularization has led to a sense of meaninglessness, or that the decline of traditional communities and societies has meant an increase in anomie. (The sophisticated hedonist, too, should take note: one way to gain a firmer sense that one's life is worthwhile, a sense that may be important to realizing various values in one's own life, is to overcome alienation from others.)

Drawing upon our earlier discussion of two kinds of hedonism, let us now distinguish two kinds of consequentialism. *Subjective consequentialism* is the view that whenever one faces a choice of actions, one should attempt to determine which act of those available would most promote the good, and should then try to act accordingly. One is behaving as subjective consequentialism requires – that is, leading a *subjectively consequentialist life* – to the extent that one uses and follows a distinctively consequentialist mode of decision-making, consciously aiming at the overall good and conscientiously using the best available information with the greatest possible rigor. *Objective consequentialism* is the view that the criterion of the rightness of an act or course of action is whether it in fact would most promote the good of those acts available to the agent. Subjective consequentialism, like subjective hedonism, is a view that prescribes following a particular mode of deliberation in action; objective consequentialism, like objective hedonism, concerns the outcomes actually brought about, and thus deals with the question of deliberation only in terms of the tendencies of certain forms of decision-making to promote appropriate outcomes. Let us reserve the expression *objectively consequentialist act* (or *life*) for those acts (or that life) of those available to the agent that would bring about the best outcomes. To complete the parallel, let us say that a *sophisticated consequentialist* is someone who has a standing commitment to leading an objectively consequentialist life, but who need not set special stock in any particular form of decision-making and therefore does not necessarily seek to lead a subjectively consequentialist life. Juan, it might be argued (if the details were filled in), is a sophisticated consequentialist, since he seems to believe he should act for the best but does not seem to feel it appropriate to bring a consequentialist calculus to bear on his every act.

Is it bizarre, or contradictory, that being a sophisticated consequentialist may involve rejecting subjective consequentialism? After all, doesn't an adherent of subjective consequentialism also seek to lead an objectively consequentialist life? He may, but then he is mistaken in thinking that this means he should always undertake a distinctively consequentialist deliberation when faced with a choice. To see his mistake, we need only consider some examples.

It is well known that in certain emergencies, the best outcome requires action so swift as to preclude consequentialist deliberation. Thus a sophisticated consequentialist has reason to inculcate in himself certain dispositions to act rapidly in obvious emergencies. The disposition is not a mere reflex, but a developed pattern of action deliberately acquired. A simple example, but it should dispel the air of paradox.

Many decisions are too insignificant to warrant consequentialist deliberation ("Which shoelace should I do up first?") or too predictable in outcome ("Should I meet my morning class today as scheduled or should I linger over the newspaper?"). A famous old conundrum for consequentialism falls into a similar category: before I deliberate about an act, it seems I must decide how much time would be optimal to allocate for this deliberation; but then I must first decide how much time would be optimal to allocate for this time-allocation decision; but before that I must decide how much time would be optimal to allocate for *that* decision; and so on. The sophisticated consequentialist can block this paralyzing regress by noting that often the best thing to do is not to ask questions about time allocation at all; instead, he may develop standing dispositions to give more or less time to decisions depending upon their perceived importance, the amount of information available, the predictability of his choice, and so on. I think we all have dispositions of this sort, which account for our patience with some prolonged deliberations but not others.

There are somewhat more intriguing examples that have more to do with psychological interference than mere time efficiency: the timid, put-upon employee who knows that if he deliberates about whether to ask for a raise he will succumb to his timidity and fail to demand what he actually deserves; the self-conscious man who knows that if, at social gatherings, he is forever wondering how he should act, his behavior will be awkward and unnatural, contrary to his goal of acting naturally and appropriately; the tightrope walker who knows he must not reflect on the value of keeping his concentration; and so on. People can learn to avoid certain characteristically self-defeating lines of thought – just as the tennis player in an earlier example learned to avoid thinking constantly about winning – and the sophisticated consequentialist may learn that consequentialist deliberation is in a variety of cases self-defeating, so that other habits of thought should be cultivated.

The sophisticated consequentialist need not be deceiving himself or acting in bad faith when he avoids consequentialist reasoning. He can fully recognize that he is developing the dispositions he does because they are necessary for promoting the good. Of course, he cannot be preoccupied with this fact all the while, but then one cannot be *preoccupied* with anything without this interfering with normal or appropriate patterns of thought and action.

To the list of cases of interference we may add John, whose all-purpose willingness to look at things by subjective consequentialist lights prevents the realization in him and in his relationships with others of values that he would recognize to be crucially important.

Bernard Williams has said that it shows consequentialism to be in grave trouble that it may have to usher itself from the scene as a mode of decision-making in a number of important areas of life. Though I think he has exaggerated the extent to which we would have to exclude consequentialist considerations from our lives in order to avoid disastrous results, it is fair to ask: If maximizing the good were in fact to require that consequentialist reasoning be *wholly* excluded, would this refute consequentialism? Imagine an all-knowing demon who controls the fate of the world and who visits unspeakable punishment upon man to the extent that he does not employ a Kantian morality. (Obviously, the demon is not himself a Kantian.) If such a demon existed, sophisticated consequentialists would have reason to convert to Kantianism, perhaps even to make whatever provisions could be made to erase consequentialism from the human memory and prevent any resurgence of it.

Does this possibility show that objective consequentialism is self-defeating? On the contrary, it shows that objective consequentialism has the virtue of not blurring the distinction between the *truth-conditions* of an ethical theory

and its *acceptance-conditions* in particular contexts, a distinction philosophers have generally recognized for theories concerning other subject matters. It might be objected that, unlike other theories, ethical theories must meet a condition of publicity, roughly to the effect that it must be possible under all circumstances for us to recognize a true ethical theory as such and to promulgate it publicly without thereby violating that theory itself. Such a condition might be thought to follow from the social nature of morality. But any such condition would be question-begging against consequentialist theories, since it would require that one class of actions – acts of adopting or promulgating an ethical theory – *not* be assessed in terms of their consequences. Moreover, I fail to see how such a condition could emanate from the social character of morality. To prescribe the adoption and promulgation of a mode of decision-making regardless of its consequences seems to me radically detached from human concerns, social or otherwise. If it is argued that an ethical theory that fails to meet the publicity requirement could under certain conditions endorse a course of action leading to the abuse and manipulation of man by man, we need only reflect that no psychologically possible decision procedure can guarantee that its widespread adoption could never have such a result. A "consequentialist demon" might increase the amount of abuse and manipulation in the world in direct proportion to the extent that people act according to the categorical imperative. Objective consequentialism (unlike certain deontological theories) has valuable flexibility in permitting us to take consequences into account in assessing the appropriateness of certain modes of decision-making, thereby avoiding any sort of self-defeating decision procedure worship.

A further objection is that the lack of any direct link between objective consequentialism and a particular mode of decision-making leaves the view too vague to provide adequate guidance in practice. On the contrary, objective consequentialism sets a definite and distinctive criterion of right action, and it becomes an empirical question (though not an easy one) which modes of decision-making should be employed and when. It would be a mistake for an objective consequentialist to attempt to tighten the connection between his criterion of rightness and any particular mode of decision-making: someone who recommended a particular mode of decision-making regardless of consequences would not be a hard-nosed, non-evasive objective consequentialist, but a self-contradicting one.

7 Contrasting Approaches

The seeming "indirectness" of objective consequentialism may invite its confusion with familiar indirect consequentialist theories, such as rule-consequentialism. In fact, the subjective/ objective distinction cuts across the rule/act distinction, and there are subjective and objective forms of both rule- and act-based theories. Thus far, we have dealt only with subjective and objective forms of act-consequentialism. By contrast, a *subjective rule*-consequentialist holds (roughly) that in deliberation we should always attempt to determine which act, of those available, conforms to that set of rules general acceptance of which would most promote the good; we then should attempt to perform this act. An *objective rule*-consequentialist sets actual conformity to the rules with the highest acceptance value as his criterion of right action, recognizing the possibility that the best set of rules might in some cases – or even always – recommend that one not perform rule-consequentialist deliberation.

Because I believe this last possibility must be taken seriously, I find the objective form of rule-consequentialism more plausible. Ultimately, however, I suspect that rule-consequentialism is untenable in either form, for it could recommend acts that (subjectively or objectively) accord with the best set of rules even when these rules are *not* in fact generally accepted, and when as a result these acts would have devastatingly bad consequences. "Let the rules with greatest acceptance utility be followed, though the heavens fall!" is no more plausible than "*Fiat justitia, ruat coelum!*" – and a good bit less ringing. Hence,

the arguments in this article are based entirely upon act-consequentialism.

Indeed, once the subjective/objective distinction has been drawn, an act-consequentialist can capture some of the intuitions that have made rule- or trait-consequentialism appealing. Surely part of the attraction of these indirect consequentialisms is the idea that one should have certain traits of character, or commitments to persons or principles, that are sturdy enough that one would at least sometimes refuse to forsake them even when this refusal is known to conflict with making some gain – perhaps small – in total utility. Unlike his subjective counterpart, the objective act-consequentialist is able to endorse characters and commitments that are sturdy in just this sense.

To see why, let us first return briefly to one of the simple examples of section 6. A sophisticated act-consequentialist may recognize that if he were to develop a standing disposition to render prompt assistance in emergencies without going through elaborate act-consequentialist deliberation, there would almost certainly be cases in which he would perform acts worse than those he would have performed had he stopped to deliberate, for example, when his prompt action is misguided in a way he would have noticed had he thought the matter through. It may still be right for him to develop this disposition, for without it he would act rightly in emergencies still less often – a quick response is appropriate much more often than not, and it is not practically possible to develop a disposition that would lead one to respond promptly in exactly those cases where this would have the best results. While one can attempt to cultivate dispositions that are responsive to various factors which might indicate whether promptness is of greater importance than further thought, such refinements have their own costs and, given the limits of human resources, even the best cultivated dispositions will sometimes lead one astray. The objective act-consequentialist would thus recommend cultivating dispositions that will sometimes lead him to violate his own criterion of right action. Still, he will not, as a trait-consequentialist would, shift his criterion and say that an act is right if it stems from the traits it would be best overall to have (given the limits of what is humanly achievable, the balance of costs and benefits, and so on). Instead, he continues to believe that an act may stem from the dispositions it would be best to have, and yet be wrong (because it would produce worse consequences than other acts available to the agent in the circumstances).

This line of argument can be extended to patterns of motivation, traits of character, and rules. A sophisticated act-consequentialist should realize that certain goods are reliably attainable – or attainable at all – only if people have well-developed characters; that the human psyche is capable of only so much self-regulation and refinement; and that human perception and reasoning are liable to a host of biases and errors. Therefore, individuals may be more likely to act rightly if they possess certain enduring motivational patterns, character traits, or prima facie commitments to rules in addition to whatever commitment they have to act for the best. Because such individuals would not consider consequences in all cases, they would miss a number of opportunities to maximize the good; but if they were instead always to attempt to assess outcomes, the overall result would be worse, for they would act correctly less often.

We may now strengthen the argument to show that the objective act-consequentialist can approve of dispositions, characters, or commitments to rules that are sturdy in the sense mentioned above, that is, that do not merely supplement a commitment to act for the best, but sometimes override it, so that one knowingly does what is contrary to maximizing the good. Consider again Juan and Linda, whom we imagine to have a commuting marriage. They normally get together only every other week, but one week she seems a bit depressed and harried, and so he decides to take an extra trip in order to be with her. If he did not travel, he would save a fairly large sum that he could send OXFAM to dig a well in a drought-stricken village. Even reckoning in Linda's uninterrupted malaise, Juan's guilt, and any ill-effects on their relationship, it may be that for Juan to contribute the fare to OXFAM would produce better consequences overall than the unscheduled trip. Let us suppose that Juan knows this, and that he could stay home and write the check if he tried. Still, given Juan's character, he in fact will not try to perform this more beneficial act but will travel to see Linda instead. The objective act-consequentialist will say that Juan performed the wrong act on this occasion. Yet he may also say that if Juan had had a character that would have led him to perform the better act (or made him more inclined to do so), he would have had to have been less devoted to Linda. Given the ways Juan can affect the world, it may be that if he were less devoted to Linda his overall contribution to human well-being would be less in the end, perhaps because he would become more cynical and self-centered. Thus it may be that Juan should have (should develop, encourage, and so on) a character such that he sometimes knowingly and deliberately acts contrary to his objective consequentialist duty. Any other character, of those actually available to him, would lead him to depart still further from an objectively consequentialist life. The issue is not whether staying home would *change* Juan's character – for we may suppose that it would not – but whether he would in fact decide to stay home if he had that character, of those available, that would lead him to perform the most beneficial overall sequence of acts. In some cases, then, there will exist an objective act-consequentialist argument for developing and sustaining characters of a kind Sidgwick and others have thought an act-consequentialist must condemn.

8   Demands and Disruptions

Before ending this discussion of consequentialism, let me mention one other large problem involving alienation that has seemed uniquely troubling for consequentialist theories and that shows how coming to terms with problems of alienation may be a social matter as well as a matter of individual psychology. Because consequentialist criteria of rightness are linked to maximal contribution to the good, whenever one does not perform the very best act one can, one is "negatively responsible" for any shortfall in total well-being that results. Bernard Williams has argued that to accept such a burden of responsibility would force most of us to abandon or be prepared to abandon many of our most basic individual commitments, alienating ourselves from the very things that mean the most to us.

To be sure, objective act-consequentialism of the sort considered here is a demanding and potentially disruptive morality, even after allowances have been made for the psychological phenomena thus far discussed and for the difference between saying an act is wrong and saying that the agent ought to be blamed for it. But just *how* demanding or disruptive it would be for an individual is a function – as it arguably should be – of how bad the state of the world is, how others typically act, what institutions exist, and how much that individual is capable of doing. If wealth were more equitably distributed, if political systems were less repressive and more responsive to the needs of their citizens, and if people were more generally prepared to accept certain responsibilities, then individuals' everyday lives would not have to be constantly disrupted for the sake of the good.

For example, in a society where there are no organized forms of disaster relief, it may be the case that if disaster were to strike a particular region, people all over the country would be obliged to make a special effort to provide aid. If, on the other hand, an adequate system of publicly financed disaster relief existed, then it probably would be a very poor idea for people to interrupt their normal lives and attempt to help – their efforts would probably be uncoordinated, ill-informed, an interference with skilled relief work, and economically disruptive (perhaps even damaging to the society's ability to pay for the relief effort).

By altering social and political arrangements we can lessen the disruptiveness of moral demands on our lives, and in the long run achieve better results than freelance good-doing. A consequentialist theory is therefore likely to recommend that accepting negative responsibility is more a matter of supporting certain social and political arrangements (or rearrangements) than

of setting out individually to save the world. Moreover, it is clear that such social and political changes cannot be made unless the lives of individuals are psychologically supportable in the meanwhile, and this provides substantial reason for rejecting the notion that we should abandon all that matters to us as individuals and devote ourselves solely to net social welfare. Finally, in many cases what matters most is *perceived* rather than actual demandingness or disruptiveness, and this will be a relative matter, depending upon normal expectations. If certain social or political arrangements encourage higher contribution as a matter of course, individuals may not sense these moral demands as excessively intrusive.

To speak of social and political changes is, of course, to suggest eliminating the social and political preconditions for a number of existing projects and relationships, and such changes are likely to produce some degree of alienation in those whose lives have been disrupted. To an extent such people may be able to find new projects and relationships as well as maintain a number of old projects and relationships, and thereby avoid intolerable alienation. But not all will escape serious alienation. We thus have a case in which alienation will exist whichever course of action we follow – either the alienation of those who find the loss of the old order disorienting, or the continuing alienation of those who under the present order cannot lead lives expressive of their individuality or goals. It would seem that to follow the logic of Williams's position would have the unduly conservative result of favoring those less alienated in the present state of affairs over those who might lead more satisfactory lives if certain changes were to occur. Such conservatism could hardly be warranted by a concern about alienation if the changes in question would bring about social and political preconditions for a more widespread enjoyment of meaningful lives. For example, it is disruptive of the ground projects of many men that women have begun to demand and receive greater equality in social and personal spheres, but such disruption may be offset by the opening of more avenues of self-development to a greater number of people.

In responding to Williams's objection regarding negative responsibility, I have focused more on the problem of disruptiveness than the problem of demandingness, and more on the social than the personal level. More would need to be said than I am able to say here to come fully to terms with his objection, although some very general remarks may be in order. The consequentialist starts out from the relatively simple idea that certain things seem to matter to people above all else. His root conception of moral rightness is therefore that it should matter above all else whether people, in so far as possible, actually realize these ends.[5] Consequentialist moralities of the sort considered here undeniably set a demanding standard, calling upon us to do more for one another than is now the practice. But this standard plainly does not require that most people lead intolerable lives for the sake of some greater good: the greater good is empirically equivalent to the best possible lives for the largest possible number of people. Objective consequentialism gives full expression to this root intuition by setting as the criterion of rightness actual contribution to the realization of human value, allowing practices and forms of reasoning to take whatever shape this requires. It is thus not equivalent to requiring a certain, alienated way of thinking about ourselves, our commitments, or how to act.

Samuel Scheffler has recently suggested that one response to the problems Williams raises about the impersonality and demandingness of consequentialism could be to depart from consequentialism at least far enough to recognize as a fundamental moral principle an agent-centered prerogative, roughly to the effect that one is not always obliged to maximize the good, although one is always permitted to do so if one wishes. This prerogative would make room for agents to give special attention to personal projects and commitments. However, the argument of this article, if successful, shows there to be a firm place in moral practice for prerogatives that afford such room even if one accepts a fully consequentialist fundamental moral theory.

[...]

Notes

1 The loss in question need not be a loss of something of value, and a fortiori need not be a bad thing overall: there are some people, institutions, or cultures alienation from which would be a boon. Alienation is a more or less troubling phenomenon depending upon what is lost; and in the cases to be considered, what is lost is for the most part of substantial value. It does not follow, as we will see in section 5, that in all such cases alienation is a bad thing on balance. Moreover, I do not assume that the loss in question represents an actual *decline* in some value as the result of a separation coming into being where once there was none. It seems reasonable to say that an individual can experience a loss in being alienated from nature, for example, without assuming that he was ever in communion with it, much as we say it is a loss for someone never to receive an education or never to appreciate music. Regrettably, various relevant kinds and sources of alienation cannot be discussed here. A general, historical discussion of alienation may be found in Richard Schacht, *Alienation* (Garden City, NY: Doubleday, 1971).

2 This is not to say that no questions arise about whether Helen's (or John's) feelings and attitudes constitute the fullest sort of affection, as will be seen shortly.

3 A few remarks are needed. First, I will say that an act is available to an agent if he would succeed in performing it if he tried. Second, here and elsewhere in this article I mean to include quite "thick" descriptions of actions, so that it may be part of an action that one perform it with a certain intention or goal. In the short run (but not so much the long run) intentions, goals, motives, and the like are usually less subject to our deliberate control than overt behavior – it is easier to say "I'm sorry" than to say it and mean it. This, however, is a fact about the relative availability of acts to the agent at a given time, and should not dictate what is to count as an act. Third, here and elsewhere I ignore for simplicity's sake the possibility that more than one course of action may be maximally valuable. And fourth, for reasons I will not enter into here, I have formulated objective hedonism in terms of actual outcomes rather than expected values (relative to the information available to the agent). One could make virtually the same argument using an expected value formulation.

4 To my knowledge, the best-developed method for justifying claims about intrinsic value involves

thought-experiments of a familiar sort, in which, for example, we imagine two lives, or two worlds, alike in all but one respect, and then attempt to determine whether rational, well-informed, widely-experienced individuals would (when vividly aware of both alternatives) be indifferent between the two or have a settled preference for one over the other. Since no one is ideally rational, fully informed, or infinitely experienced, the best we can do is to take more seriously the judgments of those who come nearer to approximating these conditions. Worse yet: the best we can do is to take more seriously the judgments of those we *think* better approximate these conditions. (I am not supposing that facts or experience somehow entail values, but that in rational agents, beliefs and values show a marked mutual influence and coherence.) We may overcome some narrowness if we look at behavior and preferences in other societies and other epochs, but even here we must rely upon interpretations colored by our own beliefs and values. Within the confines of this article I must leave unanswered a host of deep and troubling questions about the nature of values and value judgments. Suffice it to say that there is no reason to think that we are in a position to give anything but a tentative list of intrinsic goods.

It becomes a complex matter to describe the psychology of intrinsic value. For example, should we say that one values a relationship of solidarity, say, a friendship, *because it is* a friendship? That makes it sound as if it were somehow instrumental to the realization of some abstract value, friendship. Surely this is a misdescription. We may be able to get a clearer idea of what is involved by considering the case of happiness. We certainly do not value a particular bit of experienced happiness because it is instrumental in the realization of the abstract goal, happiness – we value the experience for its own sake because it is a happy experience. Similarly, a friendship is itself the valued thing, the thing of a valued kind. Of course, one can say that one values friendship and therefore seeks friends, just as one can say one values happiness and therefore seeks happy experiences. But this locution must be contrasted with what is being said when, for example, one talks of seeking *things that make one happy.* Friends are not "things that make one achieve friendship" – they partially constitute friendships, just as particular happy experiences partially constitute happiness for an individual. Thus taking friendship as an intrinsic value does not entail viewing particular friendships instrumentally.

5   I appealed to this "root conception" in rejecting rule-consequentialism in section 7. Although consequentialism is often condemned for failing to provide an account of morality consistent with respect for persons, this root conception provides the basis for a highly plausible notion of such respect. I doubt, however, that any fundamental ethical dispute between consequentialists and deontologists can be resolved by appeal to the idea of respect for persons. The deontologist has his notion of respect – e.g. that we not use people in certain ways – and the consequentialist has *his* – e.g. that the good of every person has an equal claim upon us, a claim unmediated by any notion of right or contract, so that we should do the most possible to bring about outcomes that actually advance the good of persons. For every consequentially justified act of manipulation to which the deontologist can point with alarm there is a deontologically justified act that fails to promote the well-being of some person(s) as fully as possible to which the consequentialist can point appalled. Which notion takes "respect for persons" more seriously? There may be no non-question-begging answer, especially once the consequentialist has recognized such things as autonomy or respect as intrinsically valuable.

Duty

19   Duty and Categorical Rules

Immanuel Kant

Transition from the Common Rational Knowledge of Morality to the Philosophical

Nothing can possibly be conceived in the world, or even out of it, which can be called good, without qualification, except a Good Will. Intelligence, wit, judgment, and the other *talents* of the mind, however they may be named, or courage, resolution, perseverance, as qualities of temperament, are undoubtedly good and desirable in many respects; but these gifts of nature may also become extremely bad and mischievous if the will which is to make use of them, and which, therefore, constitutes what is called *character*, is not good. It is the same with the *gifts of fortune*. Power, riches, honor, even health, and the general well-being and contentment with one's condition which is called *happiness*, inspire pride, and often presumption, if there is not a good will to correct the influence of these on the mind, and with this also to rectify the whole principle of acting, and adapt it to its end. The sight of a being who is not adorned with a single feature of a pure and good will, enjoying unbroken prosperity, can never give pleasure to an impartial rational spectator. Thus a good will appears to constitute the indispensable condition even of being worthy of happiness.

From "Fundamental Principles of the Metaphysic of Morals," in *Kant's Critique of Practical Reason and Other Works on the Theory of Ethics*, 6th edn, trans. Thomas Kingsmill Abbott (London: Longmans, 1909), pp. 9–22 and 29–59. Reprinted with permission.

There are even some qualities which are of service to this good will itself, and may facilitate its action, yet which have no intrinsic unconditional value, but always presuppose a good will, and this qualifies the esteem that we justly have for them, and does not permit us to regard them as absolutely good. Moderation in the affections and passions, self-control, and calm deliberation are not only good in many respects, but even seem to constitute part of the intrinsic worth of the person; but they are far from deserving to be called good without qualification, although they have been so unconditionally praised by the ancients. For without the principles of a good will, they may become extremely bad; and the coolness of a villain not only makes him far more dangerous, but also directly makes him more abominable in our eyes than he would have been without it.

A good will is good not because of what it performs or effects, not by its aptness for the attainment of some proposed end, but simply by virtue of the volition, that is, it is good in itself, and considered by itself is to be esteemed much higher than all that can be brought about by it in favor of any inclination, nay, even of the sum-total of all inclinations. Even if it should happen that, owing to special disfavor of fortune, or the niggardly provision of a stepmotherly nature, this will should wholly lack power to accomplish its purpose, if with its greatest efforts it should yet achieve nothing, and there should remain only the good will (not, to be sure, a mere wish, but the summoning of all means in our power), then, like a jewel, it would still shine by its own light, as a thing which has its whole value in itself. Its usefulness or fruitlessness can neither add to nor take away anything from this value. It would be, as it were, only the setting to enable us to handle it the more conveniently in common commerce, or to attract to it the attention of those who are not yet connoisseurs, but not to recommend it to true connoisseurs, or to determine its value. . . .

We have then to develop the notion of a will which deserves to be highly esteemed for itself, and is good without a view to anything further, a notion which exists already in the sound natural understanding, requiring rather to be cleared up than to be taught, and which in estimating the value of our actions always takes the first place, and constitutes the condition of all the rest. In order to do this, we will take the notion of duty, which includes that of a good will, although implying certain subjective restrictions and hindrances. These, however, far from concealing it, or rendering it unrecognizable, rather bring it out by contrast, and make it shine forth so much the brighter.

I omit here all actions which are already recognized as inconsistent with duty, although they may be useful for this or that purpose, for with these the question whether they are done *from duty* cannot arise at all, since they even conflict with it. I also set aside those actions which really conform to duty, but to which men have *no* direct *inclination*, performing them because they are impelled thereto by some other inclination. For in this case we can readily distinguish whether the action which agrees with duty is done *from duty*, or from a selfish view. It is much harder to make this distinction when the action accords with duty, and the subject has besides a *direct* inclination to it. For example, it is always a matter of duty that a dealer should not overcharge an inexperienced purchaser; and whenever there is much commerce the prudent tradesman does not overcharge, but keeps a fixed price for everyone, so that a child buys of him as well as any other. Men are thus *honestly* served; but this is not enough to make us believe that the tradesman has so acted from duty and from principles of honesty: his own advantage required it; it is

out of the question in this case to suppose that he might besides have a direct inclination in favor of the buyers, so that, as it were, from love he should give no advantage to one over another. Accordingly the action was done neither from duty nor from direct inclination, but merely with a selfish view.

On the other hand, it is a duty to maintain one's life; and, in addition, everyone has also a direct inclination to do so. But on this account the often anxious care which most men take for it has no intrinsic worth, and their maxim has no moral import. They preserve their life *as duty requires* no doubt, but not *because duty requires.* On the other hand, if adversity and hopeless sorrow have completely taken away the relish for life; if the unfortunate one, strong in mind, indignant at his fate rather than desponding or dejected, wishes for death, and yet preserves his life without loving it – not from inclination or fear, but from duty – then his maxim has a moral worth.

To be beneficent when we can is a duty; and besides this, there are many minds so sympathetically constituted that, without any other motive of vanity or self-interest, they find a pleasure in spreading joy around them, and can take delight in the satisfaction of others so far as it is their own work. But I maintain that in such a case an action of this kind, however proper, however amiable it may be, has nevertheless no true moral worth, but is on a level with other inclinations, e.g. the inclination to honor, which, if it is happily directed to that which is in fact of public utility and accordant with duty, and consequently honorable, deserves praise and encouragement, but not esteem. For the maxim lacks the moral import, namely, that such actions be done *from duty*, not from inclination. Put the case that the mind of that philanthropist was clouded by sorrow of his own, extinguishing all sympathy with the lot of others, and that while he still has the power to benefit others in distress, he is not touched by their trouble because he is absorbed with his own; and now suppose that he tears himself out of this dead insensibility, and performs the action without any inclination to it, but simply from duty, then first has his action its genuine moral worth. Further still; if nature has put little sympathy in the heart of this or that man; if he, supposed to be an upright man, is by temperament cold and indifferent to the sufferings of others, perhaps because in respect of his own he is provided with the special gift of patience and fortitude, and supposes, or even requires, that others should have the same – and such a man would certainly not be the meanest product of nature – but if nature had not specially framed him for a philanthropist, would he not still find in himself a source from whence to give himself a far higher worth than that of a good-natured temperament could be? Unquestionably. It is just in this that the moral worth of the character is brought out which is incomparably the highest of all, namely, that he is beneficent, not from inclination, but from duty.

To secure one's own happiness is a duty, at least indirectly; for discontent with one's condition, under a pressure of many anxieties and amidst unsatisfied wants, might easily become a great *temptation to transgression of duty*. But here again, without looking to duty, all men have already the strongest and most intimate inclination to happiness, because it is just in this idea that all inclinations are combined in one total. But the precept of happiness is often of such a sort that it greatly interferes with some inclinations, and yet a man cannot form any definite and certain conception of the sum of satisfaction of all of them which is called happiness. It is not then to be wondered at that a single inclination, definite both as to what it promises and as to the time within which it can be gratified, is often able to overcome such a fluctuating idea, and that a gouty patient, for instance, can choose to enjoy what he likes, and to suffer what he may, since, according to his calculation, on this occasion at least, he has [only] not sacrificed the enjoyment of the present moment to a possible mistaken expectation of a happiness which is supposed to be found in health. But even in this case, if the general desire for happiness did not influence his will, and supposing that in his particular case health was not a necessary element in this calculation, there yet remains in this, as in all other cases, this law, namely, that he would promote

his happiness not from inclination but from duty, and by this would his conduct first acquire true moral worth.

It is in this manner, undoubtedly, that we are to understand those passages of Scripture also in which we are commanded to love our neighbor, even our enemy. For love, as an affection, cannot be commanded, but beneficence for duty's sake may; even though we are not impelled to it by any inclination – nay, are even repelled by a natural and unconquerable aversion. This is *practical* love, and not *pathological* – a love which is seated in the will, and not in the propensions of sense – in principles of action and not of tender sympathy; and it is this love alone which can be commanded.

The second[1] proposition is: That an action done from duty derives its moral worth, *not from the purpose* which is to be attained by it, but from the maxim by which it is determined, and therefore does not depend on the realization of the object of the action, but merely on the *principle of volition* by which the action has taken place, without regard to any object of desire. It is clear from what precedes that the purposes which we may have in view in our actions, or their effects regarded as ends and springs of the will, cannot give to actions any unconditional or moral worth. In what, then, can their worth lie, if it is not to consist in the will and in reference to its expected effect? It cannot lie anywhere but in the *principle of the will* without regard to the ends which can be attained by the action. For the will stands between its a priori principle, which is formal, and its a posteriori spring, which is material, as between two roads, and as it must be determined by something, it follows that it must be determined by the formal principle of volition when an action is done from duty, in which case every material principle has been withdrawn from it.

The third proposition, which is a consequence of the two preceding, I would express thus: *Duty is the necessity of acting from respect for the law.* I may have *inclination* for an object as the effect of my proposed action, but I cannot have respect for it, just for this reason, that it is an effect and not an energy of will. Similarly, I cannot have respect for inclination, whether my own or another's; I can at most, if my own, approve it; if another's, sometimes even love it; i.e. look on it as favorable to my own interest. It is only what is connected with my will as a principle, by no means as an effect – what does not subserve my inclination, but overpowers it, or at least in case of choice excludes it from its calculation – in other words, simply the law of itself, which can be an object of respect, and hence a command. Now an action done from duty must wholly exclude the influence of inclination, and with it every object of the will, so that nothing remains which can determine the will except objectively the *law*, and subjectively *pure respect* for this practical law, and consequently the maxim[2] that I should follow this law even to the thwarting of all my inclinations.

Thus the moral worth of an action does not lie in the effect expected from it, nor in any principle of action which requires to borrow its motive from this expected effect. For all these effects – agreeableness of one's condition, and even the promotion of the happiness of others – could have been also brought about by other causes, so that for this there would have been no need of the will of a rational being; whereas it is in this alone that the supreme and unconditional good can be found. The pre-eminent good which we call moral can therefore consist in nothing else than *the conception of law* in itself, *which certainly is only possible in a rational being*, so far as this conception, and not the expected effect, determines the will. This is a good which is already present in the person who acts accordingly, and we have not to wait for it to appear first in the result.[3] . . .

Transition from Popular Moral Philosophy to the Metaphysic of Morals

. . . Everything in nature works according to laws. Rational beings alone have the faculty of acting according *to the conception* of laws, that is according to principles, i.e. have a *will*. Since the deduction of actions from principles requires *reason*, the will is nothing but practical reason. If reason infallibly determines the will, then the actions of such a being which are recognized as objectively necessary are subjectively necessary also, i.e. the will is a faculty to choose *that only* which reason independent of inclination recognizes as practically necessary, i.e. as good. But if reason of itself does not sufficiently determine the will, if the latter is subject also to subjective conditions (particular impulses) which do not always coincide with the objective conditions; in a word, if the will does not *in itself* completely accord with reason (which is actually the case with men), then the actions which objectively are recognized as necessary are subjectively contingent, and the determination of such a will according to objective laws is *obligation*, that is to say, the relation of the objective laws to a will that is not thoroughly good is conceived as the determination of the will of a rational being by principles of reason, but which the will from its nature does not of necessity follow.

The conception of an objective principle, in so far as it is obligatory for a will, is called a command (of reason), and the formula of the command is called an Imperative.

All imperatives are expressed by the word *ought* [or *shall*], and thereby indicate the relation of an objective law of reason to a will, which from its subjective constitution is not necessarily determined by it (an obligation). They say that something would be good to do or to forbear, but they say it to a will which does not always do a thing because it is conceived to be good to do it. That is practically *good*, however, which determines the will by means of the conceptions of reason, and consequently not from subjective causes, but objectively, that is on principles which are valid for every rational being as such. It is distinguished from the *pleasant*, as that which influences the will only by means of sensation from merely subjective causes, valid only for the sense of this or that one, and not as a principle of reason, which holds for every one.[4]

A perfectly good will would therefore be equally subject to objective laws (viz. laws of good), but could not be conceived as *obliged* thereby to act lawfully, because of itself from its subjective constitution it can only be determined by the conception of good. Therefore no imperatives hold for the Divine will, or in general for a *holy* will; *ought* is here out of place, because the volition is already of itself necessarily in unison with the law. Therefore imperatives are only formulae to express the relation of objective laws of all volition to the subjective imperfection of the will of this or that rational being, e.g. the human will.

Now all *imperatives* command either *hypothetically* or *categorically*. The former represent the practical necessity of a possible action as means to something else that is willed (or at least which one might possibly will). The categorical imperative would be that which represented an action as necessary of itself without reference to another end, i.e. as objectively necessary.

Since every practical law represents a possible action as good, and on this account, for a subject who is practically determinable by reason, necessary, all imperatives are formulae determining an action which is necessary according to the principle of a will good in some respects. If now the action is good only as a means *to something else*, then the imperative is *hypothetical*; if it is conceived as good *in itself* and consequently as being necessarily the principle of a will which of itself conforms to reason, then it is *categorical*.

Thus the imperative declares what action possible by me would be good, and presents the practical rule in relation to a will which does not forthwith perform an action simply because it is good, whether because the subject does not always know that it is good, or because, even if it know this, yet its maxims might be opposed to the objective principles of practical reason.

Accordingly the hypothetical imperative only says that the action is good for some purpose, *possible* or *actual*. In the first case it is a Problematical, in the second an Assertorial practical principle. The categorical imperative which declares an action to be objectively necessary in itself without reference to any purpose, i.e. without any other end, is valid as an Apodictic (practical) principle.

Whatever is possible only by the power of some rational being may also be conceived as a possible purpose of some will; and therefore the principles of action as regards the means necessary to attain some possible purpose are in fact infinitely numerous. All sciences have a practical part, consisting of problems expressing that some end is possible for us, and of imperatives directing how it may be attained. These may, therefore, be called in general imperatives of Skill. Here there is no question whether the end is rational and good, but only what one must do in order to attain it. The precepts for the physician to make his patient thoroughly healthy, and for a poisoner to ensure certain death, are of equal value in this respect, that each serves to effect its purpose perfectly. Since in early youth it cannot be known what ends are likely to occur to us in the course of life, parents seek to have their children taught a *great many things*, and provide for their *skill* in the use of means for all sorts of arbitrary ends, of none of which can they determine whether it may not perhaps hereafter be an object to their pupil, but which it is at all events *possible* that he might aim at; and this anxiety is so great that they commonly neglect to form and correct their judgment on the value of the things which may be chosen as ends.

There is *one* end, however, which may be assumed to be actually such to all rational beings (so far as imperatives apply to them, viz. as dependent beings), and, therefore, one purpose which they not merely *may* have, but which we may with certainty assume that they all actually *have* by a natural necessity, and this is *happiness*. The hypothetical imperative which expresses the practical necessity of an action as means to the advancement of happiness is Assertorial. We are not to present it as necessary for an uncertain and merely possible purpose, but for a purpose which we may presuppose with certainty and a priori in every man, because it belongs to his being. Now skill in the choice of means to his own greatest wellbeing may be called *prudence* [5] in the narrowest sense. And thus the imperative which refers to the choice of means to one's own happiness, i.e. the precept of prudence, is still always *hypothetical*; the action is not commanded absolutely, but only as means to another purpose.

Finally, there is an imperative which commands a certain conduct immediately, without having as its condition any other purpose to be attained by it. This imperative is Categorical. It concerns not the matter of the action, or its intended result, but its form and the principle of which it is itself a result; and what is essentially good in it consists in the mental disposition, let the consequence be what it may. This imperative may be called that of Morality.

There is a marked distinction also between the volitions on these three sorts of principles in the *dissimilarity* of the obligation of the will. In order to mark this difference more clearly, I think they would be most suitably named in their order if we said they are either *rules* of skill, or *counsels* of prudence, or *commands* (*laws*) of morality. For it is *law* only that involves the conception of an *unconditional* and objective necessity, which is consequently universally valid; and commands are laws which must be obeyed, that is, must be followed, even in opposition to inclination. *Counsels*, indeed, involve necessity, but one which can only hold under a contingent subjective condition, viz. they depend on whether this or that man reckons this or that as part of his happiness; the categorical imperative, on the contrary, is not limited by any condition, and as being absolutely, although practically, necessary, may be quite properly called a command. We might also call the first kind of imperatives *technical* (belonging to art), the second *pragmatic* [6] (to welfare), the third *moral* (belonging to free conduct generally, that is, to morals).

Now arises the question, how are all these imperatives possible? This question does not seek to know how we can conceive the accomplishment of the action which the imperative ordains, but merely how we can conceive the obligation of the will which the imperative expresses. No special explanation is needed to show how an imperative of skill is possible. Whoever wills the end, wills also (so far as reason decides his conduct) the means in his power which are indispensably necessary thereto. This proposition is, as regards the volition, analytical for, in willing an object as my effect, there is already thought the causality of myself as an acting cause, that is to say, the use of the means; and the imperative educes from the conception of volition of an end the conception of actions necessary to this end.

Synthetical propositions must no doubt be employed in defining the means to a proposed end; but they do not concern the principle, the act of the will, but the object and its realization. E.g., that in order to bisect a line on an unerring principle I must draw from its extremities two intersecting arcs; this no doubt is taught by mathematics only in synthetical propositions; but if I know that it is only by this process that the intended operation can be performed, then to say that if I fully will the operation, I also will the action required for it, is an analytical proposition; for it is one and the same thing to conceive something as an effect which I can produce in a certain way, and to conceive myself as acting in this way.

If it were only equally easy to give a definite conception of happiness, the imperatives of prudence would correspond exactly with those of skill, and would likewise be analytical. For in this case as in that, it could be said, whoever wills the end, wills also (according to the dictate of reason necessarily) the indispensable means thereto which are in his power. But, unfortunately, the notion of happiness is so indefinite that although every man wishes to attain it, yet he never can say definitely and consistently what it is that he really wishes and wills. The reason of this is that all the elements which belong to the notion of happiness are altogether empirical, i.e. they must be borrowed from experience, and nevertheless the idea of happiness requires an absolute whole, a maximum of welfare in my present and all future circumstances. Now it is impossible that the most clear-sighted and at the same time most powerful being (supposed finite) should frame to himself a definite conception of what he really wills in this. Does he will riches, how much anxiety, envy, and snares might he not thereby draw upon his shoulders? Does he will knowledge and discernment, perhaps it might prove to be only an eye so much the sharper to show him so much the more fearfully the evils that are now concealed from him, and that cannot be avoided, or to impose more wants on his desires, which already give him concern enough. Would he have long life? Who guarantees to him that it would not be a long misery? Would he at least have health? How often has uneasiness of the body restrained from excesses into which perfect health would have allowed one to fall? And so on. In short, he is unable, on any principle, to determine with certainty what would make him truly happy; because to do so he would need to be omniscient. We cannot therefore act on any definite principles to secure happiness, but only on empirical counsels, e.g. of regimen, frugality, courtesy, reserve, etc., which experience teaches do, on the average, most promote well-being. Hence it follows that the imperatives of prudence do not, strictly speaking, command at all, that is, they cannot present actions objectively as practically *necessary;* that they are rather to be regarded as counsels (*consilia*) than precepts (*praecepta*) of reason, that the problem to determine certainly and universally what action would promote the happiness of a rational being is completely insoluble, and consequently no imperative respecting it is possible which should, in the strict sense, command to do what makes happy; because happiness is not an ideal of reason but of imagination, resting solely on empirical grounds, and it is vain to expect that these should define an action by which one could attain the totality of a series of consequences which is really endless. This imperative of prudence would, however, be an analytical proposition if we assume that the means to happiness could be certainly assigned; for it is distinguished from the imperative of skill only by this, that in the latter the end is merely possible, in the former it is given; as, however, both only ordain the means to that which we suppose to be willed as an end, it follows that the imperative which ordains the willing of the means to him who wills the end is in both cases analytical. Thus there is no difficulty in regard to the possibility of an imperative of this kind either.

On the other hand, the question, how the imperative of *morality* is possible, is undoubtedly one, the only one, demanding a solution, as this is not at all hypothetical, and the objective necessity which it presents cannot rest on any hypothesis, as is the case with the hypothetical imperatives. Only here we must never leave out of consideration that we *cannot* make out *by any*

example, in other words empirically, whether there is such an imperative at all; but it is rather to be feared that all those which seem to be categorical may yet be at bottom hypothetical. For instance, when the precept is: Thou shalt not promise deceitfully; and it is assumed that the necessity of this is not a mere counsel to avoid some other evil, so that it should mean: Thou shalt not make a lying promise, lest if it become known thou shouldst destroy thy credit, but that an action of this kind must be regarded as evil in itself, so that the imperative of the prohibition is categorical; then we cannot show with certainty in any example that the will was determined merely by the law, without any other spring of action, although it may appear to be so. For it is always possible that fear of disgrace, perhaps also obscure dread of other dangers, may have a secret influence on the will. Who can prove by experience the non-existence of a cause when all that experience tells us is that we do not perceive it? But in such a case the so-called moral imperative, which as such appears to be categorical and unconditional, would in reality be only a pragmatic precept, drawing our attention to our own interests, and merely teaching us to take these into consideration.

We shall therefore have to investigate a priori the possibility of a categorical imperative, as we have not in this case the advantage of its reality being given in experience, so that [the elucidation of] its possibility should be requisite only for its explanation, not for its establishment. In the meantime it may be discerned beforehand that the categorical imperative alone has the purport of a practical law: all the rest may indeed be called *principles* of the will but not laws, since whatever is only necessary for the attainment of some arbitrary purpose may be considered as in itself contingent, and we can at any time be free from the precept if we give up the purpose: on the contrary, the unconditional command leaves the will no liberty to choose the opposite; consequently it alone carries with it that necessity which we require in a law.

Secondly, in the case of this categorical imperative or law of morality, the difficulty (of discerning its possibility) is a very profound one. It is an a priori synthetical practical proposition;[7] and as there is so much difficulty in discerning the possibility of speculative propositions of this kind, it may readily be supposed that the difficulty will be no less with the practical.

In this problem we will first inquire whether the mere conception of a categorical imperative may not perhaps supply us also with the formula of it, containing the proposition which alone can be a categorical imperative; for even if we know the tenor of such an absolute command, yet how it is possible will require further special and laborious study, which we postpone to the last section.

When I conceive a hypothetical imperative, in general I do not know beforehand what it will contain until I am given the condition. But when I conceive a categorical imperative, I know at once what it contains. For as the imperative contains besides the law only the necessity that the maxims[8] shall conform to this law, while the law contains no conditions restricting it, there remains nothing but the general statement that the maxim of the action should conform to a universal law, and it is this conformity alone that the imperative properly represents as necessary.

There is therefore but one categorical imperative, namely, this: *Act only on that maxim whereby thou canst at the same time will that it should become a universal law*.

Now if all imperatives of duty can be deduced from this one imperative as from their principle, then, although it should remain undecided whether what is called duty is not merely a vain notion, yet at least we shall be able to show what we understand by it and what this notion means.

Since the universality of the law according to which effects are produced constitutes what is properly called *nature* in the most general sense (as to form), that is the existence of things so far as it is determined by general laws, the imperative of duty may be expressed thus: *Act as if the maxim of the action were to become by thy will a universal law of nature*.

We will now enumerate a few duties, adopting the usual division of them into duties to ourselves and to others, and into perfect and imperfect duties.[9]

1. A man reduced to despair by a series of misfortunes feels wearied of life, but is still so far in possession of his reason that he can ask himself whether it would not be contrary to his duty to himself to take his own life. Now he inquires whether the maxim of his actions could become a universal law of nature. His maxim is: From self-love I adopt it as a principle to shorten my life when its longer duration is likely to bring more evil than satisfaction. It is asked then simply whether this principle founded on self-love can become a univesal law of nature. Now we see at once that a system of nature of which it should be a law to destroy life by means of the very feeling whose special nature it is to impel to the improvement of life would contradict itself, and therefore could not exist as a system of nature; hence that maxim cannot possibly exist as a universal law of nature, and consequently would be wholly inconsistent with the supreme principle of all duty.

2. Another finds himself forced by necessity to borrow money. He knows that he will not be able to repay it, but sees also that nothing will be lent to him, unless he promises stoutly to repay it in a definite time. He desires to make this promise, but he has still so much conscience as to ask himself: Is it not unlawful and inconsistent with duty to get out of a difficulty in this way? Suppose, however, that he resolves to do so, then the maxim of his action would be expressed thus: When I think myself in want of money, I will borrow money and promise to repay it, although I know that I never can do so. Now this principle of self-love or of one's own advantage may perhaps be consistent with my whole future welfare; but the question now is, Is it right? I change then the suggestion of self-love into a universal law, and state the question thus: How would it be if my maxim were a universal law? Then I see at once that it could never hold as a universal law of nature, but would necessarily contradict itself. For supposing it to be a universal law that everyone when he thinks himself in a diffi-

culty should be able to promise whatever he pleases, with the purpose of not keeping his promise, the promise itself would become impossible, as well as the end that one might have in view in it, since no one would consider that anything was promised to him, but would ridicule all such statements as vain pretenses.

3. A third finds in himself a talent which with the help of some culture might make him a useful man in many respects. But he finds himself in comfortable circumstances, and prefers to indulge in pleasure rather than to take pains in enlarging and improving his happy natural capacities. He asks, however, whether his maxim of neglect of his natural gifts, besides agreeing with his inclination to indulgence, agrees also with what is called duty. He sees then that a system of nature could indeed subsist with such a universal law although men (like the South Sea Islanders) should let their talents rest, and resolve to devote their lives merely to idleness, amusement, and propagation of their species – in a word, to enjoyment; but he cannot possibly *will* that this should be a universal law of nature, or be implanted in us as such by a natural instinct. For, as a rational being, he necessarily wills that his faculties be developed, since they serve him, and have been given him, for all sorts of possible purposes.

4. A fourth, who is in prosperity, while he sees that others have to contend with great wretchedness and that he could help them, thinks: What concern is it of mine? Let everyone be as happy as Heaven pleases, or as he can make himself; I will take nothing from him nor even envy him, only I do not wish to contribute anything to his welfare or to his assistance in distress! Now no doubt if such a mode of thinking were a universal law, the human race might very well subsist, and doubtless even better than in a state in which everyone talks of sympathy and goodwill, or even takes care occasionally to put it into practice, but, on the other side, also cheats when he can, betrays the rights of men, or

otherwise violates them. But although it is possible that a universal law of nature might exist in accordance with that maxim, it is impossible to *will* that such a principle should have the universal validity of a law of nature. For a will which resolved this would contradict itself, inasmuch as many cases might occur in which one would have need of the love and sympathy of others, and in which, by such a law of nature, sprung from his own will, he would deprive himself of all hope of the aid he desires.

These are a few of the many actual duties, or at least what we regard as such, which obviously fall into two classes on the one principle that we have laid down. We must be *able to will* that a maxim of our action should be a universal law. This is the canon of the moral appreciation of the action generally. Some actions are of such a character that their maxim cannot without contradiction be even *conceived* as a universal law of nature, far from it being possible that we should *will* that it *should* be so. In others this intrinsic impossibility is not found, but still it is impossible to *will* that their maxim should be raised to the universality of a law of nature, since such a will would contradict itself. It is easily seen that the former violate strict or rigorous (inflexible) duty; the latter only laxer (meritorious) duty. Thus it has been completely shown by these examples how all duties depend as regards the nature of the obligation (not the object of the action) on the same principle.

If now we attend to ourselves on occasion of any transgression of duty, we shall find that we in fact do not will that our maxim should be a universal law, for that is impossible for us; on the contrary, we will that the opposite should remain a universal law, only we assume the liberty of making an *exception* in our own favor or (just for this time only) in favor of our inclination. Consequently if we considered all cases from one and the same point of view, namely, that of reason, we should find a contradiction in our own will, namely, that a certain principle should be objectively necessary as a universal law, and yet subjectively should not be universal, but admit of exceptions. As, however, we at one moment regard our action from the point of view of a will wholly conformed to reason, and then again look at the same action from the point of view of a will affected by inclination, there is not really any contradiction, but an antagonism of inclination to the precept of reason, whereby the universality of the principle is changed into a mere generality, so that the practical principle of reason shall meet the maxim half way. Now, although this cannot be justified in our own impartial judgment, yet it proves that we do really recognize the validity of the categorical imperative and (with all respect for it) only allow ourselves a few exceptions, which we think unimportant and forced from us. . . .

Supposing, however, that there were something *whose existence* has *in itself* an absolute worth, something which, being *an end in itself*, could be a source of definite laws, then in this and this alone would lie the source of a possible categorical imperative, i.e. a practical law.

Now I say: man and generally any rational being *exists* as an end in himself, *not merely as a means* to be arbitrarily used by this or that will, but in all his actions, whether they concern himself or other rational beings, must be always regarded at the same time as an end. All objects of the inclinations have only a conditional worth; for if the inclinations and the wants founded on them did not exist, then their object would be without value. But the inclinations themselves being sources of want are so far from having an absolute worth for which they should be desired, that, on the contrary, it must be the universal wish of every rational being to be wholly free from them. Thus the worth of any object which is *to be acquired* by our action is always conditional. Beings whose existence depends not on our will but on nature's, have nevertheless, if they are rational beings, only a relative value as means, and are therefore called things; rational beings, on the contrary, are called *persons*, because their very nature points them out as ends in themselves, that is as something which must not be used merely as means, and so far therefore restricts freedom of action (and is an object of respect). These, therefore, are not merely subjective

ends whose existence has a worth *for us* as an effect of our action, but *objective ends*, that is things whose existence is an end in itself: an end moreover for which no other can be substituted, which they should subserve *merely* as means, for otherwise nothing whatever would possess *absolute worth*; but if all worth were conditioned and therefore contingent, then there would be no supreme practical principle of reason whatever.

If then there is a supreme practical principle or, in respect of the human will, a categorical imperative, it must be one which, being drawn from the conception of that which is necessarily an end for everyone because it is *an end in itself*, constitutes an *objective* principle of will, and can therefore serve as a universal practical law. The foundation of this principle is: *rational nature exists as an end in itself*. Man necessarily conceives his own existence as being so: so far then this is a *subjective* principle of human actions. But every other rational being regards its existence similarly, just on the same rational principle that holds for me: so that it is at the same time an objective principle, from which as a supreme practical law all laws of the will must be capable of being deduced. Accordingly the practical imperative will be as follows: *So act as to treat humanity whether in thine own person or in that of any other, in every case as an end withal, never as means only*. We will now inquire whether this can be practically carried out.

To abide by the previous examples:

Firstly, under the head of necessary duty to oneself: He who contemplates suicide should ask himself whether his action can be consistent with the idea of humanity *as an end in itself*. If he destroys himself in order to escape from painful circumstances, he uses a person merely as *a mean* to maintain a tolerable condition up to the end of life. But a man is not a thing, that is to say, something which can be used merely as means, but must in all his actions be always considered as an end in himself. I cannot, therefore, dispose in any way of a man in my own person so as to mutilate, to damage or kill him. It belongs to ethics proper to define this principle more precisely, so as to avoid all misunderstanding, e.g. as to the amputation of the limbs in order to preserve myself; as to exposing my life to danger with a view to preserve it, etc. This question is therefore omitted here.)

Secondly, as regards necessary duties, or those of strict obligation, toward others; he who is thinking of making a lying promise to others will see at once that he would be using another man *merely as a mean*, without the latter containing at the same time the end in himself. For he whom I propose by such a promise to use for my own purposes cannot possibly assent to my mode of acting toward him, and therefore cannot himself contain the end of this action. This violation of the principle of humanity in other men is more obvious if we take in examples of attacks on the freedom and property of others. For then it is clear that he who transgresses the rights of men intends to use the person of others merely as means, without considering that as rational beings they ought always to be esteemed also as ends, that is, as beings who must be capable of containing in themselves the end of the very same action.

Thirdly, as regards contingent (meritorious) duties to oneself; it is not enough that the action does not violate humanity in our own person as an end in itself, it must also *harmonize with* it. Now there are in humanity capacities of greater perfection which belong to the end that nature has in view in regard to humanity in ourselves as the subject: to neglect these might perhaps be consistent with the *maintenance* of humanity as an end in itself, but not with the *advancement* of this end.

Fourthly, as regards meritorious duties toward others: the natural end which all men have is their own happiness. Now humanity might indeed subsist, although no one should contribute anything to the happiness of others, provided he did not intentionally withdraw anything from it; but after all, this would only harmonize negatively, not positively, with *humanity as an end in itself*, if everyone does not also endeavor, as far as in him lies, to forward the ends of others. For the ends of any subject which is an end in himself, ought as far as possible to be *my* ends also, if that conception is to have its *full* effect with me. . . .

Looking back now on all previous attempts to discover the principle of morality, we need not wonder why they all failed. It was seen that man was bound to laws by duty, but it was not observed that the laws to which he is subject are *only those of his own giving*, though at the same time they are *universal*. And that he is only bound to act in conformity with his own will; a will, however, which is designed by nature to give universal laws. For when one has conceived man only as subject to a law (no matter what), then this law required some interest, either by way of attraction or constraint, since it did not originate as a law from *his own* will, but this will was according to a law obliged by *something else* to act in a certain manner. Now by this necessary consequence all the labor spent in finding a supreme principle of *duty* was irrevocably lost. For men never elicited duty, but only a necessity of acting from a certain interest. Whether this interest was private or otherwise, in any case the imperative must be conditional, and could not by any means be capable of being a moral command. I will therefore call this the principle of *Autonomy* of the will, in contrast with every other which I accordingly reckon as *Heteronomy*.

The conception of every rational being as one which must consider itself as giving in all the maxims of its will universal laws, so as to judge itself and its actions from this point of view – this conception leads to another which depends on it and is very fruitful, namely, that of a *kingdom of ends*.

By a *kingdom* I understand the union of different rational beings in a system by common laws. Now since it is by laws that ends are determined as regards their universal validity, hence, if we abstract from the personal differences of rational beings, and likewise from all the content of their private ends, we shall be able to conceive all ends combined in a systematic whole (including both rational beings as ends in themselves, and also the special ends which each may propose to himself), that is to say, we can conceive a kingdom of ends, which on the preceding principles is possible.

For all rational beings come under the *law* that each of them must treat itself and all others *never merely as means*, but in every case *at the same time as ends in themselves.* Hence results a systematic union of rational beings by common objective laws, i.e. a kingdom which may be called a kingdom of ends, since what these laws have in view is just the relation of these beings to one another as ends and means. It is certainly only an ideal.

A rational being belongs as a *member* to the kingdom of ends when, although giving universal laws in it, he is also himself subject to these laws. He belongs to it *as sovereign* when, while giving laws, he is not subject to the will of any other.

A rational being must always regard himself as giving laws either as member or as sovereign in a kingdom of ends which is rendered possible by the freedom of will. He cannot, however, maintain the latter position merely by the maxims of his will, but only in case he is a completely independent being without wants and with unrestricted power adequate to his will. . . .

We can now end where we started at the beginning, namely, with the conception of a will unconditionally good. *That will* is *absolutely good* which cannot be evil – in other words, whose maxim, if made a universal law, could never contradict itself. This principle, then, is its supreme law: Act always on such a maxim as thou canst at the same time will to be a universal law; this is the sole condition under which a will can never contradict itself; and such an imperative is categorical. Since the validity of the will as a universal law for possible actions is analogous to the universal connection of the existence of things by general laws, which is the formal notion of nature in general, the categorical imperative can also be expressed thus; *Act on maxims which can at the same time have for their object themselves as universal laws of nature.* Such then is the formula of an absolutely good will.

Rational nature is distinguished from the rest of nature by this, that it sets before itself an end. This end would be the matter of every good will. But since in the idea of a will that is absolutely good without being limited by any condition (of attaining this or that end) we must abstract wholly from every end *to be effected* (since this would make every will only relatively good), it follows

that in this case the end must be conceived, not as an end to be effected, but as an *independently* existing end. Consequently it is conceived only negatively, i.e. as that which we must never act against, and which, therefore, must never be regarded merely as means, but must in every volition be esteemed as an end likewise. Now this end can be nothing but the subject of all possible ends, since this is also the subject of a possible absolutely good will; for such a will cannot without contradiction be postponed to any other object. This principle: So act in regard to every rational being (thyself and others), that he may always have place in thy maxim as an end in himself, is accordingly essentially identical with this other; Act upon a maxim which, at the same time, involves its own universal validity for every rational being. For that in using means for every end I should limit my maxim by the condition of its holding good as a law for every subject, this comes to the same thing as that the fundamental principle of all maxims of action must be that the subject of all ends, i.e. the rational being himself, be never employed merely as means, but as the supreme condition restricting the use of all means, that is in every case as an end likewise.

It follows incontestably that, to whatever laws any rational being may be subject, he being an end in himself must be able to regard himself as also legislating universally in respect of these same laws, since it is just this fitness of his maxims for universal legislation that distinguishes him as an end in himself; also it follows that this implies his dignity (prerogative) above all mere physical beings, that he must always take his maxims from the point of view which regards himself, and likewise every other rational being, as lawgiving beings (on which account they are called persons). In this way a world of rational beings (*mundus intelligibilis*) is possible as a kingdom of ends, and this by virtue of the legislation proper to all persons as members. Therefore every rational being must so act as if he were by his maxims in every case a legislating member in the universal kingdom of ends. The formal principle of these maxims is: So act as if thy maxim were to serve likewise as the universal law (of all rational beings). A kingdom of ends is thus only possible on the analogy of a kingdom of nature, the former, however, only by maxims, that is self-imposed rules, the latter only by the laws of efficient causes acting under necessitation from without. Nevertheless, although the system of nature is looked upon as a machine, yet so far as it has reference to rational beings as its ends, it is given on this account the name of a kingdom of nature. Now such a kingdom of ends would be actually realized by means of maxims conforming to the canon which the categorical imperative prescribes to all rational beings, *if they were universally followed*. But although a rational being, even if he punctually follows this maxim himself, cannot reckon upon all others being therefore true to the same, nor expect that the kingdom of nature and its orderly arrangements shall be in harmony with him as a fitting member, so as to form a kingdom of ends to which he himself contributes, that is to say, that it shall favor his expectation of happiness, still that law: Act according to the maxims of a member of a merely possible kingdom of ends legislating in it universally, remains in its full force, inasmuch as it commands categorically. And it is just in this that the paradox lies; that the mere dignity of man as a rational creature, without any other end or advantage to be attained thereby, in other words, respect for a mere idea, should yet serve as an inflexible precept of the will, and that it is precisely in this independence of the maxim on all such springs of action that its sublimity consists; and it is this that makes every rational subject worthy to be a legislative member in the kingdom of ends: for otherwise he would have to be conceived only as subject to the physical law of his wants. And although we should suppose the kingdom of nature and the kingdom of ends to be united under one sovereign, so that the latter kingdom thereby ceased to be a mere idea and acquired true reality, then it would no doubt gain the accession of a strong spring, but by no means any increase of its intrinsic worth. For this sole absolute lawgiver must, notwithstanding this, be always conceived as estimating the worth of rational beings only by their disinterested behavior, as prescribed to themselves

from that idea [the dignity of man] alone. The essence of things is not altered by their external relations, and that which, abstracting from these, alone constitutes the absolute worth of man, is also that by which he must be judged, whoever the judge may be, and even by the Supreme Being. *Morality*, then, is the relation of actions to the autonomy of the will, that is, to the potential universal legislation by its maxims. An action that is consistent with the autonomy of thewill is *permitted*; one that does not agree therewith is *forbidden*. A will whose maxims necessarily coincide with the laws of autonomy is a *holy* will, good absolutely. The dependence of a will not absolutely good on the principle of autonomy (moral necessitation) is obligation. This, then, cannot be applied to a holy being. The objective necessity of actions from obligation is called *duty*.

From what has just been said, it is easy to see how it happens that although the conception of duty implies subjection to the law, we yet ascribe a certain *dignity* and sublimity to the person who fulfills all his duties. There is not, indeed, any sublimity in him, so far as he is *subject* to the moral law; but inasmuch as in regard to that very law he is likewise a *legislator*, and on that account alone subject to it, he has sublimity. We have also shown above that neither fear nor inclination, but simply respect for the law, is the spring which can give actions a moral worth. Our own will, so far as we suppose it to act only under the condition that its maxims are potentially universal laws, this ideal will which is possible to us is the proper object of respect; and the dignity of humanity consists just in this capacity of being universally legislative, though with the condition that it is itself subject to this same legislation.

Notes

1   The first proposition was that to have moral worth an action must be done from duty.
2   A *maxim* is the subjective principle of volition. The objective principle (i.e. that which would also serve subjectively as a practical principle to all rational beings if reason had full power over the faculty of desire) is the practical *law*.
3   It might be here objected to me that I take refuge

behind the word *respect* in an obscure feeling, instead of giving a distinct solution of the question by a concept of the reason. But although respect is a feeling, it is not a feeling *received* through influence, but is *self-wrought* by a rational concept, and, therefore, is specifically distinct from all feelings of the former kind, which may be referred either to inclination or fear. What I recognize immediately as a law for me, I recognize with respect. This merely signifies the consciousness that my will is *subordinate* to a law, without the intervention of other influences on my sense. The immediate determination of the will by the law, and the consciousness of this, is called *respect*, so that this is regarded as an *effect* of the law on the subject, and not as the *cause* of it. Respect is properly the conception of a worth which thwarts my self-love. Accordingly it is something which is considered neither as an object of inclination nor of fear, although it has something analogous to both. The *object* of respect is the *law* only, and that, the law which we impose on *ourselves*, and yet recognize as necessary in itself. As a law, we are subjected to it without consulting self-love; as imposed by us on ourselves, it is a result of our will. In the former aspect it has an analogy to fear, in the latter to inclination. Respect for a person is properly only respect for the law (of honesty, etc.) of which he gives us an example. Since we also look on the improvement of our talents as a duty, we consider that we see in a person of talents, as it were, the *example of a law* (viz. to become like him in this by exercise), and this constitutes our respect. All so-called moral *interest* consists simply in *respect* for the law.

4 The dependence of the desires on sensations is called inclination, and this accordingly always indicates a *want*. The dependence of a contingently determinable will on principles of reason is called an *interest*. This, therefore, is found only in the case of a dependent will which does not always of itself conform to reason; in the Divine will we cannot conceive any interest. But the human will can also *take an interest* in a thing without therefore acting *from interest*. The former signifies the *practical* interest in the action, the latter the *pathological* in the object of the action. The former indicates only dependence of the will on principles of reason in themselves; the second, dependence on principles of reason for the sake of inclination, reason supplying only the practical rules how the requirement of the inclination may be satisfied. In the first case the action interests me; in the second the object of the action (because it is pleasant to me). We have seen in the first section that in an action done from duty we must look not to the interest in the object, but only to that in the action itself, and in its rational principle (viz. the law).

5 The word *prudence* is taken in two senses: in the one it may bear the name of knowledge of the world, in the other that of private prudence. The former is a man's ability to influence others so as to use them for his own purposes. The latter is the sagacity to combine all these purposes for his own lasting benefit. This latter is properly that to which the value even of the former is reduced, and when a man is prudent in the former sense, but not in the latter, we might better say of him that he is clever and cunning, but, on the whole, imprudent.

6 It seems to me that the proper signification of the word *pragmatic* may be most accurately defined in this way. For *sanctions* are called pragmatic which flow properly, not from the law of the states as necessary enactments, but from precaution for the general welfare. A history is composed pragmatically when it teaches prudence, i.e. instructs the world how it can provide for its interests better, or at least as well as the men of former time.

7 I connect the act with the will without presupposing any condition resulting from any inclination, but a priori, and therefore necessarily (though only objectively, i.e. assuming the idea of a reason possessing full power over all subjective motives). This is accordingly a practical proposition which does not deduce the willing of an action by mere analysis from another already presupposed (for we have not such a perfect will), but connects it immediately with the conception of the will of a rational being, as something not contained in it.

8 A maxim is a subjective principle of action, and must be distinguished from the *objective principle*, namely, practical law. The former contains the practical rule set by reason according to the conditions of the subject (often its ignorance or its inclinations), so that it is the principle on which the subject *acts*; but the law is the objective principle valid for every rational being, and is the principle on which it *ought to act* that is an imperative.

9 It must be noted here that I reserve the division of duties for a future *metaphysic of morals*, so that I give it here only as an arbitrary one (in order to arrange my examples). For the rest, I understand by a perfect duty one that admits no exception in favor of inclination, and then I have not merely external but also internal perfect duties. This is

contrary to the use of the word adopted in the schools; but I do not intend to justify it here, as it is all one for my purpose whether it is admitted or not. [*Perfect* duties are usually understood to be those which can be enforced by external law; *imperfect*, those which cannot be enforced. They are also called respectively *determinate* and *indeterminate*, *officio juris* and *officio virtutis*.]

---

20   Kantian Ethics

Fred Feldman

Sometimes our moral thinking takes a decidedly non-utilitarian turn. That is, we often seem to appeal to a principle that is inconsistent with the whole utilitarian standpoint. One case in which this occurs clearly enough is the familiar tax-cheat case. A person decides to cheat on his income tax, rationalizing his misbehavior as follows: "The government will not be injured by the absence of my tax money. After all, compared with the enormous total they take in, my share is really a negligible sum. On the other hand, I will be happier if I have the use of the money. Hence, no one will be injured by my cheating, and one person will be better off. Thus, it is better for me to cheat than it is for me to pay."

In response to this sort of reasoning, we may be inclined to say something like this: "Perhaps you are right in thinking that you will be better off if you cheat. And perhaps you are right in thinking that the government won't even know the difference. Nevertheless, your act would be wrong. For if everyone were to cheat on his income taxes, the government would soon go broke. Surely you can see that you wouldn't want others to act in the way you propose to act. So you shouldn't act in that way." While it may not be clear that this sort of response would be decisive, it should be clear that this is an example of a sort of response that is often given.

From *Introductory Ethics* (Englewood Cliffs, NJ: Prentice-Hall, 1978), pp. 97–9, 101–17. Reprinted with permission.

There are several things to notice about this response. For one, it is not based on the view that the example of the tax cheat will provoke everyone else to cheat too. If that were the point of the response, then the response might be explained on the basis of utilitarian considerations. We could understand the responder to be saying that the tax cheater has miscalculated his utilities. Whereas he thinks his act of cheating has high utility, in fact it has low utility because it will eventually result in the collapse of the government. It is important to recognize that the response presented above is not based upon any such utilitarian considerations. This can be seen by reflecting on the fact that the point could just as easily have been made in this way: "Of course, very few other people will know about your cheating, and so your behavior will not constitute an example to others. Thus, it will not provoke others to cheat. Nevertheless, your act is wrong. For if everyone were to cheat as you propose to do, then the government would collapse. Since you wouldn't want others to behave in the way you propose to behave, you should not behave in that way. It would be wrong to cheat."

Another thing to notice about the response in this case is that the responder has not simply said, "What you propose to do would be cheating; hence, it is wrong." The principle in question is not simply the principle that cheating is wrong. Rather, the responder has appealed to a much more general principle, which seems to be something like this: If you wouldn't want everyone else to act in a certain way, then you shouldn't act in that way yourself.

This sort of general principle is in fact used quite widely in our moral reasoning. If someone proposes to remove the pollution-control devices from his automobile, his friends are sure to say "What if everyone did that?" They would have in mind some dire consequences for the quality of the air, but their point would not be that the removal of the pollution-control device by one person will in fact cause others to remove theirs, and will thus eventually lead to the destruction of the environment. Their point, rather, is that if their friend would not want others to act in the way he proposes to act, then it would be wrong for him to act in that way. This principle is also used against the person who refrains from giving to charity; the person who evades the draft in time of national emergency; the person who tells a lie in order to get out of a bad spot; and even the person who walks across a patch of newly seeded grass. In all such cases, we feel that the person acts wrongly not because his actions will have bad results, but because he wouldn't want others to behave in the way he behaves.

A highly refined version of this non-utilitarian principle is the heart of the moral theory of Immanuel Kant.[1] In his *Groundwork of the Metaphysic of Morals*,[2] Kant presents, develops, and defends the thesis that something like this principle is the "supreme principle of morality." Kant's presentation is rather complex; in parts, it is very hard to follow. Part of the trouble arises from his use of a rather unfamiliar technical vocabulary. Another source of trouble is that Kant is concerned with establishing a variety of other points in this little book, and some of these involve fairly complex issues in metaphysics and epistemology. Since our aim here is simply to present a clear, concise account of Kant's basic moral doctrine, we will have to ignore quite a bit of what he says in the book.

Kant formulates his main principle in a variety of different ways. All of the members of the following set of formulations seem to have a lot in common:

I ought never to act except in such a way that my maxim should become a universal law.[3]

Act only on that maxim through which you can at the same time will that it should become a universal law![4]

Act as if the maxim of your action were to become through your will a universal law of nature.[5]

We must be able to will that a maxim of our action should become a universal law – this is the general canon for all moral judgment of action.[6]

Before we can evaluate this principle, which Kant calls the *categorical imperative*, we have to devote some attention to figuring out what it is supposed to mean. To do this, we must answer a variety of questions. What is a maxim? What is meant by "universal law"? What does Kant mean by "will"? Let us consider these questions in turn.

Maxims

In a footnote, Kant defines *maxim* as "a subjective principle of volition."[7] This definition is hardly helpful. Perhaps we can do better. First, however, a little background.

Kant apparently believes that when a person engages in genuine action, he always acts on some sort of general principle. The general principle will explain what the person takes himself to be doing and the circumstances in which he takes himself to be doing it. For example, if I need money, and can get some only by borrowing it, even though I know I won't be able to repay it, I might proceed to borrow some from a friend. My maxim in performing this act might be, "Whenever I need money and can get it by borrowing it, then I will borrow it, even if I know I won't be able to repay it."

Notice that this maxim is *general*. If I adopt it, I commit myself to behaving in the described way *whenever* I need money and the other conditions are satisfied. In this respect, the maxim serves to formulate a general principle of action rather than just some narrow reason applicable in just one case![8] So a maxim must describe some general sort of situation, and then propose some form of action for the situation. To adopt a maxim is to commit yourself to acting in the described way whenever the situation in question arises.

It seems clear that Kant holds that every action has a maxim, although he does not explicitly state this view. When we speak of an action here, we mean a concrete, particular action, or *act-token*, rather than an *act-type*. Furthermore, we must distinguish between genuine actions and what we may call "mere bodily movements." It would be absurd to maintain that a man who scratches himself in his sleep is acting on the maxim "When I itch, I shall scratch." His scratching is a mere bodily movement, and has no maxim. A man who deliberately sets out to borrow some money from a friend, on the other hand, does perform an action. And according to our interpretation of Kant, his action must have a maxim.

It would be implausible to maintain that before we act, we always consciously formulate the maxim of our action. Most of the time we simply go ahead and perform the action without giving any conscious thought to what we're doing, or what our situation is. We're usually too intent on getting the job done. Nevertheless, if we are asked after the fact, we often recognize that we actually were acting on a general policy, or maxim. For example, if you are taking a test, and you set about to answer each question correctly, you probably won't give any conscious thought to your maxim. You will be too busy thinking about the test. But if someone were to ask you to explain what you are doing and to explain the policy upon which you are doing it, you might then realize that in fact you have been acting a maxim. Your maxim may be, "Whenever I am taking an academic test, and I believe I know the correct answers, I shall give what I take to be the correct answers." So a person may act on a maxim even though she hasn't consciously entertained it.

In one respect, the maxim of action may be inaccurate: it does not so much represent the actual situation of the action as it does the situation the agent takes himself to be in. Suppose, for example, that I have a lot of money in my savings account but I have forgotten all about it. I take myself to be broke. When I go out to borrow some money from a friend, my maxim might be, "When I am broke and can get money in no other way, I shall borrow some from a friend." In this case, my maxim does not apply to my actual situation. For my actual situation is not one in which I am broke. Yet the maxim does apply to the situation I take myself to be in. For I believe that I am broke, and I believe that I can get money in no other way. So it is important to recognize that a maxim is a general policy statement that describes the sort of situation the agent takes himself to be in when he performs an action, and the sort of action he takes himself to be performing. In fact, both the situation and the action may be different from what the agent takes them to be.

Another point about maxims that should be recognized is this. Externally similar actions may in fact have radically different maxims. Here is an elaborated version of an example given by Kant that illustrates this point.[9] Suppose there are two grocers, Mr Grimbley and Mr Hughes. Mr Grimbley's main goal in life is to get rich. After careful consideration, he has decided that in the long run he'll make more money if he gains a reputation for treating his customers fairly. In other words, he believes that "honesty is the best policy – because it pays." Hence, Mr Grimbley scrupulously sees to it that every customer gets the correct change. When Mr Grimbley gives correct change to a customer, he acts on this maxim:

(M_1) When I can gain a good business reputation by giving correct change, I shall give correct change.

Mr Hughes, on the other hand, has decided that it would be morally wrong to cheat his customers. This decision has moved him to adopt the policy of always giving the correct change. He doesn't care whether his honest dealings will in the long run contribute to an increase in sales. Even if he were to discover that honesty in business dealings does not pay, he would still treat his customers honestly. So Mr Hughes apparently acts on some maxim such as this:

(M_2) When I can perform a morally right act by giving correct change, I shall give correct change.

Mr Grimbley's overt act of giving correct change to a customer looks just like Mr Hughes's overt act of giving correct change to a customer. Their customers cannot tell, no matter how closely they observe the behavior of Mr Grimbley and Mr Hughes, what their maxims are. However, as we have seen, the actions of Mr Grimbley are associated with a maxim radically different from that associated with the actions of Mr Hughes.

For our purposes, it will be useful to introduce a concept that Kant does not employ. This is the concept of the *generalized form* of a maxim. Suppose I decide to go to sleep one night and my maxim in performing this act is this:

(M_3) Whenever I am tired, I shall sleep.

My maxim is stated in such a way as to contain explicit references to me. It contains two occurrences of the word "I." The generalized form of my maxim is the principle we would get if we were to revise my maxim so as to make it applicable to everyone. Thus, the generalized form of my maxim is this:

(GM_3) Whenever anyone is tired, he will sleep.

In general, then, we can represent the form of a maxim in this way:

(M) Whenever I am ____ , I shall ____ .

Actual maxims have descriptions of situations in the first blank and descriptions of actions in the second blank. The generalized form of a maxim can be represented in this way:

(GM) Whenever anyone is ____ , she will ____ .

So much, then, for maxims. Let us turn to our second question, "What is meant by universal law?"

Universal Law

When, in the formulation of the categorical imperative, Kant speaks of "universal law," he seems to have one or the other of two things in mind. Sometimes he seems to be thinking of a *universal law of nature*, and sometimes he seems to be thinking of a *universal law of freedom*.

A *law of nature* is a fully general statement that describes not only how things are, but how things always *must* be. Consider this example: If the temperature of a gas in an enclosed container is increased, then the pressure will increase too. This statement accurately describes the behavior of gases in enclosed containers. Beyond this, however, it describes behavior that is, in a certain sense, necessary. The pressure not only *does* increase, but it *must* increase if the volume remains the same and the temperature is increased. This "must" expresses not logical or moral necessity, but "physical necessity." Thus, a law of nature is a fully general statement that expresses a physical necessity.

A *universal law of freedom* is a universal principle describing how all people ought to act in a certain circumstance. It does not have to be a legal enactment – it needn't be passed by Congress or signed by the president. Furthermore, some universal laws of freedom are not always followed – although they should be. If in fact it is true that all promises ought to be kept, then this principle is a universal law of freedom: If anyone has made a promise, he keeps it. The "must" in a statement such as "If you have made a promise, then you must keep it" does not express logical or physical necessity. It may be said to express moral necessity. Using this concept of moral necessity, we can say that a universal law of freedom is a fully general statement that expresses a moral necessity.

Sometimes Kant's categorical imperative is stated in terms of universal laws of nature, and sometimes in terms of universal laws of freedom.

We will consider the "law of nature" version, since Kant appeals to it in discussing some fairly important examples.

Willing

To will that something be the case is more than to merely wish for it to be the case. A person might wish that there would be peace everywhere in the world. Yet knowing that it is not within his power to bring about this wished-for state of affairs, he might refrain from willing that there be peace everywhere in the world. It is not easy to say just what a person does when he wills that something be the case. According to one view, willing that something be the case is something like commanding yourself to make it be the case. So if I will my arm to go up, that would be something like commanding myself to raise my arm. The Kantian concept of willing is a bit more complicated, however. According to Kant, it makes sense to speak of willing something to happen, even if that something is not an action. For example, we can speak of someone willing that everyone keep their promises.

Some states of affairs are impossible. They simply cannot occur. For example, consider the state of affairs of your jumping up and down while remaining perfectly motionless. It simply cannot be done. Yet a sufficiently foolish or irrational person might will that such a state of affairs occur. That would be as absurd as commanding someone else to jump up and down while remaining motionless. Kant would say of a person who has willed in this way that his will has "contradicted itself." We can also put the point by saying that the person has willed inconsistently.

Inconsistency in willing can arise in another, somewhat less obvious way. Suppose a person has already willed that he remain motionless. He does not change this volition, but persists in willing that he remain motionless. At the same time, however, he begins to will that he jump up and down. Although each volition is self-consistent, it is inconsistent to will both of them at the same time. This is a second way in which inconsistency in willing can arise.

It may be the case that there are certain things that everyone must always will. For example, we may have to will that we avoid intense pain. Anyone who wills something that is inconsistent with something everyone must will, thereby wills inconsistently.

Some of Kant's examples suggest that he held that inconsistency in willing can arise in a third way. This form of inconsistency is a bit more complex to describe. Suppose a person wills to be in Boston on Monday and also wills to be in San Francisco on Tuesday. Suppose, furthermore, that because of certain foul-ups at the airport it will be impossible for her to get from Boston to San Francisco on Tuesday. In this case, Kant would perhaps say that the person has willed inconsistently.

In general, we can say that a person wills inconsistently if he wills that p be the case and he wills that q be the case and it is impossible for p and q to be the case together.

The Categorical Imperative

With all this as background, we may be in a position to interpret the first version of Kant's categorical imperative. Our interpretation is this:

(CI_1) An act is morally right if and only if the agent of the act can consistently will that the generalized form of the maxim of the act be a law of nature.

We can simplify our formulation slightly by introducing a widely used technical term. We can say that a maxim is *universalizable* if and only if the agent who acts upon it can consistently will that its generalized form be a law of nature. Making use of this new term, we can restate our first version of the categorical imperative as follows:

(CI_1') An act is morally right if and only if its maxim is universalizable.

As formulated here, the categorical imperative is a statement of necessary and sufficient conditions for the moral rightness of actions. Some commentators have claimed that Kant did not intend his principle to be understood in this way. They have suggested that Kant meant it to be understood merely as a necessary but not sufficient condition for morally right action. Thus, they would prefer to formulate the imperative in some way such as this:

(CI_1'') An act is morally right only if its maxim is universalizable.

Understood in this way, the categorical imperative points out one thing to avoid in action. That is, it tells us to avoid actions whose maxims cannot be universalized. But it does not tell us the distinguishing feature of the actions we should perform. Thus, it does not provide us with a criterion of morally right action. Since Kant explicitly affirms that his principle is "the supreme principle of morality," it is reasonable to suppose that he intended it to be taken as a statement of necessary and sufficient conditions for morally right action. In any case, we will take the first version of the categorical imperative to be CI_1, rather than CI_1''.

It is interesting to note that other commentators have claimed that the categorical imperative isn't a criterion of right action at all. They have claimed that it was intended to be understood as a criterion of correctness for maxims.[10] These commentators might formulate the principle in this way:

(CI_1''') A maxim is normally acceptable if and only if it is universalizable.

This interpretation is open to a variety of objections. In the first place, it is not supported by the text. Kant repeatedly states that the categorical imperative is the basic principle by which we are to evaluate actions.[11] Furthermore, when he presents his formulations of the categorical imperative, he generally states it as a principle about the moral rightness of action. Finally, it is somewhat hard to see why we should be interested in a principle such as CI_1'''. For it does not constitute a theory about right action, or good per-

sons, or anything else that has traditionally been a subject of moral enquiry. CI_1, on the other hand, competes directly with act utilitarianism, rule utilitarianism, and other classical moral theories.

In order to gain a better insight into the workings of the categorical imperative, it may be worthwhile to compare it with a doctrine with which it is sometimes confused – the golden rule. The golden rule has been formulated in a wide variety of ways.[12] Generally, however, it looks something like this:

(GR) An act is morally right if and only if, in performing it, the agent refrains from treating others in ways in which he would not want the others to treat him.

According to GR, then, if you wouldn't want others to lie to you, it is wrong to lie to them. If you would want others to treat you with respect, then it is right to treat others with respect.

Kant explicitly rejects the view that his categorical imperative is equivalent to the golden rule.[13] He points out a number of respects in which the two doctrines differ. For one, GR is not applicable to cases in which only one person is involved. Consider suicide. When a person commits suicide, he does not "treat others" in any way; he only "treats himself." Hence, when a person commits suicide, he does not treat others in ways in which he would not want the others to treat him. Therefore, under GR, anyone who commits suicide performs a morally right act. CI_1, on the other hand, may not yield this result. For if a person commits suicide, he does so on a maxim, whether other people are involved or not. Either his maxim is universalizable, or it is not. If it is not, CI_1 entails that his action is not right. If it is, CI_1 entails that his action is right. In this respect, CI_1 is clearly distinct from GR.

Kant also hints at another aspect in which the two doctrines differ. Suppose a person considers herself to be utterly self-sufficient. She feels that she has no need of aid from others. GR then has nothing to say against her refraining from extending any kindness to others. After all, she has no objection to being treated in this unkind way by them. So GR entails that her behavior is morally right. CI_1, on the other hand, has no such consequence. Whether this person is willing to be mistreated by others or not, it may still be irrational of her to will that it be a law of nature that no one help anyone else. If so, CI_1 rules out uncharitableness, whether the agent likes it or not.

Similar considerations apply to masochists, whose behavior is not adequately guided by GR. After all, we surely don't want to allow the masochist to torture others simply on the grounds that he wouldn't object to being tortured by them! The unusual desires of masochism do not pose any special threat to CI_1.

So the main difference between GR and CI_1 seems to be this: According to GR, what makes an act right is the fact that the agent would not object to "having it done to himself." This opens the door to incorrect results in cases in which the agent, for some unexpected reason, would not object to being mistreated. According to CI_1, what makes an act right is the fact that the agent's maxim in performing it can be universalized. Thus, even if he would not object to being mistreated by others, his mistreatment of them may be wrong simply because it would be *irrational* to will that everyone should mistreat others in the same way.

Kant's Four Examples

In a very famous passage in chapter 2 of the *Groundwork*, Kant presents four illustrations of the application of the categorical imperative.[14] In each case, in Kant's opinion, the act is morally wrong and the maxim is not universalizable. Thus, Kant holds that his theory implies that each of these acts is wrong. If Kant is right about this, then he has given us four positive instances of his theory. That is, he has given us four cases in which his theory yields correct results. Unfortunately, the illustrations are not entirely persuasive.

Kant distinguishes between "duties to self" and "duties to others." He also distinguishes between "perfect" and "imperfect" duties. This gives him four categories of duty: "perfect to self," "perfect to others," "imperfect to self," and "imperfect to others." Kant gives one example of each type of duty. By "perfect duty," Kant says he means a duty "which admits of no exception in the interests of inclination."[15] Kant seems to have in mind something like this: If a person has a perfect duty to perform a certain kind of action, then he must *always* do that kind of action when the opportunity arises. For example, Kant apparently holds that we must always perform the (negative) action of refraining from committing suicide. This would be a perfect duty. On the other hand, if a person has an imperfect duty to do a kind of action, then he must at least *sometimes* perform an action of that kind when the opportunity arises. For example, Kant maintains that we have an imperfect duty to help others in distress. We should devote at least some of our time to charitable activities, but we are under no obligation to give all of our time to such work.

The perfect/imperfect distinction has been drawn in a variety of ways – none of them entirely clear. Some commentators have said that if a person has a perfect duty to do a certain action, *a*, then there must be someone else who has a corresponding right to demand that *a* be done. This seems to be the case in Kant's second example, but not in his first example. Thus, it isn't clear that we should understand the concept of perfect duty in this way. Although the perfect/imperfect distinction is fairly interesting in itself, it does not play a major role in Kant's theory. Kant introduces the distinction primarily to ensure that his examples will illustrate different kinds of duty.

Kant's first example illustrates the application of CI_1 to a case of perfect duty to oneself – the alleged duty to refrain from committing suicide. Kant describes the miserable state of the person contemplating suicide, and tries to show that his categorical imperative entails that the person should not take his own life. In order to simplify our discussion, let us use the abbreviation "a_1" to refer to the act of suicide the man would commit, if he were to commit suicide. According to Kant, every act must have a maxim. Kant tells us the maxim of a_1: "From self-love I make it my principle to shorten my life if its continuance threatens more evil than it promises pleasure."[16] Let us simplify and clarify this maxim, understanding it as follows:

(M(a₁)) When continuing to live will bring me more pain than pleasure, I shall commit suicide out of self-love.

The generalized form of this maxim is as follows:

(GM(a₁)) Whenever continuing to live will bring anyone more pain than pleasure, he will commit suicide out of self-love.

Since Kant believes that suicide is wrong, he attempts to show that his moral principle, the categorical imperative, entails that a₁ is wrong. To do this, of course, he needs to show that the agent of a₁ cannot consistently will that GM(a₁) be a law of nature. Kant tries to show this in the following passage:

> . . . a system of nature by whose law the very same feeling whose function is to stimulate the furtherance of life should actually destroy life would contradict itself and consequently could not subsist as a system of nature. Hence this maxim cannot possibly hold as a universal law of nature and is therefore entirely opposed to the supreme principle of all duty.[17]

The general outline of Kant's argument is clear enough:

Suicide Example
(1) GM(a₁) cannot be a law of nature.
(2) If GM (a₁) cannot be a law of nature, then the agent of a₁ cannot consistently will that GM(a₁) be a law of nature.
(3) a₁ is morally right if and only if the agent of a₁ can consistently will that GM(a₁) be a law of nature.
(4) Therefore, a₁ is not morally right.

In order to determine whether Kant really has shown that his theory entails that a₁ is not right, let us look at this argument more closely. First of all, for our purposes we can agree that the argument is valid. If all the premises are true, then the argument shows that the imagined act of suicide would not be right. CI₁, here being used as premise (3), would thus be shown to imply that a₁ is not right.

Since we are now interested primarily in seeing how Kant makes use of CI₁, we can withhold judgment on the merits of it for the time being.

The second premise seems fairly plausible. For although an irrational person could probably will almost anything, it surely would be difficult for a perfectly rational person to will that something be a law of nature if that thing could not be a law of nature. Let us grant, then, that it would not be possible for the agent to consistently will that GM(a₁) be a law of nature if in fact GM(a₁) could not be a law of nature.

The first premise is the most troublesome. Kant apparently assumes that "self-love" has as its function the stimulation of the furtherance of life. Given this, he seems to reason that self-love cannot also contribute sometimes to the destruction of life. Perhaps Kant assumes that a given feeling cannot have two "opposite" functions. However, if GM(a₁) were a law of nature, self-love would have to contribute toward self-destruction in some cases. Hence, Kant seems to conclude, GM(a₁) cannot be a law of nature. And so we have our first premise.

If this is Kant's reasoning, it is not very impressive. In the first place, it is not clear why we should suppose that self-love has the function of stimulating the furtherance of life. Indeed, it is not clear why we should suppose that self-love has any function at all! Second, it is hard to see why self-love can't serve two "opposite" functions. Perhaps self-love motivates us to stay alive when continued life would be pleasant, but motivates us to stop living when continued life would be unpleasant. Why should we hold this to be impossible?

So it appears that Kant's first illustration is not entirely successful. Before we turn to the second illustration, however, a few further comments may be in order. First, some philosophers would say that it is better that Kant's argument failed here. Many moralists would take the following position: Kant's view about suicide is wrong. The act of suicide out of self-love, a_1, is morally blameless. In certain circumstances suicide is each person's "own business." Thus, these moralists would say that if the categorical imperative did imply that a_1 is morally wrong, as Kant tries to show, then Kant's theory would be defective. But since Kant was not entirely successful in showing that his theory had this implication, the theory has not been shown to have any incorrect results.

A second point to notice about the suicide example is its scope. It is important to recognize that in this passage Kant has not attempted to show that suicide is always wrong. Perhaps Kant's personal view is that it is never right to commit suicide. However, in the passage in question he attempts to show only that a certain act of suicide, one based on a certain maxim, would be wrong. For all Kant has said here, other acts of suicide, done according to other maxims, might be permitted by the categorical imperative.

Let us turn now to the second illustration. Suppose I find myself hard-pressed financially and I decide that the only way in which I can get some money is by borrowing it from a friend. I realize that I will have to promise to repay the money, even though I won't in fact be able to do so. For I foresee that my financial situation will be even worse later on than it is at present. If I perform this action, a_2, of borrowing money on a false promise, I will perform it on this maxim:

($M(a_2)$)   When I need money and can get some by borrowing it on a false promise, then I shall borrow the money and promise to repay, even though I know that I won't be able to repay.

The generalized form of my maxim is this:

($GM(a_2)$))   Whenever anyone needs money and can get some by borrowing it on a false promise, then he will borrow the money and promise to repay, even though he knows that he won't be able to repay.

Kant's view is that I cannot consistently will

that $GM(a_2)$ be a law of nature. This view emerges clearly in the following passage:

> . . . I can by no means will a universal law of lying; for by such a law there could properly be no promises at all, since it would be futile to profess will for future action to others who would not believe my profession or who, if they did so over-hastily, would pay me back in like coin; and consequently my maxim, as soon as it was made a universal law, would be bound to annul itself.[18]

It is important to be clear about what Kant is saying here. He is not arguing against lying on the grounds that if I lie, others will soon lose confidence in me and eventually won't believe my promises. Nor is he arguing against lying on the grounds that my lie will contribute to a general practice of lying, which in turn will lead to a breakdown of trust and the destruction of the practice of promising. These considerations are basically utilitarian. Kant's point is more subtle. He is saying that there is something covertly self-contradictory about the state of affairs in which, as a law of nature, everyone makes a false promise when in need of a loan. Perhaps Kant's point is this: Such a state of affairs is self-contradictory because, on the one hand, in such a state of affairs everyone in need would borrow money on a false promise, and yet, on the other hand, in that state of affairs no one could borrow money on a false promise – for if promises were always violated, who would be silly enough to loan any money?

Since the state of affairs in which everyone in need borrows money on a false promise is covertly self-contradictory, it is irrational to will it to occur. No one can consistently will that this state of affairs should occur. But for me to will that $GM(a_2)$ be a law of nature is just for me to will that this impossible state of affairs occur. Hence, I cannot consistently will that the generalized form of my maxim be a law of nature. According to CI_1, my act is not right unless I can consistently will that the generalized form of its maxim be a law of nature. Hence, according to CI_1, my act of borrowing the money on the false promise is not morally right.

We can restate the essentials of this argument much more succinctly:

Lying-Promise Example

(1) $GM(a_2)$ cannot be a law of nature.

(2) If $GM(a_2)$ cannot be a law of nature, then I cannot consistently will that $GM(a_2)$ be a law of nature.

(3) a_2 is morally right if and only if I can consistently will that $GM(a_2)$ be a law of nature.

(4) Therefore, a_2 is not morally right.

The first premise is based upon the view that it would somehow be self-contradictory for it to be a law of nature that everyone in need makes a lying promise. For in that (allegedly impossible) state of affairs there would be promises, since those in need would make them, and there would also not be promises, since no one would believe that anyone was really committing himself to future payment by the use of the words "I promise." So, as Kant says, the generalized form of the maxim "annuls itself." It cannot be a law of nature.

The second premise is just like the second premise in the previous example. It is based on the idea that it is somehow irrational to will that something be the case if in fact it is impossible for it to be the case. So if it really is impossible for $GM(a_2)$ to be a law of nature, then it would be irrational of me to will that it be so. Hence, I cannot consistently will that the generalized form of my maxim be a law of nature. In other words, I cannot consistently will that it be a law of nature that whenever anyone needs money and can get some on a false promise, then he will borrow some and promise to repay, even though he knows that he won't be able to repay.

The third premise of the argument is the categorical imperative. If the rest of the argument is acceptable, then the argument as a whole shows that the categorical imperative, together with these other facts, implies that my lying promise would not be morally right. This would seem to be a reasonable result.

Some readers have apparently taken this example to show that according to Kantianism, it is always wrong to make a false promise. Indeed, Kant himself may have come to this conclusion. Yet if we reflect on the argument for a moment, we will see that the view of these readers is surely not the case. At best, the argument shows only that one specific act of making a false promise would be wrong. That one act is judged to be wrong because its maxim allegedly cannot be universalized. Other acts of making false promises would have to be evaluated independently. Perhaps it will turn out that every act of making a false promise has a maxim that cannot be universalized. If so, CI_1 would imply that they are all wrong. So far, however, we have been given no reason to suppose that this is the case.

Other critics would insist that Kant hasn't even succeeded in showing that a_2 is morally wrong. They would claim that the first premise of the argument is false. Surely it could be a law of nature that everyone will make a false promise when in need of money, they would say. If people borrowed money on false promises rarely enough, and kept their word on other promises, then no contradiction would arise. There would then be no reason to support that "no one would believe he was being promised anything, but would laugh at utterances of this kind as empty shams."[19]

Let us turn, then, to the third example. Kant now illustrates the application of the categorical imperative to a case of imperfect duty to oneself. The action in question is the "neglect of natural talents." Kant apparently holds that it is wrong for a person to let all of his natural talents go to waste. Of course, if a person has several natural talents, he is not required to develop all of them. Perhaps Kant considers this to be an imperfect duty partly because a person has the freedom to select which talents he will develop and which he will allow to rust.

Kant imagines the case of someone who is comfortable as he is and who, out of laziness, contemplates performing the act, a_3, of letting all his talents rust. His maxim in doing this would be

($M(a_3)$) When I am comfortable as I am, I shall let my talents rust.

When generalized, the maxim becomes

GM(a_3)) Whenever anyone is comfortable as he is, he will let his talents rust.

Kant admits that GM(a_3) could be a law of nature. Thus, his argument in this case differs from the arguments he produced in the first two cases. Kant proceeds to outline the reasoning by which the agent would come to see that it would be wrong to perform a_3:

> He then sees that a system of nature could indeed always subsist under such a universal law, although (like the South Sea Islanders) every man should let his talents rust and should be bent on devoting his life solely to idleness, indulgence, procreation, and, in a word, to enjoyment. Only he cannot possibly *will* that this should become a universal law of nature or should be implanted in us as such a law by a natural instinct. For as a rational being he necessarily wills that all his powers should be developed, since they serve him, and are given him, for all sorts of possible ends.[20]

Once again, Kant's argument seems to be based on a rather dubious appeal to natural purposes. Allegedly, nature implanted our talents in us for all sorts of purposes. Hence, we necessarily will to develop them. If we also will to let them rust, we are willing both to develop them (as we must) and to refrain from developing them. Anyone who wills both of these things obviously wills inconsistently. Hence, the agent cannot consistently will that his talents rust. This, together with the categorical imperative, implies that it would be wrong to perform the act, a_3, of letting one's talents rust.

The argument can be put as follows:

Rusting-talents example

(1) Everyone necessarily wills that all his talents be developed.
(2) If everyone necessarily wills that all his talents be developed, then the agent of a_3 cannot consistently will that GM(a_3) be a law of nature.

(3) a_3 is morally right if and only if the agent of a_3 can consistently will that GM(a_3) be a law of nature.
(4) Therefore a_3 is not morally right.

This argument seems even less persuasive than the others. In the quoted passage Kant himself presents a counter-example to the first premise. The South Sea Islanders, according to Kant, do not will to develop their talents. This fact, if it is one, is surely inconsistent with the claim that we all necessarily will that all our talents be developed. Even if Kant is wrong about the South Sea Islanders, his first premise is still extremely implausible. Couldn't there be a rational person who, out of idleness, simply does not will to develop his talents? If there could not be such a person, then what is the point of trying to show that we are under some specifically moral obligation to develop all our talents?

Once again, however, some philosophers may feel that Kant would have been worse off if his example had succeeded. These philosophers would hold that we in fact have no moral obligation to develop our talents. If Kant's theory had entailed that we have such an obligation, they would insist, then that would have shown that Kant's theory is defective.

In Kant's fourth illustration the categorical imperative is applied to an imperfect duty to others – the duty to help others who are in distress. Kant describes a man who is flourishing and who contemplates performing the act, a_4, of giving nothing to charity. His maxim is not stated by Kant in this passage, but it can probably be formulated as follows:

(M(a_4)) When I'm flourishing and others are in distress, I shall give nothing to charity.

When generalized, this maxim becomes

(GM(a_4)) Whenever anyone is flourishing and others are in distress, he will give nothing to charity.

As in the other example of imperfect duty, Kant acknowledges that GM(a_4) could be a law of nature. Yet he claims once again that the agent cannot consistently will that it be a law of nature. He explains this by arguing as follows:

> For a will which decided in this way would be in conflict with itself, since many a situation might arise in which the man needed love and sympathy from others, and in which, by such a law of nature sprung from his own will, he would rob himself of all hope of the help he wants for himself.[21]

Kant's point here seems to be this: The day may come when the agent is no longer flourishing. He may need charity from others. If that day does come, then he will find that he wills that others give him such aid. However, in willing that $GM(a_4)$ be a law of nature, he has already willed that no one should give charitable aid to anyone. Hence, on that dark day, his will will contradict itself. Thus, he cannot consistently will that $GM(a_4)$ be a law of nature. This being so, the categorical imperative entails that a_4 is not right.

If this is Kant's reasoning, then his reasoning is defective. For we cannot infer from the fact that the person *may* someday want aid from others, that he in fact already is willing inconsistently when he wills today that no one should give aid to anyone. The main reason for this is that that dark day may not come, in which case no conflict will arise. Furthermore, as is pretty obvious upon reflection, even if that dark day does arrive, the agent may steadfastly stick to his general policy. He may say, "I didn't help others when they were in need, and now that I'm in need I don't want any help from them." In this way he would avoid having inconsistent policies. Unless this attitude is irrational, which it does not seem to be, Kant's fourth example is unsuccessful.

More Examples

It should be clear, then, that Kant has not provided us with a clear, persuasive example of the application of the categorical imperative. In light of this, some may feel that the categorical imperative is a worthless doctrine. Such a harsh judgment would probably be premature. For in the first place, Kant surely would have been worse off if he had succeeded in showing that suicide, or letting your talents rust, are invariably wrong. The normative status of these acts is hardly as obvious as Kant suggests. In the second place, the failure of Kant's illustrations may be due in part to his choice of some rather strange maxims, and to the fact that he presupposed some questionable views about the purposes of nature. Let us attempt to develop a more plausible illustration of the application of the categorical imperative.

In attempting to develop such an example, we should turn to the sort of case in which the categorical imperative stands the greatest chance of working correctly. This would be a case in which an agent proposes to take unfair advantage of his neighbors. It would be a case in which others, out of regard for the common good, have generously refrained from performing a certain kind of act, even though many of them might like to do such an act. Our agent, however, finds that he can get away with the act. The crucial feature of this case is that the agent cannot consistently will that the others act in the way he proposes to act. For if they all were to try to act in this way, that would destroy his opportunity for so acting.

Here is a good example of this sort of case. Primarily out of laziness, Miss Perkins, a college student, buys a term paper for her ethics course and submits it as her own work. Miss Perkins deals with a skillful term paper manufacturer, so she is assured of getting a very high grade. There is no chance that she will be found out. Most of us would say that regardless of its utility, Miss Perkins's act is morally wrong. She should not deceive her instructor and take advantage of her fellow students in this way. What does the categorical imperative say?

Let us call Miss Perkins's act of submitting the phony term paper "a_5," and let us suppose that her maxim in performing a_5 is

> $(M(a_5))$ When I need a term paper for a course and don't feel like writing one, I shall buy a term paper and submit it as my own work.

The generalized form of her maxim is

(GM(a_5)) Whenever anyone needs a term paper for a course and doesn't feel like writing one, she will buy one and submit it as her own work.

According to Kant's doctrine, a_5 is morally right only if Miss Perkins can consistently will that GM(a_5) be a law of nature. So to see if a_5 is right, we must determine whether Miss Perkins can consistently will that everyone needing a term paper but not feeling like writing one should submit a store-bought one.

It is reasonable to suppose that Miss Perkins cannot will that GM(a_5) be a law of nature. For consider what would happen if GM(a_5) were a law of nature, and everyone needing a term paper but not feeling like writing one were therefore to submit a store-bought one. Clearly, college instructors would soon realize that they were reading work not produced by their students. The instructors would have to deal with the problem – perhaps by resorting to a system under which each student would be required to take a final oral exam instead of submitting a term paper. If some such alteration in the course requirements were instituted, Miss Perkins would lose her opportunity to get a good grade by cheating. Thus, she surely does not will that any such change in the system should occur. She prefers to have the system remain as it is. Since it is clear that some such change would occur if GM(a_5) were a law of nature, Miss Perkins cannot consistently will that GM(a_5) be a law of nature. Thus, according to CI$_1$, her act is not right.

The essentials of this example are simple. Miss Perkins wills that the system remain as it is – thus providing her with the opportunity to take advantage of her instructor and her fellow students. She recognizes that if everyone were to submit a store-bought term paper, the system would be changed. Hence, she cannot consistently will that everyone should submit a store-bought term paper. In other words, she cannot consistently will that GM(a_5) be a law of nature. CI$_1$, together with this fact, entails that a_5 is morally wrong.

One of the most troubling aspects of this ex-ample is that it is pretty easy to see how the categorical imperative can be short-circuited. That is, it is pretty easy to see how Miss Perkins can make Kant's doctrine yield the result that her act is morally right. She needs only to change her maxim in a fairly trivial way:

(M(a_6)) When I need a term paper for a course, and I don't feel like writing one, and no change in the system will occur if I submit a store-bought one, then I shall buy a term paper and submit it as my own work.

M(a_6) differs from M(a_5) in only one respect. M(a_6) contains the extra phrase "and no change in the system will occur if I submit a store-bought one." But this little addition makes a big difference to the argument. We found that Miss Perkins could not consistently will that GM(a_5) be a law of nature. For if she willed that GM(a_5) be a law of nature, she would, indirectly, will that the system be changed. But she already willed that the system remain as it is. However, no such argument applies to GM(a_6). For it appears that if GM(a_6) were a law of nature, the system would not be changed. Apparently, then, Miss Perkins can consistently will that GM(a_6) be a law of nature. Hence, according to CI$_1$, her act of submitting a store-bought term paper, if performed under M(a_6) rather than under M(a_5), would be morally acceptable. This seems wrong.

The categorical imperative, interpreted as CI$_1$, yields incorrect results in another sort of case too. Consider a man who has a large amount of money in a savings account. He decides that he will wait until the stock market index reaches 1,000 and then take all of his money out of the bank. This act seems quite acceptable from the moral point of view. However, it seems that CI$_1$ yields the odd result that the act is morally wrong. Let us consider why this is so.

We can call the man's act of removing his money from the bank "a_7." The maxim of a_7 is

(M(a_7)) When the stock market index reaches 1,000, I shall withdraw all my money from the bank.

The generalized form of $M(a_7)$ is

($GM(a_7)$) Whenever the stock market index reaches 1,000, everyone shall withdraw all of their money from the bank.

It should be clear that the man cannot consistently will that $GM(a_7)$ be a law of nature. For, banks have loaned out most of the money deposited in them. If everyone came to withdraw their savings from their bank, banks would soon run out of money. Not everyone can withdraw simultaneously. Hence, $GM(a_7)$ cannot be a law of nature. Thus, the agent cannot consistently will that it be so. CI_1 entails, together with this fact, that it would not be right for the man to withdraw his own money under this maxim. Surely, there is something wrong with a moral theory that has this result.

This same problem arises in any number of cases. Whenever, for some irrelevant reason, an otherwise innocent maxim cannot be universalized, CI_1 yields the result that the act is wrong. So if a person acts on the maxim, for example, of not becoming a doctor, he acts wrongly. For he surely could not will that *everyone* should refrain from becoming a doctor. As a rational being, he recognizes that there must be some doctors. Similarly, if a person acts on the maxim of always using adequate contraceptive devices when engaging in sexual intercourse, she acts wrongly, according to this interpretation of CI_1. For if everyone were to do what she does, there would soon be no human race at all. This, Kant would think, is something no rational agent can consistently will.

These absurd results show that there is a very deep problem with CI_1. The problem, in general, is that there are many different reasons why a maxim may fail to be universalizable. Some of these reasons have nothing whatever to do with morality. Yet, as far as can be discerned from the text of the *Groundwork*, Kant nowhere attempts to distinguish between innocent-but-non-universalizable maxims, on the one hand, and evil-and-non-universalizable ones, on the other. Without such a distinction, CI_1 yields obviously incorrect results in innumerable cases.

So we can conclude that there are very serious problems with CI_1. Perhaps CI_1 is not an adequate interpretation of Kant's categorical imperative. Perhaps a more adequate version of that doctrine would not have these unsatisfactory results. However, if CI_1 is not Kant's theory, then it is very hard to see what Kant's theory might be.

Notes

1 Immanuel Kant (1724–1804) is one of the greatest Continental philosophers. He produced quite a few philosophical works of major importance. *The Critique of Pure Reason* (1781) is perhaps his most famous work.

2 Kant's *Grundlegung zur Metaphysik der Sitten* (1785) has been translated into English many times. All references here are to Immanuel Kant, *Groundwork of the Metaphysic of Morals*, translated and analysed by H. J. Paton (New York: Harper & Row, 1964).

3 Kant, *Groundwork*, p. 70.

4 Ibid., p. 88

5 Ibid., p. 89.

6 Ibid., p. 91.

7 Ibid., p. 69n.

8 In some unusual cases, it may accidentally happen that the situation to which the maxim applies can occur only once, as, for example, in the case of successful suicide. Nevertheless, the maxim is general in form.

9 Kant, *Groundwork*, p. 65.

10 See, for example, Robert Paul Wolff, *The Autonomy of Reason* (New York: Harper & Row, 1973), p. 163.

11 This is stated especially clearly on p. 107 of the *Groundwork*.

12 For an interesting discussion of various formulations of the golden rule, see Marcus Singer, "The Golden Rule," in Paul Edwards (ed.), *The Encyclopedia of Philosophy* (New York: Macmillan, Free Press, 1967), vol. 3, pp. 365–7.

13 Kant, *Groundwork*, p. 97n.

14 Ibid., pp. 89–91.

15 Ibid., p. 89n.

16 Ibid., p. 89.

17 Ibid.

18 Ibid., p. 71.

19 Ibid.

20 Ibid.

21 Ibid., p. 91.

21　Kant on Dealing with Evil

Christine M. Korsgaard

One of the great difficulties with Kant's moral philosophy is that it seems to imply that our moral obligations leave us powerless in the face of evil. Kant's theory sets a high ideal of conduct and tells us to live up to that ideal regardless of what other persons are doing. The results may be very bad. But Kant says that the law "remains in full force, because it commands categorically" (*G*, 438–9/57).[1] The most well-known example of this "rigorism," as it is sometimes called, concerns Kant's views on our duty to tell the truth.

In two passages in his ethical writings, Kant seems to endorse the following pair of claims about this duty: first, one must never under any circumstances or for any purpose tell a lie; second, if one does tell a lie one is responsible for all the consequences that ensue, even if they were completely unforeseeable.

One of the two passages appears in the *Metaphysical Principles of Virtue*. There Kant classifies lying as a violation of a perfect duty to oneself. In one of the casuistical questions, a servant, under instructions, tells a visitor the lie that his master is not at home. His master, meanwhile, sneaks off and commits a crime, which would have been prevented by the watchman sent to arrest him. Kant says:

> Upon whom . . . does the blame fall? To be sure, also upon the servant, who here violated a duty to himself by lying, the consequence of which will now be imputed to him by his own conscience. (*MMV*, 431/93)

The other passage is the infamous one about the murderer at the door from the essay, "On a Supposed Right to Lie from Altruistic Motives."

From *Philosophy and Public Affairs*, vol. 15 (1986), pp. 420–40. Reprinted with permission.

Here Kant's claims are more extreme, for he says that the liar may be held legally as well as ethically responsible for the consequences, and the series of coincidences he imagines is even more fantastic:

> After you have honestly answered the murderer's question as to whether his intended victim is at home, it may be that he has slipped out so that he does not come in the way of the murderer, and thus that the murder may not be committed. But if you had lied and said he was not at home when he had really gone out without your knowing it, and if the murderer had then met him as he went away and murdered him, you might justly be accused as the cause of his death. For if you had told the truth as far as you knew it, perhaps the murderer might have been apprehended by the neighbors while he searched the house and thus the deed might have been prevented. (*SRL*, 427/348)

Kant's readers differ about whether Kant's moral philosophy commits him to the claims he makes in these passages. Unsympathetic readers are inclined to take them as evidence of the horrifying conclusions to which Kant was led by his notion that the necessity in duty is rational necessity – as if Kant were clinging to a logical point in the teeth of moral decency. Such readers take these conclusions as a defeat for Kant's ethics, or for ethical rationalism generally; or they take Kant to have confused principles which are merely general in their application and prima facie in their truth with absolute and universal laws. Sympathetic readers are likely to argue that Kant here mistook the implications of his own theory, and to try to show that, by careful construction and accurate testing of the maxim on which this liar acts, Kant's conclusions can be blocked by his own procedures.

Sympathetic and unsympathetic readers alike have focused their attention on the implications of the first formulation of the categorical imperative, the Formula of Universal Law. The *Foundations of the Metaphysics of Morals* contains two other sets of terms in which the categorical imperative is formulated: the treatment of humanity as an end in itself, and autonomy, or legislative membership in a Kingdom of Ends. My treatment of the issue falls into three parts. First, I want to argue that Kant's defenders are right in thinking that, when the case is treated under the Formula of Universal Law, this particular lie can be shown to be permissible. Second, I want to argue that when the case is treated from the perspective provided by the Formulas of Humanity and the Kingdom of Ends, it becomes clear why Kant is committed to the view that lying is wrong in every case. But from this perspective we see that Kant's rigorism about lying is not the result of a misplaced love of consistency or legalistic thinking. Instead, it comes from an attractive ideal of human relations which is the basis of his ethical system. If Kant is wrong in his conclusion about lying to the murderer at the door, it is for the interesting and important reason that morality itself sometimes allows or even requires us to do something that from an ideal perspective is wrong. The case does not impugn Kant's ethics as an *ideal* system. Instead, it shows that we need special principles for dealing with evil. My third aim is to discuss the structure that an ethical system must have in order to accommodate such special principles.

Universal Law

The Formula of Universal Law tells us never to act on a maxim that we could not at the same time will to be a universal law. A maxim which cannot even be conceived as a universal law without contradiction is in violation of a strict and perfect duty, one which assigns us a particular action or omission. A maxim which cannot be willed as universal law without contradicting the will is in violation of a broad and imperfect duty, one which assigns us an end, but does not tell us

what or how much we should do toward it. Maxims of lying are violations of perfect duty, and so are supposed to be the kind that cannot be conceived without contradiction when universalized.

The sense in which the universalization of an immoral maxim is supposed to "contradict" itself is a matter of controversy. On my reading, which I will not defend here, the contradiction in question is a "practical" one: the universalized maxim contradicts itself when the efficacy of the action as a method of achieving its purpose would be undermined by its universal practice.[2] So, to use Kant's example, the point against false promising as a method of getting ready cash is that if everyone attempted to use false promising as a method of getting ready cash, false promising would no longer *work* as a method of getting ready cash, since, as Kant says, "no one would believe what was promised to him but would only laugh at any such assertion as vain pretense" (*G*, 422/40).

Thus the test question will be: could this action be the universal method of achieving this purpose? Now when we consider lying in general, it looks as if it could not be the universal method of doing anything. For lies are usually efficacious in achieving their purposes because they deceive, but if they were universally practiced they would not deceive. We believe what is said to us in a given context because most of the time people in that context say what they really think or intend. In contexts in which people usually say false things – for example, when telling stories that are jokes – we are not deceived. If a story that is a joke and is false counts as a lie, we can say that a lie in this case is not wrong, because the universal practice of lying in the context of jokes does not interfere with the *purpose* of jokes, which is to amuse and does not depend on deception. But in most cases lying falls squarely into the category of the sort of action Kant considers wrong: actions whose efficacy depends upon the fact that most people do not engage in them, and which therefore can only be performed by someone who makes an exception of himself (*G*, 424/42).

When we try to apply this test to the case of the murderer at the door, however, we run into a difficulty. The difficulty derives from the fact that there is probably already deception in the case. If murderers standardly came to the door and said: "I wish to murder your friend – is he here in your house?" then perhaps the universal practice of lying in order to keep a murderer from his victim would not work. If everyone lied in these circumstances the murderer would be aware of that fact and would not be deceived by your answer. But the murderer is not likely to do this, or, in any event, this is not how I shall imagine the case. A murderer who expects to conduct his business by asking questions must suppose that you do not know who he is and what he has in mind.[3] If these are the circumstances, and we try to ascertain whether there could be a universal practice of lying in these circumstances, the answer appears to be yes. The lie will be efficacious even if universally practiced. But the reason it will be efficacious is rather odd: it is because the murderer supposes you do not know what circumstances you are in – that is, that you do not know you are addressing a murderer – and so does not conclude from the fact that people in those circumstances always lie that *you* will lie.

The same point can be made readily using Kant's publicity criterion (*PP*, 381–3/129–31). Can we announce in advance our intention of lying to murderers without, as Kant says, vitiating our own purposes by publishing our maxims (*PP*, 383/131)? Again the answer is yes. It does not matter if you say publicly that you will lie in such a situation, for the murderer supposes that you do not know you are in that situaion.[4]

These reflections might lead us to believe, then, that Kant was wrong in thinking that it is never all right to lie. It is permissible to lie to deceivers in order to counteract the intended results of their deceptions, for the maxim of lying to a deceiver is universalizable. The deceiver has, so to speak, placed himself in a morally unprotected position by his own deception. He has created a situation which universalization cannot reach.

Humanity

When we apply the Formula of Humanity, how-
ever, the argument against lying that results applies to any lie whatever. The formula runs:

> Act so that you treat humanity, whether in your own person or in that of another, always as an end and never as a means only. (*G*, 429/47)

In order to use this formula for casuistical purposes, we need to specify what counts as treating humanity as an end. "Humanity" is used by Kant specifically to refer to the capacity to determine ends through rational choice (*G*, 437/56; *MMV*, 392/50). Imperfect duties arise from the obligation to make the exercise, preservation, and development of this capacity itself an end. The perfect duties – that is, the duties of justice, and, in the realm of ethics, the duties of respect – arise from the obligation to make each human being's capacity for autonomous choice the condition of the value of every other end.

In his treatment of the lying promise case under the Formula of Humanity, Kant makes the following comments:

> For he whom I want to use for my own purposes by means of such a promise cannot possibly assent to my mode of acting against him and cannot contain the end of this action in himself . . . he who transgresses the rights of men intends to make use of the persons of others merely as means, without considering that as rational beings, they must always be esteemed at the same time as ends, i.e. only as beings who must be able to contain in themselves the end of the very same action. (*G*, 429–30/48)

In these passages, Kant uses two expressions that are the key to understanding the derivation of perfect duties to others from the Formula of Humanity. One is that the other person "cannot possibly assent to my mode of acting toward him" and the second is that the other person cannot "contain the end of this action in himself." These phrases provide us with a test for perfect duties to others: an action is contrary to perfect duty if it is not possible for the other to assent to it or to hold its end.

It is important to see that these phrases do not mean simply that the other person *does not* or *would not* assent to the transaction or that she does not happen to have the same end I do, but strictly that she *cannot* do so: that something makes it impossible. If what we cannot assent to means merely what we are likely to be annoyed by, the test will be subjective and the claim that the person does not assent to being used as a means will sometimes be false. The object you steal from me may be the gift I intended for you, and we may both have been motivated by the desire that you should have it. And I may care about you too much or too little to be annoyed by the theft. For all that, this must be a clear case of your using me as a mere means.[5]

So it must not be merely that your victim will not like the way you propose to act, that this is psychologically unlikely, but that something makes it impossible for her to assent to it. Similarly, it must be argued that something makes it impossible for her to hold the end of the very same action. Kant never spells out why it is impossible, but it is not difficult to see what he has in mind.

People cannot *assent* to a way of acting when they are given no chance to do so. The most obvious instance of this is when coercion is used. But it is also true of deception: the victim of the false promise cannot assent to it because he doesn't know it is what he is being offered. But even when the victim of such conduct does happen to know what is going on, there is a sense in which he cannot assent to it. Suppose, for example, that you come to me and ask to borrow some money, falsely promising to pay it back next week, and suppose that by some chance I know perfectly well that your promise is a lie. Suppose also that I have the same end you do, in the sense that I want you to have the money, so that I turn the money over to you anyway. Now here I have the same end that you do, and I tolerate your attempts to deceive me to the extent that they do not prevent my giving you the money. Even in this case I cannot really assent to the transaction *you* propose. We can imagine the case in a number of different ways. If I call your bluff openly and say "never mind that nonsense, just take this money" then what I am doing is not accepting a false promise, but giving you a hand-

out, and scorning your promise. The nature of the transaction is changed: now it is not a promise but a handout. If I don't call you on it, but keep my own counsel, it is still the same. I am not accepting a false promise. In this case what I am doing is *pretending* to accept your false promise. But there is all the difference in the world between actually doing something and pretending to do it. In neither of these cases can I be described as accepting a false promise, for in both cases I fix it so that it is something else that is happening. My knowledge of what is going on makes it *impossible* for me to accept the deceitful promise in the ordinary way.

The question whether another can assent to your way of acting can serve as a criterion for judging whether you are treating her as a mere means. We will say that knowledge of what is going on and some power over the proceedings are the conditions of possible assent; without these, the concept of assent does not apply. This gives us another way to formulate the test for treating someone as a mere means: suppose it is the case that if the other person knows what you are trying to do and has the power to stop you, then what you are trying to do cannot be what is really happening. If this is the case, the action is one that by its very nature is impossible for the other to assent to. You cannot wrest from me what I freely give to you; and if I have the power to stop you from wresting something from me and do not use it, I am in a sense freely giving it to you. This is of course not intended as a legal point: the point is that any action which depends for its nature and efficacy on the other's ignorance or powerlessness fails this test. Lying clearly falls into this category of action: it only deceives when the other does not know that it is a lie.[6]

A similar analysis can be given of the possibility of holding the end of the very same action. In cases of violation of perfect duty, lying included, the other person is unable to hold the end of the very same action because the way that you act prevents her from *choosing* whether to contribute to the realization of that end or not. Again, this is obviously true when someone is forced to contribute to an end, but it is also true in cases of deception. If you give a lying promise to get some money, the other person is invited to think that the end she is contributing to is your temporary possession of the money: in fact, it is your permanent possession of it. It doesn't matter whether that would be all right with her if she knew about it. What matters is that she never gets a chance to choose the end, not knowing that it is to be the consequence of her action.[7]

According to the Formula of Humanity, coercion and deception are the most fundamental forms of wrongdoing to others – the roots of all evil. Coercion and deception violate the conditions of possible assent, and all actions which depend for their nature and efficacy on their coercive or deceptive character are ones that others cannot assent to. Coercion and deception also make it impossible for others to choose to contribute to our ends. This in turn makes it impossible, according to Kant's value theory, for the ends of such actions to be good. For on Kant's view "what we call good must be, in the judgment of every reasonable man, an object of the faculty of desire" (C_2, 60/62–3). If your end is one that others cannot choose – not because of what they want, but because they are not in a position to choose – it cannot, as the end of that action, be good. This means that in any cooperative project – whenever you need the decisions and actions of others in order to bring about your end – everyone who is to contribute must be in a position to *choose* to contribute to the end.

The sense in which a good end is an object for everyone is that a good end is in effect one that everyone, in principle, and especially everyone who contributes to it, gets to cast a vote on. This voting, or legislation, is the prerogative of rational beings; and the ideal of a world in which this prerogative is realized is the Kingdom of Ends.

The Kingdom of Ends

The Kingdom of Ends is represented by the kingdom of nature; we determine moral laws by considering their viability as natural laws. On Kant's view, the will is a kind of causality (*G*, 446/64).

A person, an end in itself, is a free cause, which is to say a first cause. By contrast, a thing, a means, is a merely mediate cause, a link in the chain. A first cause is, obviously, the initiator of a causal chain, hence a real determiner of what will happen. The idea of deciding for yourself whether you will contribute to a given end can be represented as a decision whether to initiate that causal chain which constitutes your contribution. Any action which prevents or diverts you from making this initiating decision is one that treats you as a mediate rather than a first cause; hence as a mere means, a thing, a tool. Coercion and deception both do this. And deception treats you as a mediate cause in a specific way: it treats your reason as a mediate cause. The false promiser thinks: if I tell her I will pay her back next week, then she will choose to give me the money. Your reason is worked, like a machine: the deceiver tries to determine what levers to pull to get the desired results from you. Physical coercion treats someone's person as a tool; lying treats someone's *reason* as a tool. This is why Kant finds it so horrifying; it is a direct violation of autonomy.

We may say that a tool has two essential characteristics: it is there to be used, and it does not control itself – its nature is to be directed by something else. To treat someone as a mere means is to treat her as if these things were true of her. Kant's treatment of our duties to others in the *Metaphysical Principles of Virtue* is sensitive to *both* characteristics. We are not only forbidden to use another as a mere means to our private purposes. We are also forbidden to take attitudes toward her which involve regarding her as not in control of herself, which is to say, as not using her reason.

This latter is the basis of the duties of respect. Respect is violated by the vices of calumny and mockery (*MMV*, 466–8/131–3): we owe to others not only a practical generosity toward their plans and projects – a duty of aid – but also a generosity of attitude toward their thoughts and motives. To treat another with respect is to treat him as if he were using his reason and as far as possible as if he were using it well. Even in a case where someone evidently *is* wrong or mistaken, we ought to suppose he must have what he takes to be good reasons for what he believes or what he does. This is not because, as a matter of fact, he probably does have good reasons. Rather, this attitude is something that we *owe* to him, something that is his right. And he cannot forfeit it. Kant is explicit about this:

> Hereupon is founded a duty to respect man even in the logical use of his reason: not to censure someone's errors under the name of absurdity, inept judgment, and the like, but rather to suppose that in such an inept judgment there must be something true, and to seek it out. . . . Thus it is also with the reproach of vice, which must never burst out in complete contempt or deny the wrongdoer all moral worth, because on that hypothesis he could never be improved either – and this latter is incompatible with the idea of man, who as such (as a moral being) can never lose all predisposition to good.   (*MMV*, 463–4/128–9)

To treat others as ends in themselves is always to address and deal with them as rational beings. Every rational being gets to reason out, for herself, what she is to think, choose, or do. So if you need someone's contribution to your end, you must put the facts before her and ask for her contribution. If you think she is doing something wrong, you may try to convince her by argument but you may not resort to tricks or force. The Kingdom of Ends is a democratic ideal, and poor judgment does not disqualify anyone for citizenship. In the *Critique of Pure Reason*, Kant says:

> Reason depends on this freedom for its very existence. For reason has no dictatorial authority; its verdict is always simply the agreement of free citizens, of whom each one must be permitted to express, without let or hindrance, his objections or even his veto.[8]

This means that there cannot be a good reason for taking a decision out of someone else's hands. It is a rational being's prerogative, as a first cause, to have a share in determining the destiny of things.

This shows us in another way why lying is for Kant a paradigm case of treating someone as a mere means. Any attempt to control the actions and reactions of another by any means except an appeal to reason treats her as a mere means, because it attempts to reduce her to a mediate cause. This includes much more than the utterance of falsehoods. In the *Lectures on Ethics*, Kant says "whatever militates against frankness lowers the dignity of man" (*LE*, 231).[9] It is an everyday temptation, even (or perhaps especially) in our dealings with those close to us, to withhold something, or to tidy up an anecdote, or to embellish a story, or even just to place a certain emphasis, in order to be sure of getting the reaction we want.[10] Kant holds the Socratic view that any sort of persuasion that is aimed at distracting its listener's attention from either the reasons that she ought to use or the reasons the speaker thinks she will use is wrong.[11]

In light of this account it is possible to explain why Kant says what he does about the liar's responsibility. In a Kantian theory our responsibility has definite boundaries: each person as a first cause exerts some influence on what happens, and it is your part that is up to you. If you make a straightforward appeal to the reason of another person, your responsibility ends there and the other's responsibility begins. But the liar tries to take the consequences out of the hands of others; he, and not they, will determine what form their contribution to destiny will take. By refusing to share with others the determination of events, the liar takes the world into his own hands, and makes the events his own. The results, good or bad, are imputable to him, at least in his own conscience. It does not follow from *this*, of course, that this is a risk one will never want to take.

Humanity and the Universal Law

If the foregoing casuistical analyses are correct, then applying the Formula of Universal Law and the Formula of Humanity lead to different answers in the case of lying to the murderer at the door. The former seems to say that this lie is permissible, but the latter says that coercion and deception are the most fundamental forms of wrongdoing. In a Kingdom of Ends coercive and deceptive methods can never be used.

This result impugns Kant's belief that the formulas are equivalent. But it is not necessary to conclude that the formulas flatly say different things, and are unrelated except for a wide range of coincidence in their results. For one thing, lying to the murderer at the door was not shown to be permissible in a straightforward manner: the maxim did not so much pass as evade universalization. For another, the two formulas can be shown to be expressions of the same basic theory of justification. Suppose that your maxim is in violation of the Formula of Universal Law. You are making an exception of yourself, doing something that everyone in your circumstances could not do. What this means is that you are treating the reason *you* have for the action as if it were stronger, had more justifying force, than anyone else's exactly similar reason. You are then acting as if the fact that it was in particular *your* reason, and not just the reason of a human being, gave it special weight and force. This is an obvious violation of the idea that it is your humanity – your power of rational choice – which is the condition of all value and which therefore gives your needs and desires the justifying force of *reasons.* Thus, any violation of the Formula of Universal Law is also a violation of the Formula of Humanity. This argument, of course, only goes in one direction: it does not show that the two formulas are equivalent. The Formula of Humanity is stricter than the Formula of Universal Law – but both are expressions of the same basic theory of value: that your rational nature is the source of justifying power of your reasons, and so of the goodness of your ends.

And although the Formula of Humanity gives us reason to think that all lies are wrong, we can still give an account in the terms it provides of what vindicates lying to a liar. The liar tries to use your reason as a means – your honesty as a tool. You do not have to passively submit to being used as a means. In the *Lectures on Ethics,* this is the line that Kant takes. He says:

> If we were to be at all times punctiliously truthful we might often become victims of the wick-

edness of others who were ready to abuse our truthfulness. If all men were well-intentioned it would not only be a duty not to lie, but no one would do so because there would be no point in it. But as men are malicious, it cannot be denied that to be punctiliously truthful is often dangerous . . . if I cannot save myself by maintaining silence, then my lie is a weapon of defence. (*LE*, 228)

The common thought that lying to a liar is a form of self-defence, that you can resist lies with lies as you can resist force with force, is according to this analysis correct.[12] This should not be surprising, for we have seen that deception and coercion are parallel. Lying and the use of force are attempts to undercut the two conditions of possible assent to actions and of autonomous choice of ends, namely, knowledge and power. So, although the Formula of Universal Law and the Formula of Humanity give us different results, this does not show that they simply express different moral outlooks. The relation between them is more complex than that.

Two Casuistical Problems

Before I discuss this relation, however, I must take up two casuistical problems arising from the view I have presented so far. First, I have argued that we *may* lie to the murderer at the door. But most people think something stronger: that we ought to lie to the murderer – that we will have done something wrong if we do not. Second, I have argued that it is permissible to lie to a deceiver in order to counter the deception. But what if someone lies to you for a good end, and, as it happens, you know about it? The fact that the murderer's *end* is evil has played no direct role in the arguments I have given so far. We have a right to resist liars and those who try to use force because of their methods, not because of their purposes. In one respect this is a virtue of my argument. It does not license us to lie or to use violence against persons *just* because we think their purposes are bad. But it looks as if it may license us to lie to liars whose purposes are good. Here is a case: suppose someone comes to your door and pretends to be taking a survey of some sort.[13] In fact, this person is a philanthropist who wants to give his money to people who meet certain criteria, and this is his way of discovering appropriate objects for his beneficence. As it happens, you know what is up. By lying, you could get some money, although you do not in fact meet his criteria. The argument that I derived from the Formula of Universal Law about lying to the murderer applies here. Universalizing the lie to the philanthropist will not destroy its efficacy. Even if it is a universal law that everyone will lie in these circumstances, the philanthropist thinks you do not know you are in these circumstances. By my argument, it is permissible to lie in this case. The philanthropist, like the murderer, has placed himself in a morally unprotected position by his own deception.

Start with the first casuistical problem. There are two reasons to lie to the murderer at the door. First, we have a duty of mutual aid. This is an imperfect duty of virtue, since the law does not say exactly what or how much we must do along these lines. This duty gives us *a* reason to tell the lie. Whether it makes the lie imperative depends on how one understands the duty of mutual aid, on how one understands the "wideness" of imperfect duties.[14] It may be that on such an urgent occasion, the lie is imperative. Notice that if the lie were impermissible, this duty would have no force. Imperfect duties are always secondary to perfect ones. But if the lie is permissible, this duty will provide a reason, whether or not an imperative one, to tell the lie.

The second reason is one of self-respect. The murderer wants to make you a tool of evil; he regards your integrity as a useful sort of predictability. He is trying to use you, and your good will, as a means to an evil end. You owe it to humanity in your own person not to allow your honesty to be used as a resource for evil. I think this would be a perfect duty of virtue; Kant does not say this specifically, but in his discussion of servility (the avoidance of which is a perfect duty of virtue) he says "Do not suffer your rights to be trampled underfoot by others with impunity" (*MMV*, 436/99).

Both of these reasons spring from duties of

virtue. A person with a good character will tell the lie. Not to tell it is morally bad. But there is no duty of justice to tell the lie. If we do not tell it, we cannot be punished, or, say, treated as an accessory to the murder. Kant would insist that even if the lie ought to be told this does not mean that the punctiliously truthful person who does not tell it is somehow implicated in the murder. It is the murderer, not the truthful person, who commits this crime. Telling the truth cannot be part of the crime. On Kant's view, persons are not supposed to be responsible for managing each other's conduct. If the lie were a duty of justice, we would be responsible for that.

These reflections will help us to think about the second casuistical problem, the lie to the philanthropist. I think it does follow from the line of argument I have taken that the lie cannot be shown to be impermissible. Although the philanthropist can hardly be called evil, he is doing something tricky and underhanded, which on Kant's view is wrong. He should not use this method of getting the information he wants. This is especially true if the reason he does not use a more straightforward method is that he assumes that if he does, people will lie to him. We are not supposed to base our actions on the assumption that other people will behave badly. Assuming this does not occur in an institutional context, and you have not sworn that your remarks were true, the philanthropist will have no recourse to justice if you lie to him.[15] But the reasons that favor telling the lie that exist in the first case do not exist here. According to Kant, you do not have a duty to promote your own happiness. Nor would anyone perform such an action out of self-respect. This is, in a very trivial way, a case of dealing with evil. But you can best deal with it by telling the philanthropist that you know what he is up to, perhaps even that you find it sneaky. This is *because* the ideal that makes his action a bad one is an ideal of straightforwardness in human relations. This would also be the best way to deal with the murderer, if it *were* a way to deal with a murderer. But of course it is not.

Ideal and Non-ideal Theory

I now turn to the question of what structure an ethical theory must have in order to accommodate this way of thinking. In *A Theory of Justice*, John Rawls proposes a division of moral philosophy into ideal and non-ideal theory.[16] In that work, the task of ideal theory is to determine "what a perfectly just society would be like," while non-ideal theory deals with punishment, war, opposition to unjust regimes, and compensatory justice (sec. 2, pp. 8–9). Since I wish to use this feature of Rawls's theory for a model, I am going to sketch his strategy for what I will call a double-level theory.

Rawls identifies two conceptions of justice, which he calls the general conception and the special conception (secs 11, 26, 39, 46). The general conception tells us that all goods distributed by society, including liberty and opportunity, are to be distributed equally unless an unequal distribution is to the advantage of everyone, and especially those who fall on the low side of the inequality (sec. 13). Injustice, according to the general conception, occurs whenever there are inequalities that are not to the benefit of everyone (sec. 11, p. 62). The special conception in its most developed form removes liberty and opportunity from the scope of this principle and says they must be distributed equally, forbidding tradeoffs of these goods for economic gains. It also introduces a number of priority rules, for example, the priority of liberty over all other considerations, and the priority of equal opportunity over economic considerations (secs 11, 46, 82).

Ideal theory is worked out under certain assumptions. One is strict compliance: it is assumed that everyone will act justly. The other, a little harder to specify, is that historical, economic, and natural conditions are such that realization of the ideal is feasible. Our conduct toward those who do not comply, or in circumstances which make the immediate realization of a just state of affairs impossible, is governed by the principles of non-ideal theory. Certain ongoing natural conditions which may always prevent the full realization of the ideal state of affairs also belong to non-ideal theory: the problems of dealing with the seriously ill or mentally disturbed, for instance, belong in this category. For purposes of constructing ideal theory, we assume that everyone is "rational and able to manage their own affairs" (sec. 39, p. 248). We also assume in ideal theory that there are no massive historic injustices, such as the oppression of blacks and women, to be corrected. The point is to work out our ideal view of justice on the assumption that people, nature, and history will behave themselves so that the ideal can be realized, and then to determine – in light of that ideal – what is to be done in actual circumstances when they do not. The special conception is not applied without regard to circumstances. Special principles will be used in non-ideal conditions.

Non-ideal conditions exist when, or to the extent that, the special conception of justice cannot be realized effectively. In these circumstances our conduct is to be determined in the following way: the special conception becomes a goal, rather than an ideal to live up to; we are to work toward the conditions in which it is feasible. For instance, suppose there is a case like this: widespread poverty or ignorance due to the level of economic development is such that the legal establishment of equal liberties makes no real difference to the lot of the disadvantaged members of society. It is an empty formality. On the other hand, some inequality, temporarily instituted, would actually tend to foster conditions in which equal liberty could become a reality for everyone. In these circumstances, Rawls's double-level theory allows for the temporary inequality (secs 11, 39). The priority rules give us guidance as to which features of the special conception are most urgent. These are the ones that we should be striving to achieve as soon as possible. For example, if formal equal opportunity for blacks and women is ineffective, affirmative action measures may be in order. If some people claim that this causes inefficiency at first, it is neither here nor there, since equality of opportunity has priority over efficiency. The special conception may also tell us which of our non-ideal options is least bad, closest to ideal conduct. For instance, civil disobedience is better than resorting to violence not only because violence is bad in itself, but because of the way in which civil disobedience expresses the democratic principles of the just society it aspires to bring about (sec. 59). Finally, the general conception of justice commands categorically. In sufficiently bad circumstances none of the characteristic features of the special conception may be realizable. But there is no excuse *ever* for violation of the general conception. If inequalities are not benefiting those on the lower end of them in some way, they are simply oppression. The general conception, then, represents the point at which justice becomes uncompromising.[17]

A double-level theory can be contrasted to two types of single-level theory, both of which in a sense fail to distinguish the way we should behave in ideal and non-ideal conditions, but which are at opposite extremes. A consequentialist theory such as utilitarianism does not really distinguish ideal from non-ideal conditions. Of course, the utilitarian can see the difference between a state of affairs in which everyone can be made reasonably happy and a state of affairs in which the utilitarian choice must be for the "lesser of evils," but it is still really a matter of degree. In principle we do not know what counts as a state in which everyone is "as happy as possible" absolutely. Instead, the utilitarian wants to make everyone as happy as possible relative to the circumstances, and pursues this goal regardless of how friendly the circumstances are to human happiness. The difference is not between ideal and non-ideal states of affairs but simply between better and worse states of affairs.

Kant's theory as he understood it represents the other extreme of single-level theory. The standard of conduct he sets for us is designed for an ideal state of affairs: we are always to act as if we were living in a Kingdom of Ends, regardless of possible disastrous results. Kant is by no means dismissive toward the distressing problems caused by the evil conduct of other human beings and the unfriendliness of nature to human ideals, but his solution to these problems is different. He finds in them grounds for a morally motivated religious faith in God.[18] Our rational motive for belief in a moral author of the world derives from our rational need for grounds for hope that these problems will be resolved. Such an author would have designed the laws of nature so that, in ways that are not apparent to us, our moral actions and efforts do tend to further the realization of an actual Kingdom of Ends. With faith in God, we can trust that a Kingdom of Ends will be the consequence of our actions as well as the ideal that guides them.

In his *Critique of Utilitarianism*, Bernard Williams spells out some of the unfortunate consequences of what I am calling single-level theories.[19] According to Williams, the consequentialist's commitment to doing whatever is necessary to secure the best outcome may lead to violations of what we would ordinarily think of as integrity. There is no kind of action that is so mean or so savage that it can *never* lead to a better outcome than the alternatives. A commitment to always securing the best outcome never allows you to say "bad consequences or not, this is not the sort of thing I do; I am not that sort of person." And no matter how mean or how savage the act required to secure the best outcome is, the utilitarian thinks that you will be irrational to regret that you did it, for you will have done what is in the straightforward sense the right thing.[20] A Kantian approach, by defining a determinate *ideal* of conduct to live up to rather than setting a *goal* of action to strive for, solves the problem about integrity, but with a high price. The advantage of the Kantian approach is the definite sphere of responsibility. Your share of the responsibility for the way the world is is well-defined and limited, and if you act as you ought, bad outcomes are not your responsibility. The trouble is that in cases such as that of the murderer at the door it seems grotesque simply to say that I have done my part by telling the truth and the bad results are not my responsibility.

The point of a double-level theory is to give us both a definite and well-defined sphere of responsibility for everyday life and some guidance, at least, about when we may or must take the responsibility of violating ideal standards. The commonsense approach to this problem uses an intuitive quantitative measure: we depart from our ordinary rules and standards of conduct when the consequences of following them would be "very bad." This is unhelpful for two reasons. First, it leaves us on our own about determining *how* bad. Second, the attempt to justify it leads down a familiar consequentialist slippery slope: if very bad consequences justify a departure from ordinary norms, why do not slightly bad consequences justify such a departure? A double-level theory substitutes something better than this rough quantitative measure. In Rawls's theory, for example, a departure from equal liberty cannot be justified by the fact that the consequences of liberty are "very bad" in terms of mere efficiency. This does not mean that an endless amount of inefficiency will be tolerated, because presumably at some point the inefficiency may interfere with the effectiveness of liberty. One might put the point this way: the measure of "very bad" is not entirely intuitive but rather, bad enough to interfere with the reality of liberty. Of course this is not an algorithmic criterion and cannot be applied without judgment, but it is not as inexact as a wholly intuitive quantitative measure, and, importantly, does not lead to a consequentialist slippery slope.

Another advantage of a double-level theory is the explanation it offers of the other phenomenon Williams is concerned about: that of regret for doing a certain kind of action even if in the circumstances it was the "right" thing. A double-level theory offers an account of at least some of the occasions for this kind of regret. We will regret having to depart from the ideal standard of conduct, for we identify with this standard and think of our autonomy in terms of it. Regret for an action we would not do under ideal circumstances seems appropriate even if we have done what is clearly the right thing.[21]

[. . .]

Conclusion

If the account I have given is correct, the resources of a double-level theory may be available to the Kantian. The Formula of Humanity and its corollary, the vision of a Kingdom of Ends, provide an ideal to live up to in daily life as well as a long-term political and moral goal for humanity. But it is not feasible always to live up to this ideal, and where the attempt to live up to it would make you a tool of evil, you should not do so. In evil circumstances, but only then, the Kingdom of Ends can become a goal to seek rather than an ideal to live up to, and this will provide us with some guidance. The Kantian priorities – of justice over the pursuit of obligatory ends, and of respect over benevolence – still help us to see what matters most. And even in the worst circumstances, there is always the Formula of Universal Law, telling us what we must not in any case do. For whatever bad circumstances may drive us to do, we cannot possibly be justified in doing something which others in those same circumstances could not also do. The Formula of Universal Law provides the point at which morality becomes uncompromising.

Let me close with some reflections about the extent to which Kant himself might have agreed with this modification of his views. Throughout this essay, I have portrayed Kant as an uncompromising idealist, and there is much to support this view. But in the historical and political writings, as well as in the *Lectures on Ethics*, we find a somewhat different attitude. This seems to me to be especially important. Kant believes that the Kingdom of Ends on earth, the highest political good, can only be realized in a condition of peace (*MMJ*, 354–5/127–9). But he does not think that this commits a nation to a simple pacifism that would make it the easy victim of its enemies. Instead, he draws up laws of war in which peace functions not as an uncompromising ideal to be lived up to in the present, but as a long-range goal which guides our conduct even when war is necessary (*PP*, 343–8/85–91; *MMJ*, 343–51/114–25). If a Kantian can hold such a view for the conduct of nations, why not for that of individuals? If this is right, the task of Kantian moral philosophy is to draw up for individuals something analogous to Kant's laws of war: special principles to use when dealing with evil.

Notes

1 Where I cite or refer to any of Kant's works more than once, I have inserted the reference into the text. The following abbreviations are used:

G   *Foundations of the Metaphysics of Morals* (1785). The first page number is that of the Prussian Academy Edition Volume IV; the second is that of the translation by Lewis White Beck (Indianapolis: Bobbs-Merrill Library of Liberal Arts, 1959).

C_2 *Critique of Practical Reason* (1788). Prussian Academy Volume V; Lewis White Beck's translation (Indianapolis: Bobbs-Merrill Library of Liberal Arts, 1956).

MMV   *The Metaphysical Principles of Virtue* (1797). Prussian Academy Volume VI; James Ellington's translation in *Immanuel Kant: Ethical Philosophy* (Indianapolis: Hackett, 1983).

MMJ   *The Metaphysical Elements of Justice* (1797). Prussian Academy Volume VI; John Ladd's translation (Indianapolis: Bobbs-Merrill Library of Liberal Arts, 1965).

PP   *Perpetual Peace* (1795). Prussian Academy Volume VIII, translation by Lewis White Beck in *On History*, edited by Lewis White Beck (Indianapolis: Bobbs-Merrill Library of Liberal Arts, 1963).

SRL   "On a Supposed Right to Lie from Altruistic Motives" (1797). Prussian Academy Volume VIII; translation by Lewis White Beck in *Immanuel Kant: Critique of Practical Reason and Other Writings in Moral Philosophy* (Chicago: University of Chicago Press, 1949; reprint, New York: Garland Publishing Company, 1976).

E   *Lectures on Ethics* (1775–1780). Edited by Paul Menzer from the notes of Theodor Friedrich Brauer, using the notes of Gottlieb Kutzner and Christian Mrongovius; translated by Louis Infield (London: Methuen & Co., Ltd., 1930; reprint, New York: Harper Torchbooks, 1963; current reprint, Indianapolis: Hackett Publishing Co., 1980).

2 I defend it in "Kant's Formula of Universal Law," *Pacific Philosophical Quarterly*, 66, nos 1 and 2 (January/April 1986), pp. 24–47.

3 I am relying here on the assumption that when people ask us questions, they give us some account of themselves and of the context in which the questions are asked. Or, if they don't, it is because they are relying on a context that is assumed. If someone comes to your door looking for someone, you assume that there is a family emergency or some such thing. I am prepared to count such reliance as deception if the questioner knows about it and uses it, thinking that we would refuse to answer his questions if we knew the real context to be otherwise. Sometimes people ask me, "Suppose the murderer just asks whether his friend is in your house, without saying anything about why he wants to know?" I think that, in our culture anyway, people do not *just ask* questions of each other about anything except the time of day and directions for getting places. After all, the reason why refusal to answer is an unsatisfactory way of dealing with this case is that it will almost inevitably give rise to suspicion of the truth, and this is because people normally answer such questions. Perhaps if we did live in a culture in which people regularly *just asked* questions in the way suggested, refusal to answer would be commonplace and would not give rise to suspicion; it would not even be considered odd or rude. Otherwise there would be no way to maintain privacy.

4 In fact, it will now be the case that if the murderer supposes that you suspect him, he is not going to ask you, knowing that you will answer so as to deceive him. Since we must avoid the silly problem about the murderer being able to deduce the truth from his knowledge that you will speak falsely, what you announce is that you will say whatever is necessary in order to conceal the truth. There is no reason to suppose that you will be mechanical about this. You are not going to be a reliable source of information. The murderer will therefore seek some other way to locate his victim.

On the other hand, suppose that the murderer does, contrary to my supposition, announce his real intentions. Then the arguments that I have given do not apply. In this case, I believe your only recourse is refusal to answer (whether or nor the victim is in your house, or you know his whereabouts). If an answer is extorted from you by force you may lie, according to the argument I will give later in this article.

5 Kant himself takes notice of this sort of problem in a footnote to this passage in which he criticizes Golden-Rule type principles for, among other things, the sort of subjectivity in question: such principles cannot establish the duty of beneficence, for insurance, because "many a man would gladly consent that others should not benefit him, provided only that he might be excused from showing benevolence to them" (*G*, 430n./48n.).

6 Sometimes it is objected that someone could assent to being lied to in advance of the actual occasion of the lie, and that in such a case the deception might still succeed. One can therefore agree to be deceived. I think it depends what circumstances are envisioned. I can certainly agree to remain uninformed about something, but this is not the same as agreeing to be deceived. For example, I could say to my doctor: "Don't tell me if I am fatally ill, even if I ask." But if I then do ask the doctor whether I am fatally ill, I cannot be certain whether she will answer me truthfully. Perhaps what's being envisioned is that I simply agree to be lied to, but not about anything, in particular. Will I then trust the person with whom I have made this odd agreement?

7 A similar conclusion about the way in which the Formula of Humanity makes coercion and deception wrong is reached by Onora O'Neill in "Between Consenting Adults," *Philosophy & Public Affairs*, 14, no. 3 (Summer 1985), pp. 252–77.

8 *Immanuel Kant's "Critique of Pure Reason,"* trans. Norman Kemp Smith (New York: St Martin's Press, 1965) A738–9/B766–7, p. 593.

9 It is perhaps also relevant that in Kant's discussion of perfect moral friendship the emphasis is not on good will toward one another, but on complete confidence and openness. See *MMV*, 471–2/138–9.

10 Some evidence that Kant is concerned with this sort of thing may be found in the fact that he identifies two meanings of the word "prudence" (*Klugheit*); "The former sense means the skill of a man in having an influence on others so as to use them for his own purposes. The latter is the ability to unite all these purposes to his own lasting advantage" (*G*, 416n./33n.). A similar remark is found in *Anthropology from a Pragmatic Point of View* (1798). See the translation by Mary J. Gregor (The Hague: Martinus Nijhoff, 1974), p. 183; Prussian Academy Edition Volume VII, p. 322.

11 I call this view Socratic because of Socrates' concern with the differences between reason and persuasion and, in particular, because in the *Apology*, he makes a case for the categorical duty of straightforwardness. Socrates and Plato are also concerned with a troublesome feature of this moral view that Kant neglects. An argument must come packaged in some sort of presentation, and one may well object that it is impossible to make a straightforward presentation of a case to someone who is close to or admires you, without emphasis, without style, without taking some sort of advantage of whatever it is about you that has your listener's attention in the first place. So how can we avoid the non-rational influence of others? I take it that most obviously in the *Symposium*, but also in other dialogues concerned with the relation of love and teaching such as the *Phaedrus*, Plato is at work on the question whether you can use your sex appeal to draw another's attention to the reasons he has for believing or doing things, rather than as a distraction that aids your case illicitly.

12 Of course you may also resist force with lies, if resisting it with force is not an option for you. This gives rise to a question about whether these options are on a footing with each other. In many cases, lying will be the better option. This is because when you use coercion you risk doing injury to the person you coerce. Injuring people unnecessarily is wrong, a wrong that should be distinguished from the use of coercion. When you lie you do not risk doing this extra wrong. But Kant thinks that lying is in itself worse than coercion, because of the peculiarly direct way in which it violates autonomy. So it should follow that if you can deal with the murderer by coercion, this is a *better* option than lying. Others seem to share this intuition. Cardinal John Henry Newman, responding to Samuel Johnson's claim that he would lie to a murderer who asked which way his victim had gone, suggests that the appropriate thing to do is "to knock the man down, and to call out for the police" (*Apologia Pro Vita Sua: Being a History of His Religious Opinions* [London: Longmans, Green, 1880], p. 361. I am quoting from Sissela Bok, *Lying* [New York: Vintage Books, 1979], p. 42). If you can do it without seriously hurting the murderer, it is, so to speak, cleaner just to kick him off the front porch than to lie. This treats the *murderer himself* more like a human being than lying to him does.

13 I owe this example to John Koethe.

14 For a discussion of this question see Barbara Herman, "Mutual Aid and Respect for Persons," *Ethics*, 94 (July 1984), pp. 577–602.

15 In the *Lectures on Ethics*, Kant takes the position that you may lie to someone who lies to or bullies you as long as you don't say specifically that your words will be true. He claims this is not lying, because such a person should not expect you to tell the truth (*LE*, pp. 227, 229).

16 John Rawls, *A Theory of Justice* (Cambridge, MA: Harvard University Press, 1971). Section and page numbers referring to this work will appear in the text.

17 In a non-ideal case, one's actions may be guided by a more instrumental style of reasoning than in ideal theory. Bur non-ideal theory is not a form of consequentialism. There are two reasons for this. One is that the goal set by the ideal is not just one of good consequences, but of a just state of affairs. If a consequentialist view is one that defines right action entirely in terms of good consequences (which are not themselves defined in terms of considerations of rightness or justice), then non-ideal theory is not consequentialist. The second reason is that the ideal will also guide our choice among non-ideal alternatives, importing criteria for this choice other than effectiveness. I would like to thank Alan Gewirth for prompting me to clarify my thoughts on this matter, and David Greenstone for helping me to do so.

18 See the "Dialectic of Pure Practical Reason" of the *Critique of Practical Reason*, and the *Critique of Teleological Judgment*, sec. 87.

19 Bernard Williams, in *Utilitarianism For and Against*, by J. J. C. Smart and Bernard Williams (Cambridge: Cambridge University Press, 1973), pp. 75–150.

20 Williams also takes this issue up in "Ethical Consistency," originally published in the Supplementary Volumes to the *Proceedings of the Aristotelian Society*, XXXIX (1965) and reprinted in his collection, *Problems of the Self* (Cambridge: Cambridge University Press, 1973), pp. 166–86.

21 It is important here to distinguish two kinds of exceptions. As Rawls points out in "Two Conceptions of Rules" (*The Philosophical Review* 64 [January 1965]), a practice such as promising may have certain exceptions built into it. Everyone who has learned the practice understands that the obligation to keep the promise is cancelled if one of these obtains. When one breaks a promise because this sort of exception obtains, regret would be inappropriate and obsessive. And these sorts of exceptions may occur even in "ideal" circumstances. The kind of exception one makes when dealing with evil should be distinguished from exceptions built into practices.

---

22 Libertarianism

John Hospers

The political philosophy that is called libertarianism (from the Latin *libertas*, liberty) is the doctrine that every person is the owner of his own life, and that no one is the owner of anyone else's life: and that consequently every human being has the right to act in accordance with his own choices, unless those actions infringe on the

From *The Libertarian Alternative,* ed. Tibor Machan (Chicago, IL: Nelson-Hall, 1974). Reprinted by permission.

equal liberty of other human beings to act in accordance with their choices.

There are several other ways of stating the same libertarian thesis:

(1) *No one is anyone else's master, and no one is anyone else's slave.*   Since I am the one to decide how my life is to be conducted just as you decide about yours, I have no right (even if I had the power) to make you my slave and be your master, nor have you the right to become the master

by enslaving me. Slavery is *forced* servitude, and since no one owns the life of anyone else, no one has the right to enslave another. Political theories past and present have traditionally been concerned with who should be the master (usually the king, the dictator, or government bureaucracy) and who should be the slaves, and what the extent of the slavery should be. Libertarianism holds that no one has the right to use force to enslave the life of another, or any portion or aspect of that life.

(2) *Other men's lives are not yours to dispose of.* I enjoy seeing operas; but operas are expensive to produce. Opera-lovers often say, "The state (or the city, etc.) should subsidize opera, so that we can all see it. Also it would be for people's betterment, cultural benefit, etc." But what they are advocating is nothing more or less than legalized plunder. They can't pay for the productions themselves, and yet they want to see opera, which involves a large number of people and their labor; so what they are saying in effect is, "Get the money through legalized force. Take a little bit more out of every worker's paycheck every week to pay for the operas we want to see." But I have no right to take by force from the workers' pockets to pay for what I want.

Perhaps it would be better if he *did* go to see opera – then I should try to convince him to go voluntarily. But to take the money from him forcibly, because in my opinion it would be good for *him*, is still seizure of his earnings, which is plunder.

Besides, if I have the right to force him to help pay for my pet projects, hasn't he equally the right to force me to help pay for his? Perhaps he in turn wants the government to subsidize rock-and-roll, or his new car, or a house in the country? If I have the right to milk him, why hasn't he the right to milk me? If I can be a moral cannibal, why can't he too?

We should beware of the inventors of utopias. They would remake the world according to their vision – with the lives and fruits of the labor of *other* human beings. Is it someone's utopian vision that others should build pyramids to beautify the landscape? Very well, then other men should provide the labor; and if he is in a position of political power, and he can't get men to do it voluntarily, then he must *compel* them to "cooperate" – i.e. he must enslave them.

A hundred men might gain great pleasure from beating up or killing just one insignificant human being; but other men's lives are not theirs to dispose of. "In order to achieve the worthy goals of the next five-year-plan, we must forcibly collectivize the peasants . . ."; but other men's lives are not theirs to dispose of. Do you want to occupy, rent-free, the mansion that another man worked for twenty years to buy? But other men's lives are not yours to dispose of. Do you want operas so badly that everyone is forced to work harder to pay for their subsidization through taxes? But other men's lives are not yours to dispose of. Do you want to have free medical care at the expense of other people, whether they wish to provide it or not? But this would require them to work longer for you whether they want to or not, and other men's lives are not yours to dispose of. . . .

(3) *No human being should be a non-voluntary mortgage on the life of another.* I cannot claim your life, your work, or the products of your effort as mine. The fruit of one man's labor should not be fair game for every freeloader who comes along and demands it as his own. The orchard that has been carefully grown, nurtured, and harvested by its owner should not be ripe for the plucking for any bypasser who has a yen for the ripe fruit. The wealth that some men have produced should not be fair game for looting by government, to be used for whatever purposes its representatives determine, no matter what their motives in so doing may be. The theft of your money by a robber is not justified by the fact that he used it to help his injured mother.

It will already be evident that libertarian doctrine is embedded in a view of the rights of man. Each human being has the right to live his life as he chooses, compatibly with the equal right of all other human beings to live their lives as they choose.

All man's rights are implicit in the above statement. Each man has the right to life: any attempt by others to take it away from him, or even to injure him, violates this right, through the use of coercion against him. Each man has the right to liberty: to conduct his life in accordance with the alternatives open to him without coercive action by others. And every man has the right to property: to work to sustain his life (and the lives of whichever others he chooses to sustain, such as his family) and to retain the fruits of his labor.

People often defend the rights of life and liberty but denigrate property rights, and yet the right to property is as basic as the other two: indeed, without property rights no other rights are possible. Depriving you of property is depriving you of the means by which you live. . . .

I have no right to decide how *you* should spend your time or your money. I can make that decision for myself, but not for you, my neighbor. I may deplore your choice of lifestyle, and I may talk with you about it provided you are willing to listen to me. But I have no right to use force to change it. Nor have I the right to decide how you should spend the money you have earned. I may appeal to you to give it to the Red Cross, and you may prefer to go to prize-fights. But that is your decision, and however much I may chafe about it I do not have the right to interfere forcibly with it, for example by robbing you in order to use the money in accordance with *my* choices. (If I have the right to rob you, have you also the right to rob me?)

When I claim a right, I carve out a niche, as it were, in my life, saying in effect, "This activity I must be able to perform without interference from others. For you and everyone else, this is off limits." And so I put up a "no trespassing" sign, which marks off the area of my right. Each individual's right is his "no trespassing" sign in relation to me and others. I may not encroach upon his domain any more than he upon mine, without my consent. Every right entails a duty, true – but the duty is only that of *forbearance* – that is, of *refraining* from violating the other person's right. If you have a right to life, I have no right to take your life; if you have a right to the products of your labor (property), I have no right to take it from you without your consent. The non-violation of these rights will not

guarantee you protection against natural catastrophes such as floods and earthquakes, but it will protect you against the aggressive activities *of other men*. And rights, after all, have to do with one's relations to other human beings, not with one's relations to physical nature.

Nor were these rights created by government; governments – some governments, obviously not all – *recognize* and *protect* the rights that individuals already have. Governments regularly forbid homicide and theft; and, at a more advanced stage, protect individuals against such things as libel and breach of contract. . . .

The *right to property* is the most misunderstood and unappreciated of human rights, and it is one most constantly violated by governments. "Property" of course does not mean only real estate; it includes anything you can call your own – your clothing, your car, your jewelry, your books and papers.

The right of property is not the right to just *take* it from others, for this would interfere with *their* property rights. It is rather the right to work for it, to obtain non-coercively, the money or services which you can present in voluntary exchange.

The right to property is consistently underplayed by intellectuals today, sometimes even frowned upon, as if we should feel guilty for upholding such a right in view of all the poverty in the world. But the right to property is absolutely basic. It is your hedge against the future. It is your assurance that what you have worked to earn will still be there and be yours, when you wish or need to use it, especially when you are too old to work any longer.

Government has always been the chief enemy of the right to property. The officials of government, wishing to increase their power, and finding an increase of wealth an effective way to bring this about seize some or all of what a person has earned – and since government has a monopoly of physical force within the geographical area of the nation, it has the power (but not the right) to do this. When this happens, of course, every citizen of that country is insecure: he knows that no matter how hard he works the government can swoop down on him at any time and confiscate his earnings and possessions. A person sees his life savings wiped out in a moment when the tax-collectors descend to deprive him of the fruits of his work; or, an industry which has been fifty years in the making and cost millions of dollars and millions of hours of time and planning, is nationalized overnight. Or the government, via inflation, cheapens the currency, so that hard-won dollars aren't worth anything any more. The effect of such actions, of course, is that people lose hope and incentive: if no matter how hard they work the government agents can take it all away, why bother to work at all, for more than today's needs? Depriving people of property is *depriving them of the means by which they live* – the freedom of the individual citizen to do what he wishes with his own life and to plan for the future. Indeed only if property rights are respected is there any point to planning for the future and working to achieve one's goals. *Property rights are what makes long-range planning possible* – the kind of planning which is a distinctively human endeavor, as opposed to the day-by-day activity of the lion who hunts, who depends on the supply of game tomorrow but has no real insurance against starvation in a day or a week. Without the right to property, the right to life itself amounts to little: how can you sustain your life if you cannot plan ahead? and how can you plan ahead if the fruits of your labor can at any moment be confiscated by government? . . .

Indeed, the right to property may well be considered second only to the right to life. Even the freedom of speech is limited by considerations of property. If a person visiting in your home behaves in a way undesired by you, you have every right to evict him; he can scream or agitate elsewhere if he wishes, but not in your home without your consent. Does a person have a right to shout obscenities in a cathedral? No, for the owners of the cathedral (presumably the Church) have not allowed others on their property for that purpose; one may go there to worship or to visit, but not just for any purpose one wishes. Their property right is prior to your or my wish to scream or expectorate or write graffiti on their building. Or, to take the stock example, does a person have a right to shout "Fire!" falsely in a

crowded theater? No, for the theater owner has permitted others to enter and use his property only for a specific purpose, that of seeing a film or watching a stage show. If a person heckles or otherwise disturbs other members of the audience, he can be thrown out. (In fact, he can be removed for any reason the owner chooses, provided his admission money is returned.) And if he shouts "Fire!" when there is no fire, he may be endangering other lives by causing a panic or a stampede. The right to free speech doesn't give one the right to say anything anywhere; it is circumscribed by property rights.

Again, some people seem to assume that the right to free speech (including written speech) means that they can go to a newspaper publisher and demand that he print in his newspaper some propaganda or policy statement for their political party (or other group). But of course they have no right to the use of his newspaper. Ownership of the newspaper is the product of his labor, and he has a right to put into his newspaper whatever he wants, for whatever reason. If he excludes material which many readers would like to have in, perhaps they can find it in another newspaper or persuade him to print it himself (if there are enough of them, they will usually do just that). Perhaps they can even cause his newspaper to fail. But as long as he owns it, he has the right to put in it what he wishes; what would a property right be if he could not do this? They have no right to place their material in his newspaper without his consent – not for free, nor even for a fee. Perhaps other newspapers will include it, or perhaps they can start their own newspaper (in which case they have a right to put in it what they like). If not, an option open to them would be to mimeograph and distribute some handbills.

In exactly the same way, no one has a right to "free television time" unless the owner of the television station consents to give it; it is his station, he has the property rights over it, and it is for him to decide how to dispose of his time. He may not decide wisely, but it is his right to decide as he wishes. If he makes enough unwise decisions, and courts enough unpopularity with the viewing public or the sponsors, he may have to go out of business; but as he is free to make his own decisions, so is he free to face their consequences. (If the government owns the television station, then government officials will make the decisions, and there is no guarantee of *their* superior wisdom. The difference is that when "the government" owns the station, you are forced to help pay for its upkeep through your taxes, whether the bureaucrat in charge decides to give you television time or not.)

"But why have *individual* property rights? Why not have lands and houses owned by everybody together?" Yes, this involves no violation of individual rights, as long as everybody consents to this arrangement and no one is forced to join it. The parties to it may enjoy the communal living enough (at least for a time) to overcome certain inevitable problems: that some will work and some not, that some will achieve more in an hour than others can do in a day, and still they will all get the same income. The few who do the most will in the end consider themselves "workhorses" who do the work of two or three or twelve, while the others will be "freeloaders" on the efforts of these few. But as long as they can get out of the arrangement if they no longer like it, no violation of rights is involved. They got in voluntarily, and they can get out voluntarily; no one has used force.

"But why not say that everybody owns everything? That we *all* own everything there is?"

To some this may have a pleasant ring – but let us try to analyze what it means. If everybody owns everything, then everyone has an equal right to go everywhere, do what he pleases, take what he likes, destroy if he wishes, grow crops or burn them, trample them under, and so on. Consider what it would be like in practice. Suppose you have saved money to buy a house for yourself and your family. Now suppose that the principle, "everybody owns everything," becomes adopted. Well then, why shouldn't every itinerant hippie just come in and take over, sleeping in your beds and eating in your kitchen and not bothering to replace the food supply or clean up the mess? After all, it belongs to all of us, doesn't it? So we have just as much right to it as you, the buyer, have. What happens if we *all* want to sleep in the bedroom and there's not room for all of us? Is it the strongest who wins?

What would be the result? Since no one would be responsible for anything, the property would soon be destroyed, the food used up, the facilities non-functional. Beginning as a house that *one* family could use, it would end up as a house that *no one* could use. And if the principle continued to be adopted, no one would build houses any more – or anything else. What for? They would only be occupied and used by others, without remuneration.

Suppose two men are cast ashore on an island and they agree that each will cultivate half of it. The first man is industrious and grows crops and builds a shelter, making the most of the situation with which he is confronted. The second man, perhaps thinking that the warm days will last forever, lies in the sun, picks coconuts while they last, and does a minimum of work to sustain himself. At the time of harvest, the second man has nothing to harvest, nor does he assist the first man in his labors. But later when there is a dearth of food on the island, the second man comes to the first man and demands half of the harvest as his right. But of course he has no right to the product of the first man's labors. The first man may freely choose to give part of his harvest to the second out of charity rather than see him starve; but that is just what it is – charity, not the second man's right.

How can any of man's rights be violated? Ultimately, only by the use of force. I can make suggestions to you, I can reason with you, entreat you (if you are willing to listen), but I cannot *force* you without violating your rights; only by forcing you do I cut the cord between your free decisions and your actions. Voluntary relations between individuals involve no deprivation of rights, but murder, assault, and rape do, because in doing these things I make you the unwilling victim of my actions. A man's beating his wife involves no violation of rights if she *wanted* to be beaten. *Force is behavior that requires the unwilling involvement of other persons.*

Thus the use of force need not involve the use of physical violence. If I trespass on your property or dump garbage on it, I am violating your property rights, as indeed I am when I steal your watch; although this is not force in the sense of violence, it *is* a case of your being an unwilling victim of my action. Similarly, if you shout at me so that I cannot be heard when I try to speak, or blow a siren in my ear, or start a factory next door which pollutes my land, you are again violating my rights (to free speech, to property); I am, again, an unwilling victim of your actions. Similarly, if you steal a manuscript of mine and publish it as your own, you are confiscating a piece of my property and thus violating my right to keep what is the product of my labor. Of course, if I give you the manuscript with permission to sign your name to it and keep the proceeds, no violation of rights is involved – any more than if I give you permission to dump garbage on my yard.

According to libertarianism, the role of government should be limited to the retaliatory use of force against those who have initiated its use. It should not enter into any other areas, such as religion, social organization, and economics.

Government

Government is the most dangerous institution known to man. Throughout history it has violated the rights of men more than any individual or group of individuals could do: it has killed people, enslaved them, sent them to forced labor and concentration camps, and regularly robbed and pillaged them of the fruits of their expended labor. Unlike individual criminals, government has the power to arrest and try; unlike individual criminals, it can surround and encompass a person totally, dominating every aspect of one's life, so that one has no recourse from it but to leave the country (and in totalitarian nations even that is prohibited). Government throughout history has a much sorrier record than any individual, even that of a ruthless mass murderer. The signs we see on bumper stickers are chillingly accurate: "Beware: the Government Is Armed and Dangerous."

The only proper role of government, according to libertarians, is that of the protector of the citizen against aggression by other individuals. The government, of course, should never initiate aggression; its proper role is as the embodi-

ment of the *retaliatory* use of force against anyone who initiates its use.

If each individual had constantly to defend himself against possible aggressors, he would have to spend a considerable portion of his life in target practice, karate exercises, and other means of self-defense, and even so he would probably be helpless against groups of individuals who might try to kill, maim, or rob him. He would have little time for cultivating those qualities which are essential to civilized life, nor would improvements in science, medicine, and the arts be likely to occur. The function of government is to take this responsibility off his shoulders: the government undertakes to defend him against aggressors and to punish them if they attack him. When the government is effective in doing this, it enables the citizen to go about his business unmolested and without constant fear for his life. To do this, of course, government must have physical power – the police, to protect the citizen from aggression within its borders, and the armed forces, to protect him from aggressors outside. Beyond that, the government should not intrude upon his life, either to run his business, or adjust his daily activities, or prescribe his personal moral code.

Government, then, undertakes to be the individual's protector; but historically governments have gone far beyond this function. Since they already have the physical power, they have not hesitated to use it for purposes far beyond that which was entrusted to them in the first place. Undertaking initially to protect its citizens against aggression, it has often itself become an aggressor – a far greater aggressor, indeed, than the criminals against whom it was supposed to protect its citizens. Governments have done what no private citizen can do: arrest and imprison individuals without a trial and send them to slave labor camps. Government must have power in order to be effective – and yet the very means by which alone it can be effective make it vulnerable to the abuse of power, leading to managing the lives of individuals and even inflicting terror upon them.

What then should be the function of government? In a word, the *protection of human rights*.

1. *The right to life.* Libertarians support all such legislation as will protect human beings against the use of force by others, for example, laws against killing, attempting killing, maiming, beating, and all kinds of physical violence.
2. *The right to liberty.* There should be no laws compromising in any way freedom of speech, of the press, and peaceable assembly. There should be no censorship of ideas, books, films, or of anything else by government.
3. *The right to property.* Libertarians support legislation that protects the property rights of individuals against confiscation, nationalization, eminent domain, robbery, trespass, fraud and misrepresentation, patent and copyright, libel and slander.

Someone has violently assaulted you. Should he be legally liable? Of course. He has violated one of your rights. He has knowingly injured you and since he has initiated aggression against you he should be made to expiate.

Someone has negligently left his bicycle on the sidewalk where you trip over it in the dark and injure yourself. He didn't do it intentionally; he didn't mean you any harm. Should he be legally liable? Of course; he has, however unwittingly, injured you, and since the injury is caused by him and you are the victim, he should pay.

Someone across the street is unemployed. Should you be taxed extra to pay for his expenses? Not at all. You have not injured him, you are not responsible for the fact that he is unemployed (unless you are a senator or bureaucrat who agitated for further curtailing of business, which legislation passed, with the result that your neighbor was laid off by the curtailed business). You may voluntarily wish to help him out, or better still, try to get him a job to put him on his feet again; but since you have initiated no aggressive act against him, and neither purposely nor accidentally injured him in any way, you should not be legally penalized for the fact of his unemployment. (Actually, it is just such penalties that increase unemployment.)

One man, *A*, works hard for years and finally earns a high salary as a professional man. A second man, *B*, prefers not to work at all, and to spend wastefully what money he has (through inheritance), so that after a year or two he has nothing left. At the end of this time he has a long siege of illness and lots of medical bills to pay. He demands that the bills be paid by the government – that is, by the taxpayers of the land, including Mr *A*.

But of course *B* has no such right. He chose to lead his life in a certain way – that was his voluntary decision. One consequence of that choice is that he must depend on charity in case of later need. Mr *A* chose not to live that way. (And if everyone lived like Mr *B*, on whom would he depend in case of later need?) Each has a right to live in the way he pleases, but each must live with the consequences of his own decision (which, as always, fall primarily on himself). He cannot, in time of need, claim *A*'s beneficence as his right.

If a house-guest of yours starts to carve his initials in your walls and break up your furniture, you have a right to evict him, and call the police if he makes trouble. If someone starts to destroy the machinery in a factory, the factory-owner is also entitled to evict him and call the police. In both cases, persons other than the owner are permitted on the property only under certain conditions, at the pleasure of the owner. If those conditions are violated, the owner is entitled to use force to set things straight. The case is exactly the same on a college or university campus: if a campus demonstrator starts breaking windows, occupying the president's office, and setting fire to a dean, the college authorities are certainly within their rights to evict him forcibly; one is permitted on the college grounds only under specific conditions, set by the administration: study, peaceful student activity, even political activity if those in charge choose to permit it. If they do not choose to permit peaceful political activity on campus, they may be unwise, since a campus is after all a place where all sides of every issue should get discussed, and the college that doesn't permit this may soon lose its reputation and its students. All the same, the college official who does not permit it is quite within his rights; the students do not own the campus, nor do the hired troublemakers imported from elsewhere. In the case of a privately owned college, the owners, or whoever they have delegated to administer it, have the right to make the decisions as to who shall be permitted on the campus and under what conditions. In the case of a state university or college, the ownership problem is more complex: one could say that the "government" owns the campus or that "the people" do since they are the taxpayers who support it; but in either case, the university administration has the delegated task of keeping order, and until they are removed by the state administration or the taxpayers, it is theirs to decide who shall be permitted on campus, and what non-academic activities will be permitted to their students on the premises.

Property rights can be violated by physical trespass, of course, or by anyone entering on your property for any reason without your consent. (If you *do* consent to having your neighbor dump garbage on your yard, there is no violation of your rights.) But the physical trespass of a person is only a special case of violation of property rights. Property rights can be violated by soundwaves, in the form of a loud noise, or the sounds of your neighbor's hi-fi set while you are trying to sleep. Such violations of property rights are of course the subject of action in the courts.

But there is another violation of property rights that has not thus far been honored by the courts; this has to do with the effects of *pollution* of the atmosphere.

From the beginnings of modern air pollution, the courts made a conscious decision not to protect, for example, the orchards of farmers from the smoke of nearby factories or locomotives. They said, in effect, to the farmers: yes, your private property is being invaded by this smoke, but we hold that "public policy" is more important than private property, and public policy holds factories and locomotives to be good things. These goods were allowed to override the defense of property rights – with our consequent headlong rush into pollution disaster. The remedy is both "radical" and crystal clear, and it has nothing to do with multi-billion dollar palliative programs at the expense of the taxpayers which do not even meet the real issue. The remedy is simply to enjoin anyone from injecting pollutants into the air, and thereby invading the rights of persons and property. Period. The argument that such an injunction prohibition would add to the costs of industrial production is as reprehensible as the pre-Civil War argument that the abolition of slavery would add to the costs of growing cotton, and therefore should not take place. For this means that the polluters are able to impose the high costs of pollution upon those whose property rights they are allowed to invade with impunity.[1]

What about automobiles, the chief polluters of the air? One can hardly sue every automobile owner. But one can sue the manufacturers of automobiles who do not install anti-smog devices on the cars which they distribute – and later (though this is more difficult), owners of individual automobiles if they discard the equipment or do not keep it functional.

The violation of rights does not apply only to air-pollution. If someone with a factory upstream on a river pollutes the river, anyone living downstream from him, finding his water polluted, should be able to sue the owner of the factory. In this way the price of adding the anti-pollutant devices will be the owner's responsibility, and will probably be added to the cost of the products which the factory produces and thus spread around among all consumers, rather than the entire cost being borne by the users of the river in the form of polluted water, with the consequent impossibility of fishing, swimming, and so on. In each case, pollution would be stopped at the source rather than having its ill effects spread around to numerous members of the population.

What about property which you do not work to earn, but which you *inherit* from someone else? Do you have a right to that? You have no right to it until someone decides to give it to you. Consider the man who willed it to you; it was his, he had the right to use and dispose of it as *he* saw fit; and if he decided to give it to you, this is a windfall for you, but it was only the exercise of *his* right. Had the property been seized by the government at the man's death, or distributed among numerous other people designated by the government, it would have been a violation of his rights: for he, who worked to earn and sustain it, would not have been able to dispose of it according to his own judgment. If he doesn't have the right to determine who shall have it, who does?

What about the property status of your intellectual activity, such as inventions you may devise and books you write? These, of course, are your property also; they are the products of your mind; you worked at them, you created them. Prior to that, they did not exist. If you worked five years to write a book, and someone stole it and published it as his own, receiving royalties from its sales, he would have stolen your property just as surely as if he had robbed your home. The same is true if someone used and sold without your permission an invention which was the product of your labor and ingenuity.

The role of government with respect to this issue, at least most governments of the Western world, is a proper one: government protects the products of your labor from the moment they materialize. Copyright law protects your writings from piracy. In the United States, one's writings are protected for a period of twenty-seven years, and another twenty-seven if one applies for renewal of the copyright. In most other countries, they are protected for a period of fifty years after the author's death, permitting both himself and his surviving heirs to reap the fruits of his labor. After that they enter the "public domain" – that is, anyone may reprint them without your or your heirs' permission. Patent law protects your inventions for a limited period, which varies according to the type of invention. In no case are you forced to avail yourself of this protection; you need not apply for patent or copyright coverage if you do not wish to do so. But the protection of your intellectual property is there, in case you wish to use it.

What about the property status of the airwaves? Here the government's position is far more questionable. The government now claims ownership of the airwaves, leasing them to individuals and corporations. The government renews leases or refuses them depending on whether the programs satisfy authorities in the Federal Communications Commission. The official position is that "we all own the airwaves": but since only one party can broadcast on a certain frequency at a certain time without causing chaos, it is simply a fact of reality that everyone cannot use it. In fact the government decides who shall use the airwaves and one courts its displeasure only at the price of a revoked license. One can write without government approval, but one cannot use the airwaves without the approval of government.

What policy should have been observed with regard to the airwaves? Much the same as the policy that was followed in the case of the Homestead Act, when the lands of the American West were opening up for settlement. There was a policy of "first come, first served," with the government parceling out a certain acreage for each individual who wanted to claim the land as his own. There was no charge for the land, but if a man had not used it and built a dwelling during the first two-year period, it was assumed that he was not homesteading and the land was given to the next man in line. The airwaves too could have been given out on a "first come, first served" basis. The first man who used a given frequency would be its owner, and the government would protect him in the use of it against trespassers. If others wanted to use the same frequency, they would have to buy it from the first man, if he was willing to sell, or try to buy another, just as one now does with the land.

Laws may be classified into three types: (1) laws protecting individuals against themselves, such as laws against fornication and other sexual behavior, alcohol, and drugs; (2) laws protecting individuals against aggressions by other individuals, such as laws against murder, robbery, and fraud; (3) laws requiring people to help one another; for example, all laws which rob Peter to pay Paul, such as welfare.

Libertarians reject the first class of laws totally. Behavior which harms no one else is strictly the individual's own affair. Thus, there should be no laws against becoming intoxicated, since whether or not to become intoxicated is the individual's own decision: but there should be laws against driving while intoxicated, since the drunken driver is a threat to every other motorist on the highway (drunken driving falls into type 2). Similarly, there should be no laws against drugs (except the prohibition of sale of drugs to minors) as long as the taking of these drugs poses no threat to anyone else. Drug addiction is a psychological problem to which no present solution exists. Most of the social harm caused by addicts, other than to themselves, is the result of thefts which they perform in order to continue their habit – and then the *legal* crime is the theft, not the addiction. The actual cost of heroin is about ten cents a shot; if it were legalized, the enormous traffic in illegal sale and purchase of it would stop, as well as the accompanying proselytization to get new addicts (to make more money for the pusher) and the thefts performed by addicts who often require eighty dollars a day just to keep up the habit. Addiction would not stop, but the crimes would: it is estimated that 75 percent of the burglaries in New York City today are performed by addicts, and all these crimes could be wiped out at one stroke through the legalization of drugs. (Only when the taking of drugs could be shown to constitute a threat to *others*, should it be prohibited by law. It is only laws protecting people against *themselves* that libertarians oppose.)

Laws should be limited to the second class only: aggression by individuals against other individuals. These are laws whose function is to protect human beings against encroachment by others; and this, as we have seen, is (according to libertarianism) the sole function of government.

Libertarians also reject the third class of laws totally: no one should be forced by law to help others, not even to tell them the time of day if requested, and certainly not to give them a portion of one's weekly paycheck. Governments, in the guise of humanitarianism, have given to some by taking from others (charging a "handling fee" in the process, which, because of the government's waste and inefficiency, sometimes is several hundred percent). And in so doing they have decreased incentive, violated the rights of individuals and lowered the standard of living of almost everyone.

All such laws constitute what libertarians call *moral cannibalism*. A cannibal in the physical sense is a person who lives off the flesh of other human beings. A *moral* cannibal is one who believes he has a right to live off the "spirit" of other human beings – who believes that he has a moral claim on the productive capacity, time, and effort expended by others.

It has become fashionable to claim virtually everything that one needs or desires as one's *right*. Thus, many people claim that they have a right to a job, the right to free medical care, to free food and clothing, to a decent home, and so on. Now if one asks, apart from any specific context, whether it would be desirable if everyone had these things, one might well say yes. But there is a gimmick attached to each of them: *At whose expense?* Jobs, medical care, education, and so on, don't grow on trees. These are goods and services *produced only by men*. Who then is to provide them, and under what conditions?

If you have a right to a job, who is to supply it? Must an employer supply it even if he doesn't want to hire you? What if you are unemployable, or incurably lazy? (If you say "the government must supply it," does that mean that a job must be created for you which no employer needs done, and that you must be kept in it regardless of how much or little you work?) If the employer is forced to supply it at his expense even if he doesn't need you, then isn't *he* being enslaved to that extent? Whatever happened to *his* right to conduct his life and his affairs in accordance with his choices?

If you have a right to free medical care, then, since medical care doesn't exist in nature as wild apples do, some people will have to supply it to you for free: that is, they will have to spend their time and money and energy taking care of you whether they want to or not. What ever happened to *their* right to conduct their lives as they see fit? Or do you have a right to violate theirs? Can there be a right to violate rights?

All those who demand this or that as a "free service" are consciously or unconsciously evading the fact that there is in reality no such thing as free services. All man-made goods and services are the result of human expenditure of time and effort. There is no such thing as "something for nothing" in this world. If you demand something free, you are demanding that other men give their time and effort to you without compensation. If they voluntarily choose to do this, there is no problem; but if you demand that they be *forced* to do it, you are interfering with their right not to do it if they so choose. "Swimming in this pool ought to be free!" says the indignant passerby. What he means is that others should build a pool, others should provide the material, and still others should run it and keep it in functioning order, so that *he* can use it without fee. But what right has he to the expenditure of *their* time and effort? To expect something "for free" is to expect it *to be paid for by others* whether they choose to or not.

Many questions, particularly about economic matters, will be generated by the libertarian account of human rights and the role of government. Should government have no role in assisting the needy, in providing social security, in legislating minimum wages, in fixing prices and putting a ceiling on rents, in curbing monopolies, in erecting tariffs, in guaranteeing jobs, in managing the money supply? To these and all similar questions the libertarian answers with an unequivocal no.

"But then you'd let people go hungry!" comes the rejoinder. This, the libertarian insists, is precisely what would not happen; with the restrictions removed, the economy would flourish as never before. With the controls taken off business, existing enterprises would expand and new ones would spring into existence satisfying more and more consumer needs; millions more people would be gainfully employed instead of subsisting on welfare, and all kinds of research and production, released from the stranglehold of government, would proliferate, fulfilling man's needs and desires as never before. It has always been so whenever government has permitted men to be free traders on a free market. But *why* this is so, and how the free market is the best solution to all problems relating to the material aspect of man's life, is another and far longer story.

Notes

1 Murray Rothbard, "The Great Ecology Issue," *The Individualist*, vol. 2, no. 2 (Feb 1970), p. 5.

---

23   Welfare Liberalism

John Rawls

My aim is to present a conception of justice which generalizes and carries to a higher level of abstraction the familiar theory of the social contract as found, say, in Locke, Rousseau, and Kant.[1] In order to do this we are not to think of the original contract as one to enter a particular society or to set up a particular form of government. Rather, the guiding idea is that the

From *A Theory of Justice* (Cambridge, MA: The Belknap Press of Harvard University Press, 1971), pp. 11–22, 60–5, 150–6, 252–7, 302–3. Reprinted by permission.

principles of justice for the basic structure of society are the object of the original agreement. They are the principles that free and rational persons concerned to further their own interests would accept in an initial position of equality as defining the fundamental terms of their association. These principles are to regulate all further agreements; they specify the kinds of social cooperation that can be entered into and the forms of government that can be established. This way of regarding the principles of justice I shall call justice as fairness.

Thus we are to imagine that those who engage in social cooperation choose together, in one joint act, the principles which are to assign basic rights and duties and to determine the division of social benefits. Men are to decide in advance how they are to regulate their claims against one another and what is to be the foundation charter of their society. Just as each person must decide by rational reflection what constitutes his good – that is, the system of ends which it is rational for him to pursue – so a group of persons must decide once and for all what is to count among them as just and unjust. The choice which rational men would make in this hypothetical situation of equal liberty, assuming for the present that this choice problem has a solution, determines the principles of justice.

In justice as fairness the original position of equality corresponds to the state of nature in the traditional theory of the social contract. This original position is not, of course, thought of as an actual historical state of affairs, much less as a primitive condition of culture. It is understood as a purely hypothetical situation characterized so as to lead to a certain conception of justice.[2] Among the essential features of this situation is that no one knows his place in society, his class position or social status, nor does any one know his fortune in the distribution of natural assets and abilities, his intelligence, strength, and the like. I shall even assume that the parties do not know their conceptions of the good or their special psychological propensities. The principles of justice are chosen behind a veil of ignorance. This ensures that no one is advantaged or disadvantaged in the choice of principles by the outcome of natural chance or the contingency of social circumstances. Since all are similarly situated and no one is able to design principles to favor his particular condition, the principles of justice are the result of a fair agreement or bargain. For given the circumstances of the original position, the symmetry of everyone's relations to each other, this initial situation is fair between individuals as moral persons; that is, as rational beings with their own ends and capable, I shall assume, of a sense of justice. The original position is, one might say, the appropriate initial status quo, and thus the

fundamental agreements reached in it are fair. This explains the propriety of the name "justice as fairness"; it conveys the idea that the principles of justice are agreed to in an initial situation that is fair. The name does not mean that the concepts of justice and fairness are the same, any more than the phrase "poetry as metaphor" means that the concepts of poetry and metaphor are the same.

Justice as fairness begins, as I have said, with one of the most general of all choices which persons might make together, namely, with the choice of the first principles of a conception of justice which is to regulate all subsequent criticism and reform of institutions. Then, having chosen a conception of justice, we can suppose that they are to choose a constitution and a legislature to enact laws, and so on, all in accordance with the principles of justice initially agreed upon. Our social situation is just if it is such that by this sequence of hypothetical agreements we would have contracted into the general system of rules which defines it. Moreover, assuming that the original position does determine a set of principles (that is, that a particular conception of justice would be chosen), it will then be true that whenever social institutions satisfy these principles those engaged in them can say to one another that they are cooperating on terms to which they would agree if they were free and equal persons whose relations with respect to one another were fair. They could all view their arrangements as meeting the stipulations which they would acknowledge in an initial situation that embodies widely accepted and reasonable constraints on the choice of principles. The general recognition of this fact would provide the basis for a public acceptance of the corresponding principles of justice. No society can, or course, be a scheme of cooperation which men enter voluntarily in a literal sense; each person finds himself placed at birth in some particular position in some particular society, and the nature of this position materially affects his life prospects. Yet a society satisfying the principles of justice as fairness comes as close as a society can to being a voluntary scheme, for it meets the principles which free and equal persons would assent to under circumstances that are fair. In this sense its members are autonomous and the obligations they recognize self-imposed.

One feature of justice as fairness is to think of the parties in the initial situation as rational and mutually disinterested. This does not mean that the parties are egoists; that is, individuals with only certain kinds of interests, say in wealth, prestige, and domination. But they are conceived as not taking an interest in one another's interests. They are to presume that even their spiritual aims may be opposed, in the way that the aims of those of different religions may be opposed. Moreover, the concept of rationality must be interpreted as far as possible in the narrow sense, standard in economic theory, of taking the most effective means to given ends. I shall modify this concept to some extent . . . but one must try to avoid introducing into it any controversial ethical elements. The initial situation must be characterized by stipulations that are widely accepted.

In working out the conception of justice as fairness one main task clearly is to determine which principles of justice would be chosen in the original position. To do this we must describe this situation in some detail and formulate with care the problem of choice which it presents. It may be observed, however, that once the principles of justice are thought of as arising from an original agreement in a situation of equality, it is an open question whether the principle of utility would be acknowledged. Offhand it hardly seems likely that persons who view themselves as equals, entitled to press their claims upon one another, would agree to a principle which may require lesser life prospects for some simply for the sake of a greater sum of advantages enjoyed by others. Since each desires to protect his interests, his capacity to advance his conception of the good, no one has a reason to acquiesce in an enduring loss for himself in order to bring about a greater net balance of satisfaction. In the absence of strong and lasting benevolent impulses, a rational man would not accept a basic structure merely because it maximized the algebraic sum of advantages irrespective of its permanent effects on his own basic rights and interests. Thus it seems that the principle of utility is incompatible with

the conception of social cooperation among equals for mutual advantage. It appears to be inconsistent with the idea of reciprocity implicit in the notion of a well-ordered society. Or, at any rate, so I shall argue.

I shall maintain instead that the persons in the initial situation would choose two rather different principles: the first requires equality in the assignment of basic rights and duties, while the second holds that social and economic inequalities (for example, inequalities of wealth and authority) are just only if they result in compensating benefits for everyone, and in particular for the least advantaged members of society. These principles rule out justifying institutions on the grounds that the hardships of some are offset by a greater good in the aggregate. It may be expedient but it is not just that some should have less in order that others may prosper. But there is no injustice in the greater benefits earned by a few provided that the situation of persons not so fortunate is thereby improved. The intuitive idea is that since everyone's well-being depends upon a scheme of cooperation without which no one could have a satisfactory life, the division of advantages should be such as to draw forth the willing cooperation of everyone taking part in it, including those less well situated. Yet this can be expected only if reasonable terms are proposed. The two principles mentioned seem to be a fair agreement on the basis of which those better endowed, or more fortunate in their social position, neither of which we can be said to deserve, could expect the willing cooperation of others when some workable scheme is a necessary condition of the welfare of all.[3] Once we decide to look for a conception of justice that nullifies the accidents of natural endowment and the contingencies of social circumstance as counters in quest for political and economic advantage, we are led to these principles. They express the result of leaving aside those aspects of the social world that seem arbitrary from a moral point of view.

The problem of the choice of principles, however, is extremely difficult. I do not expect the answer I shall suggest to be convincing to everyone. It is, therefore, worth noting from the outset that justice as fairness, like other contract views, consists of two parts: (1) an interpretation of the initial situation and of the problem of choice posed there, and (2) a set of principles which, it is argued, would be agreed to. One may accept the first part of the theory (or some variant thereof), but not the other, and conversely. The concept of the initial contractual situation may seem reasonable although the particular principles proposed are rejected. To be sure, I want to maintain that the most appropriate conception of this situation does lead to principles of justice contrary to utilitarianism and perfectionism, and therefore that the contract doctrine provides an alternative to these views. Still, one may dispute this contention even though one grants that the contractarian method is a useful way of studying ethical theories and of setting forth their underlying assumptions.

Justice as fairness is an example of what I have called a contract theory. Now there may be an objection to the term "contract" and related expressions, but I think it will serve reasonably well. Many words have misleading connotations which at first are likely to confuse. The terms "utility" and "utilitarianism" are surely no exception. They too have unfortunate suggestions which hostile critics have been willing to exploit; yet they are clear enough for those prepared to study utilitarian doctrine. The same should be true of the term "contract" applied to moral theories. As I have mentioned, to understand it one has to keep in mind that it implies a certain level of abstraction. In particular, the content of the relevant agreement is not to enter a given society or to adopt a given form of government, but to accept certain moral principles. Moreover, the undertakings referred to are purely hypothetical: a contract view holds that certain principles would be accepted in a well-defined initial situation.

The merit of the contract terminology is that it conveys the idea that principles of justice may be conceived as principles that would be chosen by rational persons, and that in this way conceptions of justice may be explained and justified. The theory of justice is a part, perhaps the most significant part, of the theory of rational choice. Furthermore, principles of justice deal with conflicting claims upon the advantages won by social cooperation; they apply to the relations among several persons or groups. The word "contract" suggests this plurality as well as the condition that the appropriate division of advantages must be in accordance with principles acceptable to all parties. The condition of publicity for principles of justice is also connoted by the contract phraseology. Thus, if these principles are the outcome of an agreement, citizens have a knowledge of the principles that others follow. It is characteristic of contract theories to stress the public nature of political principles. Finally there is the long tradition of the contract doctrine. Expressing the tie with this line of thought helps to define ideas and accords with natural piety. There are then several advantages in the use of the term "contract." With due precautions taken, it should not be misleading.

A final remark. Justice as fairness is not a complete contract theory. For it is clear that the contractarian idea can be extended to the choice of more or less an entire ethical system; that is, to a system including principles for all the virtues and not only for justice. Now for the most part I shall consider only principles of justice and others closely related to them; I make no attempt to discuss the virtues in a systematic way. Obviously if justice as fairness succeeds reasonably well, a next step would be to study the more general view suggested by the name "rightness as fairness." But even this wider theory fails to embrace all moral relationships, since it would seem to include only our relations with other persons and to leave out of account how we are to conduct ourselves toward animals and the rest of nature. I do not contend that the contract notion offers a way to approach these questions, which are certainly of the first importance; and I shall have to put them aside. We must recognize the limited scope of justice as fairness and of the general type of view that it exemplifies. How far its conclusions must be revised once these other matters are understood cannot be decided in advance.

The Original Position and Justification

I have said that the original position is the appropriate initial status quo which insures that the fundamental agreements reached in it are fair. This fact yields the name "justice as fairness." It is clear, then, that I want to say that one conception of justice is more reasonable than another, or justifiable with respect to it, if rational persons in the initial situation would choose its principles over those of the other for the role of justice. Conceptions of justice are to be ranked by their acceptability to persons so circumstanced. Understood in this way the question of justification is settled by working out a problem of deliberation: we have to ascertain which principles it would be rational to adopt given the contractual situation. This connects the theory of justice with the theory of rational choice.

If this view of the problem of justification is to succeed, we must, of course, describe in some detail the nature of this choice problem. A problem of rational decision has a definite answer only if we know the beliefs and interests of the parties, their relations with respect to one another, the alternatives between which they are to choose, the procedure whereby they make up their minds, and so on. As the circumstances are presented in different ways, correspondingly different principles are accepted. The concept of the original position, as I shall refer to it, is that of the most philosophically favored interpretation of this initial choice situation for the purposes of a theory of justice.

But how are we to decide what is the most favored interpretation? I assume, for one thing, that there is a broad measure of agreement that principles of justice should be chosen under certain conditions. To justify a particular description of the initial situation one shows that it incorporates these commonly shared presumptions. One argues from widely accepted but weak premises to more specific conclusions. Each of the presumptions should by itself be natural and plausible; some of them may seem innocuous or even trivial. The aim of the contract approach is to establish that taken together they impose significant bounds on acceptable principles of justice. The ideal outcome would be that these conditions determine a unique set of principles; but I shall be satisfied if they suffice to rank the main traditional conceptions of social justice.

One should not be misled, then, by the somewhat unusual conditions which characterize the original position. The idea here is simply to make vivid to ourselves the restrictions that it seems reasonable to impose on arguments for principles of justice, and therefore on these principles themselves. Thus it seems reasonable and generally acceptable that no one should be advantaged or disadvantaged by natural fortune or social circumstances in the choice of principles. It also seems widely agreed that it should be impossible to tailor principles to the circumstances of one's own case. We should ensure further that particular inclinations and aspirations, and persons' conceptions of their good, do not affect the principles adopted. The aim is to rule out those principles that it would be rational to propose for acceptance, however little the chance of success, only if one knew certain things that are irrelevant from the standpoint of justice. For example, if a man knew that he was wealthy, he might find it rational to advance the principle that various taxes for welfare measures be counted unjust; if he knew that he was poor, he would most likely propose the contrary principle. To represent the desired restrictions one imagines a situadon in which everyone is deprived of this sort of information. One excludes the knowledge of those contingencies which sets men at odds and allows them to be guided by their prejudices. In this manner the veil of ignorance is arrived at in a natural way. This concept should cause no difficulty if we keep in mind the constraints on arguments that it is meant to express. At any time we can enter the original position, so to speak, simply by following a certain procedure; namely, by arguing for principles of justice in accordance with these restrictions.

It seems reasonable to suppose that the parties in the original position are equal. That is, all have the same rights in the procedure for choosing principles; each can make proposals, submit reasons for their acceptance, and so on. Obviously the purpose of these conditions is to represent equality between human beings as moral persons, as creatures having a conception of their good and capable of a sense of justice. The basis of equality is taken to be similarity in these two respects. Systems of ends are not ranked in value, and each man is presumed to have the requisite ability to understand and to act upon whatever principles are adopted. Together with the veil of ignorance, these conditions define the principles of justice as those which rational persons concerned to advance their interests would consent to as equals when none are known to be advantaged or disadvantaged by social and natural contingencies.

There is, however, another side to justifying a particular description of the original position. This is to see if the principles which would be chosen match our considered convictions of justice or extend them in an acceptable way. We can note whether applying these principles would lead us to make the same judgments about the basic structure of society which we now make intuitively and in which we have the greatest confidence; or whether, in cases where our present judgments are in doubt and given with hesitation, these principles offer a resolution which we can affirm on reflection. There are questions which we feel sure must be answered in a certain way. For example, we are confident that religious intolerance and racial discrimination are unjust. We think that we have examined these things with care and have reached what we believe is an impartial judgment not likely to be distorted by an excessive attention to our own interests. These convictions are provisional fixed points which we presume any conception of justice must fit. But we have much less assurance as to what is the correct distribution of wealth and authority. Here we may be looking for a way to remove our doubts. We can check an interpretation of the initial situation, then, by the capacity of its principles to accommodate our firmest convictions and to provide guidance where guidance is needed.

In searching for the most favored description of this situation we work from both ends. We begin by describing it so that it represents generally shared and preferably weak conditions. We then see if these conditions are strong enough to yield a significant set of principles. If not, we look for further premises equally reasonable. But if so, and these principles match our considered convictions of justice, then so far well and good. But presumably there will be discrepancies. In this case we have a choice. We can either modify the account of the initial situation or we can revise our existing judgments, for even the judgments we take provisionally as fixed points are liable to revision. By going back and forth, sometimes altering the conditions of the contractual circumstances, at others withdrawing our judgments and conforming them to principle, I assume that eventually we shall find a description of the initial situation that both expresses reasonable conditions and yields principles which match our considered judgments duly pruned and adjusted. This state of affairs I refer to as reflective equilibrium.[4] It is an equilibrium because at last our principles and judgments coincide; and it is reflective since we know to what principles our judgments conform and the premises of their derivation. At the moment everything is in order. But this equilibrium is not necessarily stable. It is liable to be upset by further examination of the conditions which should be imposed on the contractual situation and by particular cases which may lead us to revise our judgments. Yet for the time being we have done what we can to render coherent and to justify our convictions of social justice. We have reached a conception of the original position.

I shall not, of course, actually work through this process. Still, we may think of the interpretation of the original position that I shall present as the result of such a hypothetical course of reflection. It represents the attempt to accommodate within one scheme both reasonable philosophical conditions on principles as well as our considered judgments of justice. In arriving at the favored interpretation of the initial situation there is no point at which an appeal is made to self-evidence in the traditional sense either of general conceptions or particular convictions. I do not claim for the principles of justice proposed that they are necessary truths or derivable from such truths. A conception of justice cannot be deduced from self-evident premises or conditions on principles; instead, its justification is a matter of the mutual support of many considerations, of everything fitting together into one coherent view.

A final comment. We shall want to say that certain principles of justice are justified because they would be agreed to in an initial situation of equality. I have emphasized that this original position is purely hypothetical. It is natural to ask why, if this agreement is never actually entered into, we should take any interest in these principles, moral or otherwise. The answer is that the conditions embodied in the description of the original position are ones that we do in fact accept. Or if we do not, then perhaps we can be persuaded to do so by philosophical reflection. Each aspect of the contractual situation can be given supporting grounds. Thus what we shall do is to collect together into one conception a number of conditions on principles that we are ready upon due consideration to recognize as reasonable. These constraints express what we are prepared to regard as limits on fair terms of social cooperation. One way to look at the idea of the original position, therefore, is to see it as an expository device which sums up the meaning of these conditions and helps us to extract their consequences. On the other hand, this conception is also an intuitive notion that suggests its own elaboration, so that led on by it we are drawn to define more clearly the standpoint from which we can best interpret moral relationships. We need a conception that enables us to envision our objective from afar: the intuitive notion of the original position is to do this for us. . . .

Two Principles of Justice

I shall now state in a provisional form the two principles of justice that I believe would be chosen in the original position. In this section I wish to make only the most general comments, and therefore the first formulation of these principles is tentative. As we go on I shall run through several formulations and approximate step by step

the final statement to be given much later. I believe that doing this allows the exposition to proceed in a natural way.

The first statement of the two principles reads as follows:

> First: each person is to have an equal right to the most extensive basic liberty compatible with a similar liberty for others.

> Second: social and economic inequalities are to be arranged so that they are both (a) reasonably expected to be to everyone's advantage, and (b) attached to positions and offices open to all.

There are two ambiguous phrases in the second principle, namely "everyone's advantage" and "open to all." Determining their sense more exactly will lead to a second formulation of the principle. . . .

By way of general comment, these principles primarily apply, as I have said, to the basic structure of society. They are to govern the assignment of rights and duties and to regulate the distribution of social and economic advantages. As their formulation suggests, these principles presuppose that the social structure can be divided into two more or less distinct parts, the first principle applying to the one, the second to the other. They distinguish between those aspects of the social system that define and secure the equal liberties of citizenship and those that specify and establish social and economic inequalities. The basic liberties of citizens are, roughly speaking, political liberty (the right to vote and to be eligible for public office) together with freedom of speech and assembly; liberty of conscience and freedom of thought; freedom of the person along with the right to hold (personal) property; and freedom from arbitrary arrest and seizure as defined by the concept of the rule of law. These liberties are all required to be equal by the first principle, since citizens of a just society are to have the same basic rights.

The second principle applies, in the first approximation, to the distribution of income and wealth and to the design of organizations that make use of differences in authority and responsibility, or chains of command. While the distribution of wealth and income need not be equal, it must be to everyone's advantage, and at the same time, positions of authority and offices of command must be accessible to all. One applies the second principle by holding positions open, and then, subject to this constraint, arranges social and economic inequalities so that everyone benefits.

These principles are to be arranged in a serial order with the first principle prior to the second. This ordering means that a departure from the institutions of equal liberty required by the first principle cannot be justified by, or compensated for, by greater social and economic advantages. The distribution of wealth and income, and the hierarchies of authority, must be consistent with both the liberties of equal citizenship and equality of opportunity.

It is clear that these principles are rather specific in their content, and their acceptance rests on certain assumptions that I must eventually try to explain and justify. A theory of justice depends upon a theory of society in ways that will become evident as we proceed. For the present, it should be observed that the two principles (and this holds for all formulations) are a special case of a more general conception of justice that can be expressed as follows:

> All social values – liberty and opportunity, income and wealth, and the bases of self-respect – are to be distributed equally unless an unequal distribution of any, or all, of these values is to everyone's advantage.

Injustice, then, is simply inequalities that are not to the benefit of all. Of course, this conception is extremely vague and requires interpretation.

As a first step, suppose that the basic structure of society distributes certain primary goods, that is, things that every rational man is presumed to want. These goods normally have a use whatever a person's rational plan of life. For simplicity, assume that the chief primary goods at the disposition of society are rights and liberties, powers and opportunities, income and wealth. (Later on

. . . the primary good of self-respect has a central place.) These are the social primary goods. Other primary goods such as health and vigor, intelligence and imagination, are natural goods; although their possession is influenced by the basic structure, they are not so directly under its control. Imagine, then, a hypothetical initial arrangement in which all the social primary goods are equally distributed: everyone has similar rights and duties, and income and wealth are evenly shared. This state of affairs provides a benchmark for judging improvements. If certain inequalities of wealth and organizational powers would make everyone better off than in this hypothetical starting situation, then they accord with the general conception.

Now it is possible, at least theoretically, that by giving up some of their fundamental liberties men are sufficiently compensated by the resulting social and economic gains. The general conception of justice imposes no restrictions on what sort of inequalities are permissible; it only requires that everyone's position be improved. We need not suppose anything so drastic as consenting to a condition of slavery. Imagine instead that men forgo certain political rights when the economic returns are significant and their capacity to influence the course of policy by the exercise of these rights would be marginal in any case. It is this kind of exchange which the two principles as stated rule out; being arranged in serial order they do not permit exchanges between basic liberties and economic and social gains. The serial ordering of principles expresses an underlying preference among primary social goods. When this preference is rational so likewise is the choice of these principles in this order.

In developing justice as fairness I shall, for the most part, leave aside the general conception of justice and examine instead the special case of the two principles in serial order. The advantage of this procedure is that from the first the matter of priorities is recognized and an effort made to find principles to deal with it. One is led to attend throughout to the conditions under which the acknowledgment of the absolute weight of liberty with respect to social and economic advantages, as defined by the lexical order of the two principles, would be reasonable. Offhand, this ranking appears extreme and too special a case to be of much interest; but there is more justification for it than would appear at first sight. Or at any rate, so I shall maintain. . . . Furthermore, the distinction between fundamental rights and liberties and economic and social benefits marks a difference among primary social goods that one should try to exploit. It suggests an important division in the social system. Of course, the distinctions drawn and the ordering proposed are bound to be at best only approximations. There are surely circumstances in which they fail. But it is essential to depict clearly the main lines of a reasonable conception of justice; and under many conditions, anyway, the two principles in serial order may serve well enough. When necessary we can fall back on the more general conception.

The fact that the two principles apply to institutions has certain consequences. Several points illustrate this. First of all, the rights and liberties referred to by these principles are those that are defined by the public rules of the basic structure. Whether men are free is determined by the rights and duties established by the major institutions of society. Liberty is a certain pattern of social forms. The first principle simply requires that certain sorts of rules, those defining basic liberties, apply to everyone equally and that they allow the most extensive liberty compatible with a like liberty for all. The only reason for circumscribing the rights defining liberty and making men's freedom less extensive than it might otherwise be is that these equal rights as institutionally defined would interfere with one another.

Another thing to bear in mind is that when principles mention persons, or require that everyone gain from an inequality, the reference is to representative persons holding the various social positions, or offices, or whatever, established by the basic structure. Thus in applying the second principle I assume that it is possible to assign an expectation of well-being to representative individuals holding these positions. This expectation indicates their life prospects as viewed from their social station. In general, the expectations of representative persons depend upon the distribution of rights and duties throughout the basic structure. When this changes, expectations change. I assume, then, that expectations are connected: by raising the prospects of the representative man in one position we presumably increase or decrease the prospects of representative men in other positions. Since it applies to institutional forms, the second principle (or rather the first part of it) refers to the expectations of representative individuals. As I shall discuss below, neither principle applies to distributions of particular goods to particular individuals who may be identified by their proper names. The situation where someone is considering how to allocate certain commodities to needy persons who are known to him is not within the scope of the principles. They are meant to regulate basic institutional arrangements. We must not assume that there is much similarity from the standpoint of justice between an administrative allotment of goods to specific persons and the appropriate design of society. Our common sense intuitions for the former may be a poor guide to the latter.

Now the second principle insists that each person benefit from permissible inequalities in the basic structure. This means that it must be reasonable for each relevant representative man defined by this structure, when he views it as a going concern, to prefer his prospects with the inequality, to his prospects without it. One is not allowed to justify differences in income or organizational powers on the ground that the disadvantages of those in one position are outweighed by the greater advantages of those in another. Much less can infringements of liberty be counterbalanced in this way. Applied to the basic structure, the principle of utility would have us maximize the sum of expectations of representative men (weighted by the number of persons they represent, on the classical view); and this would permit us to compensate for the losses of some by the gains of others. Instead the two principles require that everyone benefit from economic and social inequalities.

The Reasoning Leading to the Two Principles of Justice

It will be recalled that the general conception of justice as fairness requires that all primary social goods be distributed equally unless an unequal distribution would be to everyone's advantage. No restrictions are placed on exchanges of these goods and therefore a lesser liberty can be compensated for by greater social and economic benefits. Now looking at the situation from the standpoint of one person selected arbitrarily, there is no way for him to win special advantages for himself. Nor, on the other hand, are there grounds for his acquiescing in special disadvantages. Since it is not reasonable for him to expect more than an equal share in the division of social goods, and since it is not rational for him to agree to less, the sensible thing for him to do is to acknowledge as the first principle of justice one requiring an equal distribution. Indeed, this principle is so obvious that we would expect it to occur to anyone immediately.

Thus, the parties start with a principle establishing equal liberty for all, including equality of opportunity, as well as an equal distribution of income and wealth. But there is no reason why this acknowledgment should be final. If there are inequalities in the basic structure that work to make everyone better off in comparison with the benchmark of initial equality, why not permit them? The immediate gain which a greater equality might allow can be regarded as intelligently invested in view of its future return. If, for example, these inequalities set up various incentives which succeed in eliciting more productive efforts, a person in the original position may look upon them as necessary to cover the costs of training and to encourage effective performance. One might think that ideally individuals should want to serve one another. But since the parties are assumed not to take an interest in one another's interests, their acceptance of these inequalities is only the acceptance of the relations in which men stand in the circumstances of justice. They have no grounds for complaining of one another's motives. A person in the original position would, therefore, concede the justice of these inequalities. Indeed, it would be shortsighted of him not to do so. He would hesitate to agree to these regularities only if he would be dejected by the bare knowledge or perception that others were better situated; and I have assumed that the parties decide as if they are not moved by envy. In order to make the principle regulating inequalities determinate, one looks at the system from the standpoint of the least advantaged representative man. Inequalities are permissible when they maximize, or at least all contribute to, the long-term expectations of the least fortunate group in society.

Now this general conception imposes no constraints on what sorts of inequalities are allowed, whereas the special conception, by putting the two principles in serial order (with the necessary adjustments in meaning), forbids exchanges between basic liberties and economic and social benefits. I shall not try to justify this ordering here. . . . But roughly, the idea underlying this ordering is that if the parties assume that their basic liberties can be effectively exercised, they will not exchange a lesser liberty for an improvement in economic well-being. It is only when social conditions do not allow the effective establishment of these rights that one can concede their limitation; and these restrictions can be granted only to the extent that they are necessary to prepare the way for a free society. The denial of equal liberty can be defended only if it is necessary to raise the level of civilization so that in due course these freedoms can be enjoyed. Thus in adopting a serial order we are in effect making a special assumption in the original position, namely, that the parties know that the conditions of their society, whatever they are, admit the effective realization of the equal liberties. The serial ordering of the two principles of justice eventually comes to be reasonable if the general conception is consistently followed. This lexical ranking is the long-run tendency of the general view. For the most part I shall assume that the requisite circumstances for the serial order obtain.

It seems clear from these remarks that the two principles are at least a plausible conception of justice. The question, though, is how one is to argue for them more systematically. Now there are several things to do. One can work out their consequences for institutions and note their implications for fundamental social policy. In this way they are tested by a comparison with our considered judgments of justice. . . . But one can also try to find arguments in their favor that are decisive from the standpoint of the original position. In order to see how this might be done, it is useful as a heuristic device to think of the two principles as the maximin solution to the problem of social justice. There is an analogy between the two principles and the maximin rule for choice under uncertainty.[5] This is evident from the fact that the two principles are those a person would choose for the design of a society in which his enemy is to assign him his place. The maximin rule tells us to rank alternatives by their worst possible outcomes: we are to adopt the alternative the worst outcome of which is superior to the worst outcomes of the others. The persons in the original position do not, of course, assume that their initial place in society is decided by a malevolent opponent. As I note below, they should not reason from false premises. The veil of ignorance does not violate this idea, since an absence of information is not misinformation. But that the two principles of justice would be chosen if the parties were forced to protect themselves against such a contingency explains the sense in which this conception is the maximin solution. And this analogy suggests that if the original position has been described so that it is rational for the parties to adopt the conservative attitude expressed by this rule, a conclusive argument can indeed be constructed for these principles. Clearly the maximin rule is not, in general, a suitable guide for choices under uncertainty. But it is attractive in situations marked by certain special features. My aim, then, is to show that a good case can be made for the two principles based on the fact that the original position manifests these features to the fullest possible degree, carrying them to the limit, so to speak.

Consider the gain-and-loss table below. It represents the gains and losses for a situation which is not a game of strategy. There is no one playing against the person making the decision; instead

he is faced with several possible circumstances which may or may not obtain. Which circumstances happen to exist does not depend upon what the person choosing decides or whether he announces his moves in advance. The numbers in the table are monetary values (in hundreds of dollars) in comparison with some initial situation. The gain (g) depends upon the individual's decision (d) and the circumstances (c). Thus $g = f(d,c)$. Assuming that there are three possible decisions and three possible circumstances, we might have this gain-and-loss table.

Decisions	Circumstances		
	C1	C2	C3
d1	-7	8	12
d2	-8	7	14
d3	5	6	8

The maximin rule requires that we make the third decision. For in this case the worst that can happen is that one gains five hundred dollars, which is better than the worst for the other actions. If we adopt one of these we may lose either eight or seven hundred dollars. Thus, the choice of d_3 maximizes $f(d,c)$ for that value of c which for a given d, minimizes f. The term "maximin" means the *maximum minimorum*; and the rule directs our attention to the worst that can happen under any proposed course of action, and to decide in the light of that.

Now there appear to be three chief features of situations that give plausibility to this unusual rule.[6] First, since the rule takes no account of the likelihoods of the possible circumstances, there must be some reason for sharply discounting estimates of these probabilities. Offhand, the most natural rule of choice would seem to be to compute the expectation of monetary gain for each decision and then to adopt the course of action with the highest prospect. (This expectation is defined as follows: let us suppose that g_{ij} represent the numbers in the gain-and-loss table, where i is the row index and j is the column index; and let p_j, $j = 1, 2, 3$, be the likelihoods of the circumstances, with $\Sigma p_j = 1$. Then the expectation for the ith decision is equal to $\Sigma p_j g_{ij}$.) Thus it must be, for example, that the situation is one in which a knowledge of likelihoods is impossible, or at best extremely insecure. In this case it is unreasonable not to be skeptical of probabilistic calculations unless there is no other way out, particularly if the decision is a fundamental one that needs to be justified to others.

The second feature that suggests the maximin rule is the following: the person choosing has a conception of the good such that he cares very little, if anything, for what he might gain above the minimum stipend that he can, in fact, be sure of by following the maximin rule. It is not worthwhile for him to take a chance for the sake of a further advantage, especially when it may turn out that he loses much that is important to him. This last provision brings in the third feature; namely, that the rejected alternatives have outcomes that one can hardly accept. The situation involves grave risks. Of course these features work most effectively in combination. The paradigm situation for following the maximin rule is when all three features are realized to the highest degree. This rule does not, then, generally apply, nor of course is it self-evident. Rather, it is a maxim, a rule of thumb, that comes into its own in special circumstances. Its application depends upon the qualitative structure of the possible gains and losses in relation to one's conception of the good, all this against a background in which it is reasonable to discount conjectural estimates of likelihoods.

It should be noted, as the comments on the gain-and-loss table say, that the entries in the table represent monetary values and not utilities. This difference is significant since for one thing computing expectations on the basis of such objective values is not the same thing as computing expected utility and may lead to different results. The essential point, though, is that in justice as fairness the parties do not know their conception of the good and cannot estimate their utility in the ordinary sense. In any case, we want to go behind *de facto* preferences generated by given conditions. Therefore expectations are based upon an index of primary goods and the parties make their choice accordingly. The entries in the example are in terms of money and not utility to indicate this aspect of the contract doctrine.

Now, as I have suggested, the original position has been defined so that it is a situation in which the maximin rule applies. In order to see this, let us review briefly the nature of this situation with these three special features in mind. To begin with, the veil of ignorance excludes all but the vaguest knowledge of likelihoods. The parties have no basis for determining the probable nature of their society, or their place in it. Thus they have strong reasons for being wary of probability calculations if any other course is open to them. They must also take into account the fact that their choice of principles should seem reasonable to others, in particular their descendants, whose rights will be deeply affected by it. There are further grounds for discounting that I shall mention as we go along. For the present it suffices to note that these considerations are strengthened by the fact that the parties know very little about the gain-and-loss table. Not only are they unable to conjecture the likelihoods of the various possible circumstances, they cannot say much about what the possible circumstances are, much less enumerate them and foresee the outcome of each alternative available. Those deciding are much more in the dark than the illustration by a numerical table suggests. It is for this reason that I have spoken of an analogy with the maximin rule.

Several kinds of arguments for the two principles of justice illustrate the second feature. Thus, if we can maintain that these principles provide a workable theory of social justice, and that they are compatible with reasonable demands of efficiency, then this conception guarantees a satisfactory minimum. There may be, on reflection, little reason for trying to do better. Thus much of the argument . . . is to show, by their application to the main questions of social justice, that the two principles are a satisfactory conception. These details have a philosophical purpose. Moreover, this line of thought is practically decisive if we can establish the priority of liberty, the lexical ordering of the two principles. For this priority implies that the persons in the original position have no desire to try for greater gains at the expense of the equal liberties. The minimum assured by the two principles in lexical order is not one that the parties wish to jeopardize for the sake of greater economic and social advantages. . . .

Finally, the third feature holds if we can assume that other conceptions of justice may lead to institutions that the parties would find intolerable. For example, it has sometimes been held that under some conditions the utility principle (in either form) justifies, if not slavery or serfdom, at any rate serious infractions of liberty for the sake of greater social benefits. We need not consider here the truth of this claim, or the likelihood that the requisite conditions obtain. For the moment, this contention is only to illustrate the way in which conceptions of justice may allow for outcomes which the parties may not be able to accept. And having the ready alternative of the two principles of justice which secure a satisfactory minimum, it seems unwise, if not irrational, for them to take a chance that these outcomes are not realized.

So much, then, for a brief sketch of the features of situations in which the maximin rule comes into its own and of the way in which the arguments for the two principles of justice can be subsumed under them. . . .

The Final Formulation of the Principles of Justice

. . . I now wish to give the final statement of the two principles of justice for institutions. For the sake of completeness, I shall give a full statement including earlier formulations.

First principle
Each person is to have an equal right to the most extensive total system of equal basic liberties compatible with a similar system of liberty for all.

Second principle
Social and economic inequalities are to be arranged so that they are both:
(a) to the greatest benefit of the least advantaged, consistent with the just savings principle, and

(b) attached to offices and positions open to all under conditions of fair equality of opportunity.

First priority rule (the priority of liberty)
The principles of justice are to be ranked in lexical order and therefore liberty can be restricted only for the sake of liberty. There are two cases:
(a) a less extensive liberty must strengthen the total system of liberty shared by all;
(b) a less than equal liberty must be acceptable to those with the lesser liberty.

Second priority rule (the priority of justice over efficiency and welfare)
The second principle of justice is lexically prior to the principle of efficiency and to that of maximizing the sum of advantages; and fair opportunity is prior to the difference principle. There are two cases:
(a) an inequality of opportunity must enhance the opportunities of those with the lesser opportunity;
(b) an excessive rate of saving must on balance mitigate the burden of those bearing this hardship.

General conception
All social primary goods – liberty and opportunity, income and wealth, and the bases of self-respect – are to be distributed equally unless an unequal distribution of any or all of these goods is to the advantage of the least favored.

By way of comment, these principles and priority rules are no doubt incomplete. Other modifications will surely have to be made, but I shall not further complicate the statement of the principles. It suffices to observe that when we come to non-ideal theory, we do not fall back straightway upon the general conception of justice. The lexical ordering of the two principles, and the valuations that this ordering implies, suggest priority rules which seem to be reasonable enough in many cases. By various examples I have tried to illustrate how these rules can be used and to indicate their plausibility. Thus the ranking of the principles of justice in ideal theory reflects back and guides the application of these principles to non-ideal situations. It identifies which limitations need to be dealt with first. The drawback of the general conception of justice is that it lacks the definite structure of the two principles in serial order. In more extreme and tangled instances of non-ideal theory there may be no alternative to it. At some point the priority of rules for non-ideal cases will fail; and indeed, we may be able to find no satisfactory answer at all. But we must try to postpone the day of reckoning as long as possible, and try to arrange society so that it never comes. . . .

The Kantian Interpretation

Kant held, I believe, that a person is acting autonomously when the principles of his action are chosen by him as the most adequate possible expression of his nature as a free and equal rational being. The principles he acts upon are not adopted because of his social position or natural endowments, or in view of the particular kind of society in which he lives or the specific things that he happens to want. To act on such principles is to act heteronomously. Now the veil of ignorance deprives the persons in the original position of the knowledge that would enable them to choose heteronomous principles. The parties arrive at their choice together as free and equal rational persons knowing only that those circumstances obtain which give rise to the need for principles of justice.

To be sure, the argument for these principles does add in various ways to Kant's conception. For example, it adds the feature that the principles chosen are to apply to the basic structure of society; and premises characterizing this structure are used in deriving the principles of justice. But I believe that this and other additions are natural enough and remain fairly close to Kant's doctrine, at least when all of his ethical writings are viewed together. Assuming, then, that the reasoning in favor of the principles of justice is correct, we can say that when persons act on these principles they are acting in accordance with principles that they would choose as rational and independent persons in an original position of equality. The principles of their actions do not depend upon social or natural contingencies, nor do they reflect the bias of the particulars of their plan of life or the aspirations that motivate them. By acting from these principles persons express their nature as free and equal rational beings subject to the general conditions of human life. For to express one's nature as a being of a particular kind is to act on the principles that would be chosen if this nature were the decisive determining element. Of course, the choice of the parties in the original position is subject to the restrictions of that situation. But when we knowingly act on the principles of justice in the ordinary course of events, we deliberately assume the limitations of the original position. One reason for doing this, for persons who can do so and want to, is to give expression to one's nature.

The principles of justice are also categorical imperatives in Kant's sense. For by a categorical imperative Kant understands a principle of conduct that applies to a person in virtue of his nature as a free and equal rational being. The validity of the principle does not presuppose that one has a particular desire or aim. Whereas a hypothetical imperative by contrast does assume this: it directs us to take certain steps as effective means to achieve a specific end. Whether the desire is for a particular thing, or whether it is for something more general, such as certain kinds of agreeable feelings or pleasures, the corresponding imperative is hypothetical. Its applicability depends upon one's having an aim which one need not have as a condition of being a rational human individual. The argument for the two principles of justice does not assume that the parties have particular ends, but only that they desire certain primary goods. These are things that it is rational to want whatever else one wants. Thus given human nature, wanting them is part of being rational; and while each is presumed to have some conception of the good, nothing is known about his final ends. The preference for primary goods is derived, then, from only the most general assumptions about rationality and the conditions of human life. To act from the principles of justice is to act from categorical imperatives in the sense that they apply to us whatever in particular our aims are. This simply reflects the fact that no such contingencies appear as premises in their derivation.

We may note also that the motivational assumption of mutual disinterest accords with Kant's notion of autonomy, and gives another reason for this condition. So far this assumption has been used to characterize the circumstances of justice and to provide a clear conception to guide the reasoning of the parties. We have also seen that the concept of benevolence, being a second-order notion, would not work out well. Now we can add that the assumption of mutual disinterest is to allow for freedom in the choice of a system of final ends.[7] Liberty in adopting a conception of the good is limited only by principles that are deduced from a doctrine which imposes no prior constraints on these conceptions. Presuming mutual disinterest in the original position carries out this idea. We postulate that the parties have opposing claims in a suitably general sense. If their ends were restricted in some specific way, this would appear at the outset as an arbitrary restriction on freedom. Moreover, if the parties were conceived as altruists, or as pursuing certain kinds of pleasures, then the principles chosen would apply, as far as the argument would have shown, only to persons whose freedom was restricted to choices compatible with altruism or hedonism. As the argument now runs, the principles of justice cover all persons with rational plans of life, whatever their content, and these principles represent the appropriate restrictions on freedom. Thus it is possible to say that the constraints on conceptions of the good are the result of an interpretation of the contractual situation that puts no prior limitations on what men may desire. There are a variety of reasons, then, for the motivational premise of mutual disinterest. This premise is not only a matter of realism about the circumstances of justice or a way to make the theory manageable. It also connects up with the Kantian idea of autonomy. . . .

The original position may be viewed, then, as a procedural interpretation of Kant's conception of autonomy and the categorical imperative. The principles regulative of the kingdom of ends are those that would be chosen in this position, and the description of this situation enables us to explain the sense in which acting from these principles expresses our nature as free and equal rational persons. No longer are these notions purely transcendent and lacking explicable connections with human conduct, for the procedural conception of the original position allows us to make these ties. . . .

Notes

1 As the text suggests, I shall regard Locke's *The Second Treatise of Government*, Rousseau's *Social Contract*, and Kant's ethical works beginning with *The Foundations of the Metaphysics of Morals* as definitive of the contract tradition. For all of its greatness, Hobbes's *Leviathan* raises special problems. A general historical survey is provided by J. W. Gough, *The Social Contract*, 2nd edn (Oxford: The Clarendon Press, 1957), and Otto Gierke, *Natural Law and the Theory of Society*, trans. with an introduction by Ernest Barker (Cambridge: Cambridge University Press, 1934). A presentation of the contract view as primarily an ethical theory is to be found in G. R. Grice, *The Grounds of Moral Judgment* (Cambridge: Cambridge University Press, 1967). . . .

2 Kant is clear that the original agreement is hypothetical. See *The Metaphyics of Morals*, pt I (Rechtslehre), especially §§ 47, 52; and pt II of the essay "Concerning the Common Saying: This May Be True in Theory But It Does Not Apply in Practice," in *Kant's Political Writings*, ed. Hans Reiss and trans. by H. B. Nisbet (Cambridge: Cambridge University Press, 1970), pp. 73–87. See Georges Vlachos, *La Pensée politique de Kant* (Paris: Presses Universitaires de France, 1962), pp. 326–35; and J. G. Murphy, *Kant: The Philosophy of Right* (London: Macmillan, 1970), pp.109–12, 133–6, for a further discussion.

3 For the formulation of this intuitive idea I am indebted to Allan Gibbard.

4 The process of mutual adjustment of principles and considered judgments is not peculiar to moral philosophy. See Nelson Goodman, *Fact, Fiction, and Forecast* (Cambridge, MA: Harvard University Press, 1955), pp. 65–8, for parallel remarks con-

cerning the justification of the principles of deductive and inductive inference.

5 An accessible discussion of this and other rules of choice under uncertainty can be found in W. J. Baumol, *Economic Theory and Operations Analysis*, 2nd edn (Englewood Cliffs, NJ: Prentice-Hall, 1965), ch. 24. Baumol gives a geometric interpretation of these rules, including the diagram used

... to illustrate the difference principle. See pp. 558–62. See also R. D. Luce and Howard Raiffa, *Games and Decisions* (New York: John Wiley, 1957), ch. XIII, for a fuller account.

6 Here I borrow from William Fellner, *Probability and Profit* (Homewood, IL: Richard D. Irwin, 1965), pp. 140–2, where these features are noted.

7 For this point I am indebted to Charles Fried.

---

24 From Liberty to Welfare

James P. Sterba

The central contrast between libertarians and socialists is usually put this way: Libertarians take the ideal of liberty to be the ultimate political ideal from which they think it follows that only a minimal or night watchman state can be justified, whereas socialists take the ideal of equality to be the ultimate political ideal from which they think it follows that only a state that socializes the means of production can be justified. Libertarians, however, tend to agree with socialists that when the ideal of equality is interpreted in the manner favored by socialists, it would justify a socialist state. Libertarians simply contend that the socialist interpretation of the ideal of equality is morally contestable. Why not interpret the ideal in the manner favored by libertarians as equality before the law or equality of basic rights so that the ideal is at least consistent with, if not required by, the libertarian's own ideal of liberty? Why not indeed! But obviously an analogous question could be directed at libertarians. Why not interpret the ideal of liberty in the manner favored by socialists as a positive rather than a negative ideal so that it would justify the

greater equality in the distribution of goods and resources that is characteristic of a socialist state?

To either of these questions, no convincing answer seems forthcoming. Both the interpretations of the ideals of liberty and equality favored by libertarians and those favored by socialists appear morally contestable. Consequently, the dispute between libertarians and socialists seems irresolvable. I wish to argue, however, that this is not the case. I will show that the dispute can be resolved, for all practical purposes, by proceeding from premises that libertarians endorse to a conclusion that socialists endorse. Specifically, I will argue that libertarians, given their ideal of liberty, must be socialists because they must endorse the equality in the distribution of goods and resources required by a socialist state.

I

To see that this is the case, suppose we interpret the ideal of liberty as a negative ideal in the manner favored by libertarians, rather than as a positive ideal in the manner favored by socialists.[1] So understood, liberty is the absence of interference by other people from doing what one wants or is able to do. Interpreting their ideal in this way, libertarians claim to derive a number of more specific requirements, in particular, a right to life;

A longer version of this article has appeared as "Reconciling Liberty and Equality, or Why Libertarians must be Socialists" in *Liberty and Equality*, edited by Larry May and Jonathan Schonsheck (Boston, MA: MIT Press, 1997).

a right to freedom of speech, press, and assembly; and a right to property. Here it is important to observe that the libertarian's right to life is not a right to receive from others the goods and resources necessary for preserving one's life; it is simply a right not to be killed unjustly. Correspondingly, the libertarian's right to property is not a right to receive from others the goods and resources necessary for one's welfare, but rather a right to acquire goods and resources either by initial acquisition or by voluntary agreement.

Of course, libertarians would allow that it would be nice of the rich to share their surplus goods and resources with the poor. Nevertheless, according to libertarians, such acts of charity should not be coercively required. For this reason, libertarians are opposed to coercively supported welfare programs. By contrast, socialists would certainly interpret their ideal of equality to require not only coercively supported welfare programs, but also considerable equality in the distribution of goods and resources as well.

In order to see why libertarians are mistaken about what their ideal requires, consider a typical conflict situation between the rich and the poor. In this situation, the rich have more than enough goods and resources to satisfy their basic needs.[2] By contrast, the poor lack the goods and resources to meet their most basic needs even though they have tried all the means available to them that libertarians regard as legitimate for acquiring such goods and resources. Under such circumstances, libertarians usually maintain that the rich should have the liberty to use their resources to satisfy their luxury needs if they so wish. Libertarians recognize that this liberty might well be enjoyed at the expense of the satisfaction of the most basic needs of the poor; they just think that liberty always has priority over other political ideals, and since they assume that the liberty of the poor is not at stake in such conflict situations, it is easy for them to conclude that the rich should not be required to sacrifice their liberty so that the basic needs of the poor may be met.

Of course, libertarians allow that it would be nice of the rich to share their surplus goods and resources with the poor. Nevertheless, according to libertarians, such acts of charity cannot be required because the liberty of the poor is not thought to be at stake in such conflict situations.

In fact, however, the liberty of the poor *is* at stake in such conflict situations. What is at stake is the liberty of the poor not to be interfered with in taking from the surplus possessions of the rich what is necessary to satisfy their basic needs.[3]

Needless to say, libertarians would want to deny that the poor have this liberty. But how could they justify such a denial? As this liberty of the poor has been specified, it is not a positive right to receive something but a negative right of non-interference. Nor will it do for libertarians to appeal to a right to life or a right to property to rule out such a liberty because on the view under consideration liberty is basic and all other rights are derived from a right to liberty.[4] Clearly, what libertarians must do is recognize the existence of such a liberty and then claim that it conflicts with other liberties of the rich. But when libertarians see that this is the case, they are often genuinely surprised – one might even say rudely awakened – for they had not previously seen the conflict between the rich and the poor as a conflict of liberties.[5]

When the conflict between the rich and the poor is viewed as a conflict of liberties, either we can say that the rich should have the liberty not to be interfered with in using their surplus goods and resources for luxury purposes, or we can say that the poor should have the liberty not to be interfered with in taking from the rich what they require to meet their basic needs. If we choose one liberty, we must reject the other. What needs to be determined, therefore, is which liberty is morally preferable: the liberty of the rich or the liberty of the poor.

Two principles

In order to see that the liberty of the poor not to be interfered with in taking from the surplus resources of the rich what is required to meet their basic needs is morally preferable to the liberty of the rich not to be interfered with in using their surplus goods and resources for luxury purposes, we need to appeal to one of the most fundamental principles of morality, one that is common to all political perspectives. This is the "Ought" Implies "Can" Principle:

> People are not morally required to do what they lack the power to do or what would involve so great a sacrifice that it would be unreasonable to ask them to perform such an action, and/or in the case of severe conflicts of interest, unreasonable to require them to perform such an action.

For example, suppose I promised to attend a departmental meeting on Friday, but on Thursday I am involved in a serious car accident that leaves me in a coma. Surely it is no longer the case that I ought to attend the meeting, now that I lack the power to do so. Or suppose instead that on Thursday I develop a severe case of pneumonia for which I am hospitalized. Surely, I could legitimately claim that I cannot attend the meeting, on the grounds that the risk to my health involved in attending is a sacrifice that it would be unreasonable to ask me to bear. Or suppose the risk to my health from having pneumonia is not so serious that it would be unreasonable to ask me to attend the meeting (a supererogatory request), it might still be serious enough to be unreasonable to require my attendance at the meeting (a demand that is backed up by blame or coercion).

Now applying the "ought" implies "can" principle to the case at hand, it seems clear that the poor have it within their power willingly to relinquish such an important liberty as the liberty not to be interfered with in taking from the rich what they require to meet their basic needs. Nevertheless, it would be unreasonable to ask or require them to make so great a sacrifice. In the extreme case, it would involve asking or requiring the poor to sit back and starve to death. Of course, the poor may have no real alternative to relinquishing this liberty. To do anything else may involve worse consequences for themselves and their loved ones and may invite a painful death. Accordingly, we may expect that the poor would acquiesce, albeit unwillingly, to a political system that denies them the right to welfare sup-

ported by such a liberty, at the same time that we recognize that such a system imposes an unreasonable sacrifice upon the poor – a sacrifice that we cannot morally blame the poor for trying to evade.[6] Analogously, we might expect that a woman whose life was threatened would submit to a rapist's demands, at the same time that we recognize the utter unreasonableness of those demands.

By contrast, it would not be unreasonable to ask and require the rich to sacrifice the liberty to meet some of their luxury needs so that the poor can have the liberty to meet their basic needs.[7] Naturally, we might expect that the rich, for reasons of self-interest and past contribution, might be disinclined to make such a sacrifice. We might even suppose that the past contribution of the rich provides a good reason for not sacrificing their liberty to use their surplus for luxury purposes. Yet, unlike the poor, the rich could not claim that relinquishing such a liberty would involve so great a sacrifice that it would be unreasonable to ask and require them to make it; unlike the poor, the rich could be morally blameworthy for failing to make such a sacrifice.

Notice that by virtue of the "ought" implies "can" principle, this argument establishes that:

(1a) Because it would be unreasonable to ask or require the poor to sacrifice the liberty not to be interfered with when taking from the surplus goods and resources of the rich what is necessary to meet their basic needs, (1b) it is not the case that the poor are morally required to make such a sacrifice.

(2a) Because it would not be unreasonable to ask and require rich to sacrifice the liberty not to be interfered with when using their surplus goods and resources for luxury purposes, (2b) it may be the case that the rich are morally required to make such a sacrifice.

What the argument does not establish is that it is the case that the rich are *morally required* to sacrifice (some of) their surplus so that the basic needs of the poor can be met. To clearly establish that conclusion, we need to appeal to a principle, which is, in fact, simply the contrapositive of the "ought" implies "can" principle. It is the Conflict Resolution Principle:

> What people are morally required to do is what is either reasonable to ask them to do, or in the case of severe conflicts of interest, reasonable to require them to do.

While the "ought" implies "can" principle claims that if any action is *not reasonable to ask or require* a person to do, all things considered, that action is *not morally required* for that person, all things considered [−R(A v Re) → −MRe], the conflict resolution principle claims that if any action is *morally required* for a person to do all things considered, that action is *reasonable to ask or require* that person to do, all things considered [MRe → R(A v Re)].

This conflict resolution principle accords with the generally accepted view of morality as a system of reasons for resolving interpersonal conflicts of interest. Of course, morality is not limited to such a system of reasons. Most surely it also includes reasons of self-development. All that is being claimed by the principle is that moral resolutions of interpersonal conflicts of interest cannot be contrary to reason to ask everyone affected to accept or, in the case of severe interpersonal conflicts of interest, unreasonable to require everyone affected to accept. The reason for the distinction between the two kinds of cases is that when interpersonal conflicts of interest are not severe, moral resolutions must still be reasonable to ask everyone affected to accept but they need not be reasonable to *require* everyone affected to accept. This is because not all moral resolutions can be justifiably enforced; only moral resolutions of severe interpersonal conflicts of interest can and *should* be justifiably enforced. Furthermore, the reason moral resolutions of severe interpersonal conflicts of interest should be enforced is that if the parties are simply asked but not required to abide by a moral resolution in such cases of conflict, then it is likely that the stronger party will violate the resolution and that would be unreasonable to ask or require the weaker party to accept.

When we apply the conflict resolution principle to our example of severe conflict between the rich and the poor, there are three possible moral resolutions:

I   A moral resolution that would require the rich to sacrifice the liberty not to be interfered with when using their surplus goods and resources for luxury purposes so that the poor can have the liberty not to be interfered with when taking from the surplus resources of the rich what is necessary to meet their basic needs.

II   A moral resolution that would require the poor to sacrifice the liberty not to be interfered with when taking from the surplus goods and resources of the rich what is necessary to meet their basic needs so that the rich can have the liberty not to be interfered with when using their surplus resources for luxury purposes.

III A moral resolution that would require the rich and the poor to accept the results of a power struggle in which both the rich and the poor are at liberty to appropriate and use the surplus goods and resources of the rich.

Applying our previous discussion of the "ought" implies "can" principle to these three possible moral resolutions, it is clear that 1a (it would be unreasonable to ask or require the poor . . .) rules out II, but 2a (it would not be unreasonable to ask and require the rich . . .) does not rule out I. But what about III? Some libertarians have contended that III is the proper resolution of severe conflicts of interest between the rich and the poor.[8] But a resolution, like III, that sanctions the results of a power struggle between the rich and the poor, is a resolution that, by and large, favors the rich over the poor. So all things considered, it would be no more reasonable to require the poor to accept III, than it would be to require them to accept II. This means that only I satisfies the conflict resolution principle by being a resolution that is reasonable to require everyone affected to accept. Consequently, if we assume that, however else we specify the requirements of morality, they cannot violate the "ought" implies "can" principle or the conflict resolution principle, it follows that, despite what libertarians claim, the basic right to liberty endorsed by them, as determined by a weighing of the relevant competing liberties according to these two principles, actually favors the liberty of the poor over the liberty of the rich.[9]

Yet couldn't libertarians object to this conclusion, claiming that it would be unreasonable to require the rich to sacrifice the liberty to meet some of their luxury needs so that the poor could have the liberty to meet their basic needs? As has been pointed out, libertarians don't usually see the situation as a conflict of liberties. But suppose they did. How plausible would such an objection be? Not very plausible at all.

Consider: What are libertarians going to say about the poor? Isn't it clearly unreasonable to require the poor to sacrifice the liberty to meet their basic needs so that the rich can have the liberty to meet their luxury needs? Isn't it clearly unreasonable to require the poor to sit back and starve to death? If it is, then there is no resolution of this conflict that would be reasonable to require both the rich and the poor to accept. But that would mean that libertarians could not be putting forth a moral resolution, because according to the conflict resolution principle, in cases of severe conflict of interest, a moral resolution resolves conflicts of interest in ways that it would be reasonable to require everyone affected to accept. Therefore, as long as libertarians think of themselves as putting forth a moral resolution for cases of severe conflict of interest, they cannot allow that it would be unreasonable *both* to require the rich to sacrifice the liberty to meet some of their luxury needs in order to benefit the poor and to require the poor to sacrifice the liberty to meet their basic needs in order to benefit the rich. But I submit that if one of these requirements is to be judged reasonable, then, by any neutral assessment, it must be the requirement that the rich sacrifice the liberty to meet some of their luxury needs so that the poor can have the liberty to meet their basic needs. There is no other plausible resolution if libertarians intend to be putting forth a moral resolution.

It should also be noted that this case for restricting the liberty of the rich depends upon the willingness of the poor to take advantage of whatever opportunities are available to them to engage in mutually beneficial work, so that failure of the poor to take advantage of such opportunities would normally cancel or at least significantly reduce the obligation of the rich to restrict their own liberty for the benefit of the poor.[10] In addition, the poor would be required to return the equivalent of any surplus possessions they have taken from the rich once they are able to do so and still satisfy their basic needs. Nor would the poor be required to keep the liberty to which they are entitled. They could give up part of it, or all of it, or risk losing it on the chance of gaining a greater share of liberties or other social goods.[11] Consequently, the case for restricting the liberty of the rich for the benefit of the poor is neither unconditional nor inalienable.

Of course, there will be cases in which the poor fail to satisfy their basic needs, not because of any direct restriction of liberty on the part of the rich but because the poor are in such dire need that they are unable even to attempt to take from the rich what they require to meet their basic needs. In such cases, the rich would not be performing any act of commission that would prevent the poor from taking what they require. Yet, even in such cases, the rich would normally be performing acts of commission that would prevent other persons from taking part of the rich's own surplus possessions and using it to aid the poor. And when assessed from a moral point of view, restricting the liberty of these allies or agents of the poor would not be morally justified for the very same reason that restricting the liberty of the poor to meet their own basic needs would not be morally justified: it would not be reasonable to require all of those affected to accept such a restriction of liberty.

In brief, I have argued that a libertarian ideal of liberty can be seen to support a right to welfare through an application of the "ought" implies "can" principle and the conflict resolution principle to conflicts of liberty between the rich and the poor. In this interpretation of libertarianism, these principles support a right to welfare by favoring the liberty of the poor over the liberty of the rich. In another interpretation of libertarianism (developed elsewhere), these principles support this right to welfare by favoring a conditional right to property over an unconditional right to property.[12] In either interpretation, what is crucial to the derivation of this right is the claim that it would be unreasonable to require the poor to deny their basic needs and accept anything less than this right to welfare as the condition for their willing cooperation.

Now it might be objected that the right to welfare that this argument establishes from libertarian premises is not the same as the right to welfare endorsed by socialists. This is correct. We could mark this difference by referring to the right that this argument establishes as "a negative welfare right" and by referring to the right endorsed by socialists as "a positive welfare right." The significance of this difference is that a person's negative welfare right can be violated only when other people through acts of commission interfere with its exercise, whereas a person's positive welfare right can be violated not only by such acts of commission but by acts of omission as well. None the less, this difference will have little practical import. For in recognizing the legitimacy of negative welfare rights, libertarians will come to see that virtually any use of their surplus possessions is likely to violate the negative welfare rights of the poor by preventing the poor from rightfully appropriating (some part of) their surplus goods and resources. So in order to ensure that they will not be engaging in such wrongful actions, it will be incumbent on them to set up institutions guaranteeing adequate positive welfare rights for the poor. Only then will they be able to legitimately use any remaining surplus possessions to meet their own non-basic needs. Furthermore, in the absence of adequate positive welfare rights, the poor, either acting by themselves or through their allies or agents, would have some discretion in determining when and how to exercise their negative welfare rights.[13] In order not to be subject to that discretion, libertarians will tend to favor the only morally legitimate way of preventing the exercise of such rights: They will set up institutions guaranteeing

adequate positive welfare rights that will then take precedence over the exercise of negative welfare rights. For these reasons, recognizing the negative welfare rights of the poor will ultimately lead libertarians to endorse the same sort of welfare institutions favored by socialists.

II

Now it is possible that libertarians convinced to some extent by the previous argument might want to accept a right to welfare but then deny that this would lead to anything like a socialist state. After all, the fundamental rights recognized by libertarians are universal rights, that is, rights possessed by all people, not just those who live in certain places or at certain times. Of course, to claim that these rights are universal rights does not mean that they are universally recognized. Obviously, the fundamental rights that flow from the libertarian ideal have not been universally recognized. Rather, to claim that they are universal rights, despite their spotty recognition, implies only that they ought to be recognized at all times and places by people who have or could have had good reasons to recognize these rights, whether or not they actually did or do so. Nor need these universal rights be unconditional. This is particularly true in the case of the right to welfare, which, I have argued, is conditional on people doing all that they legitimately can to provide for themselves. In addition, this right is conditional on there being sufficient goods and resources available so that everyone's welfare needs can be met. So where people do not do all that they can to provide for themselves or where there are not sufficient goods and resources available, people simply do not have a right to welfare. Still, libertarians might grant that there are universal rights, even a right to welfare, that can be supported by the libertarian ideal of liberty but still deny that such rights lead to a socialist rather than a welfare state. But to see why this is not the case, consider what would be required to recognize a universal right to welfare.

Consider that at present there is probably a sufficient worldwide supply of goods and resources to meet the normal costs of satisfying the basic nutritional needs of all existing persons. According to former US Secretary of Agriculture, Bob Bergland:

> For the past 20 years, if the available world food supply had been evenly divided and distributed, each person would have received more than the minimum number of calories.[14]

Other authorities have made similar assessments of the available world food supply.

Needless to say, the adoption of a policy of supporting a right to welfare for all existing persons would necessitate significant changes, especially in developed countries. For example, the large percentage of the US population whose food consumption clearly exceeds even an adequately adjusted poverty index would have to substantially alter their eating habits. In particular, they would have to reduce their consumption of beef and pork in order to make more grain available for direct human consumption. (Presently the amount of grain fed to American livestock is as much as all the people of China and India eat in a year.) Thus, at least the satisfaction of some of the non-basic needs of the more advantaged in developed countries would have to be forgone if the basic nutritional needs of all existing persons in developing and underdeveloped countries are to be met. Of course, meeting the long-term basic nutritional needs of these societies will require other kinds of aid including appropriate technology and training and the removal of trade barriers favoring developed societies.[15] Furthermore, to raise the standard of living in developing and underdeveloped countries will require substantial increases in the consumption of energy and other resources. But such an increase would have to be matched by a substantial decrease in the consumption of these goods in developed countries; otherwise, global ecological disaster would result from increased global warming, ozone depletion, and acid rain, lowering virtually everyone's standard of living.[16]

In addition, once the basic nutritional needs of future generations are also taken into account,

the satisfaction of the non-basic needs of the more advantaged in developed countries would have to be further restricted in order to preserve the fertility of cropland and other food-related natural resources for the use of future generations. Obviously, the only assured way to guarantee the energy and resources necessary for the satisfaction of the basic needs of future generations is to set aside resources that would otherwise be used to satisfy the non-basic needs of existing generations.

Once basic needs other than nutritional needs are taken into account as well, still further restrictions would be required. For example, it has been estimated that presently a North American uses fifty times more goods and resources than a person living in India. This means that in terms of resource consumption the North American continent's population is the equivalent of 12.5 billion Indians. So unless we assume that basic goods and resources – such as arable land, iron, coal, oil, and so forth – are in unlimited supply, then this unequal consumption would have to be radically altered if the basic needs of distant peoples and future generations are to be met. Accordingly, recognizing a universal right to welfare applicable both to distant peoples and to future generations would lead to an equal sharing of goods and resources over place and time. In short, socialist equality is the consequence of recognizing a universal libertarian right to welfare.

In brief, I have argued that when a libertarian ideal of liberty is correctly interpreted, it leads to a universal right to welfare, and further that the recognition of this universal right to welfare leads to the equality in the distribution of goods and resources that is characteristic of a socialist state. Of course, the libertarian ideal, unlike the socialist ideal, does not directly pursue the goal of (substantive) equality.[17] Nevertheless, I contend that the practical effect of both ideals is much the same.

Notes

I would like to thank Joan Callahan, David Duquette, Joseph Ellin, Sidney Geldin, Carol Gould, Larry May,

Jan Narveson, David Phillips, Jonathan Schonsheck, and Carl Wellman for helpful comments on earlier versions of this paper.

1   See John Hospers, *Libertarianism* (Los Angeles, CA: Nash Press, 1971).

2   Basic needs, if not satisfied, lead to significant lacks or deficiencies with respect to a standard of mental and physical well-being, Thus, a person's needs for food, shelter, medical care, protection, companionship, and self-development are, at least in part, needs of this sort. For a discussion of basic needs, see *How to Make People Just* (Totowa, NJ: Rowman and Littlefield, 1988), pp. 45–8.

3   It is not being assumed here that the surplus possessions of the rich are either justifiably or unjustifiably possessed by the rich. Moreover, according to libertarians, it is an assessment of the liberties involved that determines whether the possession is justifiable or not.

4   There is another interpretation of libertarianism according to which a particular set of rights are basic and liberty is interpreted as the absence of interference with these rights. But, as I have argued elsewhere, the same sort of argument works against both forms of libertarianism. For this other interpretation, see "From Liberty to Welfare," *Ethics* (1994), and my *How to Make People Just*, ch. 5.

5   See John Hospers, *Libertarianism* (Los Angeles, CA: Nash Publishing, 1971), ch. 7, and Tibor Machan, *Human Rights and Human Liberties* (Chicago, IL: Nelson-Hall, 1975), pp. 231ff.

6   See James P. Sterba, "Is there a Rationale for Punishment?" *American Journal of Jurisprudence*, 29 (1984), pp. 29–43.

7   By the liberty of the rich to meet their luxury needs I continue to mean the liberty of the rich not to be interfered with when using their surplus possessions for luxury purposes. Similarly, by the liberty of the poor to meet their basic needs I continue to mean the liberty of the poor not to be interfered with when taking what they require to meet their basic needs from the surplus possessions of the rich.

8   See, for example, Eric Mack, "Individualism, Rights and the Open Society," *The Libertarian Alternative*, edited by Tibor Machan (Chicago, IL: Nelson-Hall, 1974).

9   Since the conflict resolution principle is the contrapositive of the "ought" implies "can" principle, whatever logically follows from the one principle logically follows from the other; nevertheless, by first appealing to the one principle and then the other, as I have here, I maintain that the conclusions that I derive can be seen to follow more clearly.

10 The employment opportunities offered to the poor must be honorable and supportive of self-respect. To do otherwise would be to offer the poor the opportunity to meet some of their basic needs at the cost of denying some of their other basic needs.

11 The poor cannot, however, give up the liberty to which their children are entitled.

12 For this other interpretation, see note 4.

13 When the poor are acting collectively in conjunction with their agents and allies to exercise their negative welfare rights, they will want, in turn, to institute adequate positive welfare rights to secure a proper distribution of the goods and resources they are acquiring.

14 Bob Bergland, "Attacking the Problem of World Hunger," *The National Forum* (1979) vol. 69, no. 2, p. 4.

15 Henry Shue, *Basic Rights* (Princeton, NJ: Princeton University Press, 1980), ch. 7.

16 For a discussion of these causal connections, see Cheryl Silver, *One Earth One Future* (Washington, DC: National Academy Press, 1990); Bill McKibben, *The End of Nature* (New York: Anchor Books, 1989); Jeremy Leggett, ed., *Global Warming* (New York: Oxford University Press, 1990); Lester Brown (ed.), *The World Watch Reader* (New York: Nelson, 1991).

17 Here I agree with Narveson that there are formal notions of equality, like equality before the law and equality of basic rights, that libertarians will frequently aim to achieve.

Virtue

25   The Virtuous Life

Aristotle

Book I, Chapter 1

Every science and every investigation, and likewise every practical pursuit and undertaking, appears to aim at some good: and consequently the good has been well defined as the object at which all things aim. It is true that a certain variety can be observed among the ends aimed at; sometimes the mere activity of practising the pursuit is the object of pursuing it, whereas in other cases the end aimed at is some product over and above the pursuit itself; and in the pursuits that aim at certain objects besides their mere practice, those products are essentially superior in value to the activities that produce them. But as there are numerous pursuits and sciences and branches of knowledge, it follows that the ends at which they aim are correspondingly numerous. Medicine aims at producing health, naval architecture at building ships, strategic science at winning victories, economics at acquiring wealth. And many pursuits of this sort are subordinate to some single faculty – for instance bit-making and the other departments of the harness trade are subordinate to the art of horsemanship, and the latter together with every other military activity to the science of strategies, and similarly other arts to different arts again. Now in all these cases the ends of the master sciences are of higher value than the objects of the subordinate ones, the latter being only pursued for the sake of the former. Nor does it make any difference whether

From *Nichomachean Ethics* (Oxford: Blackwell, 1989), I. 1–5, 7, 10, 13; II. 1–2, 6–9. Reprinted with permission.

the end aimed at by the pursuit is the mere activity of pursuing it or something else besides this, as in the case of the sciences mentioned.

If, therefore, among the ends at which our conduct aims there is one which we will for its own sake, whereas we will the other ends only for the sake of this one, and if we do not choose everything for the sake of some other thing – that would clearly be an endless process, making all desire futile and idle – it is clear that this one ultimate end will be the good, and the greatest good. Then will not a knowledge of this ultimate end be of more than theoretic interest? Will it not also have great practical importance for the conduct of life? Shall we not be more likely to attain our needs if like archers we have a target before us to aim at? If this be so, an attempt must be made to ascertain at all events in outline what precisely this supreme good is, and under which of the theoretical or practical sciences it falls.

Now it would be agreed that it must be the subject of the most authoritative of the sciences – the one that is in the fullest sense of the term a master-craft. This term clearly describes the science of politics, since it is that which ordains which of the sciences ought to exist in states and what branches of knowledge the various classes of citizens must study and up to what point; we observe that even the most highly esteemed faculties, such as strategies and domestic economy and oratory, are subordinate to political science. As then this science employs the rest of the sciences, and as it moreover lays down laws prescribing what people are to do and what things they are to abstain from, the end of political science must comprise the ends of the other sciences. Consequently the good of man must be the subject pursued by the science of politics. No doubt it is true that the good is the same for the individual and for the state; but still the good of the state is manifestly a greater and more perfect object both to ascertain and to secure. To procure the good of only a single individual is better than nothing; but to effect the good of a nation or a state is a nobler and more divine achievement.

This then being the object of our present investigation, it is in a sense the science of politics.

The present investigation therefore, as directed to these objects, may be termed Political Science.

Our treatment of this science will be adequate if it achieves the degree of accuracy that is appropriate to the subject. The same amount of precision is not requisite in every department of philosophy, any more than in every product of the arts and crafts. Questions of right and of justice, which are the matters investigated by Political Science, involve much difference of opinion and much uncertainty; indeed this has given rise to the view that such things are mere conventions, and not realities in the order of nature. There is a similar uncertainty as to the meaning of the term 'good', owing to the fact that good things may often lead to harmful consequences; before now people have been ruined by wealth, and courage has been the undoing of others. Therefore in dealing with subjects and starting from conceptions so indefinite we must be content to obtain no more than a rough outline of the truth, and to reach conclusions which, like the matters dealt with and the principles postulated, have merely general validity. And accordingly the reader likewise must accept the various views propounded in the same spirit. It is the mark of an educated mind to expect that degree of precision in each department which the nature of the subject allows: to demand rigorous demonstration from a political orator is on a par with accepting plausible probabilities from a mathematician. Also a man judges correctly about matters that are within his personal knowledge,

and of these he is a competent student. Consequently while a specialist can make judgements as to his own particular subject it requires a person of all-round education to form competent judgements about things in general. That is why a young man is not a competent student of political science,[1] because he has had no practical experience of the affairs of life, which supply the premises and form the subjects of political theory. Moreover, as he is liable to be guided by his emotions it will be waste of time for him to attend lectures on Ethics. He will get no profit from them, inasmuch as the real object of ethical instruction is not to impart knowledge but to influence conduct. Nor does it make any difference whether the student is young in years or immature in character; his deficiency is not a matter of age but is due to his living his life and pursuing his various aims under the guidance of emotion. For the immature, ethical study is of no value, any more than it is for persons deficient in self-control; but those who regulate their aims and guide their conduct by principle may derive great benefit from the science.

So much by way of preface in regard to the student and to the manner in which our discourse is to be received and the object which we have in view.

To resume: inasmuch as all study and all deliberate action is aimed at some good object, let us state what is the good which is in our view the aim of political science, and what is the highest of the goods obtainable by action.

Now as far as the name goes there is virtual agreement about this among the vast majority of mankind. Both ordinary people and persons of trained mind define the good as happiness. But as to what constitutes happiness opinions differ; the answer given by ordinary people is not the same as the verdict of the philosopher. Ordinary men identify happiness with something obvious and visible, such as pleasure or wealth or honour – everybody gives a different definition, and sometimes the same person's own definition alters: when a man has fallen ill he thinks that happiness is health, if he is poor he thinks it is wealth. And when people realize their own ignorance they regard with admiration those who propound some grand theory that is above their heads. The view has been held by some thinkers[2] that besides the many good things alluded to above there also exists something that is good in itself, which is the fundamental cause of the goodness of all the others.

Now to review the whole of these opinions would perhaps be a rather thankless task. It may be enough to examine those that are most widely held, or that appear to have some considerable argument in their favour.

But it is important for us to realize that there is a difference between lines of argument which proceed *from* first principles and those that lead *to* first principles. This was a point properly raised by Plato, who used to ask the question whether the right method is to work down from, or work up to, first principles – just as on a racecourse the runners are either going out from the start to the turning-point at the end of the track or coming back to the finish. A line of argument necessarily starts from something known; but the term 'known' has two meanings: some things are known to us, other things are known absolutely. Now presumably we for our part are bound to start from things known to us. Consequently in order to be a competent student of questions of right and justice and of political matters in general, the pupil must himself have been trained in good habits of conduct; for one has to start from facts; and if these be sufficiently clear there will be no need for reasons in addition. The student trained in right conduct knows the principles already, or can easily acquire them. As for one who has neither qualification, let him listen to the verses of Hesiod:

Best is the man who can himself advise;
He too is good who hearkeneth to the wise.
But whoso, being witless, cannot heed
Another's wisdom, is a dolt indeed![3]

But to resume. To judge by men's mode of living, the mass of mankind think that good and happiness consist in pleasure, and consequently are content with a life of mere enjoyment. There are in fact three principal modes of life – the one just mentioned, the life of active citizenship, and the life of contemplation. The masses, being utterly servile, obviously prefer the life of mere cattle; and indeed they have some reason for this, inasmuch as many men of high station share the tastes of Sardanapallus.[4] The better people, on the other hand, and men of action, give the highest value to honour, since honour may be said to be the object aimed at in a public career. Nevertheless, it would seem that honour is a more superficial thing than the good which we are in search of, because honour seems to depend more on the people who render it than on the person who receives it, whereas we dimly feel that good must be something inherent in oneself and inalienable. Moreover men's object in pursuing honour appears to be to convince themselves of their own worth; at all events they seek to be honoured by persons of insight and by people who are well acquainted with them, and to be honoured for their merit. It therefore seems that at all events in the opinions of these men goodness is more valuable than honour, and probably one may suppose that it has a better claim than honour to be deemed the end at which the life of politics aims. But even virtue appears to lack completeness as an end, inasmuch as it seems to be possible to possess it while one is asleep or living a life of perpetual inactivity, and moreover one can be virtuous and yet suffer extreme sorrow and misfortune; but nobody except for the sake of maintaining a paradox would call a man happy in those circumstances.

However, enough has been said on this topic which has indeed been sufficiently discussed in popular treatises.[5]

The third life is the life of contemplation, which we shall consider later.

The life of money-making is a cramped way of living, and clearly wealth is not the good we are in search of, as it is only valuable as a means to something else. Consequently a stronger case might be made for the objects previously specified, because they are valued for their own sake; but even they appear to be inadequate, although a great deal of discussion has been devoted to them.

What then is the precise nature of the practicable good which we are investigating? It appears to be one thing in one occupation or profession and another in another: the object pursued in medicine is different from that of military science, and similarly in regard to the other activities. What definition of the term 'good' then is applicable to all of them? Perhaps 'the object for the sake of attaining which all the subsidiary activities are undertaken'. The object pursued in the practice of medicine is health, in a military career victory, in architecture a building – one thing in one pursuit and another in another, but in every occupation and every pursuit it is the end aimed at, since it is for the sake of this that the subsidiary activities in all these pursuits are undertaken. Consequently if there is some one thing which is the end and aim of all practical activities whatsoever, that thing, or if there are several, those things, will constitute the practicable good.

Our argument has therefore come round again by a different route to the point reached before. We must endeavour to render it yet clearer.

Now the objects at which our actions aim are manifestly several, and some of these objects, for instance, money, and instruments in general, we adopt as means to the attainment of something else. This shows that not all the objects we pursue are final ends. But the greatest good manifestly is a final end. Consequently if there is only one thing which is final, that will be the object for which we are now seeking, or if there are several, it will be that one among them which possesses the most complete finality.

Now a thing that is pursued for its own sake we pronounce to be more final than one pursued as a means to some other thing, and a thing that is never desired for the sake of something else we call more final than those which are desired for the sake of something else as well as for their own sake. In fact the absolutely final is something that is always desired on its own account and never as a means for obtaining something else. Now this description appears to apply in the highest degree to happiness, since we always desire happiness for its own sake and never on account of something else; whereas honour and pleasure and intelligence and each of the virtues,

though we do indeed desire them on their own account as well, for we should desire each of them even if it produced no external result, we also desire for the sake of happiness, because we believe that they will bring it to us, whereas nobody desires happiness for the sake of those things, nor for anything else but itself.

The same result seems to follow from a consideration of the subject of self-sufficiency, which is felt to be a necessary attribute of the final good. The term self-sufficient denotes not merely being sufficient for oneself alone, as if one lived the life of a hermit, but also being sufficient for the needs of one's parents and children and wife, and one's friends and fellow-countrymen in general, inasmuch as man is by nature a social being.

Yet we are bound to assume some limit in these relationships, since if one extends the connection to include one's children's children and friends' friends, it will go on *ad infinitum*. But that is a matter which must be deferred for later consideration. Let us define self-sufficiency as the quality which makes life to be desirable and lacking in nothing even when considered by itself; and this quality we assume to belong to happiness. Moreover when we pronounce happiness to be the most desirable of all things, we do not mean that it stands as one in a list of good things – were it so, it would obviously be more desirable in combination with even the smallest of the other goods, inasmuch as that addition would increase the total of good, and of two good things the larger must always be the more desirable.

Thus it appears that happiness is something final and complete in itself, as being the aim and end of all practical activities whatever.

Possibly, however, the student may feel that the statement that happiness is the greatest good is a mere truism, and he may want a clearer explanation of what the precise nature of happiness is. This may perhaps be achieved by ascertaining what is the proper function of man. In the case of flute-players or sculptors or other artists, and generally of all persons who have a particular work to perform, it is felt that their good and their well-being are found in that work. It may be supposed that this similarly holds good in the case of a human being, if we may assume that there is some work which constitutes the proper function of a human being as such. Can it then be the case that whereas a carpenter and a shoemaker have definite functions or businesses to perform, a man as such has none, and is not designed by nature to perform any function? Should we not rather assume that, just as the eye and hand and foot and every part of the body manifestly have functions assigned to them, so also there is a function that belongs to a man, over and above all the special functions that belong to his members? If so, what precisely will that function be? It is clear that the mere activity of living is shared by man even with the vegetable kingdom, whereas we are looking for some function that belongs specially to man. We must therefore set aside the vital activity of nutrition and growth. Next perhaps comes the life of the senses; but this also is manifestly shared by the horse and the ox and all the animals. There remains therefore what may be designated the practical life of the rational faculty.

But the term 'rational' life has two meanings: it denotes both the mere possession of reason, and its active exercise. Let us take it that we here mean the latter, as that appears to be the more proper signification of the term. Granted then that the special function of man is the active exercise of the mind's faculties in accordance with rational principle, or at all events not in detachment from rational principle, and that the function of anything, for example, a harper, is generally the same as the function of a good specimen of that thing, for example a good harper (the specification of the function merely being augmented in the latter case with the statement of excellence – a harper is a man who plays the harp, a good harper one who plays the harp well) – granted, I say, the truth of these assumptions, it follows that the good of man consists in the active exercise of the faculties in conformity with excellence or virtue, or if there are several virtues, in conformity with the best and most perfect among them.

Moreover, happiness requires an entire lifetime. One swallow does not make a summer, nor does a single fine day; and similarly one day or a brief period of prosperity does not make a man supremely fortunate and happy.

Let this then stand as a first sketch of the good, since perhaps our right procedure is to begin by drawing a preliminary outline, and then to fill in the details later on. Given a good outline to start with, it would seem to be within anybody's capacity to carry on, and to put in all the details. In discovering these time is a good collaborator; and that is in fact the way in which advances in the arts and crafts have actually been achieved, as anybody is capable of filling in the gaps.

It is also important to bear in mind the warning already given, that we must not expect the same degree of accuracy in every department of study, but only so much precision as corresponds with the nature of the particular subject and is proper to the enquiry in hand. A carpenter and a mathematician employ different methods of finding a right angle; the carpenter only aims at such degree of accuracy as is necessary for his work, but the mathematician must arrive at the essential nature and qualities of a right angle, inasmuch as he is a student of truth. In other matters also therefore one must follow the same method, in order that the main task in hand may not be outbalanced by side issues. Nor should we in the case of everything alike expect a statement of the cause *why* the thing is so; in some cases it is enough if we achieve a satisfactory demonstration of the fact *that* it is so. This holds good in regard to first principles: the fact *is* a first principle, a point to start from.

Moreover, first principles are apprehended in various ways, some by the method of induction, some by direct intuition and some by a sort of familiarization: different methods are used in different cases, and we must endeavour to arrive at each first principle by the method appropriate to its particular nature. Also extreme care must be taken to define the first principles correctly, as they have a most important influence on the subsequent course of the argument. To make a right beginning is more than half the battle, and to start from the right first principle throws light straight away on many of the problems under investigation.

Accordingly, we must examine our first principle[6] not only as a logical conclusion deduced from given premises but also in the light of the opinions currently put forward with regard to it, inasmuch as if a theory is correct, all the data of experience will be in harmony with it, but if it is false they are quickly found to clash with it.

Goods then have been classified in three groups – external goods, goods of the body and goods of the mind; and of these we pronounce the goods of the mind to be good in the most important sense and in the highest degree. But our definition of happiness identifies it with goods of the mind, and so is at all events supported by the classification of good referred to, which has held the field for a long time and is accepted by philosophers.

Our theory is also correct in speaking of the aim and end as consisting in particular modes of conduct or activities, since this classes happiness among the goods of the mind and not among external goods. And it is in agreement with the popular phrase describing the happy man as a man who 'lives well' or 'does well', since our formula virtually defines happiness as a form of good living and good conduct.

Indeed the happy man as we describe him appears to possess all the qualifications that are deemed requisite for happiness. Some people identify happiness with virtue, others with prudence or wisdom of some kind, and others with these things or one of them accompanied by pleasure, or not devoid of pleasure; others also include material prosperity. Some of these definitions are widely held and have been current for a long time; others are put forward by a few eminent thinkers. It is not reasonable to suppose that either can be entirely mistaken, but it is probable that the accepted definitions are at least partly, or indeed mainly, correct.

Now our formula agrees with the view that identifies happiness with excellence, or with some particular virtue, inasmuch as activity conforming with excellence presupposes excellence in the agent. Perhaps however it makes an important difference whether the greatest good is judged to consist in possessing excellence or in employing it – whether it is classed as a quality of character or as the exercise of a quality in action. A man may possess a good quality without its producing any good effect, for instance when he is asleep or has in some other way ceased to function; but active virtue cannot be inoperative, since if present it will necessarily be exercised in action, and in good action. The garlands at the Olympic games are not awarded to the handsomest and strongest men present but to the handsomest and strongest who enter for the competitions, as it is among these that the winners are found. Similarly it is people who act rightly that win distinction and credit in life.

Moreover the life of active virtue is intrinsically pleasant. To feel pleasure is a psychological, not a physical experience; and when a man is described as being a 'lover' of so and so, it means that the thing in question gives him pleasure: for instance a lover of horses derives pleasure from a horse, and a lover of the theatre from a play; and similarly a lover of justice derives pleasure from just actions, and a lover of virtue from good actions in general. In most cases people's pleasures conflict with one another, because they are not natural pleasures; but lovers of what is noble take pleasure in things that are by nature pleasant, and such is virtuous conduct, so that it is intrinsically pleasant as well as pleasant to them.

In consequence of this their life has no need of pleasure as an external appendage; it contains pleasures within itself. For in addition to what has been said, if a man does not enjoy performing noble actions he is not a good man at all. Nobody would call a man just who did not enjoy acting justly, nor liberal if he did not enjoy acting liberally, and similarly with the other virtues. But if this is so, actions in conformity with virtue will be intrinsically pleasant. Moreover, they are also good and noble; and good and noble in the highest degree, inasmuch as the virtuous man must be a good judge of these matters, and his judgement is as we have said.

Consequently happiness is at once the best and the noblest and the pleasantest thing there is, and these qualities do not exist in separate compartments, as is implied by the inscription at Delos:

The noblest thing is justice, health the best,
But getting your desire the pleasantest.

For all these qualities are combined in the highest activities, and it is these activities or the best one among them which according to our definition constitutes happiness. All the same it is manifest that happiness requires external goods in addition, since it is impossible, or at all events difficult, to perform noble actions without resources. Many of them require the aid of friends and of wealth and power in the state. Also a lack of such advantages as good birth or a fine family of children or good looks is a blot on a man's supreme felicity. A very ugly man or one of low birth or without children cannot be classed as completely happy; and still less perhaps can a man whose children or friends are utterly base, or though worthy have died.

As we said then, happiness seems to require prosperity of this kind in addition; and this has led some people to identify happiness with good fortune.

This leads to the question whether happiness is something that can be acquired by study or by a course of training, or whether it comes to us by divine dispensation, or merely by chance.

Now if there is any other thing that comes to men as a gift of providence, it is reasonable to hold that happiness is given us by the gods, and more so than any other of man's possessions inasmuch as it is the best of them all. This however is perhaps a matter that belongs more properly to another line of enquiry. But even if happiness is not sent by the gods but acquired by virtue or by some process of study or training, it is nevertheless among the most divine things that exist; for it would seem that the prize of virtue must be the highest aim and end, and something divine and supremely felicitous.

It would also be something that is widely distributed, since everybody not incapable of virtue could acquire it by means of study and by effort. And if happiness thus acquired is a better thing than prosperity due to fortune, it is reasonable to assume that it can be won in this way, inasmuch as nature's order is planned on the best

lines possible, as likewise are works of art and the various products of design, and especially those of the highest form of design. For the greatest and noblest of all matters to be attributable to mere chance would seem too great a violation of the harmony of things.

This definition of happiness also throws light on our question how happiness may be attained. We pronounced it to be the active exercise of the faculties on certain lines; whereas goods of the other kinds are only requisite as a foundation, or else serviceable as auxiliaries and for their utility as instruments.

Moreover this would be in agreement with what we said at the outset, when we laid it down that the end at which statesmanship aims is the highest good, and that the statesman's chief concern is to produce a certain type of character in the citizens, namely to make them good men and capable of noble action. This justifies our refusal to apply the term 'happy' to an ox, or a horse or any other animal, inasmuch as no animal is capable of taking part in activity of the kind indicated. For this reason a child also cannot be happy in the proper sense, as he is not old enough to engage in conduct of this nature. When we speak of children as happy we are merely congratulating them on their promise for the future. For happiness, as we said, complete excellence is requisite; and also a life prolonged to its full limit, inasmuch as in the course of a lifetime a great many reverses and accidents of all sorts may occur, and it is possible that the most prosperous man may encounter severe misfortunes in old age, as legend tells us was the case with Priam in the tale of Troy. No one applies the term happy to one who encounters such disasters and comes to such a miserable end as Priam.

Must we then pronounce no other human being either to be happy as long as he is alive? Must we, as Solon[7] puts it, 'first see the end'? And if we are indeed to make that rule, is it really true that a man can be happy when he is dead? Is not that a very curious thing to assert, especially for us who define happiness as a form of activity? If on the other hand we refuse to speak of a dead man as happy, and if Solon does not mean this, but that only when a man is dead, and not before, is it safe to congratulate him as finally beyond the reach of evils and misfortunes, yet even this is open to question. It is generally believed that both good and evil can befall a man when he is dead, just as they can happen to one who is still alive without his being aware of them – for instance, the bestowal of honour and of dishonour, and the successes and misfortunes of his children and descendants. In regard to these moreover a difficulty arises; it is possible that a man may have lived in complete happiness till old age and have made an equally happy end, but that then a number of reverses may befall his descendants, some of whom may be good men and may enjoy a life in accordance with their deserts, but others the contrary; and these descendants may obviously stand in any degree of proximity to the ancestor in question. Now it would be strange if a dead man's condition altered together with that of his descendants, and if he became happy and miserable in turn; but it would also be strange if no cognizance at all of people's fortunes reached their forebears, even over a limited period.

However, we must return to the previous question raised, whether it is possible to pronounce a man happy before his death, as that may perhaps throw light on the problem before us now. It may be essential to see how a man's life ends, and perhaps even then he cannot be congratulated as being happy but only as having been happy previously. Yet surely it is paradoxical to say that happiness does not really belong to him at the time when he is in fact happy, and to refuse to call people happy while they are alive, on the ground that fortune may change, but we think of happiness as something stable and not easily liable to change, whereas the wheel of fortune often turns full circle in the same person's experience. It is clear that if we are to wait attendance on the changes of fortune we shall frequently apply the terms happy and miserable to the same person by turns, and so make out our happy man to be

Chameleon-hued, built on no firm foundation.

Or is it a complete mistake merely to wait in attendance on fortune? Good and evil do not consist in fortune's vicissitudes, although these do form a part of life, as we said. Happiness is controlled by activities in conformity with virtue and unhappiness by their opposite.

Moreover the difficulty now raised affords further support to our definition. No human actions possess such a degree of permanence as the active exercise of virtue. This appears to be more permanent than our possession of the various branches of knowledge; and even of these the most permanent are the more honourable, because men blest by fortune find their life in them most fully and most continuously. This indeed seems to be the reason why knowledge of this kind when once acquired is not easily forgotten. . . .

May we not then confidently define the happy man as 'the man who is engaged in virtuous activities and who is adequately equipped with external goods'? Or ought we to add, 'and who is destined to continue to live thus not for some chance period but throughout his whole lifetime, and to end his life correspondingly'? We must add this proviso because the future is hidden from us, and happiness as we define it is an aim and end, something possessing complete finality of every sort and kind. If this is so, it will be possible to ascribe felicity to persons still living who possess and are destined to continue to possess the blessings specified above – though of course we mean felicity on the human level. . . .

Happiness then we define as the active exercise of the mind in conformity with perfect goodness or virtue. It will therefore be necessary to investigate the nature of virtue, as to do so will contribute to our understanding the nature of happiness. Moreover it appears that the true statesman must have made a special study of virtue, because it is his aim to make the citizens good and law-abiding men. As an example of this we have the law-givers of Crete and of Sparta, and the other founders of constitutions recorded in history. But if the investigation of the nature of virtue is a duty of statesmanship, that investigation will clearly fit in with the original plan of this treatise.

Now obviously the virtue which we have to investigate is human virtue, inasmuch as the good and the happiness which we set out to discover were human good and human happiness. And by human virtue we mean not bodily excellence but goodness of the mind; and happiness also we define as an activity of the mind. This being so, it is clearly necessary for the statesman to have some acquaintance with psychology – just as the doctor in order to cure an affection of the eye or any other part of the body must know their anatomical structure. This background of science is even more essential for the statesman, inasmuch as statesmanship is a higher and more honourable profession than medicine; and even physicians of a high standard give a great deal of time to studying anatomy and physiology. Consequently the student of politics must study psychology, though he must study it for its bearing on politics, and only so far as is sufficient to throw light on the matters which fall to him to consider. To pursue it to a greater degree of precision would be a more laborious task than his purpose requires.

Notes to Book I, Chapter 1

1　This dictum floated down to Shakespeare, *Troilus and Cressida* II, ii 165:

> Most like young men, whom Aristotle thought unfit to hear moral philosophy.

2　Plato and the Academy.
3　From *Works and Days*, an early agricultural epic.
4　A mythical Assyrian king; two versions of his epitaph are recorded, one containing the words 'Eat, drink, play, since all else is not worth that snap of the fingers,' the other ending 'I have what I ate, and the delightful deeds of wantonness and love in which I shared; but all my wealth is vanished.'
5　There follows a technical refutation, omitted in this version, of Plato's Theory of Ideas as a basis for ethics.
6　I.e., the definition of happiness given above.
7　Herodotus I, 30–3. The famous sage visited Croesus, king of Sardis, and was shown his treasures, but refused to call him the happiest of mankind while he was still alive and therefore still liable to misfortune. 'It is necessary to see the end of every matter, and to discover how it is going to turn out; for to many men God has given a glimpse of prosperity and then has destroyed them root and branch.'

Book I, Chapter 2

Virtue, then, falls into two divisions, intellectual excellence and goodness of character. A good intellect is chiefly produced and fostered by education, and consequently requires experience and time, but moral goodness is formed mainly by training in habit. This shows that none of the moral virtues are implanted in us by nature, because natural characteristics can never be altered by training: for instance, a stone, which naturally moves downward, could not be trained to move upward even if one tried to accustom it to do so by throwing it up into the air ten thousand times; nor can a flame be trained to move downward, nor anything else that naturally acts in one way be educated to act in another way. Consequently the virtues are not formed in us by nature, but they result from our natural capacity to acquire them when that capacity has been developed by training.

Moreover in the case of the endowments given us by nature, we first receive the power of using them and exercise these powers in action subsequently. This is clear in the case of the sense-faculties: we did not acquire our sight and hearing by repeatedly seeing and hearing things, but the other way round: we started in possession of those senses and then began to use them, we did not acquire them by using them. But we acquire the virtues by first acting virtuously, just as in the case of the arts and crafts: we learn these by actually doing the things that we shall have to do when we have learnt them – for instance men become builders by building houses and harpers by playing the harp. Similarly by acting justly we become just, by acting temperately we become self-controlled, and by acting bravely we become courageous.

This is confirmed by what occurs in the state. Lawgivers make the citizens good by training them in good habits – at least that is every legislator's intention; and those who fail as legislators are those who do not establish a good system of education. In this lies the difference between a good constitution and a bad one.

Moreover all excellence is both produced and destroyed by the same means. This is the case with the arts and crafts; both good harpers and bad harpers are made by playing on the harp, and the same with building and all the other trades – a man will become a good builder by building well and a bad one by building badly. Were this not so, there would be no need of a period of apprenticeship, but people would all be born either good tradesmen or else bad ones.

Similarly with the virtues: it is by actually transacting business with our fellow-citizens that some of us become honest and others dishonest; it is by encountering danger and forming a habit of being frightened or else of keeping up our courage that some of us become brave men and others cowards; and the same is the case in regard to indulging the appetites and giving way to anger – people become self-controlled and gentle, or self-indulgent and passionate, from behaving in the one way or in the other in the fields of conduct concerned. To sum up, habits of character are formed as the result of conduct of the same kind. Consequently it is essential for us to give a certain quality to our actions, since differences of conduct produce differences of character. Hence the formation of habits, good or bad, from early childhood up is not a matter of small moment; on the contrary it is something of very great or more truly speaking of the supremest importance.

The present investigation then, unlike our other studies, is not undertaken for the purpose of attaining knowledge in the abstract – we are not pursuing it in order to learn what virtue is but in order to become virtuous; otherwise it would be of no value. We are therefore bound to carry the enquiry further, and to ascertain the rules that govern right conduct, since, as we have said, our conduct determines our characters.

The rule of acting in conformity with right principle is generally accepted, and may be taken for granted. Let us also take it as agreed that ethics is not an exact science, any more than are medicine and the art of navigation; and consequently the rules of conduct that it lays down are only of general validity, and their application must vary with the circumstances of the particular occasion, and be modified by the discretion of the agent.

The first point to have in view then is that in matters of conduct both excess and deficiency are essentially detrimental. It is the same here as in the case of bodily health and strength. Our strength is impaired by taking too much exercise, and also by taking too little; and similarly too much and too little food and drink injure our health, while the right amount produces health and increases it and preserves it. This also applies to self-control and courage and the other virtues. The man who runs away from every danger and never stands his ground becomes a coward, and the man who is afraid of nothing whatever and walks into everything becomes foolhardy; and similarly one who partakes of every pleasure and refrains from no gratification becomes self-indulgent, while one who shuns all pleasures becomes a boor and a dullard. It follows that self-control and courage are impaired by excess and by deficiency and are preserved by moderation. . . .

. . . In the case of every whole that is divisible into parts, it is possible to take a larger or a smaller share of it, or an equal share; and those amounts may be measured either in relation to the thing itself or in relation to us. I mean that whereas the middle of an object is the point equally distant from each of its extremities, which is one and the same for everybody, the medium quantity in its relation to us is the amount that is not excessive and not deficient, and this is not the same for everybody. For instance, if ten is many and two is few, to take the actual middle amount between them gives six (because 6 is the arithmetical mean between 2 and 10: $6 - 2 = 10 - 6$); but a medium quantity relative to us cannot be arrived at in this way. For instance, supposing that for an athlete in training ten pounds of food is too large a ration and two pounds too small, the trainer will not necessarily advise six pounds, as possibly that will be too large or too small an allowance for the particular person – a small ration for a Milo[1] but a large one for a novice in athletics; and the same applies to the amount of running or wrestling prescribed in training. This is how every expert avoids excess and deficiency and adopts the middle amount – not the exact half of the object he is dealing with, but a medium quantity in relation to the person concerned.

Such then is the manner in which every kind of skill operates successfully, by looking to the middle point and making its products conform with it. This accounts for the remark commonly made about successful productions, that you cannot take anything away from them or add anything to them. The implication is that excess and deficiency impair excellence, and a middle quantity secures it. If then we are right in saying that good craftsmen when at work keep their eyes fixed on a middle point, and if virtue, no less than nature herself, surpasses all the arts and crafts in accuracy and excellence, it follows that excellence will be the faculty of hitting a middle point. I refer to moral excellence or virtue; and this is concerned with emotions and actions, in which it is possible to have excess, or deficiency, or a medium amount. For instance you can feel either more or less than a moderate amount of fear and boldness, and of desire and anger and pity, and of pleasant or painful emotions generally; and in both cases the feelings will be wrong. But to feel these emotions at the right time and on the right occasion and towards the right people and for the right motives and in the right manner is a middle course, and the best course; and this is the mark of goodness. And similarly there is excess and deficiency or a middle amount in the case of actions. Now it is with emotions and actions that virtue is concerned; excess and deficiency in them are wrong, and a middle amount receives praise and achieves success, both of which are marks of virtue. It follows that virtue is a sort of middle state, in the sense that it aims at the middle.

Moreover, though it is possible to go wrong in many ways (according to the conjecture of the Pythagorean school evil is a property of the infinite and good of the finite), it is only possible to go right in one way:

Goodness is one, but badness manifold[2].

This is why to go wrong is easy but to go right difficult; it is easy to miss the target but difficult to hit it. Here then is another reason why vice is a matter of excess and deficiency and virtue a middle state.

It follows that virtue is a fixed quality of the will, consisting essentially in a middle state – middle in relation to ourselves, and as determined by principle, by the standard that a man of practical wisdom would apply. And it is a middle state between two vices, one of excess and one of deficiency: and this in view of the fact that vices either exceed or fall short of the right amount in emotions or actions, whereas virtue ascertains the mean and chooses that. Consequently while in its essence and by the principle defining its fundamental nature virtue is a middle state, in point of excellence and rightness it is an extreme.

But not every action or every emotion admits of a middle state: the very names of some of them suggest wickedness – for instance spite,[3] shamelessness, envy, and among actions, adultery, theft, murder; all of these and similar emotions and actions are blamed as being wicked intrinsically and not merely when practised to excess or insufficiently. Consequently it is not possible ever to feel or commit them rightly: they are always wrong, nor are the qualifications 'well' or 'ill' applicable to them – for instance, you cannot commit adultery with the right woman and at the right time and in the right place: the mere commission of adultery with any woman anywhere at any time is an offence. Similarly it is equally erroneous to think that there can be a middle amount and an excess and a deficiency of injustice or cowardice or self-indulgence, as that would mean that you can have a medium quantity of excess and deficiency or too much excess or too little deficiency. So just as there is no such thing as an excess or a deficiency of self-control and courage, because in these the middle is in a sense the top point, so there can be no middle amount or excess or deficiency of self-indulgence or cowardice, but actions of that sort however committed are an offence. There is no such thing as a medium amount of excess or deficiency, nor an excessive or insufficient amount of observance of a mean.

It is not enough, however, merely to give a general definition of moral goodness; it is necessary to show how our definition applies to particular virtues. In theories of conduct although general principles have a wider application, particular rules are more accurate, inasmuch as actual conduct deals with particular cases, and theory must be in agreement with these. Let us then take the particular virtues and vices from the diagram.[4]

The middle state as regards fear and boldness is courage. Excessive fearlessness has no name (as is the case with many types of character); excessive boldness is called rashness, and excessive fear and insufficient boldness cowardice.

In regard to pleasure, and in a less degree to pain, the middle state is self-control,[5] and the excess self-indulgence.[6] Persons deficient in sensibility to pleasure are scarcely to be found, so that this class has no recognized name; they may however be called insensitive.

The middle disposition in respect of giving and getting money is liberality; the excess and the deficiency are extravagance and meanness, both of these vices in opposite ways displaying both excess and deficiency – the extravagant man exceeds in spending money and is deficient in acquiring it, and the mean man exceeds in acquiring money but is deficient in spending it.

We are for the present giving a description of these characters in outline only, as that is sufficient for our present purpose. A more detailed account of them will be given later.

There are also other dispositions in regard to money – the middle state called munificence (which is not the same as liberality, as munificence is concerned with large sums of money whereas liberality is displayed in dealing with minor amounts), the excess which is tasteless vulgarity and the deficiency shabbiness in the use of money; the differences between the two latter will be stated later, and also two extremes corresponding with liberality.

The middle state in regard to honour and dishonour is pride;[7] the excess is called conceit and the deficiency lack of spirit. There is another middle state which stands in the same relation to pride as that which was described as existing between generosity and munificence: pride being concerned with high honours, the state indicated is similarly concerned with minor honours. These also may be desired in a proper manner, or more than is proper, or less. The man who covets them to excess is called ambitious and the man who is too little desirous of them unambitious; but there is no name for the person in between, who has a proper desire for such honours. Consequently the two extremes both lay claim to the middle place; and in fact in our ordinary use of the words we sometimes call a man of middle character in this respect ambitious and sometimes unambitious: both words are occasionally employed as terms of approval.

The reason for this ambiguity will be stated later. For the present let me speak about the remaining characters, in pursuance of our plan.

There are also excess and deficiency and a middle disposition in regard to anger, but there are virtually no accepted names to denote them. However, we speak of the person of intermediate character in regard to anger as good-tempered, so let us call the middle state good temper; while of the two extremes the man who exceeds may be called irascible and his vice irascibility, and for the man who is deficient perhaps we may use the term spiritless, and call his deficiency lack of spirit.

There are also three other middle dispositions which somewhat resemble one another and yet are really distinct, as although they all are concerned with our daily intercourse with our fellows in conversation and in conduct, they differ in that one is a matter of sincerity in social intercourse and the others denote agreeableness, displayed either in hours of relaxation or in the business of life. These dispositions must also be dealt with, to bring it home to us that in all affairs the middle course is to be commended and the extremes are neither commendable nor right, but reprehensible.

These dispositions also for the most part have

no names attached to them, but for the sake of clearness and to enable the reader to follow us more easily we must attempt to invent terms of our own to denote them, as we have done for the other dispositions.

In regard to sincerity, the middle person may be called frank and the middle disposition frankness. To exaggerate one's own merits is boastfulness and the person possessing that quality a boaster; to deprecate oneself is mock-modesty and the man who does so is mock-modest. In respect of being pleasant in giving amusement the middle person is witty and his characteristic wit; the excess is buffoonery and its possessor a boor. In regard to pleasantness in the affairs of life in general, one who is agreeable in the proper way is kindly and the middle state of character kindliness; one who is agreeable to excess is obsequious if it is for no interested motive and a toady if he hopes to get something out of it; one who is deficient in kindliness and always disagreeable in intercourse may be called churlish or surly.

There are also middle dispositions in respect of the emotions. In these also one man is said to be of a middle character, another excessive. There is the bashful man who is ashamed of everything, whereas another is deficient or entirely devoid of the emotion in question, who is impudent; while the middle character is called modest; though modesty is not a virtue, 'modest' is a term of commendation.

Righteous indignation is the middle state between envy and malice in regard to pain or pleasure at what happens to one's neighbours. The righteously indignant man is distressed when they prosper undeservedly; the jealous man goes further, and feels aggrieved at any prosperity of others; the malicious man is so far from feeling distress at other people's misfortunes that they give him actual pleasure.

There are then three kinds of dispositions, two of them vices, one a vice of excess and the other a vice of deficiency, and one a virtue, which is a middle state, and each of the three dispositions is in a manner opposed to both of the others: the extremes are the opposites of each other and the middle one is the opposite of each of the extremes – because just as in mathematics a is greater than $a - b$ and less than $a + \beta$, similarly middle dispositions of character are excessive as compared with the deficiencies and deficient as compared with the excesses. This holds good both of emotions and of actions. A brave man appears rash when compared with a coward and cowardly when compared with a rash man; and similarly a self-controlled man seems self-indulgent in comparison with a man insensitive to pleasure and pain but insensitive in comparison with a self-indulgent one, and a generous man extravagant in comparison with a mean man and mean in comparison with a spendthrift. Because of this people at either extreme push the man in the middle over to the other extreme – cowards call brave men rash and rash men call them cowardly, and similarly with the other types of character. But although the two extreme dispositions are opposed in this way to the middle one, it is the two extremes that are most widely opposed, as these are further away from each other than they are from the middle – just as in mathematics, if x, y and z are in descending order of magnitude, $x - z$ is greater than $x - y$ or $y - z$; and the things farthest apart from each other are defined as absolute opposites, so that the farther apart things are the more contrary they are.

Moreover in some cases there appears to be some resemblance between one of the extremes and the middle point – for instance, rashness is somewhat like courage and extravagance like liberality; whereas the extremes are most unlike each other. But it is things that are furthest apart from each other that are defined as contraries, so that things that are farther apart are more contrary.

In some cases there is more opposition between the deficiency and the middle point, in other cases between the excess and the middle – for example, the special opposite of courage is not rashness, which is the excess, but cowardice, which is the deficiency, and the special opposite of self-control is not insensitiveness, the deficiency, but extravagance, the excess. Of this there are two causes, one arising out of the facts of the case. If one of the two extremes appears to be closer than the other to the middle and to resemble it more, we do not consider it but rather the other one as the opposite of the middle. For instance, rashness seems to be more like courage and nearer to it and cowardice seems more unlike it; consequently we consider cowardice rather than rashness to be the opposite of courage, for the qualities that are farther away from the middle seem more contrary to it. The other cause is due to ourselves. The things to which we are more prone by our own nature seem more opposite to the middle: for instance, we are disposed by nature to enjoy pleasure, and consequently we are more liable to self-indulgence than we are to insensitiveness. So we speak of the things we are disposed by our nature to lapse into as more contrary to what is right: and consequently self-indulgence, which is a vice of excess, seems more contrary than insensitiveness to self-control.

It has now been shown that moral goodness is a middle state, and in what sense this is so – namely, that it is intermediate between two vices, one a vice of excess and the other a vice of deficiency; and that it holds this position in virtue of its quality of aiming to hit the middle point in emotions and in actions.

A consequence of this is that to be virtuous is no easy task. It is difficult to hit the middle point in anything – for instance, it takes a mathematician to find the centre of a circle. And similarly anybody can get angry – that is easy enough; and so is giving and spending money, but to bestow our money on the proper person and in the proper amount and at the proper time and for the proper motive and in the proper manner – all this is not within everybody's capacity, nor is it easy. Consequently right conduct is rare and praiseworthy and noble. The first rule in aiming at a middle course is to keep well away from that extreme which is the more opposite to it, as Calypso advises:[8]

Steer the ship wide of yonder spray and surge.

For of two extreme courses one is a greater mistake than the other. Inasmuch then as to hit the mean is extremely difficult, we must sail the second best way,[9] as they say, and the best method of doing this will be the one that we describe.

The second rule is to notice what are the errors to which we are ourselves most prone. Some of us have a natural tendency to one fault and others to another, and we can discover what our tendencies are from the pleasure or pain that different things give us. Then we must drag ourselves away in the opposite direction: to steer clear of our besetting error will bring us into the middle course. This is how carpenters straighten out timber that is warped.

And thirdly we must in everything keep a most careful watch on pleasant things and pleasant feelings. When mistress Pleasure is on her trial, we the jury have been tampered with. Our attitude towards her must be that of the Elders of Troy towards Helen;[10] on all occasions we must apply to Pleasure their remarks about Helen. We shall be less liable to go wrong if we just send her about her business.

These then, to sum up the matter, are the measures that will best enable us to hit the middle point. No doubt it is a difficult thing to do, especially in particular cases – for instance, it is difficult to define the conditions that justify getting angry: how we ought to show anger, and against whom, and on what occasion, and for how long. In fact we do sometimes praise those who are deficient in anger and call them good-tempered, and sometimes we applaud the hot-tempered for what we call their manliness.

A small departure from the right amount, either in the direction of excess or of deficiency, is not censured, though a wider divergence is bound to be noticed. Still it is not easy to give a formula defining the limit – *how wide* a divergence is reprehensible. No more indeed is any other matter of direct observation easy to define; such questions of degree depend on the particular circumstances, and can only be judged by intuition.

This much then is clear, that the middle course in everything is commendable, but that we should diverge sometimes towards excess and sometimes towards deficiency, as that is the easiest way of hitting the middle course, which is the right one.

Notes to Book I, Chapter 2

1   A famous wrestler.
2   A quotation from an unknown poem.
3   *Schadenfreude*, delight in the misfortunes of other people.
4   It appears that the lecturer here exhibited a table in which the virtues in the various fields of emotion and action were displayed as lying halfway between the two extremes of excess and deficiency in each. This is developed in detail in the latter part of chapter III and in chapter IV.
5   The Greek term, literally 'soundmindedness', was represented in Latin by *temperantia*, and is commonly rendered 'temperance'.
6   The usual translation 'profligacy' is too strong. The adjective means literally 'unchastized', and it was applied to naughty children.
7   The Greek term means literally 'greatness of soul', but that expression bears a different shade of meaning in English from what it suggests in Greek. It was rendered in Latin by *magnanimitas*, but our 'magnanimity' again is different. As is seen in Book VI, the Greek word means lofty and dignified pride, justified by real distinction of character and position.
8   I.e., advises the helmsman of Odysseus sailing through the Straits of Messina between Scylla and Charybdis, *Odyssey* XII, 219: but as a matter of fact it was Circe who had warned Odysseus, and the line quoted is Odysseus's order to his crew.
9   I.e. when the wind drops or is contrary, lower sail and take to the oars. Compare our phrase 'Shanks's mare', meaning having to walk.
10 *Iliad* III, 156ff. 'No one can quarrel with the Trojans and the well-greaved Achaeans for enduring sorrow so long with such a woman as the prize. Truly she is fair of face as the immortal goddesses. But albeit she is so fair, nevertheless, let her depart on shipboard, and not remain to plague us and our children hereafter.'

26   Non-Relative Virtues: An Aristotelian Approach

Martha Nussbaum

> All Greeks used to go around armed with swords.
> Thucydides, *History of the Peloponnesian War*

> The customs of former times might be said to be too simple and barbaric. For Greeks used to go around armed with swords; and they used to buy wives from one another, and there are surely other ancient customs that are extremely stupid. (For example, in Cyme there is a law about homicide, that if a man prosecuting a charge can produce a certain number of witnesses from among his own relations, the defendant will automatically be convicted of murder.) In general, all human beings seek not the way of their ancestors, but the good.
> Aristotle, *Politics* 1268a39ff.

From *Midwest Studies in Philosophy*, vol. XIII (Notre Dame, IN: University of Notre Dame Press). Reprinted by permission.

> One may also observe in one's travels to distant countries the feelings of recognition and affiliation that link every human being to every other human being.
> Aristotle, *Nichomachean Ethics* 1155a21–22

I

The virtues are attracting increasing interest in contemporary philosophical debate. From many different sides one hears of a dissatisfaction with ethical theories that are remote from concrete human experience. Whether this remoteness results from the utilitarian's interest in arriving at a universal calculus of satisfactions or from a Kantian concern with universal principles of broad generality, in which the names of particular contexts, histories, and persons do not occur, remoteness is now being seen by an increasing number of moral philosophers as a defect in an approach to ethical questions. In the search for an alternative approach, the concept of virtue is playing a prominent role. So, too, is the work of Aristotle, the greatest defender of an ethical approach based on the concept of virtue. For Aristotle's work seems, appealingly, to combine rigor with concreteness, theoretical power with sensitivity to the actual circumstances of human life and choice in all their multiplicity, variety, and mutability.

But on one central point there is a striking divergence between Aristotle and contemporary virtue theory. To many current defenders of an ethical approach based on the virtues, the return to the virtues is connected with a turn toward relativism – toward, that is, the view that the only appropriate criteria of ethical goodness are local ones, internal to the traditions and practices of each local society or group that asks itself questions about the good. The rejection of general algorithms and abstract rules in favor of an account of the good life based on specific modes of virtuous action is taken, by writers as otherwise diverse as Alasdair MacIntyre, Bernard Williams, and Philippa Foot,[1] to be connected with the abandonment of the project of rationally justifying a single norm of flourishing life for and to all human beings and with a reliance, instead, on norms that are local both in origin and in application.

The positions of all of these writers, where relativism is concerned, are complex; none unequivocally endorses a relativist view. But all connect virtue ethics with a relativist denial that ethics, correctly understood, offers any transcultural norms, justifiable with reference to reasons of universal human validity, with reference to which we may appropriately criticize different local conceptions of the good. And all suggest that the insights we gain by pursuing ethical questions in the Aristotelian virtue-based way lend support to relativism.

For this reason it is easy for those who are interested in supporting the rational criticism of local traditions and in articulating an idea of ethical progress to feel that the ethics of virtue can

give them little help. If the position of women, as established by local traditions in many parts of the world, is to be improved, if traditions of slave holding and racial inequality, if religious intolerance, if aggressive and warlike conceptions of manliness, if unequal norms of material distribution are to be criticized in the name of practical reason, this criticizing (one might easily suppose) will have to be done from a Kantian or utilitarian viewpoint, not through the Aristotelian approach.

This is an odd result, where Aristotle is concerned. For it is obvious that he was not only the defender of an ethical theory based on the virtues, but also the defender of a single objective account of the human good, or human flourishing. This account is supposed to be objective in the sense that it is justifiable with reference to reasons that do not derive merely from local traditions and practices, but rather from features of humanness that lie beneath all local traditions and are there to be seen whether or not they are in fact recognized in local traditions. And one of Aristotle's most obvious concerns is the criticism of existing moral traditions, in his own city and in others, as unjust or repressive, or in other ways incompatible with human flourishing. He uses his account of the virtues as a basis for this criticism of local traditions: prominently, for example, in Book II of the *Politics*, where he frequently argues against existing social forms by pointing to ways in which they neglect or hinder the development of some important human virtue.[2] Aristotle evidently believes that there is no incompatibility between basing an ethical theory on the virtues and defending the singleness and objectivity of the human good. Indeed, he seems to believe that these two aims are mutually supportive.

Now the fact that Aristotle believes something does not make it true. (Though I have sometimes been accused of holding that position!) But it does, on the whole, make that something a plausible *candidate* for the truth, one deserving our most serious scrutiny. In this case, it would be odd indeed if he had connected two elements in ethical thought that are self-evidently incompatible, or in favor of whose connectedness and compatibility there is nothing interesting to be said. The purpose of this paper is to establish that Aristotle does indeed have an interesting way of connecting the virtues with a search for ethical objectivity and with the criticism of existing local norms, a way that deserves our serious consideration as we work on these questions. Having described the general shape of the Aristotelian approach, we can then begin to understand some of the objections that might be brought against such a non-relative account of the virtues, and to imagine how the Aristotelian could respond to those objections.

II

The relativist, looking at different societies, is impressed by the variety and the apparent non-comparability in the lists of virtues she encounters. Examining the different lists, and observing the complex connections between each list and a concrete form of life and a concrete history, she may well feel that any list of virtues must be simply a reflection of local traditions and values, and that, virtues being (unlike Kantian principles or utilitarian algorithms) concrete and closely tied to forms of life, there can in fact be no list of virtues that will serve as normative for all these varied societies. It is not only that the specific forms of behavior recommended in connection with the virtues differ greatly over time and place, it is also that the very areas that are singled out as spheres of virtue, and the manner in which they are individuated from other areas, vary so greatly. For someone who thinks this way, it is easy to feel that Aristotle's own list, despite its pretensions to universality and objectivity, must be similarly restricted, merely a reflection of one particular society's perceptions of salience and ways of distinguishing. At this point, relativist writers are likely to quote Aristotle's description of the "great-souled" person, the *megalopsuchos*, which certainly contains many concrete local features and sounds very much like the portrait of a certain sort of Greek gentleman, in order to show that Aristotle's list is just as culture-bound as any other.[3]

But if we probe further into the way in which

Aristotle in fact enumerates and individuates the virtues, we begin to notice things that cast doubt upon the suggestion that he has simply described what is admired in his own society. First of all, we notice that a rather large number of virtues and vices (vices especially) are nameless, and that, among the ones that are not nameless, a good many are given, by Aristotle's own account, names that are somewhat arbitrarily chosen by Aristotle, and do not perfectly fit the behavior he is trying to describe.[4] Of such modes of conduct he writes, "Most of these are nameless, but we must try . . . to give them names in order to make our account clear and easy to follow" (*NE* 1108a16–19). This does not sound like the procedure of someone who is simply studying local traditions and singling out the virtue names that figure most prominently in those traditions.

What *is* going on becomes clearer when we examine the way in which he does, in fact, introduce his list. For he does so, in the *Nicomachean Ethics*,[5] by a device whose very straightforwardness and simplicity has caused it to escape the notice of most writers on this topic. What he does, in each case, is to isolate a sphere of human experience that figures in more or less any human life, and in which more or less any human being will have to make *some* choices rather than others, and act in *some* way rather than some other. The introductory chapter enumerating the virtues and vices begins from an enumeration of these spheres (*NE* 2.7); and each chapter on a virtue in the more detailed account that follows begins with "Concerning *x* . . ." or words to this effect, where "*x*" names a sphere of life with which all human beings regularly and more or less necessarily have dealings.[6] Aristotle then asks: What is it to choose and respond well within that sphere? What is it, on the other hand, to choose defectively? The "thin account" of each virtue is that it is whatever it is to be stably disposed to act appropriately in that sphere. There may be, and usually are, various competing specifications of what acting well, in each case, in fact comes to. Aristotle goes on to defend in each case some concrete specifications, producing, at the end, a full or "thick" definition of the virtue.

Here are the most important spheres of experience recognized by Aristotle, along with the names of their corresponding virtues:[7]

Sphere	Virtue
1. Fear of important damages, esp. death	courage
2. Bodily appetites and their pleasures	moderation
3. Distribution of limited resources	justice
4. Management of one's personal property, where others are concerned	generosity
5. Management of personal property, where hospitality is concerned	expansive hospitality
6. Attitudes and actions with respect to one's own worth	greatness of soul
7. Attitude to slights and damages	mildness of temper
8. "Association and living together and the fellowship of words and actions"	
(a) truthfulness in speech	truthfulness
(b) social association of a playful kind	easy grace (contrasted with coarseness, rudeness, insensitivity)
(c) social association more generally	nameless, but a kind of friendliness (contrasted with irritability and grumpiness)
9. Attitude to the good and ill fortune of others	proper judgment (contrasted with enviousness, spitefulness, etc.)
10. Intellectual life	the various intellectual virtues (such as perceptiveness, knowledge, etc.)
11. The planning of one's life and conduct	practical wisdom

There is, of course, much more to be said about this list, its specific members, and the names Aristotle chooses for the virtue in each case, some of which are indeed culture-bound. What I want, however, to insist is the care with which Aristotle articulates his general approach, beginning from a characterization of a sphere of universal experience and choice, and introducing the virtue name as the name (as yet undefined) of whatever it is to choose appropriately in that area of experience. On this approach, it does not seem possible to say, as the relativist wishes to, that a given society does not contain anything that corresponds to a given virtue. Nor does it seem to be an open question, in the case of a particular agent, whether a certain virtue should or should not be included in his or her life – except in the sense that she can always choose to pursue the corresponding deficiency instead. The point is that everyone makes some choices and acts somehow or other in these spheres: if not properly, then improperly. Everyone has *some* attitude and behavior toward her own death; toward her bodily appetites and their management; toward her property and its use; toward the distribution of social goods; toward telling the truth; toward being kindly or not kindly to others; toward cultivating or not cultivating a sense of play and delight; and so on. No matter where one lives one cannot escape these questions, so long as one is living a human life. But then this means that one's behavior falls, willy nilly, within the sphere of the Aristotelian virtue, in each case. If it is not appropriate, it is inappropriate; it cannot be off the map altogether. People will of course disagree about what the appropriate ways of acting and reacting in fact *are*. But in that case, as Aristotle has set things up, they are arguing about the same thing, and advancing competing specifications of the same virtue. The reference of the virtue term in each case is fixed by the sphere of experience – by what we shall from now on call the "grounding experiences." The thin or "nominal definition" of the virtue will be, in each case, that it is whatever it is that being disposed to choose and respond well consists in, in that sphere. The job of ethical theory will be to search for the best further specification corresponding to this nominal definition, and to produce a full definition.

III

We have begun to introduce considerations from the philosophy of language. We can now make the direction of the Aristotelian account clearer by considering his own account of linguistic indicating (referring) and defining, which guides his treatment of both scientific and ethical terms, and of the idea of progress in both areas.[8]

Aristotle's general picture is as follows. We begin with some experiences – not necessarily our own, but those of members of our linguistic community, broadly construed.[9] On the basis of these experiences, a word enters the language of the group, indicating (referring to) whatever it is that is the content of those experiences. Aristotle gives the example of thunder.[10] People hear a noise in the clouds, and they then refer to it, using the word "thunder." At this point, it may be that nobody has any concrete account of the noise or any idea about what it really is. But the experience fixes a subject for further inquiry. From now on, we can refer to thunder, ask "What is thunder?" and advance and assess competing theories. The thin or, we might say, "nominal definition" of thunder is "That noise in the clouds, whatever it is." The competing explana-

tory theories are rival candidates for correct full or thick definition. So the explanation story citing Zeus' activities in the clouds is a false account of the very same thing of which the best scientific explanation is a true account. There is just one debate here, with a single subject.

So too, Aristotle suggests, with our ethical terms. Heraclitus, long before him, already had the essential idea, saying, "They would not have known the name of justice, if these things did not take place."[11] "These things," our source for the fragment informs us, are experiences of injustice – presumably of harm, deprivation, inequality. These experiences fix the reference of the corresponding virtue word. Aristotle proceeds along similar lines. In the *Politics* he insists that only human beings, and not either animals or gods, will have our basic ethical terms and concepts (such as just and unjust, noble and base, good and bad), because the beasts are unable to form the concepts, and gods lack the experiences of limit and finitude that give a concept such as justice its point.[12] In the *Nicomachean Ethics* enumeration of the virtues, he carries the line of thought further, suggesting that the reference of the virtue terms is fixed by spheres of choice, frequently connected with our finitude and limitation, that we encounter in virtue of shared conditions of human existence.[13] The question about virtue usually arises in areas in which human choice is both non-optional and somewhat problematic. (Thus, he stresses, there is no virtue involving the regulation of listening to attractive sounds or seeing pleasing sights.) Each family of virtue and vice or deficiency words attaches to some such sphere. And we can understand progress in ethics, like progress in scientific understanding, to be progress in finding the correct fuller specification of a virtue, isolated by its thin or "nominal" definition. This progress is aided by a perspicuous mapping of the sphere of the grounding experiences. When we understand more precisely what problems human beings encounter in their lives with one another, what circumstances they face in which choice of some sort is required, we will have a way of assessing competing responses to those problems, and we will begin to understand what it might be to act well in the face of them.

Aristotle's ethical and political writings provide many examples of how such progress (or, more generally, such a rational debate) might go. We find argument against Platonic asceticism, as the proper specification of moderation (appropriate choice and response *vis-à-vis* the bodily appetites) and the consequent proneness to anger over slights, that was prevalent in Greek ideals of maleness and in Greek behavior, together with a defense of a more limited and controlled expression of anger, as the proper specification of the virtue that Aristotle calls "mildness of temper." (Here Aristotle evinces some discomfort with the virtue term he has chosen, and he is right to do so, since it certainly loads the dice heavily in favor of his concrete specification and against the traditional one.)[14] And so on for all the virtues.

In an important section of *Politics* II, part of which forms one of the epigraphs to this paper, Aristotle defends the proposition that laws should be revisable and not fixed by pointing to evidence that there is progress toward greater correctness in our ethical conceptions, as also in the arts and sciences. Greeks used to think that courage was a matter of waving swords around; now they have (the *Ethics* informs us) a more inward and a more civic and communally attuned understanding of proper behavior toward the possibility of death. Women used to be regarded as property, bought and sold; now this would be thought barbaric. And in the case of justice as well we have, the *Politics* passage claims, advanced toward a more adequate understanding of what is fair and appropriate. Aristotle gives the example of an existing homicide law that convicts the defendant automatically on the evidence of the prosecutor's relatives (whether they actually witnessed anything or not, apparently). This, Aristotle says, is clearly a stupid and unjust law; and yet it once seemed appropriate – and, to a tradition-bound community, must still be so. To hold tradition fixed is then to prevent ethical progress. What human beings want and seek is not conformity with the past, it is the good. So our systems of law should make it possible for them to progress beyond the past, when they have agreed that a change is good. (They should not, however, make change too easy, since it is no easy matter to see one's way to the good, and tradition is frequently a sounder guide than current fashion.)

In keeping with these ideas, the *Politics* as a whole presents the beliefs of the many different societies it investigates not as unrelated local norms, but as competing answers to questions of justice and courage (and so on) with which all the societies (being human) are concerned, and in response to which they are all trying to find what is good. Aristotle's analysis of the virtues gives him an appropriate framework for these comparisons, which seem perfectly appropriate inquiries into the ways in which different societies have solved common human problems.

In the Aristotelian approach it is obviously of the first importance to distinguish two stages of the inquiry: the initial demarcation of the sphere of choice, of the "grounding experiences" that fix the reference of the virtue term; and the ensuing more concrete inquiry into what appropriate choice, in that sphere, *is*. Aristotle does nor always do this carefully, and the language he has to work with is often not helpful to him. We do not have much difficulty with terms like "moderation" and "justice" and even "courage," which seem vaguely normative but relatively empty, so far, of concrete moral content. As the approach requires, they can serve as extension-fixing labels under which many competing specifications may be investigated. But we have already noticed the problem with "mildness of temper," which seems to rule out by fiat a prominent contender for the appropriate disposition concerning anger. And much the same thing certainly seems to be true of the relativists' favorite target, *megalopsuchia*, which implies in its very name an attitude to one's own worth that is more Greek than universal. (For example, a Christian will feel that the proper attitude to one's own worth requires understanding one's lowness, frailty, and sinfulness. The virtue of humility requires considering oneself *small*, not great.) What we ought to get at this point in the inquiry is a word for the proper behavior toward anger and offense and a word for the proper behavior toward one's worth that are more truly neutral among the competing specifications, referring only to the sphere of experience within which we wish to determine what is appropriate. Then we could regard the competing conceptions as rival accounts of one and the same thing, so that, for example, Christian humility would be a rival specification of the same virtue whose Greek specification is given in Aristotle's account of *megalopsuchia*, namely, the proper way to behave toward the question of one's own worth.

And in fact, oddly enough, if one examines the evolution in the use of this word from Aristotle through the Stoics to the Christian fathers, one can see that this is more or less what happened, as "greatness of soul" became associated, first, with Stoic emphasis on the supremacy of virtue and the worthlessness of externals, including the body, and, through this, with the Christian denial of the body and of the worth of earthly life.[15] So even in this apparently unpromising case, history shows that the Aristotelian approach not only provided the materials for a single debate but actually succeeded in organizing such a debate, across enormous differences of both place and time.

Here, then, is a sketch for an objective human morality based upon the idea of virtuous action – that is, of appropriate functioning in each human sphere. The Aristotelian claim is that, further developed, it will retain virtue morality's immersed attention to actual human experiences, while gaining the ability to criticize local and traditional moralities in the name of a more inclusive account of the circumstances of human life, and of the needs for human functioning that these circumstances call forth.

IV

This proposal will encounter many objections. The concluding sections of this paper will present three of the most serious and will sketch the lines along which the Aristotelian conception might proceed in formulating a reply. To a great extent these objections are not imagined or confronted by Aristotle himself, but his position seems capable of confronting them.

The first objection concerns the relationship between singleness of problem and singleness of solution. Let us grant for the moment that the Aristotelian approach has succeeded in coherently isolating and describing areas of human experience and choice that form, so to speak, the *terrain* of the virtues, and in giving thin definitions of each of the virtues as whatever it is that consists in choosing and responding well within that sphere. Let us suppose that the approach succeeds in doing this in a way that embraces many times and places, bringing disparate cultures together into a single debate about the good human being and the good human life. Different cultural accounts of good choice within the sphere in question in each case are now seen not as untranslatably different forms of life, but as competing answers to a single general question about a set of shared human experiences. Still, it might be argued, what has been achieved is, at best, a single discourse or debate about virtue. It has not been shown that this debate will have, as Aristotle believes, a single answer. Indeed, it has not even been shown that the discourse we have set up will have the form of a *debate* at all, rather than that of a plurality of culturally specific narratives, each giving the thick definition of a virtue that corresponds to the experience and traditions of a particular group. There is an important disanalogy with the case of thunder, on which the Aristotelian so much relies in arguing that our questions will have a single answer. For in that case what is given in experience is the definiendum itself, so that experiences establish a rough extension, to which any good definition must respond. In the case of the virtues, things are more indirect. What is given in experience across groups is only the *ground* of virtuous action, the circumstances of life to which virtuous action is an appropriate response. Even if these grounding experiences are shared, that does not tell us that there will be a shared appropriate response.

In the case of thunder, furthermore, the conflicting theories are clearly put forward as competing candidates for the truth; the behavior of those involved in the discourse suggests that they are indeed, as Aristotle says, searching "not for the way of their ancestors, but for the good." And it seems reasonable in that case for them to do so. It is far less clear, where the virtues are concerned (the objector continues), that a unified practical solution is either sought by the actual participants or a desideratum for them. The Aristotelian proposal makes it possible to conceive of a way in which the virtues might be non-relative. It does not, by itself, answer the question of relativism.

The second objection goes deeper. For it questions the notion of spheres of shared human experience that lies at the heart of the Aristotelian approach. The approach, says this objector, seems to treat the experiences that ground the virtues as in some way primitive, given, and free from the cultural variation that we find in the plurality of normative conceptions of virtue. Ideas of proper courage may vary, but the fear of death is shared by all human beings. Ideas of moderation may vary, but the experiences of hunger, thirst, and sexual desire are (so the Aristotelian seems to claim) invariant. Normative conceptions introduce an element of cultural interpretation that is not present in the grounding experiences, which are, for that very reason, the Aristotelian's starting point.

But, the objector continues, such assumptions are naive. They will not stand up either to our best account of experience or to a close examination of the ways in which these so-called grounding experiences have in fact been differently constructed by different cultures. In general, first of all, our best accounts of the nature of experience, even perceptual experience, inform us that there is no such thing as an "innocent eye" that receives an uninterpreted "given." Even sense-perception is interpretive, heavily influenced by belief, teaching, language, and in general by social and contextual features. There is a very real sense in which members of different societies do not see the same sun and stars, encounter the same plants and animals, hear the same thunder.

But if this seems to be true of human experience of nature, which was the allegedly unproblematic starting point for Aristotle's ac-

count of naming, it is all the more plainly true, the objector claims, in the area of the human good. Here it is only a very naive and historically insensitive moral philosopher who would say that the experience of the fear of death or the experience of bodily appetites is a human constant. Recent anthropological work on the social construction of the emotions,[16] for example, has shown to what extent the experience of fear has learned and culturally variant elements. When we add that the object of the fear in which the Aristotelian takes an interest is death, which has been so variously interpreted and understood by human beings at different times and in different places, the conclusion that the "grounding experience" is an irreducible plurality of experiences, highly various and in each case deeply infused with cultural interpretation, becomes even more inescapable.

Nor is the case different with the apparently less complicated experience of the bodily appetites. Most philosophers who have written about the appetites have treated hunger, thirst, and sexual desire as human universals, stemming from our shared animal nature. Aristotle himself was already more sophisticated, since he insisted that the object of appetite is "the apparent good" and that appetite is therefore something interpretive and selective, a kind of intentional awareness.[17] But he does not seem to have reflected much about the ways in which historical and cultural differences could shape that awareness. The Hellenistic philosophers who immediately followed him did so reflect, arguing that the experience of sexual desire and of many forms of the desire for food and drink are, at least in part, social constructs, built up over time on the basis of a social teaching about value that is external to start with, but that enters so deeply into the perceptions of the individual that it actually forms and transforms the experience of desire.[18] Let us take two Epicurean examples. People are taught that to be well fed they require luxurious fish and meat, that a simple vegetarian diet is not enough. Over time, the combination of teaching with habit produces an appetite for meat, shaping the individual's perceptions of the objects before him. Again, people are taught that what sexual relations are all about is a romantic union or fusion with an object who is seen as exalted in value, or even as perfect. Over time, this teaching shapes sexual behavior and the experience of desire, so that sexual arousal itself responds to this culturally learned scenario.[19]

This work of social criticism has recently been carried further by Michel Foucault in his *History of Sexuality*.[20] This work has certain gaps as a history of Greek thought on this topic, but it does succeed in establishing that the Greeks saw the problem of the appetites and their management in an extremely different way from the way of twentieth-century Westerners. To summarize two salient conclusions of his complex argument, the Greeks did not single out the sexual appetite for special treatment; they treated it alongside hunger and thirst, as a drive that needed to be mastered and kept within bounds. Their central concern was with self-mastery, and they saw the appetites in the light of this concern. Furthermore, where the sexual appetite is concerned, they did not regard the gender of the partner as particularly important in assessing the moral value of the act. Nor did they identify or treat as morally salient a stable disposition to prefer partners of one sex rather than the other. Instead, they focused on the general issue of activity and passivity, connecting it in complex ways with the issue of self-mastery.

Work like Foucault's – and there is a lot of it in various areas, some of it very good – shows very convincingly that the experience of bodily desire, and of the body itself, has elements that vary with cultural and historical change. The names that people call their desires and themselves as subjects of desire, the fabric of belief and discourse into which they integrate their ideas of desiring, all this influences, it is clear, not only their reflection about desire, but also their experience of desire itself. Thus, for example, it is naive to treat our modern debates about homosexuality as continuations of the very same debate about sexual activity that went on in the Greek world.[21] In a very real sense there was no "homosexual experience" in a culture that did not contain our emphasis on the gender of the object, our emphasis on the subjectivity of inclination and the

permanence of appetitive disposition, our particular ways of problematizing certain forms of behavior.

If we suppose that we can get underneath this variety and this constructive power of social discourse in at least one case – namely, with the universal experience of bodily pain as a bad thing – even here we find subtle arguments against us. For the experience of pain seems to be embedded in a cultural discourse as surely as the closely related experiences of the appetites; and significant variations can be alleged here as well. The Stoics already made this claim against the Aristotelian virtues. In order to establish that bodily pain is not bad by its very nature, but only by cultural tradition, the Stoics had to provide some explanation for the ubiquity of the belief that pain is bad and of the tendency to shun it. This explanation would have to show that the reaction was learned rather than natural, and to explain why, in the light of this fact, it is learned so widely. This they did by pointing to certain features in the very early treatment of infants. As soon as an infant is born, it cries. Adults, assuming that the crying is a response to its pain at the unaccustomed coldness and harshness of the place where it finds itself, hasten to comfort it. This behavior, often repeated, teaches the infant to regard its pain as a bad thing – or, better, teaches it the concept of pain, which includes the notion of badness, and teaches it the forms of life its society shares concerning pain. It is all social teaching, they claim, though this usually escapes our notice because of the early and non-linguistic nature of the teaching.[22]

These and related arguments, the objector concludes, show that the Aristotelian idea that there is a single non-relative discourse about human experiences such as mortality or desire is a naive idea. There is no such bedrock of shared experience, and thus no single sphere of choice within which the virtue is the disposition to choose well. So the Aristotelian project cannot even get off the ground.

Now the Aristotelian confronts a third objector, who attacks from a rather different direction. Like the second, she charges that the Aristotelian has taken for a universal and necessary feature of human life an experience that is contingent on certain non-necessary historical conditions. Like the second, she argues that human experience is much more profoundly shaped by non-necessary social features than the Aristotelian has allowed. But her purpose is not simply, like the second objector's, to point to the great variety of ways in which the "grounding experiences" corresponding to the virtues are actually understood and lived by human beings. It is more radical still. It is to point out that we could imagine a form of human life that does not contain these experiences – or some of them – at all, in any form. Thus the virtue that consists in acting well in that sphere need not be included in an account of the human good. In some cases, the experience may even be a sign of *bad* human life, and the corresponding virtue, therefore, no better than a form of non-ideal adaptation to a bad state of affairs. The really good human life, in such a case, would contain neither the grounding deficiency nor the remedial virtue.

This point is forcefully raised by some of Aristotle's own remarks about the virtue of generosity. One of his points against societies that eliminate private ownership is that they have thereby done away with the opportunity for generous action, which requires having possessions of one's own to give to others.[23] This sort of remark is tailor-made for the objector, who will immediately say that generosity, if it really rests upon the experience of private possession, is a dubious candidate indeed for inclusion in a purportedly non-relative account of the human virtues. If it rests upon a "grounding experience" that is non-necessary and is capable of being evaluated in different ways, and of being either included or eliminated in accordance with that evaluation, then it is not the universal the Aristotelian said it was.

Some objectors of the third kind will stop at this point, or use such observations to support the second objector's relativism. But in another prominent form this argument takes a non-relativist direction. It asks us to assess the "grounding experiences" against an account of human flourishing, produced in some independent man-

ner. If we do so, the objector urges, we will discover that some of the experiences are remediable deficiencies. The objection to Aristotelian virtue ethics will then be that it limits our social aspirations, getting us to regard as permanent and necessary what we might in fact improve to the benefit of all human life. This is the direction in which the third objection to the virtues was pressed by Karl Marx, its most famous proponent.[24] According to Marx's argument, a number of the leading bourgeois virtues are responses to defective relations of production. Bourgeois justice, generosity, etc. presuppose conditions and structures that are non-ideal and that will be eliminated when communism is achieved. And it is not only the current *specification* of these virtues that will be superseded with the removal of deficiency. It is the virtues themselves. It is in this sense that communism leads human beings beyond ethics.

Thus the Aristotelian is urged to inquire into the basic structures of human life with the daring of a radical political imagination. It is claimed that when she does so she will see that human life contains more possibilities than are dreamed of in her list of virtues.

V

Each of these objections is profound. To answer any one of them adequately would require a treatise. But we can still do something at this point to map out an Aristotelian response to each one, pointing the direction in which a fuller reply might go.

The first objector is right to insist on the distinction between singleness of framework and singleness of answer, and right, again, to stress that in constructing a debate about the virtues based on the demarcation of certain spheres of experience we have not yet answered any of the "What is x?" questions that this debate will confront. We have not even said very much about the structure of the debate itself, beyond its beginnings – about how it will both use and criticize traditional beliefs, how it will deal with conflicting beliefs, how it will move critically from the "way of one's ancestors" to the "good" – in short, about whose judgments it will trust. I have addressed some of these issues, again with reference to Aristotle, in two other papers,[25] but much more remains to be done. At this point, however, we can make four observations to indicate how the Aristotelian might deal with some of the objector's concerns here. First, the Aristotelian position that I wish to defend need not insist, in every case, on a single answer to the request for a specification of a virtue. The answer might well turn out to be a disjunction. The process of comparative and critical debate will, I imagine, eliminate numerous contenders – for example, the view of justice that prevailed in Cyme. But what remains might well be a (probably small) plurality of acceptable accounts. These accounts may or may not be capable of being subsumed under a single account of greater generality. Success in the eliminative task will still be no trivial accomplishment. For example, if we should succeed in ruling out conceptions of the proper attitude to one's own human worth that are based on a notion of original sin, this would be moral work of enormous significance, even if we got no further than that in specifying the positive account.

Second, the general answer to a "What is x?" question in any sphere may well be susceptible of several or even of many concrete specifications, in connection with other local practices and local conditions. For example, the normative account where friendship and hospitality are concerned is likely to be extremely general, admitting of many concrete "fillings." Friends in England will have different customs, where regular social visiting is concerned, from friends in ancient Athens. And yet both sets of customs can count as further specifications of a general account of friendship that mentions, for example, the Aristotelian criteria of mutual benefit and well-wishing, mutual enjoyment, mutual awareness, a shared conception of the good, and some form of "living together."[26] Sometimes we may want to view such concrete accounts as optional alternative specifications, to be chosen by a society on the basis of reasons of ease and convenience. Sometimes, on the other hand, we may

want to insist that this account gives the only legitimate specification of the virtue in question for that concrete context; in that case, the concrete account could be viewed as a part of a longer or fuller version of the single normative account. The decision between these two ways of regarding it will depend upon our assessment of its degree of non-arbitrariness for its context (both physical and historical), its relationship to other non-arbitrary features of the moral conception of that context, and so forth.

Third, whether we have one or several general accounts of a virtue, and whether this account or these accounts do or do not admit of more concrete specifications relative to ongoing cultural contexts, the particular choices that the virtuous person, under this conception, makes will always be a matter of being keenly responsive to the local features of his or her concrete context. So in this respect, again, the instructions the Aristotelian gives to the person of virtue do not differ from one part of what a relativist would recommend. The Aristotelian virtues involve a delicate balancing between general rules and the keen awareness of particulars, in which process, as Aristotle stresses, the perception of the particular takes priority. It takes priority in the sense that a good rule is a good summary of wise particular choices and not a court of last resort. Like rules in medicine and in navigation, ethical rules should be held open to modification in the light of new circumstances; and the good agent must therefore cultivate the ability to perceive and correctly describe his or her situation finely and truly, including in this perceptual grasp even those features of the situation that are not covered under the existing rule.

I have written a good deal elsewhere on this idea of the "priority of the particular," exactly what it does and does not imply, in exactly what ways the particular perception is and is not prior to the general rule. Those who want clarification on this central topic will have to turn to those writings.[27]

What I want to stress here is that Aristotelian particularism is fully compatible with Aristotelian objectivity. The fact that a good and virtuous decision is context-sensitive does not imply that it is right only *relative* to, or *inside*, a limited context, any more than the fact that a good navigational judgment is sensitive to particular weather conditions shows that it is correct only in a local or relational sense. It is right absolutely, objectively, from anywhere in the human world, to attend to the particular features of one's context; and the person who so attends and who chooses accordingly is making, according to Aristotle, the humanly correct decision, period. If another situation ever should arise with all the same morally relevant features, including contextual features, the same decision would again be absolutely right.[28]

Thus the virtue-based morality can capture a great deal of what the relativist is after and still lay claim to objectivity. In fact, we might say that the Aristotelian virtues do better than the relativist virtues in explaining what people are actually doing when they scrutinize the features of their context carefully, looking at both the shared and the non-shared features with an eye to what is best. For as Aristotle says, people who do this are usually searching for the good, not just for the way of their ancestors. They are prepared to defend their decisions as good or right, and to think of those who advocate a different course as disagreeing about what is right, not just narrating a different tradition.

Finally, we should point out that the Aristotelian virtues, and the deliberations they guide, unlike some systems of moral rules, remain always open to revision in the light of new circumstances and new evidence. In this way, again, they contain the flexibility to local conditions that the relativist would desire, but, again, without sacrificing objectivity. Sometimes the new circumstances may simply give rise to a new concrete specification of the virtue as previously defined; in some cases it may cause us to change our view about what the virtue itself is. All general accounts are held provisionally, as summaries of correct decisions and as guides to new ones. This flexibility, built into the Aristotelian procedure, will again help the Aristotelian account to answer the questions of the relativist, without relativism.

VI

We must now turn to the second objection. Here, I believe, is the really serious threat to the Aristotelian position. Past writers on virtue, including Aristotle himself, have lacked sensitivity to the ways in which different traditions of discourse, different conceptual schemes, articulate the world, and also to the profound connections between the structure of discourse and the structure of experience itself. Any contemporary defense of the Aristotelian position must display this sensitivity, responding somehow to the data that the relativist historian or anthropologist brings forward.

The Aristotelian should begin, it seems to me, by granting that with respect to any complex matter of deep human importance there is no "innocent eye" – no way of seeing the world that is entirely neutral and free of cultural shaping. The work of philosophers such as Putnam, Goodman, and Davidson[29] – following, one must point out, from the arguments of Kant and, I believe, from those Aristotle himself[30] – have shown convincingly that even where sense-perception is concerned, the human mind is an active and interpretive instrument and that its interpretations are a function of its history and its concepts, as well as of its innate structure. The Aristotelian should also grant, it seems to me, that the nature of human world-interpretations is holistic and that the criticism of them must, equally well, be holistic. Conceptual schemes, like languages, hang together as whole structures, and we should realize, too, that a change in any single element is likely to have implications for the system as a whole.

But these two facts do not imply, as some relativists in literary theory and in anthropology tend to assume, that all world interpretations are equally valid and altogether non-comparable, that there are no good standards of assessment and "anything goes." The rejection of the idea of ethical truth as correspondence to an altogether uninterpreted reality does not imply that the whole idea of searching for the truth is an old-fashioned error. Certain ways in which people see the world can still be criticized exactly as Aristotle criticized them: as stupid, pernicious, and false. The standards used in such criticisms must come from inside human life. (Frequently they will come from the society in question itself, from its own rationalist and critical traditions.) And the inquirer must attempt, prior to criticism, to develop an inclusive understanding of the conceptual scheme being criticized, seeing what motivates each of its parts and how they hang together. But there is so far no reason to think that the critic will not be able to reject the institution of slavery or the homicide law of Cyme as out of line with the conception of virtue that emerges from reflection on the variety of different ways in which human cultures have had the experiences that ground the virtues.

The "grounding experiences" will not, the Aristotelian should concede, provide precisely a single language – neutral bedrock on which an account of virtue can be straightforwardly and unproblematically based. The description and assessment of the ways in which different cultures have constructed these experiences will become one of the central tasks of Aristotelian philosophical criticism. But the relativist has, so far, shown no reasons why we could not, at the end of the day, say that certain ways of conceptualizing death are more in keeping with the totality of our evidence and with the totality of our wishes for flourishing life than others; that certain ways of experiencing appetitive desire are for similar reasons more promising than others.

Relativists tend, furthermore, to understate the amount of attunement, recognition, and overlap that actually obtains across cultures, particularly in the areas of the grounding experiences. The Aristotelian in developing her conception in a culturally sensitive way, should insist, as Aristotle himself does, upon the evidence of such attunement and recognition. Despite the evident differences in the specific cultural shaping of the grounding experiences, we do recognize the experiences of people in other cultures as similar to our own. We do converse with them about matters of deep importance, understand them, allow ourselves to be moved by them. When we read Sophocles' *Antigone*, we see a good deal that seems strange to us; and we have not read

the play well if we do not notice how far its conceptions of death, womanhood, and so on differ from our own. But it is still possible for us to be moved by the drama, to care about its people, to regard their debates as reflections upon virtue that speak to our own experience, and their choices as choices in spheres of conduct in which we too must choose. Again, when one sits down at a table with people from other parts of the world and debates with them concerning hunger or just distribution or in general the quality of human life, one does find, in spite of evident conceptual differences, that it is possible to proceed as if we are all talking about the same human problem; and it is usually only in a context in which one or more of the parties is intellectually committed to a theoretical relativist position that this discourse proves impossible to sustain. This sense of community and overlap seems to be especially strong in the areas that we have called the areas of the grounding experiences. And this, it seems, supports the Aristotelian claim that those experiences can be a good starting point for ethical debate.

Furthermore, it is necessary to stress that hardly any cultural group today is as focused upon its own internal traditions and as isolated from other cultures as the relativist argument presupposes. Cross-cultural communication and debate are ubiquitous facts of contemporary life. Our experience of cultural interaction indicates that in general the inhabitants of different conceptual schemes do tend to view their interaction in the Aristotelian and not the relativist way. A traditional society, confronted with new technologies and sciences, and the conceptions that go with them, does not, in fact, simply fail to understand them or regard them as totally alien incursions upon a hermetically sealed way of life. Instead, it assesses the new item as a possible contributor to flourishing life, making it comprehensible to itself and incorporating elements that promise to solve problems of flourishing. Examples of such assimilation, and the debate that surrounds it,[31] suggest that the parties do, in fact, recognize common problems and that the traditional society is perfectly capable of viewing an external innovation as a device to solve a problem that it shares with the innovating society. The parties do, in fact, search for the good, not the way of their ancestors; only traditionalist anthropologists insist, nostalgically, on the absolute presentation of the ancestral.

And this is so even when cross-cultural discourse reveals a difference at the level of the conceptualization of the grounding experiences. Frequently the effect of work like Foucault's, which reminds us of the non-necessary and non-universal character of one's own ways of seeing in some such area, is precisely to prompt a critical debate in search of the human good. It is difficult, for example, to read Foucault's observations about the history of our sexual ideas without coming to feel that certain ways in which the Western contemporary debate on these matters has been organized, as a result of some combination of Christian morality with nineteenth-century pseudo-science, are especially silly, arbitrary, and limiting, inimical to a human search for flourishing. Foucault's moving account of Greek culture, as he himself insists in a preface,[32] provides not only a sign that someone once thought differently, but also evidence that it is possible for us to think differently. Foucault announced that the purpose of his book was to "free thought" so that it could think differently, imagining new and more fruitful possibilities. And close analysis of spheres of cultural discourse, which stresses cultural differences in the spheres of the grounding experiences, is being combined, increasingly, in current debates about sexuality and related matters, with the critique of existing social arrangements and attitudes, and with the elaboration of a new norm of human flourishing. There is no reason to think this combination incoherent.[33]

As we pursue these possibilities, the basic spheres of experience identified in the Aristotelian approach will no longer, we have said, be seen as spheres of *uninterpreted* experience. But we have also insisted that there is much family relatedness and much overlap among societies. And certain areas of relatively greater universality can be specified here, on which we should insist as we proceed to areas that are more varied in their cultural expression. Not without a sensi-

tive awareness that we are speaking of something that is experienced differently in different contexts, we can none the less identify certain features of our common humanity, closely related to Aristotle's original list, from which our debate might proceed.

1. *Mortality.* No matter how death is understood, all human beings face it and (after a certain age) know that they face it. This fact shapes every aspect of more or less every human life.

2. *The Body.* Prior to any concrete cultural shaping, we are born with human bodies, whose possibilities and vulnerabilities do not as such belong to one culture rather than any other. Any given human being might have belonged to any culture. The experience of the body is culturally influenced; but the body itself, prior to such experience, provides limits and parameters that ensure a great deal of overlap in what is going to be experienced, where hunger, thirst, desire, the five senses are concerned. It is all very well to point to the cultural component in these experiences. But when one spends time considering issues of hunger and scarcity, and in general of human misery, such differences appear relatively small and refined, and one cannot fail to acknowledge that "there are no known ethnic differences in human physiology with respect to metabolism of nutrients. Africans and Asians do not burn their dietary calories or use their dietary protein any differently from Europeans and Americans. It follows then that dietary requirements cannot vary widely as between different races."[34] This and similar facts should surely be focal points for debate about appropriate human behavior in this sphere. And by beginning with the body, rather than with the subjective experience of desire, we get, furthermore, an opportunity to criticize the situation of people who are so persistently deprived that their *desire* for good things has actually decreased. This is a further advantage of the Aristotelian approach, when contrasted with approaches to choice

that stop with subjective expressions of preference.

3. *Pleasure and pain.* In every culture, there is a conception of pain; and these conceptions, which overlap very largely with one another, can be plausibly seen as grounded in universal and pre-cultural experience. The Stoic story of infant development is highly implausible; the negative response to bodily pain is surely primitive and universal, rather than learned and optional, however much its specific "grammar" may be shaped by later learning.

4. *Cognitive capability.* Aristotle's famous claim that "all human beings by nature reach out for understanding"[35] seems to stand up to the most refined anthropological analysis. It points to an element in our common humanity that is plausibly seen, again, as grounded independently of particular acculturation, however much it is later shaped by acculturation.

5. *Practical reason.* All human beings, whatever their culture, participate (or try to) in the planning and managing of their lives, asking and answering questions about how one should live and act. This capability expresses itself differently in different societies, but a being who altogether lacked it would not be likely to be acknowledged as a human being, in any culture.[36]

6. *Early infant development.* Prior to the greatest part of specific cultural shaping, though perhaps not free from all shaping, are certain areas of human experiences and development that are broadly shared and of great importance for the Aristotelian virtues: experiences of desire, pleasure, loss, one's own finitude, perhaps also of envy, grief, gratitude. One may argue about the merits of one or another psychoanalytical account of infancy. But it seems difficult to deny that the work of Freud on infant desire and of Klein on grief, loss, and other more complex emotional attitudes has identified spheres of human experience that are to a large extent common to all humans, regardless of their particular society. All humans begin as hungry babies, perceiving their own helplessness, their alternating closeness to and distance from those on whom they depend, and so forth. Melanie Klein records a conversation with an anthropologist in which an event that at first looked (to Western eyes) bizarre was interpreted by Klein as the expression of a universal pattern of mourning. The anthropologist accepted her interpretation.[37]

7. *Affiliation.* Aristotle's claim that human beings as such feel a sense of fellowship with other human beings, and that we are by nature social animals, is an empirical claim, but it seems to be a sound one. However varied our specific conceptions of friendship and love are, there is a great point in seeing them as overlapping expressions of the same family of shared human needs and desires.

8. *Humor.* There is nothing more culturally varied than humor, and yet, as Aristotle insists, some space for humor and play seems to be a need of any human life. The human being was not called the "laughing animal" for nothing; it is certainly one of our salient differences from almost all animals, and (in some form or other) a shared feature, I somewhat boldly assert, of any life that is going to be counted as fully human.

This is just a list of suggestions, closely related to Aristotle's list of common experiences. One could subtract some of these items and/or add others. But it seems plausible to claim that in all these areas we have a basis for further work on the human good. We do not have a bedrock of completely uninterpreted "given" data, but we do have nuclei of experience around which the construction of different societies proceeds. There is no Archimedean point here, and no pure access to unsullied "nature" – even, here, human nature – as it is in and of itself. There is just human life as it is lived. But in life as it is lived, we do find a family of experiences, clustering around certain foci, which can provide reasonable starting points for cross-cultural reflection.

VII

The third objection raises, at bottom, a profound conceptual question: What is it to inquire about the *human* good? What circumstances of existence go to define what it is to live the life of a *human being*, and not some other life? Aristotle likes to point out that an inquiry into the human good cannot, on pain of incoherence, end up describing the good of some other being, say a god, a good, that on account of our circumstances, it is impossible for us to attain (cf. *NE* 1159a10–12, 1166a18–23). Which circumstances then? The virtues are defined relatively to certain problems and limitations, and also to certain endowments. Which ones are sufficiently central that their removal would make us into different beings, and open up a wholly new and different debate about the good? This question is itself part of the ethical debate we propose. For there is no way to answer it but ask ourselves which elements of our experience seem to us so important that they count, for us, as part of who we are. I discuss Aristotle's attitude to this question elsewhere, and I shall simply summarize here.[38] It seems clear, first of all, that our mortality is an essential feature of our circumstances as human beings. An immortal being would have such a different form of life, and such different values and virtues, that it does not seem to make sense to regard that being as part of the same search for good. Essential, too, will be our dependence upon the world outside of us: some sort of need for food, drink, the help of others. On the side of abilities, we would want to include cognitive functioning and the activity of practical reasoning as elements of any life that we would regard as human. Aristotle argues, plausibly, that we would want to include sociability as well, some sensitivity to the needs of and pleasure in the company of other beings similar to ourselves.

But it seems to me that the Marxian question remains, as a deep question about human forms of life and the search for the human good. For one certainly can imagine forms of human life that do not contain the holding of private property – and, therefore, not those virtues that have to do with its proper management. And this means that it remains an open question whether these virtues ought to be regarded as virtues, and kept upon our list. Marx wished to go much further, arguing that communism would remove the need for justice, courage, and most of the bourgeois virtues. I think we might be skeptical here. Aristotle's general attitude to such transformations of life is to suggest that they usually have a tragic dimension. If we remove one sort of problem – say, by removing private property – we frequently do so by introducing another – say, the absence of a certain sort of freedom of choice, the freedom that makes it possible to do fine and generous actions for others. If things are complex even in the case of generosity, where we can rather easily imagine the transformation that removes the virtue, they are surely far more so in the cases of justice and courage. And we would need a far more detailed description than Marx ever gives us of the form of life under communism, before we would be able even to begin to see whether this form of life has in fact transformed things where these virtues are concerned, and whether it has or has not introduced new problems and limitations in their place.

In general it seems that all forms of life, including the imagined life of a god, contain boundaries and limits.[39] All structures, even that of putative limitlessness, are closed to something, cut off from something – say, in that case, from the specific value and beauty inherent in the struggle against limitation. Thus it does not appear that we will so easily get beyond the virtues. Nor does it seem to be so clearly a good thing for human life that we should.

VIII

The best conclusion to this sketch of an Aristotelian program for virtue ethics was written by Aristotle himself, at the end of his discussion of human nature in *Nicomachean Ethics* I:

> So much for our outline sketch for the good. For it looks as if we have to draw an outline first, and fill it in later. It would seem to be open to anyone to take things further and to articu-

late the good parts of the sketch. And time is a good discoverer or ally in such things. That's how the sciences have progressed as well: it is open to anyone to supply what is lacking. (*NE* 1098a20–6)

Notes

This paper was motivated by questions discussed at the WIDER conference on Value and Technology, summer 1986, Helsinki. I would like to thank Steve and Frédérique Marglin for provoking some of these arguments, with hardly any of which they will agree. I also thank Dan Brock for his helpful comments, and Amartya Sen for many discussions of these issues.

1   A. MacIntyre, *After Virtue* (Notre Dame, IN, 1981); P. Foot, *Virtues and Vices* (Los Angeles, 1978); B. Williams, *Ethics and the Limits of Philosophy* (Cambridge, MA, 1985) and Tanner Lectures, Harvard, 1983. See also M. Walzer, *Spheres of Justice* (New York, 1983) and Tanner Lectures, Harvard, 1985.
2   For examples of this, see Nussbaum, "Nature, Function, and Capability: Aristotle on Political Distribution," circulated as a WIDER working paper, and in *Oxford Studies in Ancient Philosophy* (1988) and also, in an expanded version, in the Proceedings of the 12th Symposium Aristotelicum.
3   See, for example, Williams, *Ethics and the Limits*, 34–6; Stuart Hampshire, *Morality and Conflict* (Cambridge, MA, 1983), 150ff.
4   For "nameless" virtues and vices, see *NE* 1107b1–2, 1107b8, 1107b30–1, 1108a17, 1119a10–11, 1126b20, 1127a12, 1127a14; for recognition of the unsatisfactoriness of names given, see 1107b8, 1108a5–6, 1108a20ff. The two categories are largely overlapping, on account of the general principles enunciated at 1108a16–19, that where there is no name a name should be given, unsatisfactory or not.
5   It should be noted that this emphasis on spheres of experience is not present in the *Eudemian Ethics*, which begins with a list of virtues and vices. This seems to me a sign that that treatise expresses a more primitive stage of Aristotle's thought on the virtues – whether earlier or not.
6   For statements with *peri*, connecting virtues with spheres of life, see 1115a6–7, 1117a29–30, 1117b25, 27, 1119b23, 1122a19, 1122b34, 1125b26, 1126b13; and *NE* 2.7 throughout. See also the related usages at 1126b11, 1127b32.
7   My list here inserts justice in a place of prominence. (In the *NE* it is treated separately, after all the other virtues, and the introductory list defers it for that later examination.) I have also added at the end of the list categories corresponding to the various intellectual virtues discussed in *NE* 6, and also to *phronesis* or practical wisdom, discussed in 6 as well. Otherwise the order and wording of my list closely follows 2.7, which gives the program for the more detailed analyses of 3.5–4.
8   For a longer account of this, with references to the literature and to related philosophical discussions, see Nussbaum, *The Fragility of Goodness* (Cambridge, MA, 1986), ch. 8.
9   Aristotle does not worry about questions of translation in articulating this idea; for some worries about this, and an Aristotelian response, see below sections IV and VI.
10   *Posterior Analytics*, 2.8, 93a21ff.; see *Fragility*, ch. 4, 8.
11   Heraclitus, fragment DK B23; see Nussbaum, "*Psuche* in Heraclitus, II," *Phronesis* 17 (1972): 153–70.
12   See *Politics* 1.2. 1253a1–18; that discussion does not deny the virtues to gods explicitly, but this denial is explicit at *NE* 1145a25–7 and 1178b10ff.
13   Aristotle does not make the connection with his account of language explicit, but his project is one of defining the virtues, and we would expect him to keep his general view of defining in mind in this context. A similar idea about the virtues, and experience of a certain sort as a possible basis for a non-relative account, is developed, without reference to Aristotle, in a review of P. Foot's *Virtues and Vices* by N. Sturgeon, *Journal of Philosophy*, 81 (1984), pp. 326–33.
14   1108a5, where Aristotle says that the virtues and the corresponding person are "pretty much nameless," and says "Let us call . . ." when he introduces the names. See also 1125b29, 1126a3–4.
15   See John Procope, *Magnanimity* (1987); also R.-A. Gauthier, *Magnanimité* (Paris, 1951).
16   See, for example, *The Social Construction of the Emotions*, edited by Rom Harré (Oxford, 1986).
17   See Nussbaum, *Aristotle's De Motu Animalium* (Princeton, NJ, 1976), notes on ch. 6, and *Fragility*, ch. 9.
18   A detailed study of the treatment of these ideas in the three major Hellenistic schools was presented in Nussbaum, *The Therapy of Desire: Theory and Practice in Hellenistic Ethics*, The Martin Classical Lectures 1986, and forthcoming.

19 The relevant texts are discussed in Nussbaum, *The Therapy*, chs 4–6. See also Nussbaum, "Therapeutic Arguments: Epicurus and Aristotle," in *The Norms of Nature*, edited by M. Schofield and G. Striker (Cambridge, 1986), pp. 314–74.

20 M. Foucault, *Histoire de la sexualité*, vols 2 and 3 (Paris, 1984).

21 See the papers by D. Halperin and J. Winkler in *Before Sexuality*, edited by D. Halperin, J. Winkler, and F. Zeitlin, forthcoming (Princeton).

22 The evidence for this part of the Stoic view is discussed in Nussbaum, *The Therapy*.

23 *Politics* 1263b11ff.

24 For a discussion of the relevant passages, see S. Lukes, *Marxism and Morality* (Oxford, 1987). For an acute discussion of these issues I am indebted to an exchange between Alan Ryan and Stephen Lukes at the Oxford Philosophical Society, March 1987.

25 *Fragility*, ch. 8, and "Internal Criticism and Indian Rationalist Traditions," the latter co-authored with Amartya Sen, in *Relativism*, edited by M. Krausz (Notre Dame, IN, 1988) and a WIDER Working Paper.

26 See *Fragility*, ch. 12.

27 Fragility, ch. 10, "The Discernment of Perception," *Proceedings of the Boston Area Colloquium in Ancient Philosophy*, 1 (1985), pp. 151–201; "Finely Aware and Richly Responsible: Moral Awareness and the Moral Task of Literature," *Journal of Philosophy*, 82 (1985), pp. 516–29, reprinted in expanded form in *Philosophy and the Question of Literature*, edited by A. Cascardi (Baltimore, 1987).

28 I believe, however, that some morally relevant features, in the Aristotelian view, may be features that are not, even in principle, replicable in another context. See "The Discernment," and *Fragility*, ch. 10.

29 See H. Putnam, *Reason, Truth, and History* (Cambridge, 1981); *The Many Faces of Realism*, The Carus Lectures, forthcoming; and *Meaning and the Moral Sciences* (London, 1979); N. Goodman, *Languages of Art* (Indianapolis, 1968) and *Ways of World-Making* (Indianapolis, 1978); D. Davidson, *Inquiries into Truth and Interpretation* (Oxford, 1984).

30 On his debt to Kant, see Putnam, *The Many Faces*; on Aristotle's "internal realism," see Nussbaum, *Fragility*, ch. 8.

31 C. Abeysekera, paper presented at Value and Technology Conference, WIDER 1986.

32 Foucault, *Histoire*, vol. 2, preface.

33 This paragraph expands remarks made in a commentary on papers by D. Halperin and J. Winkler at the conference on "Homosexuality in History and Culture" at Brown University, February 1987. The combination of historically sensitive analysis with cultural criticism was forcefully developed at the same conference in Henry Abelove's "Is Gay History Possible?" (forthcoming).

34 C. Gopalan, "Undernutrition: Measurement and Implications," paper prepared for the WIDER Conference on Poverty, Undernutrition, and Living Standards, Helsinki, 27–31 July 1987, and forthcoming in the volume of Proceedings, edited by S. Osmani.

35 *Metaphysics* 1.1.

36 See Nussbaum, "Nature, Function, and Capability," where this Aristotelian view is compared with Marx's views on human functioning.

37 M. Klein, in Postscript to "Our Adult World and its Roots in Infancy," in *Envy, Gratitude and Other Works 1946–1963* (London, 1984), pp. 247–63.

38 "Aristotle on Human Nature and the Foundations of Ethics," forthcoming in a volume of essays on the work of Bernard Williams, edited by R. Harrison and J. Altham (Cambridge). This paper will be a WIDER Working Paper.

39 See *Fragility*, ch. 11.

27   The Nature of Virtues

Alasdair MacIntyre

[It might be suggested] that even within the relatively coherent tradition of thought which I have sketched there are just too many different and incompatible conceptions of a virtue for there to be any real unity to the concept or indeed to the history. Homer, Sophocles, Aristotle, the New Testament, and medieval thinkers differ from each other in too many ways. They offer us different virtues; and they have different and incompatible theories of the virtues. If we were to consider later Western writers on the virtues, the list of differences and incompatibilities would be enlarged still further: and if we extended our enquiry to Japanese, say, or American Indian cultures, the differences would become greater still. It would be all too easy to conclude that there are a number of rival and alternative conceptions of the virtues, but, even within the tradition which I have been delineating, no single core conception.

The case for such a conclusion could not be better constructed than by beginning from a consideration of the very different lists of items which different authors in different times and places have included in their catalogues of virtues. Some of these catalogues – Homer's, Aristotle's, and the New Testament's – I have already noticed at greater or lesser length. Let me at the risk of some repetition recall some of their key features and then introduce for further comparison the catalogues of two later Western writers, Benjamin Franklin and Jane Austen.

The first example is that of Homer. At least some of the items in a Homeric list of the *aretai* would clearly not be counted by most of us nowadays as virtues at all, physical strength being the most obvious example. To this it might be re-

From *After Virtue*, rev. edn (Notre Dame, IN: University of Notre Dame Press, 1984). Reprinted with permission.

plied that perhaps we ought not to translate the word *aretê* in Homer by our word "virtue," but instead by our word "excellence"; and perhaps, if we were so to translate it, the apparently surprising difference between Homer and ourselves would at first sight have been removed. For we could allow without any kind of oddity that the possession of physical strength is the possession of an excellence. But in fact we would not have removed, but instead would merely have relocated, the difference between Homer and ourselves. For we would now seem to be saying that Homer's concept of an *aretê*, an excellence, is one thing and that our concept of a virtue is quite another since a particular quality can be an excellence in Homer's eyes, but not a virtue in ours and vice versa.

But of course it is not that Homer's list of virtues differs only from our own; it also notably differs from Aristotle's. And Aristotle's of course also differs from our own. For one thing, as I noticed earlier, some Greek virtue-words are not easily translated into English or rather out of Greek. Moreover, consider the importance of friendship as a virtue in Aristotle's list – how different from us! Or the place of *phronêsis* – how different from Homer and from us! The mind receives from Aristotle the kind of tribute which the body receives from Homer. But it is not just the case that the difference between Aristotle and Homer lies in the inclusion of some items and the omission of others in their respective catalogues. It turns out also in the way in which those catalogues are ordered, in which items are ranked as relatively central to human excellence and which marginal.

Moreover the relationship of virtues to the social order has changed. For Homer the paradigm of human excellence is the warrior; for Aristotle it is the Athenian gentleman. Indeed according to Aristotle certain virtues are only available to those of great riches and of high social status; there are virtues which are unavailable to the poor man, even if he is a free man. And those virtues are on Aristotle's view ones central to human life: magnanimity – and once again, any translation of *megalopsuchia* is unsatisfactory – and munificence are not just virtues, but important virtues within the Aristotelian scheme.

At once it is impossible to delay the remark that the most striking contrast with Aristotle's catalogue is to be found neither in Homer's nor in our own, but in the New Testament's. For the New Testament not only praises virtues of which Aristotle knows nothing – faith, hope, and love – and says nothing about virtues such as *phronêsis* which are crucial for Aristotle, but it praises at least one quality as a virtue which Aristotle seems to count as one of the vices relative to magnanimity, namely humility. Moreover since the New Testament quite clearly sees the rich as destined for the pains of Hell, it is clear that the key virtues cannot be available to them; yet they *are* available to slaves. And the New Testament of course differs from both Homer and Aristotle not only in the items included in its catalogue, but once again in its rank ordering of the virtues.

Turn now to compare all three lists of virtues considered so far – the Homeric, the Aristotelian, and the New Testament's – with two much later lists, one which can be compiled from Jane Austen's novels and the other which Benjamin Franklin constructed for himself. Two features stand out in Jane Austen's list. The first is the importance that she allots to the virtue which she calls "constancy," a virtue about which I shall say more in a later chapter [of *After Virtue*]. In some ways constancy plays a role in Jane Austen analogous to that of *phronêsis* in Aristotle; it is a virtue the possession of which is a prerequisite for the possession of other virtues. The second is the fact that what Aristotle treats as the virtue of agreeableness (a virtue for which he says there is no name) she treats as only the simulacrum of a genuine virtue – the genuine virtue in question is the one she calls amiability. For the man who practices agreeableness does so from considera-

tions of honor and expediency, according to Aristotle; whereas Jane Austen thought it possible and necessary for the possessor of that virtue to have a certain real affection for people as such. (It matters here that Jane Austen is a Christian.) Remember that Aristotle himself had treated military courage as a simulacrum of true courage. Thus we find here yet another type of disagreement over the virtues; namely, one as to which human qualities are genuine virtues and which mere simulacra.

In Benjamin Franklin's list we find almost all the types of difference from at least one of the catalogues we have considered and one more. Franklin includes virtues which are new to our consideration such as cleanliness, silence, and industry; he clearly considers the drive to acquire itself a part of virtue, whereas for most ancient Greeks this is the vice of *pleonexia*; he treats some virtues which earlier ages had considered minor as major, but he also redefines some familiar virtues. In the list of thirteen virtues which Franklin compiled as part of his system of private moral accounting, he elucidates each virtue by citing a maxim obedience to which *is* the virtue in question. In the case of chastity the maxim is "Rarely use venery but for health or offspring – never to dullness, weakness, or the injury of your own or another's peace or reputation." This is clearly not what earlier writers had meant by "chastity."

We have therefore accumulated a startling number of differences and incompatibilities in the five stated and implied accounts of the virtues. So the question which I raised at the outset becomes more urgent. If different writers in different times and places, but all within the history of Western culture, include such different sets and types of items in their lists, what grounds have we for supposing that they do indeed aspire to list items of one and the same kind, that there is any shared concept at all? A second kind of consideration reinforces the presumption of a negative answer to this question. It is not just that each of these five writers lists different and differing kinds of items; it is also that each of these lists embodies, is the expression of a different theory about what a virtue is.

In the Homeric poems a virtue is a quality the manifestation of which enables someone to do exactly what their well-defined social role requires. The primary role is that of the warrior king and that Homer lists those virtues which he does becomes intelligible at once when we recognize that the key virtues therefore must be those which enable a man to excel in combat and in the games. It follows that we cannot identify the Homeric virtues until we have first identified the key social roles in Homeric society and the requirements of each of them. The concept of *what anyone filling such-and-such a role ought to do* is prior to the concept of a virtue; the latter concept has application only via the former.

On Aristotle's account matters are very different. Even though some virtues are available only to certain types of people, none the less virtues attach not to men as inhabiting social roles, but to man as such. It is the *telos* of man as a species which determines what human qualities are virtues. We need to remember however that although Aristotle treats the acquisition and exercise of the virtues as means to an end, the relationship of means to end is internal and not external. I call a means internal to a given end when the end cannot be adequately characterized independently of a characterization of the means. So it is with the virtues and the *telos* which is the good life for man on Aristotle's account. The exercise of the virtues is itself a crucial component of the good life for man. This distinction between internal and external means to an end is not drawn by Aristotle himself in the *Nicomachean Ethics*, as I noticed earlier, but it is an essential distinction to be drawn if we are to understand what Aristotle intended. The distinction *is* drawn explicitly by Aquinas in the course of his defense of St Augustine's definition of a virtue, and it is clear that Aquinas understood that in drawing it he was maintaining an Aristotelian point of view.

The New Testament's account of the virtues, even if it differs as much as it does in content from Aristotle's – Aristotle would certainly not have admired Jesus Christ and he would have been horrified by St Paul – does have the same logical and conceptual structure as Aristotle's account. A virtue is, as with Aristotle, a quality the exercise of which leads to the achievement of the human *telos*. The good for man is of course a supernatural and not only a natural good, but supernature redeems and completes nature. Moreover the relationship of virtues as means to the end which is human incorporation in the divine kingdom of the age to come is internal and not external, just as it is in Aristotle. It is of course this parallelism which allows Aquinas to synthesize Aristotle and the New Testament. A key feature of this parallelism is the way in which the concept of *the good life for man* is prior to the concept of a virtue in just the way in which on the Homeric account the concept of a social role was prior. Once again it is the way in which the former concept is applied which determines how the latter is to be applied. In both cases the concept of a virtue is a secondary concept.

The intent of Jane Austen's theory of the virtues is of another kind. C. S. Lewis has rightly emphasized how profoundly Christian her moral vision is and Gilbert Ryle has equally rightly emphasized her inheritance from Shaftesbury and from Aristotle. In fact her views combine elements from Homer as well, since she is concerned with social roles in a way that neither the New Testament nor Aristotle are. She is therefore important for the way in which she finds it possible to combine what are at first sight disparate theoretical accounts of the virtues. But for the moment any attempt to assess the significance of Jane Austen's synthesis must be delayed. Instead we must notice the quite different style of theory articulated in Benjamin Franklin's account of the virtues.

Franklin's account, like Aristotle's, is teleological; but unlike Aristotle's, it is utilitarian. According to Franklin in his *Autobiography* the virtues are means to an end, but he envisages the means-ends relationship as external rather than internal. The end to which the cultivation of the virtues ministers is happiness, but happiness understood as success, prosperity in Philadelphia and ultimately in heaven. The virtues are to be useful and Franklin's account continuously stresses utility as a criterion in individual cases: "Make no expense but to do good to others or yourself;

i.e. waste nothing." "Speak not but what may benefit others or yourself. Avoid trifling conversation" and, as we have already seen, "Rarely use venery but for health or offspring. . . ." When Franklin was in Paris he was horrified by Parisian architecture: "Marble, porcelain, and gilt are squandered without utility."

We thus have at least three very different conceptions of a virtue to confront: a virtue is a quality which enables an individual to discharge his or her social role (Homer); a virtue is a quality which enables an individual to move towards the achievement of the specifically human *telos*, whether natural or supernatural (Aristotle, the New Testament, and Aquinas); a virtue is a quality which has utility in achieving earthly and heavenly success (Franklin). Are we to take these as three different rival accounts of the same thing? Or are they instead accounts of three different things? Perhaps the moral structures in archaic Greece, in fourth-century Greece, and in eighteenth-century Pennsylvania were so different from each other that we should treat them as embodying quite different concepts, whose difference is initially disguised from us by the historical accident of an inherited vocabulary which misleads us by linguistic resemblance long after conceptual identity and similarity have failed. Our initial question has come back to us with redoubled force.

Yet although I have dwelt upon the prima facie case for holding that the differences and incompatibilities between different accounts at least suggest that there is no single, central, core conception of the virtues which might make a claim for universal allegiance, I ought also to point out that each of the five moral accounts which I have sketched so summarily does embody just such a claim. It is indeed just this feature of those accounts that makes them of more than sociological or antiquarian interest. Every one of these accounts claims not only theoretical, but also an institutional hegemony. For Odysseus the Cyclopes stand condemned because they lack agriculture, an *agora* and *themis*. For Aristotle the barbarians stand condemned because they lack the *polis* and are therefore incapable of politics. For New Testament Christians there is no salvation outside the apostolic church. And we know that Benjamin Franklin found the virtues more at home in Philadelphia than in Paris and that for Jane Austen the touchstone of the virtues is a certain kind of marriage and indeed a certain kind of naval officer (that is, a certain kind of *English* naval officer).

The question can therefore now be posed directly: are we or are we not able to disentangle from these rival and various claims a unitary core concept of the virtues of which we can give a more compelling account than any of the other accounts so far? I am going to argue that we can in fact discover such a core concept and that it turns out to provide the tradition of which I have written the history with its conceptual unity. It will indeed enable us to distinguish in a clear way those beliefs about the virtues which genuinely belong to the tradition from those which do not. Unsurprisingly perhaps it is a complex concept, different parts of which derive from different stages in the development of the tradition. Thus the concept itself in some sense embodies the history of which it is the outcome.

One of the features of the concept of a virtue which has emerged with some clarity from the argument so far is that it always requires for its application the acceptance for some prior account of certain features of social and moral life in terms of which it has to be defined and explained. So in the Homeric account the concept of a virtue is secondary to that of *a social role*, in Aristotle's account it is secondary to that of *the good life for man* conceived as the *telos* of human action, and in Franklin's much later account it is secondary to that of utility. What is it in the account which I am about to give which provides in a similar way the necessary background against which the concept of a virtue has to be made intelligible? It is in answering this question that the complex, historical, multi-layered character of the core concept of virtue becomes clear. For there are no less than three stages in the logical development of the concept which have to be identified in order, if the core conception of a virtue is to be understood, and each of these stages has its own conceptual background. The first stage requires a background account of what I shall call a practice, the second an account of what I have already characterized as the narrative order of a single human life and the third an account a good deal fuller than I have given up to now of what constitutes a moral tradition. Each later stage presupposes the earlier, but not vice versa. Each earlier stage is both modified by and reinterpreted in the light of, but also provides an essential constituent of each later stage. The progress in the development of the concept is closely related to, although it does not recapitulate in any straightforward way, the history of the tradition of which it forms the core.

In the Homeric account of the virtues – and in heroic societies more generally – the exercise of a virtue exhibits qualities which are required for sustaining a social role and for exhibiting excellence in some well-marked area of social practice: to excel is to excel at war or in the games, as Achilles does, in sustaining a household, as Penelope does, in giving counsel in the assembly, as Nestor does, in the telling of a tale, as Homer himself does. When Aristotle speaks of excellence in human activity, he sometimes though not always refers to some well-defined type of human practice: flute-playing, or war, or geometry. I am going to suggest that this notion of a particular type of practice as providing the arena in which the virtues are exhibited and in terms of which they are to receive their primary, if incomplete, definition is crucial to the whole enterprise of identifying a core concept of the virtues. I hasten to add two caveats however.

The first is to point out that my argument will not in any way imply that virtues are *only* exercised in the course of what I am calling practices. The second is to warn that I shall be using the word "practice" in a specially defined way which does not completely agree with current ordinary usage, including my own previous use of that word. What am I going to mean by it?

By a "practice" I am going to mean any coherent and complex form of socially established cooperative human activity through which goods internal to that form of activity are realized in the course of trying to achieve those standards of excellence which are appropriate to, and partially definitive of, that form of activity, with the result that human powers to achieve excellence, and human conceptions of the ends and goods involved, are systematically extended. Tic-tac-toe is not an example of a practice in this sense, nor is throwing a football with skill; but the game of football is, and so is chess. Bricklaying is not a practice; architecture is. Planting turnips is not a practice; farming is. So are the enquiries of physics, chemistry, and biology, and so is the work of the historian, and so are painting and music. In the ancient and medieval worlds the creation and sustaining of human communities – of households, cities, nations – is generally taken to be a practice in the sense in which I have defined it. Thus the range of practices is wide: arts, sciences, games, politics in the Aristotelian sense, the making and sustaining of family life, all fall under the concept. But the question of the precise range of practices is not at this stage of the first importance. Instead let me explain some of the key terms involved in my definition, beginning with the notion of goods internal to a practice.

Consider the example of a highly intelligent seven-year-old child whom I wish to teach to play chess, although the child has no particular desire to learn the game. The child does however have a very strong desire for candy and little chance of obtaining it. I therefore tell the child that if the child will play chess with me once a week I will give the child 50 cents worth of candy; moreover I tell the child that I will always play in such a way that it will be difficult, but not impossible, for the child to win and that, if the child wins, the child will receive an extra 50 cents worth of candy. Thus motivated the child plays and plays to win. Notice however that, so long as it is the candy alone which provides the child with a good reason for playing chess, the child has no reason not to cheat and every reason to cheat, provided he or she can do so successfully. But, so we may hope, there will come a time when the child will find in those goods specific to chess, in the achievement of a certain highly particular kind of analytical skill, strategic imagination, and competitive intensity, a new set of reasons, reasons now not just for winning on a particular occasion, but for trying to excel in whatever way the game of chess demands. Now if the child cheats, he or she will be defeating not me, but himself or herself.

There are thus two kinds of good possibly to be gained by playing chess. On the one hand there are those goods externally and contingently attached to chess-playing and to other practices by the accidents of social circumstance – in the case of the imaginary child candy, in the case of real adults such goods as prestige, status, and money. There are always alternative ways for achieving such goods, and their achievement is never to be had *only* by engaging in some particular kind of practice. On the other hand there are the goods internal to the practice of chess which cannot be had in any way but by playing chess or some other game of that specific kind. We call them internal for two reasons: first, as I have already suggested, because we can only specify them in terms of chess or some other game of that specific kind and by means of examples from such games (otherwise the meagerness of our vocabulary for speaking of such goods forces us into such devices as my own resort to writing of "a certain highly particular kind of"); and secondly because they can only be identified and recognized by the experience of participating in the practice in question. Those who lack the relevant experience are incompetent thereby as judges of internal goods.

This is clearly the case with all the major examples of practices: consider for example – even if briefly and inadequately – the practice of portrait painting as it developed in Western Europe from the late Middle Ages to the eighteenth century. The successful portrait painter is able to achieve many goods which are in the sense just defined external to the practice of portrait painting – fame, wealth, social status, even a measure of power and influence at courts upon occasion. But those external goods are not to be confused with the goods which are internal to the practice. The internal goods are those which result from an extended attempt to show how Wittgenstein's dictum "The human body is the best picture of the human soul" (*Investigations*, p. 178e) might be made to become true by teaching us "to regard . . . the picture on our wall as the object itself (the men, landscape and so on)

depicted there" (p. 205e) in a quite new way. What is misleading about Wittgenstein's dictum as it stands is its neglect of the truth in George Orwell's thesis "At fifty everyone has the face he deserves." What painters from Giotto to Rembrandt learnt to show was how the face at any age may be revealed as the face that the subject of a portrait deserves.

Originally in medieval paintings of the saints the face was an icon: the question of a resemblance between the depicted face of Christ or St Peter and the face that Jesus or Peter actually possessed at some particular age did not even arise. The antithesis to this iconography was the relative naturalism of certain fifteenth-century Flemish and German painting. The heavy eyelids, the coifed hair, the lines around the mouth undeniably represent some particular woman, either actual or envisaged. Resemblance has usurped the iconic relationship. But with Rembrandt there is, so to speak, synthesis: the naturalistic portrait is now rendered as an icon, but an icon of a new and hitherto inconceivable kind. Similarly in a very different kind of sequence mythological faces in a certain kind of seventeenth-century French painting become aristocratic faces in the eighteenth century. Within each of these sequences at least two different kinds of good internal to the painting of human faces and bodies are achieved.

There is first of all the excellence of the products, both the excellence in performance by the painters and that of each portrait itself. This excellence – the very verb "excel" suggests it – has to be understood historically. The sequences of development find their point and purpose in a progress towards and beyond a variety of types and modes of excellence. There are of course sequences of decline as well as of progress, and progress is rarely to be understood as straightforwardly linear. But it is in participation in the attempts to sustain progress and to respond creatively to problems that the second kind of good internal to the practices of portrait painting is to be found. For what the artist discovers within the pursuit of excellence in portrait painting – and what is true of portrait painting is true of the practice of the fine arts in general – is the good of a certain kind of life. That life may not constitute the whole of life for someone who is a painter by a very long way or it may at least for a period, Gauguin-like, absorb him or her at the expense of almost everything else. But it is the painter's living out of a greater or lesser part of his or her life *as a painter* that is the second kind of good internal to painting. And judgment upon these goods requires at the very least the kind of competence that is only to be acquired either as a painter or as someone willing to learn systematically what the portrait painter has to teach.

A practice involves standards of excellence and obedience to rules as well as the achievement of goods. To enter into a practice is to accept the authority of those standards and the inadequacy of my own performance as judged by them. It is to subject my own attitudes, choices, preferences, and tastes to the standards which currently and partially define the practice. Practices of course, as I have just noticed, have a history: games, sciences, and arts all have histories. Thus the standards are not themselves immune from criticism, but none the less we cannot be initiated into a practice without accepting the authority of the best standards realized so far. If, on starting to listen to music, I do not accept my own incapacity to judge correctly, I will never learn to hear, let alone to appreciate, Bartok's last quartets. If, on starting to play baseball, I do not accept that others know better than I when to throw a fast ball and when not, I will never learn to appreciate good pitching let alone to pitch. In the realm of practices the authority of both goods and standards operates in such a way as to rule out all subjectivist and emotivist analyses of judgment. De gustibus *est* disputandum.

We are now in a position to notice an important difference between what I have called internal and what I have called external goods. It is characteristic of what I have called external goods that when achieved they are always some individual's property and possession. Moreover characteristically they are such that the more someone has of them, the less there is for other people. This is sometimes necessarily the case, as with power and fame, and sometimes the case by reason of contingent circumstance as with money.

External goods are therefore characteristically objects of competition in which there must be losers as well as winners. Internal goods are indeed the outcome of competition to excel, but it is characteristic of them that their achievement is a good for the whole community who participate in the practice. So when Turner transformed the seascape in painting or W. G. Grace advanced the art of batting in cricket in a quite new way their achievement enriched the whole relevant community.

But what does all or any of this have to do with the concept of the virtues? It turns out that we are now in a position to formulate a first, even if partial and tentative definition of a virtue: *A virtue is an acquired human quality the possession and exercise of which tends to enable us to achieve those goods which are internal to practices and the lack of which effectively prevents us from achieving any such goods.* Later this definition will need amplification and amendment. But as a first approximation to an adequate definition it already illuminates the place of the virtues in human life. For it is not difficult to show for a whole range of key virtues that without them the goods internal to practices are barred to us, but not just barred to us generally, barred in a very particular way.

It belongs to the concept of a practice as I have outlined it – and as we are all familiar with it already in our actual lives, whether we are painters or physicists or quarterbacks or indeed just lovers of good painting or first-rate experiments or a well-thrown pass – that its goods can only be achieved by subordinating ourselves within the practice in our relationship to other practitioners. We have to learn to recognize what is due to whom; we have to be prepared to take whatever self-endangering risks are demanded along the way; and we have to listen carefully to what we are told about our own inadequacies and to reply with the same carefulness for the facts. In other words we have to accept as necessary components of any practice with internal goods and standards of excellence the virtues of justice, courage, and honesty. For not to accept these, to be willing to cheat as our imagined child was willing to cheat in his or her early days at chess, so far bars us from achieving the standards of excellence or the goods internal to the practice that it renders the practice pointless except as a device for achieving external goods.

We can put the same point in another way. Every practice requires a certain kind of relationship between those who participate in it. Now the virtues are those goods by reference to which, whether we like it or not, we define our relationships to those other people with whom we share the kind of purposes and standards which inform practices. Consider an example of how reference to the virtues has to be made in certain kinds of human relationship.

A, B, C, and D are friends in that sense of friendship which Aristotle takes to be primary: they share in the pursuit of certain goods. In my terms they share in a practice. D dies in obscure circumstances. A discovers how D died and tells the truth about it to B while lying to C. C discovers the lie. What A cannot then intelligibly claim is that he stands in the same relationship of friendship to both B and C. By telling the truth to one and lying to the other he has partially defined a difference in the relationship. Of course it is open to A to explain this difference in a number of ways: perhaps he was trying to spare C pain or perhaps he is simply cheating C. But some difference in the relationship now exists as a result of the lie. For their allegiance to each other in the pursuit of common goods has been put in question.

Just as, so long as we share the standards and purposes characteristic of practices, we define our relationship to each other, whether we acknowledge it or not, by reference to standards of truthfulness and trust, so we define them too by reference to standards of justice and of courage. If A, a professor, gives B and C the grades that their papers deserve, but grades D because he is attracted by D's blue eyes or is repelled by D's dandruff, he has defined his relationship to D differently from his relationship to the other members of the class, whether he wishes it or not. Justice requires that we treat others in respect of merit or desert according to uniform and impersonal standards: to depart from the standards of justice in some particular instance defines

our relationship with the relevant person as in some way special or distinctive.

The case with courage is a little different. We hold courage to be a virtue because the care and concern for individuals, communities, and causes which is so crucial to so much in practices requires the existence of such a virtue. If someone says that he cares for some individual, community, or cause, but is unwilling to risk harm or danger on his, her, or its own behalf, he puts in question the genuineness of his care and concern. Courage, the capacity to risk harm or danger to oneself, has its role in human life because of this connection with care and concern. This is not to say that a man cannot genuinely care and also be a coward. It is in part to say that a man who genuinely cares and has not the capacity for risking harm or danger has to define himself, both to himself and to others, as a coward.

I take it then that from the standpoint of those types of relationship without which practices cannot be sustained truthfulness, justice, and courage – and perhaps some others – are genuine excellences, are virtues in the light of which we have to characterize ourselves and others, whatever our private moral standpoint or our society's particular codes may be. For this recognition that we cannot escape the definition of our relationships in terms of such goods is perfectly compatible with the acknowledgment that different societies have and have had different codes of truthfulness, justice, and courage. Lutheran pietists brought up their children to believe that one ought to tell the truth to everybody at all times, whatever the circumstances or consequences, and Kant was one of their children. Traditional Bantu parents brought up their children not to tell the truth to unknown strangers, since they believed that this could render the family vulnerable to witchcraft. In our culture many of us have been brought up not to tell the truth to elderly great-aunts who invite us to admire their new hats. But each of these codes embodies an acknowledgment of the virtue of truthfulness. So it is also with varying codes of justice and of courage.

Practices then might flourish in societies with very different codes; what they could not do is flourish in societies in which the virtues were not valued, although institutions and technical skills serving unified purposes might well continue to flourish. (I shall have more to say about the contrast between institutions and technical skills mobilized for a unified end, on the one hand, and practices on the other, in a moment.) For the kind of cooperation, the kind of recognition of authority and of achievement, the kind of respect for standards and the kind of risk-taking which are characteristically involved in practices demand for example fairness in judging oneself and others – the kind of fairness absent in my example of the professor, a ruthless truthfulness without which fairness cannot find application – the kind of truthfulness absent in my example of A, B, C, and D – and willingness to trust the judgments of those whose achievement in the practice gives them an authority to judge which presupposes fairness and truthfulness in those judgments, and from time to time the taking of self-endangering and even achievement-endangering risks. It is no part of my thesis that great violinists cannot be vicious or great chess-players mean-spirited. Where the virtues are required, the vices also may flourish. It is just that the vicious and mean-spirited necessarily rely on the virtues of others for the practices in which they engage to flourish and also deny themselves the experience of achieving those internal goods which may reward even not very good chess-players and violinists.

To situate the virtues any further within practices it is necessary now to clarify a little further the nature of a practice by drawing two important contrasts. The discussion so far I hope makes it clear that a practice, in the sense intended, is never just a set of technical skills, even when directed towards some unified purpose and even if the exercise of those skills can on occasion be valued or enjoyed for their own sake. What is distinctive in a practice is in part the way in which conceptions of the relevant goods and ends which the technical skills serve – and every practice does require the exercise of technical skills – are transformed and enriched by these extensions of human powers and by that regard for its own internal goods which are partially definitive of each particular practice or type of practice. Prac-

tices never have a goal or goals fixed for all time – painting has no such goal nor has physics – but the goals themselves are transmuted by the history of the activity. It therefore turns out not to be accidental that every practice has its own history and a history which is more and other than that of the improvement of the relevant technical skills. This historical dimension is crucial in relation to the virtues.

To enter into a practice is to enter into a relationship not only with its contemporary practitioners, but also with those who have preceded us in the practice, particularly those whose achievements extended the reach of the practice to its present point. It is thus the achievement, and *a fortiori* the authority, of a tradition which I then confront and from which I have to learn. And for this learning and the relationship to the past which it embodies the virtues of justice, courage, and truthfulness are prerequisite in precisely the same way and for precisely the same reasons as they are in sustaining present relationships within practices.

It is not only of course with sets of technical skills that practices ought to be contrasted. Practices must not be confused with institutions. Chess, physics, and medicine are practices; chess clubs, laboratories, universities, and hospitals are institutions. Institutions are characteristically and necessarily concerned with what I have called external goods. They are involved in acquiring money and other material goods: they are structured in terms of power and status, and they distribute money, power, and status as rewards. Nor could they do otherwise if they are to sustain not only themselves, but also the practices of which they are the bearers. For no practices can survive for any length of time unsustained by institutions. Indeed so intimate is the relationship of practices to institutions – and consequently of the goods external to the goods internal to the practices in question – that institutions and practices characteristically form a single causal order in which the ideals and the creativity of the practice are always vulnerable to the acquisitiveness of the institution, in which the cooperative care for common goods of the practice is always vulnerable to the competitiveness of the institution. In this context the essential function of the virtues is clear. Without them, without justice, courage, and truthfulness, practices could not resist the corrupting power of institutions.

Yet if institutions do have corrupting power, the making and sustaining of forms of human community – and therefore of institutions – itself has all the characteristics of a practice, and moreover of a practice which stands in a peculiarly close relationship to the exercise of the virtues in two important ways. The exercise of the virtues is itself apt to require a highly determinate attitude to social and political issues; and it is always within some particular community with its own specific institutional forms that we learn or fail to learn to exercise the virtues. There is of course a crucial difference between the way in which the relationship between moral character and political community is envisaged from the standpoint of liberal individualist modernity and the way in which that relationship was envisaged from the standpoint of the type of ancient and medieval tradition of the virtues which I have sketched. For liberal individualism a community is simply an arena in which individuals each pursue their own self-chosen conception of the good life, and political institutions exist to provide that degree of order which makes such self-determined activity possible. Government and law are, or ought to be, neutral between rival concepts as of the good life for man, and hence, although it is the task of government to promote law-abidingness, it is on the liberal view no part of the legitimate function of government to inculcate any one moral outlook.

By contrast, on the particular ancient and medieval view which I have sketched political community not only requires the exercise of the virtues for its own sustenance, but it is one of the tasks of parental authority to make children grow up so as to be virtuous adults. The classical statement of this analogy is by Socrates in the *Crito*. It does not of course follow from an acceptance of the Socratic view of political community and political authority that we ought to assign to the modern state the moral function which Socrates assigned to the city and its laws.

Indeed the power of the liberal individualist standpoint partly derives from the evident fact that the modern state is indeed totally unfitted to act as moral educator of any community. But the history of how the modern state emerged is of course itself a moral history. If my account of the complex relationship of virtues to practices and to institutions is correct, it follows that we shall be unable to write a true history of practices and institutions unless that history is also one of the virtues and vices. For the ability of a practice to retain its integrity will depend on the way in which the virtues can be and are exercised in sustaining the institutional forms which are the social bearers of the practice. The integrity of a practice causally requires the exercise of the virtues by at least some of the individuals who embody it in their activities: and conversely the corruption of institutions is always in part at least an effect of the vices.

The virtues are of course themselves in turn fostered by certain types of social institution and endangered by others. Thomas Jefferson thought that only in a society of small farmers could the virtues flourish; and Adam Ferguson with a good deal more sophistication saw the institutions of modern commercial society as endangering at least some traditional virtues. It is Ferguson's type of sociology which is the empirical counterpart of the conceptual account of the virtues which I have given, a sociology which aspires to lay bare the empirical, causal connection between virtues, practices, and institutions. For this kind of conceptual account has strong empirical implications; it provides an explanatory scheme which can be tested in particular cases. Moreover my thesis has empirical content in another way; it does entail that without the virtues there could be a recognition only of what I have called external goods and not at all of internal goods in the context of practices. And in any society which recognized only external goods competitiveness would be the dominant and even exclusive feature. We have a brilliant portrait of such a society in Hobbes's account of the state of nature; and Professor Turnbull's report of the fate of the Ik suggests that social reality does in the most horrifying way confirm both my thesis and Hobbes's.

Virtues then stand in a different relationship to external and to internal goods. The possession of the virtues – and not only of their semblance and simulacra – is necessary to achieve the latter; yet the possession of the virtues may perfectly well hinder us in achieving external goods. I need to emphasize at this point that external goods genuinely are goods. Not only are they characteristic objects of human desire, whose allocation is what gives point to the virtues of justice and of generosity, but no one can despise them altogether without a certain hypocrisy. Yet notoriously the cultivation of truthfulness, justice, and courage will often, the world being what it contingently is, bar us from being rich or famous or powerful. Thus although we may hope that we can not only achieve the standards of excellence and the internal goods of certain practices by possessing the virtues *and* become rich, famous, and powerful, the virtues are always a potential stumbling block to this comfortable ambition. We should therefore expect that, if in a particular society the pursuit of external goods were to become dominant, the concept of the virtues might suffer first attrition and then perhaps something near total effacement, although simulacra might abound.

The time has come to ask the question of how far this partial account of a core conception of the virtues – and I need to emphasize that all that I have offered so far is the first stage of such an account – is faithful to the tradition which I delineated. How far, for example, and in what ways is it Aristotelian? It is – happily – not Aristotelian in two ways in which a good deal of the rest of the tradition also dissents from Aristotle. First, although this account of the virtues is teleological, it does not require any allegiance to Aristotle's metaphysical biology. And secondly, just because of the multiplicity of human practices and the consequent multiplicity of goods in the pursuit of which the virtues may be exercised – goods which will often be contingently incompatible and which will therefore make rival claims upon our allegiance – conflict will not spring solely from flaws in individual character. But it was just on these two matters that Aristotle's account of the virtues seemed most vulnerable;

hence if it turns out to be the case that this socially teleological account can support Aristotle's general account of the virtues as well as does his own biologically teleological account, these differences from Aristotle himself may well be regarded as strengthening rather than weakening the case for a generally Aristotelian standpoint.

There are at least three ways in which the account that I have given *is* clearly Aristotelian. First it requires for its completion a cogent elaboration of just those distinctions and concepts which Aristotle's account requires: voluntariness, the distinction between the intellectual virtues and the virtues of character, the relationship of both to natural abilities and to the passions and the structure of practical reasoning. On every one of these topics something very like Aristotle's view has to be defended, if my own account is to be plausible.

Secondly my account can accommodate an Aristotelian view of pleasure and enjoyment, whereas it is interestingly irreconcilable with any utilitarian view and more particularly with Franklin's account of the virtues. We can approach these questions by considering how to reply to someone who, having considered my account of the differences between goods internal to and goods external to a practice enquired into which class, if either, does pleasure or enjoyment fall? The answer is, "Some types of pleasure into one, some into the other."

Someone who achieves excellence in a practice, who plays chess or football well or who carries through an enquiry in physics or an experimental mode in painting with success, characteristically enjoys his achievement and his activity in achieving. So does someone who, although not breaking the limit of achievement, plays or thinks or acts in a way that leads towards such a breaking of limit. As Aristotle says, the enjoyment of the activity and the enjoyment of achievement are not the ends at which the agent aims, but the enjoyment supervenes upon the successful activity in such a way that the activity achieved and the activity enjoyed are one and the same state. Hence to aim at the one is to aim at the other; and hence also it is easy to confuse the pursuit of excellence with the pursuit of enjoyment *in this specific sense*. This particular confusion is harmless enough; what is not harmless is the confusion of enjoyment *in this specific sense* with other forms of pleasure.

For certain kinds of pleasure are of course external goods along with prestige, status, power, and money. Not all pleasure is the enjoyment supervening upon achieved activity; some is the pleasure of psychological or physical states independent of all activity. Such states – for example that produced on a normal palate by the closely successive and thereby blended sensations of Colchester oyster, cayenne pepper, and Veuve Cliquot – may be sought as external goods, as external rewards which may be purchased by money or received in virtue of prestige. Hence the pleasures are categorized neatly and appropriately by the classification into internal and external goods.

It is just this classification which can find no place within Franklin's account of the virtues which is framed entirely in terms of external relationships and external goods. Thus although by this stage of the argument it is possible to claim that my account does capture a conception of the virtues which is at the core of the particular ancient and medieval tradition which I have delineated, it is equally clear that there is more than one possible conception of the virtues and that Franklin's standpoint and indeed any utilitarian standpoint is such that to accept it will entail rejecting the tradition and vice versa.

One crucial point of incompatibility was noted long ago by D. H. Lawrence. When Franklin asserts, "Rarely use venery but for health or offspring . . . ," Lawrence replies, "Never *use* venery." It is of the character of a virtue that in order that it be effective in producing the internal goods which are the rewards of the virtues it should be exercised without regard to consequences. For it turns out to be the case that – and this is in part at least one more empirical factual claim – although the virtues are just those qualities which tend to lead to the achievement of a certain class of goods, none the less unless we practice them irrespective of whether in any particular set of contingent circumstances they will produce those goods or not, we cannot possess them at all. We cannot be genuinely courageous or truthful and be so only on occasion. Moreover, as we have seen, cultivation of the virtues always may and often does hinder the achievement of those external goods which are the mark of worldly success. The road to success in Philadelphia and the road to heaven may not coincide after all.

Furthermore we are now able to specify one crucial difficulty for *any* version of utilitarianism – in addition to those which I noticed earlier. Utilitarianism cannot accommodate the distinction between goods internal to and goods external to a practice. Not only is that distinction marked by none of the classical utilitarians – it cannot be found in Bentham's writings nor in those of either of the Mills or of Sidgwick – but internal goods and external goods are not commensurable with each other. Hence the notion of summing goods – and *a fortiori* in the light of what I have said about kinds of pleasure and enjoyment the notion of summing happiness – in terms of one single formula or conception of utility, whether it is Franklin's or Bentham's or Mill's, makes no sense. None the less we ought to note that although *this* distinction is alien to J. S. Mill's thought, it is plausible and in no way patronizing to suppose that something like this is the distinction which he was trying to make in *Utilitarianism* when he distinguished between "higher" and "lower" pleasures. At the most we can say "something like this"; for J. S. Mill's upbringing had given him a limited view of human life and powers, had unfitted him, for example, for appreciating games just because of the way it had fitted him for appreciating philosophy. None the less the notion that the pursuit of excellence in a way that extends human powers is at the heart of human life is instantly recognizable as at home in not only J. S. Mill's political and social thought, but also in his and Mrs Taylor's life. Were I to choose human exemplars of certain of the virtues as I understand them, there would of course be many names to name, those of St Benedict and St Francis of Assisi and St Theresa *and* those of Frederick Engels and Eleanor Marx and Leon Trotsky among them. But that of John Stuart Mill would have to be there as certainly as any other.

Thirdly my account is Aristotelian in that it links evaluation and explanation in a characteristically Aristotelian way. From an Aristotelian standpoint to identify certain actions as manifesting or failing to manifest a virtue or virtues is never only to evaluate; it is also to take the first step towards explaining why those actions rather than some others were performed. Hence for an Aristotelian quite as much as for a Platonist the fate of a city or an individual can be explained by citing the injustice of a tyrant or the courage of its defenders. Indeed without allusion to the place that justice and injustice, courage and cowardice play in human life very little will be genuinely explicable. It follows that many of the explanatory projects of the modern social sciences, a methodological canon of which is the separation of "the facts" from all evaluation, are bound to fail. For the fact that someone was or failed to be courageous or just cannot be recognized as "a fact" by those who accept that methodological canon. The account of the virtues which I have given is completely at one with Aristotle's on this point. But now the question may be raised: your account may be in many respects Aristotelian, but is it not in some respects false? Consider the following important objection.

I have defined the virtues partly in terms of their place in practices. But surely, it may be suggested, some practices – that is, some coherent human activities which answer to the description of what I have called a practice – are evil. So in discussion by some moral philosophers of this type of account of the virtues it has been suggested that torture and sadomasochistic sexual activities might be examples of practices. But how can a disposition be a virtue if it is the kind of disposition which sustains practices and some practices issue in evil? My answer to this objection falls into two parts.

First I want to allow that there *may* be practices – in the sense in which I understand the concept – which simply *are* evil. I am far from convinced that there are, and I do not in fact believe that either torture or sadomasochistic sexuality answer to the description of a practice which my account of the virtues employs. But I do not want to rest my case on this lack of conviction, especially since it is plain that as a matter of contingent fact many types of practice may on particular occasions be productive of evil. For the range of practices includes the arts, the sciences and certain types of intellectual and athletic games. And it is at once obvious that any of these may under certain conditions be a source of evil: the desire to excel and to win can corrupt, a man may be so engrossed by his painting that he neglects his family, what was initially an honorable resort to war can issue in savage cruelty. But what follows from this?

It certainly is not the case that my account entails *either* that we ought to excuse or condone such evils *or* that whatever flows from a virtue is right. I do have to allow that courage sometimes sustains injustice, that loyalty has been known to strengthen a murderous aggressor and that generosity has sometimes weakened the capacity to do good. But to deny this would be to fly in the face of just those empirical facts which I invoked in criticizing Aquinas' account of the unity of the virtues. That the virtues need initially to be defined and explained with reference to the notion of a practice thus in no way entails approval of all practices in all circumstances. That the virtues – as the objection itself presupposed – *are* defined not in terms of good and right practices, but of practices, does not entail or imply that practices as actually carried through at particular times and places do not stand in need of moral criticism. And the resources for such criticism are not lacking. There is in the first place no inconsistency in appealing to the requirements of a virtue to criticize a practice. Justice may be initially defined as a disposition which in its particular way is necessary to sustain practices; it does not follow that in pursuing the requirements of a practice violations of justice are not to be condemned. Moreover I already pointed out in chapter 12 [of *After Virtue*] that a morality of virtues requires as its counterpart a conception of moral law. Its requirements too have to be met by practices. But, it may be asked, does not all this imply that more needs to be said about the place of practices in some larger moral context? Does not this at least suggest that there is more to the core concept of a virtue than can be spelled out in terms of practices? I have after all emphasized that the scope of any virtue in human life extends beyond the practices in terms of which it is initially defined. What then is the place of the virtues in the larger arenas of human life?

I stressed earlier that any account of the virtues in terms of practices could only be a partial and first account. What is required to complement it? The most notable difference so far between my account and any account that could be called Aristotelian is that although I have in no way restricted the exercise of the virtues to the context of practices, it is in terms of practices that I have located their point and function. Whereas Aristotle locates that point and function in terms of the notion of a type of whole human life which can be called good. And it does seem that the question "What would a human being lack who lacked the virtues?" must be given a kind of answer which goes beyond anything which I have said so far. For such an individual would not merely fail *in a variety of particular ways* in respect of the kind of excellence which can be achieved through participation in practices and in respect of the kind of human relationship required to sustain such excellence. His own life *viewed as a whole* would perhaps be defective; it would not be the kind of life which someone would describe in trying to answer the question, "What is the best kind of life for this kind of man or woman to live?" And that question cannot be answered without at least raising Aristotle's own question, "What is the good life for man?" Consider three ways in which human life informed only by the conception of the virtues sketched so far would be defective.

It would be pervaded, first of all, by *too many* conflicts and *too much* arbitrariness. I argued earlier that it is a merit of an account of the virtues in terms of a multiplicity of goods that it allows for the possibility of tragic conflict in a way in which Aristotle's does not. But it may also produce even in the life of someone who is virtuous and disciplined too many occasions when one allegiance points in one direction, another in another. The claims of one practice may be incompatible with another in such a way that one may find oneself oscillating in an arbitrary way,

rather than making rational choices. So it seems to have been with T. E. Lawrence. Commitment to sustaining the kind of community in which the virtues can flourish may be incompatible with the devotion which a particular practice – of the arts, for example – requires. So there may be tensions between the claims of family life and those of the arts – the problem that Gauguin solved or failed to solve by fleeing to Polynesia, or between the claims of politics and those of the arts – the problem that Lenin solved or failed to solve by refusing to listen to Beethoven.

If the life of the virtues is continuously fractured by choices in which one allegiance entails the apparently arbitrary renunciation of another, it may seem that the goods internal to practices do after all derive their authority from our individual choices; for when different goods summon in different and in incompatible directions, "I" have to choose between their rival claims. The modern self with its criterionless choices apparently reappears in the alien context of what was claimed to be an Aristotelian world. This accusation might be rebutted in part by returning to the question of why both goods and virtues do have authority in our lives and repeating what was said earlier in this chapter. But this reply would only be partly successful: the distinctively modern notion of choice would indeed have reappeared, even if with a more limited scope for its exercise than it has usually claimed.

Secondly, without an overriding conception of the *telos* of a whole human life, conceived as a unity, our conception of certain individual virtues has to remain partial and incomplete. Consider two examples. Justice, on an Aristotelian view, is defined in terms of giving each person his or her due or desert. To deserve well is to have contributed in some substantial way to the achievement of those goods, the sharing of which and the common pursuit of which provide foundations for human community. But the goods internal to practices, including the goods internal to the practice of making and sustaining forms of community, need to be ordered and evaluated in some way if we are to assess relative desert. Thus any substantive application of an Aristotelian concept of justice requires an understanding of goods and of the good that goes beyond the multiplicity of goods which inform practices. As with justice, so also with patience. Patience is the virtue of waiting attentively without complaint, but not of waiting thus for anything at all. To treat patience as a virtue presupposes some adequate answer to the question: waiting for what? Within the context of practices a partial, although for many purposes adequate, answer can be given: the patience of a craftsman with refractory material, of a teacher with a slow pupil, of a politician in negotiations, are all species of patience. But what if the material is just too refractory, the pupil too slow, the negotiations too frustrating? Ought we always at a certain point just to give up in the interests of the practice itself? The medieval exponents of the virtue of patience claimed that there are certain types of situation in which the virtue of patience requires that I do not ever give up on some person or task, situations in which, as they would have put it, I am required to embody in my attitude to that person or task something of the patient attitude of God towards his creation. But this could only be so if patience served some overriding good, some *telos* which warranted putting other goods in a subordinate place. Thus it turns out that the content of the virtue of patience depends upon how we order various goods in a hierarchy and *a fortiori* on whether we are able rationally so to order these particular goods.

I have suggested so far that unless there is a *telos* which transcends the limited goods of practices by constituting the good of a whole human life, the good of a human life conceived as a unity, it will *both* be the case that a certain subversive arbitrariness will invade the moral life *and* that we shall be unable to specify the context of certain virtues adequately. These two considerations are reinforced by a third: that there is at least one virtue recognized by the tradition which cannot be specified at all except with reference to the wholeness of a human life – the virtue of integrity or constancy. "Purity of heart," said Kierkegaard, "is to will one thing." This notion of singleness of purpose in a whole life can have no application unless that of a whole life does. . . .

28   A Critique of Virtue-Based Ethical Systems

William Frankena

Morality and Cultivation of Traits

Our present interest, then, is not in moral principles nor in non-moral values, but in moral values, in what is morally good or bad. Throughout its history morality has been concerned about the cultivation of certain dispositions, or traits, among which are "character" and such "virtues" (an old-fashioned but still useful term) as hon-

From *Ethics*, 2nd edn (Englewood Cliffs, NJ: Prentice-Hall, 1973), pp. 63–71. Reprinted by permission.

esty, kindness, and conscientiousness. Virtues are dispositions or traits that are not wholly innate; they must all be acquired, at least in part, by teaching and practice, or, perhaps, by grace. They are also traits of "character", rather than traits of "personality" like charm or shyness, and they all involve a tendency to do certain kinds of action in certain kinds of situations, not just to think or feel in certain ways. They are not just abilities or skills, like intelligence or carpentry, which one may have without using.

In fact, it has been suggested that morality is or should be conceived as primarily concerned, not with rules or principles . . . but with the cultivation of such dispositions or traits of character. Plato and Aristotle seem to conceive of morality in this way, for they talk mainly in terms of virtues and the virtuous, rather than in terms of what is right or obligatory. Hume uses similar terms, although he mixes in some non-moral traits like cheerfulness and wit along with moral ones like benevolence and justice. More recently, Leslie Stephen stated the view in these words:

> . . . morality is internal. The moral law . . . has to be expressed in the form, "be this," not in the form, "do this" . . . the true moral law says "hate not," instead of "kill not". . . . the only mode of stating the moral law must be as a rule of character.[1]

Ethics of Virtue

Those who hold this view are advocating an *ethics of virtue* or being, in opposition to an ethics of duty, principle, or doing, and we should note here that, although the ethical theories criticized or defended . . . were all stated as kinds of ethics of duty, they could also be recast as kinds of ethics of virtue. The notion of an ethics of virtue is worth looking at here, not only because it has a long history but also because some spokesmen of the "the new morality" seem to espouse it. What would an ethics of virtue be like? It would, of course, not take deontic judgments or principles as basic in morality, as we have been doing; instead, it would take as basic aretaic judgments like "That was a courageous deed," "His action was virtuous," or "Courage is a virtue," and it would insist that deontic judgments are either derivative from such aretaic ones or can be dispensed with entirely. Moreover, it would regard aretaic judgments about actions as secondary and as based on aretaic judgments about agents and their motives or traits, as Hume does when he writes:

> . . . when we praise any actions, we regard only the motives that produced them. . . . The external performance has no merit. . . . all virtuous actions derive their merit only from virtuous motives.[2]

For an ethics of virtue, then, what is basic in morality is judgments like "Benevolence is a good motive," "Courage is a virtue," "The morally good man is kind to everyone" or, more simply and less accurately, "Be loving!" – not judgments or principles about what our duty is or what we ought to do. But of course, it thinks that its basic instructions will guide us, not only about what to be, but also about what to do. . . .

On Being and Doing: Morality of Traits vs. Morality of Principles

We may now return to the issue posed by the quotation from Stephen, though we cannot debate it as fully as we should. To be or to do, that is the question. Should we construe morality as primarily a following of certain principles or as primarily a cultivation of certain dispositions and traits? Must we choose? It is hard to see how a morality of principles can get off the ground except through the development of dispositions to act in accordance with its principles, else all motivation to act on them must be of an *ad hoc* kind, either prudential or impulsively altruistic. Moreover, morality can hardly be content with a mere conformity to rules, however willing and self-conscious it may be, unless it has no interest in the spirit of its law but only in the letter. On the other hand, one cannot conceive of traits of character except as including dispositions and tendencies to act in certain ways in certain circumstances. Hating involves being disposed to kill or harm, being just involves tending to do just acts (acts that conform to the principle of justice) when the occasion calls. Again, it is hard to see how we could know what traits to encourage or inculcate if we did not subscribe to principles, for example, to the principle of utility, or to those of benevolence and justice.

I propose therefore that we regard the morality of duty and principles and the morality of virtues or traits of character not as rival kinds of morality between which we must choose, but as two complementary aspects of the same morality. Then, for every principle there will be a morally good trait, often going by the same name, consisting of a disposition or tendency to act according to it; and for every morally good trait there will be a principle defining the kind of action in which it is to express itself. To parody a famous dictum of Kant's, I am inclined to think that principles without traits are impotent and traits without principles are blind.

Even if we adopt this double-aspect conception of morality, in which principles are basic, we may still agree that morality does and must put a premium on *being* honest, conscientious, and so forth. If its sanctions or sources of motivation are not to be entirely external (for example, the prospect of being praised, blamed, rewarded, or punished by others) or adventitious (for example, a purely instinctive love of others), if it is to have adequate "internal sanctions," as Mill called them, then morality must foster the development of such dispositions and habits as have been mentioned. It could hardly be satisfied with a mere conformity to its principles even if it could provide us with fixed principles of actual duty. For such a conformity might be motivated entirely by extrinsic or non-moral considerations, and would then be at the mercy of these other considerations. It could not be counted on in a moment of trial. Besides, since morality cannot provide us with fixed principles of actual duty but only with principles of prima facie duty, it cannot be content with the letter of its law, but must foster in us the dispositions that will sustain us in the hour of decision when we are choosing between conflicting principles of prima facie duty or trying to revise our working rules of right and wrong.

There is another reason why we must cultivate certain traits of character in ourselves and others, or why we must be certain sorts of persons. Although morality is concerned that we act in certain ways, it cannot take the hard line of insisting that we act in precisely those ways, even if those ways could be more clearly defined. We cannot praise and blame or apply other sanctions to an agent simply on the ground that he has or has not acted on conformity with certain principles. It would not be right. Through no fault of his own, the agent may not have known all the relevant facts. What action the principles of morality called for in the situation may not have been clear to him, again through no fault of his own, and he may have been honestly mistaken about his duty. Or his doing what he ought to have done might have carried with it an intolerable sacrifice on his part. He may even have been simply incapable of doing it. Morality must therefore recognize various sorts of excuses and extenuating circumstances. All it can really insist on, then, except in certain critical cases, is that we develop and manifest fixed dispositions to find out what the right thing is and to do it if possible. In this sense a person must "be this" rather than "do this." But it must be remembered that "being" involves at least *trying* to "do." Being without doing, like faith without works, is dead.

At least it will be clear from this discussion that an ethics of duty or principles also has an important place for the virtues and must put a premium on their cultivation as a part of moral education and development. The place it has for virtue and/or the virtues is, however, different from that accorded them by an ethics of virtue. Talking in terms of the theory defended . . . , which was an ethics of duty, we may say that, if we ask for *guidance* about what to do or not do, then the answer is contained, at least primarily, in two deontic principles and their corollaries, namely, the principles of beneficence and equal treatment. Given these two deontic principles, plus the necessary clarity of thought and factual knowledge, we can know what we morally ought to do or not do, except perhaps in cases of conflict between them. We also know that we should cultivate two virtues, a disposition to be beneficial (i.e. benevolence) and a disposition to treat people equally (justice as a trait). But the point of acquiring these virtues is not further guidance or instruction; the function of the virtues in an ethics of duty is not to tell us what to do but to ensure that we will do it willingly in whatever situations we may face. In an ethics of virtue, on the other hand, the virtues play a dual role – they must not only move us to do what we do, they must also tell us what to do. To parody Alfred Lord Tennyson:

> Theirs not (only) to do or die,
> Theirs (also) to reason why.

Moral Ideals

This is the place to mention ideals, which are among what we called the ingredients of morality. One may, perhaps, identify moral ideals with moral principles, but, more properly speaking, moral ideals are ways of being rather than of doing. Having a moral ideal is wanting to be a person of a certain sort, wanting to have a certain trait of character rather than others, for example, moral courage or perfect integrity. That is why the use of exemplary persons like Socrates, Jesus, or Martin Luther King has been such an important part of moral education and self-development, and it is one of the reasons for the writing and reading of biographies or of novels and epics in which types of moral personality are portrayed, even if they are not all heroes or saints. Often such moral ideals of personality go beyond what can be demanded or regarded as obligatory, belonging among the things to be praised rather than required, except as one may require them of oneself. It should be remembered, however, that not all personal ideals are moral ones. Achilles, Hercules, Napoleon, and Prince Charming may all be taken as ideals, but the ideals they represent are not moral ones, even though they may not be immoral ones either. Some ideals, e.g. those of chivalry, may be partly moral and partly non-moral. There is every reason why one should pursue non-moral as well as moral ideals, but there is no good reason for confusing them.

When one has a moral ideal, wanting to be a certain sort of moral person, one has at least some motivation to live in a certain way, but one also has something to guide him in living. Here the idea of an ethics of virtue may have a point. One may, of course, take as one's ideal that of being a good man who always does his duty from a sense of duty, perhaps gladly, and perhaps even going a second mile on occasion. Then one's guidance clearly comes entirely from one's rules and principles of duty. However, one may also have an ideal that goes beyond anything that can be regarded by others or even oneself as strict duty or obligation, a form or style of personal being that may be morally good or virtuous, but it is not morally required of one. An ethics of virtue seems to provide for such an aspiration more naturally than an ethics of duty or principle, and perhaps an adequate morality should at least contain a region in which we can follow such an idea, over and beyond the region in which we are to listen to the call of duty. There certainly should be moral heroes and saints who go beyond the merely good man, if only to serve as an inspiration to others to be better and do more than they would otherwise be or do. Granted all this, however, it still seems to me that, if one's ideal is truly a moral one, there will be nothing in it that is not covered by the principles of beneficence and justice conceived as principles of what we ought to do in the wider sense referred to earlier.

Dispositions to Be Cultivated

Are there any other moral virtues to be cultivated besides benevolence and justice? No cardinal ones, of course. In this sense our answer to Socrates' question whether virtue is one or many is that it is two. We saw, however, that the principles of beneficence and equality have corollaries like telling the truth, keeping promises, etc. It follows that character traits like honesty and fidelity are virtues, though subordinate ones, and should be acquired and fostered. There will then be other virtues corresponding to other corollaries of our main principles. Let us call all of these virtues, cardinal and non-cardinal, first-order moral virtues. Besides first-order virtues like these, there are certain other moral virtues that ought also to be cultivated, which are in a way more abstract and general and may be called second-order virtues. Conscientiousness is one such virtue; it is not limited to a certain sector of the moral life, as gratitude and honesty are, but is a virtue covering the whole of the moral life. Moral courage, or courage when moral issues are at stake, is another such second-order virtue; it belongs to all sectors of the moral life. Others that overlap with these are integrity and good-will, understanding good-will in Kant's sense of respect for the moral law.

In view of what was said . . . , we must list two other second-order traits: a disposition to find out and respect the relevant facts and a disposition to think clearly. These are not just abilities but character traits; one might have the ability to think intelligently without having a disposition to use it. They are therefore virtues, though they are intellectual virtues, not moral ones. Still, though their role is not limited to the moral life, they are necessary to it. More generally speaking, we should cultivate the virtue Plato called wisdom and Aristotle practical wisdom, which they thought of as including all of the intellectual abilities and virtues essential to the moral life.

Still other second-order qualities, which may be abilities rather than virtues, but which must be cultivated for moral living, and so may, perhaps, best be mentioned here, are moral autonomy, the ability to make moral decisions and to revise one's principles if necessary, and the ability to realize vividly, in imagination and feeling, the "inner lives" of others. Of these second-order qualities, the first two have been referred to on occasion and will be again, but something should be said about the last.

If our morality is to be more than a conformity to internalized rules and principles, if it is to include and rest on an understanding of the point of these rules and principles, and certainly if it is to involve *being* a certain kind of person and not merely *doing* certain kinds of things, then we must somehow attain and develop an ability to be aware of others as persons, as important to themselves as we are to ourselves, and to have a lively and sympathetic representation in imagination of their interests and of the effects of our actions on their lives. The need for this is particularly stressed by Josiah Royce and William James. Both men point out how we usually go our own busy and self-concerned ways, with only an external awareness of the presence of others, much as if they were things, and without any realization of their inner and peculiar worlds of personal experience; and both emphasize the need and possibility of a "higher vision of an inner significance" which pierces this "certain blindness in human beings" and enables us to realize the existence of others in a wholly different way, as we do our own.

> What then is thy neighbor? He too is a mass of states, of experiences, thoughts and desire, just as concrete, as thou art. . . . Dost thou believe this? Art thou sure what it means? This is for thee the turning-point of thy whole conduct toward him.

These are Royce's quaint old-fashioned words. Here are James's more modern ones.

> This higher vision of an inner significance in what, until then, we had realized only in the dead external way, often comes over a person suddenly; and, when it does so, it makes an epoch in his history.

Royce calls this more perfect recognition of our neighbors "the moral insight" and James says that its practical consequence is "the well-known democratic respect for the sacredness of individuality." It is hard to see how either a benevolent (loving) or a just (equalitarian) disposition could come to fruition without it. To quote James again,

> We ought, all of us, to realize each other in this intense, pathetic, and important way.

Doing this is part of what is involved in fully taking the moral point of view.

Two Questions

We can now deal with the question, sometimes raised, whether an action is to be judged right or wrong because of its results, because of the principle it exemplifies, or because the motive, intention, or trait of character involved is morally good or bad. The answer, implied in what was said [earlier], is that an action is to be judged *right* or *wrong* by reference to a principle or set of principles. Even if we say it is right or wrong because of its effects, this means that it is right or wrong by the principle of utility or some other teleological principle. But an act may also be said to be *good* or *bad*, praiseworthy or blameworthy, noble or despicable, and so on, and then the moral quality ascribed to it will depend on the agent's motive, intention, or disposition in doing it.

Another important question here is: What is moral goodness? When is a person morally good and when are his actions, dispositions, motives or intentions morally good? Not just when he does what is actually right, for he may do what is right from bad motives, in which case he is not morally good, or he may fail to do what is right though sincerely trying to do it, in which case he is not morally bad. Whether he and his actions are morally good or not depends, not on the rightness of what he does or on its consequences, but on his character or motives; so far the statement quoted from Hume is certainly correct. But when are his motives and dispositions morally good? Some answer that a person and his actions are morally good if and only if they are motivated wholly by a sense of duty or a desire to do what is right; the Stoics and Kant sometimes seem to take this extreme view. Others hold that a man and his actions are morally good if and only if they are motivated primarily by a sense of duty or desire to do what is right, though other motives may be present too; still others contend, with Aristotle, that they are at any rate not morally good unless they are motivated at least in part by such a sense or desire. A more responsible view, to my mind, is that a man and his actions are morally good if it is at least true that, whatever his actual motives in acting are, his sense of duty or desire to do the right is so strong in him that it would keep him trying to do his duty anyway.

Actually, I find it hard to believe that no dispositions or motivations are good or virtuous from the moral point of view except those that include a will to do the right as such. It is more plausible to distinguish two kinds of morally good dispositions or traits of character, first, those that are usually called moral virtues and do include a will to do the right, and second, others like purely natural kindliness or gratefulness, which, while they are non-moral, are still morality-supporting, since they dispose us to do such actions as morality requires and even to perform deeds, for example, in the case of motherly love, which are well beyond the call of duty.

It has even been alleged that conscientiousness or moral goodness in the sense of a disposition to act from a sense of duty alone is not a good thing or not a virtue – that it is more desirable to have people acting from motives like friendship, gratitude, honor, love, and the like, than from a dry or driven sense of obligation. There is something to be said for this view, though it ignores the nobility of great moral courage and of the higher reaches of moral idealism. But even if conscientiousness or good will is not the only thing that is unconditionally good, as Kant believed, or the greatest of intrinsically good things, as Ross thought, it is surely a good thing from the moral point of view. For an ethics of duty at any rate, it must be desirable that people do what is right for its own sake, especially if they do it gladly, as a gymnast may gladly make the right move just because it is right.

Notes

1 Leslie Stephen, *The Science of Ethics* (New York: G. P. Putnam's Sons, 1882), pp. 155, 158.
2 David Hume, *Treatise of Human Nature* (1739), Book III, Part II, opening of Sec. I.

29   Are Virtues No More than Dispositions to Obey Moral Rules?

Walter Schaller

Recent interest in the virtues has prompted re-consideration of certain questions concerning their place and function within ethical theory. On the one side of the debate are philosophers (Alasdair MacIntyre prominent among them) who argue that the virtues properly occupy center stage in morality and that the "function and authority of rules" can only be understood by reference to the virtues. On the other side are proponents of the prevailing wisdom: the moral rules are "the primary concept of the moral life" and the virtues are derived from them, for morality is concerned, first and foremost, with right and wrong conduct, with how persons ought to act.[1]

In addition to the general question of the relative importance of duties and virtue within ethical theory, there are more specific ones about the relationship between duties and virtues: Do aretaic judgments (about the goodness or virtuousness of persons) presuppose prior deontic judgments (about the rightness of actions)? Is it possible, in other words, to judge that an action is selfish, or unkind, or disrespectful, but not wrong; or does the fact that an action manifests a vice imply that it also violates some moral rule?

I shall argue that the prevailing or Standard View of the connection between virtues and duties is false; it purports to represent the nature of all moral virtues *vis-à-vis* the moral rules, but there are some virtues which are recalcitrant: they do not conform to its analysis. After summarizing the central tenets of the Standard View, I shall argue that the virtues of benevolence, gratitude, and self-respect cannot be conceived as the Standard View requires; they do not stand in the prescribed relation to the moral rules, nor is their

From *Philosophy*, 20 (July 1990), pp. 1–2. Reprinted with permission.

moral significance or value limited in the way the Standard View supposes.

The Standard View

What I have been calling the Standard View consists of the following three theses:

1. Moral rules require persons to perform or omit certain actions (act-types), and these actions can be performed by persons who lack no less than by those who possess the various virtues. On this analysis, the rule against lying, for example, can be obeyed perfectly well even by persons who lack the virtue of honesty or veracity. One's motives in obeying the rule are irrelevant to whether one has fulfilled its requirements;

2. The moral virtues are, fundamentally and essentially, dispositions to obey the moral rules, i.e. to perform or omit certain actions.[2] Thus the heart of the virtue of honesty is a disposition to obey the moral rule which forbids telling lies, and at the core of the virtue of honesty is a disposition to obey the moral rule which forbids telling lies, and at the core of the virtue of benevolence is a disposition to perform those actions that fulfill the duty of beneficence; and

3. The moral virtues have only instrumental or derivative value: individuals who possess the virtues are more likely to do what is right – i.e. to obey the moral rules – than are people who lack such dispositions. Certain dispositions or character traits are *virtues*, therefore, just because they motivate right conduct, and others are *vices*, because they motivate wrong actions.

Contemporary statements and defenses of the Standard View abound.[3] In *The Moral Rules* Bernard Gert defends the first two theses: moral rules are, he says, "primarily concerned with actions" and a moral virtue is "any character trait that involves unjustifiably obeying the moral rules or following moral ideals." Thus, "the degree to which one has a particular moral virtue or vice is determined by the extent to which one unjustifiably breaks the corresponding moral rule."[4]

In his response to MacIntyre's own controversial critique of the Standard View in *After Virtue*, Alan Gewirth explicitly argues for all three theses, contending that

1. The moral rules concern only actions and not dispositions;
2. "To have a moral virtue is to be disposed to act as moral rules direct," on the ground that "moral virtues derive their contents from the requirements set by moral rules"; and
3. "These virtues are good to have precisely because persons who have them are more likely to do what the Principle of Generic Consistency requires," i.e. to act in accordance with the fundamental principle of morality.[5]

And finally, even though the nature of the virtues is far from the central concerns of *A Theory of Justice*, John Rawls too accepts the Standard View: "The virtues are . . . related families of dispositions and propensities regulated by a higher-order desire . . . to act from the corresponding moral principle." They are "habitual attitudes leading us to act on certain principles of right."[6]

How accurate is the Standard View? Does it withstand scrutiny when applied to three particular virtues?

The Duty of Beneficence

What I shall argue in this section is that the duty of beneficence cannot be satisfactorily formulated in accordance with the first thesis of the Standard View – that the moral rules command only

certain act-types – and, consequently, the virtue of benevolence is inaccurately characterized by the second and third theses.

The claim that beneficence is a duty – and not merely supererogatory – should elicit little dissent: we *ought* to help people in need. But when we try to formulate this duty as a "moral rule for conduct" (to borrow Alan Gewirth's phrase), well-known difficulties surface. Some formulations – "Help everyone who needs help" – are clearly too strong, too demanding. Others are more plausible but otherwise flawed. The rule "Help other people as much as possible" raises the question: how much is "possible"? It is possible to give all of one's money to the poor and homeless, but doing so would surely go beyond the requirements of this duty.

Other formulations of the duty in terms of obligatory actions are inadequate because they allow persons too much latitude or discretion. The rule "One ought to help other people sometimes, to some extent"[7] is flawed for just this reason: it fails to capture the fact that on some occasions the refusal to help another person is wrong (e.g. when a drowning child can be rescued with no danger to the rescuer). And even if it is true that people who fulfill the duty of beneficence have acted beneficently "sometimes, to some extent," that way of stating the duty is inadequate as a general moral rule as a normative guide to conduct (for an individual who helps one other person once a year has acted in conformity with that rule but it is most unlikely to have satisfied the duty).

Notice, furthermore, that if the duty of beneficence cannot be stated successfully as a rule for action,[8] then the *virtue* of benevolence cannot be defined in accordance with the second thesis of the Standard View, namely, as a disposition to obey such a rule.

Given the problems that confront the attempt to conceive of the duty of beneficence in accordance with the Standard View, let us consider a different approach. Instead of defining the virtue in terms of the duty and trying to formulate the duty as an action-guiding rule sufficiently fine-grained to tell us when, how much, how often, and toward whom we ought to act beneficently, suppose the duty is conceived as requiring persons to cultivate – to seek to acquire – the virtue of benevolence, to become benevolent persons, in other words.[9]

Understanding the duty of beneficence in this way does not solve all the problems that have plagued attempts to define it along the lines of the Standard View. In particular, there is still no rule or decision-procedure for determining when, or how much, or whom one must help. But that is simply because, as Kant and Mill (among others) have pointed out, beneficence is an imperfect duty, which allows persons a certain latitude (though not in every case) in deciding how to *act* in fulfilling it. The very nature of the duty precludes a precise general statement of how persons are required to act. Nevertheless, formulating the duty in terms of the virtue does solve some of the problems – both theoretical and practical – that have undermined alternative, more traditional formulations.

First, the objections to requiring persons to *act* beneficently "as much as possible" do not extend to the obligation to develop the virtue of benevolence as much as possible. What the latter duty requires is that people become ever more willing to help those who are in need, to become less and less indifferent to human suffering. (Whether one actually does – and ought to – act beneficently in a particular case will depend upon the total circumstances, e.g. whether there are overriding reasons for not helping, whether one is capable of providing the requisite assistance, etc.).

Second, consider the case of the infant drowning in a shallow pool who could be easily rescued. Someone who had a policy of acting beneficently "sometimes, to some extent" could callously walk past this child without violating that policy; but letting that child drown is clearly inconsistent with possessing the virtue of benevolence. Not trying to save that infant would thus be prima facie evidence (of a very compelling sort) that one lacks the virtue of benevolence. In short, since there should be no doubt that one has a duty to rescue a child in such straits, formulating the general duty of beneficence in terms of the virtue yields a conclusion more in conformity with our intuitions about what ought to be done than do formulations of the duty in terms of obligatory actions.

Third, if the duty of beneficence is explicated in terms of actions some of which are optional, then an individual's refusal to perform a particular helping act which (unlike saving the drowning baby) is not obligatory provides no reason by itself for concluding that that person is not fulfilling the duty satisfactorily. If Alex, for example, obstinately refused to perform a simple helping action which would cost him little in terms of time, money, or effort, yet which he is not duty-bound to perform, his selfish refusal may indicate a shortcoming[10] in his character (in the sense that he has not acted as the perfectly virtuous person would act), but, according to the Standard View, he has not acted wrongly. A negative aretaic judgment might be in order, but not a negative deontic judgment.

But if Alex has a duty to cultivate a benevolent disposition, then his selfish refusal to perform this particular action is at least prima facie evidence of a failure to fulfill that duty (for selfishness is incompatible with benevolence). On this interpretation of the duty of beneficence, there is not a sharp division between virtue and duty: the aretaic judgments that are properly made about a person bear on the question whether he has fulfilled his duties.

Furthermore, on the present interpretation of this duty, a later generous action does not excuse or "make up for" an earlier selfish one. A person can at best only partially overcome the prima facie implication of selfishness arising from a selfish action by subsequently carrying out a benevolent one. Thus, Alex's refusal to help Jack at t_1 does not cease to be a selfish action – and a sign of his lack of benevolence – just because he helps Jill at t_2. To be sure, the fact that Alex does help Jill after having failed to lend a hand to Jack indicates that he is less selfish than if he ignored Jill's needs too. But even if the good of the latter action outweighs the harm resulting from the former, this does not justify or excuse the earlier action. (Compare this to the way that a baseball player can compensate for a costly fielding error or strikeout by hitting a game-winning home run later; the latter action erases the negative effects of the former.)

Fourth, for the person who has cultivated the virtue of benevolence, the question whether she *ought* to help a needy individual on a given occasion will often be subordinated to, or even displaced by, the question whether this is a person whom she is *able* to help. Non-benevolent persons will tend to ask whether they "have to" perform a given beneficent action and may often seek reasons or excuses not to. But the more one possesses the virtue of benevolence, the less will the fact that a particular action is not, strictly speaking, obligatory count as a reason not to perform it. The benevolent person will *want* to help people in need and will look for ways to overcome whatever obstacles might stand in the way of providing the needed aid or assistance.

Formulating the duty of beneficence in terms of the character trait of benevolence thus has the virtue of providing a middle path between the two extremes rejected above (that one ought to help other people "sometimes, to some extent," and that individuals must help others as much as possible).

The argument to this point has been that the duty of beneficence cannot be adequately formulated consistent with the first two theses of the Standard View. Next I want to show that the third thesis must also be rejected (or at least revised). It holds that the virtues have only instrumental value: people who possess them are more likely to obey the moral rules for the simple reason that the virtues just are dispositions to obey those rules. Moreover (and this is the point I want to stress), a person who lacks a particular virtue is not thereby disabled from fulfilling completely and satisfactorily the correlative duty. Good character is not required for right conduct.

In treating the virtues as having only instrumental value, the Standard View overlooks the fact that on some occasions a person who lacks the virtues of benevolence or sympathy is thereby unable to provide the kind of assistance that another person needs.[11] For what is required in such circumstances is not some external good or service – which could be supplied by persons acting from duty, or even from self-interest – but sympathy itself (or love, compassion, or some other altruistic emotion). In these cases the needy individual will not be benefited except by the action of someone who *is* sympathetic and who *feels* compassion, i.e. someone who possess these virtues. Possessing the virtue is thus not good or necessary simply as a motive for an independently specified act of beneficence; on the contrary, the beneficent action itself is not possible except for one who is motivated by benevolence, sympathy, or some other altruistic emotion.[12]

The Virtue of Gratitude[13]

The Standard View also fails to describe accurately either the virtue or the duty of gratitude. On that view it should be possible (1) to formulate a "rule for conduct" obedience to which will fully satisfy the duty, and (2) for persons who lack the virtue to satisfy the duty (by obeying the rule from say, the motive of duty).

Let us consider the second claim first. Recall that with respect to beneficence, it is possible for a non-benevolent (even a selfish) person to perform beneficent actions. There is nothing problematic about acting beneficently from the motive of duty. But gratitude is different, for what constitutes an act of gratitude is the motive from which it is done (along with the beliefs and attitudes of the agent). In order to perform an act of gratitude, one must *be* grateful (at least on that occasion, though not necessarily in the sense of having the virtue as an enduring character trait). Duty cannot serve as a substitute or back-up motive without altering the nature of the action being performed.

Now it is of course possible to perform what *appear* to be acts of gratitude even if one lacks the virtue, even if one is not grateful for the favor or benefit one has received. Moreover, we should agree that if someone has done you a favor, or voluntarily benefited you in some way, then you generally ought to act *as if* you are grateful even if you are not. The only thing worse than an insincere show of gratitude is no show of gratitude (even if the former is pure show and the latter is genuine). There is something to be said for keeping up appearances in morality no less than in etiquette.

So let us grant that it is possible to formulate a "rule for action" concerning gratitude to the effect that whenever one is the beneficiary of another's benevolence, one has a duty to express gratitude, to act as if one is grateful, even at the cost of insincerity. This is a rule which persons who are ungrateful (who lack the virtue) can fulfill as well as those who are grateful – just as the Standard View's first thesis requires.

But the fact that such a rule for behavior can be formulated does not imply that the duty of gratitude is fulfilled simply by obeying it. On the contrary, in acting "gratefully" from some other motive, one does not so much fulfill that duty as avoid the greater wrong of acting as if one is ungrateful, of appearing to have the vice of ingratitude.

In short, the duty of gratitude cannot be stated satisfactorily as a moral rule for action; on the contrary, in order to fulfill it, one must possess the virtue of gratitude. And from this requirement it follows that the second thesis of the Standard View is also false as regards gratitude: This virtue is not simply a disposition to obey a moral rule for action. It consists rather in having certain beliefs, feelings, and attitudes toward, and about, one's benefactors (and, of course, in acting in the appropriate ways).

Finally, gratitude's value as a virtue is not merely instrumental. For although it will typically serve as a motive for acts of gratitude,[14] its value does not lie solely in its utility as a motive. In so far as the duty of gratitude can be understood in Kantian terms as following from the more general duty to regard or value – to respect – persons as ends in themselves, it follows that what this duty requires first and foremost is that persons *appreciate* the favor that has been done them and that they do not regard their benefactor as existing solely to provide such favors (i.e. merely as an instrument for promoting their happiness). The value of acts of gratitude thus lies less in the benefits they confer upon the original benefactor than in the fact that they are evidence of certain beliefs and attitudes (e.g. of respect) on the part of the agent. The value of

grateful acts is derived from the value of the virtue of gratitude, and not conversely (as the Standard View suggests).

The Virtue of Self-respect

The Kantian idea that self-respect is a moral virtue, even a duty, does not command widespread acceptance these days. Yet, despite the various objections that can be – and have been – raised against it (that there are no duties to oneself, for example), it is not such an unreasonable idea. For just as other people ought to be respected because of their autonomy and rationality, so individuals ought to respect themselves for the same reasons. Following Kant's analysis of the Principle of Humanity, it is clear that persons are capable of acting in ways which are inconsistent with their own capacity for autonomy: they can fail to value and treat themselves as ends just as they can fail to treat others as ends.

In the interests of brevity I shall not attempt a full defense of the Kantian doctrine of respect and self-respect. Instead, drawing upon Thomas E. Hill, Jr.'s well-known account of servility and self-respect,[15] I shall argue that *if* self-respect is a virtue (and a duty), it provides a third counterexample to the Standard View.

If the Standard View were true with respect to self-respect, then it should be possible (in accordance with the first thesis) to formulate a moral rule for action which could be obeyed even by persons who lack this virtue, indeed, even by persons who have the opposite trait of servility. But no such rule is possible, for servility and self-respect are fundamentally matters of attitude and belief, not merely of conduct. Whether an action counts as servile, for example, depends less upon *what* the agent does than upon his or her beliefs, attitudes, and reasons for performing the action. The Deferential Wife – to take the best-known of Hill's three examples of servility – is not servile merely because of what she does (namely, defer to her husband's preferences), for deference is not the same as servility, but rather because of her reasons for deferring, because of the beliefs and attitudes she has about her own moral rights, worth, and status. Like the Uncle Tom and the Self-Deprecator (Hill's other two examples of servile character types), the Deferential Wife has a tendency "to deny or disavow" her moral rights; she fails to "understand or acknowledge" her rights and place as an equal within the moral community.

In short, the virtue of self-respect does not conform to the Standard View's first thesis for the same reason the virtue of gratitude did not: in neither case can a sharp distinction be drawn between motive and action. Just as a grateful action is one motivated by the virtue of gratitude, so a self-respecting action (or, more accurately, an action exhibiting self-respect) is one which is done from that virtue. Consequently, no rule for action concerning self-respect can be formulated which could be obeyed by persons who lack self-respect. If there is a *duty* of self-respect, it must be understood not in terms of a rule of action but rather on the model of gratitude, as a duty to seek to cultivate the virtue of self-respect.

Furthermore, in the absence of such a rule for action, the virtue of self-respect cannot be merely a disposition to obey such a rule (as the second thesis requires). Instead, the virtue must consist in having the appropriate beliefs and attitudes about one's moral worth, dignity, and rights (as well as in acting in accordance with them). And from this it follows, just as it did for gratitude, that the virtue of self-respect cannot be of merely instrumental value.

Conclusions

1. Not all virtues are alike. Some conform to the Standard View, but others do not. With respect to the latter group, the Standard View gets the relationship between duties and virtues backwards: in each of these cases, since the kind of action in question cannot (always) be carried out by persons who lack the virtue – by persons acting from the motive of duty, for example – possessing the virtue is of central, not of secondary or derivative, importance. Persons lacking the virtue of sympathy cannot respond helpfully to people who need sympathy, and individuals who lack the virtues of gratitude and self-respect can at best only imitate the actions called for by those duties. For these reasons the duties of beneficence, gratitude, and self-respect are best interpreted, not simply as duties to perform certain actions, but as duties to cultivate a virtue, to develop certain character traits. (This is not to deny that one cannot fulfill these duties without also acting.)

2. Neither the moral rules nor the virtues stand alone at the heart of moral theory. On the one hand, not all virtues can be analyzed as dispositions to fulfill duties which are *prior* to and more *basic* than those virtues; on the other hand, I do not wish to defend a full-fledged ethics of virtue which expels the moral rules and the concept of duty from ethical theory altogether.

3. Without denying that ethics is fundamentally practical, that it is essentially concerned with conduct, I would argue that it is not concerned *just* with (external) conduct. More specifically, the moral importance of the virtues is not exhausted by their relation to conduct (even if that relation is more complex and multidimensional than the Standard View allows). Consider the virtue of gratitude again. Typically, one who is the recipient of another's generosity is under an obligation to *do* something, if at all possible, in return (if only to say "Thank you"). And of course, one should also *be* grateful: the point of the action is to demonstrate the fact of one's gratitude.

But with a little imagination we could sketch a case in which one person (let's call her Pat) does a small but nevertheless not insignificant favor for another person (call her Chris), and the debt of gratitude which Chris incurs by accepting the favor is completely discharged if Chris simply *is* grateful and does not do or say anything to manifest her gratitude. The "moral order" is restored if (1) Chris *acknowledges* (to herself) that Pat's action shows that she values Chris and Chris's happiness, and (2) Chris *appreciates* Pat's favor, or at least appreciates the fact that another person values her enough to do such a favor.

Such a conclusion is possible because the duty of gratitude is essentially a duty to respect other persons. The fact that one is grateful for a favor shows that one does not regard one's benefactor merely as an instrument of one's own happiness. And the duty of respect is not limited to conduct: besides being obligated to *treat* persons with respect, we ought also to *regard* or *value* them as ends and not merely as means. It is for this reason that Chris is able to satisfy the duty of gratitude simply by *being* grateful. The duty of respect, and thus the duty of gratitude, do not always require any further action.

Notes

1   Quoted phrases in this paragraph are from Alasdair MacIntyre, *After Virtue* (Notre Dame: University of Notre Dame Press, 1981), pp. 112, 239.

2   I am grateful to Robert C. Roberts for the observation (addressed to an earlier version of this paper read at the Central Division meetings of the APA) that it is unexceptional to say (as I had) that virtues are (among other things) dispositions to obey moral rules, but that saying they are *nothing but* such dispositions (which is what I clearly intended to imply) is obviously false. The virtue of honesty incorporates a number of dispositions (e.g. dispositions to feel guilt if one lies, or to feel revulsion at the lies told by others), and not simply a disposition to honest behavior.

While Roberts is right to point out the internal complexity of the virtues, the point I was making is unaffected. For what is the value of a disposition to feel guilt except that such guilt is instrumental in preventing further acts of lying, or that it shows that the person who lied still respects the rule he has broken. These other dispositions are part of the virtue only because they support the central and more fundamental disposition to act as the rule requires. Their value, in other words, must be cashed out in terms of the value of the rule for action, as the third thesis states.

3   In addition to the statements of the Standard View cited in notes 4–7, see also John Kilcullen, "Utilitarianism and Virtue," *Ethics*, 93 (1983). The leading exponent is, of course, Kant (at least as he has traditionally been interpreted); I have argued elsewhere (see note 9 below), however, that Kant is best interpreted as a critic of the Standard View.

4   Bernard Gert, *The Moral Rules* (New York: Harper and Row, 1966), pp. 153, 155, 156. For Gert, it should be noted, one does not possess a virtue just because (as a sufficient condition) one obeys the corresponding moral rule. Being honest or benevolent or kind (to name three virtues) also requires acting for the right reasons or having the right motives. But this is still consistent with the first thesis of the Standard View.

5   Alan Gewirth, *Reason and Morality* (Chicago: University of Chicago Press, 1978), p. 339, and "Rights and Virtues," *Review of Metaphysics*, 38 (1985), pp. 739–62.

6   John Rawls, *A Theory of Justice* (Cambridge, MA: Harvard University Press, 1971), pp. 192, 437.

7   For this formulation see Thomas E. Hill, Jr., "Kant on Imperfect Duty and Supererogation," *Kant-Studien* 62 (1971), p. 56.

8   Admittedly, I have not surveyed all attempts to formulate the duty of beneficence in terms of obligatory actions. A more complete argument would need to cover a wider range of alternative formulations.

9   I have argued for this interpretation of Kant's duties of virtue in "Sympathy and Moral Worth in Kant's Ethics," *Southern Journal of Philosophy* (Winter 1987) and in "Kant's Architectonic of Duty," *Philosophy and Phenomenological Research* (December 1987).

10   I adopt the notion of a shortcoming from an insightful article by Gregory W. Trianosky, "Supererogation, Wrongdoing, and Vice: On the Autonomy of the Ethics of Virtue," *Journal of Philosophy*, 83 (1986), pp. 26–40. Trianosky writes that "the deliberate omission of a supererogatory act on a given occasion entails that the agent's motivational structure on that occasion falls short of what the ideal, dully virtuous person would display" and thus reveals a shortcoming (p. 31).

11   This has been argued by a number of critics of Kant's doctrine of moral worth. See, for example, Lawrence Blum, *Friendship, Altruism, and Morality* (London: Routledge and Kegan Paul, 1980), pp. 37–8, 142–3.

A word of caution against a possible misunderstanding. The argument is not merely that sympathy or benevolence is sometimes necessary as a motive for beneficent action (although that is true), for that implies that the action can be conceived independently of the motive. Rather, the argument here is that on occasion a person lacking the virtue is unable to perform the needed action, for what is needed is an action done from a certain motive. To speak of the motive as distinct from the action is in these cases misleading, for the action confers a good only because it is done from that motive. If carried out from, say, the motive of duty, the good to the recipient would be far less.

12 Tolstoy's short story, "The Death of Ivan Ilych," illustrates how people who lack sympathy and compassion are handicapped when confronted with certain kinds of human need. Toward the end of the story, when Ivan is near death, Tolstoy writes:

> He saw that no one felt for him, because no one even wished to grasp his position. Only Gerasim recognized it and pitied him. . . . And so Ivan Ilych felt at ease only with him. . . . Gerasim alone did not lie; everything showed that he alone understood the facts of the case and did not consider it necessary to disguise them, but simply felt sorry for his emaciated and enfeebled master. . . . And in Gerasim's attitude toward him there was something akin to what he wished for, and so that attitude comforted him. (*The Death of Ivan Ilych and Other Stories* (New York: New American Library, 1960), p. 138)

Gerasim cannot save Ivan from death; all he can do is sympathize with (in this translation, pity) him; none the less, Ivan finds this beneficial. It is, one might say, just what the doctor ordered (or should have ordered) but could not himself provide.

This scene illustrates that in addition to his "impersonal" or external needs (which could be provided for equally well by his family, his doctor, or even by a competent stranger), Ivan felt the need for someone else – for another human being – to understand that he was dying and to have sympathy or pity for him. Far from having instrumental value (as a means to, or motive for, providing something else which Ivan wanted), Gerasim's ca-

pacity for sympathy was essential to his ability to comfort Ivan. For what Ivan needed was sympathy itself, not those things which result from actions that happen to be motivated by sympathy.

13 The following account of gratitude draws on Fred Berger, "Gratitude," *Ethics*, 85 (1985), pp. 298–305, and A. D. M. Walter, "Gratefulness and Gratitude," *Proceedings of The Aristotelian Society*, 81 (1980–1), pp. 39–55.

Berger argues that "expressions of gratitude are demonstrations of a complex of belief, feelings, and attitudes"; in particular, that (1) we believe that our benefactor *intended* to benefit us ("gratitude is a response to the benevolence of others"); (2) we recognize the value of the benefactor's act; (3) we do not regard our benefactor "as having the value only of an instrument of [our] welfare," i.e. we respect him or her; and (4) we appreciate the favor, gift, or benefit.

Walker, while taking issue with Berger's account at several points, is in agreement on the fundamental point that "the distinctive feature of the grateful return is its motivation, that the grateful return must be made from a desire to favour one's benefactor because he has favoured oneself and be accompanied by good will" (p. 51).

14 In fact, to speak of the virtue as a motive for action is redundant: an act of gratitude just is an action motivated by gratitude. The motive is not something distinct from the action such that one could perform that kind of action from a different motive.

15 "Servility and Self-Respect," *The Monist*, 57 (1973), pp. 87–104. See also Marcia Baron, "Servility, Critical Deference, and the Deferential Wife," *Philosophical Studies*, 48 (1985), pp. 393–400, and Hill, "Self-Respect Revisited," *Tulane Studies in Philosophy*, vol. 31 (New Orleans: Tulane University, 1982), pp. 129–37.

30 Ancient Ethics and Modern Morality

Julia Annas

It is no news to moral philosophers that it is extremely hard to define morality, at least convincingly. Those of us who do ancient philosophy face a further problem. When we study Plato's *Republic*, Aristotle's *Ethics*, the Stoics and Epicureans, it's not at all obvious that these famous figures in moral philosophy are talking about morality at all. They all take it for granted, for a start, that the main focus of their enquiry is the agent's happiness; and this doesn't sound much like morality. We explain at this point, of course, that they are not talking about happiness as we understand that, but about *eudaimonia*, and that *eudaimonia* is the satisfactory, well-lived life. But a little reflection shows that this doesn't help, or at least that it doesn't help as much as one might have hoped; it still doesn't sound much like morality. And this initial feeling of unease is only reinforced when we find other differences, such as that in ancient ethics the good of others enters in as part of one's own good, justice is a virtue of character rather than being introduced *via* the rights of others, and so on.

We study the ancient theories, then, but sometimes with some doubt as to what they are theories of. We tend in fact to talk of ancient *ethics*, not ancient morality, and we do the same for modern theories containing elements that are prominent in the ancient ones: thus we talk of virtue ethics, not virtue morality. There is a fairly widespread attitude that ancient theories of virtue and the good life are concerned not with what we take to be morality, but with something different, an alternative which can be labelled ethics.[1]

Recently the issue has been sharpened by Bernard Williams.[2] The ancients did indeed, Williams claims, lack our notion of morality – and were better off without it, since it is confused and in many ways objectionable. However, one need not be hostile to morality to think that ancient ethics is an alternative to modern morality, rather than part of the same endeavour. We might have taken a wrong turning, but there again we might have made progress.[3] There are, moreover, a variety of possible viewpoints as to how central to our own outlook morality is. We might find ancient ethics useful to us in our own attempts to produce moral theory; but equally we might find it attractive but irrelevant, perhaps not really available at all in the modern age.

Whatever we do with the contrast, it is widely taken that there *is* such a contrast; ancient ethics is another country, and they do things differently there – and think differently about them. I am not convinced that this contrast, as it is commonly conceived, exists. Of course there are important differences, but they do not compel us to deny that ancient ethics is also ancient morality.

Because of the difficulty of demarcating the notion of morality, we are, I think, guaranteed to make no progress if we try first to define morality and then see how it measures up against what we find in the ancient theories. A more tractable project is to examine prominent features of morality which, it is alleged, we do *not* find when we examine the ancient theories. The result will fall short of a complete account, but it does at least constitute progress in showing whether or not ancient ethics and modern morality can be taken to be, as wholes, so distinct as to be alternatives.

From *Philosophical Perspectives*, 6 (1992), pp. 119–36. Reprinted with permission.

Moral and Non-moral Reasons

The most prominent feature of modern moral theories that we fail to find in the ancient ones is the thought that moral and non-moral reasons are different in kind. Moral reasons have a special, compelling force, for when properly appreciated they have a special status in our deliberations: they override or silence all non-moral considerations. Of course, stated thus blankly the difference between moral and non-moral reasons can seem quite mysterious; it is more plausible if it is taken to be a formal one. Moral reasons will then be taken to acquire their force from the fact that they recommend themselves to our reason by being, for example, universalizable without contradiction.

Ancient Greek lacks words or concepts corresponding at all closely to those of the moral and non-moral. Further, no ethical theory suggests that practical reasons come in two kinds, which, just as a ground-floor fact, have basically different kinds of force. Rather, all the ancient theories claim that the good person is marked by possession of *phronēsis*, practical wisdom or practical intelligence, which is an undivided excellence in reasoning over one's life as a whole. Aristotle in chapter 5 of book VI of the *Nicomachean Ethics* says that it is characteristic of someone with this excellence 'to be good at deliberating about what is good and expedient for himself, not in particular matters . . . but about the kinds of thing that conduce to living well in general'. He instances Pericles and other successful politicians, not the most obvious kind of moral exemplar to the modern mind.

Since ancient theories don't distinguish moral reasons as a special kind of reason, *a fortiori* they don't distinguish them as a special kind of reason by their form. We can even go further: ancient theories show no particular interest in the form of ethical reasoning as such. There is a modern preoccupation with 'the correct form of moral reasoning'; commonly it is assumed that there is such a thing, the only question being, what it is (rule-following, calculating consequences, etc.). But in ancient theories there is no kind of reasoning, employing which ensures ethical correctness.[4]

Given all this, it may be tempting to conclude, with Williams, that '[Greek ethical thought] basically lacks the concept of *morality* altogether, in the sense of a class of reasons or demands which are vitally different from other kinds of reason or demand'.[5] But this would be premature.

If we ask what the point is of distinguishing moral from non-moral reasons, we find something that has a striking likeness. For the point is to show that moral reasons have a special place in our deliberations. Suppose I consider an action in terms of how much it would cost, how long it would take, and so on. Then I find out that it is dishonest. This is not just another consideration to be taken into account and weighed against the others. If I understand what dishonesty is, this reason just stops the deliberating; for this kind of reason does not outweigh, but overrides or silences the other kinds.[6] Of course I may do it anyway; to understand what morality requires is one thing, to do it another. The point is rather that to consider this fact, of dishonesty, as though it were merely another reason like the others, possibly to be outweighed by profit-making, is to misconceive what dishonesty is. Moral reasons are special just because of this role they have in our deliberations: they silence or override other kinds of reason just because of the kind of reason that they are.[7]

But now we don't find a difference with ancient virtue ethics. For all ancient theories think exactly the same way about the fact that the action is dishonest: this is a consideration which is not just weighed up against the profit and time expended, but which sweeps them aside; and to think otherwise is to misconstrue what dishonesty is.

The Stoics make this point in the clearest and most uncompromising way. Only virtue, they say, is good; other things that we desire should be called not good but 'indifferent'. This does not mean that we have no more reason to go for them than not; it simply marks the difference between virtue and everything else. Some things, like health and wealth, are natural advantages, and it is rational for us to seek them; these are 'preferred indifferents', illness and poverty being 'dispreferred' since nothing is bad but vice. Along with this goes a whole set of new vocabulary; thus only virtue is 'chosen', while health, wealth, etc. are 'selected'. The point of all this is to stress the special role of virtue in our reasoning; if we have to use different words for virtue and for other things which we conventionally call good, then there is an initial barrier to our thoughtlessly treating them as considerations all of which are on a par.

'We judge health to be worthy of a kind of value, but we do not judge it a good, and we do not think there to be any value so great as to be preferred to virtue. . . . Compare the way the light of a lamp is obscured and overpowered by the light of the sun, and the way a drop of honey is lost in the extent of the Aegean sea; compare adding a penny to the riches of Croesus and taking one step on the journey from here to India – if the final good is what the Stoics say it is, it is necessary for all the value of bodily things to be obscured and overwhelmed, indeed to be destroyed, by the brilliance and the extent of virtue.'[8]

The analogies suggest two points. On the one hand, virtue is not straightforwardly incommensurable with other things, in the sense of not being on the same scale at all. A penny has the same kind of value (monetary) as Croesus' riches; one step does get you *some* of the way to India. On the other hand, there is a difference so marked that seriously to compare these items shows a lack of understanding of what they are. Someone who seriously congratulated herself on the progress she had made towards getting to India after taking one step would be showing lack of understanding of what one step is and what the journey to India is; someone who seriously counted a penny as the first step towards a billion-dollar fortune likewise. Similarly, while we can at the intuitive level talk of virtue, health and so on as considerations all of which have value in an agent's life, seriously to compare the value of money as against that of honesty, say, shows a misconstrual of what money is and of what honesty is.

This is less familiar to us than the distinction between moral and non-moral reasons, both because the ancients do not pose the issue in terms of different kinds of reason and because they do pose it in terms of the ways we can and cannot compare virtue and other kinds of thing. (In particular, we find in the ancient sources less stress on overridingness in cases of conflict, doubtless because of the fact that in ancient discussions less stress is put on conflict and disagreement.)[9] None the less, we could easily reformulate the ancient point as a point about the kinds of reason that the virtues give rise to. And even without reformulation the distinctions seem congruent, for their point is the same: they are emphasizing a feature of our practical deliberation, the fact that one kind of consideration, if rightly understood, cannot simply be weighed up against the other kinds, but knocks them out of the running. Of course the reasons that modern theories give as to *why* dishonesty is to be avoided will be different from the ancient reasons; modern theories may point to alleged formal features of reasons deriving from honesty, whereas ancient theories will point us towards analysis of the nature of the virtue of honesty. But there is agreement on the main point: dishonesty is not just another reason to be factored in, it is a consideration which stops the others in their tracks and sends us back to square one.

Admittedly the Stoics are the only school who insist so uncompromisingly on the difference between the value of virtue and the value of any other kind of thing. Aristotle does not insist that virtue is marked off from other kinds of thing that we seek in this way, and later his followers, the Peripatetics, defined their position against that of the Stoics by saying that virtue and other kinds of natural advantage are all good, ridiculing the Stoics for saying that things that we all rationally seek are not good. Aristotle is thus not in as strong a position as the Stoics are to mark off the special deliberative role of virtue. None the less, Aristotle insists in different ways that virtue has special kinds of benefit which other goods do not. The virtuous person will take pleasure in being virtuous, even if it leads to disadvantages, or even to wounds and death; thus he is not losing anything by his virtuous activity that can be balanced against the value of virtue. Thus virtue has a special place in relation to the other goods.[10]

Aristotle also describes virtuous action in ways which bring it close to other modern characterizations of what is done for a moral reason. The virtuous person does the virtuous action for its own sake,[11] and because it is *kalon*, 'fine' or 'noble'.[12] The *kalon* is the aim of virtue.[13] Alexander of Aphrodisias, the later commentator on Aristotle, puts the point more precisely: 'Virtue does everything for the sake of the *kalon qua kalon*, for virtue is such as to do things that are *kala* in the field of action.'[14] The virtuous action is done for its own sake, without ulterior motive, as is commonly taken to be true of an action done for a moral reason. And it is done with the *kalon* as its aim, rather than benefit or pleasure, which are the other characteristic human aims.[15] Aristotle does not, in the *Ethics*, further analyse the *kalon*. It is distinguished not only from what is pleasant and beneficial but also from what is necessary,[16] but we learn little more about it; Aristotle assumes that it motivates the virtuous person, and that this is something that we can recognize. It can be analysed in different ways, which we cannot examine here,[17] but what matters for the present issue is that Aristotle clearly recognizes that the virtuous person does the virtuous act for its own sake, and that this is a distinctive kind of motivation.

Again we seem to have agreement with the demands of modern morality rather than disagreement, since moral reasons are commonly taken to have just these features: to act for a moral reason is to do the action for its own sake and not for any further motive, and it also involves a distinct kind of motivation. Thus in different ways Aristotle and the Stoics seem to agree with modern theories of morality. Aristotle's position is the weaker (hence it is no surprise that it is his theory which is most often invoked in contrasts with modern morality).[18]

The Stoics have the sharpest and most satisfactory position about virtue, though other schools have a weaker view along similar lines; but in both cases there seems no reason to deny that the role of virtue in our deliberations is essentially that which modern theories take morality to have. Only Epicurus does not mark off the deliberative role of virtue in even the weaker way; but just this point forms a standard ancient *criticism* of him.[19] And if this kind of force in our deliberations is taken to be characteristic, or even definitive of morality, the ancient theories seem to be telling us something about morality.

Moral Responsibility

In modern moral philosophy it is a cliché that 'ought implies can', that moral appraisal implies moral responsibility, where this in turn implies that the agent was in some way free not to do what is in question. Ancient ethics, it is often claimed, is by contrast less concerned about this; ethical appraisal is sometimes handed out in cases where the agent was not in this way free not so to act. Sometimes this is put as a point about 'moral luck': the agent can be morally held to account for actions which it was not in her power to avoid doing. If one accepts this claim, one will indeed tend to think that ancient ethics is not modern morality, since it is central to all going modern theories that if one was not free not to do the action one cannot be morally held to account for it.

This point is often buttressed by pointing out that the Greek word *aretē* (and the same goes for the Latin *virtus*) does not mean 'virtue'; it means 'excellence', and can apply to what makes a house or a horse an excellent house or horse. From this point it is often inferred that even for humans the *aretai* are not the virtues. (Some modern translations reflect this belief.)[20] Virtues are states where we are concerned with particularly moral appraisal, and judge that the person can be praised or blamed and hence is morally responsible for what he did. But if the *aretai* are just the human excellences, there will be no division of kind between being brave or just and excellences like being healthy or handsome, no way of marking off an area of peculiarly moral appraisal where it is assumed that the agent is morally responsible.

This charge against ancient ethics is a venerable one, and can be found in Hume's fourth appendix to his *Enquiry Concerning the Principles of Morals*. Hume claims there that even in

English we do not make a marked distinction between what are usually called the moral virtues and other kinds of non-moral excellence, a claim rebutted by Sidgwick.[21] More to our present point, Hume claims that 'the ancient moralists, the best models, made no material distinction among the different species of mental endowments and defects, but treated all alike under the appellation of virtues and vices', and, 'In general, we may observe, that the distinction of voluntary or involuntary was little regarded by the ancients in their moral reasonings.' It was, he claims, only with the incursion of religion, specifically Christianity, into moral philosophy that philosophers began to be obsessed by the question of voluntariness.

Hume's analysis, and its accompanying diagnosis, have been often repeated, so it is worth pointing out that what Hume says is quite false. Aristotle devotes a prominent part of book III of the *Nicomachean Ethics* to discussing the conditions for voluntariness, precisely because this is needed in an enquiry into virtue, since 'praise and blame are bestowed on what is voluntary, pardon and sometimes pity on what is involuntary'.[22] Further, what is true of Aristotle remains true for all the ancient schools: virtue requires voluntariness, the free exercise of choice to act one way rather than another. Nothing could be less true than the claim that the ancients were uninterested in the difference between this kind of state and a state like health or beauty.

What of the point about *aretē*, however? It is true that *aretē* means 'excellence', not 'virtue'. But it is quite compatible with this that the excellences of a human life should be the virtues, indeed what we might call the moral virtues. And this is in fact what we find. We might, of course, disagree that this is the form an excellent human life should take. But the human *aretai*, from Plato onwards, are routinely taken to be courage, 'temperance' (moderation and self-control), practical intelligence and justice, with the other virtues as subdivisions of these.[23] And if we look more closely at courage, justice and so on, we cannot doubt that they are not regarded as being on a par with natural endowments, nor are they simply regarded as some among a lot of desirable dispositions. They are dispositions *to do the ethically right thing*, and as such involve the agent's choice, and presuppose that this is voluntary.

By the time of the Stoics we find it explicitly recognized, and enshrined in technical terminology, that the virtues are special kinds of excellence or *aretē*, precisely because they involve choice and are, as they say, 'reasoned', based on accepting certain principles:

'As for *aretē*, it is in one sense generally anything's reaching completion. So it is with a statue. And there is the unreasoned kind, like health, and the reasoned kind, like intelligence. Hecaton says . . . that the *aretai* that involve knowledge and are reasoned are those whose constitution is formed from principles,[24] like intelligence and justice; unreasoned are those that are observed to be co-extensive with those constituted from principles, such as health and strength.'[25]

Indeed, the use of *aretē* or *virtus* for the moral virtues of a person came to be seen as the standard or primary use, and the application to statues and horses as secondary, as we can see from later passages, where *virtutes voluntariae* are said to be *virtutes* in the proper sense of the word,[26] and where it is claimed that *aretē* is actually ambiguous because it can be used both of the virtues of a person, which are developed by accepting moral principles, and of aptitudes and natural excellences.[27]

No understanding is gained, then, by translating *aretē* as 'excellence', or by pointing to *aretē* as applied to statues and healthy bodies. Indeed, understanding is lost. For the *aretai* that concern ethics are courage, justice, etc.; and these are precisely different from the statue and health uses in that they do presuppose a freely choosing and developing agent.

It is certainly true that in some ancient texts we find reflected a belief in 'moral luck' – in tragedy, for example. But it is striking that we do not find it in ancient moral *theory*. The main reason for this seems to be that ancient moral theory is centrally concerned with the virtues, and the virtues are, as we have seen, reasoned states presupposing freedom of choice. Ancient moral theory in fact is committed to being *critical* of the acceptance of 'moral luck' in other areas of ancient intellectual life, and in very similar ways to those in which modern moral theories are committed to being critical of such an acceptance in areas of modern intellectual life. Thus it would be a mistake to think that deontological and consequentialist theories are committed to rejecting moral luck, while virtue ethics is not; it finds precisely the same problem that they do. It is sometimes claimed[28] that it is a profound mistake to reject the notion of 'moral luck'. If this is so, it is a mistake on the part of ethical theory generally, as opposed to pre-reflective ethical beliefs. It is not a mistake of modern as opposed to ancient ethical theory.[29]

Scope

Reflection on Aristotle's list of virtues has often suggested to modern readers (especially those who read no ancient ethics but Aristotle's) that there is a fundamental difference of scope between modern morality and the ancient ethics of virtue. Aristotle's virtues range over areas of life that we would not at all naturally take to be the domain of morality. Thus Aristotle opposes the virtue of 'temperance' or self-control in bodily pleasures such as those of eating, drinking and sex not just to self-indulgence, in his terms the 'excess', but also to the 'defect', *anaisthēsia*, the disposition not to enjoy food, drink and sex as much as one should. (This disposition, he remarks, is rarely encountered.) He also sketches large-scale social virtues, such as that of paying for public works in a tasteful and appropriate manner. If we are to take him to be talking about virtue in a sense which is recognizably moral, then we seem forced to absurd conclusions such as that not enjoying food is a moral vice, or that tasteful expenditure is a moral virtue. And similar conclusions follow for many of Aristotle's virtues.

This criticism can be partially deflected, whatever else we say about it, by the point that Aristotle's list of virtues is rather unusual. His successors revert to Plato's habit of regarding virtue as consisting of the four 'cardinal' virtues,

subdivided. So Aristotle is at least not typical. Further, his theory of virtue as a mean, which directs many of his distinctions, was likewise unusual, and it, not a view about virtue in general, is responsible for some of his odder views, such as the status of *anaisthēsia*. But even taking this into account the fact remains that Aristotle talks of virtues covering areas of life which we would not be inclined to bring under morality.

There are other responses, however, than the usual one of claiming that Aristotle's virtues are not concerned with morality. For it might be that Aristotle is prepared to moralize more of everyday life than we are. Perhaps he thinks that indifference to food and sex is not (always) a blank physical given, but an insensitivity which involves or flows from a moral insensitivity. And perhaps tastefulness in public expenditure, and the large-scale public virtues generally, are matters of moral concern, either in their results or in their origin or both. The plausibility of this thesis about Aristotle obviously depends on a detailed account of all Aristotle's virtues, which cannot be done here; but the general strategy is clear enough.

Is this an absurd position? All the ancient ethical schools accepted the assumption that ethics is not a distinct compartment in one's life. Taste, style, and social behaviour generally are not neutral matters, indifferent between the good and the bad: because of the centrality of character, ethical differences will affect all aspects of your life. Most ethical theories do not follow Aristotle by structuring actual virtues for all aspects of social life. Aristotle is unusual, and arguably overambitious, in trying to work out these matters in detail as part of a theory of virtue. But the other schools do not disagree with Aristotle's point that the possession or otherwise of the virtues makes a great difference to how one spends money, enjoys food, makes jokes and so on. Your ethical stage of development is relevant in your life as a whole, in every aspect of your interactions with others.

Does this contrast with morality? Only if morality is compartmentalized in our lives, if our stage of moral development has little or nothing to do with the way we live the rest of our lives. And while some hold that this can be the case, it is not obviously true. In fact quite compelling arguments can be put forward to show that it is not true – arguments effectively articulated by Bradley. As he puts it,

> It is . . . an error to suppose that in what is called human life there remains any region which has not been moralized . . . . The character shows itself in every trifling detail of life; we can not go in to amuse ourselves while we leave it outside the door with our dog; it is ourself, and our moral self, being not mere temper or in-born disposition, but the outcome of a series of acts of will.[30]

We may reject this; and Bradley is not typical of modern moral theory here, which in general ignores the problem. But it certainly ought not to be taken for granted that morality can be restricted to part of one's life only. And if we take this point we may find it a matter of detail whether, with Aristotle, we take it that areas of social life demarcate distinct virtues, or, with the other schools, that the virtues, more narrowly defined, affect one's conduct in all areas of social life.[31]

Actions and Agents

Williams characterizes morality as a system of thought making *obligation* primary, indeed the only form of moral requirement.[32] He points out that if we try to reduce all aspects of the moral life to the holding of obligations, we shall find the account drastically impoverished. While this is certainly true, one might well doubt whether modern moral theories really are characterized quite as strongly as Williams suggests by the primacy of obligation. Consequentialists, for example, think that what matters is maximizing good consequences of some kind; even if they think that this is what one ought to do, they are often not happy with the idea of starting from such notions as obligation and duty.

A weaker position captures what has widely been felt to be an important difference, one summed up by calling modern morality *act-cen-tred*. The thought is this: morality is primarily a matter of how one ought to act, what one ought to do. Morality starts from what are called our intuitions, the judgements we pre-reflectively make about what we ought to do. It examines the ways we come to make those judgements and the kinds of grounds that we consider relevant. The task of moral theory is to clarify to ourselves, and make more rigorous, our ways of coming to decide what we ought to do. Some forms of moral theory aim to produce a decision procedure – a mechanical way of finding out what to do, which is to be so constructed as to come to the right results. But even theories which fall short of this tend to take as their primary aim that of improving our ability to decide what to do.

By contrast, ancient ethics does not see this as its aim; relatedly, it does not spend time on tasks which are important to modern theories, such as studying hard cases. Ancient theories have been labelled *agent-centred*; they take their primary aim to be that of delineating the good person and of helping us to understand what constitutes the good life. Assuming that we all seek the good life, they examine what it consists in; and they ask what it is about certain of our dispositions that makes them virtues, and how possessing these helps one to achieve the best life.

Broadly stated in this way, the contrast is obviously right. But it needs some refinement. Modern theories don't just seek decision procedures; especially if they have revisionary views as to what the right thing to do is, they have to examine the relation between doing the right thing and being the kind of person who will do the right thing. And ancient theories don't just discuss virtue and the good life; they also discuss what is the right thing to do. They can hardly avoid this, since a virtue is a disposition to do the right thing. In fact a little reflection shows that no sensible theory could be act- or agent-centred in the sense of *just* considering acts or agents; all theories have to consider both.

The contrast, then, must lie in the relative importance that ancient and modern theories give to acts and agents. And it at first seems that we still have a striking contrast. For modern theories tend to take questions about what one should do to be the primary ones, in that it is only when these are in hand that one can consider the question of what kind of person to be. The good person, to put it crudely, is the person who is so disposed as to do the right thing; but we find out what the right thing to do is independently, without appeal to what the good person is. Thus, since virtue notions will not help us to discover or clarify what the right thing to do is, they will be secondary in moral theory. By contrast, ancient theories are seen as taking virtue notions to be primary, and questions of right action to be secondary. The important point for ancient ethics will be to establish what the virtuous person is like; the right thing to do will just be what the virtuous person would do, and thus will be a secondary issue.

It is widely accepted that there is something like this contrast between ancient and modern theories. Indeed, it is often made the basis for criticisms of ancient theories, on the grounds that they have nothing to say about right conduct that is not trivial.[33] For if one is faced by a difficult decision, and is told that the right thing to do is what the virtuous person would do, one does not feel much helped.

However, the more one looks at this alleged contrast, the shakier it seems to be. Few modern theories are so crude as to work out a decision procedure for action and then simply define the good or ideal agent as the person who applies that procedure. For if an account of right action is to be an account of how people act rightly, some account of how people are and ought to be has to be fed into it; it is pointless to develop it in a void. What use could a theory be as a *moral* theory if nobody could internalize it and act on it?[34] And on the other side, ancient theories do not develop an account of what the virtuous person is in the void, adding that right action is just what this person would produce. Rather, the virtuous person is the person with developed dispositions to do the right thing. We have to have some idea of what the right thing to do is in order so much as to get going a notion of a *virtue*, as opposed to some other kind of disposition. In fact it is obvious on reflection that any ethical theory has to say something by way of criticism and clarification of our intuitive views on both rightness of action and goodness of people.

In the end there does remain a difference. For modern theories often demand that particular answers to hard cases be built into the theory itself, in such a way that all one needs is to feed in a fairly simple description of a particular problem for the theory to produce an answer to it. Ancient theories, on the other hand, are more impressed by the complexity and difficulty of particular situations. The completely virtuous person will be able to come to particular decisions which do justice to all features of a particular situation, because he has internalized the ethical theory; but the decisions are not themselves part of the theory.

(It should be added, however, that this is the ideal; you and I, not being completely virtuous, are best advised to follow the best available rules or principles, rather than relying on the capacity we have developed to make particular judgements. So for unideal people the gap between ancient and modern closes somewhat.)

Sometimes modern morality is characterized by its emphasis on rules, as a guide to right acting, and ancient ethics is held up as a more humane alternative, more interested in developing good dispositions, since it is interested in people. Rule-following is often supposed to be of interest only if one is concerned only or primarily about acts. But moral rules clearly have a place in both kinds of theory. Moral rules are a guide to acting rightly; but just for that reason they are the way to develop a virtuous disposition. Aristotle says little about rules, being more interested in the following of virtuous models, and so rules are often under-stressed in modern discussions of ancient ethics. But the Stoics make a fairly large place for rule-following within the development of virtue. It is true that in an ethics of virtue rule-following will not be, on its own, enough to make one virtuous. But then few modern theories would hold that rule-following on its own is enough to make one act rightly either.

Myself and Others

Ancient ethical theory begins by specifying what, really, when I understand it, is my 'final end' or 'final good'. It is taken for granted that each of us does have a final good – an overall good which we seek to bring about in all we do. It is also assumed that this is happiness, though this point is regarded as trivial and settling nothing; real debate centres on how one's final good is to be informatively specified. Epicurus claims that it is pleasure; Aristotle and the Stoics disagree as to whether it requires only the development of virtue, or some material advantages as well. Thus ethical enquiry takes place within a framework in which the fundamental ethical question which faces me is, how I shall achieve my own final good.

This is, to put it mildly, not the fundamental ethical question in modern theories. The fact that these tend to characterize morality in terms of concern for others, whereas ancient ethics begins from concern with oneself, shows that there is certainly a contrast here. And if one takes a basic and non-derivative concern for others to be definitive of morality, one will, as is often done, take the contrast to show that ancient ethics is not morality, or at best is grossly defective as morality. But again the supposed contrast is a slippery one.

It is still sometimes claimed that, because ancient ethical theory works to answer the question, what constitutes my final good, that it is egoistic; in pursuing my own final good I am pursuing my own self-interest. This claim is mistaken. For what ancient theory demands that I develop, in pursuing my final good, are the *virtues*, and these include justice, courage and the like. Some of them have a direct connection with the good of others, for example justice. All of them involve at least having a disposition to do the right thing, where this is established independently of the agent's own interests. An ethics of virtue is at most formally self-centred, since its framework is that of the agent's own final end; its content can be fully as other-regarding as that of other ethical theories.

None the less, the idea persists that ancient ethics, since its framework is that of the agent's final end, is at bottom egoistic. This has, I think, two main sources, one confused, the other not, but in the end mistaken. The confusion comes from the thought that if the good of others is introduced into the agent's own final good, it cannot really be the good of *others*, but must in some way be reduced to what matters *to the agent*. But why must this be the case? Perhaps the thought is that the good of others must matter to me *because* it is the good of others, not because it is part of my own good. But no ancient theorist would dispute this. The good of others does not matter to me because it is part of my own good; it matters to me because it is the good of others. This is quite compatible with its being part of my overall final good. The second thought does not undermine the first.

A more creditable objection goes as follows: If ethics begins from the question, what my final good is, then this can indeed include *philia* or friendship, caring for particular other people for their own sake. It can even include justice understood as a concern for fair dealing. But it cannot extend to impartiality, the thought that I matter, from the moral point of view, merely as one among others, and should give my interests no more weight than those of anybody else. And impartiality is required by (many, at least) modern moral theories.[35]

This is an interesting claim, but false. Not all ancient theories demand that I think of myself as merely one person among others from the ethical point of view, but Stoicism does. The Stoics think that a rational person will naturally be led to extend her rational concern to all other people (rational people at least) until she is impartial between her own interests and those of 'the remotest Mysian', that is, someone living in a far-off country of whom she has no personal knowledge at all, and to whom she has no personal links.[36] They draw conclusions from this which were attacked by ancient critics in much the way that Williams has attacked Kantian theories. In a shipwreck, for example, where there is one plank and each of two people wanting to be saved, the Stoic view is that the person who ought to have the plank is the morally worthier. If both are equally morally worthy, they will use a fair random procedure. An ancient critic attacks this on the ground that in such a case each person would in fact save himself; to claim that he ought to be impartial between his own interests and those of others, and settle the matter by appeal only to considerations of ethical worth, appeals to motivations that people don't in fact have.[37] The Stoics, that is, do exactly what is supposed not to be possible: they take ethics to be an examination of what constitutes the agent's good, and claim that ethical development leads the agent eventually to do two things. One is to see morality as not just one of her concerns, but as a concern that override all her other concerns. The other is to see morality as a perspective from which one is impartial between one's own concerns and interests and those of other people concerned. We may find it strange that eudaimonism can accommodate these thoughts, but it is part of the data of ancient ethics that it can.

It is true that not all ancient theories think that this kind of impartiality between one's own interests and those of anyone else *is* demanded by ethical considerations. Aristotle's account of justice, for example, does not make the demand of impartiality between oneself and all others that the Stoic account does. Theories that derive from Aristotle do not make this a requirement of morality generally or even of justice in particular; they start from the agent's concern for the good of particular other people and tend to stop when a group of people is reached with whom the agent has a feeling of community, such as the citizens of one's city-state. The important point here is that while impartiality between one's own interests and those of any other rational human was not taken for granted as a requirement of morality or even of justice in ancient theories, the idea was familiar and a matter of debate. A eudaimonistic form of ethics does not prevent the agent from reaching this impartial viewpoint.

So we cannot deny that ancient theories are moral theories on the grounds that they do not recognize that morality requires impartiality; some of them do, and it is a topic of argument. And since in recent years there has been debate as to whether modern theories are right to re-

quire impartiality of this kind, any division of principle seems to evaporate.

Conclusion

My account has been sketchy and partial. But I hope that I have at least isolated, and tried to meet, a common line of thought. There are indeed large differences between ancient and modern ethical thought, and it is easy to be over-impressed by them, and to conclude that, since our notion of what morality is must answer to our own type of theory, we have to regard the ancient theories not as moral theories, but something different. I have tried to focus on the main reasons for thinking this, and the reasons for rejecting them.

My project may seem to have been an irenic one; I have been trying to reconcile positions that are often taken to be hopelessly diverse. I have done so by way of minimizing differences: what appear to be competing positions turn out not to be in competition, since they are doing the same thing in different ways. But this does not leave everything where it was before. For it undermines two attitudes to ancient ethical theories, and to modern theories that hark back to ancient texts. One is the hostile attitude that the ancient theories are simply outdated: they are inadequate to cope with the problems that modern moral theories have to deal with.[38] I hope I have shown that this attitude rests on some mistakes about ancient ethical theories. But there is another attitude, equally harmful, I think, of romantic nostalgia: the feeling that it would be nicer if we could shed the problem-area that we have and go back to a very different set of problems, that ethics would be a kinder, gentler place if we could forget about hard cases and talk about friendship and the good life instead. Like much nostalgia, this is misplaced.

Both of these attitudes neutralize the ancient theories as answers to our problems: whether *passé* or inspiring, these theories are seen as out of our reach, not applicable to the moral problems we now have. But if what I have suggested is right, ancient ethics is not so easily disposed of. The possibility remains open that one of the competing ancient theories might have just as much chance as the modern competitors of being, not just interesting, or edifying, but a true theory of morality.

Notes

This paper has been read at the University of Arizona, Columbia University, the University of Oklahoma, Brown University, Johns Hopkins University, Brigham Young University and the political thought seminar at Princeton University. I have benefited from comments on each occasion, and apologize to the numerous people whose questions and problems have greatly helped me to clarify the issues, but whose individual contributions I can no longer accurately distinguish. I am grateful for written comments from Michael Slote and Jonathan Kandell. The need for reflecting on these issues arises from a book I am writing on the intellectual structure of Greek ethical theory, *The Morality of Happiness* (Oxford University Press, forthcoming).

1   I take it that in everyday language 'ethics' and 'morality' are used interchangeably. There seems at any rate to be no single principled difference between them. The use of 'ethics' to label an alternative distinct from morality is the product of certain assumptions made when discussing ethical theory, and I have used it in conformity with those assumptions. I do not know of any general argument to establish the difference; hence my opponent in this paper is not one single argued position, but a set of assumptions which are widespread in discussions of ancient philosophy, though possibly no one would explicitly subscribe to all the assumptions I criticize here.

2   In the chapter 'Philosophy' in M. I. Finley, *The Legacy of Greece* (Oxford: Oxford University Press, 1981); also in *Ethics and the Limits of Philosophy* (London: Fontana/Collins, 1985). My criticisms of Williams are not aimed at his own position in the book, but merely at his historical claims about ancient ethics.

3   Bernard Williams in his Sather Lectures labels as 'progressivist' the idea that we have outgrown ancient ethics, that we now have more mature responses to the problems in question.

4   Rather, what is important in Greek ethical theory is the difference between the beginner and the ethically developed person. This is commonly seen on the model of a beginner in a craft, who is dependent on following rules and models, and the expert, who has internalized the principles of the craft and need not follow rules and models so rigidly. (Whether, however, this amounts to a difference in the form of ethical reasoning between beginner and expert is a difficult matter, and may well differ between the different schools.)

5   'Philosophy', p. 251.

6   For the silencing metaphor see J. McDowell, 'The Role of *Eudaimonia* in Aristotle's Ethics', in A. Rorty (ed.), *Essays on Aristotle's Ethics* (Berkeley/Los Angeles/London: University of California Press 1980), pp. 359–76.

7   To avert misunderstanding: this is what I take the intuitive notion of a moral reason to be. I am not providing a theoretical defence of it against theories which would try to weaken or erase the difference.

8   *De Finibus*, III 44–5.

9   For the Stoics, virtue is the *technē* or skill which is exercised in putting non-moral advantages (the 'indifferents') to use. This conception of the relation of moral to non-moral value is strikingly different from a conception which assumes from the start that they are likely to come into conflict, as John Cooper has emphasized to me. None the less it is compatible with considerations of virtue having what I have called the special deliberative role.

10   It is necessary for happiness, since without it the other goods cannot be appreciated at their true worth, but not sufficient, since external goods are needed also. See my article, 'Aristotle on Virtue and Happiness', *University of Dayton Review* (Winter 1988–9), pp. 7–22, and the relevant parts of my book *The Morality of Happiness*, where I argue that this position is inherently unstable.

11   E.g. 1105 a 31–2.

12   E.g. 1116 a 11.

13   1115 b 11–13. For a more detailed account of the occurrences of these phrases, see the excellent article by T. Irwin, 'Aristotle's Conception of Morality', in *Proceedings of the Boston Area Ancient Philosophy Colloquium*, vol. 1 (1985), 115–43. See also 'The *Kalon* in the Aristotelian Ethics', by J. Owens, in *Studies in Aristotle*, ed. D. O'Meara (Catholic University of America Press, 1981).

14   *De Anima*, II 154.30–2.

15   1104 b 30–1105 a 1.

16   See Irwin, 'Aristotle's Conception', pp. 125–6.

17   Compare Owens, who understands it as 'the in-

trinsic obligatory character of moral goodness' with Irwin, who explicates it, via passages from the *Rhetoric*, as essentially connected with the good of others.

18 The stronger Stoic position implies something like the Aristotelian, but not the other way around. The question, whether Aristotle really recognizes the nature of moral reasons, thus depends on how strong you take the contrast between moral and other reasons to be. I have assumed that intuitively we suppose the stronger view, but have not here defended this assumption.

19 See *De Finibus*, II 44ff. Epicurus is often interpreted as giving virtue only instrumental value as a means to producing pleasure. I have argued that Epicurus is driven by various constraints into allowing virtue intrinsic value (see my 'Epicurus on Pleasure and Happiness', *Philosophical Topics*, XV (1987), pp. 5–21, and the relevant parts of my book (see above).

20 For example, the revised Oxford translation (ed. J. Barnes, Princeton, 1984), which replaces 'virtue' by 'excellence' throughout. This produces the odd result that people interested to see what Aristotle has contributed to 'virtue ethics' find in this translation that he has nothing to say about virtue. J. O. Urmson, *Aristotle's Ethics* (Blackwell, 1988), pp. 26ff, explicitly defends the translation 'excellence' rather than 'virtue' on the grounds that Aristotle is not making 'hopelessly wrong' claims about moral virtue, but is concerned with acting effortlessly and with enjoyment, as a result of one's character.

21 *The Methods of Ethics*, III ii.

22 Hume, we should note, says that 'We need only peruse the titles of chapters in Aristotle's Ethics to be convinced' that Aristotle's virtues are not restricted to what is voluntary; there is little sign that Hume perused the actual chapters. Indeed, while Hume is clearly at home with ancient literature, history and oratory, his grip on ancient philosophy is surprisingly weak.

23 Aristotle is the exception; his list of virtues includes these, but is wider and messier. Concentration on Aristotle's ethics has tended to obscure the extent to which these four are in the ancient world quite standard. Even later versions of Aristotelian ethics conform more to the standard pattern.

24 The word is *theorēmata*. This is used by the Stoics for mathematical theorems, but also for the principles which give structure to any craft or skill (cf. the passages in von Arnim, *Stoicorum Veterum Fragmenta*, III 214, where *logos . . . kata ta theorēmata* is distinguished from mere habituation; also III 278, 295). Virtue for the Stoics is a skill, so its 'theorems' are the principles which structure a virtue, the rules or principles which you have to accept to be dispositionally brave, just and so on. (There is no implication that the agent's moral reasoning has a deductive or mathematical structure.)

25 Diogenes Laertius, VII 90. Cf. also the parallel passage in Arius Didymus and the account of Stoic ethics in Stobaeus, *Eclogae* II, 62.15–63.5.

26 *De Finibus*, V 36–38, in a description of Antiochus' ethical theory.

27 Alexander of Aphrodisias, *De Anima* II 155 24–8.

28 Influentially by Martha Nussbaum, in *The Fragility of Goodness* (Cambridge University Press, 1986).

29 And of course I have not in the least shown whether it is a mistake or not.

30 *Ethical Studies*, 2nd edn (Oxford University Press, 1962), Essay VI, pp. 217–18.

31 The latter is certainly more plausible, as we can see from the difficulties we tend to find with Aristotle's more 'social' virtues. We can presume that the later schools shared these difficulties, and that this explains why they took the alternative course.

32 *Ethics and the Limits of Philosophy*, ch. 10.

33 See R. Louden, 'On Some Vices of Virtue Ethics', *American Philosophical Quarterly*, 1984 (reprinted in R. Kruschwitz and R. Roberts, *The Virtues*, N.Y.: Wadsworth, 1987) for a trenchant statement of this.

34 Some modern versions of consequentialism do not recognize this constraint, distinguishing the role of a moral theory as motivating and as justifying. I do not think that this move is as successful as often thought, but cannot argue that here.

35 This issue is discussed more fully in the relevant part of my book (see above), and also in 'The Good Life and the Good Lives of Others', forthcoming in *Social Philosophy and Policy*.

36 Plato has Socrates use 'the remotest Mysian' as a proverbial expression for someone far off and unknown to us, at *Theaetetus*, 209b. The Anonymous Commentator on the *Theaetetus*, probably first century BC, of whose work we possess a substantial papyrus fragment, uses it as an example in an ethical context (cols 5–6) when discussing the Stoic theory.

37 The Anonymous Commentator (see n.36 above). The shipwreck example is in fact fragmentary in the Commentary, though the author's view is clear enough from the substantial objections which do remain, and from the parallel passage in Cicero's *de Officiis* III 89–90.

38 This attitude is often accompanied by the romantic thought that modern moral philosophy faces problems that are unprecedented, and that our ways of dealing with them owe little or nothing to past traditions.

PART FOUR

CHALLENGES TO MORALITY

Postmodernism: Morality from Whose Cultural Perspective?

Feminism: How is Gender Relevant to Morality?

31 Equality for Men and Women

Musonius Rufus

That Man is Born with an Inclination Toward Virtue

All of us, he used to say, are so fashioned by nature that we can live our lives free from error and nobly; not that one can and another cannot, but all. The clearest evidence of this is the fact that lawgivers lay down for all alike what may be done and forbid what may not be done, exempting from punishment no one who disobeys or docs wrong, not the young nor the old, not the strong nor the weak, not anyone whomsoever. And yet if the whole notion of virtue were something that came to us from without, and we shared no part of it by birth, just as in activities pertaining to the other arts no one who has not learned the art is expected to be free from error, so in like manner in things pertaining to the conduct of life it would not be reasonable to expect anyone to be free from error who had not learned virtue, seeing that virtue is the only thing that saves us from error in daily living. Now in the care of the sick we demand no one but the physician to be free from error, and in handling the lyre no one but the musician, and in managing the helm no one but the pilot, but in the conduct of life it is no longer only the philosopher whom we expect to be free from error, though he alone would seem to be the only one concerned with the study of virtue, but all men alike, including those who have never given any attention to virtue. Clearly, then, there is no explanation for this other than that the human being is born with an inclination toward virtue. And this indeed is strong evidence of the presence of goodness in our nature, that all speak of themselves as having virtue and being good. For take the common man; when asked whether he is stupid or intelligent, not one will confess to being stupid; or again, when asked whether he is just or unjust, not one will say that he is unjust. In the same way, if one asks him whether he is temperate or intemperate, he replies at once that he is temperate; and finally, if one asks whether he is good or bad, he would say that he is good, even though he can name no teacher of virtue or mention any study or practice of virtue he has ever made. Of what, then, is this evidence if not of the existence of an innate inclination of the human soul toward goodness and nobleness, and of the presence of the seeds of virtue in each one of us? Moreover, because it is entirely to our advantage to be good, some of us deceive ourselves into thinking that we are really good, while others of us are ashamed to admit that we are not. Why then pray, when one who has not learned letters or music or gymnastics never claims to have knowledge of these arts nor makes any pretence of knowing them, and is quite unable even to name a teacher to whom he went, why, I say, does everyone profess that he has virtue? It is because none of those other skills is natural to man, and no human being is born with a natural facility for them, whereas an inclination toward virtue is inborn in each one of us.

From *Discourses* II–IV. Reprinted by permission of the Department of Classics, Yale University.

That Women Too Should Study Philosophy

When someone asked him if women too should study philosophy, he began to discourse on the theme that they should, in somewhat the following manner. Women as well as men, he said, have received from the gods the gift of reason, which we use in our dealings with one another and by which we judge whether a thing is good or bad, right or wrong. Likewise the female has the same senses as the male; namely sight, hearing, smell, and the others. Also both have the same parts of the body, and one has nothing more than the other. Moreover, not men alone, but women too, have a natural inclination toward virtue and the capacity for acquiring it, and it is the nature of women no less than men to be pleased by good and just acts and to reject the opposite of these. If this is true, by what reasoning would it ever be appropriate for men to search out and consider how they may lead good lives, which is exactly the study of philosophy, but inappropriate for women? Could it be that it is fitting for men to be good, but not for women? Let us examine in detail the qualities which are suitable for a woman who would lead a good life, for it will appear that each one of them would accrue to her most readily from the study of philosophy. In the first place, a woman must be a good housekeeper, that is a careful accountant of all that pertains to the welfare of her house and capable of directing the household slaves. It is my contention that these are the very qualities which would be present particularly in the woman who studies philosophy, since obviously each of them is a part of life, and philosophy is nothing other than knowledge about life, and the philosopher, as Socrates said, quoting Homer, is constantly engaged in investigating precisely this: 'Whatsoever of good and of evil is wrought in thy halls.' But above all a woman must be chaste and self-controlled; she must, I mean, be pure in respect of unlawful love, exercise restraint in other pleasures, not be a slave to desire, not be contentious, not lavish in expense, nor extravagant in dress. Such are the works of a virtuous woman, and to them I would add yet these: to control her tem-per, not to be overcome by grief, and to be superior to uncontrolled emotion of every kind. Now these are the things which the teachings of philosophy transmit, and the person who has learned them and practises them would seem to me to have become a well-ordered and seemly character, whether man or woman. Well then, so much for self-control. As for justice, would not the woman who studies philosophy be just, would she not be a blameless life-partner, would she not be a sympathetic helpmate, would she not be an untiring defender of husband and children, and would she not be entirely free of greed and arrogance? And who better than the woman trained in philosophy – and she certainly of necessity if she has really acquired philosophy – would be disposed to look upon doing a wrong as worse than suffering one (as much worse as it is the baser), and to regard being worsted as better than gaining an unjust advantage? Moreover, who better than she would love her children more than life itself? What woman would be more just than such a one? Now as for courage, certainly it is to be expected that the educated woman will be more courageous than the uneducated, and one who has studied philosophy than one who has not; and she will not therefore submit to anything shameful because of fear of death or unwillingness to face hardship, and she will not be intimidated by anyone because he is of noble birth, or powerful, or wealthy, no, not even if he be the tyrant of her city. For in fact she has schooled herself to be high-minded and to think of death not as an evil and life not as a good, and likewise not to shun hardship and never for a moment to seek ease and indolence. So it is that such a woman is likely to be energetic, strong to endure pain, prepared to nourish her children at her own breast, and to serve her husband with her own hands, and willing to do things which some would consider no better than slaves' work. Would not such a woman be a great help to the man who married her, an ornament to her relatives, and a good example for all who know her? Yes, but I assure you, some will say, that women who associate with philosophers are bound to be arrogant for the most part and presumptuous, in that abandoning their own households and turning to the company of men they practise speeches, talk like sophists, and analyse syllogisms, when they ought to be sitting at home spinning. I should not expect the women who study philosophy to shirk their appointed tasks for mere talk any more than men, but I maintain that their discussions should be conducted for the sake of their practical application. For as there is no merit in the science of medicine unless it conduces to the healing of man's body, so if a philosopher has or teaches reason, it is of no use if it does not contribute to the virtue of man's soul. Above all, we ought to examine the doctrine which we think women who study philosophy ought to follow; we ought to see if the study which presents modesty as the greatest good can make them presumptuous, if the study which is a guide to the greatest self-restraint accustoms them to live heedlessly, if what sets forth intemperance as the greatest evil does not teach self-control, if what represents the management of a household as a virtue does not impel them to manage well their homes. Finally, the teachings of philosophy exhort the woman to be content with her lot and to work with her own hands.

Should Daughters Receive the Same Education as Sons?

Once when the question arose as to whether or not sons and daughters ought to be given the same education, he remarked that trainers of horses and dogs make no distinction in the training of the male and the female; for female dogs are taught to hunt just as the males are, and one can see no difference in the training of mares, if they are expected to do a horse's work, and the training of stallions. In the case of man, however, it would seem to be felt necessary to employ some special and exceptional training and education for males over females, as if it were not essential that the same virtues should be present in both alike, in man and woman, or as if it were possible to arrive at the same virtues, not through the same, but through different instruction. And yet that there is not one set of virtues for a man and another for a woman is easy to

perceive. In the first place, a man must have understanding and so must a woman, or what pray would be the use of a foolish man or woman? Then it is essential for one no less than the other to live justly, since the man who is not just would not be a good citizen, and the woman would not manage her household well if she did not do it justly; but if she is unjust she will wrong her husband like Eriphyle in the story. Again, it is recognized as right for a woman in wedlock to be chaste, and so is it likewise for a man; the law, at all events, decrees the same punishment for committing adultery as for being taken in adultery. Gluttony, drunkenness and other related vices, which are vices of excess and bring disgrace upon those guilty of them, show that self-control is most necessary for every human being, male and female alike; for the only way of escape from wantonness is through self-control; there is no other. Perhaps someone may say that courage is a virtue appropriate to men only. That is not so. For a woman too of the right sort must have courage and be wholly free of cowardice, so that she will neither be swayed by hardships nor by fear; otherwise, how will she be said to have self-control, if by threat or force she can be constrained to yield to shame? Nay more, it is necessary for women to be able to repel attack, unless indeed they are willing to appear more cowardly than hens and other female birds which fight with creatures much larger than themselves to defend their young. How then should women not need courage? That women have some prowess in arms the race of the Amazons demonstrated when they defeated many tribes in war. If, therefore, something of this courage is lacking in other women, it is due to lack of use and practice rather than because they were not endowed with it. If then men and women are born with the same virtues, the same type of training and education must, of necessity, befit both men and women. For with every animal and plant whatsoever, proper care must be bestowed upon it to produce the excellence appropriate to it. Is it not true that, if it were necessary under like circumstances for a man and a woman to be able to play the flute, and if, furthermore, both had to do so in order to earn a living, we should give them both exactly the same thorough training in flute playing; and similarly if it were necessary for either to play the harp? Well then, if it is necessary for both to be proficient in the virtue which is appropriate to a human being, that is for both to be able to have understanding, and self-control, and courage, and justice, the one no less than the other, shall we not teach them both alike the art by which a human being becomes good? Yes, certainly we must do that and nothing else. 'Come now,' I suppose someone will say, 'do you expect that men should learn spinning the same as women, and that women should take part in gymnastic exercises the same as men?' No, that I should not demand. But I do say that, since in the human race man's constitution is stronger and woman's weaker, tasks should be assigned which are suited to the nature of each; that is the heavier tasks should be given to the stronger and lighter ones to the weaker. Thus spinning and indoor work would be more fitting for women than for men, while gymnastics and outdoor work would be more suitable for men. Occasionally, however, some men might more fittingly handle certain of the lighter tasks and what is generally considered women's work, and again, women might do heavier tasks which seem more appropriate for men whenever conditions of strength, need or circumstance warranted. For all human tasks, I am inclined to believe, are a common obligation and are common for men and women, and none is necessarily appointed for either one exclusively, but some pursuits are more suited to the nature of one, some to the other, and for this reason some are called men's work and some women's. But whatever things have reference to virtue, these one would properly say are equally appropriate to the nature of both, inasmuch as we agree that virtues are in no respect more fitting for the one than the other. Hence I hold it reasonable that the things which have reference to virtue ought to be taught to male and female alike; and furthermore that straight from infancy they ought to be taught that this is right and that is wrong, and that it is the same for both

alike; that this is helpful, that is harmful, that one must do this, one must not do that. From this training understanding is developed in those who learn, boys and girls alike, with no difference. Then they must be inspired with a feeling of shame toward all that is base. When these two qualities have been created within them, man and woman are of necessity self-controlled. And most of all the child who is trained properly, whether boy or girl, must be accustomed to endure hardship, not to fear death, not to be disheartened in the face of any misfortune; he must in short be accustomed to every situation which calls for courage. Now courage, it was demonstrated above, should be present in women too. Furthermore to shun selfishness and to have high regard for fairness and, being a human being, to wish to help and to be unwilling to harm one's fellow men is the noblest lesson, and it makes those who learn it just. What reason is there why it is more appropriate for a man to learn this? Certainly if it is fitting for women to be just, it is necessary for both to learn the same lessons which are in the highest degree appropriate to the character of each and supremely important. If it happens that a man knows a little something about a certain skill and a woman not, or again she knows something and he not, that suggests no difference in the education of either. But about the all-important things let not one know and the other not, but let them know the same things. If you ask me what doctrine produces such an education, I shall reply that as without philosophy no man would be properly educated, so no woman would be. I do not mean that women should possess technical skill and acuteness in argument. It would be quite superfluous, since they will use philosophy for the ends of their life as women. Even in men I do not prize this accomplishment too highly. I only urge that they should acquire from philosophy goodness in conduct and nobility of character. Now in very truth philosophy is training in nobility of character and nothing else.

32   What Do Women Want in a Moral Theory?

Annette C. Baier

When I finished reading Carol Gilligan's *In a Different Voice*," I asked myself the obvious question for a philosopher reader, namely what differences one should expect in the moral philosophy done by women, supposing Gilligan's sample of women representative, and supposing her analysis of their moral attitudes and moral development to be correct. Should one expect them to want to produce moral theories, and if so, what sort of moral theories? How will any moral theories they produce differ from those produced by men?

Obviously one does not have to make this an entirely a priori and hypothetical question. One can look and see what sort of contributions women have made to moral philosophy. Such a look confirms, I think, Gilligan's findings. What one finds *is* a bit different in tone and approach from the standard sort of moral philosophy as done by men following in the footsteps of the great moral philosophers (all men). Generalizations are extremely rash, but when I think of Philippa Foot's work on the moral virtues, of Elizabeth Anscombe's work on intention and on modern moral philosophy, of Iris Murdoch's philosophical writings, of Ruth Barcan Marcus' work on moral dilemmas, of the work of the radical feminist moral philosophers who are not content with orthodox Marxist lines of thought, of Jenny Teichman's book on Illegitimacy, of Susan Wolf's recent articles, of Claudia Card's essay on mercy, Sabina Lovilbond's recent book, Gabriele Taylor's work on pride, love and on integrity, Cora Diamond's and Mary Midgeley's work on our attitude to animals, Sissela Bok's work on lying and on secrecy, Virginia Held's work, the work of Alison Jaggar, Marilyn Frye, and many

others, I seem to hear a different voice from the standard moral philosopher's voice. I hear the voice Gilligan heard, made reflective and philosophical. What women want in moral philosophy is what they are providing. And what they are providing seems to me to confirm Gilligan's theses about women. One has to be careful here, of course, for not all important contributions to moral philosophy by women fall easily into the Gilligan stereotype, nor its philosophical extension. Nor has it been only women who recently have been proclaiming discontent with the standard approach in moral philosophy, and trying new approaches. Michael Stocker, Alasdair MacIntyre, Ian Hacking when he assesses the game-theoretic approach to morality,[1] all should be given the status of honorary women, if we accept the hypothesis that there are some moral insights which for whatever reason women seem to attain more easily or more reliably than men do. Still, exceptions confirm the rule, so I shall proceed undaunted by these important exceptions to my generalizations.

If Hacking is right, preoccupation with prisoners' dilemma is a big boys' game, and a pretty silly one too. It is, I think, significant that women have not rushed into the field of game-theoretic moral philosophy, and that those who have dared enter that male locker room have said distinctive things there. Edna Ullman Margalit's book *The Emergence of Norms* put prisoners' dilemma in its limited moral place. Supposing that at least part of the explanation for the relatively few women in this field is disinclination rather than disability, one might ask if this disinclination also extends to a disinclination for the construction of moral theories. For although we find out what sort of moral philosophy women want by looking to see what they have provided, if we do that for moral theory, the answer we get seems to be

From *Noûs*, vol. 19 (1985), pp. 53–63. Reprinted by permission.

"none." For none of the contributions to moral philosophy by women really count as moral theories, nor are seen as such by their authors.

Is it that reflective women, when they become philosophers, want to do without moral theory, want no part in the construction of such theories? To conclude this at this early stage, when we have only a few generations of women moral philosophers to judge from, would be rash indeed. The term "theory" can be used in wider and narrower ways, and in its widest sense a moral theory is simply an internally consistent fairly comprehensive account of what morality is and when and why it merits our acceptance and support. In that wide sense, a moral theory is something it would take a skeptic, or one who believes that our intellectual vision is necessarily blurred or distorted when we let it try to take in too much, to be an anti-theorist. Even if there were some truth in the latter claim, one might compatibly with it still hope to build up a coherent total account by a mosaic method, assembling a lot of smaller-scale works until one had built up a complete account – say taking the virtues or purported virtues one by one until one had a more or less complete account. But would that sort of comprehensiveness in one's moral philosophy entitle one to call the finished work a moral theory? If it does, then many women moral philosophers today can be seen as engaged in moral theory construction. In the weakest sense of "theory," namely coherent near-comprehensive account, then there are plenty of incomplete theories to be found in the works of women moral philosophers. And in *that* sense of theory, most of what are recognized as the current moral theories are also incomplete, since they do not purport to be yet really comprehensive. Wrongs to animals and wrongful destruction of our physical environment are put to one side by Rawls, and in most "liberal" theories there are only hand waves concerning our proper attitude to our children, to the ill, to our relatives, friends and lovers.

Is comprehensiveness too much to ask of a moral theory? The paradigm examples of moral theories – those that are called by their authors "moral theories," are distinguished not by the comprehensiveness of their internally coherent account, but by the sort of coherence which is aimed at over a fairly broad area. Their method is not the mosaic method, but the broad brushstroke method. Moral theories, as we know them, are, to change the art form, vaults rather than walls – they are not built by assembling painstakingly-made brick after brick. In *this* sense of theory, namely a fairly tightly systematic account of a fairly large area of morality, with a key stone supporting all the rest, women moral philosophers have not yet, to my knowledge, produced moral theories, nor claimed that they have.

Leaving to one side the question of what good purpose (other than good clean intellectual fun) is served by such moral theories, and supposing for the sake of argument that women can, if they wish, systematize as well as the next man, and if need be systematize in a mathematical fashion as well as the next mathematically minded moral philosopher, then what key concept, or guiding *motif*, might hold together the structure of a moral theory hypothetically produced by a reflective woman, Gilligan-style, who has taken up moral theorizing as a calling? What would be a suitable central question, principle, or concept, to structure a moral theory which might accommodate those moral insights women tend to have more readily than men, and to answer those moral questions which, it seems, worry women more than men? I hypothesized that the women's theory, expressive mainly of women's insights and concerns, would be an ethics of love, and this hypothesis seems to be Gilligan's too, since she has gone on from *In a Different Voice* to write about the limitations of Freud's understanding of love as women know it.[2] But presumably women theorists will be like enough to men to want their moral theory to be acceptable to all, so acceptable both to reflective women and to reflective men. Like any good theory, it will need not to ignore the partial truth of previous theories. So it must accommodate both the insights men have more easily than women, and those women have more easily than men. It should swallow up its predecessor theories. Women moral theorists, if any, will have this very great advantage over the men whose theories theirs supplant, that they can stand on the shoulders of men moral theorists, as no man has yet been able to stand on the shoulders of any woman moral theorist. There can be advantages, as well as handicaps, in being latecomers. So women theorists will need to connect their ethics of love with what has been the men theorists' preoccupation, namely obligation.

The great and influential moral theorists have in the modern era taken *obligation* as the key and the problematic concept, and have asked what justifies treating a person as morally bound or obliged to do a particular thing. Since to be bound is to be unfree, by making obligation central one at the same time makes central the question of the justification of coercion, of forcing or trying to force someone to act in a particular way. The concept of obligation as justified limitation of freedom does just what one wants a good theoretical concept to do – to divide up the field (as one looks at different ways one's freedom may be limited, freedom in different spheres, different sorts and versions and levels of justification) and at the same time hold the subfields together. There must in a theory be some generalization and some specification or diversification, and a good rich key concept guides on both in recognizing the diversity and in recognizing the unity in it. The concept of obligation has served this function very well for the area of morality it covers, and so we have some fine theories about that area. But as Aristotelians and Christians, as well as women, know, there is a lot of morality *not* covered by that concept, a lot of very great importance even for the area where there are obligations.

[In the next section, omitted here, I discuss responsibility for forming new members of the moral community to be capable of taking obligations seriously, and also discuss military duties. I attempt to show that current theories of obligation, especially contractarian ones, fail to yield conclusions compatible with their own principles on who is to do the ruthless human destruction and the loving human reproduction we depend on having done, so these theories are at best incomplete and at worst incoherent or in bad faith.]

Granted that the men's theories of obligation need supplementation, to have much chance of integrity and coherence, and that the women's hypothetical theories will want to cover obligation as well as love, then what concept brings them together? My tentative answer is – the concept of appropriate trust, oddly neglected in moral theory. This concept also nicely mediates between reason and feeling, those tired old candidates for moral authority, since to trust is neither quite to believe something about the trusted, nor necessarily to feel any emotion towards them – but to have a belief-informed and action-influencing attitude. To make it plausible that the neglected concept of appropriate trust is a good one for the enlightened moral theorist to make central, I need to show, or begin to show, how it could include obligation, indeed shed light on obligations and their justification, as well as include love and the other moral concerns of Gilligan's women, and many of the topics women moral philosophers have chosen to address, mosaic fashion. I would also need to show that it could connect all of these in a way which holds out promise both of synthesis and of comprehensive moral coverage. A moral theory which looked at the conditions for proper trust of all the various sorts we show, and at what sorts of reasons justify inviting such trust, giving it, and meeting it, would, I believe, not have to avoid turning its gaze on the conditions for the survival of the practices it endorses, so it could avoid that unpleasant choice many current liberal theories seem to have – between incoherence and bad faith. I do not pretend that we will easily agree once we raise the questions I think we should raise, but at least we may have a language adequate to the expression of both men's and women's moral viewpoints.

My trust in the concept of trust is based in part on my own attempts to restate and consider what was right and what was wrong with men's theories, especially Hume's, which I consider the best of the lot. There I found myself reconstructing his account of the artifices of justice as an account of the progressive enlargement of a climate of trust, and found that a helpful way to see it. It has some textual basis, but is nevertheless a reconstruction, and one I found, immodestly, an improvement. So it is because I have tried the concept, and explored its dimensions a bit – the variety of goods we may trust others not to take from us, the variety of sorts of security or insurance we have when we do, the sorts of defenses or potential defenses we lay down when we trust, the various conditions for reasonable trust of various types – that I am hopeful about its power as a theoretical not just an exegetical tool. I also found myself needing to use it, when I made a brief rash attempt at that women's topic, caring (invited in by a man philosopher,[3] I should say). That it does generalize some central moral features both of the recognition of binding obligations and moral virtues, and of loving, as well as of other important relations between persons, such as teacher–pupil, confider–confidante, worker to co-worker in the same cause, professional to client, I am reasonably sure. Indeed it is fairly obvious that love, the main moral phenomenon women want attended to, involves trust, so I anticipate little quarrel when I claim that, if we had a moral theory spelling out the conditions for appropriate trust and distrust, that would include a morality of love in all its variants – parental love, love of children for their parents, love of family members, love of friends, of lovers in the strict sense, of co-workers, of one's country, and its figureheads, of exemplary heroines and heroes, of goddesses and gods.

Love and loyalty demand maximal trust of one sort, and maximal trustworthiness, and in investigating the conditions for maximal trust and maximal risk we must think about the ethics of love. More controversial may be my claim that the ethics of obligation will also be covered. I see it as covered since to recognize a set of obligations is to trust some group of persons to instill them, to demand that they be met, possibly to levy sanctions if they are not, and this is to trust persons with very significant coercive power over others. Less coercive but still significant power is possessed by those shaping our conception of the virtues, and expecting us to display them, approving when we do, disapproving and perhaps shunning us when we do not. Such coercive and manipulative power over others requires justification, and is justified only if we have reason to trust those who have it to use it properly, and to use the discretion which is always given when trust is given in a way which serves the purpose of the whole system of moral control, and not merely self-serving or morally improper purposes. Since the question of the justification of coercion becomes, at least in part, the question of the wisdom of trusting the coercers to do their job properly, the morality of obligation, in as far as it reduces to the morality of coercion, is covered by the morality of proper trust. Other forms of trust may also be involved, but trusting enforcers with the use of force is the most problematic form of trust involved.

The coercers and manipulators are, to some extent, all of us, so to ask what our obligations are and what virtues we should exhibit is to ask what it is reasonable to trust us to demand, expect, and contrive to get, from one another. It becomes, in part, a question of what powers we can in reason trust ourselves to exercise properly. But self-trust is a dubious or limited case of trust, so I prefer to postpone the examination of the concept of proper self-trust at least until proper trust of others is more clearly understood. Nor do we distort matters too much if we concentrate on those cases where moral sanctions and moral pressure and moral manipulation is not self-applied but applied to others, particularly by older persons to younger persons. Most moral pressuring that has any effects goes on in childhood and early youth. Moral sanctions may continue to be applied, formally and informally, to adults, but unless the criminal courts apply them it is easy enough for adults to ignore them, to brush them aside. It is not difficult to become a sensible knave, and to harden one's heart so that one is insensible to the moral condemnation of one's victims and those who sympathize with them. Only if the pressures applied in the morally formative stage have given one a heart that rebels against the thought of such ruthless independence of what others think will one see any reason *not* to ignore moral condemnation, not to treat it as mere powerless words and breath. Condemning sensible knaves is as much a waste of breath as arguing with them – all we can sensibly do is to try to protect their children against their influence, and ourselves against their knavery. Adding to the criminal law will not be the way to do the latter, since such moves will merely challenge sensible knaves to find new knavish exceptions and loopholes, not protect us from sensible knavery. Sensible knaves are precisely those who exploit us without breaking the law. So the whole question of when moral pressure of various sorts, formative, reformative, and punitive, ought to be brought to bear by whom is subsumed under the question of whom to trust when and with what, and for what good reasons.

In concentrating on obligations, rather than virtues, modern moral theorists have chosen to look at the cases where more trust is placed in enforcers of obligations than is placed in ordinary moral agents, the bearers of the obligations. In taking, as contractarians do, contractual obligations as the model of obligations, they concentrate on a case where the very minimal trust is put in the obligated person, and considerable punitive power entrusted to the one to whom the obligation is owed (I assume here that Hume is right in saying that when we promise or contract, we formally subject ourselves to the penalty, in case of failure, of never being trusted as a promisor again). This is an interesting case of the allocation of trust of various sorts, but it surely distorts our moral vision to suppose that *all* obligations, let alone all morally pressured expectations we impose on others, conform to that abnormally coercive model. It takes very special conditions for it to be safe to trust persons to inflict penalties on other persons, conditions in which either we can trust the penalizers to have the virtues necessary to penalize wisely and fairly, or else we can rely on effective threats to keep unvirtuous penalizers from abusing their power – that is to say, rely on others to coerce the first coercers into proper behavior. But that reliance too will either be trust, or will have to rely on threats from coercers of the coercers of coercers, and so on. Morality on this model becomes a nasty, if intellectually intriguing, game of mutual mutually corrective threats. The central question of who should deprive whom of what freedom soon becomes the question of whose anger should be dreaded by whom (the theory of obligation) supplemented perhaps by an afterthought on whose favor should be courted by whom (the theory of the virtues).

Undoubtedly some important part of morality does depend in part on a system of threats and bribes, at least for its survival in difficult conditions when normal goodwill and normally virtuous dispositions may be insufficient to motivate the conduct required for the preservation and justice of the moral network of relationships. But equally undoubtedly life will be nasty, emotionally poor, and worse than brutish (even if longer), if that is all morality is, or even if that coercive structure of morality is regarded as the backbone, rather than as an available crutch, should the main support fail. For the main support has to come from those we entrust with the job of rearing and training persons so that they can be trusted in various ways, some trusted with extraordinary coercive powers, some with public decision-making powers, all trusted as parties to promise, most trusted by some who love them and by one or more willing to become co-parents with them, most trusted by dependent children, dependent elderly relatives, sick friends, and so on. A very complex network of a great variety of sorts of trust structures our moral relationships with our fellows, and if there is a *main* support to this network it is the trust we place in those who respond to the trust of new members of the moral community, namely to children, and prepare them for new forms of trust.

A theory which took as its central question "Who should trust whom with what, and why?" would not have to forgo the intellectual fun and games previous theorists have had with the various paradoxes of morality – curbing freedom to increase freedom, curbing self-interest the better to satisfy self-interest, not aiming at happiness in order to become happier. For it is easy enough to get a paradox of trust, to accompany or, if I am right, to generalize the paradoxes of freedom, self-interest and hedonism. To trust is to make oneself or let oneself be more vulnerable than one might have been to harm from others – to give them an opportunity to harm one, in the confidence that they will not take it, because they have no good reason to.[4] Why would one take such a risk? For risk it always is, given the partial opaqueness to us of the reasoning and motivation of those we trust and with whom we cooperate. Our confidence may be, and quite often is, misplaced. That is what we risk when we trust. If the best reason to take such a risk is the expected gain in security which comes from a climate of trust, then in trusting we are always giving up security to get greater security, exposing our throats so that others become accustomed to not biting. A moral theory which made proper trust its central concern could have its own categorical imperative, could replace obedience to self-made laws and freely-chosen restraint on freedom with security-increasing sacrifice of security, distrust in the promoters of a climate of distrust, and so on.

Such reflexive use of one's central concept, negative or affirmative, is an intellectually satisfying activity which is bound to have appeal to those system-lovers who want to construct moral theories, and it may help them design their theory in an intellectually pleasing manner. But we should beware of becoming hypnotized by our slogans, or of sacrificing truth to intellectual elegance. Any theory of proper trust should not *prejudge* the questions of when distrust is proper. We might find more objects of proper distrust than just the contributors to a climate of reasonable distrust, just as freedom should be restricted not just to increase human freedom but to protect human life from poisoners and other killers. I suspect, however, that all the objects of reasonable distrust are more reasonably seen as falling into the category of ones who contribute to a decrease in the scope of proper trust, than can all who are reasonably coerced be seen as themselves guilty of wrongful coercion. Still, even if all proper trust turns out to be for such persons and on such matters as will increase the scope or stability of a climate of reasonable trust, and all proper distrust for such persons and on such matters as increase the scope of reasonable distrust, overreliance on such nice reflective formulae can distract us from asking all the questions about trust which need to be asked, if an ad-

equate moral theory is to be constructed around that concept. These questions should include when to *respond* to trust with *un*trustworthiness, when and when not to invite trust, as well as when to give and refuse trust. We should not assume that promiscuous trustworthiness is any more a virtue than is undiscriminating distrust. It is appropriate trustworthiness, appropriate trustingness, appropriate encouragement to trust, which will be virtues, as will be judicious untrustworthiness, selective refusal to trust, discriminating discouragement of trust.

Women are particularly well placed to appreciate these last virtues, since they have sometimes needed them to get into a position to even consider becoming moral theorizers. The long exploitation and domination of women by men depended on men's trust in women and women's trustworthiness to play their allotted role and so to perpetuate their own and their daughters' servitude. However keen women now are to end the lovelessness of modern moral philosophy, they are unlikely to lose sight of the cautious virtue of appropriate distrust, or of the tough virtue of principled betrayal of the exploiters' trust.

Gilligan's girls and women saw morality as a matter of preserving valued ties to others, of preserving the conditions for that care and mutual care without which human life becomes bleak, lonely, and after a while, as the mature men in her study found, not self-affirming, however successful in achieving the egoistic goals which had been set. The boys and men saw morality as a matter of finding workable traffic rules for self-assertors, so that they not needlessly frustrate one another, and so that they could, should they so choose, cooperate in more positive ways to mutual advantage. Both for the women's sometimes unchosen and valued ties with others, and for the men's mutual respect as sovereigns and subjects of the same minimal moral traffic rules (and for their more voluntary and more selective associations of profiteers) trust is important. Both men and women are concerned with cooperation, and the dimensions of trust-distrust structure the different cooperative relations each emphasize. The various considerations which arise when we try to defend an answer to any question about the appropriateness of a particular form of cooperation with its distinctive form of trust or distrust, that is when we look into the terms of all sorts of cooperation, at the terms of trust in different cases of trust, at what are fair terms and what are trust-enhancing and trust-preserving terms are suitably many and richly interconnected. A moral theory (or family of theories) that made trust its central problem could do better justice to men's and women's moral intuitions than do the going men's theories. Even if we don't easily agree on the answer to the question of who should trust whom with what, who should accept and who should meet various sorts of trust, and why, these questions might enable us better to morally reason together than we can when the central moral questions are reduced to those of whose favor one must court and whose anger one must dread. But such programmatic claims as I am making will be tested only when women standing on the shoulders of men, or

men on the shoulders of women, or some theorizing Tiresias, actually work out such a theory. I am no Tiresias, and have not foresuffered all the labor pains of such a theory. I aim here only to fertilize.

Notes

1 Ian Hacking, "Winner Take Less," a review of *The Evolution of Cooperation* by Robert Axelrod, *New York Review of Books*, vol. XXX, no. 11 (June 28, 1984).

2 Carol Gilligan, "The Conquistador and the Dark Continent: Reflections on the Psychology of Love," *Daedalus*, Summer 1984.

3 "Caring About Caring," a response to Harry Frankfurt's "The Importance of What We Care About," both in *Matters of the Mind, Synthese*, vol. 53, no. 2 (November 1982), pp. 257–90. My paper will also be included in *Postures of the Mind*, University of Minnesota Press (1985).

4 I defend this claim about trust in "Trust and Anti-trust," *Ethics* (1986).

---

33   Feminist Transformations of Moral Theory

Virginia Held

If we turn to the history of philosophy, including the history of ethics, we can see that it has been constructed from male points of view and has been built on assumptions and concepts that are by no means gender-neutral.[1] Lorraine Code points out the significance of the way feminists characteristically begin with different concerns and give different emphases to the issues we consider: "Starting points and focal points shape the impact of theoretical discussion."[2] Far from merely providing additional insights that can be incorporated into traditional theory, feminist

From *Philosophy and Phenomenological Research*, 50 (1990), pp. 321–44. Reprinted with permission.

explorations often require radical transformations of existing fields of inquiry and theory.[3] From a feminist point of view, moral theory, along with almost all theory, will have to be transformed to take adequate account of the experience of women.

Bias in the History of Ethics

Consider the ideals embodied in the phrase "the man of reason." As Genevieve Lloyd has told the story, what has been taken to characterize the man of reason may have changed from historical period to historical period, but in each, the character ideal of the man of reason has been constructed in conjunction with a rejection of whatever has been taken to be characteristic of the feminine. "Rationality," Lloyd writes, "has been conceived as transcendence of the 'feminine,' and the 'feminine' itself has been partly constituted by its occurrence within this structure."[4]

This has, of course, fundamentally affected the history of philosophy and of ethics. The split between reason and emotion is one of the most familiar of philosophical conceptions. The advocacy of reason "controlling" unruly emotion, of rationality guiding responsible human action against the blindness of passion, has a long and highly influential history, almost as familiar to non-philosophers as to philosophers. Lloyd sums it up:

> From the beginnings of philosophical thought, femaleness was symbolically associated with what Reason supposedly left behind – the dark powers of the earth goddesses, immersion in unknown forces associated with mysterious female powers. The early Greeks saw women's capacity to conceive as connecting them with the fertility of Nature. As Plato later expressed the thought, women "imitate the earth."[5]

In asserting its claims and winning its status in human history, Reason was thought to have to conquer the female forces of Unreason. Reason and clarity of thought were early associated with maleness, and as Lloyd says, "What had to be shed in developing culturally prized rationality was, from the start, symbolically associated with femaleness." In later Greek philosophical thought, the form/matter distinction was articulated with a similar hierarchical and gendered association. Maleness was aligned with active, determinate, and defining form; femaleness with mere passive, indeterminate, and inferior matter. Plato, in the *Timaeus*, compared the defining aspect of form with the father, and indefinite matter with the mother; Aristotle also compared the form/matter distinction with the male/female distinction. To quote Lloyd again, "This comparison . . . meant that the very nature of knowledge was implicitly associated with the ex-

trusion of what was symbolically associated with the feminine."[6]

The associations among Reason, form, knowledge, and maleness have persisted in various guises and have permeated what has been thought to be moral knowledge as well as what has been thought to be scientific knowledge and what has been thought to be the practice of morality. The associations between the philosophical concepts and gender cannot be merely dropped and the concepts retained regardless of gender, because gender has been built into them in such a way that without it, they will have to be different concepts. As feminists repeatedly show, if the concept of "human" were built on what we think about "woman" rather than what we think about "man," it would be a very different concept. Ethics, thus, has not been a search for universal, or truly human guidance, but a gender-biased enterprise.

Other distinctions and associations have supplemented and reinforced the identification of reason with maleness, and of the irrational with the female; on this and other grounds "man" has been associated with the human, "woman" with the natural. Prominent among distinctions reinforcing the latter view has been that between the public and the private. Again, these provide as familiar and entrenched a framework as do reason and emotion, and they have been as influential for non-philosophers as for philosophers. It has been supposed that in the public realm man transcends his animal nature and creates human history. As citizen, he creates government and law; as warrior, he protects society by his willingness to risk death; and as artist or philosopher, he overcomes his human mortality. Here, in the public realm, morality should guide human decisions. In the household, in contrast, it has been supposed that women merely "reproduce" life as natural, biological matter. Within the household, the "natural" needs of man for food and shelter are served, and new instances of the biological creature that man is are brought into being. But what is distinctively human and what transcends any given level of development to create human progress have been thought to occur elsewhere.

This contrast was made explicit in Aristotle's conceptions of polls and household; it has continued to affect the basic assumptions of a remarkably broad swath of thought ever since. In ancient Athens, women were confined to the household; the public sphere was literally a male domain. The associations of the public, historically male sphere with the distinctively human, and of the household, historically a female sphere, with the merely natural and repetitious, have persisted, even though women have been permitted to venture into public space. These associations have deeply affected moral theory, which has often supposed the transcendent, public domain to be relevant to the foundations of morality in ways that the natural behavior of women in the household could not be.

To take some representative examples, David Heyd, in his discussion of supererogation, dismisses a mother's sacrifice for her child as an example of the supererogatory because it belongs, in his view, to "the sphere of natural relationships and instinctive feelings (which lie outside morality)."[7] J. O. Urmson had earlier taken a similar position, saying, "Let us be clear that we are not now considering cases of natural affection, such as the sacrifice made by a mother for her child; such cases may be said with some justice *not to fall under the concept of morality*" (emphasis added).[8] And in his article "Distrusting Economics," Alan Ryan argues persuasively about the questionableness of economics and other branches of the social sciences built on the assumption that human beings are rational, self-interested calculators. He discusses various examples of behavior, such as that of men in wartime, which is not self-interested and which shows the assumption to be false; but nowhere in the article is there any mention of the activity of mothering, which would seem to be a fertile locus for doubts about the usual picture of rational man.[9] Although Ryan does not provide the kind of explicit reason offered by Heyd and Urmson for omitting mothering from consideration as relevant to his discussion, it is difficult to understand the omission without a comparable assumption being implicit here, as it so often is elsewhere. Without feminist insistence on the relevance for morality of the experience in mothering, this context is largely ignored by moral theorists. And yet from a gender-neutral point of view, how can this vast and fundamental domain of human experience possibly be imagined to lie "outside morality"?

The result of the distinction between public and private, as usually formulated, has been to privilege the points of view of men in the public domains of state and law, and later in the marketplace, and to discount the experience of women. Mothering has been conceptualized as a primarily biological activity, even when performed by human beings, and virtually no moral theory in the history of ethics has taken mothering, as experienced by women, seriously as a source of moral insight, until feminists in recent years began to.[10] Women have been seen as emotional rather than rational beings, and thus incapable of full moral personhood. Women's behavior has been interpreted as either "natural" and driven by instinct, and thus as irrelevant to morality and to the construction of moral principles, or it has been interpreted, at best, as in need of instruction and supervision by males better able to know what morality requires and better able to live up to its demands.

The Hobbesian conception of reason is very different from the Platonic or Aristotelian conceptions before it and from the conceptions of Rousseau or Kant or Hegel later; all have in common the habit of ignoring and disparaging the experience and reality of women. Consider Hobbes's account of man in the state of nature contracting with other men to establish society. These men hypothetically come into existence fully formed and independent of one another, and decide either to enter civil society or stay outside of it. As Christine Di Stefano writes, "What we find in Hobbes's account is a vital concern with the survival of a gendered subject conceived in modern masculine terms. . . . In the state of nature, Hobbes's masculine egoism carries the day . . . the specifically gendered dimension of this egoism is underscored by a radical atomism erected on the denial of maternity."[11]

In *The Citizen*, where Hobbes gave his first systematic exposition of the state of nature, he asks us to "consider men as if but even now sprung out of the earth, and suddenly, like mushrooms, come to full maturity, without all kind of engagement with each other."[12] Di Stefano points out that it is an incredible feature of Hobbes's state of nature that the men in it "are not born of, much less nurtured by, women, or anyone else" and that to abstract from the complex web of human reality an abstract man for rational perusal, Hobbes has "expunged human reproduction and early nurturance from his account of basic human nature and primordial human relations. Such a descriptive strategy ensures that Hobbes can present a thoroughly atomistic subject."[13]

From the point of view of women's experience, such a subject or self is unbelievable and misleading, even as a theoretical construct. The manmade political Leviathan Hobbes erects on these foundations "is effectively composed," Di Stefano writes, "of a body politic of social orphans who have socially acculturated themselves." Hence, Hobbesian man "bears the tell-tale signs of a modern masculinity in extremis: identity through opposition, denial of reciprocity, repudiation of the (m)other in oneself and in relation to oneself."[14]

Rousseau and Kant and Hegel paid homage respectively to the emotional power, the aesthetic sensibility, and the familial concerns of women. But since in their views morality must be based on rational principle and since women were incapable of full rationality, or a degree or kind of rationality comparable to that of men, women were deemed to be inherently wanting in morality. For Rousseau, women must be trained from childhood to submit to the will of men lest their sexual power lead both men and women to disaster. For Kant, women were thought incapable of achieving full moral personhood, and women lose all charm if they try to behave like men by engaging in rational pursuits. For Hegel, women's moral concern for our families could be admirable in its proper place, but it is a threat to the more universal aims to which men, as members of the state, should aspire.[15]

These images of the feminine as what must be overcome if knowledge and morality are to be achieved, of female experience as naturally irrelevant to morality, and of women as inherently deficient moral creatures are all built into the history of ethics. Examining these images, feminists find that they are not the incidental or merely idiosyncratic suppositions of a few philosophers whose views on many topics depart far from the ordinary anyway; they are the nearly uniform reflection in philosophical and ethical theory of patriarchal attitudes pervasive throughout human history. Or they are exaggerations of ordinary male experience, which exaggerations then reinforce rather than temper other conceptions and institutions reflective of male domination. At any rate, they distort the actual experience of many men as well as women. Annette Baier has speculated why it is that moral philosophy has so seriously overlooked the trust among human beings that in her view is an utterly central aspect of moral life. "The great moral theorists in our tradition," she says, "not only are all men, they are mostly men who had minimal adult dealings with (and so were then minimally influenced by) women." For the most part they were "clerics, misogynists, and puritan bachelors," and thus it is not surprising that they focus their philosophical attention "so single-mindedly on cool, distanced relations between more or less free and equal adult strangers."[16]

As feminists, we deplore the male domination that so much of philosophy and moral theory reflect. But we recognize that the problem requires more than changing patriarchal attitudes, for moral theory as so far developed is incapable of correcting itself without almost total transformation. It cannot simply absorb the gender that has been "left behind," even if both genders want it to. To continue to build morality on rational principles opposed to the emotions and to include women among the rational will leave no one to reflect the promptings of the heart, which promptings can be moral rather than merely instinctive. To simply bring women into the public and male domain of the polls will leave no one to speak for the household. Its values have been hitherto unrecognized, but they are often moral values. Or to continue to seek contractual restraints on the pursuits of self-interest by atomistic individuals and to have women join men in devotion to these pursuits will leave no one involved in the nurturance of children and cultivation of social relations, which nurturance and cultivation can be of the greatest moral import.

There are very good reasons for women not to want simply to be accorded entry as equals into the enterprise of morality as so far developed. In a recent survey of types of feminist moral theory, Kathryn Morgan laments that "many women who engage in philosophical reflection are acutely aware of the masculine nature of the profession and tradition, and feel their own moral concerns as women silenced or trivialized in virtually all the official settings that define the practice."[17] Clearly women should not agree, as the price of admission to the masculine realm of traditional morality, to abandon our own moral concerns as women.

And so we are trying to shape new moral theory. Understandably, we are not yet ready to offer fully developed feminist moral theories. But we can suggest some directions our project is taking. As Morgan points out, there is not likely to be a "star" feminist moral theorist on the order of a Rawls or a Nozick:

> There will be no individual singled out for two reasons. One reason is that vital moral and theoretical conversations are taking place on a large dialectical scale as the feminist community struggles to develop a feminist ethic. The second reason is that this community of feminist theoreticians is calling into question the very model of the individualized autonomous self presupposed by a star-centered male-dominated tradition. . . . We experience it as a common labour, a common task.[18]

Promising dialogues are proceeding on feminist approaches to moral theory. As Alison Jaggar makes clear in her useful overview, there is no unitary view of ethics that can be identified as "feminist ethics." Feminist approaches to ethics share a commitment to "rethinking ethics with a view to correcting whatever forms of male bias it may contain." While those who develop these approaches are "united by a shared project, they diverge widely in their view as to how this project is to be accomplished."[19]

Not all feminists, by any means, agree that there are distinctive feminist virtues or values. Some are especially skeptical of the attempt to give positive value to such traditional "feminine virtues" as a willingness to nurture, or an affinity with caring, or reluctance to seek independence. They see this approach as playing into the hands of those who would confine women to traditional roles.[20] Other feminists are skeptical of all claims about women as such, emphasizing that women are divided by class and race and sexual orientation in ways that make any conclusions drawn from "women's experience" dubious.[21]

Still, it is possible, I think, to discern some focal points in current feminist attempts to transform ethics into an acceptable theoretical and practical activity. In the glimpse I have presented of bias in the history of ethics, I focused on what, from a feminist point of view, are three of its most questionable aspects: the split between reason and emotion and the devaluation of emotion; the public/private distinction and the relegation of the private to the natural; and the concept of the self as constructed from a male point of view. In the remainder of this chapter, I will examine further how some feminists are exploring these topics. We are showing that previous treatment of them has been distorted, and we are trying to re-envision the realities and recommendations with which these aspects of moral theorizing should deal.

Reason and Emotion

In the area of moral theory in the modern era, the priority accorded to reason has taken two major forms. On the one hand has been the Kantian, or Kantian-inspired, search for very general, abstract, deontological, universal moral principles by which rational beings should be guided. Kant's Categorical Imperative is a prime example. It suggests that all moral problems can be handled by applying an impartial, pure, rational principle to particular cases. It requires that we try to see what the general features of the problem before us are and that we apply to the problem an abstract principle or rules derivable from it. This procedure, it is said, should be adequate for all moral decisions. We should thus be able to act as reason recommends, and resist yielding to emotional inclinations and desires in conflict with our rational wills.

On the other hand, the priority accorded to reason in the modern era has taken a Utilitarian form. The Utilitarian approach, reflected in rational choice theory, recognizes that persons have desires and interests, and suggests rules of rational choice for maximizing the satisfaction of these desires and interests. While some philosophers in the tradition espouse egoism, especially of an intelligent and long-term kind, many do not. They begin, however, with assumptions that what is morally relevant are the gains and losses of utility to theoretically isolable individuals and that morality should aim to maximize the satisfaction of individuals. Rational calculation about such an outcome will, in this view, provide moral recommendations to guide all our choices. Like the Kantian approach, the utilitarian approach relies on abstract general principles or rules to be applied to particular cases. And it holds that although emotion is, in fact, the source of our desires for certain objectives, the task of morality should be to instruct us on how to pursue those objectives most rationally. Emotional attitudes toward moral issues themselves interfere with rationality and should be disregarded.

Although the conceptions of what the judgments of morality should be based on and how reason should guide moral decision are different in Kantian and utilitarian approaches, they share a reliance on a highly abstract, universal principle as the appropriate source of moral guidance, and they share the view that moral problems are to be solved by the application of such an abstract principle to particular cases. Both admire the rules of reason to be appealed to in moral contexts, and both denigrate emotional responses to moral issues.

Many feminist philosophers have questioned whether the reliance on abstract rules, rather than the adoption of more context-respectful approaches, can possibly be adequate for dealing with moral problems, especially as women experience them. Though Kantians may hold that

complex rules can be elaborated for specific contexts, there is nevertheless an assumption in this approach that the more abstract the reasoning applied to a moral problem, the more satisfactory. And utilitarians suppose that one highly abstract principle, the Principle of Utility, can be applied to every moral problem no matter what the context.

A genuinely universal or gender-neutral moral theory would be one that would take account of the experience and concerns of women as fully as it would take account of the experience and concerns of men. When we focus on women's experience of moral problems, however, we find that they are especially concerned with actual relationships between embodied persons and with what these relationships seem to require. Women are often inclined to attend to rather than to dismiss the particularities of the context in which a moral problem arises. And we often pay attention to feelings of empathy and caring to help us decide what to do rather than relying as fully as possible on abstract rules of reason.

Margaret Walker, for instance, contrasts feminist moral "understanding" with traditional moral "knowledge." She sees the components of the former as involving "attention, contextual and narrative appreciation, and communication in the event of moral deliberation." This alternative moral epistemology holds that "the adequacy of moral understanding decreases as its form approaches generality through abstraction."[22]

The work of psychologists such as Carol Gilligan has led to a clarification of what may be thought of as tendencies among women to approach moral issues differently from men. Rather than seeking solutions to moral problems by applying abstract rules of justice to particular cases, many of the women studied by Gilligan were concerned with preserving actual human relationships and with expressing care for those for whom they felt responsible. Their moral reasoning was typically more embedded in a context of particular others than was the reasoning of a comparable group of men.[23] One should not equate tendencies women in fact display with feminist views, since the former may well be the result of the sexist, oppressive conditions in which women's lives have been lived. But many feminists see our own consciously considered experience as lending confirmation to such psychological studies.

Feminist philosophers are in the process of re-evaluating the place of emotion in morality in at least two respects. First, many think morality requires the development of the moral emotions, in contrast to moral theories emphasizing the primacy of reason. As Annette Baier observes, the rationalism typical of traditional moral theory will be challenged when we pay attention to the role of parent:

> It might be important for father figures to have rational control over their violent urges to beat to death the children whose screams enrage them, but more than control of such nasty passions seems needed in the mother or primary parent, or parent-substitute, by most psychological theories. They need to love their children, not just to control their irritation.[24]

So the emphasis in traditional theories on rational control over the emotions, rather than on cultivating desirable forms of emotion, is challenged by feminist approaches to ethics.

Second, emotion will be respected rather than dismissed by many feminist moral philosophers in the process of gaining moral understanding. The experience and practice out of which we can expect to develop feminist moral theory will include embodied feeling as well as thought. In an overview of a vast amount of writing, Kathryn Morgan states that "feminist theorists begin ethical theorizing with embodied, gendered subjects who have particular histories, particular communities, particular allegiances, and particular visions of human flourishing. The starting point involves valorizing what has frequently been most mistrusted and despised in the western philosophical tradition."[25] Foremost among the elements being re-evaluated are women's emotions. The "care" of the alternative feminist approach to morality appreciates rather than rejects emotion, and such caring relationships cannot be understood in terms of abstract rules or moral reasoning. And the "weighing" so often needed between the conflicting claims of some relationships and others cannot be settled by deduction or rational calculation. A feminist ethic will not just acknowledge emotion, as do utilitarians, as giving us the objectives toward which moral rationality can direct us; it will embrace emotion as providing at least a partial basis for morality itself and certainly for moral understanding.

Trust is essential for at least some segments of morality.[26] Achieving and maintaining trusting, caring relationships is quite different from acting in accord with rational principles or satisfying the individual desires of either self or other. Caring, empathy, feeling for others, being sensitive to each other's feelings – all may be better guides to what morality requires in actual contexts than may abstract rules of reason or rational calculation.

The fear that a feminist ethic will be a relativistic "situation ethic" is misplaced. Some feelings can be as widely shared as are rational beliefs, and feminists do not see their views as reducible to "just another attitude." In her discussion of the differences between feminist medical ethics and non-feminist medical ethics, Susan Sherwin shows why feminists reject the mere case-by-case approach that prevails in non-feminist medical ethics. This approach also rejects the excessive reliance on abstract rules characteristic of standard ethics, and in this way resembles feminist ethics. But the very focus on cases in isolation rules out attending to general features in the institutions and practices of medicine that, among other faults, systematically contribute to the oppression of women.[27] The difference of approach can be seen in the treatment of issues in the new reproductive technologies that may further decrease the control of women over reproduction.

This difference is not one of substance alone; Sherwin shows its implications for method as well. With respect to reproductive technologies one can see clearly the deficiencies of the case-by-case approach: what needs to be considered is not only choice as seen in the purely individualistic terms of this approach, but control at a more general level and how such control affects the structure of gender in society. Thus, a feminist perspective does not always counsel attention to specific cases versus appeal to general considerations, as some sort of methodological rule. But the general considerations are often not the purely abstract ones of traditional and standard moral theory; they are the general features and judgments to be made about cases in actual (which means, so far, male-dominated) societies. A feminist evaluation of a moral problem should never omit the political elements involved; and it is likely to recognize that political issues cannot be dealt with adequately in purely abstract terms any more than can moral issues.

The liberal tradition in social and moral philosophy argues that in a pluralistic society and even more clearly in a pluralistic world, we cannot agree on our visions of the good life, on what is the best kind of life for human beings, but we can hope to agree on the minimal conditions for justice, for coexistence within a framework allowing us to pursue our visions of the good life.[28] Many feminists contend that the commitment to justice needed for agreement *in actual conditions* on even minimal requirements of justice is as likely to demand relational feelings as a rational recognition of abstract principles. Human beings can and do care – and are capable of caring far more than most do at present – about the suffering of children quite distant from them, about the prospects for future generations, and about the well-being of the globe. The mutually disinterested rational individualists of the liberal tradition would seem unlikely to care enough to take the actions needed to achieve moral decency at a global level, or environmental sanity for decades hence, since they seem unable to represent caring relationships within the family and among friends. Annette Baier puts it thus:

> A moral theory, it can plausibly be claimed, cannot regard concern for new and future persons as an optional charity left for those with a taste for it. If the morality the theory endorses is to sustain itself, it must provide for its own continuers, not just take out a loan on a carefully encouraged maternal instinct or on the enthusiasm of a self-selected group of environmentalists, who make it their business or hobby to be concerned with what we are doing to mother earth.[29]

The possibilities as well as the problems (and we are well aware of some of them) in a feminist re-envisioning of emotion and reason need to be further developed, but we can already see that the views of non-feminist moral theory are unsatisfactory.

The Public and the Private

A second questionable aspect of the history of ethics is its conception of the distinction between the public and the private. As with the split between reason and emotion, feminists are showing how gender bias has distorted previous conceptions of these spheres, and we are trying to offer more appropriate understandings of "private" morality and "public" life.

Feminists reject the implication that what occurs in the household occurs as if on an island beyond politics. In fact, the personal is highly affected by the political power beyond, from legislation about abortion to the greater earning power of men, to the interconnected division of labor by gender both within and beyond the household, to the lack of adequate social protection for women against domestic violence.[30] Of course we recognize that the family is not identical with the state, and we still need concepts for thinking about the private and the personal, the public and the political; but we do know they will have to be very different from the traditional concepts.

Feminists have also criticized deeper assumptions about what is distinctively human and what is "natural" in the public and private aspects of human life, and what is meant by "natural" in connection with women.[31] Consider the associations that have traditionally been built up: the public realm is seen as the distinctively human realm in which man transcends his animal nature, while the private realm of the household is seen as the natural region in which women merely reproduce the species. These associations are extraordinarily pervasive in standard concepts and theories, in art and thought and cultural ideals, and especially in politics. So entrenched is this way of thinking that it was reflected even in

Simone de Beauvoir's pathbreaking feminist text *The Second Sex*, published in 1949.[32] Here, as elsewhere, feminists have had to transcend our own early searches for our own perspectives.

Dominant patterns of thought have seen women as primarily mothers, and mothering as the performance of a primarily biological function. Then it has been supposed that while engaging in political life is a specifically human activity, women are engaged in an activity which is not specifically human. Women accordingly have been thought to be closer to nature than men, to be enmeshed in a biological function involving processes more like those in which other animals are involved than like the rational discussion of the citizen in the polls, or the glorious battles of noble soldiers, or the trading and rational contracting of "economic man."[33] The total or relative exclusion of women from the domain of public life has thus been seen as either fitting or inevitable.

The view that women are more determined by biology than are men is still extraordinarily prevalent. From a feminist perspective it is highly questionable. Human mothering is a far different activity from the mothering engaged in by other animals, as different as the work and speech of men is from what might be thought of as the "work" and "speech" of other animals. Of course all human beings are animal as well as human. But to whatever extent it is appropriate to recognize a difference between "man" and other animals, so is it appropriate to recognize a comparable difference between "woman" and other animals, and between the activities – including mothering – engaged in by women and the behavior of other animals.

Human mothering shapes language and culture, it forms human social personhood, it develops morality. Animal behavior can be highly complex, but it does not have built into it any of the consciously chosen aims of morality. In creating human social persons, human mothering is different in kind from merely propagating a species. And human mothering can be fully as creative an activity as those activities traditionally thought of as distinctively human, because to create *new* persons and new types of *persons* can surely be as creative, as to make new objects, products, or institutions. *Human* mothering is no more "natural" or "primarily biological" than is any human activity.

Consider nursing an infant, often thought of as the epitome of a biological process with which mothering is associated and women are identified. There is no more reason to think of human nursing as simply biological than it is to think this way of, say, a businessman's lunch. Eating is a biological process, but what and how and with whom we eat are thoroughly cultural. Whether and how long and with whom a woman nurses an infant are also human, cultural matters. If men transcend the natural by conquering new territory and trading with their neighbors and making deals over lunch to do so, women can transcend the natural by choosing not to nurse their children when they could, or choosing to nurse them when their culture tells them not to, or singing songs to their infants as they nurse, or nursing in restaurants to overcome the prejudices against doing so, or thinking human thoughts as they nurse, and so forth. Human culture surrounds and characterizes the activity of nursing as it does the activities of eating or governing or writing or thinking.

We are continually being presented with images of the humanly new and creative as occurring in the public realm of the polls or in the realms of marketplace or of art and science outside the household. The very term "reproduction" suggests mere repetition, the bringing into existence of repeated instances of the same human animal. But human reproduction is not repetition. This is not to suggest that bringing up children in the interstices of patriarchal families, in society structured by institutions supporting male dominance, can achieve the potential of transformation latent in the activity of human mothering. But the activity of creating new social persons and new kinds of persons is potentially the most transformative human activity of all. And it suggests that morality should concern itself first of all with this activity, with what its norms and practices ought to be, and with how the institutions and arrangements throughout society and the world ought to be structured to facilitate the right kinds of development of the best kinds of new persons. The flourishing of children ought to be at the very center of moral and social and political and economic and legal thought, rather than, as at present, at the periphery, if attended to at all.

Revised conceptions of public and private have significant implication for our conceptions of human beings and relationships between them. Some feminists suggest that instead of interpreting human relationships on the model of the impersonal "public" sphere, as standard political and moral theory has so often done, we might consider interpreting them on the model of the "private," or of what these relationships could be imagined to be like in postpatriarchal society. The traditional approach is illustrated by those who generalize, to regions of human life other than the economic, assumptions about "economic man" in contractual relations with other men. It sees such impersonal, contractual relations as paradigmatic, even, on some views, for moral theory. Many feminists, in contrast, consider the realm of what has been misconstrued as the "private" as offering guidance to what human beings and their relationships should be like in regions beyond those of family and friendship as well as in more intimate contexts. Sara Ruddick looks at the implications of the practice of mothering for the conduct of peace politics. Marilyn Friedman and Lorraine Code consider friendship, especially as women understand it, as a possible model for human relationships.[34] Others see society as non-contractual rather than as contractual.

Clearly, a reconceptualization is needed of the ways in which every human life is entwined with both personal and social components. Feminist theorists are rethinking and reorganizing the private and the public, the personal and the political, and thus morality.

The Concept of Self

Let me turn now to the third aspect of the history of ethics which I discussed and which feminists are re-envisioning: the concept of self. A major emphasis in a feminist approach to morality is the recognition that more attention must be paid to the domain between the self as ego, as self-interested individual, and the universal, everyone, others in general. Traditionally, ethics has dealt with these poles of individual self and universal all. Often it has called for impartiality against the partiality of the egoistic self; sometimes it has defended egoism against claims for a universal perspective. But most standard moral theory has hardly noticed as morally significant the intermediate realm of family relations and relations of friendship, of group ties and neighborhood concerns, especially from the point of view of women.

When it has noticed this intermediate realm it has often seen its attachments as threatening to the aspirations of the man of reason or as subversive of "true" morality. In seeing the problems of ethics as problems of reconciling the interests of the self with what would be right or best for "everyone," standard ethics has neglected the moral aspects of the concern and sympathy that people actually feel for particular others, and what moral experience in this intermediate realm suggests for an adequate morality.

The region of "particular others" is a distinct domain, where what can be seen to be artificial and problematic are the very egoistic "self" and the universal "all others" of standard moral theory. In the domain of particular others, the self is already constituted to an important degree by relations with others, and these relations may be much more salient and significant than the interests of any individual self in isolation.[35] The "others" in the picture, however, are not the "all others," or "everyone," of traditional moral theory; they are not what a universal point of view or a view from nowhere could provide.[36] They are, characteristically, actual flesh-and-blood other human beings for whom we have actual feelings and with whom we have real ties.

From the point of view of much feminist theory, the individualistic assumptions of liberal theory and of most standard moral theory are suspect.[37] Even if we were freed from the debilitating aspects of dominating male power to "be ourselves" and to pursue our own interests, we would, as persons, still have ties to other persons, and we would at least in part be constituted by such ties. Such ties would be part of what we inherently are. We are, for instance, the daughter or son of given parents or the mother or father of given children, and we carry with us at least some ties to the racial or ethnic or national group within which we developed into the persons we are.

If we look at the realities of the relation between mothering person (who can be female or male) and child, we can see that what we value in the relation cannot be broken down into individual gains and losses for the individual members in the relation. Nor can it be understood in universalistic terms. Self-development apart from the relation may be much less important than the satisfactory development of the relation. What matters may often be the health and growth and development of the relation-and-its-members in ways that cannot be understood in the individualistic terms of standard moral theories designed to maximize the satisfaction of self-interest. Neither can the universalistic terms of moral theories grounded in what would be right for "all rational beings" or "everyone" handle what has moral value in the relation between mothering person and child.

Feminism is, of course, not the only locus of criticism of the individualistic and abstractly universalistic features of liberalism and of standard moral theory. Marxists and communitarians also see the self as constituted by its social relations. But in their usual form Marxist and communitarian criticisms pay no more attention than liberalism and standard moral theory to the experience of women, to the context of mothering, or to friendship as women experience it.[38] Some non-feminist criticisms, such as offered by Bernard Williams, of the impartiality required by standard moral theory, stress how a person's identity may be formed by personal projects in ways that do not satisfy universal norms yet ought to be admired. Such views still interpret morality from the point of view of an individual and his project, not a social relationship such as that between mothering person and child. And non-feminist criticisms in terms of traditional com-munities and their moral practices, as seen for instance in the work of Stuart Hampshire and Alasdair MacIntyre, often take traditional gender roles as given or else provide no basis for a radical critique of them.[39] There is no substitute, then, for feminist exploration of the area between ego and universal, as women experience this area, or for the development of a refocused concept of relational self that could be acceptable from a feminist point of view.

Relationships can be evaluated as trusting or mistrustful, mutually considerate or selfish, harmonious or stressful, and so forth. Where trust and consideration are appropriate, which is not always, we can find ways to foster them. But to understand and evaluate relationships and to encourage them to be what they can be at their best require us to look at relationships between actual persons and to see what both standard moral theories and their non-feminist critics often miss. To be adequate, moral theories must pay attention to the neglected realm of particular others in the actual relationships and actual contexts of women's experience. In doing so, problems of individual self-interest versus universal rules may recede to a region more like background, out-of-focus insolubility, or relative unimportance. The salient problems may then be seen to be how we ought best to guide or to maintain or to reshape the relationships, both close and more distant, that we have, or might have, with actual other human beings. Particular others can be actual children in need in distant continents or the anticipated children of generations not yet even close to being born. But they are not "all rational beings" or "the greatest number," and the self that is in relationships with particular others and is shaped to a significant degree by such relations is not a self whose ego must be pitted against abstract, universal claims.

The concept of a relational self is evolving within feminist thought. Among the interesting inquiries it is leading to is the work being done at the Stone Center at Wellesley College.[40] Psychologists there have posited a self-in-relation theory and are conducting empirical inquiries to try to establish how the female self develops. In working with a theory that a female relational self develops through a mutually empathetic mother–daughter bond, they have been influenced by Jean Baker Miller's re-evaluation of women's psychological qualities as strengths rather than weaknesses. In 1976, Miller identified women's "great desire for affiliation" as one such strength. Nancy Chodorow's *Reproduction of Mothering*, published in 1978, has also had a significant influence on the work done at the Stone Center, as it has on much feminist inquiry.[41] Chodorow argued that a female sense of self is reproduced by a structure of parenting in which mothers are the primary caretakers and that sons and daughters develop differently in relation to a parent of the same sex, or a parent of different sex, as primary caretaker. Daughters come to define themselves as connected to or in relation with others. Sons, in contrast, come to define themselves as separate from or less connected with others. An implication often drawn from Chodorow's work is that parenting should be shared equally by fathers and mothers so that children of either sex can develop with caretakers of both same and different sex.

In 1982, Carol Gilligan offered her view of the "different voice" with which girls and women express their understanding of moral problems.[42] Like Miller and Chodorow, Gilligan valued tendencies found especially in women to affiliate with others and to interpret their moral responsibilities in terms of their relationships with others. In all, to value autonomy and individual independence over care and concern for relationships was seen as an expression of male bias. Psychologists at the Stone Center have tried to elaborate on and to study a feminist conception of the relational self. In a series of working papers, researchers and clinicians have explored the implications of the conception of the relational self for various issues in women's psychology (for example, power, anger, work inhibitions, violence, eating patterns) and for therapy.

The self as conceptualized in these studies is seen as having both a need for recognition and a need to understand the other, and these needs are seen as compatible. They are created in the context of mother–child interaction and are satisfied in a mutually empathetic relationship. This does not require a loss of self, but a relationship of mutuality in which self and other both express an understanding of each other's subjectivity. Both give and take in a way that not only contributes to the satisfaction of their needs as individuals but also affirms the "larger relational unit" they compose.[43] Maintaining this larger relational unit then becomes a goal, and maturity is seen not in terms of individual autonomy but in terms of competence in creating and sustaining relations of empathy and mutual intersubjectivity.

The Stone Center psychologists contend that the goal of mutuality is rarely achieved in adult male–female relationships because of the traditional gender system, which leads men to seek autonomy and power over others and to undervalue the caring and relational connectedness that is expected of women. Women rarely receive the nurturing and empathetic support they provide. Accordingly, these psychologists look to the interaction that occurs in mother–daughter relationships as the best source of insight into the promotion of the healthy relational self. This research provides an example of exploration into a refocused, feminist conception of the self and into empirical questions about its development.

In a quite different field, that of legal theory, a refocused concept of self is leading to re-examination of such concepts as property and autonomy and the role these have played in political theory and in constitutional law. For instance, the legal theorist Jennifer Nedelsky questions the imagery that is dominant in constitutional law and in our conceptions of property: the imagery of a bounded self, a self contained within boundaries and having rights to property inside a wall – rights to exclude others and to exclude government. The boundary metaphor, she argues, obscures and distorts our thinking about human relationships and what is valuable in them: "The boundedness of selves may seem to be a self-evident truth, but I think it is a wrong-headed and destructive way of conceiving of the human creatures law and government are created for." In the domain of the self's relation to the state, the central problem, she argues, is not "maintaining a sphere into which the state cannot penetrate, but fostering autonomy when people are already within the sphere of state control or responsibility." What we can from a feminist perspective think of as the male "separative self" seems on an endless quest for security behind such walls of protection as those of property. Property focuses the quest for security "in ways that are paradigmatic of the efforts of separative selves to protect themselves through boundaries."[44] But surely property is a social construction, not a thing; it requires the involvement of the state to define what it is and to defend it. Only constructive relationships can provide what we seek to assure through the concept of property.

In a discussion of autonomy, Nedelsky recognizes that of course feminists are centrally concerned with the freedom and autonomy to live our own lives. But, she argues, to express these concerns we need a language that will also reflect "the equally important feminist precept that any good theorizing will start with people in their social contexts. And the notion of social context must take seriously its constitutive quality; social context cannot simply mean that individuals will, of course, encounter one another." The problem, then, is how to combine the claim that social relations are a large part of what we are with the value of self-determination. Liberalism has been the source of our language of freedom and self-determination, but it lacks the ability to express comprehension of "the reality we know: the centrality of relationships in constituting the self."[45]

In developing a new conception of autonomy that avoids positing self-sufficient and thus highly artificial individuals, Nedelsky points out, first, that "the capacity to find one's own law can develop only in the context of relations with others (both intimate and more broadly social) that nurture this capacity," and, second, that "the 'content' of one's own law is comprehensible only with reference to shared social norms, values, and concepts."[46] She sees the traditional liberal view of the self as implying that the most perfectly autonomous man is the most perfectly isolated, and this she finds pathological.

Instead of developing autonomy through images of walls around one's property, as does the Western liberal tradition and as does United States constitutional law, Nedelsky suggests that "the most promising model, symbol, or metaphor for autonomy is not property, but childrearing. There we have encapsulated the emergence of autonomy through relationship with other. . . . Interdependence [is] a constant component of autonomy."[47] And she goes on to examine how law and bureaucracies can foster autonomy within relationships between citizen and government. This does not entail extrapolating from intimate relations to large-scale ones; rather, the insights gained from experience with the context of childrearing allow us to recognize the relational aspects of autonomy. In work such as Nedelsky's we can see how feminist reconceptualizations of the self can lead to the rethinking of fundamental concepts even in terrains such as law, thought by many to be quite distant from such disturbances.

To argue for a view of the self as relational does not mean that women need to remain enmeshed in the ties by which we are constituted. Increasingly, women are breaking free from oppressive relationships with parents, with the communities in which we grew up, and with men – relationships in which we defined ourselves through the traditional and often stifling expectations of others.[48] These quests for self have often involved wrenching instability and painful insecurity. But the quest has been for a new and more satisfactory relational self, not for the self-sufficient individual of liberal theory. Many might share the concerns expressed by Alison Jaggar that disconnecting ourselves from particular others, as ideals of individual autonomy seem to presuppose we should, might render us *in*capable of morality, rather than capable of it if, as so many feminists think, "an ineliminable part of morality consists in responding emotionally to particular others."[49]

I have examined three topics on which feminist philosophers and feminists in other fields are thinking anew about where we should start and how we should focus our attention in ethics. Feminist reconceptualizations and recommendations concerning the relation between reason and emotion, the distinction between public and private, and the concept of the self are providing insights deeply challenging to standard moral theory. The implications of this work are that we need an almost total reconstruction of social and political and economic and legal theory in all their traditional forms as well as a reconstruction of moral theory and practice at more comprehensive, or fundamental, levels.

Notes

1 See, e.g., Cheshire Calhoun, "Justice, Care, Gender Bias," *Journal of Philosophy* 85 (September 1988): 451–63.

2 Lorraine Code, "Second Persons," in *Science, Morality and Feminist Theory*, ed. M. Hanen and K. Nielsen, 360.

3 See, e.g., Sue Rosenberg Zalk and Janice Gordon-Kelter, eds, *Revolutions in Knowledge: Feminism in the Social Sciences* (Boulder, CO: Westview Press, 1992).

4 Genevieve Lloyd, *The Man of Reason: "Male" and "Female" in Western Philosophy* (Minneapolis: University of Minnesota Press, 1984), 104. For detailed argument that the association between reason and maleness is fundamental and lasting rather than incidental and expendable, see Phyllis Rooney, "Gendered Reason: Sex Metaphor and Conceptions of Reason," *Hypatia* 6 (Summer 1991): 77–103.

5 G. Lloyd, *Man of Reason*, 2.

6 G. Lloyd, *Man of Reason*, 3, 4. For a feminist view of how reason and emotion in the search for knowledge might be re-evaluated, see Alison M. Jaggar, "Love and Knowledge: Emotion in Feminist Epistemology," *Inquiry* 32 (June 1989): 151–76.

7 David Heyd, *Supererogation: Its Status in Ethical Theory* (New York: Cambridge University Press, 1982), 134.

8 J. O. Urmson, "Saints and Heroes," in *Essays in Moral Philosophy*, ed. A. I. Melden (Seattle: University of Washington Press, 1958), 202. I am indebted to Marcia Baron for pointing out this example and the preceding one in her "Kantian Ethics and Supererogation," *Journal of Philosophy* 84 (May 1987): 237–62.

9 Alan Ryan, "Distrusting Economics," *New York Review of Books*, 18 May 1989, 25–7. For a different treatment, see Jane Mansbridge, ed., *Beyond Self-Interest* (Chicago: University of Chicago Press, 1990).

10 Pioneering works are Joyce Trebilcot, ed., *Mothering: Essays in Feminist Theory* (Totowa, NJ: Rowman and Allanheld, 1984); and S. Ruddick, *Maternal Thinking*.

11 Christine Di Stefano, *Configurations of Masculinity: A Feminist Perspective on Modern Political Theory* (Ithaca, NY: Cornell University Press, 1991), 81–3.

12 Thomas Hobbes, *The Citizen: Philosophical Rudiments Concerning Government and Society*, ed. B. Gert (Garden City, NY: Doubleday, 1972), 205.

13 C. Di Stefano, *Configurations of Masculinity*, 84.

14 C. Di Stefano, *Configurations of Masculinity*, 92, 104.

15 For examples of relevant passages, see Mary Mahowald, ed., *Philosophy of Woman: Classical to Current Concepts* (Indianapolis: Hackett, 1978); and Linda Bell, ed., *Visions of Women* (Clifton, NJ: Humana Press, 1985). For discussion, see Susan Moller Okin, *Women in Western Political Thought* (Princeton: Princeton University Press, 1979); and Lorenne Clark and Lynda Lange, eds, *The Sexism of Social and Political Theory: Women and Reproduction from Plato to Nietzsche* (Toronto: University of Toronto Press, 1979).

16 A. Baier, "Trust and Anti-Trust," 247–8.

17 K. Morgan, "Strangers in a Strange Land."

18 Kathryn Pauly Morgan, "Women and Moral Madness," in *Science, Morality and Feminist Theory*, ed. M. Hanen and K. Nielsen, 223.

19 Alison M. Jaggar, "Feminist Ethics: Some Issues for the Nineties," *Journal of Social Philosophy* 20 (Spring–Fall 1989): 91. See also Alison M. Jaggar, "Feminist Ethics," in *Feminist Ethics*, ed. C. Card.

20 One well-argued statement of this position is Barbara Houston, "Rescuing Womanly Virtues: Some Dangers of Moral Reclamation," in *Science, Morality and Feminist Theory*, ed. M. Hanen and K. Nielsen.

21 See E. Spelman, *Inessential Woman*. See also Sarah Lucia Hoagland, *Lesbian Ethics: Toward New Value* (Palo Alto, CA: Institute of Lesbian Studies, 1989); and Katie Geneva Cannon, *Black Womanist Ethics* (Atlanta, GA: Scholars Press, 1988).

22 M. Walker, "Moral Understandings," 19, 20. See also I. Young, "Impartiality and the Civic Public."

23 See C. Gilligan, *In a Different Voice*; and E. Kittay and D. Meyers, eds, *Women and Moral Theory*. See also Joan C. Tronto, "Beyond Gender Difference to a Theory of Care," *Signs* 12 (Summer

1987): 644–63.

24 A. Baier, "The Need for More than Justice," 55.

25 K. Morgan, "Strangers in a Strange Land," 2.

26 See A. Baier, "Trust and Anti-Trust"; and Laurence Thomas, "Trust, Affirmation, and Moral Character: A Critique of Kantian Morality," in *Identity, Character, and Morality: Essays in Moral Psychology*, ed. Owen Flanagan and Amélie Oksenberg Rorty (Cambridge, MA: MIT Press, 1990).

27 S. Sherwin, "Feminist and Medical Ethics."

28 See John Rawls, "Justice as Fairness: Political not Metaphysical," *Philosophy and Public Affairs* 14 (Summer 1985): 251–75; Rawls, "The Priority of Right and Ideas of the Good," *Philosophy and Public Affairs* 17 (Fall 1988): 251–76; Rawls, "The Idea of Overlapping Consensus," *Oxford Journal of Legal Studies* 7 (Spring 1987): 1–25; Ronald Dworkin, "Liberalism," in *Public and Private Morality*, ed. Stuart Hampshire (Cambridge, Eng.: Cambridge University Press, 1978). See also Charles Larmore, *Patterns of Moral Complexity* (Cambridge, Eng.: Cambridge University Press, 1987).

29 A. Baier, "The Need for More than Justice," 53–4.

30 See Linda Nicholson, *Gender and History: The Limits of Social Theory in the Age of the Family* (New York: Columbia University Press, 1986); and Jean Bethke Elshtain, *Public Man, Private Woman* (Princeton: Princeton University Press, 1981). See also C. Pateman, *The Sexual Contract*.

31 See S. Okin, *Women in Western Political Thought*; and A. Jaggar, *Feminist Politics*.

32 Simone de Beauvoir, *The Second Sex*, trans. H. Parshley (New York: Bantam, 1953).

33 See Sherry B. Ortner, "Is Female to Male as Nature Is to Culture?" in *Woman, Culture, and Society*, ed. Michelle Z. Rosaldo and Louise Lamphere (Stanford, CA: Stanford University Press, 1974).

34 See Marilyn Friedman, "Feminism and Modern Friendship: Dislocating the Community," *Ethics* 99 (January 1989): 275–90; and L. Code, "Second Persons."

35 See Seyla Benhabib, "The Generalized and the Concrete Other. The Kohlberg–Gilligan Controversy and Moral Theory," in *Women and Moral Theory*, ed. E. Kittay and D. Meyers; Caroline Whitbeck, "Feminist Ontology: A Different Reality," in *Beyond Domination: New Perspectives on Women and Philosophy*, ed. Carol C. Gould

(Totowa, NJ: Rowman and Allanheld,1983); Janice Raymond, *A Passion for Friends: Toward a Philosophy of Female Affection* (Boston: Beacon Press, 1986); and Marilyn Friedman, "Individuality without Individualism: Review of Janice Raymond's *A Passion for Friends*," *Hypatia* 3 (Summer 1988): 131–7.

36 See T. Nagel, *View from Nowhere*. For a feminist critique, see S. Bordo, "Feminism, Postmodernism, and Gender-Scepticism."

37 See Naomi Scheman, "Individualism and the Objects of Psychology," in *Discovering Reality*, ed. S. Harding and M. Hintikka.

38 On Marxist theory, see L. Sargent, ed., *Women and Revolution*; A. Jaggar, *Feminist Politics*; and A. Ferguson, *Blood at the Root*. On communitarian theory, see M. Friedman, "Feminism and Modern Friendship" and "The Social Self and the Partiality Debates," in *Feminist Ethics*, ed. C. Card.

39 B. Williams, *Moral Luck*; S. Hampshire, ed., *Public and Private Morality*; Alasdair MacIntyre, *After Virtue: A Study in Moral Theory* (Notre Dame, IN: University of Notre Dame Press, 1981). For discussion, see Susan Moller Okin, *Justice, Gender, and the Family* (New York: Basic Books, 1989).

40 On the Stone Center concept of the self, see especially Jean Baker Miller, "The Development of Women's Sense of Self," Wellesley, MA: Stone Center Working Paper No. 12 (1984); Janet Surrey, "The 'Self-in-Relation': A Theory of Women's Development," Working Paper No. 13 (1985); and Judith Jordan, "The Meaning of Mutuality," Working Paper No. 23 (1986). For a feminist but critical view of this work, see Marcia Westkott, "Female Relationality and the Idealized Self," *American Journal of Psychoanalysis* 49 (September 1989): 239–50.

41 Jean Baker Miller, *Toward a New Psychology of Women* (Boston: Beacon Press, 1976); Nancy Chodorow, *The Reproduction of Mothering: Psychoanalysis and the Sociology of Gender* (Berkeley: University of California Press, 1978).

42 C. Gilligan, *In a Different Voice*.

43 J. Jordan, "The Meaning of Mutuality," 2.

44 Jennifer Nedelsky, "Law, Boundaries, and the Bounded Self," *Representations* 30 (Spring 1990): 169, 181. See also Martha Minow, *Making All the Difference: Inclusion, Exclusion, and American Law* (Ithaca, NY: Cornell University Press, 1990).

45 Jennifer Nedelsky, "Reconceiving Autonomy: Sources, Thoughts and Possibilities," *Yale Journal of Law and Feminism* 1 (Spring 1989): 9. See also Diana T. Meyers, *Self, Society, and Personal Choice* (New York: Columbia University Press, 1989). For a discussion of why feminist criticisms of the ideal of autonomy need not weaken arguments for women's reproductive rights, see Sally Markowitz, "Abortion and Feminism," *Social*

Theory and Practice 16 (Spring 1990): 1–17.
46 J. Nedelsky, "Reconceiving Autonomy," 11.
47 J. Nedelsky, "Reconceiving Autonomy," 12. See also Mari J. Matsuda, "Liberal Jurisprudence and Abstracted Visions of Human Nature," *New Mexico Law Review* 16 (Fall 1986): 613–30.
48 See M. Belenky et al., *Women's Ways of Knowing*.
49 A. Jaggar, "Feminist Ethics," 11.

34   What Can Feminists Learn about Morality from Caring?

Joan C. Tronto

Embedded in our notions of caring we can see some of the deepest dimensions of traditional gender differentiation in our society. The script runs something like this: Men care about money, career, ideas, and advancement; men show they care by the work they do, the values they hold, and the provisions they make for their families (see Ehrenreich 1983). Women care for their families, neighbors, and friends; women care for their families by doing the direct work of caring. Furthermore, the script continues, men care about more important things, whereas women care about less important.

Some writers have begun to challenge this script. Caring has been defended in the first instance as a kind of labor, the "labor of love" (Finch and Groves 1983). Others have looked behind the work involved in women's caring to the attitudes and thinking involved in it. Sara Ruddick (1980) began the rehabilitation of one part of caring with her description of "maternal thinking" as a difficult and demanding practice. Further rehabilitation of caring has taken an explicitly moral direction (Elshtain 1982). The most

From *Gender/Body/Knowledge*, ed. Alison Jaggar and Susan Bords (New Brunswick, NJ: Rutgers University Press). Reprinted with permission.

widely read work on women's moral development, Carol Gilligan's *In a Different Voice* (1982), is often associated with the language of "an ethic of care." Other writers have suggested that caring grounds women in the world in such a way that they become and should remain immune from the appeals of abstract principles (McMillan 1982) or of religion (Noddings 1984: 97).

In this essay I not only continue challenging the traditional script about men's and women's caring, but I also suggest that feminists must be careful about the direction their analysis of care takes. I shall argue that feminists cannot assume that any attribute of women is automatically a virtue worthy of feminists embracing it. Unless we adopt an uncritically profeminine position and say whatever women do is fine because women do it, we need to take a closer look at caring. In this essay I attempt to explore what a feminist approach to caring could be.

The task of disentangling feminine and feminist aspects of caring is not simple. First, we must clarify the nature of caring as understood today in the West. Then we will be in a position to evaluate how caring challenges contemporary notions in moral theory about what is desirable and virtuous. In both regards, feminine and feminist analyses of caring may overlap. In the final analysis, however, moral categories take on meaning in a broader context. Feminine analyses of caring can be distinguished in that they assume that the traditional script about caring is more or less correct. The truly transformative and feminist aspects of caring cannot be recognized unless we also revise our view of the political context in which we situate caring as a moral phenomenon.

Two Types of Caring: Caring About and Caring For

The language of caring appears in many settings in our daily language. Caring includes myriad actors and activities. Doing household tasks is taking care of the house. Doctors, nurses, and others provide medical care. We might ask whether a corporation cares for its workers. Someone might ask, who is taking care of this account? Historians care about the past. Judges care about justice. We usually assume that mothers care for their children, that nurses care for their patients, that teachers care for their students, that social workers care for their clients.

What all of these examples share can be distilled: Caring implies some kind of on-going responsibility and commitment. This notion accords with the original meaning of "care" in English, where care meant a burden; to care is to assume a burden. When a person or a group cares about something or someone, we presume that they are willing to work, to sacrifice, to spend money, to show emotional concern, and to expend energy toward the object of care. Thus, we can make sense of statements such as: he only cares about making money; she cares for her mother; this society does not care about the homeless. To the challenge, You do not care, one responds by showing some evidence of work, sacrifice, or commitment.

If caring involves a commitment, then caring must have an object. Thus, caring is necessarily relational. We say that we care for or about something or someone. We can distinguish "caring about" from "caring for" based on the objects

of caring.[1] Caring about refers to less concrete objects; it is characterized by a more general form of commitment. Caring for implies a specific, particular object that is the focus of caring. The boundaries between caring about and caring for are not so neat as these statements imply. Nonetheless, this distinction is useful in revealing something about the way we think of caring in our society because this distinction fits with the engendered category of caring in our society.

Caring for involves responding to the particular, concrete, physical, spiritual, intellectual, psychic, and emotional needs of others. The self, another person, or a group of others can provide care. For example, I take care of myself, a mother cares for the child, a nurse for hospital patients, the Red Cross for victims of the earthquake. These types of care are unified by growing out of the fact that humans have physical and psychic needs (food, grooming, warmth, comfort, etc.) that require activity to satisfy them. These needs are in part socially determined; they are also met in different societies by different types of social practices.

In our society, the particular structures involving caring for grow especially out of the family; caring professions are often construed as a buttress to, or substitute for, care that can no longer be provided within a family. The family may no longer be intact, as a result of death, divorce, distance. Or the family may not be able to provide help; some caring requires expertise. The family may be or may be seen as the source of the problem – for example, families with patterns of substance abuse, incest, violence. Increasingly, then, care has been provided for by the state or in the market. Americans eat fewer meals at home, hire housekeepers, contract for others to wait in a line for them. In response to this increasingly market-oriented version of caring, some thinkers have pulled back in horror and suggested that caring cannot be provided if it disturbs the integrity of the self–other relationship (Elshtain 1981: 30; Noddings 1984). The result is that in modern market society the illusion of caring is often preserved: providers of services are expected to feign caring (Hochschild 1983).

Caring is engendered in both market and private life. Women's occupations are the caring occupations, and women do the disproportionate amount of caretaking in the private household. To put the point simply, traditional gender roles in our society imply that men care about but women care for.

Because not all caring is moral, another distinction between caring about and caring for becomes obvious. When we wish to know if "caring about" is a moral activity, we inquire about the nature of the object of the care. To care about justice is a moral activity because justice is a moral concern; to care about one's accumulation of vacation days presumably is not a moral activity.

Caring for takes on moral significance in a different way. When we inquire about caring for, it is not enough to know the object of the care; presumably we must know something about the context of care, perhaps especially about the relationship between the caregiver and recipient of care. A dirty child is not a moral concern for most people, but we might morally disapprove of such a child's mother, who we might think has failed to meet her duty to care for her child. Note, of course, that such judgments are deeply rooted in social, classist, and cultural assumptions about mother's duties, about standards of cleanliness, and so on. The assignment of the responsibility of caring for someone, something, or some group, then might be a moral question. Thus, what typically makes "caring for" perceived as moral is not the activity *per se* but how that activity reflects upon the assigned social duties of the caretaker and who is doing the assigning.

The actual *activity* of caring for another person seems far removed from what we usually consider moral. Caring as an activity seems more tied to the realm of necessity than to the realm of freedom where moral judgments presumably have a place (see Arendt 1958; Aristotle 1981). One way in which recent theorists have tried to describe the value of caring is to deny that caring is simply banal activity devoid of judgment. Sara Ruddick (1980) describes maternal thinking as a kind of practice, that is, as a prudential activity where emotions and reason are brought to bear to raise a child. Like the theorists of care, Ruddick stresses that maternal thinking is a particular practice; the maternal thinker focuses on the single child before her or him. In order for children to grow, Ruddick explains, they must be preserved, they must grow physically and mentally, and they must be made aware of the norms and practices of the society of which they are a part. These goals will actually be in conflict in individual instances; for example, the toddler learning to climb threatens its preservation at the same time it develops its strength. Because raising children involves conflicting goals, the maternal thinker cannot simply rely upon instincts or receptivity to the child's wishes to achieve the ultimate goal of raising the child. Instead, a complex set of prudential calculations are involved, which Ruddick calls maternal thinking. Ruddick's point suggests that it might be worthwhile to explore at length the ways in which the practice of caring involves moral issues.

From the standpoint of much contemporary moral theory, caring poses a moral question only in deciding whether one ought to care, not in determining how one engages in the activity of caring. The "moral point of view," as described by moral philosophers such as William Frankena (1973), involves attributes of impartiality and universalizability. We might agree, universally, that special relationships such as being a parent entail certain duties toward our children, but this moral precept cannot then bring us any closer to how to engage in the practice of caring in a moral way. Furthermore, we often assume that morality concerns our interaction with other morally autonomous actors; in caring, the relationships between the caretakers and those cared for are often relations between unequals, where some amount of dependency exists.

Thus, in order to determine the moral dimensions of caring for others, the kind of caring most closely associated with women in our society, we must consider two aspects of caring for others. First, we must consider whether the activity of caring raises moral questions in and of itself. Second, and here a feminist analysis of caring will differ from a simply "feminine" analysis of caring, we must consider how the duties of caring for others are given moral significance in society as a whole. I shall explore these two concerns in the next two sections of this essay.

Moral Dimensions of the Activity of Caring for Others

In this section I shall suggest three ways in which caring for another raises questions about moral life. First, I shall discuss some aspects of moral life posed by the necessary attentiveness to [the] other's needs when caring for another. Second, I shall consider the way in which caring for another raises questions about authority and autonomy between carer and cared-for. And third, I shall examine how caring for another raises problems that grow out of the particularity of caring.

Attentiveness

Caring suggests an alternative moral attitude. From the perspective of caring, what is important is not arriving at the fair decision, understood as how the abstract individual in this situation would want to be treated, but at meeting the needs of particular others or preserving the relationships of care that exist (see Gilligan 1982). In this way, moral theory becomes much more closely connected to the concrete needs of others. How we come to know these needs raises several dimensions of concern for moral theory.

Knowledge. In order to engage in the practice of caring the nature of knowledge needed to act morally changes. At the most obvious level, the mode of philosophical discussion that starts from a philosopher's introspection is an inappropriate starting place to arrive at caring judgments. In the first instance one needs knowledge about others' needs, knowledge that comes from others.

It is not that contemporary moral theory ignores the needs of others, but in most moral discussion the needs of others are taken to reflect the understood needs of the thinking self if only he or she were in another's situation. In contrast, caring rests on knowledge completely pe-

culiar to the particular person being cared for. Proper action for a nurse, faced with a patient who will not finish a meal, depends upon knowing the patient's medical condition, usual eating habits, and tastes. There is no simple way one can generalize from one's own experience to what another needs.

To provide such knowledge, the caring person must devote much attention to learning what the other person might need. Accounts of caring stress that an important part of the process of caring is attentiveness to the needs of others (see Weil 1951: 72–3; Ruddick 1980: 357–8). To achieve the proper frame of mind in which to care, Noddings stresses the need to be receptive to the needs of others (1984: 24). At the moment when one wishes to care, it is impossible to be preoccupied with the self. This kind of selflessness is a key element of what Noddings calls the crucial moral question in caring, that is, how to meet the other morally.

How radically different the epistemological notion of attentiveness is from contemporary ways of thinking can be illustrated by re-examining the long-standing issue about the relationship of knowledge and interests from this perspective. Liberals commonly assume that no one knows your interests as well as you yourself do (see Mill 1975: 187). Marxists and those inspired by Marx believe that a person's interests arise out of the objective circumstances in which one finds oneself or that one can posit some universal, or nearly universal, human interests, for example, "emancipatory interests" (Marx and Engels 1978; Habermas 1971; Cohen 1978). But from the standpoint of caring, these views are equally incomplete. There is some relationship between what the cared-for thinks he or she wants and his or her true interests and needs, although it may not be a perfect correspondence. A patient in the hospital who refuses to get up may be forced to do so. A child who wishes only to eat junk food may be disappointed by parents' reluctance to meet this wish. Genuine attentiveness would presumably allow the caretaker to see through these pseudo-needs and come to appreciate what the other really needs.

Such a commitment to perceiving the genuine needs of the other, though, is not so easy. Alice Miller suggests that many parents act not so much to meet the needs of their children as to work out unmet needs they continue to carry from when they were children (Miller 1981). If a caretaker has deficient self-knowledge about his or her own needs, then there is no way to guarantee that those needs have been removed in looking to see what the other's needs are. It may be very difficult to achieve the state of attentiveness, requiring first a tremendous self-knowledge so that the caretaker does not simply transform the needs of the other into a projection of the self's own needs.[2]

The Attentive Self. To say that attentiveness requires a profound self-knowledge, though, does not yet capture how deeply attentiveness affects the self. The concern with attentiveness, with losing one's own concerns in order to see clearly the concerns of the cared-for, raises some difficult questions for the moral theory of caring: How much must one disregard one's own needs in order to be sufficiently attentive? How does one become adept at creating the condition of receptivity? If one is being solely receptive to the needs of others, how can one judge whether the needs are genuine, as serious as the one cared-for believes they are, and so on?

Furthermore, attentiveness involves a commitment of time and effort that may be made at a high price to the self. Noddings asserts that caring is not complete unless recognized by the cared-for person (1984: 73–4), but this position is clearly wrong. As Noddings herself suggests, such recognition depends upon whether the cared-for person has the capacity to respond to caring. Although a mother's child may develop what Noddings would consider the proper responsiveness to caring over time, others, such as teachers and nurses, who provide care over a shorter duration, cannot expect that their commitment will be recognized and rewarded. Nodding's argument (1984: 86) is seductive in its suggestion that we are always recognized for our sacrifices, but it is also dangerous in encouraging us to restrict caring only to those near to us

on a continuing basis. For the rest of us, though, who are willing to attempt to care at some greater distance, attentiveness has a cost.

Another potential cost to the self is that caring is risky. As Sara Ruddick notes, the contingencies of the world will often cause disasters to befall those for whom we care (Ruddick 1980: 350–1). If the self has become too committed to caring for the other, then the loss of the other may destroy the self. Thus caring cannot simply be a romanticized notion of selflessness, nor can it occur if the self remains aloof. A connection between the self and the other is necessary for the self to care, and the nature of this connection is a problem for any ethic of care.

Attentiveness and Market Relations. These questions about self–other relations and knowledge are not restricted to relations among individuals; there is a social and political dimension to attentiveness as well. I have noted that in order to be attentive to the needs of others one must relinquish the absolute primacy of the needs of the self. In this regard, attentive care is incompatible with the paradigmatic relationship of modern society, exchange (Hartsock 1983). The paradigm of market relations, of exchange, involves putting one's own interests first. It involves the assertion that one knows one's own interests best, another assumption inconsistent with the attitude of caring. It involves reducing complex relationships into terms that can be made equivalent. None of these premises is compatible with attentiveness.

The seriousness of this point depends upon whether market relationships and attentive care can coexist, and if so, how (see Lane 1986; Hardwig 1984; Walzer 1983; Schaar 1983). Theorists differ about how much the metaphors of exchange permeate all social relationships. Virtually all social relationships in modern life can be described in terms of exchange, but whether that means it is the only or the most illuminating way in which individuals conceive of those relationships is another matter.

If individuals are capable of using and discarding exchange and caring modes of thought at will, then to recognize a caring dimension provides important depth to our picture of moral life. If one cannot move easily from one mode to the other, however (see Hardwig 1984), then to suggest that caring is of value suggests several other disturbing possibilities. If people must either be predominantly caring or exchange-oriented, then the simplest way to arrange social institutions would be to create separate spheres for each mode of life. The ideological glorification of men in the cruel business world and women in the caring home is one obvious solution.

The advocate of caring might respond that if caring and market society cannot coexist, let us abolish market relations. The radicalness of this claim is immediately obvious, but the obviousness of its replacement to conduct life in a complex society is not.

Authority and autonomy

The second area where caring raises fundamental questions opposed to contemporary moral theory is another issue that grows out of caring as providing help to meet the needs of others. Because caring occurs in a situation where one person is helping to meet the concrete needs of another, caring raises questions that cannot be easily accommodated by the starting assumption in most contemporary moral philosophy that we are rational, autonomous actors. Many conditions that we usually associate with care-giving belie this view because society does not consider all people we take care of to be rational and autonomous, either in an abstract moral sense (e.g. children) or in a concrete, physical sense (e.g. a bed-ridden parent, a disabled person) (see Fisher and Galler 1988). Furthermore, if the care-giver is considered rational and autonomous, then the relationship between the parties is unequal, and relationships of authority and dependency are likely to emerge. As I noted earlier, if the care-giver's needs are themselves met by providing care, then the care-giver might desire to keep the cared-for person dependent. How should care-givers understand their authoritative position in relation to those for whom they care?

However, the image of equal adults who rely upon other equal adults for care, not exchange, once again raises questions about what it means to be rational and autonomous. Two people in an equal relationship of care share an awareness of the concrete complications of caring. To maintain such a relationship will often entail making judgments that, from a more abstract point of view, might seem questionable. Is one wrong if one refuses to move for a better job because of an on-going situation for caring? Again one is forced to consider what autonomy actually means.

Previous writers about an ethic of care vary in whether they perceive authority and autonomy as an issue. The work of Carol Gilligan and Nona Lyons is useful in that it poses the nature of autonomy as an issue. Gilligan has identified an "ethic of care" characterized by a commitment to maintaining and fostering the relationships in which one is woven (Gilligan 1982: 119). Her analysis leads her to suggest that without this dimension the account of morality found in enumeration of rights would be incomplete. Kohlberg's cognitive model of moral development, which Gilligan criticizes, stresses that a sense of the autonomous self, clearly differentiated from others, is crucial to developing a moral sense. In contrast, this ethic of care is based upon a different account of the self. Lyons's research suggests that only individuals who view themselves as connected to others, rather than as separate and objective, are able to use both an ethic of care and claims about justice to resolve real-life moral dilemmas (Lyons 1983: 140–1). Gilligan stresses that there may well be tension between the maintenance of self and of relationships; by her account moral maturity arrives when an individual can correctly balance concerns for the self and for others (Gilligan 1983: 41–5).

Noddings's approach, on the other hand, seems to leave too little autonomy to the self and is unable to discern that relations of care might also be relations of authority. Noddings analyzes care as the relationship between the one caring and the one cared-for. The essential aspect of caring is that it involves a displacement from one's own interests to the interests of the one cared-for. "Our attention, our mental engrossment is on the cared-for, not on ourselves" (Noddings 1984: 24). Caring affects both the one caring and the one cared-for. It affects the one caring because she must become engrossed in the other; it affects the cared-for because that individual's needs are met and because that individual must somehow respond and accept the care offered.

Caring challenges the view that morality starts where rational and autonomous individuals confront each other to work out the rules of moral life. Instead, caring allows us to see autonomy as a problem that people must deal with all the time, in their relations with both equals and those who either help them or depend upon them.

Particularity

Finally, let us consider how the particularity of caring challenges contemporary moral theory. Most contemporary moral theorists require universal moral judgments, that is, that if it is moral for a person to act in a given way in a given situation then it must be moral for any person so situated to act the same way[3] (Kohlberg 1981). Yet the decision we must make about how much care to provide and to whom cannot be so easily generalized or universalized. It is theoretically possible to spend all of one's time caring for others (see Blum et al.1976); the real decisions everyone will face then are decisions about both when to provide care and when to stop providing care. Because caring varies with the amount of time and kind of effort that a caring individual can expend as well as with the needs of the ones who need care, it is difficult to imagine that rules could ever be specified allowing us to claim that we had applied universal moral principles.

Consider, for example, a rule: always give aid to a person whose car is broken down on the highway. Suppose you are a non-mechanical woman alone and the stranger is a male? Always take care of your mother. Suppose she and your children rely on your income to keep the household together and caring for her will cost you your job? Thus, the moral judgments made in offering and providing care are much more complex than any set of rules can take into account. Any rule sufficiently flexible to cover all the complexities would probably have to take a form such as "do all that you can to help someone else." Such a form, though, does not serve as any guide to what morality requires. What may be "too much" care for a child to provide an elderly parent may seem too selfishly skimpy to another. This logical objection about the limits of rule-governed morality is familiar, yet it remains a practical difficulty.

The reason that rule-governed behavior is so often associated with moral life, though, is that if we are bound to follow the rules then we are bound to act impartially, not giving special favors to those nearest us. Another problem with caring from a moral point of view, then, is that we might, because of our caring relationship, provide special treatment to those closest to us and ignore others more deserving of care.

Nel Noddings pursues this problem in a disturbing way. Noddings is very restrictive about the conditions under which caring occurs. Although Noddings argues that it is natural for us to care for our children, when we extend care beyond our own children it becomes an ethical act (Noddings 1984: 79–80). Noddings also suggests that caring must take place in a limited context or it is not properly understood as caring: Noddings's description of caring is very personal; her examples include caring for cats and birds, children and husbands, students and strangers who arrive at the door. Mother–child and teacher–pupil are paradigmatic caring relationships. But any expansion of caring beyond this sphere is dangerous because caring cannot be generalized. Thus, Noddings wishes to separate caring from many of its broader social connotations; she seems to exclude caretaking from caring for:

> The danger is that caring, which is essentially nonrational in that it requires a constitutive engrossment and displacement of motivation, may gradually or abruptly be transformed into abstract problem solving. There is, then, a shift of focus from the cared-for to the "problem." Opportunities arise for self-interest, and persons entrusted with caring may lack the necessary engrossment in those to be cared for. (Noddings 1984: 25–6; compare Finch and Groves 1983)

Such caring can only be provided for a very limited number of others, and Noddings would probably exclude many relationships we might otherwise think of as caring. By Noddings's understanding of caring, nurses in hospitals do not necessarily care; indeed, by this view there are probably many mothers who would not qualify as carers. In this case, a moral question arises about the needs of the particular others we care for weighed against the needs of others more distant from us. To Noddings this problem is solved by saying that because everyone will be cared for by someone, it is not anyone else's concern to wonder about who is caring for whom in society.

To say that we should only care for those things that come within our immediate purview ignores the ways in which we are responsible for the construction of our narrow sphere. When Noddings says that she will respond with caring to the stranger at her door but not to starving children in Africa, she ignores the ways in which the modern world is intertwined and the ways in which hundreds of prior public and private decisions affect where we find ourselves and which strangers show up at our doors. In an affluent community, where affluence is maintained by such decisions as zoning ordinances, the stranger at the door is less of a threat than in a dense city, where the stranger may wish to do you harm. Perhaps Noddings would have no problem with this point because in the city you do not have to care for strangers at the door. But the question then becomes, who does? Questions about the proximity of people to us are shaped by our collective social decisions. If we decide to isolate ourselves from others, we may reduce our moral burden of caring. Yet if moral life is only understood narrowly in the context of the exhibition of caring, then we can be absolved from these broader responsibilities.

One way to answer this objection is to say that the task of moral theory is to set out what the parameters of caring should be. Such an approach would soon blend into questions of social and political life. For caring to be an on-going activity, it is necessarily bounded by the activities of daily life because the entire complex of social institutions and structures determine with whom we come into contact on a regular enough basis to establish relationships of care.[4]

If caring is used as an excuse to narrow the scope of our moral activity to be concerned only with those immediately around us, then it does have little to recommend it as a moral theory. But the question of whom we should care for is not left entirely to individuals in our society.

A Feminist Approach to Caring: Caring About What We Care For

In the second section of this essay I explored some ways in which caring challenges contemporary moral theory. In each case, I realized that caring seems to provide a richer account of people's moral lives. Nevertheless, caring seems to suffer a fatal moral flaw if we allow it to be circumscribed by deciding that we shall only care for those closest to us. From this perspective, it is hard to see how caring can remain moral, rather than becoming a way to justify inconsideration of others at the expense of those for whom we care.

To solve this problem I must return to the way in which the activity of caring is situated in contemporary society. I noted at the beginning of this essay that the problem of who should care for whom is rooted in (often questionable) social values, expectations, and institutions. We do not hold everyone (anyone?) individually responsible for the homeless. Similarly, we do not hold just anyone responsible for the appearance of a child, but we do hold her mother (and father?) responsible. Nonetheless, I can make at least one generalization about caring in this society: men care about; women care for. Thus, by definition the traditional script on caring re-enacts the division of male and female worlds into public and private. To raise the question about whether caring for is inevitably too particularistic is thus to return as well to the engendered nature of caring in our society and to a consideration of the difference between a feminist and feminine account of caring.

What does it mean to assert, as Nel Noddings

does, that caring is a "feminine" approach to ethics? For Noddings, it means the celebration and legitimation of a part of women's lives. Yet we have seen that Noddings's formulation of caring cannot be satisfying as a model for moral theory. As Genevieve Lloyd (1984) argues about reason, the category of the feminine is quite problematic (see also Gilman 1979). Femininity is constructed as the antithesis of masculinity. Thus, what is constructed as the masculine, as the normal, is constructed in opposition to what is feminine. In this case, the construction of women as tied to the more particular activity of caring for others stands in opposition to the more public and social concerns about which men care.

I can make this argument still more pointed. In so far as caring is a kind of attentiveness, it may be a reflection of a survival mechanism for women or others who are dealing with oppressive conditions, rather than a quality of intrinsic value on its own. Another way to understand caring is to see it as an ethic most appropriate for those in a subordinate social position. Just as women and others who are not in the central corridors of power in this society adopt a variety of deferential mannerisms (e.g. differences in speech, smiling, other forms of body language, etc.), so too it may have served their purposes of survival to have adopted an attitude that Noddings may approvingly call "attentiveness" but might otherwise be understood as the necessity to anticipate the wishes of one's superior.[5]

A feminine approach to caring, then, cannot serve as a starting point for a broader questioning of the proper role of caring in society. As with Temma Kaplan's (1982) description of "female consciousness," the feminine approach to caring bears the burden of accepting traditional gender divisions in a society that devalues what women do. From this perspective, caring will always remain as a corrective to morality, as an "extra" aspect of life, neither suggesting nor requiring a fundamental rethinking of moral categories.

A feminist approach to caring, in contrast, needs to begin by broadening our understanding of what caring for others means, both in terms of the moral questions it raises and in terms of the need to re-structure broader social and political institutions if caring for others is to be made a more central part of the everyday lives of everyone in society. It is beyond the scope of this essay to spell out fully a feminist theory of care, but some points seem to suggest a starting place for further analysis.

In this essay I noted the way in which caring involves moral acts not usually comprehended in the framework of contemporary moral theory. The moral relevance of attentiveness belies the adequacy of the abstract, exchange-oriented individual as the moral subject. We noted earlier that to take attentiveness seriously questions our assumptions about our autonomy, the self, our knowledge of our interests, the effectiveness of the market. These issues are already topics that feminist political and moral philosophers consider. Caring may prove an especially useful way for feminist thinkers to try to ground their thoughts on these subjects.

Feminist theory will also need to describe what constitutes good caring. We have already noted that this task will be difficult because caring is so much tied to particular circumstances. Yet we need to rethink as well how those particular circumstances are socially constructed. Perhaps the impoverishment of our vocabulary for discussing caring is a result of the way caring is privatized, thus beneath our social vision in this society. The need to rethink appropriate forms for caring also raises the broadest questions about the shape of social and political institutions in our society.

To think of the social world in terms of caring for others radically differs from our present way of conceiving of it in terms of pursuing our self-interest. Because caring emphasizes concrete connections with others, because it evokes so much of the daily stuff of women's lives, and because it stands as a fundamental critique of abstract and often seemingly irrelevant moral theory, it is worthy of the serious attention of feminist theorists.

Notes

I gratefully acknowledge in writing this essay the help I received from Annmarie Levins, Mary Dietz, George Shulman, Berenice Fisher, and Alison Jaggar.

1 Note that my distinction between caring for and caring about differs from the distinction drawn by Meyeroff (1971) and Noddings (1984). Meyeroff wishes to conflate caring for ideas with caring for people. Not only does this parallel mask the traditional gender difference, but, as will become clear later, the kinds of activities involved in caring for other people cannot be easily used in this same sense. Noddings distinguishes caring for from caring about on a dimension that tries to get at the degree of commitment. We care more for what we care for than for what we care about (1984: 86, 112), but Noddings also wishes to claim that we can care for ideas. I believe that the way I have formulated the distinction reveals more about caring and traditional assumptions of gender difference.

2 None the less, in order for caring to occur, there must be more than good intentions and undistorted communication; the acts of caring must also occur. I believe this point may help to distinguish this approach from (at least early versions of) Habermas's approach. For the criticism that Habermas's work is too intellectualized, see Henning Ottmann (1982: 86).

3 See, among other recent authors who question the dominant Kantian form of morality, Lawrence Blum (1980), Alasdair MacIntyre and Stanley Hauerwas (1983), John Kekes (1984), and Peter Winch (1972).

4 I am indebted here to Berenice Fisher's suggestion that one important element of a theory of care is the specification of the limits of caring.

5 Jack H. Nagel refined earlier analyses of power to include what C. J. Friedrich had called the "rule of anticipated reactions," the situation where "one actor, B, shapes his behavior to conform to what he believes are the desires of another actor, A, without having received explicit messages about A's wants or intentions from A or A's agents" (1975: 16). See also Dahl (1984: 24–5).

References

Arendt, H. 1958. *The Human Condition*. Chicago: University of Chicago Press.

Aristotle. 1981. *The Politics*. Harmondsworth: Penguin Books.

Blum, L. 1980. *Friendship, Altruism, and Morality*. Boston: Routledge and Kegan Paul.

Blum, L., M. Homiak, J. Housman, and N. Scheman. 1976. "Altruism and Women's Oppression." In *Women and Philosophy*, ed. C. Gould and M. W. Wartofsky. New York: G. P. Putnam.

Cohen, G. A. 1978. *Karl Marx's Theory of History: A Defence*. Princeton, NJ: Princeton University Press.

Dahl, R. A. 1984. *Modern Political Analysis*. 4th edn. Englewood Cliffs, NJ: Prentice-Hall.

Ehrenreich, B. 1983. *The Hearts of Men*. Garden City, NJ: Anchor Books.

Elshtain, J. B. 1981. *Public Man, Private Woman*. Princeton, NJ: Princeton University Press.

——. 1982. "Antigone's Daughters." *Democracy*, 2: 46–59.

Finch, J., and D. Groves, eds. 1983. *A Labour of Love: Women. Work and Caring*. London: Routledge and Kegan Paul.

Fisher, B., and R. Galler. 1988. "Friendship and Fairness: How Disability Affects Friendship Between Women." In *Women with Disabilities: Essays in Psychology, Politics and Policy*, ed. A. Asch and M. Fine. Philadelphia: Temple University Press.

Frankena, W. 1973. *Ethics*. Englewood Cliffs, NJ: Prentice-Hall.

Gilligan, C. 1982. *In a Different Voice*. Cambridge: Harvard University Press.

——. 1983. "Do the Social Sciences Have an Adequate Theory of Moral Development?" In *Social Science as Moral Inquiry*. ed. N. Haan, et al. New York: Columbia University Press.

Gilman, C. P. 1979. *Herland*. New York: Pantheon.

Habermas, J. 1971. *Knowledge and Human Interests*. Boston: Beacon Press.

Hardwig, J. 1984. "Should Women Think in Terms of Rights?" *Ethics*, 94: 441–55.

Hartsock, N. C. M. 1983. *Money, Sex and Power: Toward a Feminist Historical Materialism*. New York: Longman.

Hochschild, A. 1983. *The Managed Heart: Commercialization of Human Feeling*. Berkeley: University of California Press.

Kaplan, T. 1982. "Female Consciousness and Collective Action: The Case of Barcelona, 1910–1918." In *Feminist Theory: A Critique of Ideology*, eds N. Keohane, M. Rosaldo, B. Gelpi. Chicago: University of Chicago Press.

Kekes, J. 1984. "Moral Sensitivity." *Philosophy*, 59:3–19.

Kohlberg, L. 1981. "From *Is* to *Ought*: How to Commit the Naturalistic Fallacy and Get Away with It in the Study of Moral Development." In his *The Philosophy of Moral Development: Moral Stages and the Idea of Justice*. Vol. 1 of *Essays in Moral Development*. New York: Harper & Row.

Lane, R. E. 1986. "Market Justice, Political Justice." *American Political Science Review*, 80: 383–402.

Lloyd, G. 1984. *The Man of Reason: "Male" and "Female" in Western Philosophy*. Minneapolis: University of Minnesota Press.

Lyons, N. P. 1983. "Two Perspectives: On Self, Relationships, and Morality." *Harvard Educational Review*, 53: 125–44.

MacIntyre, A., and S. Hauerwas, eds. 1983. *Revisions: Changing Perspectives in Moral Philosophy*. Notre Dame, IN: University of Notre Dame Press.

McMillan, C. 1982. *Women, Reason, and Nature: Some Philosophical Problems With Feminism*. Princeton, NJ: Princeton University Press.

Marx, K., and F. Engels. 1978. "The German Ideology." In *The Marx-Engels Reader*, ed. R. C. Tucker. 2d edn. New York: Norton.

Meyeroff, M. 1971. *On Caring*. New York: Harper & Row.

Mill, J. S. 1975. "Considerations on Representative Government." In *Three Essays*, ed. R. Wollheim. Oxford: Oxford University Press.

Miller, A. 1981. *The Drama of the Gifted Child*. New York: Basic Books.

Nagel, J. H. 1975. *The Descriptive Analysis of Power*. New Haven, CT: Yale University Press.

Noddings, N. 1984. *Caring: A Feminine Approach to Ethics*. Berkeley: University of California Press.

Ottmann, H. 1982. "Cognitive Interests and Self-Reflection." In *Habermas: Critical Debates*, eds J. B. Thompson and D. Held. Cambridge, MA: MIT Press.

Ruddick, S. 1980. "Maternal Thinking." *Feminist Studies*, 6: 342–67.

Schaar, J. 1983. "The Question of Justice." *Raritan Review*, 3: 107–29.

Walzer, M. 1983. *Spheres of Justice*. New York: Basic Books.

Weil, S. 1951. "Reflections on the Right Use of School Studies with a View to the Love of God." In *Waiting for God*. Trans. E. Craufurd. New York: Harper.

Winch, P. 1972. *Ethics and Action*. London: Routledge and Kegan Paul.

35   Toward a Feminist Conception of Moral Reasoning

Alison Jaggar

This essay is part of a longer work in progress.[1] It is my first attempt to discuss in print some aspects of a model of moral reasoning practiced by several groups of North American feminist activists from the late 1960s until the present. I call the model "Feminist Practical Dialogue" or FPD. FPD continues the discursive tradition of moral reasoning developed by Western philosophers such as Plato, John Stuart Mill, John Rawls, and Jürgen Habermas but it suggests an alternative understanding of moral discourse, as well as alternative understandings of associated concepts such as moral subjectivity, moral community, and moral

From *Morality and Social Justice*, James P. Sterba, Alison Jaggar et al. Reprinted by permission of Rowman and Littlefield.

justification. These alternative understandings seem to me empirically, conceptually, morally, and pragmatically more satisfactory than those found in most non-feminist conceptions of moral reasoning. In this essay, I begin to explore FPD's understandings of moral discourse as well as to raise some questions about its strengths and limits. First, however, I'd like to make some comments about the sense in which I take FPD to be feminist.

Certainly not all feminists subscribe to FPD; many have other views of how moral reasoning should be practiced.[2] In addition, FPD has drawn inspiration from various non-feminist conceptions of moral reasoning and incorporates elements from these.[3] Nevertheless, FPD is feminist in a sense stronger than simply that of having been developed by self-identified feminists. Some have argued that consensual approaches to moral reasoning, of which FPD is one, come more easily to contemporary Western women than to their male counterparts since women are thought to be better listeners than men and more committed to the empowerment of others (Iannello 1992). Whether or not this is empirically true, FPD certainly incorporates features that, in Western culture, are symbolically feminine, including the values of caring for specific individuals, sharing intimate feelings, and emphasizing concrete experience over abstract ideals. But *feminine* thinking is not *feminist*, even though a reassessment of the traditionally feminine must be a part of the feminist project, and in any case FPD also embodies values, such as equality and fairness, that are associated with masculine moral thinking. Just as the incorporation of feminine values does not render FPD feminist, neither does FPD become feminist by adding masculine values to the feminine in a mix that might be called androgynous. Instead, I regard FPD as feminist primarily because it revises both feminine and masculine values in the light of a distinctively feminist commitment to ending women's subordination.

Feminist Practical Dialogue

Modern Western feminism has revolved around the complementary themes of women being silenced and women regaining their voices. It was the prohibition on women abolitionists speaking in public that sparked the emergence of nineteenth-century feminism in the United States, and the ensuing campaigns for women's suffrage may be seen as struggles to gain a voice for women in the conduct of public affairs. When North American feminism was revived in the late 1960s, it continued to be preoccupied with voice, a concern beautifully expressed by Adrienne Rich.

One of the most powerful social and political catalysts of the past decade has been the speaking of women with other women, the telling of our secrets, the comparing of wounds and the sharing of words. This hearing and saying of women has been able to break many a silence and taboo; literally to transform forever the way we see. . . . And so I begin tonight by urging each of you to take responsibility for the voicing of her experience, to take seriously the work of listening to each other and the work of speaking, whether in private dialogue or in larger groups. In order to change what is, we need to give speech to what *has been*, to imagine together what *might be*. (Rich 1979)

Speaking was not invented by contemporary feminists, of course; people have always talked with each other. Speech is a distinguishing characteristic of human beings and it is primarily through talking that we become members of a human community and acquire much of our most basic knowledge. In societies that have developed literacy, however, speech is usually thought to be less authoritative than the written word and the knowledge transmitted through oral discourse is typically regarded as suspect: as unreliable or, at best, as "folk wisdom." Nevertheless, even in advanced industrial societies speech remains an important source of insight or knowledge for some subcultural groups. Patricia Hill Collins asserts that, in the African American community, the use of dialogue continues to be vital in assessing knowledge claims. She writes: "the use of dialogue has deep roots in an African-based oral tradition and in African-American culture," and she cites the widespread use of the call-and-response discourse mode among African-Americans as illustrating the continuing importance placed on dialogue (Collins 1990: 212).

Recent feminist psychologists have claimed that North American women in general, including college-educated women of European ancestry, are more likely than their male counterparts to value discourse as a source of knowledge. They assert that women frequently "ground their epistemological premises in metaphors suggesting speaking and listening" rather than in "visual metaphors (such as equating knowledge with illumination, knowing with seeing, and truth with light)" (Belenky et al. 1986: 18). Men talk to each other too, of course, but

The differences between the women's conversation and the male bull session were strikingly reminiscent of the differences . . . noted between the play of fifth-grade girls and boys: intimate rather than impersonal, relatively informal and unstructured rather than bound by more or less explicit formal rules. Women have been practicing this kind of conversation since childhood. (Belenky et al. 1986: 114)

Given this cultural context, it is not surprising that contemporary Western feminists emphasize speaking between women as a primary means of determining feminist action and developing feminist understanding. In what follows, I offer several examples of how, over the past two decades, grass-roots activists have assigned a central role to spoken discourse. For description of the feminist discursive practices, I rely mostly, though not exclusively, on documents circulated among activists in typescript form or published by small "underground" or "alternative" presses.

Consciousness raising

"Consciousness raising," often referred to affectionately as c.r., is one of the best-known inventions of contemporary Western feminism. Reaching the height of its popularity in the late 1960s and early 1970s, consciousness raising groups are small gatherings of women meeting in private to share experiences hitherto thought of as personal. The operating assumption of the consciousness raising process is that much so-called personal experience, rather than being idiosyncratic, in fact is characterized by a number of common features frequently manifesting male dominance – hence the slogan "The personal is political." During consciousness raising sessions, participants offer first-hand accounts of specific personal experiences, describing not only who said and did what to whom but also the speakers' own emotional responses to the events. Honesty and vulnerability are valued in c.r. groups, which emphasize that no aspect of experience is too trivial for respectful attention. Questions to clarify or stimulate reflection are encouraged, but hearers are expected to be "non-judgmental,"

that is, to refrain from criticizing a speaker's conduct or disputing her account of her own experience. C.r. sessions are intended primarily to increase both the speakers' and the hearers' awareness of how women are subordinated in daily life, that is, to "raise their consciousness." The process is also designed, however, to provide emotional or moral support for individual women in order to strengthen them in resisting subordination.[4]

Feminist health care activism

Our Bodies, Our Selves is now a best-selling feminist self-help manual, published in several editions by a major publishing house, but initially it was produced by a small "underground" press, the New England Free Press, and sold for 35 cents. It was written by the Boston Women's Health Course Collective as a text for a feminist course on "health, women, and our bodies," first offered at Boston's Emmanuel College in May 1969. The first edition of *Our Bodies, Our Selves* (originally titled *Women and Their Bodies* and published in December 1970) describes how a feminist conception of healthy embodiment was developed through collective discussion.

The course planners began by sharing their own experiences and their knowledge of sickness, health, and medical care, soon discovering that "there were no 'good' doctors and we had to learn for ourselves." For more information, they went to books and to medically trained people, deciding collectively on the topics for research and how those topics should be handled. They met weekly to discuss their research, "gave support and helpful criticisms to each other and rewrote the papers." They then shared their collective knowledge with other "sisters," who "added their questions, fears, feelings, excitement." They insisted that their published results were "not final," "not static," but rather "a tool which stimulates discussion and action, which allows for new ideas and for change" (Boston Women's Health Course Collective 1971: 1).

Often, our best presentations of the course were done by a group of women (we could see a collective at work – in harmony, sharing, arguing, disagreeing) with questions throughout. . . . It was more important that we talked about our experiences, were challenged by others' experiences (often we came from very different situations), raised our questions, expressed our feelings, were challenged to act, than that we learned any specific body of material.

It was exciting to learn new facts about our bodies, but it was even more exciting to talk about how we felt about our bodies, how we felt about ourselves, how we could become more autonomous human beings, how we could act together on our collective knowledge to change the health care system for women and for all people.   (Boston Women's Health Course Collective 1971: 1–2)

In this account of its work process by the Boston Women's Health Course Collective, we find early statements of several themes that recur in later accounts of feminist process. The themes include a recognition that difference and even disagreement are not only inevitable but epistemically valuable, a willingness to acknowledge and explore people's emotional reactions, and an acceptance of technical expertise as necessary but not sufficient for an adequate understanding of women's health care needs. Above all, the themes include a conviction that, for students as well as instructors in the course, "the process that developed in the group became as important as the material we were learning." For these feminist activists, discussion was not just an efficient means to the end of acquiring new factual information about health care or even a means for developing critical evaluations of existing health care delivery systems. It was also a process that developed the moral capacities of each participant and the group as a whole.

Feminist anti-militarist activism

In another feminist enterprise, undertaken more than a decade later, anti-militarist activists developed an explicit formulation of the norms of feminist practical dialogue. This formulation can be found in the *Women's Encampment for a Future of Peace and Justice: Resource Handbook*. Inspired by the women besieging the US military base at Greenham Common in England, a feminist "peace camp" was established in the summer of 1983 at Seneca Army Depot in upstate New York. The *Women's Encampment Handbook* is a 50-page pamphlet distributed free to camp participants. It includes information on Seneca Army Depot and the surrounding area, some history of feminist activism in the region and a great deal of feminist philosophy of non-violence. It also sets out guidelines for collective decision-making by consensus.

The *Women's Encampment Handbook* echoes the aspirations of the Kantian (as opposed to the Hobbesian) contractarian tradition in stating clearly that consensus decision-making differs in principle not only from majority rule but also from bargaining. "Coercion and trade-offs are replaced with creative alternatives, and compromise with synthesis" (*Women's Encampment Handbook* 1983: 42). It also offers a brief statement of the moral presuppositions of consensus decision-making. "The fundamental right of consensus is for all people to be able to express themselves in their own words and of their own free will. The fundamental responsibility of consensus is to assure others of their right to speak and be heard" (*Women's Encampment Handbook* 1983: 42).

Most of the *Handbook*'s brief discussion is concerned less with elaborating philosophical assumptions than it is with the practical steps of moving towards consensus. In this connection, it identifies several roles that, if filled, may help consensus decision-making run smoothly. The roles include those of facilitator, recorder, and so called "vibes-watcher," the last of whom "watches and comments on individual and group feelings and patterns of participation" (*Women's Encampment Handbook* 1983: 42). The *Handbook* also lists various morally permissible alternatives if consensus cannot be reached. These are non-support, expressing reservations, standing aside, blocking and withdrawing from the group.

An especially interesting feature of the *Handbook*'s account of consensus decision-making is its statement of what is required of individuals who engage in this process. The requirements are as follows:

Responsibility: Participants are responsible for voicing their opinions, participating in the discussion, and actively implementing the agreement.

Self-discipline: Blocking consensus should only be done for principled objections. Object clearly, to the point, and without putdowns or speeches. Participate in finding an alternative solution.

Respect: Respect others and trust them to make responsible input.

Cooperation: Look for areas of agreement and common ground and build on them. Avoid competitive, right/wrong, win/lose thinking.

Struggle: Use clear means of disagreement – no putdowns. Use disagreements and arguments to learn, grow, and change. Work hard to build unity in the group, but not at the expense of the individuals who are its members. (*Women's Encampment Handbook* 1983: 42)

In striking contrast with Robert's Rules of Order, these requirements do not define specific procedures for the conduct of practical dialogue. Instead, they recommend the cultivation of certain moral attitudes or virtues and trust the reader to figure out how these attitudes or virtues should be manifested on specific occasions. They illustrate concretely what it means to pursue consensus rather than compromise, and show how, rather than fragmenting the community, the search for consensus may actually strengthen it and promote its moral development.[5]

Feminist pedagogy

The preceding examples implicitly assume that participants in feminist dialogue enjoy something approaching a peer relationship. In fact, however, relations between women are frequently characterized by inequality rather than equality and some North American feminists have ad-

dressed this fact directly.[6] One good source for reflecting on inequality is feminist pedagogy, which addresses the dialogical constraints as well as opportunities inherent in the context of an academic institution, where credentialed instructors are paid to instruct, where students pay for instruction, and where credits and grades are conferred.

Classrooms do indeed offer a space for dialogue that is relatively free from some kinds of distractions and disruptions but in which the time available for speaking is rigidly limited and there are inevitable power differences between teachers and students. These inequalities are based not just on varying experience and expertise but also on the institutionally assigned power to grade – and to some extent on the student's power as a consumer of education. In addition, and except in the most homogeneous classrooms, there are power differences among students – and conflicts that often are related to these differences. Such inequalities, combined with the introduction of course material that may be highly emotive, are likely to stimulate extremely powerful feelings that must be somehow handled in the course of classroom discussion.

Instructors of courses in feminist studies see their job as being to facilitate open dialogue in the face of these difficulties and they have worked to develop specific ways of guaranteeing respect for all present, while acknowledging the variety and limitations of each person's experience, knowledge, ability, and social power. They have sought to acknowledge speakers' thoughts and feelings respectfully without accepting them uncritically. In short, they have tried to integrate "egalitarian content and process" into a situation where people in many respects are unequal (Schniedewind 1983: 262).

Nancy Schniedewind begins her women's studies courses with interpersonal exercises for developing an "atmosphere of mutual respect, trust, and community in the classroom." She emphasizes that democratic processes among students are important for community and mutual respect," and notes that "the more aware each woman is of her use or abuse of time, attention, and power within the class, the more potentially democratic the group process" (1983: 262). She also remarks that "festive procedures are community-builders. Refreshments during breaks, a potluck dinner, and the integration of poetry and songs into the course, all catalyze energy and build community" (1983: 263). Like many other feminist teachers, Schniedewind uses various devices to foster cooperation among students and to integrate affective and practical learning with cognitive development. She suggests that pass/fail options or contract grading help both to reduce the instructor's power and to eliminate competitiveness between students (Schniedewind 1983: 268).

Schniedewind combines a strong commitment to feminist principles with a recognition of the difficulties in applying them. She endeavors to share leadership with her students but does not have "a totally egalitarian classroom." "I take more leadership and have more power than any of the students. I have found that students need an arena in which to *learn* to take responsibility for themselves and the group. For many, this is a new experience. I no longer expect that they automatically come to class with those experiences and skills" (Schniedewind 1983: 265).

Rachel Martin, a white feminist working outside academia with black women who possessed few literacy skills, also found that a necessary prerequisite to dialogue was the establishment of a sense of community with her students. Like Schniedewind and her students, Martin and her students moved toward community through sharing personal experience and forms of mutual aid such as food, sympathy, massages, and haircuts (Martin 1989).

Feminist reflections on pedagogy provide one resource for considering how open and productive dialogue may occur even in a context that sets a variety of constraints. Especially noteworthy is feminist instructors' conscious concern with establishing a sense of community as a prerequisite to dialogue, despite the inevitable presence of inequalities. Working to establish such a sense of community requires feminists to recognize in practical ways that people are not simply "talking heads." Thus, feminists attend not only to the explicit content of assertions made but also to the speaker's emotional and physical needs, providing not only an attentive ear but food, drink, haircuts, and hugs. Finally, feminist instructors remain continually conscious that even adults are not finished or complete but are constantly changing and developing. This consciousness is especially clearly articulated in Schniedewind's assertion that democracy requires more than the institution of certain rules of procedure; the ability to utilize such rules appropriately requires that people possess certain moral capacities that can be developed only by practicing them.

African American women's dialogue

My final example of feminist reliance on spoken dialogue is drawn from the work of Patricia Hill Collins who has asserted that the use of dialogue is especially characteristic of Afrocentric feminist epistemology in so far as it draws both on African American modes of gaining knowledge and on women's traditional "ways of knowing." Collins's account of black women's dialogue echoes many of the themes noted already. They include the importance of personal experience in assessing knowledge claims and the epistemic significance of emotion, characterized by Collins as part of an ethic of caring. For African American women, Collins writes, "personal expressiveness, emotions, and empathy are central to the knowledge validation process" (1990: 215). She adds that, for African American women, "Assessments of an individual's knowledge claims simultaneously evaluate an individual's character, values, and ethics." She reports that one of her classes of black women students "refused to evaluate the rationality of (a prominent Black male scholar's) written ideas without some indication of his personal credibility as an ethical human being" (1990: 218). Thus, what Collins calls "an ethic of personal accountability" is an additional dimension of an Afrocentric feminist epistemology.

Collins insists that the dialogue in which black women engage is quite different from adversarial debate. Rather than being a weapon for verbal contest, dialogue is seen instead as fundamental to the creation of community, the only context in which "people become more human and empowered" (1990: 212).

FPD as an idealization

Each of the practices described above offers a process for participants to recount their moral experience and then to reflect together critically on those accounts. While the practices differ somewhat from each other, I find them sufficiently similar to justify referring to them in the singular as FPD. In what follows, I discuss the conception of moral discourse implicit in FPD, drawing now on the work of other feminist philosophers as well as on the primary activist documents.

The conception of FPD that I discuss here is an idealization in the sense of being reconstructed from several different accounts. It is also an idealization in the sense that it focuses on the ideals that guide feminist discursive practices and the assumptions that underlie those ideals, ignoring questions about how far the ideals are ever instantiated. In fact, there is good reason to believe that in practice feminist dialogue often falls short of its own ideals. Many feminists, myself among them, can report efforts to engage in Feminist Practical Dialogue that have been painful and unproductive and "free rider" problems were reported at the Seneca Peace Encampment (Schwartz-Shea and Burrington 1990). This essay, however, is not an anthropological study of feminist culture nor an attempt either to romanticize or debunk it. Instead, it is a discussion of the philosophical assumptions and ideals implicit in one feminist model of moral reasoning.

Toward a Feminist Conception of Moral Discourse

A discursive understanding of moral reasoning is not unique to contemporary feminism. Well over a century ago, John Stuart Mill extolled the benefits of free discussion in his classic essay *On Liberty*, and he has been followed in this century by neo-Kantian contractarian theorists such as John Rawls and communicative ethicists, such as Karl

Otto Apel and Jürgen Habermas. All have offered philosophical elaborations of the persistent conviction that the most reliable understandings are likely to emerge from unconstrained discussion between people who are clear-headed and well-informed. But although FPD has arisen within the broad Western tradition of discursive approaches to justification/rationality, it offers distinctive perspectives on the crucial and contestable concepts of discursive openness, equality, freedom, and rationality.

Moral deliberation in FPD

FPDs typically do not begin with the articulation of general moral rules or principles; instead, they begin with the creation of opportunities for participants to talk about their own lives. The importance placed on first-person narrative reflects the early radical feminists' conviction that the dominant understandings of reality, in so far as they had been male-authored, had at best disregarded and at worst distorted or denied the truths of women's experience. The radical feminists of the late 1960s and early 1970s reacted to the neglect or misrepresentation of women's experience in moral and political analyses by asserting that the basis of moral and political understanding must be personal experience and the basis of feminist theory must be women's experience. In challenging accepted understandings of reality, therefore, feminists have been concerned that women begin by recounting their experience in their own terms. Rather than bracketing or disregarding their own experiences and concerns, participants in FPDs are encouraged to use them as the primary data of moral reflection. For FPDs, personal experience is a moral resource rather than a moral diversion.

First-person narratives may contribute to moral reflection in more than one way. Most obviously, they provide information about the lives of people whose situations may be very different from those of their hearers. It is a commonplace that our experience is broadened by learning about the experience of others. Of course, we may learn about other people's lives by reading or watching films or TV as well as by listening to them speak but personal interaction with a speaker makes a story especially vivid and immediate.

Listening to others recount their experience may increase our understanding of our own lives as well as those of others. It may help us to see hitherto unrecognized implications of our own actions; "helping" a disabled person without waiting for her request, for instance, may be to assume a position of power relative to her that reinforces a system of able-bodied privilege. Listening to others may also enable us to perceive commonalities in their experience and ours, a perception crucial to feminism. It has invariably been noticing similarities or patterns in the experience of different women that has precipitated the feminist recognition that many of women's supposedly "personal" problems result not from individual inadequacies but rather from social structures of male dominance (Frye 1990). With this recognition feminists become able to define as sexual harassment or date rape, for instance, moral and political problems that previously "had no name."

Although FPD begins from the assumption that the experience of every woman is equally important, it does not assume that each person's account of her own experience is authoritative or incorrigible. For this reason, it would be misleading to describe feminist moral thinking as based in any simple sense on personal experience. While personal experiences are certainly the starting point of feminist moral thinking, they are not the building blocks of feminist moral theory. Instead, the experiences are re-evaluated in a process of collective reflection that may transform the ways in which people think about their past situations and actions. To take a well-worn example, women may report enjoying male gallantry, interpreting this kind of attention as an expression of respect for women in general and themselves in particular. On further reflection, however, they may notice that this practice presupposes that women need male assistance and protection, thus covertly implying a lack of respect for their capabilities. Regardless of well-meaning intentions on both sides, men who behave gallantly toward women may then come to be seen as reinforcing

male dominance and women who welcome this attention may be seen as colluding in reinforcing male dominant attitudes.

Although FPD begins with relatively naive descriptions of personal experience, it moves inevitably to revising these accounts by considering alternative modes of conceptualization. In the new conceptualizations, different elements are selected as morally significant; for instance, in discussing situations where women receive unwanted sexual attention or where they participate reluctantly in sexual interaction, feminists often emphasize elements of coercion that have been unremarked in previous accounts. A variety of discursive strategies may be employed in persuading others to perceive things differently. They include telling "counterstories" that highlight alternative features of situations, drawing attention to analogies with other situations, using language designed to arouse moral emotions such as disgust, pride, or shame, and encouraging imaginative identification with other people. Thus, feminist moral deliberation is typically hermeneutic, concerned to reinterpret experience and social reality.

Equality and moral deference

The broadening and deepening of moral experience envisioned by FPD is obviously much less likely to occur if we talk only with those whose experiences have been similar to our own. Enlarging our moral perspective requires that we speak with people whose lives have been very different from ours. FPD is concerned to include women of various ages, physical abilities, class backgrounds, and racial or ethnic identifications, especially those women whose public silence has been the most profound. Since the few women permitted historically to participate in Western public discourse have been mostly women from the privileged classes, the most profoundly silenced women are primarily those from the working classes and other stigmatized groups, such as racial, ethnic, religious, or sexual minorities. Such women have found their voices not only muted but rendered virtually inaudible, excluded almost completely from the public discourse.

FPD assumes that it is precisely those women who may be best able to provide moral insight and even moral inspiration, especially in certain areas. Socially located on the edges or the underside of the dominant culture, such women have first-hand experience of the far-reaching and subtle as well as immediate and blatant consequences of evils such as racism and class exploitation – and often they have developed practical strategies for survival and resistance. Some feminists have asserted that the experience of less socially privileged women is not only different from that of women with more social advantages but also richer because it involves familiarity both with hegemonic and dissenting moral perspectives. Maria Lugones and Elizabeth V. Spelman write that "white/Anglo women are much less prepared for . . . dialogue with women of color than women of color are for dialogue with them in that women of color have had to learn white/ Anglo ways, self-conceptions, and conceptions of them" (1983: 577). To survive within a social system where they are at a systematic disadvantage, less privileged women must be acquainted with the dominant moral conceptualizations as well as with alternative ways of thinking. Thus, they are sometimes said to have a kind of double vision or enlarged moral understanding or critical capacity.

Because the social location of less privileged women is thought to afford them a kind of moral epistemic privilege, FPD assumes that their speech is especially deserving of respectful attention, at least in certain areas. This assumption is reminiscent of the "moral deference" that Lawrence Thomas asserts we owe to what he calls "diminished social category" people, that is, to individuals who belong to social groups that are negatively and unjustly devalued. According to Thomas, moral deference involves a presumption in favor of the person's account of her experiences (1992–3). In the context of FPD, moral deference may also involve giving special weight to the meanings that the individual from the diminished social category assigns to the behavior of others as well as herself. If she is a woman of color, for instance, her allegations of racism on the part of others must be taken especially seriously.

Is the moral deference accorded to certain participants in FPD compatible with conceptions of moral reasoning that mandate the discursive equality of each participant? Certainly moral deference entails that the burden of justification is not distributed evenly among the participants: where relations between more and less privileged women are being evaluated, for instance, there is a presumption in favor of the account given by the less privileged speaker and in the next section we shall see that special pains are taken in FPD to ensure that women from disadvantaged groups may speak and be heard. These imbalances between participants in FPD clearly violate the principle of formal equality but they may be justified as strategies for assisting participants to attain a discursive equality that is substantive rather than formal. It is plausible to regard them as a kind of discursive affirmative action, necessary to counterbalance the socially imposed obstacles to some women's full participation in dialogue.

Even though FPD presumes that the contribution of hitherto silenced women is likely to be especially valuable, it does not assume that social deprivation results inevitably in superior moral understanding. On the one hand, as Thomas notes, it may fill its victims so full of bitterness and rancor that they perceive even innocent interactions as offensive. On the other hand, Uma Narayan has pointed out that women from subordinated cultures may be especially eager to conform with or assimilate into the dominant culture. Or they may be disempowered by feelings of schizophrenia or alienation or their critical capacities may be stunted or damaged rather than enlarged. Narayan writes:

> Certain kinds of oppressive contexts, such as the contexts in which women of my grandmother's background lived, rendered their subjects entirely devoid of skills required to function as independent entities in the culture. Girls were married off barely past puberty, trained for nothing beyond household tasks and the rearing of children, and passed from economic dependency on their fathers to economic dependency on their husbands to economic dependency on their sons in old age. Their criticisms of their

lot were articulated, if at all, in terms that precluded a desire for any radical change. They saw themselves as personally unfortunate, but they did not locate the causes of their misery in larger social arrangements.   (Narayan 1989: 267–8)

She concludes,

[T]he alternative to buying into an oppressive social system need not be a celebration of exclusion and the mechanisms of marginalization. The thesis that oppression may bestow an epistemic advantage should not tempt us in the direction of idealizing or romanticizing oppression, and blind us to its real material and psychic deprivations.   (Narayan 1989: 268)

While FPD requires that socially disempowered women be heard with special respect, it does not assume that any woman is a necessarily moral expert or authority. As Donna Haraway remarks, "*how to* see from below is a problem requiring . . . much skill with bodies and language" (1988: 584). The same is presumably true for hearing from below or, to change the metaphor, from the margins. FPD is the practice that develops this skill.

Hearing other women

It is precisely because everyone's moral insight is limited that FPD emphasizes the need for interpersonal communication. But FPD is not easy; it is not simply a bunch of well-meaning people getting together and talking. Good will is necessary for the enterprise, but it is certainly not sufficient. Also required are effort, skill, and the practice of such virtues as responsibility, self-discipline, sensitivity, respect, and trust (*Women's Encampment Handbook* 1983: 42). When the participants' past experiences have been very different from each other and when their present relations are quite unequal, practicing these skills and virtues may be especially necessary – and especially difficult.

From the earliest days of consciousness raising, FPD has emphasized the need to provide a nurturant and supportive environment so that participants will feel safe enough to speak openly

of their experiences. Even when women voice their experience, however, we have seen that they cannot count on being heard. Lugones and Spelman have enumerated some of the difficulties that Hispana women face in communicating with white/Anglo women in the United States:

We and you do not talk the same language. When we talk to you we use your language: the language of your experience and of your theories. We try to use it to communicate our world of our experience. But since your language and your theories are inadequate in expressing our experiences, we only succeed in communicating our experience of exclusion. We cannot talk to you in our language because you do not understand it.   (Lugones and Spelman 1983: 575)

If white/Anglo women are to understand Hispana women, then, they must learn the Hispanas' "text." "But the text is an extraordinarily complex one: viz. our many different cultures" (Lugones and Spelman 1983: 580). Nevertheless,

if white/Anglo women are to understand our voices, they must understand our communities and us in them. . . . This learning calls for circumspection, for questioning of yourselves and your roles in your own culture. . . . This learning is then extremely hard because it requires openness (including openness to severe criticism of the white/Anglo world), sensitivity, concentration, self-questioning, circumspection. (Lugones and Spelman 1983: 581)

Lugones and Spelman go on to ask why white/Anglo feminists should undertake the difficult project of learning to hear Hispana women. They suggest that possible motives include Anglo women's desires to make reparations for the past exclusion of women of color, to make alliances with them, or to facilitate the Anglo women's own self-growth or self-expansion. Lugones and Spelman, however, reject all such motives of duty, obligation, or self-interest and conclude that "the motive of friendship remains as both the only appropriate and understandable motive" (1983: 581).

In an article published four years later, Lugones

elaborates her conception of intercultural discourse through the metaphor of " 'world'-traveling," a metaphor that explains how some women may acquire a kind of double moral vision. Lugones writes that social outsiders, such as women of color in the United States, often are forced to practice world-traveling into the mainstream, whereas white/Anglo women often fail to see women of color, even "*while we are in their midst*" (author's italics). "[T]hey ignore us, ostracize us, render us invisible, stereotype us, leave us completely alone, interpret us as crazy" (Lugones 1987: 7). Lugones remarks that these distorted perceptions are instances of what Marilyn Frye earlier had called "arrogant perception," and she herself characterizes them as failures of love.

Frye had written that those who see with arrogant eyes "organize everything seen with reference to themselves and their own interests" (Frye 1983: 67). They misrepresent the moral situation "by mislabelling the unwholesome as healthy and what is wrong as right." One who sees with a loving eye, by contrast, is "separate from the other whom she sees" (1983: 75). She "knows the independence of the other" and she "pays a certain sort of attention." She is attentive not only to the other, but also to herself, her own "interests, desires and loathings," her "projects, hungers, fears and wishes," and she is aware of how her own interests and emotions influence her perceptions of others (1983: 75).

Patrocinio Schweickart develops this theme, noting that

> Being a good listener requires attentiveness to the needs and interests of two subjectivities. It means not only getting the speaker's argument straight, but also trying to adopt his perspective, discern his assumptions and motives, identify with his feelings, feel his needs, understand what is at stake for him. In effect, the hearer must perform a service. She must put her subjectivity at the disposal of the speaker; and must cultivate and entertain, play host to, another subjectivity. At the same time, she must retain a lively sense of her own subjectivity; otherwise she risks losing the capacity for validating the speaker's claims, or of imposing her own subjective predispositions surreptitiously on the other. (Schweickart 1987: 311)

For Frye, Lugones, and Schweickart, then, seeing and hearing are complex enterprises that may be done badly or well. They are active rather than passive processes which require, according to Frye, that listeners shift their loyalties away from men and men's projects and refocus their attention and their energy on women (Frye 1983: 171–2). Such women include not only others but also oneself; self-knowledge is needed in order to hear others speak. In the context of a hierarchical, racist, and male-dominant society, seeing and hearing other women is said to require emotional and political reorientation, so that success in FPD becomes not simply a linguistic achievement but also a moral and political achievement.

This achievement is not made possible simply by the participants in the discourse committing themselves to certain abstract principles of discursive equality – or even to equal participation by representatives of certain groups.[7] Instead, FPD assumes that understanding between diverse people becomes possible only when those involved care for each other as specific individuals. It is significant that Lugones and Spelman propose the personal relation of friendship as the only appropriate motive for white/Anglo feminists to engage discursively with Hispanas and reject impersonal motivations such as duty. Only friendship, Lugones and Spelman write, will move white/Anglo women "to attain the appropriate reciprocity of care for your and our wellbeing as whole beings" (1983: 581). Similarly, in the context of a paper describing the extreme difficulty of dialogue between English and Indian university women, Ann Seller asserts that some communication ultimately was made possible by "small acts of inclusion" such as sharing *puja* or invitations to watch television (1992: 34). Ultimately, Seller writes, "I broke out of my isolation and they broke through the silence because of friendship, because of some shared political commitments and loyalties, and because sometimes we were in the same emotional world" (1992: 29). Seller insists that dialogues occur only "intermittently on the basis of common concerns" and they take place between "people, not belief systems" (1992: 33–4).

FPD's insistence that communication occurs between particular people rather than abstract individuals or group representatives reflects its commitment to a kind of caring that requires knowing people in their concrete particularity rather than as representatives of certain disadvantaged groups. Such caring may be expressed in the process of dialogue by responses such as sympathy with another's anger, encouragement to overcome her timidity, or even concern for her physical needs. In insisting on the importance of caring for participants in discourse "as whole beings," as "concrete" rather than "generalized" others, feminists endorse one crucial aspect of the feminine value of care, namely, its focus on particular individuals, and refuse to reconceptualize it in abstract "masculine" terms.[8] However, because the caring practiced in FPD is critical as well as nurturant and because it consciously addresses social and political inequalities, it should be seen as a feminist rather than feminine form of care.

FPD as nurturant rather than adversarial

The most striking contrast between FPD and non-feminist understandings of moral discourse is FPD's nurturant rather than adversarial nature. When described by non-feminist moral theorists, the process of moral discussion sounds much like litigation or, at best, like collective bargaining – even when designed to produce an outcome that is morally justified and not simply pragmatically workable. For instance, Rawls refers to the participants in his hypothetical discourse in the legal terminology of "parties." Platonic dialogues resemble verbal battles in which Socrates invariably vanquishes his opponents and images of struggle are evoked when contemporary philosophers describe philosophical debates in terms of "protagonists" and the "force" of ideas. In the Western tradition, of course, an adversarial or agonistic understanding of argument is not peculiar to the moral philosophy. George Lakoff

and Mark Johnson assert that it is common, in Western culture, to structure, perform, and talk about argument in terms derived from war (1980: 5).

FPD, by contrast distinguishes itself explicitly from adversarial debate (Collins 1990: 212). In this context, feminists strive to develop modes of discursive interaction that are not structured by warlike metaphors. They do not seek to overwhelm each other by rational arguments. Instead, through a variety of specific practices, feminists try to support each other in re-evaluating their initial conceptions of themselves and their experience, their history and culture, their relations to each other, and their perceptions of conflicting interests. In general, FPD is designed to promote an understanding and performance of moral discussion as a consciously cooperative and nurturant enterprise rather than a continuation of war by other means.

This is especially evident in the feminist insistence that moral discussion involves not only women's right to speak "in their own words and of their own free will" but also their responsibility "to assure others of their right to speak and be heard" (*Women's Encampment Handbook* 1983: 42). FPD emphasizes good listening as much as, if not more than, good speaking and is distinguished by practices designed to encourage participants to feel that their contributions are welcome and will be heard sympathetically and respectfully while still critically. Such practices recognize "the obligation to be responsive to the voice of the other, to protect and nurture fragile speech, to assume responsibility for doing 'interactive labor,' to draw out, to facilitate, to engender and cultivate the speech of the other . . ." (Schweickart 1987: 308). FPD cannot be understood, therefore, as an alternation of separate individual acts of speaking and listening – for it assumes that speaking and listening are not individual or separable acts. Often individuals would be unable to perform either of these acts unless they were encouraged and assisted to do so by by the speaking and listening activities of others.

The nurturance displayed in FPD seems to be continuous with the discursive practices of

Western women in general. Schweickart cites research findings that "men's discourse often takes on the quality of a verbal tournament," while women do more "interactive work" designed to keep conversations going (1987: 304). Thus, "women see questions as part of conversational maintenance while men see them as requests for information; (and) women explicitly acknowledge previous utterances and try to connect with them while men have no such rule and often ignore preceding comments" (1987: 304). Nurturant styles of discourse that are culturally feminine should not be interpreted as ways of compensating for supposed impairments in women's discursive competence, such as timidity or inarticulateness. Feminists reject suggestions that women's speech is "deviant in relation to a male norm . . . characterized as . . . direct, confident and straight-talking" (Mills 1992: 5). Nor, in the context of moral discussion, should nurturance be seen simply as a culturally feminine-style "cooperative" alternative to a culturally masculine "competitive" style.[9] Instead, feminists regard nurturance as indispensable for collective moral reflection that is truly free and open.

It may not be immediately evident that nurturance promotes moral reflection more effectively than competition. Indeed, it may be thought that competition is more likely to promote the kind of critical questioning necessary to evaluate moral claims thoroughly – just as competition rather than cooperation has been alleged to promote progress in science (Hull 1988). But nurturing the speech of others does not preclude disagreeing with what they say. In the early days of consciousness raising, being supportive was thought to require that no one be "judgmental," but later it became evident that nurturance and support do not require the suppression of disagreement – that disagreement, indeed, is valuable in so far as it encourages speakers to re-evaluate their accounts of their own experience. Thus, while FPD cannot countenance attempts to impose, rather than suggest, alternative ways of thinking about experience, it does recognize that sometimes it may be more nurturant and supportive to challenge than to accept a speaker's understanding even of her own life, for instance

if she is blaming herself for being the victim of assault. Moreover, failure to express disagreement may even be a sign of disrespect.

Just as being nurturant does not preclude disagreement, neither does being nurturant mean that the tone of discussion must always be saccharine sweet. Cultures and subcultures vary in what they count as acceptable or offensive gestures and language; for instance, some Jewish American and African American women report finding the discursive style of some middle- and upper-class European Americans stilted and insincere, while some European American women from middle- and upper-class backgrounds report discomfort with what they perceive as the bluntness and loudness of Jewish American or African American speech. Deborah Tannen reports that Western men commonly pursue affiliative goals through an adversarial style that would intimidate many women but does not seem to trouble men. The point of FPD is not to privilege any particular discursive style but rather to be sufficiently sensitive to varying cultural styles as to avoid intimidating, humiliating, or giving offense to other participants.

There are epistemological as well as moral reasons to avoid intimidating, humiliating, and offending others. Frightened, humiliated, or affronted people are ill-prepared for moral reflection; they are likely to be either defensively closed to alternative ways of thinking or so crushed that they cannot be critical. This is not to deny that participants in FPD sometimes experience uncomfortable or unpleasant emotions, such as uncertainty, embarrassment, anger, disappointment, or shame; as Lugones and Spelman remark, learning may be extremely hard. But inducing such emotions is not the primary goal of other participants; instead, they are inevitable concomitants of moral re-evaluation.

Reflecting on FPD reveals that Western philosophical accounts of discourse often have been male-biased. When agonistic metaphors are taken as normative and discursive cooperation is regarded as no more than a culturally feminine deviation, the conceptual truth that cooperation is integral to *all* discourse becomes obscured.

The interdependence of speaking and listening is not merely a feminist peculiarity; it is intrinsic to all productive discussion. Accounts of discourse that focus exclusively on speakers and their rights are incomplete and distorted. To describe discourse only in terms of speaking, while disregarding listening, is to rely on a mistaken view of meaning as representational and transparent, as a message packaged in language and needing only to be unwrapped by the hearer for the speaker's intention to become evident. In fact, meaning is something that listeners participate in constructing through their interpretations of utterances. Without interpretation by a listener, no communication occurs. Schweickart illustrates this point by reference to Sartre's play *No Exit*, writing: "Hell is being trapped forever in conversation not with people who disagree with you, but with people who cannot or will not be good listeners" (1987: 309).

By recognizing the complementary roles of speakers and listeners, FPD works from a more complete and less distorted understanding of discursive interaction than philosophical accounts describing discourse only in terms of speech.

Process as product

FPD simultaneously aims at consensus and recognizes that on any given occasion it may be unattainable (*Women's Encampment Handbook* 1983: 42). Even in the absence of consensus, however, feminists regard the process of moral discussion as valuable for its own sake – unlike those philosophers who portray moral reasoning as a series of procedures or logical moves designed to generate justified conclusions but who themselves remain morally neutral. FPD's conception of moral reasoning, by contrast, embodies a number of dialogical or discursive virtues that go well beyond the Kantian values of mutual equality and respect.

Different theorists provide overlapping accounts of these virtues. The *Women's Encampment Handbook* lists responsibility, self-discipline, respect, cooperation, and struggle (1983: 42). Lugones and Spelman mention courage and caring. Frye and Seller both emphasize political commitment and loyalty, while Frye adds self-

knowledge and Seller adds empathy. Schweickart notes the need for imagination, sensitivity, and the ability to balance two subjectivities. Jane Braaten offers a list of what she calls intellectual virtues that include the ability to imagine another's response to a situation, given her subjective point of view, and to imagine a world based on alternative norms and values (1990: 6–7).

Practicing these virtues is a valuable activity in itself. As Martha Nussbaum notes, "excursions of imagination and yearnings of sympathy do not serve as a means only to an intellectual knowledge that is in principle (though perhaps not in fact) separable from them" (1990: 92). She agrees with Aristotle that "the exercise of practical wisdom is itself a human excellence, an activity of intrinsic value apart from its tendency to produce virtuous actions." In the context of FPD, the practice of dialogical or discursive virtues also promotes the development of moral subjectivity and moral community, as well as moral justifiability. Consideration of these topics must await another occasion.

Some Strengths of Feminist Practical Dialogue

FPD is both continuous with and divergent from mainstream philosophical conceptions of moral reasoning. Certainly it is not unique in its interest in discursive reasoning, in its determination that the values of freedom and equality should be expressed in the process of moral discourse, or in asserting the indispensability of empirical as opposed to imaginary dialogue. However, while many components of FPD may be found in other conceptions of moral reasoning, FPD combines them in a distinctive mixture that in my view offers several advantages.

FPD is more empirically and conceptually adequate

FPD emerges from an activist rather than an academic context and thus "constructs its alternative out of the concrete and shared experiences of women, rather than out of a romantic vision of precapitalist life or abstract ideal of human nature" (Ferguson 1984: 27). Because of this, FPD presupposes an understanding of moral discourse that is empirically and conceptually richer than that found in many philosophical theories acknowledging the complexity and intrinsically cooperative nature of discourse and the opacity of meaning.

FPD expresses feminist values

Second-wave feminists have always been clear that processes are inseparable from products; in consequence, they have insisted that feminist processes must embody feminist values. The following are among the values embodied in FPD.

1. *Respect for women's moral autonomy.* FPD expresses its respect for woman's autonomy by insisting that every woman be able to participate freely and equally in moral discourse. FPD, however, construes free and equal participation in a less abstract way than most philosophical accounts of discourse, a way that recognizes the complex realities of discursive interaction. Inherent in FPD, moreover, is a standard of discursive competence that seems attainable by any woman; specifically, and unlike most philosophical accounts of ideal discourse, FPD promotes a mode of discursive interaction that does not give systematic advantages to women with more formal education or other social privileges. FPD is therefore a deeply democratic model of moral reasoning that preserves the autonomy of all participants.

2. *Respect for women's experience and insights.* Feminists have asserted for over two decades that traditional moral theory ignores or devalues women's moral experience (Gilligan 1982). FPD regards attention to women's experience as indispensable to feminist ethics but, at the same time, it does not treat as unchallengeable women's accounts and evaluations either of their own experience or the experience of others. Women, especially previously silenced women, must be treated with moral deference but not with moral obsequiousness.

3. *Care.* In addition to the symbolically masculine values of equality and reciprocity, FPD is informed by such symbolically feminine values as friendship, love, and care for concrete rather than generalized others. This certainly does not mean that manifesting anything other than positive or "vanilla" emotions violates the ideals of FPD, which recognizes that emotions such as suspicion, resentment, or hostility are inevitable and even appropriate in certain discursive contexts. However, it regards the occurrence of these emotions as compatible with care, friendship, and love which therefore, in the context of FPD, become critical rather than sentimental emotions.

The pragmatic optimism of FPD

FPD addresses not a philosophical ideal world but rather the world that we actually inhabit. By contrast, Rawlsian hypothetical dialogue is a philosophical thought experiment that addresses only the circumstances of what Rawls calls "perfect justice," while Habermas's conditions of ideal discourse are so stringent that they are quite inapplicable to daily life. Because FPD typically occurs in response to a perceived need to address specific moral problems, the recommendations it produces are likely to be more useful pragmatically than those produced by many philosophical theories. For instance, the conclusions of FPD are likely to be intuitively or motivationally acceptable to the participants, applicable in circumstances of less than perfect justice, and formulated at the level of determinacy or generality appropriate for the context.

FPD offers an alternative not only to philosophical conceptions of ideal discourse but also to a second kind of discourse mentioned in contemporary philosophical literature. This is "conversation," a way of talking that philosophers portray as free-ranging, unstructured, and involving no systematic attempt to compensate for discursive inequalities between the participants. Unlike ideal discourse, which is designed to represent the conditions of moral justification, philosophical conversations are not thought to bear any particular moral weight (Ackerman 1989; Walzer 1989–90).

Even though they are defined in opposition to each other, these two kinds of talk converge on the same unsatisfactory conclusion from the point of view of moral reasoning. Actual conversations can contribute to moral discovery, but the agreements they may produce have no particular claim to moral legitimacy, while idealized discourse is never instantiated. Both kinds of talk thus lead quickly to skepticism in practical ethics.

It is certainly understandable why philosophers should be pessimistic about the ethical possibilities of empirical discourse. In the world we presently inhabit, even the aspiration to free and equal dialogue often seems next to hopeless, let alone capable of achieving moral consensus. People in the real world are unequal in resources, time, and power, and these inequalities cause severe imbalances in most empirical discourses. Few of our actual moral discussions resemble even the relatively fair circumstances of a philosophy seminar, and many of us can testify that socially constructed inequalities set powerful constraints on our discourse even here. Moreover, even if these obstacles to egalitarian discourse could somehow be overcome, the chance of consensus emerging seems remote indeed. People in the real world have sharply divergent values; the starting point of contemporary liberal theory, indeed, is the undisputed fact that modern societies are characterized by a plurality of conceptions of the good. Even more significantly, people also have interests that conflict in very real ways – which is not to say that they do not also share some significant interests.

It is easy to see why these unfortunately familiar facts of contemporary life should generate philosophical pessimism concerning the moral possibilities of empirical discourse. Such pessimism has led at least one influential contemporary philosopher, Bruce Ackerman, to deny explicitly that morality (unlike politics) requires dialogue. He says that "a little talk may go a long way; a lot may lead nowhere." Talking to others is not, in Ackerman's view, "of supreme importance in moral self-definition" because "The key decisions are made in silence: Whom to trust? What do I really think?" He concludes that "a morally reflective person *can* permissibly cut herself off from real-world dialogue" (1989: 6).

FPD, by contrast, takes seriously the possibilities as well as the difficulties of empirical dialogue in the real world – and the moral potential as well as the moral limitations of real people. Although it is true that FPD is predicated on the assumption that everyone is fallible, it also assumes that we are all corrigible, capable of self-conscious reflection and deliberate action, of taking others' points of view and re-evaluating our own positions from their perspectives. Because FPD is designed specifically to tap the moral capacities of the participants, we can see that respect for the moral capacities of ordinary people, notably ordinary women, is inherent in this practice.

FPD thus constitutes an alternative to the two kinds of talk recognized by contemporary philosophers. In situations that are not and never will be ideal, it suggests a way in which women may talk with each other that is less than ideal but still superior to most ordinary conversations in hierarchical societies. In working to develop this alternative, the practitioners of FPD may be seen as accepting our real-life moral situation with good grace, rather than regretfully or grudgingly, and committing themselves to making the best of it. FPD offers a seemingly practicable method for promoting moral understandings that actually occur and may also claim to be morally justified.

Conclusion

Even in those relatively favorable situations where FPD can be practiced, it never guarantees moral consensus: some emotional responses may be too intransigent and some conflicts of interest too deeply entrenched. In such situations, FPD does not require us to talk forever. When talk becomes harassment, when understanding is not even on the horizon, when the need for action is urgent, FPD accepts that discussion may be abandoned – at least for the time being. However, it requires that dialogue be resumed as soon as possible. Given the inevitably limited nature of our experience and knowledge, including our limited knowledge even of our own capacities, needs, and motivations, FPD seems the best strategy currently available for improving the moral adequacy of our thinking and action.

One advantage of concentrating on the notion of empirical rather than hypothetical discourse and seeking actual rather than hypothetical consensus is that this encourages us to focus on the practical obstacles that make even domination-free communication, let alone moral consensus, so difficult to attain. Prominent among these obstacles, as we have seen, are socially constructed inequalities. We already have good reasons for working politically to reduce such inequalities, but if empirical discourse is recognized as crucial to feminist practical ethics, considerations of moral epistemology may now be added to these reasons. It becomes even clearer that moral progress is inseparable from political progress and feminist ethics from feminist politics.

FPD makes no pretense of being a tidy and unproblematic procedure, even in principle, for figuring out what we should do. Utilizing FPD is no substitute for, and indeed requires, a kind of practical – especially political – wisdom: wisdom that enables us to weigh the claims of people who are never fully rational or uncoerced, but never completely puppets either, people who are, in addition, always in some power relation respective to us. Only such wisdom can tell us when, and especially with whom, it is morally incumbent to engage in dialogue – as well as when it is necessary to end the dialogue and commit ourselves to practical action.

Notes

1   I have received helpful comments on earlier drafts from many people, including Kathy Addelson, Hazel Barnes, Sandra Bartky, Lawrence Blum, Len Boonin, Luc Bovens, Dwight Boyd, Laura Brunell, Emily Calhoun, Frank Cunningham, Annette Dula, Marlene G. Fine, Lori Gruen, Sandra Harding, Virginia Held, Dale Jamieson, Jane Kneller, Gwyn Kirk, Marcia Lind, Bill McBride, Angela Miles, Jim Nickel, Linda Nicholson, Sally Ruddick, Richard Schmitt, Anne Seller, Gary Stahl, Karsten Struhl, and Iris Young. I have also benefited from comments made by audiences at the University of To-

ronto, the University of Frankfurt, the University of Quebec, the North American Society for Social Philosophy, and the Philosophy of Education Society as well as from Sophia and from the political philosophy reading group and the women's studies work-in-progress at the University of Colorado at Boulder.

2   There is no orthodoxy in feminist ethics although it is a common mistake to identify feminist ethics with an ethics of care. In addition to several versions of an ethics of care, different feminists have proposed as models for feminist ethics the understandings of moral reasoning held by, among others, Aristotle, Hume, Kant, Hegel, Bentham, Mill, Sartre, Camus, Rawls, and Habermas.

3   For instance, the credits on the first page of the *Women's Encampment Handbook* (1983) thank "the tradition of handbooks from which some of this material has been obtained."

4   For descriptions of consciousness raising, see Arnold 1970; Gardner 1970; Hanisch 1970; Peslikis 1970; Sarachild 1970; Koedt et al. 1973; Payne 1973.

5   Space constraints do not permit me to discuss here a 1980 document circulated by the feminist battered women's movement, "A Feminist Perspective on the Ethics of Communication, Explored in the Context of an On-Going Group of Women with Decision-Making Responsibility" (Evans 1980). The author, Kit Evans, executive Director of AWAKE, National Coalition Against Domestic Violence, offers "twelve basic principles for ethical communication at any level." These principles are grounded in a clear-eyed realization of the many ways in which free and open discourse may be subverted and provide practical suggestions for avoiding such subversion. Deborah Flick brought these principles to my attention and I obtained them from the Boulder Safehouse.

6   Some Italian feminists have also experimented with ways of utilizing inequality between women as a moral resource. See especially the Milan Women's Bookstore Collective (1990).

7   John Rawls specifies that the negotiating parties in his hypothetical discourse are "representative men" (1971).

8   The distinction between "generalized" and "concrete" others is made by Seyla Benhabib (1986). Lorraine Code insists that feminist caring is not impersonal but instead requires knowing the specific situations of the putative recipients of care,

especially whether they need or want the type of care envisioned (1992).

9. Sara Mills, for instance, seems to suggest this (1992).

Bibliography

Ackerman, Bruce (1989), "Why Dialogue?" *Journal of Philosophy*, 86: 1.

Arnold, June (1970), "Consciousness-Raising." In *Women's Liberation: Blueprint for the Future*, Sookie Stambler, ed. New York: Ace, 155–61.

Baldwin, Margaret A. (1992), "Split at the Root: Prostitution and Feminist Discourses of Law Reform," *Yale Journal of Law and Feminism* 5: 47, 47–120.

Belenky, Mary Field, Blythe McVicker Clinchy, Nancy Rule Goldberger, Jill Mattuck Tarule (1986), *Women's Ways of Knowing: The Development of Self, Voice, and Mind*. New York: Basic Books.

Benhabib, Seyla (1986), "The Generalized and the Concrete Other: The Kohlberg–Gilligan Controversy and Feminist Theory." *Praxis International*, 5: 4 (January), 402–24.

Blum, Lawrence A. (1982), "Kant's and Hegel's Moral Rationalism: A Feminist Perspective." *Canadian Journal of Philosophy*, 12: 2 (June), 287–302.

Boston Women's Health Course Collective (1971), *Our Bodies, Our Selves*. Boston: New England Free Press.

Braaten, Jane (1990), "Toward a Feminist Reassessment of Intellectual Virtue." *Hypatia*, 5: 3 (Fall), 1–14.

Code, Lorraine (1992), "Who Cares? The Poverty of Objectivism for a Moral Epistemology." *Annals of Scholarship*, 19: 1–2, 1–17.

Collins, Patricia Hill (1990), *Black Feminist Thought: Knowledge, Consciousness, and the Politics of Empowerment*. Boston: Unwin Hyman.

Evans, Kit (1980), "A Feminist Perspective on the Ethics of Communication, Explored in the Context of an On-Going Group of Women with Decision-Making Responsibility." National Coalition against Domestic Violence. Unpublished manuscript.

Ferguson, Kathy E. (1984), *The Feminist Case Against Bureaucracy*. Philadelphia: Temple University Press.

Fisher, Roger, and William Ury with Bruce Patton (1981), *Getting to Yes: Negotiating Agreement Without Giving In*. Boston: Houghton Mifflin.

Fraser, Nancy (1986) "Toward a Discourse Ethic of Solidarity." *Praxis International*, 5: 4 (January), 425–9.

Friedman, Marilyn (1989), "The Impracticality of Impartiality." *Journal of Philosophy*, 86: 11 (November), 645–56.

Frye, Marilyn (1990), *The Politics of Reality: Essays in Feminist Theory*. Trumansburg, NY: Crossing Press.

Frye, Marilyn (1983), "The Possibility of Feminist Theory." In *Theoretical Perspectives on Sex Difference*, Debrel L. Rhode, ed., New Haven: Yale University Press.

Gardner, Jennifer (1970), "False Consciousness." In *Notes from the Second Year*, Shulamith Firestone, ed. New York, 82–3.

Gibson, Mary (1985), *To Breathe Freely: Risk, Consent and Air*. Totowa, NJ: Rowman and Allanheld, 141–68.

Gilligan, Carol (1982), *In a Different Voice: Psychological Theory and Women's Development*. Cambridge, MA: Harvard University Press.

Hanisch, Carol (1970), "The Personal Is Political." In *Notes from the Second Year*, Shulamith Firestone, ed. New York, 76–8.

Haraway, Donna (1988), "Situated Knowledges: The Science Question in Feminism and the Privilege of Partial Perspective." *Feminist Studies*, 14: 4 (Fall), 575–99.

Hoagland, Sara Lucia (1988), *Lesbian Ethics: Toward New Value*. Palo Alto: Institute of Lesbian Studies.

hooks, bell (1989), *Talking Back: Thinking Feminist – Thinking Back*. Boston: South End Press.

Hull, David (1988), *Science as a Process: An Evolutionary Account of the Social and Conceptual Development of Science*. Chicago: University of Chicago Press.

Iannello, Kathleen P. (1992), *Decisions without Hierarchy: Feminist Interventions in Organization Theory and Practice*. New York: Routledge.

Jaggar, Alison M. (1989), "Love and Knowledge: Emotion in Feminist Epistemology." *Inquiry*, 32, 151–76.

Koedt, Anne, Ellen Levine, and Anita Rapone (1973), "Consciousness Raising." In *Radical Feminism*, Anne Koedt, Ellen Levine, and Anita Rapone, eds. New York: Quadrangle, 280–1.

Lakoff, George, and Mark Johnson (1980), *Metaphors We Live By*. Chicago: University of Chicago Press.

Lugones, Maria (1987), "Playfulness, 'World'-Travelling, and Loving Perception." *Hypatia*, 2: 2 (Summer), 3–19.

Lugones, Maria C., and Elizabeth V. Spelman (1983), "Have We Got a Theory for You! Feminist Theory, Cultural Imperialism and the Demand for 'the Woman's Voice.'" *Hypatia*, 1: 1, 573–81.

Martin, Rachel (1989), *Literacy from the Inside Out.* Boston.

Milan Women's Bookstore Collective (1990), *Sexual Difference: A Theory of Social-Symbolic Practice.* Bloomington: University of Indiana Press.

Mills, Sara (1992), "Discourse Competence: Or How to Theorize Strong Women Speakers." *Hypatia,* 7: 2 (Spring), 4–17.

Morgan, Kathryn Paula (1987), "Women and Moral Madness." In *Science, Morality and Feminist Theory,* Marsha Hanen and Kai Nielsen, eds. Calgary: University of Calgary Press.

Narayan, Uma (1989), "The Project of Feminist Epistemology: Perspectives from a Nonwestern Feminist." In *Gender/Body/Knowledge: Feminist Reconstructions of Being and Knowing,* Alison M. Jaggar and Susan R. Bordo, eds. New Brunswick: Rutgers University Press, 256–69.

Nussbaum, Martha (1990), *Love's Knowledge.* Oxford: Oxford University Press.

Parker, Pat (1990), "For the White Person who Wants to Know how to be my Friend." In *Making Face, Making Soul: Haciendo Caras: Creative and Critical Perspectives by Women of Color,* Gloria Anzaldua, ed. San Franciso: aunt lute foundation, 297.

Payne, Carol Williams (1973), "Consciousness Raising: A Dead End?" In *Radical Feminism,* Anne Koedt, Ellen Levine, and Anita Rapone, eds. New York: Quadrangle, 282–4.

Peslikis, Irene (1970), "Resistances to Consciousness." In *Notes from the Second Year,* Shulamith Firestone, ed. New York, 81.

Piaget, Jean (1965), *The Moral Judgement of the Child.* New York: Free Press.

Rawls, John (1971), *A Theory of Justice.* Cambridge, MA: Harvard University Press.

Rich, Adrienne (1979), *On Lies, Secrets and Silences.* New York: Norton.

Sarachild, Kathie (1970), "A Program for Feminist 'Consciousness Raising'." In *Notes from the Second Year,* Shulamith Firestone, ed. New York, 78–80.

Schniedewind, Nancy (1983), "Feminist Values: Guidelines for a Teaching Methodology in Women's Studies." In *Learning Our Way: Essays in Feminist Education,* Charlotte Bunch and Sandra Pollack, eds. Trumansburg, NY: Crossing Press, 261–71.

Schwartz-Shea, Peregrine, and Debra D. Burrington (1990), "Free Riding, Alternative Organization and Cultural Feminism: The Case of Seneca Women's Peace Camp." *Women and Politics,* 10: 3, 1–37.

Schweickart, Patrocinio (1987), "Engendering Critical Discourse." In *The Current in Criticism,* Clayton Koelb and Virgil Lokke, eds. West Lafayette: Purdue University Press, 295–317.

Seller, Anne (1992), "Should the Feminist Philosopher Stay at Home?" Unpublished manuscript, February.

Spivak, Gayatri Chakravorty (1988), "Can the Subaltern Speak?" in *Marxism and the Interpretation of Culture,* Cary Nelson and Lawrence Grossberg, eds. Urbana: University of Illinois Press, 271–313.

Sterba, James P. (1988), *How to Make People Just: A Practical Reconciliation of Alternative Conceptions of Justice.* Totowa, NJ: Rowman and Allanheld.

Taylor, Charles (1991), "The Dialogical Self." In *The Interpretive Turn,* David Hiley, James F. Bowman and Richard Shusterman, eds. Ithaca: Cornell University Press.

Thomas, Lawrence (1992–3), "Moral Deference." *Philosophical Forum,* 14: 1–3, 233–50.

Walzer, Michael (1989–90), "A Critique of Philosophical Conversation." *Philosophical Forum,* 21: 1–2 (Fall–Winter), 182–96.

Women's Encampment for a Future of Peace and Justice: Resource Handbook (1983), New York: Romulus.

36   Chimpanzee Justice

Frans De Waal

The influence of the recent past is always overestimated. When we are asked to name the greatest human inventions we tend to think of the telephone, the electric light bulb and the silicon chip rather than the wheel, the plough and the taming of fire. Similarly the origins of modern society are sought in the advent of agriculture, trade and industry, whereas in fact our social history is a thousand times older than these phenomena. It has been suggested that food sharing was a strong stimulus in furthering the evolution of our tendency to reciprocal relations. Would it not be more logical to assume that social reciprocity existed earlier, and that tangible exchanges such as food sharing stem from this phenomenon?

Be this as it may, there are indications of reciprocity in the non-material behaviour of chimpanzees. This is seen, for instance, in their coalitions (A supports B, and vice versa), non-intervention alliances (A remains neutral if B does the same), sexual bargaining (A tolerates B mating after B has groomed A) and reconciliation blackmail (A refuses to have contact with B unless B 'greets' A). It is interesting that reciprocity occurs in both the negative and the positive sense. Nikkie's habit of individually punishing females who a short time before joined forces against him has already been described. In this way he repaid a negative action with another negative action. We regularly see this mechanism in operation before the group separates for the

From *Chimpanzee Politics* (Jonathan Cape: London, 1982), pp. 205–7. Reprinted by permission.

night. This is the time when differences are squared, no matter when these differences may have arisen. For example, one morning a conflict breaks out between Mama and Oor. Oor rushes to Nikkie and with wild gestures and exaggeratedly loud screams persuades him to attack her powerful opponent. Nikkie attacks Mama and Oor wins. That evening, however, a good six hours later, we hear the sound of a scuffle in the sleeping quarters. The keeper later tells me that Mama has attacked Oor in no uncertain manner. Needless to say Nikkie was nowhere in the vicinity.

[. . .]

The principle of exchange makes it possible actively to teach someone something: good behaviour is rewarded, bad behaviour is punished. A development in the relationship between Mama and Nikkie demonstrates just how complex such influencing processes can be. Their relationship is ambivalent. There are numerous indications that the two of them are very fond of each other. For example, when Mama returned to the group after an absence of over a month, she spent hours grooming Nikkie, and not Gorilla, Jimmie, Yeroen or any of the other individuals with whom she normally spends her time. And of all the children in the colony Moniek, Mama's daughter, is obviously Nikkie's favourite. But for a while it was the hostile side of their relationship which got the upper hand. This was at the beginning of Nikkie's leadership. Yeroen used to mobilize adult females against the young leader and Mama was his major ally. At the end of such incidents, when Nikkie had been reconciled with Yeroen, he would go over to Mama to punish her for the part she had played. This could take a very long time, because Mama usually punished Nikkie in return by rejecting his subsequent attempts at reconciliation. For instance, Nikkie slaps Mama, but a little later he comes back and sits down by her 'shyly' plucking at some wisps of grass. Mama pretends she has not seen him, gets up and walks off. Nikkie waits a while, then starts all over again, with his hair on end. This was clearly a phase of negative reciprocity.

As Yeroen's resistance to Nikkie decreased, Mama became more favourably inclined towards Nikkie. She still supported Yeroen, but when Nikkie made his peace with her later she no longer took any 'affective revenge' and their conflict remained brief. Later still – a process taking years – Mama reconciled her differences with Nikkie before his conflict with Yeroen had ended. One moment the two older apes were chasing after Nikkie, the next moment Mama affectionately embraced him. The conflict then continued between the two males, but Mama declined to take any further part.

In time the situation became even stranger. Nikkie began kissing Mama before or even during his display against Yeroen. This developed gradually from their reconciliations, until it took place without any preceding conflict. It could be seen as a mark of Mama's neutrality. Nikkie and Mama were showing positive reciprocity.

I have done a statistical study of the bilateral nature of coalitions by comparing how each individual intervenes in the conflicts of the others. In periods of stability such interventions are symmetrical, both in a positive sense (two individuals support each other) and in a negative sense (two individuals support each other's opponents). If we are to get a full picture of reciprocity, however, we will have to analyse more kinds of behaviour. Interventions need not necessarily be offset by other interventions. The receipt of regular support may be answered by greater tolerance towards the supporter, or by grooming. Perhaps we will eventually be able to conduct such an analysis in Arnhem. For the time being I should like to sum up as follows: chimpanzee group life is like a market in power, sex, affection, support, intolerance and hostility. The two basic rules are 'one good turn deserves another' and 'an eye for an eye, a tooth for a tooth'.

The rules are not always obeyed and flagrant disobedience may be punished. This happened once after Puist had supported Luit in chasing Nikkie. When Nikkie later displayed at Puist she turned to Luit and held out her hand to him in search of support. Luit, however, did nothing to protect her against Nikkie's attack. Immediately Puist turned on Luit, barking furiously, chased him across the enclosure and even hit him. If her fury was in fact the result of Luit's failure to help her after she had helped him, this would suggest that reciprocity among chimpanzees is governed by the same sense of moral rightness and justice as it is among humans.

37   All Animals Are Equal

Peter Singer

"Animal Liberation" may sound more like a parody of other liberation movements than a serious objective. The idea of "The Rights of Animals" actually was once used to parody the case for women's rights. When Mary Wollstonecraft, a forerunner of today's feminists, published her *Vindication of the Rights of Woman* in 1792, her views were widely regarded as absurd, and before long an anonymous publication appeared entitled *A Vindication of the Rights of Brutes*. The author of this satirical work (now known to have been Thomas Taylor, a distinguished Cambridge philosopher) tried to refute Mary Wollstonecraft's arguments by showing that they could be carried one stage further. If the argument for equality was sound when applied to women, why should it not be applied to dogs, cats, and horses? The reasoning seemed to hold for these "brutes" too; yet to hold that brutes had rights was manifestly absurd. Therefore the reasoning by which this conclusion had been reached must be unsound, and if unsound when applied to brutes, it must also be unsound when applied to women, since the very same arguments had been used in each case.

In order to explain the basis of the case for the equality of animals, it will be helpful to start with an examination of the case for the equality of women. Let us assume that we wish to defend the case for women's rights against the attack by Thomas Taylor. How should we reply?

One way in which we might reply is by saying that the case for equality between men and women cannot validly be extended to non-human animals. Women have a right to vote, for instance, because they are just as capable of making rational decisions about the future as men

From *Animal Liberation*, rev. edn. (New York: New York Review, 1990) Reprinted by permission.

are; dogs, on the other hand, are incapable of understanding the significance of voting, so they cannot have the right to vote. There are many other obvious ways in which men and women resemble each other closely, while humans and animals differ greatly. So, it might be said, men and women are similar beings and should have similar rights, while humans and non-humans are different and should not have equal rights.

The reasoning behind this reply to Taylor's analogy is correct up to a point, but it does not go far enough. There are obviously important differences between humans and other animals, and these differences must give rise to some differences in the rights that each have. Recognizing this evident fact, however, is no barrier to the case for extending the basic principle of equality to non-human animals. The differences that exist between men and women are equally undeniable, and the supporters of Women's Liberation are aware that these differences may give rise to different rights. Many feminists hold that women have the right to an abortion on request. It does not follow that since these same feminists are campaigning for equality between men and women they must support the right of men to have abortions too. Since a man cannot have an abortion, it is meaningless to talk of his right to have one. Since dogs can't vote, it is meaningless to talk of their right to vote. There is no reason why either Women's Liberation or Animal Liberation should get involved in such nonsense. The extension of the basic principle of equality from one group to another does not imply that we must treat both groups in exactly the same way, or grant exactly the same rights to both groups. Whether we should do so will depend on the nature of the members of the two groups. The basic principle of equality does not require equal or identical *treatment*; it requires equal consideration. Equal consideration for different beings may lead to different treatment and different rights.

So there is a different way of replying to Taylor's attempt to parody the case for women's rights, a way that does not deny the obvious differences between human beings and non-humans but goes more deeply into the question of equality and concludes by finding nothing absurd in the idea that the basic principle of equality applies to so-called brutes. At this point such a conclusion may appear odd; but if we examine more deeply the basis on which our opposition to discrimination on grounds of race or sex ultimately rests, we will see that we would be on shaky ground if we were to demand equality for blacks, women, and other groups of oppressed humans while denying equal consideration to non-humans. To make this clear we need to see, first, exactly why racism and sexism are wrong. When we say that all human beings, whatever their race, creed, or sex, are equal, what is it that we are asserting? Those who wish to defend hierarchical, inegalitarian societies have often pointed out that by whatever test we choose it simply is not true that all humans are equal. Like it or not we must face the fact that humans come in different shapes and sizes; they come with different moral capacities, different intellectual abilities, different amounts of benevolent feeling and sensitivity to the needs of others, different abilities to communicate effectively, and different capacities to experience pleasure and pain. In short, if the demand for equality were based on the actual equality of all human beings, we would have to stop demanding equality.

Still, one might cling to the view that the demand for equality among human beings is based on the actual equality of the different races and sexes. Although, it may be said, humans differ as individuals, there are no differences between the races and sexes as such. From the mere fact that a person is black or a woman we cannot infer anything about that person's intellectual or moral capacities. This, it may be said, is why racism and sexism are wrong. The white racist claims that whites are superior to blacks, but this is false; although there are differences among individuals, some blacks are superior to some whites in all of the capacities and abilities that could conceivably be relevant. The opponent of sexism would say the same: a person's sex is no guide to his or her abilities, and this is why it is unjustifiable to discriminate on the basis of sex.

The existence of individual variations that cut across the lines of race or sex, however, provides us with no defense at all against a more sophisticated opponent of equality, one who proposes that, say, the interests of all those with IQ scores below 100 be given less consideration than the interests of those with ratings over 100. Perhaps those scoring below the mark would, in this society, be made the slaves of those scoring higher. Would a hierarchical society of this sort really be so much better than one based on race or sex? I think not. But if we tie the moral principle of equality to the factual equality of the different races or sexes, taken as a whole, our opposition to racism and sexism does not provide us with any basis for objecting to this kind of inegalitarianism.

There is a second important reason why we ought not to base our opposition to racism and sexism on any kind of factual equality, even the limited kind that asserts that variations in capacities and abilities are spread evenly among the different races and between the sexes: we can have no absolute guarantee that these capacities and abilities really are distributed evenly, without regard to race or sex, among human beings. So far as actual abilities are concerned there do seem to be certain measurable differences both among races and between sexes. These differences do not, of course, appear in every case, but only when averages are taken. More important still, we do not yet know how many of these differences are really due to the different genetic endowments of the different races and sexes, and how many are due to poor schools, poor housing, and other factors that are the result of past and continuing discrimination. Perhaps all of the important differences will eventually prove to be environmental rather than genetic. Anyone opposed to racism and sexism will certainly hope that this will be so, for it will make the task of ending discrimination a lot easier; nevertheless, it would be dangerous to rest the case against racism and sexism on the belief that all significant differences are environmental in origin. The opponent of, say, racism who takes this line will be unable to avoid conceding that if differences in ability did after all prove to have some genetic connection with race, racism would in some way be defensible.

Fortunately there is no need to pin the case for equality to one particular outcome of a scientific investigation. The appropriate response to those who claim to have found evidence of genetically based differences in ability among the races or between the sexes is not to stick to the belief that the genetic explanation must be wrong, whatever evidence to the contrary may turn up; instead we should make it quite clear that the claim to equality does not depend on intelligence, moral capacity, physical strength, or similar matters of fact. Equality is a moral idea, not an assertion of fact. There is no logically compelling reason for assuming that a factual difference in ability between two people justifies any difference in the amount of consideration we give to their needs and interests. *The principle of the equality of human beings is not a description of an alleged actual equality among humans: it is a prescription of how we should treat human beings.*

Jeremy Bentham, the founder of the reforming utilitarian school of moral philosophy, incorporated the essential basis of moral equality into his system of ethics by means of the formula: "Each to count for one and none for more than one." In other words, the interests of every being affected by an action are to be taken into account and given the same weight as the like interests of any other being. A later utilitarian, Henry Sidgwick, put the point in this way: "The good of any one individual is of no more importance, from the point of view (if I may say so) of the Universe, than the good of any other." More recently the leading figures in contemporary moral philosophy have shown a great deal of agreement in specifying as a fundamental presupposition of their moral theories some similar requirement that works to give everyone's interests equal consideration – although these writers generally cannot agree on how this requirement is best formulated.

It is an implication of this principle of equality that our concern for others and our readiness to consider their interest ought not to depend on what they are like or on what abilities they may possess. Precisely what our concern or consideration requires us to do may vary according to the characteristics of those affected by what we do: concern for the well-being of children growing up in America would require that we teach them to read; concern for the well-being of pigs may require no more than that we leave them with other pigs in a place where there is adequate food and room to run freely. But the basic element – the taking into account of the interests of the being, whatever those interests may be – must, according to the principle of equality, be extended to all beings, black or white, masculine or feminine, human or non-human.

Thomas Jefferson, who was responsible for writing the principle of the equality of men into the American Declaration of Independence, saw this point. It led him to oppose slavery even though he was unable to free himself fully from his slaveholding background. He wrote in a letter to the author of a book that emphasized the notable intellectual achievements of Negroes in order to refute the then common view that they had limited intellectual capacities:

> Be assured that no person living wishes more sincerely than I do, to see a complete refutation of the doubts I myself have entertained and expressed on the grade of understanding allotted to them by nature, and to find that they are on a par with ourselves . . . but whatever be their degree of talent it is no measure of their rights. Because Sir Isaac Newton was superior to others in understanding, he was not therefore lord of the property or persons of others.

Similarly, when in the 1850s the call for women's rights was raised in the United States, a remarkable black feminist named Sojourner Truth made the same point in more robust terms at a feminist convention:

> They talk about this thing in the head; what do they call it? ["Intellect," whispered someone nearby.] That's it. What's that got to do with

women's rights or Negroes' rights? If my cup won't hold but a pint and yours holds a quart, wouldn't you be mean not to let me have my little half-measure full?

It is on this basis that the case against racism and the case against sexism must both ultimately rest; and it is in accordance with this principle that the attitude that we may call "speciesism," by analogy with racism, must also be condemned. Speciesism – the word is not an attractive one, but I can think of no better term – is a prejudice or attitude of bias in favor of the interests of members of one's own species and against those of members of other species. It should be obvious that the fundamental objections to racism and sexism made by Thomas Jefferson and Sojourner Truth apply equally to speciesism. If possessing a higher degree of intelligence does not entitle one human to use another for his or her own ends, how can it entitle humans to exploit non-humans for the same purpose?

Many philosophers and other writers have proposed the principle of equal consideration of interests, in some form or other, as a basic moral principle; but not many of them have recognized that this principle applies to members of other species as well as to our own. Jeremy Bentham was one of the few who did realize this. In a forward-looking passage written at a time when black slaves had been freed by the French but in the British dominions were still being treated in the way we now treat animals, Bentham wrote:

> The day *may* come when the rest of the animal creation may acquire those rights which never could have been withholden from them but by the hand of tyranny. The French have already discovered that the blackness of the skin is no reason why a human being should be abandoned without redress to the caprice of a tormentor. It may one day come to be recognized that the number of the legs, the villosity of the skin, or the termination of the *os sacrum* are reasons equally insufficient for abandoning a sensitive being to the same fate. What else is it that should trace the insuperable line? Is it the faculty of reason, or perhaps the faculty of discourse? But a full-grown horse or dog is beyond compari-

son a more rational as well as a more conversable animal, than an infant of a day or a week or even a month, old. But suppose they were otherwise, what would it avail? The question is not, Can they *reason*? nor Can they *talk*? but, Can they *suffer*?

In this passage Bentham points to the capacity for suffering as the vital characteristic that gives a being the right to equal consideration. The capacity for suffering – or more strictly, for suffering and/or enjoyment or happiness – is not just another characteristic like the capacity for language or higher mathematics. Bentham is not saying that those who try to mark "the insuperable line" that determines whether the interests of a being should be considered happen to have chosen the wrong characteristic. By saying that we must consider the interests of all beings with the capacity for suffering or enjoyment Bentham does not arbitrarily exclude from consideration any interests at all – as those who draw the line with reference to the possession of reason or language do. The capacity for suffering and enjoyment is a *prerequisite for having interests at all*, a condition that must be satisfied before we can speak of interests in a meaningful way. It would be nonsense to say that it was not in the interests of a stone to be kicked along the road by a schoolboy. A stone does not have interests because it cannot suffer. Nothing that we can do to it could possibly make any difference to its welfare. The capacity for suffering and enjoyment is, however, not only necessary, but also sufficient for us to say that a being has interests – at an absolute minimum, an interest in not suffering. A mouse, for example, does have an interest in not being kicked along the road, because it will suffer if it is.

Although Bentham speaks of "rights" in the passage I have quoted, the argument is really about equality rather than about rights. Indeed, in a different passage, Bentham famously described "natural rights" as "nonsense" and "natural and imprescriptable rights" as "nonsense upon stilts." He talked of moral rights as a shorthand way of referring to protections that people and animals morally ought to have; but the real weight of the moral argument does not rest on the assertion of the existence of the right, for this in turn has to be justified on the basis of the possibilities for suffering and happiness. In this way we can argue for equality for animals without getting embroiled in philosophical controversies about the ultimate nature of rights.

In misguided attempts to refute the arguments of this book, some philosophers have gone to much trouble developing arguments to show that animals do not have rights. They have claimed that to have rights a being must be autonomous, or must be a member of a community, or must have the ability to respect the rights of others, or must possess a sense of justice. These claims are irrelevant to the case for Animal Liberation. The language of rights is a convenient political shorthand. It is even more valuable in the era of thirty-second TV news clips than it was in Bentham's day; but in the argument for a radical change in our attitude to animals, it is in no way necessary.

If a being suffers there can be no moral justification for refusing to take that suffering into consideration. No matter what the nature of the being, the principle of equality requires that its suffering be counted equally with the like suffering – in so far as rough comparisons can be made – of any other being. If a being is not capable of suffering, or of experiencing enjoyment or happiness, there is nothing to be taken into account. So the limit of sentience (using the term as a convenient if not strictly accurate shorthand for the capacity to suffer and/or experience enjoyment) is the only defensible boundary of concern for the interests of others. To mark this boundary by some other characteristic like intelligence or rationality would be to mark it in an arbitrary manner. Why not choose some other characteristic, like skin color?

Racists violate the principle of equality by giving greater weight to the interests of members of their own race when there is a clash between their interests and the interests of those of another race. Sexists violate the principle of equality by favoring the interests of their own sex. Similarly, speciesists allow the interests of their own species to override the greater interests of members of other species. The pattern is identical in each case.

Most human beings are speciesists. The following chapters show that ordinary human beings – not a few exceptionally cruel or heartless humans, but the overwhelming majority of humans – take an active part in, acquiesce in, and allow their taxes to pay for practices that require the sacrifice of the most important interests of members of other species in order to promote the most trivial interests of our own species.

There is, however, one general defense of the practices to be described in the next two chapters that needs to be disposed of before we discuss the practices themselves. It is a defense which, if true, would allow us to do anything at all to non-humans for the slightest reason, or for no reason at all, without incurring any justifiable reproach. This defense claims that we are never guilty of neglecting the interests of other animals for one breathtakingly simple reason: they have no interests. Non-human animals have no interests, according to this view, because they are not capable of suffering. By this is not meant merely that they are not capable of suffering in all the ways that human beings are – for instance, that a calf is not capable of suffering from the knowledge that it will be killed in six months' time. That modest claim is, no doubt, true; but it does not clear humans of the charge of speciesism, since it allows that animals may suffer in other ways – for instance, by being given electric shocks, or being kept in small, cramped cages. The defense I am about to discuss is the much more sweeping, although correspondingly less plausible, claim that animals are incapable of suffering in any way at all; that they are, in fact, unconscious automata, possessing neither thoughts nor feelings nor a mental life of any kind.

Although, as we shall see in a later chapter, the view that animals are automata was proposed by the seventeenth-century French philosopher René Descartes, to most people, then and now, it is obvious that if, for example, we stick a sharp knife into the stomach of an unanesthetized dog, the dog will feel pain. That this is so is assumed by the laws in most civilized countries that prohibit wanton cruelty to animals. Readers whose common sense tells them that animals do suffer may prefer to skip the remainder of this section, moving straight on to page 347, since the pages in between do nothing but refute a position that they do not hold. Implausible as it is, though, for the sake of completeness this skeptical position must be discussed.

Do animals other than humans feel pain? How do we know? Well, how do we know if anyone, human or non-human, feels pain? We know that we ourselves can feel pain. We know this from the direct experience of pain that we have when, for instance, somebody presses a lighted cigarette against the back of our hand. But how do we know that anyone else feels pain? We cannot directly experience anyone else's pain, whether that "anyone" is our best friend or a stray dog. Pain is a state of consciousness, a "mental event," and as such it can never be observed. Behavior like writhing, screaming, or drawing one's hand away from the lighted cigarette is not pain itself; nor are the recordings a neurologist might make of activity within the brain observations of pain itself. Pain is something that we feel, and we can only infer that others are feeling it from various external indications.

In theory, we *could* always be mistaken when we assume that other human beings feel pain. It is conceivable that one of our close friends is really a cleverly constructed robot, controlled by a brilliant scientist so as to give all the signs of feeling pain, but really no more sensitive than any other machine. We can never know, with absolute certainty, that this is not the case. But while this might present a puzzle for philosophers, none of us has the slightest real doubt that our close friends feel pain just as we do. This is an inference, but a perfectly reasonable one, based on observations of their behavior in situations in which we would feel pain, and on the fact that we have every reason to assume that our friends are beings like us, with nervous systems like ours that can be assumed to function as ours do and to produce similar feelings in similar circumstances.

If it is justifiable to assume that other human beings feel pain as we do, is there any reason why a similar inference should be unjustifiable in the case of other animals?

Nearly all the external signs that lead us to infer pain in other humans can be seen in other species, especially the species most closely related to us – the species of mammals and birds. The behavioral signs include writhing, facial contortions, moaning, yelping or other forms of calling, attempts to avoid the source of pain, appearance of fear at the prospect of its repetition, and so on. In addition, we know that these animals have nervous systems very like ours, which respond physiologically as ours do when the animal is in circumstances in which we would feel pain: an initial rise of blood pressure, dilated pupils, perspiration, an increased pulse rate, and, if the stimulus continues, a fall in blood pressure. Although human beings have a more developed cerebral cortex than other animals, this part of the brain is concerned with thinking functions rather than with basic impulses, emotions, and feelings. These impulses, emotions, and feelings are located in the diencephalon, which is well developed in many other species of animals, especially mammals and birds.

We also know that the nervous systems of other animals were not artificially constructed – as a robot might be artificially constructed – to mimic the pain behavior of humans. The nervous systems of animals evolved as our own did, and in fact the evolutionary history of human beings and other animals, especially mammals, did not diverge until the central features of our nervous systems were already in existence. A capacity to feel pain obviously enhances a species' prospects of survival, since it causes members of the species to avoid sources of injury. It is surely unreasonable to suppose that nervous systems that are virtually identical physiologically, have a common origin and a common evolutionary function, and result in similar forms of behavior in similar circumstances should actually operate in an entirely different manner on the level of subjective feelings.

It has long been accepted as sound policy in science to search for the simplest possible explanation of whatever it is we are trying to explain. Occasionally it has been claimed that it is for this reason "unscientific" to explain the behavior of animals by theories that refer to the animal's conscious feelings, desires, and so on – the idea being that if the behavior in question can be explained without invoking consciousness or feelings, that will be the simpler theory. Yet we can now see that such explanations, when assessed with respect to the actual behavior of both human and non-human animals, are actually far more complex than rival explanations. For we know from our own experience that explanations of our own behavior that did not refer to consciousness and the feeling of pain would be incomplete; and it is simpler to assume that the similar behavior of animals with similar nervous systems is to be explained in the same way than to try to invent some other explanation for the behavior of non-human animals as well as an explanation for the divergence between humans and non-humans in this respect.

The overwhelming majority of scientists who have addressed themselves to this question agree. Lord Brain, one of the most eminent neurologists of our time, has said:

> I personally can see no reason for conceding mind to my fellow men and denying it to animals. . . . I at least cannot doubt that the interests and activities of animals are correlated with awareness and feeling in the same way as my own, and which may be, for aught I know, just as vivid.

The author of a book on pain writes:

> Every particle of factual evidence supports the contention that the higher mammalian vertebrates experience pain sensations at least as acute as our own. To say that they feel less because they are lower animals is an absurdity; it can easily be shown that many of their senses are far more acute than ours – visual acuity in certain birds, hearing in most wild animals, and touch in others; these animals depend more than we do today on the sharpest possible awareness of a hostile environment. Apart from the complexity of the cerebral cortex (which does not directly perceive pain) their nervous systems are almost identical to ours and their reactions to pain remarkably similar, though lacking (so far as we know) the philosophical and moral over-

tones. The emotional element is all too evident, mainly in the form of fear and anger.

In Britain, three separate expert government committees on matters relating to animals have accepted the conclusion that animals feel pain. After noting the obvious behavioral evidence for this view, the members of the Committee on Cruelty to Wild Animals, set up in 1951, said:

> . . . we believe that the physiological, and more particularly the anatomical, evidence fully justifies and reinforces the commonsense belief that animals feel pain.

And after discussing the evolutionary value of pain the committee's report concluded that pain is "of clear-cut biological usefulness" and this is "a third type of evidence that animals feel pain." The committee members then went on to consider forms of suffering other than mere physical pain and added that they were "satisfied that animals do suffer from acute fear and terror." Subsequent reports by British government committees on experiments on animals and on the welfare of animals under intensive farming methods agreed with this view, concluding that animals are capable of suffering both from straightforward physical injuries and from fear, anxiety, stress, and so on. Finally, within the last decade, the publication of scientific studies with titles such as *Animal Thought, Animal Thinking*, and *Animal Suffering: The Science of Animal Welfare* have made it plain that conscious awareness in non-human animals is now generally accepted as a serious subject for investigation.

That might well be thought enough to settle the matter; but one more objection needs to be considered. Human beings in pain, after all, have one behavioral sign that non-human animals do not have: a developed language. Other animals may communicate with each other, but not, it seems, in the complicated way we do. Some philosophers, including Descartes, have thought it important that while humans can tell each other about their experience of pain in great detail, other animals cannot. (Interestingly, this once neat dividing line between humans and other species has now been threatened by the discovery that chimpanzees can be taught a language.) But as Bentham pointed out long ago, the ability to use language is not relevant to the question of how a being ought to be treated – unless that ability can be linked to the capacity to suffer, so that the absence of a language casts doubt on the existence of this capacity.

This link may be attempted in two ways. First, there is a hazy line of philosophical thought, deriving perhaps from some doctrines associated with the influential philosopher Ludwig Wittgenstein, which maintains that we cannot meaningfully attribute states of consciousness to beings without language. This position seems to me very implausible. Language may be necessary for abstract thought, at some level anyway; but states like pain are more primitive, and have nothing to do with language.

The second and more easily understood way of linking language and the existence of pain is to say that the best evidence we can have that other creatures are in pain is that they tell us that they are. This is a distinct line of argument, for it is denying not that non-language users conceivably *could* suffer, but only that we could ever have sufficient reason to *believe* that they are suffering. Still, this line of argument fails too. As Jane Goodall has pointed out in her study of chimpanzees, *In the Shadow of Man*, when it comes to the expression of feelings and emotions language is less important than non-linguistic modes of communication such as a cheering pat on the back, an exuberant embrace, a clasp of the hands, and so on. The basic signals we use to convey pain, fear, anger, love, joy, surprise, sexual arousal, and many other emotional states are not specific to our own species. The statement "I am in pain" may be one piece of evidence for the conclusion that the speaker is in pain, but it is not the only possible evidence, and since people sometimes tell lies, not even the best possible evidence.

Even if there were stronger grounds for refusing to attribute pain to those who do not have a language, the consequences of this refusal might lead us to reject the conclusion. Human infants and young children are unable to use language.

Are we to deny that a year-old child can suffer? If not, language cannot be crucial. Of course, most parents understand the responses of their children better than they understand the responses of other animals; but this is just a fact about the relatively greater knowledge that we have of our own species and the greater contact we have with infants as compared to animals. Those who have studied the behavior of other animals and those who have animals as companions soon learn to understand their responses as well as we understand those of an infant, and sometimes better.

So to conclude: there are no good reasons, scientific or philosophical, for denying that animals feel pain. If we do not doubt that other humans feel pain we should not doubt that other animals do so too.

Animals can feel pain. As we saw earlier, there can be no moral justification for regarding the pain (or pleasure) that animals feel as less important than the same amount of pain (or pleasure) felt by humans. But what practical consequences follow from this conclusion? To prevent misunderstanding I shall spell out what I mean a little more fully.

If I give a horse a hard slap across its rump with my open hand, the horse may start, but it presumably feels little pain. Its skin is thick enough to protect it against a mere slap. If I slap a baby in the same way, however, the baby will cry and presumably feel pain, for its skin is more sensitive. So it is worse to slap a baby than a horse, if both slaps are administered with equal force. But there must be some kind of blow – I don't know exactly what it would be, but perhaps a blow with a heavy stick – that would cause the horse as much pain as we cause a baby by slapping it with our hand. That is what I mean by "the same amount of pain," and if we consider it wrong to inflict that much pain on a baby for no good reason then we must, unless we are speciesists, consider it equally wrong to inflict the same amount of pain on a horse for no good reason.

Other differences between humans and animals cause other complications. Normal adult human beings have mental capacities that will, in certain circumstances, lead them to suffer more than animals would in the same circumstances. If, for instance, we decided to perform extremely painful or lethal scientific experiments on normal adult humans, kidnapped at random from public parks for this purpose, adults who enjoy strolling in parks would become fearful that they would be kidnapped. The resultant terror would be a form of suffering additional to the pain of the experiment. The same experiments performed on non-human animals would cause less suffering since the animals would not have the anticipatory dread of being kidnapped and experimented upon. This does not mean, of course, that it would be *right* to perform the experiment on animals, but only that there is a reason, which is *not* speciesist, for preferring to use animals rather than normal adult human beings, if the experiment is to be done at all. It should be noted, however, that this same argument gives us a reason for preferring to use human infants – orphans perhaps – or severely retarded human beings for experiments, rather than adults, since infants and retarded humans would also have no idea of what was going to happen to them. So far as this argument is concerned non-human animals and infants and retarded humans are in the same category; and if we use this argument to justify experiments on non-human animals we have to ask ourselves whether we are also prepared to allow experiments on human infants and retarded adults; and if we make a distinction between animals and these humans, on what basis can we do it other than a bare-faced – and morally indefensible – preference for members of our own species ?

There are many matters in which the superior mental powers of normal adult humans make a difference: anticipation, more detailed memory, greater knowledge of what is happening, and so on. Yet these differences do not all point to greater suffering on the part of the normal human being. Sometimes animals may suffer more because of their more limited understanding. If, for instance, we are taking prisoners in wartime we can explain to them that although they must submit to capture, search, and confinement, they will not otherwise be harmed and will be set free at the conclusion of hostilities. If we capture wild animals, however, we cannot explain that we are not threatening their lives. A wild animal cannot distinguish an attempt to overpower and confine from an attempt to kill; the one causes as much terror as the other.

It may be objected that comparisons of the sufferings of different species are impossible to make and that for this reason when the interests of animals and humans clash the principle of equality gives no guidance. It is probably true that comparisons of suffering between members of different species cannot be made precisely, but precision is not essential. Even if we were to prevent the infliction of suffering on animals only when it is quite certain that the interests of humans will not be affected to anything like the extent that animals are affected, we would be forced to make radical changes in our treatment of animals that would involve our diet, the farming methods we use, experimental procedures in many fields of science, our approach to wildlife and to hunting, trapping and the wearing of furs, and areas of entertainment like circuses, rodeos, and zoos. As a result, a vast amount of suffering would be avoided.

So far I have said a lot about inflicting suffering on animals, but nothing about killing them. This omission has been deliberate. The application of the principle of equality to the infliction of suffering is, in theory at least, fairly straightforward. Pain and suffering are in themselves bad and should be prevented or minimized, irrespective of the race, sex, or species of the being that suffers. How bad a pain is depends on how intense it is and how long it lasts, but pains of the same intensity and duration are equally bad, whether felt by humans or animals.

The wrongness of killing a being is more complicated. I have kept, and shall continue to keep, the question of killing in the background because in the present state of human tyranny over other species the more simple, straightforward principle of equal consideration of pain or pleasure is a sufficient basis for identifying and protesting against all the major abuses of animals that human beings practice. Nevertheless, it is necessary to say something about killing.

Just as most human beings are speciesists in their readiness to cause pain to animals when they would not cause a similar pain to humans for the same reason, so most human beings are speciesists in their readiness to kill other animals when they would not kill human beings. We need to proceed more cautiously here, however, because people hold widely differing views about when it is legitimate to kill humans, as the continuing debates over abortion and euthanasia attest. Nor have moral philosophers been able to agree on exactly what it is that makes it wrong to kill human beings, and under what circumstances killing a human being may be justifiable.

Let us consider first the view that it is always wrong to take an innocent human life. We may call this the "sanctity of life" view. People who take this view oppose abortion and euthanasia. They do not usually, however, oppose the killing of non-human animals – so perhaps it would be more accurate to describe this view as the "sanctity of *human* life" view. The belief that human life, and only human life, is sacrosanct is a form of speciesism. To see this, consider the following example.

Assume that, as sometimes happens, an infant has been born with massive and irreparable brain damage. The damage is so severe that the infant can never be any more than a "human vegetable," unable to talk, recognize other people, act independently of others, or develop a sense of self-awareness. The parents of the infant, realizing that they cannot hope for any improvement in their child's condition and being in any case unwilling to spend, or ask the state to spend, the thousands of dollars that would be needed annually for proper care of the infant, ask the doctor to kill the infant painlessly.

Should the doctor do what the parents ask? Legally, the doctor should not, and in this respect the law reflects the sanctity of life view. The life of every human being is sacred. Yet people who would say this about the infant do not object to the killing of non-human animals. How can they justify their different judgments? Adult chimpanzees, dogs, pigs, and members of many other species far surpass the brain-damaged infant in their ability to relate to others, act independently, be self-aware, and any other capacity that could reasonably be said to give value to life. With the most intensive care possible, some severely retarded infants can never achieve the intelligence level of a dog. Nor can we appeal to the concern of the infant's parents, since they themselves, in this imaginary example (and in some actual cases) do not want the infant kept alive. The only thing that distinguishes the infant from the animal, in the eyes of those who claim it has a "right to life," is that it is, biologically, a member of the species *Homo sapiens*, whereas chimpanzees, dogs, and pigs are not. But to use *this* difference as the basis for granting a right to life to the infant and not to the other animals is, of course, pure speciesism. It is exactly the kind of arbitrary difference that the most crude and overt kind of racist uses in attempting to justify racial discrimination.

This does not mean that to avoid speciesism we must hold that it is as wrong to kill a dog as it is to kill a human being in full possession of his or her faculties. The only position that is irredeemably speciesist is the one that tries to make the boundary of the right to life run exactly parallel to the boundary of our own species. Those who hold the sanctity of life view do this, because while distinguishing sharply between human beings and other animals they allow no distinctions to be made within our own species, objecting to the killing of the severely retarded and the hopelessly senile as strongly as they object to the killing of normal adults.

To avoid speciesism we must allow that beings who are similar in all relevant respects have a similar right to life – and mere membership in our own biological species cannot be a morally relevant criterion for this right. Within these limits we could still hold, for instance, that it is worse to kill a normal adult human, with a capacity for self-awareness and the ability to plan for the future and have meaningful relations with others, than it is to kill a mouse, which presumably does not share all of these characteristics; or we might appeal to the close family and other personal ties that humans have but mice do not have to the same degree; or we might think that it is the consequences for other humans, who will be put in fear for their own lives, that makes the crucial difference; or we might think it is some combination of these factors, or other factors altogether.

Whatever criteria we choose, however, we will have to admit that they do not follow precisely the boundary of our own species. We may legitimately hold that there are some features of certain beings that make their lives more valuable than those of other beings; but there will surely be some non-human animals whose lives, by any standards, are more valuable than the lives of some humans. A chimpanzee, dog, or pig, for instance, will have a higher degree of self-awareness and a greater capacity for meaningful relations with others than a severely retarded infant or someone in a state of advanced senility. So if we base the right to life on these characteristics we must grant these animals a right to life as good as, or better than, such retarded or senile humans.

This argument cuts both ways. It could be taken as showing that chimpanzees, dogs, and pigs, along with some other species, have a right to life and we commit a grave moral offense whenever we kill them, even when they are old and suffering and our intention is to put them out of their misery. Alternatively one could take the argument as showing that the severely retarded and hopelessly senile have no right to life and may be killed for quite trivial reasons, as we now kill animals.

Since the main concern of this book is with ethical questions having to do with animals and not with the morality of euthanasia I shall not attempt to settle this issue finally. I think it is reasonably clear, though, that while both of the positions just described avoid speciesism, neither is satisfactory. What we need is some middle position that would avoid speciesism but would not make the lives of the retarded and senile as cheap as the lives of pigs and dogs now are, or make the lives of pigs and dogs so sacrosanct that we think it wrong to put them out of hopeless misery. What we must do is bring non-human animals within our sphere of moral concern and cease to treat their lives as expendable for whatever trivial purposes we may have. At the same time, once we realize that the fact that a being is a member of our own species is not in itself enough to make it always wrong to kill that being, we may come to reconsider our policy of preserving human lives at all costs, even when there is no prospect of a meaningful life or of existence without terrible pain.

I conclude, then, that a rejection of speciesism does not imply that all lives are of equal worth. While self-awareness, the capacity to think ahead and have hopes and aspirations for the future, the capacity for meaningful relations with others and so on are not relevant to the question of inflicting pain – since pain is pain, whatever other capacities, beyond the capacity to feel pain, the being may have – these capacities are relevant to the question of taking life. It is not arbitrary to hold that the life of a self-aware being, capable of abstract thought, of planning for the future, of complex acts of communication, and so on, is more valuable than the life of a being without these capacities. To see the difference between the issues of inflicting pain and taking life, consider how we would choose within our own species. If we had to choose to save the life of a normal human being or an intellectually disabled human being, we would probably choose to save the life of a normal human being; but if we had to choose between preventing pain in the normal human being or the intellectually disabled one – imagine that both have received painful but superficial injuries, and we only have enough painkiller for one of them – it is not nearly so clear how we ought to choose. The same is true when we consider other species. The evil of pain is, in itself, unaffected by the other characteristics of the being who feels the pain; the value of life is affected by these other characteristics. To give just one reason for this difference, to take the life of a being who has been hoping, planning, and working for some future goal is to deprive that being of the fulfillment of all those efforts; to take the life of a being with a mental capacity below the level needed to grasp that one is a being with a future – much less make plans for the future – cannot involve this particular kind of loss.

Normally this will mean that if we have to

choose between the life of a human being and the life of another animal we should choose to save the life of the human; but there may be special cases in which the reverse holds true, because the human being in question does not have the capacities of a normal human being. So this view is not speciesist, although it may appear to be at first glance. The preference, in normal cases, for saving a human life over the life of an animal when a choice *has* to be made is a preference based on the characteristics that normal humans have, and not on the mere fact that they are members of our own species. This is why when we consider members of our own species who lack the characteristics of normal humans we can no longer say that their lives are always to be preferred to those of other animals. In general, though, the question of when it is wrong to kill (painlessly) an animal is one to which we need give no precise answer. As long as we remember that we should give the same respect to the lives of animals as we give to the lives of those humans at a similar mental level, we shall not go far wrong.

In any case, the conclusions that are argued for in this book flow from the principle of minimizing suffering alone. The idea that it is also wrong to kill animals painlessly gives some of these conclusions additional support that is welcome but strictly unnecessary. Interestingly enough, this is true even of the conclusion that we ought to become vegetarians, a conclusion that in the popular mind is generally based on some kind of absolute prohibition on killing.

The reader may already have thought of some objections to the position I have taken in this chapter. What, for instance, do I propose to do about animals who may cause harm to human beings? Should we try to stop animals from killing each other? How do we know that plants cannot feel pain, and if they can, must we starve? To avoid interrupting the flow of the main argument I have chosen to discuss these and other objections in a separate chapter, and readers who are impatient to have their objections answered may look ahead.

The next two chapters [not reproduced here] explore two examples of speciesism in practice. I have limited myself to two examples so that I would have space for a reasonably thorough discussion, although this limit means that the book contains no discussion at all of other practices that exist only because we do not take seriously the interests of other animals – practices like hunting, whether for sport or for furs; farming minks, foxes, and other animals for their fur; capturing wild animals (often after shooting their mothers) and imprisoning them in small cages for humans to stare at; tormenting animals to make them learn tricks for circuses and tormenting them to make them entertain the audiences at rodeos; slaughtering whales with explosive harpoons, under the guise of scientific research; drowning over 100,000 dolphins annually in nets set by tuna fishing boats; shooting three million kangaroos every year in the Australian outback to turn them into skins and pet food; and generally ignoring the interests of wild animals as we extend our empire of concrete and pollution over the surface of the globe.

I shall have nothing, or virtually nothing, to say about these things, because as I indicated in the preface to this edition, this book is not a compendium of all the nasty things we do to animals. Instead I have chosen two central illustrations of speciesism in practice. They are not isolated examples of sadism, but practices that involve, in one case, tens of millions of animals, and in the other, billions of animals every year. Nor can we pretend that we have nothing to do with these practices. One of them – experimentation on animals – is promoted by the government we elect and is largely paid for out of the taxes we pay. The other – rearing animals for food – is possible only because most people buy and eat the products of this practice. That is why I have chosen to discuss these particular forms of speciesism. They are at its heart. They cause more suffering to a greater number of animals than anything else that human beings do. To stop them we must change the policies of our government, and we must change our own lives, to the extent of changing our diet. If these officially promoted and almost universally accepted forms of speciesism can be abolished, abolition of the other speciesist practices cannot be far behind.

38   The Ethics of Respect for Nature

Paul W. Taylor

Human-centered and Life-centered Systems of Environmental Ethics

In this paper I show how the taking of a certain ultimate moral attitude toward nature, which I call "respect for nature," has a central place in the foundations of a life-centered system of environmental ethics. I hold that a set of moral norms (both standards of character and rules of conduct) governing human treatment of the natural world is a rationally grounded set if and only if, first, commitment to those norms is a practical entailment of adopting the attitude of respect for nature as an ultimate moral attitude, and second, the adopting of that attitude on the part of all rational agents can itself be justified. When the basic characteristics of the attitude of respect for nature are made clear, it will be seen that a life-centered system of environmental ethics need not be holistic or organicist in its conception of the kinds of entities that are deemed the appropriate objects of moral concern and consideration. Nor does such a system require that the concepts of ecological homeostasis, equilibrium, and integrity provide us with normative principles from which could be derived (with the addition of factual knowledge) our obligations with regard to natural ecosystems. The "balance of nature" is not itself a moral norm, however important may be the role it plays in our general outlook on the natural world that underlies the attitude of respect for nature. I argue that finally it is the good (well-being, welfare) of individual organisms considered as entities having inherent worth, that determines our moral relations with the Earth's wild communities of life.

From *Environmental Ethics*. Reprinted by permission of Paul W. Taylor.

In designating the theory to be set forth as life-centered, I intend to contrast it with all anthropocentric views. According to the latter, human actions affecting the natural environment and its non-human inhabitants are right (or wrong) by either of two criteria: they have consequences which are favorable (or unfavorable) to human well-being, or they are consistent (or inconsistent) with the system of norms that protect and implement human rights. From this human-centered standpoint it is to humans and only to humans that all duties are ultimately owed. We may have responsibilities *with regard* to the natural ecosystems and biotic communities of our planet, but these responsibilities are in every case based on the contingent fact that our treatment of those ecosystems and communities of life can further the realization of human values and/or human rights. We have no obligation to promote or protect the good of non-human living things, independently of this contingent fact.

A life-centered system of environmental ethics is opposed to human-centered ones precisely on this point. From the perspective of a life-centered theory, we have prima facie moral obligations that are owed to wild plants and animals themselves as members of the Earth's biotic community. We are morally bound (other things being equal) to protect or promote their good for *their* sake. Our duties to respect the integrity of natural ecosystems, to preserve endangered species, and to avoid environmental pollution stem from the fact that these are ways in which we can make it possible for wild species populations to achieve and maintain a healthy existence in a natural state. Such obligations are due those living things out of recognition of their inherent worth. They are entirely additional to and independent of the obligations we owe to our fellow humans.

Although many of the actions that fulfill one set of obligations will also fulfill the other, two different grounds of obligation are involved. Their well-being, as well as human well-being, is something to be realized *as an end in itself.*

If we were to accept a life-centered theory of environmental ethics, a profound reordering of our moral universe would take place. We would begin to look at the whole of the Earth's biosphere in a new light. Our duties with respect to the "world" of nature would be seen as making prima facie claims upon us to be balanced against our duties with respect to the "world" of human civilization. We could no longer simply take the human point of view and consider the effects of our actions exclusively from the perspective of our own good.

The Good of a Being and the Concept of Inherent Worth

What would justify acceptance of a life-centered system of ethical principles? In order to answer this it is first necessary to make clear the fundamental moral attitude that underlies and makes intelligible the commitment to live by such a system. It is then necessary to examine the considerations that would justify any rational agent's adopting that moral attitude.

Two concepts are essential to the taking of a moral attitude of the sort in question. A being which does not "have" these concepts, that is, which is unable to grasp their meaning and conditions of applicability, cannot be said to have the attitude as part of its moral outlook. These concepts are, first, that of the good (well-being, welfare) of a living thing, and second, the idea of an entity possessing inherent worth. I examine each concept in turn.

(1) Every organism, species population, and community of life has a good of its own which moral agents can intentionally further or damage by their actions. To say that an entity has a good of its own is simply to say that, without reference to any *other* entity, it can be benefited or harmed. One can act in its overall interest or contrary to its overall interest, and environmen-

tal conditions can be good for it (advantageous to it) or bad for it (disadvantageous to it). What is good for an entity is what "does it good" in the sense of enhancing or preserving its life and well-being. What is bad for an entity is something that is detrimental to its life and well-being.[1]

We can think of the good of an individual nonhuman organism as consisting in the full development of its biological powers. Its good is realized to the extent that it is strong and healthy. It possesses whatever capacities it needs for successfully coping with its environment and so preserving its existence throughout the various stages of the normal life cycle of its species. The good of a population or community of such individuals consists in the population or community maintaining itself from generation to generation as a coherent system of generically and ecologically related organisms whose average good is at an optimum level for the given environment. (Here *average good* means that the degree of realization of the good of *individual organisms* in the population or community is, on average, greater than would be the case under any other ecologically functioning order of interrelations among those species populations in the given ecosystem.)

The idea of a being having a good of its own, as I understand it, does not entail that the being must have interests or take an interest in what affects its life for better or for worse. We can act in a being's interest or contrary to its interest without its being interested in what we are doing to it in the sense of wanting or not wanting us to do it. It may, indeed, be wholly unaware that favorable and unfavorable events are taking place in its life. I take it that trees, for example, have no knowledge or desires or feelings. Yet it is undoubtedly the case that trees can be harmed or benefited by our actions. We can crush their roots by running a bulldozer too close to them. We can see to it that they get adequate nourishment and moisture by fertilizing and watering the soil around them. Thus we can help or hinder them in the realization of their good. It is the good of trees themselves that is thereby affected. We can similarly act so as to further the good of an entire tree population of a certain species (say, all the redwood trees in a California valley) or the good of a whole community of plant life in a given wilderness area, just as we can do harm to such a population or community.

When construed in this way, the concept of a being's good is not coextensive with sentience or the capacity for feeling pain. William Frankena has argued for a general theory of environmental ethics in which the ground of a creature's being worthy of moral consideration is its sentience. I have offered some criticisms of this view elsewhere, but the full refutation of such a position, it seems to me, finally depends on the positive reasons for accepting a life-centered theory of the kind I am defending in this essay.[2]

It should be noted further that I am leaving open the question of whether machines – in particular, those which are not only goal-directed, but also self-regulating – can properly be said to have a good of their own.[3] Since I am concerned only with human treatment of wild organisms, species populations, and communities of life as they occur in our planet's natural ecosystems, it is to those entities alone that the concept "having a good of its own" will here be applied. I am not denying that other living things, whose genetic origin and environmental conditions have been produced, controlled, and manipulated by humans for human ends, do have a good of their own in the same sense as do wild plants and animals. It is not my purpose in this essay, however, to set out or defend the principles that should guide our conduct with regard to their good. It is only in so far as their production and use by humans have good or ill effects upon natural ecosystems and their wild inhabitants that the ethics of respect for nature comes into play.

(2)   The second concept essential to the moral attitude of respect for nature is the idea of inherent worth. We take that attitude toward wild living things (individuals, species populations, or whole biotic communities) when and only when we regard them as entities possessing inherent worth. Indeed, it is only because they are conceived in this way that moral agents can think of themselves as having validly binding duties, obligations, and responsibilities that are *owed* to them as their *due*. I am not at this juncture argu-

ing why they *should* be so regarded; I consider it at length below. But so regarding them is a presupposition of our taking the attitude of respect toward them and accordingly understanding ourselves as bearing certain moral relations to them. This can be shown as follows:

What does it mean to regard an entity that has a good of its own as possessing inherent worth? Two general principles are involved: the principle of moral consideration and the principle of intrinsic value.

According to the principle of moral consideration, wild living things are deserving of the concern and consideration of all moral agents simply in virtue of their being members of the Earth's community of life. From the moral point of view their good must be taken into account whenever it is affected for better or worse by the conduct of rational agents. This holds no matter what species the creature belongs to. The good of each is to be accorded some value and so acknowledged as having some weight in the deliberations of all rational agents. Of course, it may be necessary for such agents to act in ways contrary to the good of this or that particular organism or group of organisms in order to further the good of others, including the good of humans. But the principle of moral consideration prescribes that, with respect to each being an entity having its own good, every individual is deserving of consideration.

The principle of intrinsic value states that, regardless of what kind of entity it is in other respects, if it is a member of the Earth's community of life, the realization of its good is something *intrinsically* valuable. This means that its good is prima facie worthy of being preserved or promoted as an end in itself and for the sake of the entity whose good it is. In so far as we regard any organism, species population, or life community as an entity having inherent worth, we believe that it must never be treated as if it were a mere object or thing whose entire value lies in being instrumental to the good of some other entity. The well-being of each is judged to have value in and of itself.

Combining these two principles, we can now define what it means for a living thing or group of living things to possess inherent worth. To say that it possesses inherent worth is to say that its good is deserving of the concern and consideration of all moral agents, and that the realization of its good has intrinsic value, to be pursued as an end in itself and for the sake of the entity whose good it is.

The duties owed to wild organisms, species populations, and communities of life in the Earth's natural ecosystems are grounded on their inherent worth. When rational, autonomous agents regard such entities as possessing inherent worth, they place intrinsic value on the realization of their good and so hold themselves responsible for performing actions that will have this effect and for refraining from actions having the contrary effect.

The Attitude of Respect for Nature

Why should moral agents regard wild living things in the natural world as possessing inherent worth? To answer this question we must first take into account the fact that, when rational, autonomous agents subscribe to the principles of moral consideration and intrinsic value and so conceive of wild living things as having that kind of worth, such agents are *adopting a certain ultimate moral attitude toward the natural world*. This is the attitude I call "respect for nature." It parallels the attitude of respect for persons in human ethics. When we adopt the attitude of respect for persons as the proper (fitting, appropriate) attitude to take toward all persons as persons, we consider the fulfillment of the basic interests of each individual to have intrinsic value. We thereby make a moral commitment to live a certain kind of life in relation to other persons. We place ourselves under the direction of a system of standards and rules that we consider validly binding on all moral agents as such.[4]

Similarly, when we adopt the attitude of respect for nature as an ultimate moral attitude we make a commitment to live by certain normative principles. These principles constitute the rules of conduct and standards of character that are to govern our treatment of the natural world. This is, first, an *ultimate* commitment because it is not derived from any higher norm. The attitude of respect for nature is not grounded on some other, more general, or more fundamental attitude. It sets the total framework for our responsibilities toward the natural world. It can be justified, as I show below, but its justification cannot consist in referring to a more general attitude or a more basic normative principle.

Second, the commitment is a *moral* one because it is understood to be a disinterested matter of principle. It is this feature that distinguishes the attitude of respect for nature from the set of feelings and dispositions that comprise the love of nature. The latter stems from one's personal interest in and response to the natural world. Like the affectionate feelings we have toward certain individual human beings, one's love of nature is nothing more than the particular way one feels about the natural environment and its wild inhabitants. And just as our love for an individual person differs from our respect for all persons as such (whether we happen to love them or not), so love of nature differs from respect for nature. Respect for nature is an attitude we believe all moral agents ought to have simply as moral agents, regardless of whether or not they also love nature. Indeed, we have not truly taken the attitude of respect for nature ourselves unless we believe this. To put it in a Kantian way, to adopt the attitude of respect for nature is to take a stance that one wills it to be a universal law for all rational beings. It is to hold that stance categorically, as being validly applicable to every moral agent without exception, irrespective of whatever personal feelings toward nature such an agent might have or might lack.

Although the attitude of respect for nature is in this sense a disinterested and universalizable attitude, anyone who does adopt it has certain steady, more or less permanent dispositions. These dispositions, which are themselves to be considered disinterested and universalizable, comprise three interlocking sets: dispositions to seek certain ends, dispositions to carry on one's practical reasoning and deliberation in a certain way, and dispositions to have certain feelings. We may accordingly analyze the attitude of respect for nature into the following components. (a) The disposition to aim at, and to take steps to bring about, as final and disinterested ends, the promoting and protecting of the good of organisms, species populations, and life communities in natural ecosystems. (These ends are "final" in not being pursued as means to further ends. They are "disinterested" in being independent of the self-interest of the agent.) (b) The disposition to consider actions that tend to realize those ends to be prima facie obligatory *because* they have that tendency. (c) The disposition to experience positive and negative feelings toward states of affairs in the world *because* they are favorable or unfavorable to the good of organisms, species populations, and life communities in natural ecosystems.

The logical connection between the attitude of respect for nature and the duties of a life-centered system of environmental ethics can now be made clear. In so far as one sincerely takes that attitude and so has the three sets of dispositions, one will at the same time be disposed to comply with certain rules of duty (such as non-maleficence and non-interference) and with standards of character (such as fairness and benevolence) that determine the obligations and virtues of moral agents with regard to the Earth's wild living things. We can say that the actions one performs and the character traits one develops in fulfilling these moral requirements are the way one *expresses* or *embodies* the attitude in one's conduct and character. In his famous essay, "Justice as Fairness," John Rawls describes the rules of the duties of human morality (such as fidelity, gratitude, honesty, and justice) as "forms of conduct in which recognition of others as persons is manifested."[5] I hold that the rules of duty governing our treatment of the natural world and its inhabitants are forms of conduct in which the attitude of respect for nature is manifested.

The Justifiability of the Attitude of Respect for Nature

I return to the question posed earlier, which has not yet been answered: why *should* moral agents regard wild living things as possessing inherent worth? I now argue that the only way we can answer this question is by showing how adopting the attitude of respect for nature is justified for all moral agents. Let us suppose that we were able to establish that there are good reasons for adopting the attitude, reasons which are intersubjectively valid for every rational agent. If there are such reasons, they would justify anyone's having the three sets of dispositions mentioned above as constituting what it means to have the attitude. Since these include the disposition to promote or protect the good of wild living things as a disinterested and ultimate end, as well as the disposition to perform actions for the reason that they tend to realize that end, we see that such dispositions commit a person to the principles of moral consideration and intrinsic value. To be disposed to further, as an end in itself, the good of any entity in nature just because it is that kind of entity, is to be disposed to give consideration to *every* such entity and to place intrinsic value on the realization of its good. In so far as we subscribe to these two principles we regard living things as possessing inherent worth. Subscribing to the principles is what it *means* to so regard them. To justify the attitude of respect for nature, then, is to justify commitment to these principles and thereby to justify regarding wild creatures as possessing inherent worth.

We must keep in mind that inherent worth is not some mysterious sort of objective property belonging to living things that can be discovered by empirical observation or scientific investigation. To ascribe inherent worth to an entity is not to describe it by citing some feature discernible by sense perception or inferable by inductive reasoning. Nor is there a logically necessary connection between the concept of a being having a good of its own and the concept of inherent worth. We do not contradict ourselves by asserting that an entity that has a good of its own lacks inherent worth. In order to show that such an entry "has" inherent worth we must give good reasons for ascribing that kind of value to it (placing that kind of value upon it, conceiving of it to be valuable in that way). Although it is humans (persons, valuers) who must do the valuing, for the ethics of respect for nature, the value so ascribed is not a human value. That is to say, it is not a value derived from considerations regarding human well-being or human rights. It is a value that is ascribed to non-human animals and plants themselves, independently of their relationship to what humans judge to be conducive to their own good.

Whatever reasons, then, justify our taking the attitude of respect for nature as defined above are also reasons that show why we *should* regard the living things of the natural world as possessing inherent worth. We saw earlier that, since the attitude is an ultimate one, it cannot be derived from a more fundamental attitude nor shown to be a special case of a more general one. On what sort of grounds, then, can it be established?

The attitude we take toward living things in the natural world depends on the way we look at them, on what kind of beings we conceive them to be, and on how we understand the relations we bear to them. Underlying and supporting our attitude is a certain *belief system* that constitutes a particular world view or outlook on nature and the place of human life in it. To give good reasons for adopting the attitude of respect for nature, then, we must first articulate the belief system which underlies and supports that attitude. If it appears that the belief system is internally coherent and well-ordered, and if, as far as we can now tell, it is consistent with all known scientific truths relevant to our knowledge of the object of the attitude (which in this case includes the whole set of the Earth's natural ecosystems and their communities of life), then there remains the task of indicating why scientifically informed and rational thinkers with a developed capacity of reality awareness can find it acceptable as a way of conceiving of the natural world and our place in it. To the extent we can do this we provide at least a reasonable argument for accepting the belief system and the ultimate moral attitude it supports.

I do not hold that such a belief system can be *proven* to be true, either inductively or deduc-

tively. As we shall see, not all of its components can be stated in the form of empirically verifiable propositions. Nor is its internal order governed by purely logical relationships. But the system as a whole, I contend, constitutes a coherent, unified, and rationally acceptable "picture" or "map" of a total world. By examining each of its main components and seeing how they fit together, we obtain a scientifically informed and well-ordered conception of nature and the place of humans in it.

This belief system underlying the attitude of respect for nature I call (for want of a better name) "the biocentric outlook on nature." Since it is not wholly analyzable into empirically confirmable assertions, it should not be thought of as simply a compendium of the biological sciences concerning our planet's ecosystems. It might best be described as a philosophical world view, to distinguish it from a scientific theory or explanatory system. However, one of its major tenets is the great lesson we have learned from the science of ecology: the interdependence of all living things in an organically unified order whose balance and stability are necessary conditions for the realization of the good of its constituent biotic communities.

Before turning to an account of the main components of the biocentric outlook, it is convenient here to set forth the overall structure of my theory of environmental ethics as it has now emerged. The ethics of respect for nature is made up of three basic elements: a belief system, an ultimate moral attitude, and a set of rules of duty and standards of character. These elements are connected with each other in the following manner. The belief system provides a certain outlook on nature which supports and makes intelligible an autonomous agent's adopting, as an ultimate moral attitude, the attitude of respect for nature. It supports and makes intelligible the attitude in the sense that, when an autonomous agent understands its moral relations to the natural world in terms of this outlook, it recognizes the attitude of respect to be the only *suitable* or *fitting* attitude to take toward all wild forms of life in the Earth's biosphere. Living things are now viewed as *the appropriate objects of the attitude of respect* and are accordingly regarded as entities possessing inherent worth. One then places intrinsic value on the promotion and protection of their good. As a consequence of this, one makes a moral commitment to abide by a set of rules of duty and to fulfill (as far as one can by one's own efforts) certain standards of good character. Given one's adoption of the attitude of respect, one makes that moral commitment because one considers those rules and standards to be validly binding on all moral agents. They are seen as embodying forms of conduct and character structures in which the attitude of respect for nature is manifested.

This three-part complex which internally orders the ethics of respect for nature is symmetrical with a theory of human ethics grounded on respect for persons. Such a theory includes, first, a conception of oneself and others as persons, that is, as centers of autonomous choice. Second, there is the attitude of respect for persons as persons. When this is adopted as an ultimate moral attitude it involves the disposition to treat every person as having inherent worth or "human dignity." Every human being, just in virtue of her or his humanity, is understood to be worthy of moral consideration, and intrinsic value is placed on the autonomy and well-being of each. This is what Kant meant by conceiving of persons as ends in themselves. Third, there is an ethical system of duties which are acknowledged to be owed by everyone to everyone. These duties are forms of conduct in which public recognition is given to each individual's inherent worth as a person.

This structural framework for a theory of human ethics is meant to leave open the issue of consequentialism (utilitarianism) versus nonconsequentialism (deontology). That issue concerns the particular kind of system of rules defining the duties of moral agents toward persons. Similarly, I am leaving open in this paper the question of what particular kind of system of rules defines our duties with respect to the natural world.

The Biocentric Outlook on Nature

The biocentric outlook on nature has four main components. (1) Humans are thought of as members of the Earth's community of life, holding that membership on the same terms as apply to all the non-human members. (2) The Earth's natural ecosystems as a totality are seen as a complex web of interconnected elements, with the sound biological functioning of each being dependent on the sound biological functioning of the others. (This is the component referred to above as the great lesson that the science of ecology has taught us.) (3) Each individual organism is conceived of as a teleological center of life, pursuing its own good in its own way. (4) Whether we are concerned with standards of merit or with the concept of inherent worth, the claim that humans by their very nature are superior to other species is a groundless claim and, in the light of elements (1), (2), and (3) above, must be rejected as nothing more than an irrational bias in our own favor. . . .

The Denial of Human Superiority

This fourth component of the biocentric outlook on nature is the single most important idea in establishing the justifiability of the attitude of respect for nature. Its central role is due to the special relationship it bears to the first three components of the outlook. This relationship will be brought out after the concept of human superiority is examined and analyzed.[6]

In what sense are humans alleged to be superior to other animals? We are different from them in having certain capacities that they lack. But why should these capacities be a mark of superiority? From what point of view are they judged to be signs of superiority and what sense of superiority is meant? After all, various non-human species have capacities that humans lack. There is the speed of a cheetah, the vision of an eagle, the agility of a monkey. Why should not these be taken as signs of *their* superiority over humans?

One answer that comes immediately to mind is that these capacities are not as *valuable* as the human capacities that are claimed to make us superior. Such uniquely human characteristics as rational thought, aesthetic creativity, autonomy and self-determination, and moral freedom, it might be held, have a higher value than the capacities found in other species. Yet we must ask: valuable to whom, and on what grounds?

The human characteristics mentioned are all valuable to humans. They are essential to the preservation and enrichment of our civilization and culture. Clearly it is from the human standpoint that they are being judged to be desirable and good. It is not difficult here to recognize a begging of the question. Humans are claiming human superiority from a strictly human point of view, that is, from a point of view in which the good of humans is taken as the standard of judgment. All we need to do is to look at the capacities of non-human animals (or plants, for that matter) from the standpoint of *their* good to find a contrary judgment of superiority. The speed of the cheetah, for example, is a sign of its superiority to humans when considered from the standpoint of the good of its species. If it were as slow a runner as a human, it would not be able to survive. And so for all the other abilities of non-humans which further their good but which are lacking in humans. In each case the claim to human superiority would be rejected from a non-human standpoint.

When superiority assertions are interpreted in this way, they are based on judgments of *merit*. To judge the merits of a person or an organism one must apply grading or ranking standards to it. (As I show below, this distinguishes judgments of merit from judgments of inherent worth.) Empirical investigation then determines whether it has the "good-making properties" (merits) in virtue of which it fulfills the standards being applied. In the case of humans, merits may be either moral or non-moral. We can judge one person to be better than (superior to) another from the moral point of view by applying certain standards to their character and conduct. Similarly, we can appeal to non-moral criteria in judging someone to be an excellent piano player, a

fair cook, a poor tennis player, and so on. Different social purposes and roles are implicit in the making of such judgments, providing the frame of reference for the choice of standards by which the non-moral merits of people are determined. Ultimately such purposes and roles stem from a society's way of life as a whole. Now a society's way of life may be thought of as the cultural form given to the realization of human values. Whether moral or non-moral standards are being applied, then, all judgments of people's merits finally depend on human values. All are made from an exclusively human standpoint.

The question that naturally arises at this juncture is: why should standards that are based on human values be assumed to be the only valid criteria of merit and hence the only true signs of superiority? This question is especially pressing when humans are being judged superior in merit to non-humans. It is true that a human being may be a better mathematician than a monkey, but the monkey may be a better tree climber than a human being. If we humans value mathematics more than tree climbing, that is because our conception of civilized life makes the development of mathematical ability more desirable than the ability to climb trees. But is it not unreasonable to judge non-humans by the values of human civilization, rather than by values connected with what it is for a member of *that* species to live a good life? If all living things have a good of their own, it at least makes sense to judge the merits of non-humans by standards derived from *their* good. To use only standards based on human values is already to commit oneself to holding that humans are superior to non-humans, which is the point in question.

A further logical flaw arises in connection with the widely held conviction that humans are *morally* superior beings because they possess, while others lack, the capacities of a moral agent (free will, accountability, deliberation, judgment, practical reason). This view rests on a conceptual confusion. As far as moral standards are concerned, only beings that have the capacities of a moral agent can properly be judged to be either moral (morally good) or immoral (morally deficient). Moral standards are simply not applicable to beings that lack such capacities. Animals and plants cannot therefore be said to be morally inferior in merit to humans. Since the only beings that can have moral merits *or be deficient in such merits* are moral agents, it is conceptually incoherent to judge humans as superior to non-humans on the ground that humans have moral capacities while non-humans don't.

Up to this point I have been interpreting the claim that humans are superior to other living things as a grading or ranking judgment regarding their comparative merits. There is, however, another way of understanding the idea of human superiority. According to this interpretation, humans are superior to non-humans not as regards their merits but as regards their inherent worth. Thus the claim of human superiority is to be understood as asserting that all humans, simply in virtue of their humanity, have *a greater inherent worth* than other living things.

The inherent worth of an entity does not depend on its merits.[7] To consider something as possessing inherent worth, we have seen, is to place intrinsic value on the realization of its good. This is done regardless of whatever particular merits it might have or might lack, as judged by a set of grading or ranking standards. In human affairs, we are all familiar with the principle that one's worth as a person does not vary with one's merits or lack of merits. The same can hold true of animals and plants. To regard such entities as possessing inherent worth entails disregarding their merits and deficiencies, whether they are being judged from a human standpoint or from the standpoint of their own species.

The idea of one entity having more merit than another, and so being superior to it in merit, makes perfectly good sense. Merit is a grading or ranking concept, and judgments of comparative merit are based on the different degrees to which things satisfy a given standard. But what can it mean to talk about one thing being superior to another in inherent worth? In order to get at what is being asserted in such a claim it is helpful first to look at the social origin of the concept of degrees of inherent worth.

The idea that humans can possess different degrees of inherent worth originated in societies having rigid class structures. Before the rise of modern democracies with their egalitarian outlook, one's membership in a hereditary class determined one's social status. People in the upper classes were looked up to, while those in the lower classes were looked down upon. In such a society one's social superiors and social inferiors were clearly defined and easily recognized.

Two aspects of these class-structured societies are especially relevant to the idea of degrees of inherent worth. First, those born into the upper classes were deemed more worthy of respect than those born into the lower orders. Second, the superior worth of upper class people had nothing to do with their merits nor did the inferior worth of those in the lower classes rest on their lack of merits. One's superiority or inferiority entirely derived from a social position one was born into. The modern concept of a meritocracy simply did not apply. One could not advance into a higher class by any sort of moral or non-moral achievement. Similarly, an aristocrat held his title and all the privileges that went with it just because he was the eldest son of a titled nobleman. Unlike the bestowing of knighthood in contemporary Great Britain, one did not earn membership in the nobility by meritorious conduct.

We who live in modern democracies no longer believe in such hereditary social distinctions. Indeed, we would wholeheartedly condemn them on moral grounds as being fundamentally unjust. We have come to think of class systems as a paradigm of social injustice, it being a central principle of the democratic way of life that among humans there are no superiors and no inferiors. Thus we have rejected the whole conceptual framework in which people are judged to have different degrees of inherent worth. That idea is incompatible with our notion of human equality based on the doctrine that all humans, simply in virtue of their humanity, have the same inherent worth. (The belief in universal human rights is one form that this egalitarianism takes.)

The vast majority of people in modern democracies, however, do not maintain an egalitarian outlook when it comes to comparing human beings with other living things. Most people consider our own species to be superior to all other species and this superiority is understood to be a matter of inherent worth, not merit. There may exist thoroughly vicious and depraved humans who lack all merit. Yet because they are human they are thought to belong to a higher class of entities than any plant or animal. That one is born into the species *Homo sapiens* entitles one to have lordship over those who are one's inferiors, namely, those born into other species. The parallel with hereditary social classes is very close. Implicit in this view is a hierarchical conception of nature according to which an organism has a position of superiority or inferiority in the Earth's community of life simply on the basis of its genetic background. The "lower" orders of life are looked down upon and it is considered perfectly proper that they serve the interests of those belonging to the highest order, namely humans. The intrinsic value we place on the well-being of our fellow humans reflects our recognition of their rightful position as our equals. No such intrinsic value is to be placed on the good of other animals, unless we choose to do so out of fondness or affection for them. But their well-being imposes no moral requirement on us. In this respect there is an absolute difference in moral status between ourselves and them.

This is the structure of concepts and beliefs that people are committed to in so far as they regard humans to be superior in inherent worth to all other species. I now wish to argue that this structure of concepts and beliefs is completely groundless. If we accept the first three components of the biocentric outlook and from that perspective look at the major philosophical traditions which have supported that structure, we find it to be at bottom nothing more than the expression of an irrational bias in our own favor. The philosophical traditions themselves rest on very questionable assumptions or else simply beg the question. I briefly consider three of the main traditions to substantiate the point. These are classical Greek humanism, Cartesian dualism, and the Judeo-Christian concept of the Great Chain of Being.

The inherent superiority of humans over other species was implicit in the Greek definition of man as a rational animal. Our animal nature was identified with "brute" desires that need the order and restraint of reason to rule them (just as reason is the special virtue of those who rule in the ideal state). Rationality was then seen to be the key to our superiority over animals. It enables us to live on a higher plane and endows us with a nobility and worth that other creatures lack. This familiar way of comparing humans with other species is deeply ingrained in our Western philosophical outlook. The point to consider here is that this view does not actually provide an argument *for* human superiority but rather makes explicit the framework of thought that is implicitly used by those who think of humans as inherently superior to non-humans. The Greeks who held that humans, in virtue of their rational capacities, have a kind of worth greater than that of any non-rational being, never looked at rationality as but one capacity of living things among many others. But when we consider rationality from the standpoint of the first three elements of the ecological outlook, we see that its value lies in its importance for *human* life. Other creatures achieve their species-specific good without the need of rationality, although they often make use of capacities that humans lack. So the humanistic outlook of classical Greek thought does not give us a neutral (non-question-begging) ground on which to construct a scale of degrees of inherent worth possessed by different species of living things.

The second tradition, centering on the Cartesian dualism of soul and body, also fails to justify the claim to human superiority. That superiority is supposed to derive from the fact that we have souls while animals do not. Animals are mere automata and lack the divine element that makes us spiritual beings. I won't go into the now familiar criticisms of this two-substance view. I only add the point that, even if humans are composed of an immaterial, unextended soul and a material, extended body, this in itself is not a reason to deem them of greater worth than entities that are only bodies. Why is a soul substance a thing that adds value to its possessor? Unless some theological reasoning is offered here (which many, including myself, would find unacceptable on epistemological grounds), no logical connection is evident. An immaterial something which thinks is better than a material something which does not think only if thinking itself has value, either intrinsically or instrumentally. Now it is intrinsically valuable to humans alone, who value it as an end in itself, and it is instrumentally valuable to those who benefit from it, namely humans.

For animals that neither enjoy thinking for its own sake nor need it for living the kind of life for which they are best adapted, it has no value. Even if "thinking" is broadened to include all forms of consciousness, there are still many living things that can do without it and yet live what is for their species a good life. The anthropocentricity underlying the claim to human superiority runs throughout Cartesian dualism.

A third major source of the idea of human superiority is the Judeo-Christian concept of the Great Chain of Being. Humans are superior to animals and plants because their Creator has given them a higher place on the chain. It begins with God at the top, and then moves to the angels, who are lower than God but higher than humans, then to humans, positioned between the angels and the beasts (partaking of the nature of both), and then on down to the lower levels occupied by non-human animals, plants, and finally inanimate objects. Humans, being "made in God's image," are inherently superior to animals and plants by virtue of their being closer (in their essential nature) to God.

The metaphysical and epistemological difficulties with this conception of a hierarchy of entities are, in my mind, insuperable. Without entering into this matter here, I only point out that if we are unwilling to accept the metaphysics of traditional Judaism and Christianity, we are again left without good reasons for holding to the claim of inherent human superiority.

The foregoing considerations (and others like them) leave us with but one ground for the assertion that a human being, regardless of merit, is a higher kind of entity than any other living thing. This is the mere fact of the genetic makeup of the species *Homo sapiens*. But this is surely irrational and arbitrary. Why should the arrangement of genes of a certain type be a mark of superior value, especially when this fact about an organism is taken by itself, unrelated to any other aspect of its life? We might just as well refer to any other genetic makeup as a ground of superior value. Clearly we are confronted here with a wholly arbitrary claim that can only be explained as an irrational bias in our own favor.

That the claim is nothing more than a deep-seated prejudice is brought home to us when we look at our relation to other species in the light of the first three elements of the biocentric outlook. Those elements taken conjointly give us a certain overall view of the natural world and of the place of humans in it. When we take this view we come to understand other living things, their environmental conditions, and their ecological relationships in such a way as to awake in us a deep sense of our kinship with them as fellow members of the Earth's community of life. Humans and non-humans alike are viewed together as integral parts of one unified whole in which all living things are functionally interrelated. Finally, when our awareness focuses on the individual lives of plants and animals, each is seen to share with us the characteristic of being a teleological center of life striving to realize its own good in its own unique way.

As this entire belief system becomes part of the conceptual framework through which we understand and perceive the world, we come to see ourselves as bearing a certain moral relation to non-human forms of life. Our ethical role in nature takes on a new significance. We begin to look at other species as we look at ourselves, seeing them as beings which have a good they are striving to realize just as we have a good we are striving to realize. We accordingly develop the disposition to view the world from the standpoint of their good as well as from the standpoint of our own good. Now if the groundlessness of the claim that humans are inherently superior to other species were brought clearly before our minds, we would not remain intellectually neutral toward that claim but would reject it as being fundamentally at variance with our total world outlook. In the absence of any good reasons for holding it, the assertion of

human superiority would then appear simply as
the expression of an irrational and self-serving
prejudice that favors one particular species over
several million others.

Rejecting the notion of human superiority
entails its positive counterpart: the doctrine of
species impartiality. One who accepts that doctrine regards all living things as possessing inherent worth – the *same* inherent worth, since no
one species has been shown to be either "higher"
or "lower" than any other. Now we saw earlier
that, in so far as one thinks of a living thing as
possessing inherent worth, one considers it to
be the appropriate object of the attitude of respect and believes that attitude to be the only
fitting or suitable one for all moral agents to take
toward it.

Here, then, is the key to understanding how
the attitude of respect is rooted in the biocentric
outlook on nature. The basic connection is made
through the denial of human superiority. Once
we reject the claim that humans are superior either in merit or in worth to other living things,
we are ready to adopt the attitude of respect. The
denial of human superiority is itself the result of
taking the perspective on nature built into the
first three elements of the biocentric outlook.

Now the first three elements of the biocentric
outlook, it seems clear, would be found acceptable to any rational and scientifically informed
thinker who is fully "open" to the reality of the
lives of non-human organisms. Without denying our distinctively human characteristics, such
a thinker can acknowledge the fundamental respects in which we are members of the Earth's
community of life and in which the biological
conditions necessary for the realization of our
human values are inextricably linked with the
whole system of nature. In addition, the conception of individual living things as teleological
centers of life simply articulates how a scientifically informed thinker comes to understand them
as the result of increasingly careful and detailed
observations. Thus, the biocentric outlook recommends itself as an acceptable system of concepts and beliefs to anyone who is clear-minded,
unbiased, and factually enlightened, and who has
a developed capacity of reality awareness with

regard to the lives of individual organisms. This,
I submit, is as good a reason for making the moral
commitment involved in adopting the attitude
of respect for nature as any theory of environmental ethics could possibly have.

Moral Rights and the Matter of Competing Claims

I have not asserted anywhere in the foregoing
account that animals or plants have moral rights.
This omission was deliberate. I do not think that
the reference class of the concept, bearer of moral
rights, should be extended to include non-human living things. My reasons for taking this
position, however, go beyond the scope of this
paper. I believe I have been able to accomplish
many of the same ends which those who ascribe
rights to animals or plants wish to accomplish.
There is no reason, moreover, why plants and
animals, including whole species populations and
life communities, cannot be accorded *legal* rights
under my theory. To grant them legal protection could be interpreted as giving them legal
entitlement to be protected, and this, in fact,
would be a means by which a society that sub-
scribed to the ethics of respect for nature could
give public recognition to their inherent worth.

There remains the problem of competing
claims, even when wild plants and animals are
not thought of as bearers of moral rights. If we
accept the biocentric outlook and accordingly
adopt the attitude of respect for nature as our
ultimate moral attitude, how do we resolve conflicts that arise from our respect for persons in
the domain of human ethics and our respect for
nature in the domain of environmental ethics?
This is a question that cannot adequately be dealt
with here. My main purpose in this paper has
been to try to establish a base point from which
we can start working toward a solution to the
problem. I have shown why we cannot just begin with an initial presumption in favor of the
interests of our own species. It is after all within
our power as moral beings to place limits on
human population and technology with the deliberate intention of sharing the Earth's bounty

with other species. That such sharing is an ideal difficult to realize even in an approximate way does not take away its claim to our deepest moral commitment.

Notes

1 The conceptual links between an entity *having* a good, something being good *for* it, and events doing good *to* it are examined by G. H. Von Wright in *The Varieties of Goodness* (New York: Humanities Press, 1963), chs 3 and 5.

2 See W. K. Frankena, "Ethics and the Environment," in K. E. Goodpaster and K. M. Sayre, eds, *Ethics and Problems of the 21st Century* (Notre Dame: University of Notre Dame Press, 1979), 3–20. I critically examine Frankena's views in "Frankena on Environmental Ethics," *Monist*, 64: 3 (July 1981), 313–24.

3 In the light of considerations set forth in Daniel Dennett's *Brainstorms: Philosophical Essays on Mind and Psychology* (Montgomery, VT: Bradford Books, 1978), it is advisable to leave this question unsettled at this time. When machines are developed

that function in the way our brains do, we may well come to deem them proper subjects of moral consideration.

4 I have analyzed the nature of this commitment of human ethics in "On Taking the Moral Point of View," *Midwest Studies in Philosophy*, vol. 3, *Studies in Ethical Theory* (1978), 35–61.

5 John Rawls, "Justice as Fairness," *Philosophical Review*, 67 (1958), 183.

6 My criticisms of the dogma of human superiority gain independent support from a carefully reasoned essay by R. and V. Routley showing the many logical weaknesses in arguments for human-centered theories of environmental ethics. R. and V. Routley, "Against the Inevitability of Human Chauvinism," in K. E. Goodpaster and K. M. Sayre, eds, *Ethics and Problems of the 21st Century* (Notre Dame: University of Notre Dame Press, 1979), 36–59.

7 For this way of distinguishing between merit and inherent worth, I am indebted to Gregory Vlastos, "Justice and Equality," in R. Brandt, ed., *Social Justice* (Englewood Cliffs, NJ: Prentice-Hall, 1962), 31–72.

---

39   Environmental Justice

James P. Sterba

A central debate, if not the most central debate, in contemporary environmental ethics is between those who defend an anthropocentric ethics which holds that humans are superior overall to the members of other species, and those who defend a non-anthropocentric ethics which holds that the members of all species are equal. Here I propose to go some way toward resolving this debate by showing that when the most morally defensible versions of each of these perspectives are laid out, they do not lead to different practical requirements. In this way I hope to show how it is possible for defenders of anthropocentric and

Reprinted by permission of James P. Sterba.

non-anthropocentric environmental ethics, despite their theoretical disagreement concerning whether humans are superior to members of other species, to agree on a common set of principles for achieving environmental justice.

Non-anthropocentric Environmental Ethics

Consider first the non-anthropocentric perspective. In support of this, it can be argued that we have no non-question-begging grounds for regarding the members of any living species as superior to the members of any other. It allows that the members of species differ in a myriad of ways, but argues that these differences do not provide grounds for thinking that the members of any one species are superior to the members of any other. In particular, it denies that the differences between species provides grounds for thinking that humans are superior to the members of other species. Of course, the non-anthropocentric perspective recognizes that humans have distinctive traits which the members of other species lack, like rationality and moral agency. It just points out that the members of non-human species also have distinctive traits that humans lack, like the homing ability of pigeons, the speed of the cheetah, and the ruminative ability of sheep and cattle.

Nor will it do to claim that the distinctive traits that humans have are more valuable than the distinctive traits that members of other species possess because there is no non-question-begging standpoint from which to justify that claim. From a human standpoint, rationality and moral agency are more valuable than any of the distinctive traits found in non-human species, since, as humans, we would not be better off if we were to trade in those traits for the distinctive traits found in non-human species. Yet the same holds true of non-human species. Generally, pigeons, cheetahs, sheep, and cattle would not be better off if they were to trade in their distinctive traits for the distinctive traits of other species.

Of course, the members of some species might be better off if they could retain the distinctive traits of their species while acquiring one or another of the distinctive traits possessed by some other species. For example, we humans might be better off if we could retain our distinctive traits while acquiring the ruminative ability of sheep and cattle. But many of the distinctive traits of species cannot be even imaginatively added to the members of other species without substantially altering the original species. For example, in order for the cheetah to acquire the distinctive traits possessed by humans, presumably it would have to be so transformed that its paws became something like hands to accommodate its humanlike mental capabilities, thereby losing its distinctive speed, and ceasing to be a cheetah.

So possessing distinctively human traits would not be good for the cheetah. And with the possible exception of our nearest evolutionary relatives, the same holds true for the members of other species: they would not be better off having distinctively human traits. Only in fairy tales and in the world of Disney can the members of non-human species enjoy a full array of distinctively human traits. So there would appear to be no non-question-begging perspective from which to judge that distinctively human traits are more valuable than the distinctive traits possessed by other species. Judged from a non-question-begging perspective, we would seemingly have to regard the members of all species as equals.

It might be useful at this point to make my argument even more explicit. Here is one way this could be done.

(1) We should not aggress against any living being unless there are either self-evident or non-question-begging reasons for doing so. (It would be difficult to reject this principle given the various analogous principles we accept, such as the principle of formal equality: equals should be treated equally and unequals unequally.)

(2) To treat humans as superior overall to other living beings is to aggress against them by sacrificing their basic needs to meet the non-basic needs of humans. (Definition)

(3) Therefore, we should not treat humans as superior overall to other living beings unless we have either self-evident or non-question-begging reasons for doing so. (From 1 and 2)

(4) We do not have either self-evident or non-question-begging reasons for treating humans as superior overall to other living beings. (That we do not have any non-question-begging reasons for treating humans as superior overall to other living beings was established by the previous argument. That we do not have any self-evident reasons for doing so, I take it, is obvious.)

(5) Therefore, we should not treat humans as superior overall to other living beings. (From 3 and 4)

(6) Not to treat humans as superior overall to other living beings is to treat them as equal overall to other living beings. (Definition)

(7) Therefore, we should treat humans as equal overall to other living beings. (From 5 and 6)

Nevertheless, I want to go on to claim that regarding the members of all species as equals still allows for human preference in the same way that regarding all humans as equals still allows for self preference.

First of all, human preference can be justified on grounds of defense. Thus, we have

A Principle of Human Defense: actions that defend oneself and other human beings against harmful aggression are permissible even when they necessitate killing or harming animals or plants.

This Principle of Human Defense allows us to defend ourselves and other human beings from harmful aggression first against our persons and the persons of other humans beings that we are committed to or happen to care about, and second against our justifiably held property and the justifiably held property of other humans beings that we are committed to or happen to care about.

This principle is analogous to the principle of self-defense that applies in human ethics and permits actions in defense of oneself or other human beings against harmful human aggression. In the case of human aggression, however, it will sometimes be possible to effectively defend oneself and other human beings by first suffering the aggression and then securing adequate compensation later. Since in the case of non-human aggression, this is unlikely to obtain, more harmful preventive actions such as killing a rabid dog or swatting a mosquito will be justified. There are simply more ways to effectively stop aggressive humans than there are to stop aggressive non-humans.

Second, human preference can also be justified on grounds of preservation. Accordingly, we have

A Principle of Human Preservation: actions that are necessary for meeting one's basic needs or the basic needs of other human beings are permissible even when they require aggressing against the basic needs of animals and plants.

Now needs, in general, if not satisfied, lead to lacks or deficiencies with respect to various standards. The basic needs of humans, if not satisfied, lead to lacks or deficiencies with respect to a standard of a decent life. The basic needs of animals and plants, if not satisfied, lead to lacks or deficiencies with respect to a standard of a healthy life. The means necessary for meeting the basic needs of humans can vary widely from society to society. By contrast, the means necessary for meeting the basic needs of particular species of animals and plants are more invariant.

In human ethics, there is no principle that is strictly analogous to this Principle of Human Preservation. There is a principle of self-preservation in human ethics that permits actions that are necessary for meeting one's own basic needs or the basic needs of other people, even if this requires *failing to meet* (through an act of omission) the basic needs of still other people. For example, we can use our resources to feed ourselves and our family, even if this necessitates failing to meet the basic needs of people in Third World countries. But, in general, we don't have a principle that allows us to *aggress against* (through an act of commission) the basic needs of some people in order to meet our own basic needs or the basic needs of other people to whom we are committed or happen to care about. Actually, the closest we come to permitting aggressing against the basic needs of other people in order to meet our own basic needs or the basic needs of people to whom we are committed or happen to care about is our acceptance of the outcome of life and death struggles in lifeboat cases, where no one has an antecedent right to the available resources. For example, if you had to fight off others in order to secure the last place in a lifeboat for yourself or for a member of your family, we might say that you justifiably aggressed against the basic needs of those whom you fought to meet your own basic needs or the basic needs of the member of your family.

Nevertheless, our survival requires a principle of preservation that permits aggressing against the basic needs of at least some other living things whenever this is necessary to meet our own basic needs or the basic needs of other human beings. Here there are two possibilities. The first is a principle of preservation that allows us to aggress against the basic needs of both humans and non-humans whenever it would serve our own basic needs or the basic needs of other human beings. The second is the principle, given above, that allows us to aggress against the basic needs of only non-humans whenever it would serve our own basic needs or the basic needs of other human beings. The first principle does not express any general preference for the members of the human species, and thus it permits even cannibalism provided that it serves to meet our own basic needs or the basic needs of other human beings. In contrast, the second principle does express a degree of preference for the members of the human species in cases where their basic needs are at stake. Happily, this degree of preference for our own species is still compatible with the equality of all species because favoring the members of one's own species to this extent is characteristic of the members of nearly all species with which we interact and is thereby legitimated. The reason it is legitimated is that we would be required to sacrifice the basic needs of members of the human species only if the members of other species were making similar sacrifices for the sake of members of the human species. In addition, if we were to prefer consistently the basic needs of the members of other species whenever those needs conflicted with our own (or even if we do so half the time), given the characteristic behavior of the members of other species, we would soon be facing extinction, and, fortunately, we have no reason to think that we are morally required to bring about our own extinction. For these reasons, the degree of

preference for our own species found in the above Principle of Human Preservation is justified, even if we were to adopt a non-anthropocentric perspective.

Nevertheless, preference for humans can go beyond bounds, and the bounds that are compatible with a non-anthropocentric perspective are expressed by the following:

A Principle of Disproportionality: actions that meet non-basic or luxury needs of humans are prohibited when they aggress against the basic needs of animals and plants.

This principle is strictly analogous to the principle in human ethics mentioned previously that prohibits meeting some people's non-basic or luxury needs by aggressing against the basic needs of other people.

Without a doubt, the adoption of such a principle with respect to non-human nature would significantly change the way we live our lives. Such a principle is required, however, if there is to be any substance to the claim that the members of all species are equal. We can no more consistently claim that the members of all species are equal and yet aggress against the basic needs of some animals or plants whenever this serves our own non-basic or luxury needs than we can consistently claim that all humans are equal and aggress against the basic needs of some other human beings whenever this serves our non-basic or luxury needs. Consequently, if species equality is to mean anything, it must be the case that the basic needs of the members of non-human species are protected against aggressive actions which only serve to meet the non-basic needs of humans, as required by the Principle of Disproportionality.

So while a non-anthropocentric perspective allows for a degree of preference for the members of the human species, it also significantly limits that preference.

To see why these limits on preference for the members of the human species are all that is required for recognizing the equality of species, we need to understand the equality of species by analogy with the equality of humans. We need to see that just as we claim that humans are equal but treat them differently, so too we can claim that all species are equal but treat them differently. In human ethics, there are various interpretations given to human equality that allow for different treatment of humans. In ethical egoism, everyone is *equally at liberty* to pursue his or her own interests, but this allows us to always prefer ourselves to others, who are understood to be like opponents in a competitive game. In libertarianism, everyone has an *equal right to liberty*, but although this imposes some limits on the pursuit of self-interest, it is said to allow us to refrain from helping others in severe need. In welfare liberalism, everyone has an *equal right to welfare and opportunity*, but this need not commit us to providing everyone with exactly the same resources. In socialism, everyone has an *equal right* to self-development, and although this may commit us to providing everyone with the same resources, it still sanctions some degree of self-preference. So just as there are these various ways to interpret human equality that still allow us to treat humans differently, there are various ways that we can interpret species equality that allow us to treat species differently.

Now one might interpret species equality in a very strong sense, analogous to the interpretation of equality found in socialism. But the kind of species equality that I have defended is more akin to the equality found in welfare liberalism or in libertarianism than it is to the equality found in socialism. In brief, this form of equality requires that we not aggress against the basic needs of the members of other species for the sake of the non-basic needs of the members of our own species (the Principle of Disproportionality), but it permits us to aggress against the basic needs of the members of other species for the sake of the basic needs of the members of our own species (the Principle of Human Preservation), and also permits us to defend the basic and even the non-basic needs of the members of our own species against harmful aggression by members of other species (the Principle of Human Defense). In this way, I have argued that we can accept the claim of species equality, while avoiding imposing an unreasonable sacrifice on the members of our own species.

Individualism and Holism

It might be objected here that I have not yet taken into account the conflict within a non-anthropocentric ethics between holists and individualists. According to holists, the good of a species or the good of an ecosystem or the good of the whole biotic community can trump the good of individual living things.[1] According to individualists, the good of each individual living thing must be respected.[2]

Now one might think that holists would require that we abandon my Principle of Human Preservation. Yet consider. Assuming that people's basic needs are at stake, how could it be morally objectionable for them to try to meet those needs, even if this were to harm non-human individuals, or species, or whole ecosystems, or even, to some degree, the whole biotic community? Of course, we can ask people in such conflict cases not to meet their basic needs in order to prevent harm to non-human individuals or species, ecosystems or the whole biotic community. But if people's basic needs are at stake, we cannot reasonably demand that they make such a sacrifice. We could demand, of course, that people do all that they reasonably can to keep such conflicts from arising in the first place, for, just as in human ethics, many severe conflicts of interest can be avoided simply by doing what is morally required early on. Nevertheless, when people's basic needs are at stake, the individualist perspective seems incontrovertible. We cannot reasonably require people to be saints.

At the same time, when people's basic needs are not at stake, we would be justified in acting on holistic grounds to prevent serious harm to non-human individuals, or species, or ecosystems, or the whole biotic community. Obviously, it will be difficult to know when our interventions will have this effect, but when we can be reasonably sure that they will, such interventions (e.g. culling elk herds in wolf-free ranges or preserving the habitat of endangered species) would be morally permissible, and maybe even morally required.[3] This shows that it is possible to agree with individualists when the basic needs of human beings are at stake, and to agree with holists when they are not.

Yet this combination of individualism and holism appears to conflict with the equality of species by imposing greater sacrifices on the members of non-human species than it does on the members of the human species. Fortunately, appearances are deceiving here. Although the proposed resolution only justifies imposing holism when people's basic needs are not at stake, it does not justify imposing individualism at all. Rather it would simply permit individualism when people's basic needs *are* at stake. Of course, we could impose holism under all conditions. But given that this would, in effect, involve going to war against people who are simply striving to meet their own basic needs in the only way they can, as permitted by the Principle of Human Preservation, intervention in such cases would not be justified. It would involve taking away the means of survival from people, even when these means are not required for one's own survival.

Nevertheless, this combination of individualism and holism may leave animal liberationists wondering about the further implications of this resolution for the treatment of animals. Obviously, a good deal of work has already been done on this topic. Initially, philosophers taught that humanism could be extended to include animal liberation and eventually environmental concern.[4] Then Baird Callicott argued that animal liberation and environmental concern were as opposed to each other as they were to humanism.[5] The resulting conflict Callicott called "a triangular affair." Agreeing with Callicott, Mark Sagoff contended that any attempt to link together animal liberation and environmental concern would lead to "a bad marriage and a quick divorce."[6] Yet more recently, such philosophers as Mary Ann Warren have tended to play down the opposition between animal liberation and environmental concern, and even Callicott now thinks he can bring the two back together again.[7] There are good reasons for thinking that such a reconciliation is possible.

Right off, it would be good for the environment if people generally, especially people in the First World, adopted a more vegetarian diet of the sort that animal liberationists are recommending. This is because a good portion of livestock production today consumes grains that could be more effectively used for direct human consumption. For example, 90 percent of the protein, 99 percent of the carbohydrate, and 100 percent of the fiber value of grain is wasted by cycling it through livestock, and currently 64 percent of the US grain crop is fed to livestock.[8] So by adopting a more vegetarian diet, people generally, and especially people in the First World, could significantly reduce the amount of farmland that has to be kept in production to feed the human population. This, in turn, could have beneficial effects on the whole biotic community by eliminating the amount of soil erosion and environmental pollutants that result from raising livestock. For example, it has been estimated that of 85 percent of US topsoil lost from cropland, pasture, range land, and forest land is directly associated with raising livestock.[9] So, in addition to preventing animal suffering, there are these additional reasons to favor a more vegetarian diet.

But even though a more vegetarian diet seems in order, it is not clear that the interests of farm animals would be well served if all of us became complete vegetarians. Sagoff assumes that in a completely vegetarian human world people would continue to feed farm animals as before.[10] But it is not clear that we would have any obligation to do so. Moreover, in a completely vegetarian human world, we would probably need about half of the grain we now feed livestock to meet people's nutritional needs, particularly in Second and Third World countries. There simply would not be enough grain to go around. And then there would be the need to conserve cropland for future generations. So in a completely vegetarian human world, it seems likely that the population of farm animals would be decimated, relegating many of the animals that remain to zoos. On this account, it would seem to be more in the interest of farm animals generally that they be maintained under healthy conditions, and hence not in the numbers sustainable only with factory farms, but then killed relatively painlessly and eaten, rather than that they not be maintained at all. So a completely vegetarian human world would not seem to serve the interest of farm animals.

Nor, it seems, would it be in the interest of wild species who no longer have their natural predators not to be hunted by humans. Of course, where possible, it may be preferable to reintroduce natural predators. But this may not always be possible because of the proximity of farm animals and human populations, and then if action is not taken to control the populations of wild species, disaster could result for the species and their environments. For example, deer, rabbits, squirrels, quails, and ducks reproduce rapidly, and in the absence of predators can quickly exceed the carrying capacity of their environments. So it may be in the interest of certain wild species and their environments that humans intervene periodically to maintain a balance. Of course, there will be many natural environments where it is in the interest of the environment and the wild animals that inhabit it to be simply left alone. But here, too, animal liberation and environmental concern would not be in conflict. For these reasons, animal liberationists would have little reason to object to the proposed combination of individualism and holism within a non-anthropocentric environmental ethics.

Anthropocentric Environmental Ethics

Suppose, however, we were to reject the central contention of the non-anthropocentric perspective and deny that the members of all species are equal. We might claim, for example, that humans are superior because they, through culture, "realize a greater range of values" than members of non-human species or we might claim that humans are superior in virtue of their "unprecedented capacity to create ethical systems that impart worth to other lifeforms."[11] Or we might offer some other grounds for human superiority. Suppose, then, we adopt this anthropocentric perspective. What follows?

First of all, we will still need a principle of human defense. However, there is no need to adopt a different principle of human defense from the

principle favored by a non-anthropocentric perspective. Whether we judge humans to be equal or superior to the members of other species, we will still want a principle that allows us to defend ourselves and other human beings from harmful aggression, even when this necessitates killing or harming animals or plants.

Second, we will also need a principle of human preservation. But here too there is no need to adopt a different principle from the principle of human preservation favored by a non-anthropocentric perspective. Whether we judge humans to be equal or superior to the members of other species, we will still want a principle that permits actions that are necessary for meeting our own basic needs or the basic needs of other human beings, even when this requires aggressing against the basic needs of animals and plants.

The crucial question is whether we will need a different principle of disproportionality. If we judge humans to be superior to the members of other species, will we still have grounds for protecting the basic needs of animals and plants against aggressive action to meet the non-basic or luxury needs of humans?

Here it is important to distinguish between two degrees of preference that we noted earlier. First, we could prefer the basic needs of animals and plants over the non-basic or luxury needs of humans when to do otherwise would involve *aggressing against* (by an act of commission) the basic needs of animals and plants. Second, we could prefer the basic needs of animals and plants over the non-basic or luxury needs of humans when to do otherwise would involve simply *failing to meet* (by an act of omission) the basic needs of animals and plants.

Now in human ethics when the basic needs of some people are in conflict with the non-basic or luxury needs of others, the distinction between failing to meet and aggressing against basic needs seems to have little moral force. In such conflict cases, both ways of not meeting basic needs are objectionable.

But in environmental ethics, whether we adopt an anthropocentric or a non-anthropocentric perspective, we would seem to have grounds for morally distinguishing between the two cases, favoring the basic needs of animals and plants when to do otherwise would involve *aggressing against* those needs in order to meet our own non-basic or luxury needs, but not when it would involve simply *failing to meet* those needs in order to meet our own non-basic or luxury needs. This degree of preference for the members of the human species would be compatible with the equality of species in so far as members of non-human species similarly fail to meet the basic needs of members of the human species where there is a conflict of interest.

Even so, this theoretical distinction would have little practical force since most of the ways that we have of preferring our own non-basic needs over the basic needs of animals and plants actually involve aggressing against their basic needs to meet our own non-basic or luxury needs rather than simply failing to meet their basic needs.

Yet even if most of the ways that we have of preferring our own non-basic or luxury needs do involve aggressing against the basic needs of animals and plants, wouldn't human superiority provide grounds for preferring ourselves or other human beings in these ways? Or put another way, shouldn't human superiority have more theoretical and practical significance than I am allowing? Not, I claim, if we are looking for the most morally defensible position to take.

For consider: the claim that humans are superior to the members of other species, if it can be justified at all, is something like the claim that a person came in first in a race where others came in second, third, fourth, and so on. It would not imply that the members of other species are without intrinsic value. In fact, it would imply just the opposite – that the members of other species are also intrinsically valuable, although not as intrinsically valuable as humans, just as the claim that a person came in first in a race implies that the persons who came in second, third, fourth, and so on are also meritorious, although not as meritorious as the person who came in first.

This line of argument draws further support once we consider the fact that many animals and plants are superior to humans in one respect or another, e.g. the sense of smell of the wolf, or the acuity of sight of the eagle, or the survivability

of the cockroach, or the photosynthetic power of plants. So any claim of human superiority must allow for the recognition of excellences in non-human species, even for some excellences that are superior to their corresponding human excellences. In fact, it demands that recognition.

Moreover, if the claim of human superiority is to have any moral force, it must rest on non-question-begging grounds. Accordingly, we must be able to give a non-question-begging response to the non-anthropocentric argument for the equality of species. Yet for any such argument to be successful, it would have to recognize the intrinsic value of the members of non-human species. Even if it could be established that human beings have greater intrinsic value, we would still have to recognize that non-human nature has intrinsic value as well. So the relevant question is: how are we going to recognize the presumably lesser intrinsic value of non-human nature?

Now if human needs, even non-basic or luxury ones, are always preferred to even the basic needs of the members of non-human species, we would not be giving any recognition to the intrinsic value of non-human nature. But what if we allowed the non-basic or luxury needs of humans to trump the basic needs of non-human nature half the time, and half the time we allowed the basic needs of non-human nature to trump the non-basic or luxury needs of humans? Would that be enough? Certainly, it would be a significant advance over what we are presently doing. For what we are presently doing is meeting the basic needs of non-human nature, at best, only when it serves our own needs or the needs of those we are committed to or happen to care about, and that does not recognize the intrinsic value of non-human nature at all. A fifty-fifty arrangement would be an advance indeed. But it would not be enough.

The reason why it would not be enough is that the claim that humans are superior to non-human nature no more supports the practice of aggressing against the basic needs of non-human nature to satisfy our own non-basic or luxury needs than the claim that a person who came in first in a race would support the practice of aggressing against the basic needs of those who came in second, third, fourth, and so on to satisfy the non-basic or luxury needs of the person who came in first. A higher degree of merit does not translate into a right of domination, and to claim a right to aggress against the basic needs of non-human nature in order to meet our own non-basic or luxury needs is clearly to claim a right of domination. All that our superiority as humans would justify is not meeting the basic needs of non-human nature when this conflicts with our non-basic or luxury needs. What it does not justify is aggressing against the basic needs of non-human nature when this conflicts with our non-basic or luxury needs.

Objective and Subjective Value Theory

Now it might be objected that my argument so far presupposes an objective theory of value which regards things as valuable because of the qualities they actually have rather than a subjective theory of value which regards things as valuable simply because humans happen to value them. However, I contend that when both these theories are defensibly formulated, they will lead to the same practical requirements.

For consider. Suppose we begin with a subjective theory of value that regards things as valuable simply because humans value them. Of course, some things would be valued by humans instrumentally, others intrinsically, but, according to this theory, all things would have the value they have, if they have any value at all, simply because they are valued by humans either instrumentally or intrinsically.

One problem facing such a theory is why should we think that humans alone determine the value that things have? For example, why not say that things are valuable because the members of other species value them? Why not say that grass is valuable because zebras value it, and that zebras are valuable because lions value them, and so on? Or why not say, assuming God exists, that things are valuable because God values them?

Nor would it do simply to claim that we authoritatively determine what is valuable for ourselves, that non-human species authoritatively determine what is valuable for themselves, and that God authoritatively determines what is valuable for the Godhead. For what others value should at least be relevant data when authoritatively determining what is valuable for ourselves.

Another problem for a subjective theory of value is that we probably would not want to say that just anything we happen to value determines what is valuable for ourselves. For surely we would want to say that at least some of the things that people value, especially people who are evil or deficient in certain ways, are not really valuable, even for them. Merely thinking that something is valuable doesn't make it so.

Suppose, then, we modified this subjective theory of value to deal with these problems. Let the theory claim that what is truly valuable for people is what they would value if they had all the relevant information (including, where it is relevant, the knowledge of what others would value) and reasoned correctly. Of course, there will be many occasions where we are unsure that ideal conditions have been realized, unsure, that is, that we have all the relevant information and have reasoned correctly. And even when we are sure that ideal conditions have been realized, we may not always be willing to act upon what we come to value due to weakness of will.

Nevertheless, when a subjective theory of value is formulated in this way, it will have the same practical requirements as an objective theory of value that is also defensibly formulated. For an objective theory of value holds that what is valuable is determined by the qualities things actually have. But in order for the qualities things actually have to be valuable in the sense of being capable of being valued, they must be accessible to us, at least under ideal conditions, that is, they must be the sort of qualities that we would value if we had all the relevant information and reasoned correctly. But this is just what is valuable according to our modified subjective theory of value. So once a subjective theory of value and an objective theory of value are defensibly formulated in the manner I propose, they will lead us to value the same things.

Now it is important to note here that with respect to some of the things we value intrinsically, such as animals and plants, our valuing them depends simply on our ability to discover the value that they actually have based on their qualities, whereas for other things that we value intrinsically, such as our aesthetic experiences and the objects that provided us with those experiences, the value that these things have depends significantly on the way we are constituted. So that if we were constituted differently, what we value aesthetically would be different as well. Of course, the same holds true for some of the things that we value morally. For example, we morally value not killing human beings because of the way we are constituted. Constituted as we are, killing is usually bad for any human that we would kill. But suppose that we were constituted differently such that killing human beings was immensely pleasurable for those humans that we killed, following which they immediately sprang back to life asking us to kill them again. If human beings were constituted in this way, we would no longer morally value not killing. In fact, constituted in this new way, I think we would come to morally value *killing* and the relevant rule for us might be "Kill human beings as often as you can." But while such aesthetic and moral values are clearly dependent on the way we are constituted, they still are not anthropocentric in the sense that they imply human superiority. Such values can be recognized from both an anthropocentric and a non-anthropocentric perspective.

It might be objected, however, that while the intrinsic values of an environmental ethics need not be anthropocentric in the sense that they imply human superiority, these values must be anthropocentric in the sense that humans would reasonably come to hold them. This seems correct. However, appealing to this sense of anthropocentric, Eugene Hargrove has argued that not all living things would turn out to be intrinsically valuable as a non-anthropocentric environmental ethics maintains.[12] Hargrove cites as hypothetical examples of living things that would not turn out to be intrinsically valuable the creatures in the films *Alien* and *Aliens*. What is distinctive about these creatures in *Alien* and *Aliens* is that they require the deaths of many other living creatures, whomever they happen upon, to reproduce and survive as a species. Newly hatched, these creatures emerge from their eggs and immediately enter host organisms, which they keep alive and feed upon while they develop. When the creatures are fully developed, they explode out of the chest of their host organisms, killing their hosts with some fanfare. Hargrove suggests that if such creatures existed, we would not intrinsically value them because it would not be reasonable for us to do so.[13]

Following Paul Taylor, Hargrove assumes that to intrinsically value a creature is to recognize a negative duty not to destroy or harm that creature and a positive duty to protect it from being destroyed or harmed by others. Since Hargrove thinks that we would be loath to recognize any such duties with respect to such alien creatures, we would not consider them to be intrinsically valuable.

Surely it seems clear that we would seek to kill such alien creatures by whatever means are available to us. But why should that preclude our recognizing them as having intrinsic value any more than our seeking to kill any person who is engaged in lethal aggression against us would preclude our recognizing that person as having intrinsic value? To recognize something as having intrinsic value does not preclude destroying it to preserve other things that also have intrinsic value when there is good reason to do so. Furthermore, recognizing a prima facie negative duty not to destroy or harm something and a prima facie positive duty to protect it from being destroyed or harmed by others is perfectly consistent with recognizing an all-things-considered duty to destroy that thing when it is engaged in lethal aggression against us. Actually, all we are doing here is simply applying our Principle of Human Defense, and, as I have argued earlier, there is no reason to think that the application of this principle would preclude our recognizing the intrinsic value of every living being.

Still another objection that might be raised to my reconciliationist argument is that my view is too individualistic, as evidenced by the fact that my principles of environmental justice refer to individual humans, plants, and animals but not specifically to species or ecosystems. Now, I would certainly agree with Paul Taylor that all individual living beings as well as species populations can be benefited or harmed and have a good of their own, and, hence, qualify as moral subjects.[14] But Taylor goes on to deny that species themselves are moral subjects with a good of their own, because he regards "species" as a class name, and classes, he contends, have no good of their own.[15] Yet here I would disagree with Taylor because species are unlike abstract classes in that they evolve, split, bud off new species, become endangered, become extinct and have interests distinct from the interests of their members.[16] For example, a particular species of deer but not individual members of that species can have an interest in being preyed upon. Hence, species can be benefited and harmed and have a good of their own, and so should qualify on Taylor's view, as well as my own, as moral subjects. So, too, ecosystems should qualify as moral subjects since they can be benefited and harmed and have a good of their own, having features and interests not shared by their components.[17] Following Lawrence Johnson, we can go on to characterize moral subjects as living systems in a persistent state of low entropy sustained by metabolic processes for accumulating energy whose organic unity and self-identity is maintained in equilibrium by homeostatic feedback processes.[18] Thus, modifying my view in order to take into account species and ecosystems requires the following changes in my first three principles of environmental justice:

A Principle of Human Defense: actions that defend oneself and other human beings against harmful aggression are permissible even when they necessitate killing or harming individual animals or plants or even destroying whole species or ecosystems.

A Principle of Human Preservation: actions that are necessary for meeting one's basic needs or the basic needs of other human beings are permissible even when they require aggressing against the basic needs of individual animals and plants or even of whole species or ecosystem.

A Principle of Disproportionality: actions that meet non-basic or luxury needs of humans are prohibited when they aggress against the basic needs of individual animals and plants, or of whole species or ecosystems.

But while this modification is of theoretical interest since it allows that species and ecosystems as well as individuals count morally, it actually has little or no practical effect on the application of these principles. This is because, for the most part, the positive or negative impact the application of these principles would have on species and ecosystems is correspondingly reflected in the positive or negative impact the application of these principles would have on the individual members of those species or ecosystems. As a consequence, actions that are permitted or prohibited with respect to species and ecosystems according to the modified principles are already permitted or prohibited respectively through their correspondence with actions that are permitted or prohibited according to the unmodified principles.

However, this is not always the case. In fact, considerations about what benefits non-human species or subspecies as opposed to individuals of those species or subspecies have already figured in my previous argument. For example, I have argued for culling elk herds in wolf-free ranges, but this is primarily for the good of herds or species of elk and certainly not for the good of the particular elk who are being culled from those herds. I also have argued that it would be for the good of farm animals generally that they be maintained under healthy conditions, and then killed relatively painlessly and eaten, rather than that they not be maintained at all. But clearly this is an argument about what would be good for existing flocks or herds, or species or subspecies of farm animals. It is not an argument about what would be good for the existing individual farm animals who would be killed relatively painlessly and eaten. Nevertheless, for the most part, because of the coincidence between the welfare of species and ecosystems and the welfare of individual members of those species and ecosystems, the two formulations of the first three principles turn out be practically equivalent.

In sum, I have argued that whether we endorse an anthropocentric or a non-anthropocentric environmental ethics, we should favor a Principle of Human Defense, a Principle of Human Preservation, and a Principle of Disproportionality as I have interpreted them. In the past, failure to recognize the importance of a Principle of Human Defense and a Principle of Human Preservation has led philosophers to overestimate the amount of sacrifice required of humans.[19] By contrast, failure to recognize the importance of a Principle of Disproportionality has led philosophers to underestimate the amount of sacrifice required of humans.[20] I claim that taken together these three principles strike the right balance between concerns of human welfare and the welfare of non-human nature.

Notes

1 Aldo Leopold's view is usually interpreted as holistic in this sense. Leopold wrote, "A thing is right when it tends to preserve the integrity, stability and beauty of the biotic community. It is wrong when it tends otherwise." See his *A Sand County Almanac* (Oxford, 1949).

2 For a defender of this view, see Paul Taylor, *Respect For Nature* (Princeton, NJ: Princeton University Press, 1987).

3 Where it is most likely to be morally required is where our negligent actions have caused the environmental problem in the first place.

4 Peter Singer's *Animal Liberation* (New York, 1975) inspired this view.

5 Baird Callicott, "Animal Liberation: A Triangular Affair," *Environmental Ethics* (1980), 311–28.

6 Mark Sagoff, "Animal Liberation and Environmental Ethics: Bad Marriage, Quick Divorce," *Osgood Hall Law Journal* (1984), 297–307.

7 Mary Ann Warren, "The Rights of the Nonhuman World," in *Environmental Philosophy*, edited by Robert Elliot and Arran Gare (London, 1983), 109–34 and Baird Callicott, *In Defense of the Land Ethic* (Albany, 1989), ch. 3.

8 *Realities for the 90's* (Santa Cruz, 1991), 4.

9 Ibid., 5.

10 Mark Sagoff, "Animal Liberation," 301–5.

11 Holmes Rolston, *Environmental Ethics* (Philadelphia, 1988), 66–8; Murray Bookchin, *The Ecology of Freedom* (Montreal, 1991), xxxvi.

12 Eugene Hargrove, "Weak Anthropocentric Intrinsic Value," in *After Earth Day*, edited by Max Oelschlaeger (Denton, 1992),147ff.

13 Ibid., 151. Notice that there are at least two ways that x might intrinsically value y. First, x might regard y as good in itself for x or as an end in itself for x, by contrast with valuing y instrumentally. Second, x might regard the good of y as constraining the way that x can use y. This second way of intrinsically valuing y is the principal way we value human beings. It is the sense of value that Kantians are referring to when they claim that people should never be used as means only. Another way to put what I have been arguing is that we should extend this second way of intrinsically valuing to animals and plants.

14 Paul Taylor, *Respect for Nature*, 68–71 and 17.

15 Ibid., 68–71.

16 One way to think about species is as ongoing genetic lineages sequentially embodied in different organisms. See Lawrence Johnson, *A Morally Deep World* (New York: Cambridge University Press, 1991), 156; Holmes Rolston III, *Environmental Ethics*, ch. 4.

17 Ecosystems can be simple or complex, stable or unstable, and they can suffer total collapse.

18 *A Morally Deep World*, ch. 6. Happily, this definition distinguishes moral subjects (living systems) from cars, refrigerators, etc. See also Lawrence Johnson, "Toward the Moral Considerability of Species and Ecosystems," *Environmental Ethics*, 14 (1992).

19 For example, in "Animal Liberation: A Triangular Affair," Baird Callicott had defended Edward Abbey's assertion that he would sooner shoot a man than a snake.

20 For example, Eugene Hargrove argues that from a traditional wildlife perspective, the lives of individual specimens of quite plentiful non-human species count for almost nothing at all. See ch. 4 of his *Foundations of Environmental Ethics* (Prentice-Hall, 1989).

40   The Power and Promise of Ecological Feminism

Karen J. Warren

Introduction

Ecological feminism (ecofeminism) has begun to receive a fair amount of attention lately as an alternative feminism and environmental ethic. Since Françoise d'Eaubonne introduced the term *écoféminisme* in 1974 to bring attention to women's potential for bringing about an ecological revolution, the term has been used in a variety of ways. As I use the term in this paper, ecological feminism is the position that there are important connections – historical, experiential, symbolic, theoretical – between the domination of women and the domination of nature, an understanding of which is crucial to both feminism and environmental ethics. I argue that the promise and power of ecological feminism is that *it provides a distinctive framework both for reconceiving feminism and for developing an environmental ethic which takes seriously connections between the domination of women and the domination of nature.* I do so by discussing the nature of a feminist ethic and the ways in which ecofeminism provides a feminist and environmental ethic. I conclude that any feminist theory and any environmental ethic which fails to take seriously the twin and interconnected dominations of women and nature is at best incomplete and at worst simply inadequate.

Feminism, Ecological Feminism, and Conceptual Frameworks

Whatever else it is, feminism is at least the movement to end sexist oppression. It involves the elimination of any and all factors that contribute to the continued and systematic domination or subordi-

From *Environmental Ethics*. Reprinted by permission.

nation of women. While feminists disagree about the nature of and solutions to the subordination of women, all feminists agree that sexist oppression exists, is wrong, and must be abolished.

A "feminist issue" is any issue that contributes in some way to understanding the oppression of women. Equal rights, comparable pay for comparable work, and food production are feminist issues wherever and whenever an understanding of them contributes to an understanding of the continued exploitation or subjugation of women. Carrying water and searching for firewood are feminist issues wherever and whenever women's primary responsibility for these tasks contributes to their lack of full participation in decision making, income producing, or high status positions engaged in by men. What counts as a feminine issue, then, depends largely on context, particularly the historical and material conditions of women's lives.

Environmental degradation and exploitation are feminist issues because an understanding of them contributes to an understanding of the oppression of women. In India, for example, both deforestation and reforestation through the introduction of a monoculture species tree (e.g. eucalyptus) intended for commercial production are feminist issues because the loss of indigenous forests and multiple species of trees has drastically affected rural Indian women's ability to maintain a subsistence household. Indigenous forests provide a variety of trees for food, fuel, fodder, household utensils, dyes, medicines, and income-generating uses, while monoculture-species forests do not. Although I do not argue for this claim here, a look at the global impact of environmental degradation on women's lives suggests important respects in which environmental degradation is a feminist issue.

Feminist philosophers claim that some of the

most important feminist issues are *conceptual* ones: these issues concern how one conceptualizes such mainstay philosophical notions as reason and rationality, ethics, and what it is to be human. Ecofeminists extend this feminist philosophical concern to nature. They argue that, ultimately, some of the most important connections between the domination of women and the domination of nature are conceptual. To see this, consider the nature of conceptual frameworks.

A *conceptual framework* is a set of *basic* beliefs, values, attitudes, and assumptions which shape and reflect how one views oneself and one's world. It is a socially constructed lens through which we perceive ourselves and others. It is affected by such factors as gender, race, class, age, affectional orientation, nationality, and religious background.

Some conceptual frameworks are oppressive. An *oppressive conceptual framework* is one that explains, justifies, and maintains relationships of domination and subordination. When an oppressive conceptual framework is *patriarchal*, it explains, justifies, and maintains the subordination of women by men.

I have argued elsewhere that there are three significant features of oppressive conceptual frameworks: (1) value-hierarchical thinking, i.e. "up-down" thinking which places higher value, status, or prestige on what is "up" rather than on what is "down"; (2) value dualisms, i.e. disjunctive pairs in which the disjuncts are seen as oppositional (rather than as complementary) and exclusive (rather than as inclusive), and which place higher value (status, prestige) on one disjunct rather than the other (e.g. dualisms which give higher value or status to that which has historically been identified as "mind," "reason," and "male" than to that which has historically been identified as "body," "emotion," and "female"); and (3) logic of domination, i.e. a structure of argumentation which leads to a justification of subordination.

The third feature of oppressive conceptual frameworks is the most significant. A logic of domination is not *just* a logical structure. It also involves a substantive value system, since an ethical premise is needed to permit or sanction the "just" subordination of that which is subordinate. This justification typically is given on grounds of some alleged characteristic (e.g. rationality) which the dominant (e.g. men) have and the subordinate (e.g. women) lack.

Contrary to what many feminists and ecofeminists have said or suggested, there may be nothing *inherently* problematic about "hierarchical thinking" or even "value-hierarchical thinking" in contexts other than contexts of oppression. Hierarchical thinking is important in daily living for classifying data, comparing information, and organizing material. Taxonomies (e.g. plant taxonomies) and biological nomenclature seem to require some form of "hierarchical thinking." Even "value hierarchical thinking" may be quite acceptable in certain contexts. (The same may be said of "value dualisms" in non-oppressive contexts.) For example, suppose it is true that what is unique about humans is our conscious capacity to radically reshape our social environments (or "societies"), as Murray Bookchin suggests. Then one could truthfully say that humans are better equipped to radically reshape their environments than are rocks or plants – a "value-hierarchical" way of speaking.

The problem is not simply *that* value-hierarchical thinking and value dualisms are used, but *the way* in which each has been used *in oppressive conceptual frameworks* to establish inferiority and to justify subordination.[1] It is the logic of domination, coupled with value-hierarchical thinking and value dualisms, which "justifies" subordination. What is explanatorily basic, then, about the nature of oppressive conceptual frameworks is the logic of domination.

For ecofeminism, that a logic of domination is explanatorily basic is important for at least three reasons. First, without a logic of domination, a description of similarities and differences would be just that – a description of similarities and differences. Consider the claim, "Humans are different from plants and rocks in that humans can (and plants and rocks cannot) consciously and radically reshape the communities in which they live; humans are similar to plants and rocks in that they are both members of an ecological community." Even if humans are "better" than plants and rocks with respect to the conscious ability of humans to radically transform communities, one does not *thereby* get any *morally* relevant distinction between humans and non-humans, or an argument for the domination of plants and rocks by humans. To get *those* conclusions one needs to add at least two powerful assumptions, viz., (A2) and (A4) in argument A below:

(A1) Humans do, and plants and rocks do not, have the capacity to consciously and radically change the community in which they live.

(A2) Whatever has the capacity to consciously and radically change the community in which it lives is morally superior to whatever lacks this capacity.

(A3) Thus, humans are morally superior to plants and rocks.

(A4) For any x and y, if x is morally superior to y, then x is morally justified in subordinating y.

(A5) Thus, humans are morally justified in subordinating plants and rocks.

Without the two assumptions that *humans are morally superior* to (at least some) non-humans, (A2), and that *superiority justifies subordination*, (A4), all one has is some difference between humans and some non-humans. This is true even if that difference is given in terms of superiority. Thus, it is the logic of domination, (A4), which is the bottom line in ecofeminist discussions of oppression.

Second, ecofeminists argue that, at least in Western societies, the oppressive conceptual framework which sanctions the twin dominations of women and nature is a patriarchal one characterized by all three features of an oppressive conceptual framework. Many ecofeminists claim that, historically, within at least the dominant Western culture, a patriarchal conceptual framework has sanctioned the following argument B:

(B1) Women are identified with nature and the realm of the physical; men are iden-tified with the "human" and the realm of the mental.

(B2) Whatever is identified with nature and the realm of the physical is inferior to ("below") whatever is identified with the "human" and the realm of the mental; or, conversely, the latter is superior to ("above") the former.

(B3) Thus, women are inferior to ("below") men; or, conversely, men are superior to ("above") women.

(B4) For any x and y, if x is superior to y, then x is justified in subordinating y.

(B5) Thus, men are justified in subordinating women.

If sound, argument B establishes *patriarchy*, i.e. the conclusion given at (B5) that the systematic domination of women by men is justified. But according to ecofeminists, (B5) is justified by just those three features of an oppressive conceptual framework identified earlier: value-hierarchical thinking, the assumption at (B2); value dualisms, the assumed dualism of the mental and the physical at (B1) and the assumed inferiority of the physical *vis-à-vis* the mental at (B2); and a logic of domination, the assumption at (B4), the same as the previous premise (A4). Hence, according to ecofeminists, in so far as an oppressive patriarchal conceptual framework has functioned historically (within at least dominant Western culture) to sanction the twin dominations of women and nature (argument B), both argument B and the patriarchal conceptual framework, from whence it comes, ought to be rejected.

Of course, the preceding does not identify which premises of B are false. What is the status of premises (B1) and (B2)? Most, if not all, feminists claim that (B1), and many ecofeminists claim that (B2), have been assumed or asserted within the dominant Western philosophical and intellectual tradition.[2] As such, these feminists assert, as a matter of historical fact, that the dominant Western philosophical tradition has assumed the truth of (B1) and (B2). Ecofeminists, however, either deny (B2) or do not affirm (B2). Furthermore, because some ecofeminists are anxious to deny any historical identification of women with nature, some ecofeminists deny (B1) when (B1) is used to support anything other than a strictly historical claim about what has been asserted or assumed to be true within patriarchal culture – e.g. when (B1) is used to assert that women properly are identified with the realm of nature and the physical.[3] Thus, from an ecofeminist perspective, (B1) and (B2) are properly viewed as problematic though historically sanctioned claims: they are problematic precisely because of the way they have functioned historically in a patriarchal conceptual framework and culture to sanction the dominations of women and nature.

What *all* ecofeminists agree about, then, is the way in which *the logic of domination* has functioned historically within patriarchy to sustain and justify the twin dominations of women and nature.[4] Since *all* feminists (and not just ecofeminists) oppose patriarchy, the conclusion given at (B5), all feminists (including ecofeminists) must oppose at least the logic of domination, premise (B4), on which argument B rests – whatever the truth value status of (B1) and (B2) *outside* of a patriarchal context.

That *all* feminists muse oppose the logic of domination shows the breadth and depth of the ecofeminist critique of B: it is a critique not only of the three assumptions on which this argument for the domination of women and nature rests, viz., the assumptions at (B1), (B2), and (B4); it is also a critique of patriarchal conceptual frameworks generally, i.e. of those oppressive conceptual frameworks which put men "up" and women "down," allege some way in which women are morally inferior to men, and use that alleged difference to justify the subordination of women by men. Therefore, ecofeminism is necessary to *any* feminist critique of patriarchy, and, hence, necessary to feminism (a point I discuss again later).

Third, ecofeminism clarifies why the logic of domination, and any conceptual framework which gives rise to it, must be abolished in order both to make possible a meaningful notion of difference which does not breed domination and to prevent feminism from becoming a "support" movement based primarily on shared experiences.

In contemporary society, there is no one "woman's voice," no *woman* (or *human*) *simpliciter*: every woman (or human) is a woman (or human) of some race, class, age, affectional orientation, marital status, regional or national background, and so forth. Because there are no "monolithic experiences" that all women share, feminism must be a "solidarity movement" based on shared beliefs and interests rather than a "unity in sameness" movement based on shared experiences and shared victimization. In the words of Maria Lugones, "Unity – not to be confused with solidarity – is understood as conceptually tied to domination."

Ecofeminists insist that the sort of logic of domination used to justify the domination of humans by gender, racial or ethnic, or class status is also used to justify the domination of nature. Because eliminating a logic of domination is part of a feminist critique – whether a critique of patriarchy, white supremacist culture, or imperialism – ecofeminists insist that *naturism* is properly viewed as an integral part of any feminist solidarity movement to end sexist oppression and the logic of domination which conceptually grounds it.

Ecofeminism Reconceives Feminism

The discussion so far has focused on some of the oppressive conceptual features of patriarchy. As I use the phrase, the "logic of traditional feminism" refers to the location of the conceptual roots of sexist oppression, at least in Western societies, in an oppressive patriarchal conceptual framework characterized by a logic of domination. In so far as other systems of oppression (e.g. racism, classism, ageism, heterosexism) are also conceptually maintained by a logic of domination, appeal to the logic of traditional feminism ultimately locates the basic conceptual interconnections among *all* systems of oppression in the logic of domination. It thereby explains at a *conceptual* level why the eradication of sexist oppression requires the eradication of the other forms of oppression. It is by clarifying this conceptual connection between systems of oppression that a movement to end sexist oppression – traditionally the special turf of feminist theory and practice – leads to a reconceiving of feminism as *a movement to end all forms of oppression.*

Suppose one agrees that the logic of traditional feminism requires the expansion of feminism to include other social systems of domination (e.g. racism and classism). What warrants the inclusion of nature in these "social systems of domination"? Why must the logic of traditional feminism include the abolition of "naturism" (i.e. the domination or oppression of non-human nature) among the "isms" feminism must confront? The conceptual justification for expanding feminism to include ecofeminism is twofold. One basis has already been suggested: by showing that the conceptual connections between the dual dominations of women and nature are located in an oppressive and, at least in Western societies, patriarchal conceptual framework characterized by a logic of domination, ecofeminism explains how and why feminism, conceived as a movement to end sexist oppression, must be expanded and reconceived as also a movement to end naturism. This is made explicit by the following argument C:

(C1) Feminism is a movement to end sexism.

(C2) But sexism is conceptually linked with naturism (through an oppressive conceptual framework characterized by a logic of domination).

(C3) Thus, feminism is (also) a movement to end naturism.

Because, ultimately, these connections between sexism and naturism are conceptual – embedded in an oppressive conceptual framework – the logic of traditional feminism leads to the embracement of ecological feminism.

The other justification for reconceiving feminism to include ecofeminism has to do with the concepts of gender and nature. Just as conceptions of gender are socially constructed, so are conceptions of nature. Of course, the claim that women and nature are social constructions does not require anyone to deny that there are actual humans and actual trees, rivers, and plants. It simply implies that *how* women and nature are conceived is a matter of historical and social reality. These conceptions vary cross-culturally and by historical time period. As a result, any discussion of the "oppression or domination of nature" involves reference to historically specific forms of social domination of non-human nature by humans, just as discussion of the "domination of women" refers to historically specific forms of social domination of women by men. Although I do not argue for it here, an ecofeminist defense of the historical connections between the dominations of women and of nature, claims (B1) and (B2) in argument B, involves showing that within patriarchy the feminization of nature and the naturalization of women have been crucial to the historically successful subordinations of both.

If ecofeminism promises to reconceive traditional feminism in ways which include naturism as a legitimate feminist issue, does ecofeminism also promise to reconceive environmental ethics in ways which are feminist? I think so. This is the subject of the remainder of the paper.

Climbing from Ecofeminism to Environmental Ethics

Many feminists and some environmental ethicists have begun to explore the use of first-person narrative as a way of raising philosophically germane issues in ethics often lost or underplayed in mainstream philosophical ethics. Why is this so? What is it about narrative which makes it a significant resource for theory and practice in feminism and environmental ethics? Even if appeal to first-person narrative is a helpful literary device for describing ineffable experience or a legitimate social science methodology for documenting personal and social history, how is first-person narrative a valuable vehicle of argumentation for ethical decision making and theory building? One fruitful way to begin answering these questions is to ask them of a particular first-person narrative.

Consider the following first-person narrative about rock climbing:

> For my very first rock climbing experience, I chose a somewhat private spot, away from other climbers and on-lookers. After studying "the chimney," I focused all my energy on making it to the top. I climbed with intense determination, using whatever strength and skills I had to accomplish this challenging feat. By midway I was exhausted and anxious. I couldn't see what to do next – where to put my hands or feet. Growing increasingly more weary as I clung somewhat desperately to the rock, I made a move. It didn't work. I fell. There I was, dangling midair above the rocky ground below, frightened but terribly relieved that the belay rope had held me. I knew I was safe. I took a look up at the climb that remained. I was determined to make it to the top. With renewed confidence and concentration, I finished the climb to the top.
>
> On my second day of climbing, I rappelled down about 200 feet from the top of the Palisades at Lake Superior to just a few feet above the water level. I could see no one – not my belayer, not the other climbers, no one. I unhooked slowly from the rappel rope and took a deep cleansing breath. I looked all around me – really looked – and listened. I heard a cacophony of voices – birds, trickles of water on the rock before me, waves lapping against the rocks below. I closed my eyes and began to feel the rock with my hands – the cracks and crannies, the raised lichen and mosses, the almost imperceptible nubs that might provide a resting place for my fingers and toes when I began to climb. At that moment I was bathed in serenity. I began to talk to the rock in an almost inaudible, child-like way, as if the rock were my friend. I felt an overwhelming sense of gratitude for what it offered me – a chance to know myself and the rock differently, to appreciate unforeseen miracles like the tiny flowers growing in the even tinier cracks in the rock's surface, and to come to know a sense of *being in relationship* with the natural environment. It felt as if the rock and I were silent conversational partners in a longstanding friendship. I realized then that I had come to care about this cliff which was so different from me, so unmovable and invincible, independent and seemingly indiffer-ent to my presence. I wanted to be with the rock as I climbed. Gone was the determination to conquer the rock, to forcefully impose my will on it; I wanted simply to work respectfully with the rock as I climbed. And as I climbed, that is what I felt. I felt myself *caring* for this rock and feeling thankful that climbing provided the opportunity for me to know it and myself in this new way.

There are at least four reasons why use of such a first-person narrative is important to feminism and environmental ethics. First, such a narrative gives voice to a felt sensitivity often lacking in traditional analytical ethical discourse, viz., a sensitivity to conceiving of oneself as fundamentally "in relationship with" others, including the non-human environment. It is a modality which *takes relationships themselves seriously*. It thereby stands in contrast to a strictly reductionist modality that takes relationships seriously only or primarily because of the nature of the *relators* or parties to those relationships (e.g. relators conceived as moral agents, right holders, interest carriers, or sentient beings). In the rock-climbing narrative above, it is the climber's relationship with the rock she climbs which takes on special significance – which is itself a locus of value – in addition to whatever moral status or moral considerability she or the rock or any other parties to the relationship may also have.[5]

Second, such a first-person narrative gives expression to a variety of ethical attitudes and behaviors often overlooked or underplayed in mainstream Western ethics, e.g. the difference in attitudes and behaviors toward a rock when one is "making it to the top" and when one thinks of oneself as "friends with" or "caring about" the rock one climbs.[6] These different attitudes and behaviors suggest an ethically germane contrast between two different types of relationship humans or climbers may have toward a rock: an imposed conqueror-type relationship, and an emergent caring-type relationship. This contrast grows out of, and is faithful to, felt, lived experience.

The difference between conquering and caring attitudes and behaviors in relation to the natural environment provides a third reason why the use of first-person narrative is important to feminism and environmental ethics: it provides a way of conceiving of ethics and ethical meaning as *emerging out* of particular situations moral agents find themselves in, rather than as being *imposed on* those situations (e.g. as a derivation or instantiation of some predetermined abstract principle or rule). This emergent feature of narrative centralizes the importance of *voice*. When a multiplicity of cross-cultural *voices* are centralized, narrative is able to give expression to a range of attitudes, values, beliefs, and behaviors which may be overlooked or silenced by imposed ethical meaning and theory. As a reflection of and on felt, lived experiences, the use of narrative in ethics provides a stance from which ethical discourse can be held accountable to the historical, material, and social realities in which moral subjects find themselves.

Lastly, and for our purposes perhaps most importantly, the use of narrative has argumentative significance. Jim Cheney calls attention to this feature of narrative when he claims, "To contextualize ethical deliberation is, in some sense, to provide a narrative or story, from which the solution to the ethical dilemma emerges as the fitting conclusion." Narrative has argumentative force by suggesting *what counts* as an appropriate conclusion to an ethical situation. One ethical conclusion suggested by the climbing narrative is that what counts as a proper ethical attitude toward mountains and rocks is an attitude of respect and care (whatever that turns out to be or involve), not one of domination and conquest.

In an essay entitled "In and Out of Harm's Way: Arrogance and Love," feminist philosopher Marilyn Frye distinguishes between "arrogant" and "loving" perception as one way of getting at this difference in the ethical attitudes of care and conquest. Frye writes:

The loving eye is a contrary of the arrogant eye.

The loving eye knows the independence of the other. It is the eye of a seer who knows that nature is indifferent. It is the eye of one who knows that to know the seen, one must consult something other than one's own will and interests and fears and imagination. One must look at the thing. One must look and listen and check and question.

The loving eye is one that pays a certain sort of attention. This attention can require a discipline but *not* a self-denial. The discipline is one of self-knowledge, knowledge of the scope and boundary of the self. . . . In particular, it is a matter of being able to tell one's own interests from those of others and of knowing where one's self leaves off end another begins. . . .

The loving eye does not make the object of perception into something edible, does not try to assimilate it, does not reduce it to the size of the seer's desire, fear and imagination, and hence does not have to simplify. It knows the complexity of the other as something which will forever present new things to be known. The science of the loving eye would favor The Complexity Theory of Truth [in contrast to The Simplicity Theory of Truth] and presuppose The Endless Interestingness of the Universe.

According to Frye, the loving eye is not an invasive, coercive eye which annexes others to itself, but one which "knows the complexity of the other as something which will forever present new things to be known."

When one climbs a rock as a conqueror, one climbs with an arrogant eye. When one climbs with a loving eye, one constantly "must look and listen and check and question." One recognizes the rock as something very different, something perhaps totally indifferent to one's own presence, and finds in that difference joyous occasion for celebration. One knows "the boundary of the self," where the self – the "I," the climber – leaves off and the rock begins. There is no fusion of two into one, but a complement of two entities *acknowledged*, as separate, different, independent, yet *in relationship*; they are in relationship *if only* because the loving eye is perceiving it, responding to it, noticing it, attending to it.

An ecofeminist perspective about both women and nature involves this shift in attitude from "arrogant perception" to "loving perception" of the non-human world. Arrogant perception of non-humans by humans presupposes and maintains *sameness* in such a way that it expands the moral community to those beings who are thought to resemble (be like, similar to, or the same as) humans in some morally significant way. Any environmental movement or ethic based on arrogant perception builds a moral hierarchy of beings and assumes some common denominator of moral considerability in virtue of which like beings deserve similar treatment or moral consideration and unlike beings do not. Such environmental ethics are or generate a "unity in sameness." In contrast, "loving perception" presupposes and maintains *difference* – a distinction between the self and other, between human and at least some non-humans – in such a way that perception of the other as other *is* an expression of love for one who/which is recognized at the outset as independent, dissimilar, different. As Maria Lugones says, in loving perception, "Love is seen not as fusion and erasure of difference but as incompatible with them." "Unity in sameness" alone is an *erasure of difference.*

"Loving perception" of the non-human natural world is an attempt to understand what it means *for humans* to care about the non-human world, a world *acknowledged* as being independent, different, perhaps even indifferent to humans. Humans are different from rocks in important ways, even if they are also both members of some ecological community. A moral community based on loving perception of oneself *in relationship with* a rock, or with the natural environment as a whole, is one which acknowledges and respects difference, whatever "sameness" also exists. The limits of loving perception are determined only by the limits of one's (e.g. a person's, a community's) ability to respond lovingly (or with appropriate care, trust, or friendship) – whether it is to other humans or to the non-human world and elements of it.

If what I have said so far is correct, then there are very different ways to climb a mountain and *how* one climbs it and *how* one narrates the experience of climbing it matter ethically. If one climbs with "arrogant perception," with an attitude of "conquer and control," one keeps intact the very sorts of thinking that characterize a logic of domination and an oppressive conceptual framework. Since the oppressive conceptual framework which sanctions the domination of nature is a patriar-

chal one, one also thereby keeps intact, even if unwittingly, a patriarchal conceptual framework. Because the dismantling of patriarchal conceptual frameworks is a feminist issue, *how* one climbs a mountain and *how* one narrates – or tells the story – about the experience of climbing also are *feminist issues.* In this way, ecofeminism makes visible why, at a conceptual level, environmental ethics is a feminist issue.

Conclusion

I have argued in this paper that ecofeminism provides a framework for a distinctively feminist and environmental ethic. Ecofeminism grows out of the felt and theorized about connections between the domination of women and the domination of nature. As a contextualist ethic, ecofeminism refocuses environmental ethics on what nature might mean, morally speaking, *for* humans, and on how the relational attitudes of humans to others – humans as well as non-humans – sculpt both what it is to be human and the nature and ground of human responsibilities to the non-human environment. Part of what this refocusing does is to take seriously the voices of women and other oppressed persons in the construction of that ethic.

A Sioux elder once told me a story about his son. He sent his seven-year-old son to live with the child's grandparents on a Sioux reservation so that he could "learn the Indian ways." Part of what the grandparents taught the son was how to hunt the four-leggeds of the forest. As I heard the story, the boy was taught, "to shoot your four-legged brother in his hind area, slowing it down but not killing it. Then, take the four-legged's head in your hands, and look into his eyes. The eyes are where all the suffering is. Look into your brother's eyes and feel his pain. Then, take your knife and cut the four-legged under his chin, here, on his neck, so that he dies quickly. And as you do, ask your brother, the four-legged, for forgiveness for what you do. Offer also a prayer of thanks to your four-legged kin for offering his body to you just now, when you need food to eat and clothing to wear. And promise the four-legged that you will put yourself back into the earth when you die, to become nourishment for the earth, and for the sister flowers, and for the brother deer. It is appropriate that you should offer this blessing for the four-legged and, in due time, reciprocate in turn with your body in this way, as the four-legged gives life to you for your survival." As I reflect upon that story, I am struck by the power of the environmental ethic that grows out of and takes seriously narrative, context, and such values and relational attitudes as care, loving perception, and appropriate reciprocity, and doing what is appropriate in a given situation – however that notion of appropriateness eventually gets filled out. I am also struck by what one is able to see, once one begins to explore some of the historical and conceptual connections between the dominations of women and of nature. A *re-conceiving* and *re-visioning* of both feminism and environmental ethics, is, I think, the power and promise of ecofeminism.

Notes

1 It may be that in contemporary Western society, which is so thoroughly structured by categories of gender, race, class, age, and affectional orientation, that there simply is no meaningful notion of "value-hierarchical thinking" which does not function in an oppressive context. For purposes of this paper, I leave that question open.

2 Many feminists who argue for the historical point that claims (B1) and (B2) have been asserted or assumed to be true within the dominant Western philosophical tradition do so by discussion of that tradition's conceptions of reason, rationality, and science. For a sampling of the sorts of claims made within that context, see "Reason, Rationality, and Gender," ed. Nancy Tuana and Karen J. Warren, a special issue of the American Philosophical Association's *Newsletter on Feminism and Philosophy* 88, no. 2 (March 1989), 17–71. Ecofeminists who claim that (B2) has been assumed to be true within the dominant Western philosophical tradition include: Gray, *Green Paradise Lost*; Griffin, *Woman and Nature: The Roaring Inside Her*; Merchant, *The Death of Nature*; Ruether, *New Woman/New Earth*. For a discussion of some of these ecofeminist

historical accounts see Plumwood, "Ecofeminism." While I agree that the historical connection between the domination of women and the domination of nature is a crucial one, I do not argue for that claim here.

3 Ecofeminists who deny (B1) when (B1) is offered as anything other than a true, descriptive, historical claim about patriarchal culture often do so on grounds that an objectionable sort of biological determinism, or at least harmful female sex-gender stereotypes, underlie (B1). For a discussion of this "split" among those ecofeminists ("nature feminists") who assert and those ecofeminists ("social feminists") who deny (B1) as anything other than a true historical claim about how women are described in patriarchal culture, see Griscom, "On Healing the Nature/History Split."

4 I make no attempt here to defend the historically sanctioned truth of these premises.

5 Suppose, as I think is the case, that a necessary condition for the existence of a moral relationship is that at least one party to the relationship is a moral being (leaving open for our purposes what counts as a "moral being"). If this is so, then the Mona Lisa cannot properly be said to have or stand in a moral relationship with the wall on which she hangs, and a wolf cannot have or properly be said to have or stand in a moral relationship with a moose. Such a necessary-condition account leaves open the question whether *both* parties to the relationship must be moral beings. My point here is simply that however one resolves *that* question, recognition of the relationships themselves as a locus of value is a recognition of a source of value that is different from and not reducible to the values of the "moral beings" in those relationships.

6 It is interesting to note that the image of being friends with the Earth is one which cytogeneticist Barbara McClintock uses when she describes the importance of having "a feeling for the organism," "listening to the material [in this case the corn plant]," in one's work as a scientist. See Evelyn Fox Keller, "Women, Science, and Popular Mythology," in *Machina Ex Dea: Feminist Perspectives on Technology*, ed. Joan Rothschild (New York: Pergamon Press, 1983), and Evelyn Fox Keller, *A Feeling for the Organism: The Life and Work of Barbara McClintock* (San Francisco: W. H. Freeman, 1983).

Postmodernism: Morality from Whose Cultural Perspective?

---

41 Gender Inequality and Cultural Difference

Susan Moller Okin

Theories of justice are undergoing something of an identity crisis. How can they be universal, principled, founded on good reasons that all can accept, and yet take account of the many differences there are among persons and social groups? Feminists have been among the first to point out that large numbers of persons have typically been excluded from consideration in purportedly universalist theories. And some feminists have gone on to point out that many feminist theories, while taking account of sexist bias or omission, have neglected racist, heterosexist, class, religious, and other biases. Yet, joining our voices with those of others, some of us discern problems with going in the direction of formulating a theory of justice entirely by listening to every concrete individual's or group's point of view and expression of its needs. Is it possible, by taking this route, to come up with any principles at all? Is it a reliable route, given the possibility of "false consciousness"? Doesn't stressing differences, especially cultural differences, lead to a slide toward relativism? The problem that is being grappled with is an important one. There can no longer be any doubt that many voices have not been heard when most theories of justice were being shaped. But how can all the different voices express themselves and be heard and still yield a coherent and workable theory of justice? This question is one I shall (eventually) return to in this essay.

From *Political Theory*, vol. 22, no. 1 (February 1994), 5–24. Reprinted with permission.

Feminism, Difference, and Essentialism

Feminists have recently had much to say about difference. One aspect of the debate has been a continuation of an old argument – about how different women are from men, what such differences may be due to, and whether they require that laws and other aspects of public policy should treat women any differently from men.[1] Another, newer, aspect of the debate is about differences among women. It is "essentialist," some say, to talk about women, the problems of women, and especially the problems of women "as such."[2] White middle- and upper-class feminists, it is alleged, have excluded or been insensitive to not only the problems of women of other races, cultures, and religions but even those of women of other classes than their own. "Gender" is therefore a problematic category, those opposed to such essentialism say, unless always qualified by and seen in the context of race, class, ethnicity, religion, and other such differences (Childers and hooks 1990; Harris 1990; hooks 1984; Lorde 1984; Minow and Spelman 1990; Spelman 1988).

The general allegation of feminist essentialism certainly has validity when applied to some work. Feminists with such pedigrees as Harriet Taylor, Charlotte Perkins Gilman, Virginia Woolf, Simone de Beauvoir, and Betty Friedan (in *The Feminine Mystique*) all seem to have assumed, for example, that the women they were liberating would have recourse to servants. With the partial exception of Woolf, who remarks briefly on the difficult lot of maids, they did not pay attention to the servants, the vast majority of whom were also, of course, women. The tendency of many white middle- and upper-class feminists in the mid-nineteenth century to think only of women of their own class and race (some were explicitly racist) is what makes so poignant and compelling Sojourner Truth's words in her famous "Ain't I a woman?" speech.[3] However, I think, and will argue, that this problem is far less present in the works of most recent feminists. But the charges of "essentialism" seem to grow ever louder. They are summed up in Elizabeth Spelman's (1988) recent claim that "the focus on women 'as women' has addressed only one group of women – namely, white middle-class women of Western industrialized countries" (p. 4). This has come to be accepted in some circles as virtually a truism.

The claim that much recent feminist theory is essentialist comes primarily from three (to some extent, overlapping) sources – European-influenced postmodernist thought; the work of African-American and other minority feminist women in the United States and Britain; and, in particular, Spelman's recent book, *Inessential Woman* (hereafter *IW*). Postmodernism is skeptical of all universal or generalizable claims, including those of feminism. It finds concepts central to feminist thinking, such as "gender" and "woman," as illegitimate as any other category or generalization that does not stop to take account of every difference. As Julia Kristeva, for example, says,

> The belief that "one is a woman" is almost as absurd and obscurantist as the belief that "one is a man". . . . [W]e must use "we are women" as an advertisement or slogan for our demands. On a deeper level, however, a woman cannot "be"; it is something which does not even belong in the order of *being*. (quoted in Marks and de Courtivron 1981: 137)

In the same interview, she also says that, because of the very different history of Chinese women, "it is absurd to question their lack of 'sexual lib-

eration' " (in Marks and de Courtivron 1981: 140). Clearly, she thinks we could have no cross-cultural explanations of or objections to gender inequality.

Spelman argues that "the phrase 'as a woman' is the Trojan horse of feminist ethnocentrism" (*IW*: 13). The great mistakes of white middle-class feminists have been to exclude women different from themselves from their critiques or, even when they are included, to assume that, whatever their differences, their experience of sexism is the same. At best, she says, what is presented is "[a]n additive analysis [which] treats the oppression of a black woman in a society that is racist as well as sexist as if it were a further burden when in fact it is a *different burden*" (*IW*: 123; emphasis added).

These anti-essentialist arguments, however, are often long on theory and very short on empirical evidence. A large proportion of Spelman's examples of how women's experiences of oppression are different are taken from periods of slavery in ancient Greece and, especially, in the pre-Civil War South. It is not clear, though, how relevant is the obvious contrast between the experience of white slaveholders' wives and black female slaves to most issues involving the sameness or difference of forms of gender oppression today.

Apart from the paucity of relevant evidence (which I shall return to), there seem to me to be two other related problems with Spelman's general anti-essentialist argument. One is the claim that unless a feminist theorist perceives gender identity as intrinsically bound up with class, race, or other aspects of identity she ignores the effects of these other differences altogether. Spelman writes, "If gender were isolatable from other forms of identity, if sexism were isolatable from other forms of oppression, then what would be true about the relation between any man and any woman would be true about the relation between any other man and any other woman" (*IW*: 81). But this does not follow at all. One can argue that sexism is an identifiable form of oppression, many of whose effects are felt by women regardless of race or class, without at all subscribing to the view that race and class oppression are insignificant. One can still insist, for example, on the significant difference between the relation of a poor black woman to a wealthy white man and that of a wealthy white woman to a poor black man.

The second problem is that Spelman misplaces the burden of proof, which presumably affects her perception of the need for her to produce evidence for her claims. She says, "Precisely insofar as a discussion of gender and gender relations is really, even if obscurely, about a particular group of women and their relation to a particular group of men, it is unlikely to be applicable to any other group of women" (*IW*: 114). But why? Surely the burden of proof is on the critic. To be convincing, she needs to show that and how the theory accused of essentialism omits or distorts the experience of persons other than those few the theorist allegedly does take account of. This, after all, is the burden that many of the feminists Spelman considers "essentialist" have themselves taken on in critiquing "malestream" theories. One of the problems of anti-essentialist feminism (shared, I think, with much of postmodernist critique) is that it tends to substitute the cry "We're all different" for both argument and evidence.

There are, however, exceptions, and they tend to come from feminists who belong to racial minorities. One of the best critiques of feminist essentialism that I know of is that by Angela Harris (1990), in which she shows how ignorance of the specifics of a culture mars even thoroughly well-intentioned feminist analyses of women's experiences of oppression within that culture. She argues, for example, that in some respects, black women in the United States have had a qualitatively rather than simply quantitatively different experience of rape than that of white women (see esp. 1990: 594, 598–601). Even here, though, I think the anti-essentialist critique is only partly convincing. Although more concerned with evidence for the salience of differences than most anti-essentialists seem to be, Harris raises far more empirical questions than she provides answers. She provides just one example to support her assertion that black women's experience of rape is, even now, radi-

cally different from that of white women – that it is "an experience as deeply rooted in color as in gender" (p. 598).[4] Yet she, like Spelman, is as much disturbed by white feminists' saying that black women are "just like us only more so" as she is by their marginalizing black women or ignoring them altogether. As I shall argue, this "insult[ing]" conclusion – that the problems of other women are "similar to ours but more so" – is exactly the one I reach when I apply some Western feminist ideas about justice to the situations of poor women in many poor countries.

In this essay, I put anti-essentialist feminism to what I think is a reasonably tough test. In doing this, I am taking up the gauntlet that Spelman throws down. She says, referring to the body of new work about women that has appeared in many fields,

> Rather than assuming that women have something in common as women, these researchers should help us look to see whether they do. . . . Rather than first finding out what is true of some women as women and then inferring that this is true of all women . . . , we have to investigate different women's lives and see what they have in common. (*IW*: 137)

Trained as a philosopher, she does not seem to consider it appropriate to take up the challenge of actually looking at some of this empirical evidence. Having said the above, she turns back to discussing Plato. Trained as a political scientist, I shall attempt to look at some comparative evidence. I'll put some Western feminist ideas about justice and inequality to the test (drawing on my recent book and the many feminist sources I use to support some of its arguments) by seeing how well these theories – developed in the context of women in well-off Western industrialized countries – work when used to look at the very different situations of some of the poorest women in poor countries. How do our accounts and our explanations of gender inequality stand up in the face of considerable cultural and socioeconomic difference?

Differences and Similarities in Gender Oppression: Poor Women in Poor Countries

Does the assumption "that there is a generalizable, identifiable and collectively shared experience of womanhood" (Benhabib and Cornell 1987: 13) *have* any validity, or is it indeed an essentialist myth, rightly challenged by Third World women and their spokesfeminists? Do the theories devised by First World feminists, particularly our critiques of non-feminist theories of justice, have anything to say, in particular, to the poorest women in poor countries, or to those policymakers with the potential to affect their lives for better or for worse?

In trying to answer these questions, I shall address, in turn, four sets of issues, which have been addressed both by recent feminist critics of Anglo-American social and political theory and by those development scholars who have in recent years concerned themselves with the neglect or distortion of the situation of women in the countries they study. First, why and how has the issue of the inequality between the sexes been ignored or obscured for so long and addressed only so recently? Second, why is it so important that it be addressed? Third, what do we find, when we subject households or families to standards of justice – when we look at the largely hidden inequalities between the sexes? And finally, what are the policy implications of these findings?

Why attention to gender is comparatively new

In both development studies and theories of justice, there has, until recently, been a marked lack of attention to gender – and in particular to systematic inequalities between the sexes. This point has been made about theories of justice throughout the 1980s (e.g. Kearns 1983; Okin 1989b; Crosswaite 1989). In the development literature, it was first made earlier, in pioneering work by Ester Boserup, but has lately been heard loud and strong from a number of other prominent development theorists (Chen 1983; Dasgupta

1993; Sen 1990a, 1990b; Jelin 1990). In both contexts, the neglect of women and gender seems to be due primarily to two factors. The first is the assumption that the household (usually assumed to be male-headed) is the appropriate unit of analysis. The dichotomy between the public (political and economic) and the private (domestic and personal) is assumed valid, and only the former has been taken to be the appropriate sphere for development studies and theories of justice, respectively, to attend to. In ethical and political theories, the family is often regarded as an inappropriate context for justice, since love, altruism, or shared interests are assumed to hold sway within it. Alternatively, it is sometimes taken for granted that it is a realm of hierarchy and injustice. (Occasional theorists, like Rousseau, have said both!) In economics, development and other, households until recently have simply been taken for granted as the appropriate unit of analysis on such questions as income distribution. The public/private dichotomy and the assumption of the male-headed household have many serious implications for women as well as for children that are discussed below (Dasgupta 1993; Jaquette 1982: 283; Okin 1989b: 10–14, 124–33; Olsen 1983; Pateman 1983).

The second factor is the closely related failure to disaggregate data or arguments by sex. In the development literature, it seems to appear simply in this form (Chen et al. 1981: 68; Jaquette 1982: 283–4). In the justice literature, this used to be obscured by the use of male pronouns and other referents. Of late, the (rather more insidious) practice that I have called "false gender neutrality" has appeared. This consists in the use of gender-neutral terms ("he or she," "persons," and so on), when the point being made is simply invalid or otherwise false if one actually applies it to women (Okin 1989b: esp. 10–13, 45). But the effect is the same in both literatures; women are not taken into account, so the inequalities between the sexes are obscured.

The public/domestic dichotomy has serious implications for women. It not only obscures intrahousehold inequalities of resources and power, as I discuss below, but it also results in the failure to count a great deal of the work done by women as work, since all that is considered "work" is what is done for pay in the "public" sphere. All of the work that women do in bearing and rearing children, cleaning and maintaining households, caring for the old and sick, and contributing in various ways to men's work does not count as work. This is clearly one of those instances in which the situation of poor women in poor countries is not qualitatively *different* from that of most women in rich countries but, rather, "similar but worse," for even more, in some cases far more, of the work done by women (and children) in poor countries is rendered invisible, not counted, or "subsumed under men's work." The work of subsistence farming, tending to animals, domestic crafts (if not for the market), and the often arduous fetching of water and fuel are all added to the category of unrecognized work of women that already exists in richer countries.[5] Chen notes that women who do all these things "are listed [by policymakers] as housewives," even though "their tasks are as critical to the well-being of their families and to national production as are the men's" (Chen 1983: 220; see also Dasgupta 1993; Drèze and Sen 1989: ch. 4; Jaquette 1982, citing Bourgue and Warren 1979; Waring 1989).

Why does it matter?

This may seem like a silly question. Indeed, I hope it will soon be unnecessary, but it isn't – yet. I therefore argue, at the outset of *Justice, Gender, and the Family*, that the omission from theories of justice of gender, and of much of women's lives, is significant for three major reasons. Each of these reasons applies at least as much to the neglect of gender in theories of development. The first is obvious: women matter (at least they do to feminists), and their well-being matters at least as much as that of men. As scholars of development have recently been making clear, the inequalities between the sexes in a number of poor countries have not only highly detrimental but *fatal* consequences for millions of women. Sen (1990a) has recently argued that as many as one hundred million fewer women exist than might normally be expected on the

basis of male/female mortality rates in societies less devaluing of women – not only the Western industrialized world but much of sub-Saharan Africa, too (see also Dasgupta 1993; Drèze and Sen 1989: ch. 4; Drèze and Sen 1990: Introduction, 11–14; but cf. Harriss 1990; Wheeler and Abdullah 1988). So here too we can reasonably say that the issue of the neglect of women is "similar but *much* worse."

The second reason I have raised (in the US context) for the necessity for feminist critique of theories of social justice is that equality of opportunity – for women and girls but also for increasing numbers of boys – is much affected by the failure of theories of justice to address gender inequality. This is in part due to the greater extent of economic distress in female-headed households. In the United States, nearly 25 percent of children are being raised in single female-headed households, and three-fifths of all chronically poor households with children are among those supported by single women. It has been recently estimated that throughout the world one-third of households are headed by single females, with the percentage much higher in regions with significant male out-migration (Chen 1983: 221; Jaquette 1982: 271). Many millions of children are affected by the higher rate of poverty among such families.[6] Theories of justice or of economic development that fail to pay attention to gender ignore this, too.

In addition, the gendered division of labor has a serious and direct impact on the opportunities of girls and women, which crosses the lines of economic class. The opportunities of females are significantly affected by the structures and practices of family life, particularly by the fact that women are almost invariably primary caretakers, which has much impact on their availability for full-time wage work. It also results in their frequently being *over*worked, and renders them less likely than men to be considered economically valuable. This factor, too, operates "similarly but more so" within poor families in many poor countries. There, too, adult women suffer – often more severely – many of the same effects of the division of labor as do women in richer countries. But, in addition, their daughters are likely to be put to work for the household at a very young age, are much less likely to be educated and to attain literacy than are sons of the same households and, worst of all – less valued than their brothers – they have less chance of staying alive because they are more likely to be deprived of food or of health care (Dasgupta 1993; Drèze and Sen 1990: ch. 4; Sen 1990a; Papanek 1990).

Third, I have argued that the failure to address the issue of just distribution within households is significant because the family is the first, and arguably the most influential, school of moral development (Okin 1989b: esp. 17–23). It is the first environment in which we experience how persons treat each other, in which we have the potential to learn how to be just or unjust. If children see that sex difference is the occasion for obviously differential treatment, they are surely likely to be affected in their personal and moral development. They are likely to learn injustice by absorbing the messages, if male, that they have some kind of "natural" enhanced entitlement and, if female, that they are *not* equals and had better get used to being subordinated if not actually abused. So far as I know, this point was first made in the Western context by John Stuart Mill, who wrote of the "perverting influence" of the typical English family of his time – which he termed "a school of despotism" (Mill [1869] 1988: 88). I have argued that the still remaining unequal distribution of benefits and burdens between most parents in two-parent heterosexual families is likely to affect their children's developing sense of justice (Okin 1989b: e.g. 21–3, 97–101). In the context of poor countries, as Papanek (1990) notes, "Domestic groups in which age and gender difference confer power on some over others are poor environments in which to unlearn the norms of inequality" (1990: 163–5). She also notes that "given the persistence of gender-based inequalities in power, authority, and access to resources, one must conclude that socialization for gender inequality is by and large very successful" (1990: 170). When such basic goods as food and health care are unequally distributed to young children according to sex, a very strong signal about the acceptability of injustice is surely conferred. The

comparison of most families in rich countries with poor families in poor countries – where distinctions between the sexes often start earlier and are much more blatant and more harmful to girls – yields, here too, the conclusion that, in the latter case, things are not so much different as "similar but more so." Many Third World families, it seems, are even worse schools of justice and more successful inculcators of the inequality of the sexes as natural and appropriate than are their developed world equivalents. Thus there is even more need for attention to be paid to gender inequality in the former context than in the latter.

Justice in the family

What do we find when we compare some of Anglo-American feminists' findings about justice within households in their societies with recent discoveries about distributions of benefits and burdens in poor households in poor countries? Again, in many respects, the injustices of gender are quite similar.

In both situations, women's access to paid work is constrained both by discrimination and sex segregation in the workplace and by the assumption that women are "naturally" responsible for all or most of the unpaid work of the household (Bergmann 1986; Fuchs 1988; Gerson 1985; Okin 1989b: 147–52, 155–6; Sanday 1974). In both situations, women typically work longer total hours than men:

> Time-use statistics considering all work (paid and unpaid economic activity and unpaid housework) reveal that women spend more of their time working than men in all developed and developing regions except northern America and Australia, where the hours are almost equal. (United Nations Report 1991: 81 and ch. 6 passim; see also Bergmann 1986; Hochschild 1989)

In both situations, developed and less developed, vastly more of women's work is not paid and is not considered "productive."[7] Thus there is a wide gap between men's and women's *recorded* economic participation. The perception that women's work is of less worth (despite the fact that in most places they do more, and it is crucial to the survival of household members) contributes to women's being devalued and having less power both within the family and outside the household (Blumstein and Schwartz 1983; Dasgupta 1993; Drèze and Sen 1990: ch. 4; Okin 1989b: ch. 7; Sanday 1974; Sen 1990a, 1990b). This in turn adversely affects their capacity to become economically less dependent on men. Thus they become involved in "a cycle of socially caused and distinctly asymmetric vulnerability" (Okin 1989b: 138; Drèze and Sen 1989: 56–9). The devaluation of women's work, as well as their lesser physical strength and economic dependence on men, allows them to be subject to physical, sexual, and/or psychological abuse by men they live with (Gordon 1988; United Nations Report 1991: 19–20). However, in many poor countries, as I have mentioned, this power differential extends beyond the abuse and overwork of women to deprivation in terms of the feeding, health care, and education of female children – and even to their being born or not: "of 8,000 abortions in Bombay after parents learned the sex of the foetus through amniocentesis, only one would have been a boy" (United Nations Report 1991; see also Dasgupta 1993; Drèze and Sen 1989: ch. 4; Sen 1990a).

In cross-regional analyses, both Sen and Dasgupta have found correlations between the life expectancies of females relative to males and the extent to which women's work is perceived as having economic value. Thus in both rich and poor countries, women's participation in work outside the household can improve their status within the family, but this is not necessarily assured. It is interesting to compare Barbara Bergmann's (1986) analysis of the situation of "drudge wives" in the United States, who work fulltime for pay and who also perform virtually all of the household's unpaid labor, with Peggy Sanday's earlier finding that, in some Third World contexts, women who do little of the work that is considered "productive" have low status, whereas many who do a great deal of it become "virtual slaves" (Sanday 1974: 201; Bergmann 1986: 260–73).[8]

This leads us to the issue of women's economic dependence (actual and perceived). Although most poor women in poor countries work long hours each day, throughout the world they are often economically dependent on men. This, too, is "similar to but worse than" the situation of many women in richer countries. It results from so much of their work being unpaid work, so much of their paid work being poorly paid work, and, in some cases, from men's laying claim to the wages their wives and daughters earn. Feminist critics since Ester Boserup (1970) have argued that women's economic dependency on men was in many cases exacerbated by changes that development theory and development policymakers saw only as "progressive." All too ready to perceive women as dependants, mainstream theorists did not notice that technology, geographical mobility, and the conversion from subsistence to market economies were not, from the female point of view, "unalloyed benefits, but . . . processes that cut women out from their traditional economic and social roles and thrust them into the modern sector where they are discriminated against and exploited, often receiving cash incomes below the subsistence level, . . . in turn increas(ing) female dependency" (Jaquette 1982; see also Boserup 1970; Rogers, in Jaquette).[9]

In both rich and poor countries, women who are the sole economic support of families often face particular hardship. However, whereas some are, not all of the reasons for this are the same. Discrimination against women in access to jobs, pay, retention, and promotion are common to most countries, with obviously deleterious effects on female-supported families. In the United States, the average full-time working woman earns a little more than two-thirds of the pay of a full-time male worker, and three-fifths of the families with children who live in chronic poverty are single female-parent families. Many such women in both rich and poor countries also suffer from severe "time poverty."

But the situation of some poor women in poor countries is different from – as well as distinctly worse than – that of most Western women today. It is more like the situation of the latter in the nineteenth century: even when they have no other means of support, they are actually *prohibited* (by religiously based laws or oppressive cultural norms) from engaging in paid labor. Martha Chen (forthcoming) has studied closely the situation of such women in the Indian subcontinent. Deprived of the traditional economic support of a male, they are prevented from taking paid employment by rules of caste, or *purdah*. For such women, it can indeed be liberating to be helped (as they have been by outsiders like Chen) to resist the sanctions invoked against them by family elders, neighbors, or powerful social leaders. Although many forms of wage work, especially those available to women, are hardly "liberating," except in the most basic sense, women are surely distinctly less free if they are *not* allowed to engage in it, especially if they have no other means of support. Many employed women in Western industrialized countries still face quite serious disapproval if they are mothers of young children or if the family's need for their wages is not perceived as great. But at least, except in the most oppressive of families or subcultures, they are *allowed* to go out to work. By contrast, as Chen's work makes clear, the basic right to be allowed to make a much needed living for themselves and their children is still one that many women in the poorest of situations in other cultures are denied.

Here, then, is a real difference – an oppressive situation that most Western women no longer face. But to return to similarities: another that I discovered, while comparing some of our Western feminist ideas about justice with work on poor women in poor countries, has to do with the dynamics of power within the family. The differential exit potential theory that I adopt from Albert Hirschman's work to explain power within the family has recently been applied to the situation of women in poor countries (cf. Okin 1989b: ch. 7 with Dasgupta 1993 and Sen 1990b). Partha Dasgupta (1993) also uses exit theory in explaining the "not uncommon" desertion by men of their families during famines. He writes, 'The man deserts [his wife] because *his* outside option in these circumstances emerges higher in his ranking than any feasible allocation within the

household" (1993: 329). He regards the "hardware" he employs – John Nash's game-theoretic program – as "needed if we are to make any progress in what is a profoundly complex matter, the understanding of household decisions" (p. 329). But the conclusion he reaches is very similar to the one that I reach, drawing on Hirschman's theory of power and the effects of persons' differential exit potential: any factor that improves the husband's exit option or detracts from the wife's exit option thereby gives him additional voice, or bargaining power in the relationship. Likewise, anything that improves the wife's exit option – her acquisition of human or physical capital, for example – will increase her autonomy and place her in a better bargaining position in the relationship (Dasgupta 1993: 331–3; Okin 1989b: ch. 7).[10]

In the United States, recent research has shown that women's and children's economic status (taking need into account) typically deteriorates after separation or divorce, whereas the average divorcing man's economic status actually improves (McLindon 1987; Weitzman 1985; Wishik 1986). This, taken in conjunction with the exit/voice theory, implies less bargaining power for wives within marriage. In poor countries, where circumstances of severe poverty combine with a lack of paid employment opportunities for women, increasing women's dependency on men, men's power within the family – already in most cases legitimized by highly patriarchal cultural norms – seems very likely to be enhanced. Although, as Dasgupta (1993) points out, Nash's formula was not intended as a normative theory, employed in this context, the theory not only *explains* (much as does my employment of Hirschman's theory) the cyclical nature of women's lack of power within the family. It also points to the injustice of a situation in which the assumption of women's responsibility for children, their disadvantaged position in the paid workforce, and their physical vulnerability to male violence all contribute to giving them little bargaining room when their (or their children's) interests conflict with those of the men they live with, thereby in turn worsening their position relative to that of men. The whole theory, then, whether in its more or its less mathematical form, seems just as applicable to the situations of very poor women in poor countries as it is to women in quite well-off households in rich countries. Indeed, one must surely say, in this case, too, "similar but *much* worse," for the stakes are undeniably higher – no less than life or death for more than a hundred million women, as has recently been shown (Drèze and Sen 1990: ch. 4; Sen 1990a).

Policy implications

Some of the *solutions* to all these problems, which have been suggested recently by scholars addressing the situation of poor women in poor countries, closely resemble solutions proposed by Western feminists primarily concentrating on their own societies. (By "solutions to problems" I mean to refer to both what theorists and social scientists need to do to rectify their analyses and what policymakers need to do to solve the social problems themselves.) First, the dichotomization of public and domestic spheres must be strongly challenged. As Chen (1983) writes, in the context of poor rural regions, "So long as policymakers make the artificial distinction between the farm and the household, between paid work and unpaid work, between productive and domestic work, women will continue to be overlooked" (p. 220). Challenging the dichotomy will also point attention to the inequities that occur within households – various forms of abuse, including the inequitable distribution of food and health care. As Papanek (1990) argues, "Given a focus on socialization for inequality, power relations within the household – as a central theme in examining the dynamics of households – deserve special attention" (1990: 170).

Second, and following from the above, the unit of analysis both for studies and for much policymaking must be the individual, not the household.[11] Noting that, given the greater political voice of men, public decisions affecting the poor in poor countries are often "guided by male preferences, not [frequently conflicting] female needs," Dasgupta (1993) concludes that

the maximization of well-being as a model for explaining household behaviour must be rejected. . . . Even though it is often difficult to design and effect it, the target of public policy should be persons, not households. . . . Governments need to be conscious of the household as a resource allocation mechanism. (1993: 335–6)

Especially as women are even more likely in poor countries than in richer ones to be providing the sole or principal support for their households, as Chen (1983) points out, they require as much access as men to credit, skills training, labor markets, and technologies (and, I would add, equal pay for their work) (1983: 221). Policies prompting women's full economic participation and productivity are needed increasingly for the survival of their households, for women's overall socioeconomic status, and for their bargaining position within their families. As Drèze and Sen (1989) say, "important policy implications" follow from the "considerable evidence that greater involvement with outside work and paid employment does tend to go with less anti-female bias in intra-family distribution" (1989: 58). Because of the quite pervasive unequal treatment of female children in some poor countries, the need for equal treatment of women by policymakers is often far more urgent than the need of most women in richer countries – but again, the issue is not so much different as "similar but more so."

Implications for Thinking about Justice

Finally, I shall speculate briefly about two different ways of thinking about justice between the sexes, in cultures very different from ours. I have tried to show that, for feminists thinking about justice, John Rawls's theory, if revised so as to include women and the family, has a great deal to be said for it, and the veil of ignorance is particularly important (Rawls 1971; Okin 1989a, 1989b). If everyone were to speak only from his or her own point of view, it is unclear that we would come up with any principles at all. But the very presence of the veil, which hides from those in the original position any particular knowledge of the personal characteristics or social position they will have in the society for which they are designing principles of justice, forces them to take into account as many voices as possible and especially to be concerned with those of the least well-off. It enables us to reconcile the requirement that a theory of justice be universalizable with the seemingly conflicting requirement that it take account of the multiple differences among human beings.

In a recent paper, Ruth Anna Putnam (forthcoming), arguing a strongly anti-essentialist line, and accusing Rawls and myself of varying degrees of exclusionary essentialism, considers instead an "interactive" (some might call it "dialogic") feminism: "that we listen to the voices of women of color and women of a different class, and that we appropriate what we hear" (p. 21).[12] Listening and discussing have much to recommend them; they are fundamental to democracy in the best sense of the word. And *sometimes* when especially oppressed women are heard, their cry for justice is clear – as in the case of the women Martha Chen worked with, who became quite clear that being allowed to leave the domestic sphere in order to earn wages would help to liberate them. But we are not always enlightened about what is just by asking persons who seem to be suffering injustices what they want. Oppressed people have often internalized their oppression so well that they *have* no sense of what they are justly entitled to as human beings. This is certainly the case with gender inequalities. As Papanek (1990) writes, "The clear perception of disadvantages . . . requires conscious rejection of the social norms and cultural ideal that perpetuate inequalities and the use of different criteria – perhaps from another actual or idealized society – in order to assess inequality as a prelude for action" (1990: 164–5). People in seriously deprived conditions are sometimes not only accepting of them but relatively cheerful – the "small mercies" situation. Deprivations sometimes become gagged and muffled for reasons of deeply rooted ideology, among others. But it would surely be ethically deeply mistaken to attach a correspondingly small value to the loss of well-being of such people because of their survival strategy.

Coming to terms with very little is no recipe for social justice. Thus it is, I believe, quite justifiable for those not thoroughly imbued with the inegalitarian norms of a culture to come forth as its constructive critics. Critical distance, after all, does not have to bring with it detachment: *committed* outsiders can often be better analysts and critics of social injustice than those who live within the relevant culture. This is why a concept such as the original position, which aims to approximate an Archimedean point, is so valuable, at least in addition to some form of dialogue. Let us think for a moment about some of the cruelest or most oppressive institutions and practices that are or have been used to "brand" women – foot binding, clitoridectomy, and purdah. As Papanek shows, "well socialized" women in cultures with such practices internalize them as necessary to successful female development. Even though, in the case of the former two practices, these women may retain vivid memories of their own intense pain, they perpetuate the cruelties, inflicting them or at least allowing them to be inflicted on their own daughters.

Now, clearly, a theory of human flourishing, such as Nussbaum and Sen have been developing, would have no trouble delegitimizing such practices (Nussbaum 1992). But given the choice between a revised Rawlsian outlook or an "interactive feminist" one, as defined by Putnam, I'd choose the former any day, for in the latter, well-socialized members of the oppressed group are all too likely to rationalize the cruelties, whereas the men who perceive themselves as benefiting from them are unlikely to object. But behind the veil of ignorance, is it not much more likely that both the oppressors and the oppressed would have second thoughts? What Moslem man is likely to take the chance of spending his life in seclusion and dependency, sweltering in head-to-toe solid black clothing? What prerevolutionary Chinese man would cast his vote for the breaking of toes and hobbling through life, if he well might be the one with the toes and the crippled life? What man would endorse gross genital mutilation, not knowing *whose* genitals? And the women in these cultures, required to think of such practices from a male as well as a female perspective, might thereby, with a little distance, gain more notion of just how, rather than perfecting femininity, they perpetuate the subordination of women to men.

Martha Nussbaum (1992) has recently written of what happens when outsiders, instead of trying to maintain some critical distance, turn to what amounts to the worship of difference. Citing some examples of sophisticated Western scholars who, in their reverence for the integrity of cultures, defend such practices as the isolation of menstruating women and criticize Western "intrusions" into other cultures, such as the provision of typhoid vaccine, Nussbaum finds a strange and disturbing phenomenon:

> Highly intelligent people, people deeply committed to the good of women and men in developing countries, people who think of themselves as progressive and feminist and antiracist, . . . are taking up positions that converge . . . with the positions of reaction, oppression, and sexism. Under the banner of their radically and politically correct "antiessentialism" march ancient religious taboos, the luxury of the pampered husband, ill health, ignorance, and death.   (1992: 204)

As Nussbaum later concludes, "Identification need not ignore concrete local differences: in fact, at its best, it demands a searching analysis of differences, in order that the general good be appropriately realized in the concrete case. But the learning about and from the other is motivated . . . by the conviction that the other is one of us" (1992: 241).

As the work of some feminist scholars of development shows, using the concept of gender and refusing to let differences gag us or fragment our analyses does not mean that we should overgeneralize or try to apply "standardized" solutions to the problems of women in different circumstances. Chen argues for the value of a situation-by-situation analysis of women's roles and constraints before plans can be made and programs designed. And Papanek, too, shows how

helping to educate women to awareness of their oppression requires quite deep and specific knowledge of the relevant culture.

Thus I conclude that gender itself is an extremely important category of analysis and that we ought not be paralyzed by the fact that there are differences among women. So long as we are careful and develop our judgments in the light of empirical evidence, it is possible to generalize about many aspects of inequality between the sexes. Theories developed in Western contexts can clearly apply, at least in large part, to women in very different cultural contexts. From place to place, from class to class, from race to race, and from culture to culture, we find similarities in the specifics of these inequalities, in their causes and their effects, although often not in their extent or severity.

Notes

I am grateful to Elisabeth Friedman, Elisabeth Hansot Robert O. Keohane, Martha Nussbaum, and Louise Tilly for helpful comments on an earlier draft of this article.

1   This debate has been conducted mostly among feminist legal and political theorists. The legal literature is already so vast that it is difficult to summarize, and it is not relevant to this essay. For some references, see Okin (1991), ns. 1–3.

2   "Essentialism," employed in the context of feminist theory, seems to have two principal meanings. The other refers to the tendency to regard certain characteristics or capacities as "essentially" female, in the sense that they are unalterably associated with being female. Used in this second way, essentialism is very close to, if not always identical with, biological determinism. I am not concerned with this aspect of the term here.

3   In 1851, at an almost entirely white women's rights convention, Truth said,

> That man over there says women need to be helped into carriages, and lifted over ditches, and to have the best place everywhere. Nobody ever helps me into carriages, or over mud puddles, or gives me any best place! And ain't I a woman? Look at me! Look at my arm! I have ploughed, and planted, and gathered into barns, and no man could head me! And ain't I a woman? I

could work as much and eat as much as a man – when I could get it – and bear the lash as well! And ain't I a woman? I have borne thirteen children, and seen most all sold off to slavery, and when I cried out with my mother's grief, none but Jesus heard me! And ain't I a woman?

4   The example is that of the many black women (and few white women) who answered Joann Little's appeal on behalf of Delbert Tibbs, a black man who had been falsely accused of raping a white woman and sentenced to death. I do not think the example clearly supports Harris's assertion that black women have "a unique ambivalence" about rape, any more than it supports the assertion she claims to refute – that their experience is similar, but different in magnitude. Black women's present experience of rape is surely similar to that of white women in several important respects: many are raped (by acquaintances as well as by strangers), they fear being raped, they sometimes modify their behavior because of this fear, and they are victimized as witnesses at the trials of their rapists. But their experience is probably also worse because, in addition to all of this, they have to live with the knowledge and experience of black men's being victimized by false accusations, harsher sentences, and, at worst, lynchings. Only empirical research that involved asking them could show more certainly whether the oppression of black men as alleged rapists (or the history of master/slave rape, which Harris also discusses) makes black women's entire contemporary experience of rape different from that of white women.

5   However, the detailed division of labor between the sexes varies considerably from culture to culture. As Jane Mansbridge (1993) has recently written, in a discussion of "gratuitous gendering":

> Among the Aleut of North America, for example, only women are allowed to butcher animals. But among the Ingalik of North America, only men are allowed to butcher animals. Among the Suku of Africa, only the women can plant crops and only the men can make baskets. But among the Kaffa of the Circum-Mediterranean, only the men can plant crops and only the women can make baskets. (1993: 345)

Her analysis is derived from data in George P. Murdoch and Caterina Provost, "Factors in the Division of Labor by Sex: A Cross-Cultural Analysis," *Ethnology* 12 (1973): 203–25. However, the work done by women is less likely to be "outside" work and to be paid or valued.

6   Poverty is both a relative and an absolute term. The poorest households in poor countries are absolutely as well as relatively poor and can be easily pushed below subsistence by any number of natural, social, or personal catastrophes. Poverty in rich countries is more often relative poverty (although there is serious malnutrition currently in the United States for example, and drug abuse, with all its related ills, is highly correlated with poverty). Relative poverty, although not directly life-threatening, can however be very painful, especially for children living in societies that are not only highly consumer-oriented but in which many opportunities – for good health care, decent education, the development of talents, pursuit of interests, and so on – are seriously limited for those from poor families. Single parents also often experience severe "time poverty," which can have a serious impact on their children's well-being.

7   See Dasgupta (1993) on members' perceived "usefulness" affecting the allocation of goods within poor households in poor families. Western studies as well as non-Western ones show us that women's work is already likely to be regarded as less useful – even when it is just as necessary to family well-being. So when women are really made less useful (by convention or lack of employment opportunities), this problem is compounded. Dasgupta questions simple measures of usefulness, such as paid employment, in the case of girls (1993). Where young poor women are not entitled to parental assets and their outside employment opportunities are severely restricted, the only significant "employment" for them is as childbearers and housekeepers – so marriage becomes especially valued (even though its conditions may be highly oppressive).

8   There seems to be some conflicting evidence on this matter. See Papanek (1990: 166–8).

9   This seems similar to changes in the work and socioeconomic status of women in Western Europe in the sixteenth to eighteenth centuries.

10   I do not mean to imply here that most women, whether in developed or less developed societies, think about improving their exit options when making decisions about wage work and related issues. Indeed, in some cultures, women relin-

quish wage work as soon as their families' financial situation enables them to do so. But their exit option is nevertheless reduced, and their partner's enhanced, thereby in all likelihood altering the distribution of power within the family.

11 This point seems to have been first explicitly made in the context of policy by George Bernard Shaw, who argues in *The Intelligent Woman's Guide to Socialism and Capitalism* (New Brunswick, NJ: Transaction Books, 1984) that the state should require all adults to work and should allocate an equal portion of income to each – man, woman, and child.

12 As Joan Tronto has pointed out to me, the use of "appropriate" here is noteworthy, given Putnam's professed desire to treat these other women as her equals.

References

Benhabib, Seyla, and Drucilla Cornell (1987), Introduction: Beyond the politics of gender. In *Feminism as critique*. Minneapolis: University of Minnesota Press.

Bergmann, Barbara R. (1986), *The economic emergence of women*. New York: Basic Books.

Blumstein, Philip, and Pepper Schwartz (1983), *American couples*. New York: Morrow.

Boserup, Ester (1970), *Women's role in economic development*. London: Allen & Unwin.

Chen, Lincoln C., Emdadul Huq, and Stan D'Souza (1981), Sex bias in the family allocation of food and health care in rural Bangladesh. *Population and Development Review* 7: 55–70.

Chen, Martha Alter (1983), *A quiet revolution: Women in transition in rural Bangladesh*. Cambridge, MA: Schenkman.

—— (forthcoming), A matter of survival: Women's right to work in India and Bangladesh. In *Human capabilities: Men, women, and equality*, edited by Nussbaum and Glover. Oxford: Oxford University Press, 1994.

Childers, Mary, and bell hooks (1990), A conversation about race and class. In *Conflicts in feminism*, edited by Marianne Hirsch and Evelyn Fox Keller. New York: Routledge, Chapman & Hall.

Crosswaite, Jan (1989), Sex in the original position. Unpublished manuscript, Department of Philosophy, University of Auckland.

Dasgupta, Partha (1993), *An inquiry into well-being and destitution*. Oxford: Clarendon Press.

Drèze, Jean, and Amartya Sen (1989), *Hunger and public action*. Oxford: Clarendon Press.

——, eds (1990), *The political economy of hunger: Vol. 1. Entitlement and well-being*. Oxford: Clarendon Press.

Fuchs, Victor (1988), *Women's quest for economic equality*. Cambridge, MA: Harvard University Press.

Gerson, Kathleen (1985), *Hard choices: How women decide about work, career, and motherhood*. Berkeley: University of California Press.

Gordon, Linda (1988), *Heroes of their own lives*. New York: Viking.

Harris, Angela P. (1990), Race and essentialism in feminist legal theory. *Stanford Law Review* 42: 581–616.

Harriss, Barbara (1990), The intrafamilial distribution of hunger in South Asia. In *The political economy of hunger: Vol. 1. Entitlement and well-being*, edited by Jean Drèze and Amartya Sen. Oxford: Clarendon Press.

Hochschild, Arlie (1989), *The second shift: Working parents and the revolution at home*. New York: Viking.

hooks, bell (1984), *Feminist theory: From margin to center*. Boston: South End Press.

Jaquette, Jane S. (1982), Women and modernization theory: A decade of feminist criticism. *World Politics*. 34: 267–84.

Jelin, Elizabeth, ed. (1990), *Women and social change in Latin America*. London: Zed Books.

Kearns, Deborah (1983), A theory of justice and love – Rawls on the family. *Politics (Journal of the Australasian Political Studies Association)* 18 (2): 36–42.

Lorde, Audre (1984), An open letter to Mary Daly. In *Sister outsider*, edited by Audre Lorde. Trumansburg, NY: Crossing Press.

Mansbridge, Jane (1993), Feminism and democratic community. In *Democratic community*, ed. John Chapman and Ian Shapiro. New York: New York University Press.

Marks, Elaine, and Isabelle de Courtivron, eds (1981), *New French feminisms: An anthology*. New York: Schocken.

McLindon, James B. (1987), Separate but unequal: The economic disaster of divorce for women and children. *Family Law Quarterly* 12:3.

Mill, John Stuart [1869] (1988), *The subjection of women*. Reprint. Indianapolis: Hackett.

Minow, Martha, and Elizabeth V. Spelman (1990), In context. *Southern California Law Review* 63 (6): 1597–652.

Nussbaum, Martha (1992), Human functioning and social justice: In defense of Aristotelian essentialism. *Political Theory* 20: 202–46. (A version is forthcoming in *Human capabilities: Men, women, and equality*, edited by Nussbaum and Glover. Oxford: Oxford University Press, 1994.)

Okin, Susan Moller (1989a), Reason and feeling in thinking about justice. *Ethics* 99 (2): 229–49.

—— (1989b), *Justice, gender, and the family*. New York: Basic Books.

—— (1991), Sexual difference, feminism and the law. *Law and Social Inquiry*.

Olsen, Frances (1983), The family and the market: A study of ideology and legal reform. *Harvard Law Review* 96 (7).

Papanek Hanna (1990), To each less than she needs, from each more than she can do: Allocations, entitlements, and value. In Irene Tinker, ed., *Women and world development*. New York and London: Oxford University Press.

Pateman, Carole (1983), Feminist critiques of the public/private dichotomy. In *Public and private in social life*, ed. Stanley Benn and Gerald Gaus. London: Croom Helm. Also in Pateman, *The disorder of women*. Stanford, CA: Stanford University Press (1989).

Putnam, Ruth Anna (forthcoming), Why not a feminist theory of justice? Forthcoming in Nussbaum and Glover (1994).

Rawls, John (1971), *A theory of justice*. Cambridge, MA: Harvard University Press.

Sanday, Peggy R. (1974), Female status in the public domain. In Michelle Zimbalist Rosaldo and Louise Lamphere eds, *Woman, culture, and society*. Stanford. CA: Stanford University Press.

Sen, Amartya (1990a), More than 100 million women are missing. *New York Review of Books*, December 20.

—— (1990b), Gender and co-operative conflicts. In Irene Tinker, ed., *Women and world development*. New York and London: Oxford University Press.

Spelman, Elizabeth V. (1988), *Inessential woman: Problems of exclusion in feminist thought*. Boston: Beacon Press.

United Nations Report (1991), *The world's women: Trends and statistics, 1970–1990*. New York: United Nations Publication.

Waring, Marilyn (1989), *If women counted: A new feminist economics*. San Francisco: Harper & Row.

Weitzman, Lenore (1985), *The Divorce Revolution: The unexpected social and economic consequences for women and children*. New York: Free Press.

Wheeler, E. F., and M. Abdullah (1988) Food allocation within the family: Response to fluctuating food supply and food needs. In I. de Garine and G. A. Harrison, *Coping with uncertainty in food supply*. Oxford: Clarendon Press.

Wishik, Heather Ruth (1986), Economics of divorce: An exploratory study. *Family Law Quarterly* 20: 1.

42   Race/Gender and the Ethics of Difference

Jane Flax

Susan Moller Okin has recently attacked the emphasis some feminists place on differences among women. She discerns "problems with going in the direction of formulating a theory of justice entirely by listening to every concrete individual's or group's point of view."[1] Okin doubts that it is "possible, by taking this route, to come up with any principles at all. . . . Doesn't stress-

From *Political Theory*, vol. 23, no. 3 (August 1995), 500–10. Reprinted with permission.

ing differences, especially cultural differences, lead to a slide toward relativism?"[2]

Okin claims that within some circles a belief that a focus on "women" necessarily reflects only middle-class White women's experience is now accepted as a "truism." In contrast, she defends an internally undifferentiated and conflict-free concept of gender. Gender is constituted through what women share, especially their differences from, and domination by, men. Women are defined by the similarities of their inequalities across race, class, and geography. Okin claims: "One can argue that sexism is an identifiable form of oppression, many of whose effects are felt by women regardless of race or class, without at all subscribing to the view that race and class oppression are insignificant."[3]

Both claims are mistaken. Okin misunderstands the genealogy, content, and ethical consequences of discourses of differences. Discourses of difference cannot be understood outside their specific historical contexts and purposes. They represent attempts to theorize and undo relations of domination. The participants in these debates are socially situated subjects who both resist and are constructed by context-specific social relations. Without attention to difference, each person's multiple locations as authority, resister, and determined subject who articulates and is spoken by specific social vocabularies disappear. Attaining a "critical distance" may alert us to aspects of these multiple locations and their effects. However, it cannot render our judgments free of them. There is no Archimedean point available from which principles or practices of justice can be articulated or defended. Cross-cultural theorizing about justice requires attention to the particularity and partiality of conceptual vocabularies and practices and acknowledgment of the simultaneously determined and resisting qualities of each contributor.

Okin is also wrong to assume that race is extrinsic to gender. No "women" exist who have experiences of oppression (or dominance) unmarked by race and class. Within contemporary social relations, no woman or feminist theorizing can be situated "regardless of race and class." To make such claims is to misconstrue the meaning and to miscalculate the significance of race for all women and theorizing practices. Adequate theorizing about gender and justice requires attention to inequalities among women. A homogeneous dominance/oppression model cannot account for the complicated and contradictory constitution of gender.

Difference Discourses and Their Contexts

Okin traces the concern with differences to three sources: postmodernist thought, writings by African American and other minority women, and "particularly" Elizabeth Spelman's recent book *Inessential Woman* (Boston: Beacon Press, 1988). Okin very briefly mentions only one article by an African American.[4] Her primary purpose is to attack Spelman's claim that race is intrinsic, not additive, to gender. A major consequence of this claim is that "women" cannot be treated as a homogeneous category. One cannot assume that "other" (e.g. non-White) women have experiences "just like ours" (White women) only more so. Gender cannot be understood as a simple binary opposition composed of two categories: man and woman.

For Okin, the stakes are clear: can "we" say that "sexism" is a type of oppression that affects all women, irrespective of their race, sexuality, and so forth? Her implicit assumption seems to be that sexism must affect a homogeneous category in relatively uniform ways to be taken seriously as a form of injustice. Why uniform oppression of a homogeneous group is necessary for it to count as injustice is not made clear. I assume it has something to do with Okin's (Rawlsian) background assumptions about universalizability. Evidently, generalizable principles require general, unitary subjects. These subjects can be either homogeneous victims of oppression or reflective practitioners in the original position. However, it cannot be difference *per se* that blocks "our" ability to articulate just principles. Okin claims that inattention to differences between men and women causes or perpetuates injustice. Why should attention to differences among women undermine or weaken our claims to gender justice? One does not have to occupy a position of pure oppression to articulate principles or engage in practices intended to end relations of domination.

Okin argues that a central claim of difference discourses – gender is constituted and experienced differently according to race and other social positions – "lacks empirical evidence."[5] She intends to provide proof that there is a collectively shared, definitive experience of womanhood. Okin also wants to demonstrate that there are generalizable theories, especially feminist critiques of non-feminist theories of justice. These can both identify uniformities in women's experience and point toward common policies to overcome our shared oppression.

She takes as her test case "the poorest women in poor countries."[6] Presumably, if they are just like "us" (White women in rich countries) only more so, we can conclude that there is collectively shared oppression. The category "woman" will be meaningful beyond whatever differences there might be. She looks at the conditions of poor Third World women in relation to four categories – inattention to gender injustice, gender-based lack of equality of opportunity, injustice in the family, and policy implications. Her conclusion is that the conditions of poor women in poor countries are generally like those of women in the First World, only more so. Policies informed by attention to gender justice, similar to those she advocates for women in the First World, could provide solutions to these conditions.

Okin does not acknowledge or confront the dangers of enlisting poor women from other countries as evidence in a dispute among women in the First World. This appropriation replicates the objectification and asymmetries that often typify relations between women in the First and Third World. "Western feminists alone become the true 'subjects' of this counterhistory. Third world women, on the other hand, never rise above the debilitating generality of their 'object' status."[7] Okin does not seriously address the voluminous writings of racialized women in this country. To do this would require situating these debates in their specific political contexts. Even more, it requires an appreciation of the agency and authority that marginalized women assert in and through these debates.

Her analysis excludes both a primary purpose and the political genealogy of difference discourses in this country. Many participants were trying to compel White (and straight) women to pay attention to the actual, ongoing relations of domination among women in the United States

and elsewhere.[8] These writings provide extensive evidence of the complicity of White women in racial domination and the empirical differences in women's lives. They also detail the complex interweaving and inseparability of race and gender in the lives of women and men throughout American history.[9] The disproportionate attention paid to Spelman and the rapid movement of Okin's analysis to the "Third World" reflect and permit an elision of the social relations that produce discourses of difference and continue to potentiate them.

Okin does not adequately interrogate her own desire to emphasize the commonalities of women's experience and to insist that much of the shared content arises from domination by a unitary other (men). Why are such claims desirable or necessary? Who gains from these beliefs and what is obscured by them? Her exclusive focus on shared oppression obscures the equally important relations of domination between women. All women are not situated identically in relation to men, nor are men situated equally in relation to each other or to women. Such moves enable White women to ignore their complicity in, and privileges obtained from, their situatedness within relations of race, sexuality (if straight), and geographic location.

Despite Okin's emphasis on similarities among women, the structure of her text implicitly reveals one way women in the First World and "others" are not similar. She splits agency and determination so that the agency exercised by racialized and "Third World women" and the determined aspects of First World women theorists are invisible. This implies that a group of objective intellectuals exists who can locate and speak for the interests of others. This speech and analysis are not distorted by their own experiences or wishes. Location on this Archimedean point permits us to be objective, but "committed," outsiders. Accurate analysis of gender injustice requires this capacity for detachment. (Poor) women in the Third World exercise very little critical judgment. They appear all too ready to "settle for very little,"[10] while some women in the First World, despite their shared domination by men, can exercise detachment and undeter-

mined critical judgment. Such objectivity enables us to be more accurate and insightful critics
of other women's (and our own) societies than
they can be.

Okin's argument relies on the assumption that
First World women *are* outside the social relations that produce poor ones. This mistaken belief functions as a defense against acknowledging
the social practices that constitute the Western
observer and relations between observer and observed. It obscures "the complex interconnec-
tion between first and third world economies and
the profound effect of this on the lives of women
in all countries."[11] It also ignores the many indigenous forms of resistance and the many critiques of this sort of lumping together of women
from diverse cultures.[12] Constructing "Third
World" women as an unresisting and homogeneous category positions them exclusively as objects of the discourses and practices of others.

Furthermore, such positioning denies the possibility that women in the First World have much
to learn about themselves and others by seeing
through their eyes. Taking the diversity of practices, locations, and meanings seriously entails
placing Western, White women as the objects,
not just subjects, of discourse.[13] This approach is
also more congruent with a commitment to justice; it treats others as persons deserving of respect and capable of exercising authority in their
own lives and those of others. It does not presume in advance whose judgments ought to pre-
vail when differences arise.

The Inescapability of
Race/Gender

Okin fails to recognize the constituting effects
of race/gender on all Americans. This is obvious
in her remarks about the salience of slavery to
modern social relations. She says that the relevance of "the obvious contrast between the experience of white slaveholders' wives and black
female slaves to most issues involving the sameness or difference of forms of gender oppression
today"[14] is not clear to her. This view contrasts
strongly with recent writings by Black women,

for whom slavery reverberates in their history. It
is a primal tragedy that lives on in one's sense of
self, as the Holocaust does for me as a Jew. For
example, Nellie Y. McKay writes:

> Speaking specifically of the experiences of Black
> and white women in the USA, for Black women
> there is a long and painful history embedded in
> the difference that separate them from white
> women. This history begins with the first Afri-
> can slave woman who encountered a white
> woman on this continent . . . the "often *violent*
> connection pitting black female will against
> white female racism" is a condition that pen-
> etrates all of American cultural and literary con-
> sciousness.[15]

Slavery is intrinsic to the genealogy of modern Euro-American subjects. The "modern subject may be located in historically specific and
unavoidably complex configurations of individu-
alization and embodiment – black and white,
male and female, lord and bondsman.[16] How can
Whites not be affected in their thinking of themselves and Blacks by the knowledge (tacit or
overt) that a little more that a hundred years ago
many Black people were property, not persons?

While for all women, "issues of gender are always connected to race,"[17] racially unmarked
women can avoid recognizing this. Most discourse concerning racism focuses on its horrifying effects on its objects. While this is absolutely
necessary, another aspect of racism has been almost completely avoided – "the impact of racism on those who perpetuate it."[18] We must
analyze what racial ideology does to "the mind,
imagination and behavior of masters."[19] Such
analysis requires resistance to the denial by Whites
of the constituting effects of race/gender on our
subjectivities.

In this ability to ignore the effects of racism,
we differ radically from racialized women. "Under no circumstances can Black women forget
that. And although Black feminists, even radical
black feminists have been trying to impress the
significance of this truth on white feminists for
more than twenty years, some still do not understand."[20] Neither White nor Black women can
find some racially neutral space of gender iden-

tity or unity outside "the anguish of racial differences inscribed in the complexities of race, sex, rage and power in Black and white women's relationships."[21] Perhaps we could construct one, but that could only be the consequence of a long struggle that has hardly begun.

The Inseparability of Race and Gender

In contemporary America we never encounter an ungendered but raced person or a gendered but unraced one.[22] Race and gender intertwine and are inextricably, mutually constituting. Gender is always raced, and race is always gendered. Race and gender are not identical, or one thing, but mutually constituting, unstable, conflicting, constantly mutating, interdependent, and inseparable processes. Investment in one privilege can obscure these interwoven operations. Whatever separate lines of development they may have had in the past, each so blurs and bleeds into the other that only interwoven, processural concepts can begin to capture current complexities. Therefore, theorizing must employ metaphors of "creolization, mestizaje and hybridity, pollution and impurity . . . cultural mutation and restless (dis)continuity that exceed racial discourse and avoid capture by its agents."[23]

Discourses of race/gender are pervasive, intrinsic to, and necessary for social reproduction, systemic order, political legitimacy, and subjective stability and identity. Race/gender is intrinsic to the practice of contemporary American political institutions, and the state is an inevitable and central terrain on and over which race/gender struggles occur. While public law and legitimated race/gender beliefs have changed since the 1950s, the salience of race/gender in individual and collective identity construction and distributions of power has not. Race/gender is deployed to refer to and disguise "forces, events, classes, and expression of social decay and economic division far more threatening to the body politic than 'race' ever was."[24]

Whiteness, especially in its masculine forms, remains the unproblematized universal. There-

fore, it is not seen as constituting a racialized or genderized subjectivity; being White is not a delimited (and limiting) identity. Whiteness is not seen as implicated in the production of the racialized other; nor is its dependence on raced/gendered others for its own sense of identity and social locations acknowledged. One who lacks difference can attain a more universal and objective (undetermined) moral and political standpoint.

Racialized women are necessarily produced and doubly erased within this discourse. The implicit modal person is a (White) man; therefore, qua (lesser) man, racialized men have some claims to acknowledgment and power. The modal universal racialized person is masculine. Women remain the particularized, lesser but implicitly White others. Early feminist theorizing tended to replicate this double erasure, and discourses of difference articulate attempts to resist and undo it.

Ethics of Difference

Okin's argument does nothing to reduce my suspicion of internally undifferentiated concepts of gender that define "woman" in terms of shared oppression. Structurally, such views foreclose acknowledgment of many of our conflicting positions in contemporary networks of power. They also obscure what Wendy Brown calls our "wounded attachments" and the passions that often motivate them – guilt, hate, envy, fear, and resentment.[25] Privileged people's need for abstract positions is partially driven by an unconscious guilty recognition of the determining role of domination in the formation of subjectivities (our own and the oppressed). We also fear the revenge of the oppressed on whose subordination their identities and positions depend. The dependence on the other for one's own identity is denied through the construction of a subjectivity free from any empirical context or determinant. The marks and burdens of race/gender are projected on to the other, and these become the content of the other's difference. The projection of all historical material outward allows the individual to be "free" or to acquire objectivity behind a Rawlsian veil of ignorance. This freedom includes an absence of complicity in the production of others, "their" history and their oppression.

Rather than argue it is time to "move on" from a focus on differences, I claim we have hardly begun to recognize them. White women have only begun to learn to listen to the points of view of many groups and individuals. Fearful about what they might teach us about ourselves, we are often tone-deaf to the voices of others and blind to the constituting effects of "difference" in our own subjectivities and politics. Okin evidently does not hear how offensive statements like "*committed* outsiders can often be better analysts and critics of social injustice than those who live within the relevant culture"[26] might sound to those within it.

Learning to listen is a complex process in which one must rethink one's own position and try to see oneself through the eyes of others. This mode of listening is quite different from the one adopting a Rawlsian veil of ignorance supposedly makes possible. Behind the veil of ignorance one impartially takes up one point of view after the other; one imagines a variety of circumstances, relationships, or rules as binding on the self. The requisite attitude is impartiality. One isolated rule or point of view after another is taken up and investigated. None of these positions are constitutive of the self, nor is the self implicated in their existence. They come from the outside, are subjected to rational scrutiny, and are adopted or rejected depending on whether they meet the condition of universalizability. The dialogue is between reason and an external position, experience, or rule presented to it.

The mode of listening I have in mind is quite different. It requires an uncomfortable, double vision. Those who are the marked bearers of "cultural differences" have long experience with this. One must see oneself as others do. The other's view cannot be totally alien or external, since it has constituting effects. One must struggle with and against it, and the struggle becomes part of one's self. Like the effects of the unconscious, one can never fully be aware of the effects of the other's view and the relations of power that

potentiate this view and render it salient. Even ideas or aspects of subjectivity that seem exempt from the other's determination remain suspect. One can never be fully at home with, or trusting of, oneself. Decentered, partially estranged, multiple, overdetermined subjectivity is not a postmodernist conceit. Colonized and culturally, racially, or sexually defined "others" have long been familiar with it.

Persons of relative privilege do not have to adopt the double vision of subject/subjected others. Adopting such a position requires empathy and a willingness to see oneself as a contextual, situationally determined subject. One cannot be outside the relations that constitute the other; one's own identity is dependent on being in relation to her. Contrary to Okin's view, the search for, or claim of, an Archimedean point, whether via the original position or another approach, impedes rather than fosters the pursuit of justice. Attention to one's determinations, not detachment from them, alleviates the problem of "false consciousness." We need respectful engagement with others to improve our perspectives.

Constructive debate about moral principles and standards of judgment requires the prior development of trust. Trust cannot develop unless each participant gives as full an account as possible of her particular commitments and acknowledges their potential for partiality, error, or harm. That each person's locations necessarily shape and limit our view must be acknowledged. Without open acknowledgment of this and its potential problems, the others have every right to remain suspicious. Unless the critic takes responsibility for the complexity of her own motives and locations, she is not approaching others from a position of respect and equality. Denial of difference renders claims of solidarity suspect. This is especially likely for those who rightfully cannot trust people who see themselves as outside our own relations of injustice. Commonality must be a result of open, mutual struggle; it cannot be assumed.

The possibility of just practices depends on fuller recognition of our differences and their often tangled and bloody histories. Until there are honest acknowledgments of our differences, hatreds, and divisions, and the multiplicity of positions as oppressor and oppressed, the call for unity can only be read as a wish to control others and a willful act of denial of the past and current conflicts that pervade the contemporary United States. Until there are fundamental redistributions of power among races, genders, and sexualities, the cry of "too much difference" must remain suspect. Justice is undermined by domination, not difference. To have mutual futures, we must cultivate new, unplatonic loves: of diversity, conflict, and that which is not shared in common.

Notes

1   Susan Moller Okin, "Gender Inequality and Cultural Differences," *Political Theory* 22, no. 1 (1994): 5.

2   Ibid., 5.

3   Ibid., 7.

4   Okin's concentration on Spelman's book rather than on writings by racialized women repeats the erasure of racial differences within feminist discourses. For extensive critiques of such erasures within feminist discourses and practices, see Maxine Baca Zinn, Lynn Weber Cannon, Elizabeth Higginbotham, and Bonnie Thornton Dill, "The Costs of Exclusionary Practices in Women's Studies," *Signs* 11, no. 2 (1986): 290–303; Maivan Clech Lam, "Feeling Foreign in Feminism," *Signs* 19, no. 4 (1994): 865–93; Ann duCille, "The Occult of True Womanhood: Critical Demeanor and Black Feminist Studies," *Signs* 19, no. 3 (1994): 591–629.

5   Okin, "Gender Inequality," 8.

6   Ibid., 9.

7   Chandra Talpade Mohanty, "Cartographies of Struggle: Third World Women and the Politics of Feminism," *Third World Women and the Politics of Feminism*, eds. Chandra Talpade Mohanty, Ann Russo, and Lourdes Torres (Bloomington: Indiana University Press, 1991), 71–2.

8   There are far too many works on the tangled histories of relations among White women, Black women, and feminism to cite. Examples include the following: Iris Berger, Elsa Brown, and Nancy A. Hewitt, "Intersections and Collision Courses: Women, Blacks, and Workers Confront Gender, Race, and Class," *Feminist Studies* 18, no. 2 (1992): 283–327; Micheline R. Malson, Elisabeth Mudimbe-Boyi, Jean F. O'Barr, and Mary Wyer, eds, *Black Women in America: Social Science Perspectives* (Chicago: University of Chicago Press, 1988); Paula Giddings, *When and Where I Enter: The Impact of Black Women on Race and Sex in America* (New York: Bantam, 1984); Angela Y. Davis, *Women, Race & Class* (New York: Random House, 1981); Patricia Hill Collins, *Black Feminist Thought* (New York: Routledge, 1990); Hazel V. Carby, *Reconstructing Womanhood: The Emergence of the Afro-American Novelist* (New York: Oxford University Press, 1987); Barbara Smith, ed., *Home Girls: A Black Feminist Anthology* (New York: Kitchen Table Press, 1983); Biddy Martin and Chandra Talpade Mohanty, "Feminist Politics: What's Home Got to Do with It?" *Feminist Studies/Critical Studies*, ed. Teresa de Lauretis (Bloomington: Indiana University Press, 1986); bell hooks, *Yearning: Race, Gender, and Cultural Politics* (Boston: South End Press, 1990); Nellie Y. McKay, "Acknowledging Differences: Can Women Find Unity Through Diversity?" *Theorizing Black Feminisms: The Visionary Pragmatism of Black Women*, ed. Stanlie M. James and Abena P. A. Busa (New York: Routledge, 1993).

9   Patricia J. Williams, *The Alchemy of Race and Rights: Diary of a Law Professor* (Cambridge: Harvard University Press, 1991); and Toni Morrison, ed., *Race-ing Justice, En-gendering Power* (New York: Pantheon, 1992).

10 Okin, "Gender Inequality," 17.

11 Mohanty, "Cartographies of Struggle," 54.

12 See the essays in Mohanty, Russo, and Torres, *Third World Women*; in James and Busia, *Theorizing Black Feminisms*; Gayatri Chakravorty Spivak, "Subaltern Studies: Deconstructing Historiography," *In Other Worlds* (New York: Routledge, 1988), 197–221; Gita Sen and Lourdes Beneria, "Accumulation, Reproduction, and Women's Role in Economic Development: Boserup Revisited," *Signs* 7, no. 2 (1981): 279–98; and Aihwa Ong, *Spirits of Resistance and Capitalist Discipline: Factory Women in Malaysia* (Albany: SUNY Press, 1987).

13 Chandra Talpade Mohanty, "Under Western Eyes: Feminist Scholarship and Colonial Discourses," *Third World Women*, eds Mohanty, Russo, and Torres; Mervat Hatem, "The Politics of Sexuality and Gender in Segregated Patriarchal Systems: The Case of 18th and 19th Century Egypt," *Feminist Studies* 12, no. 2 (1986): 251–74; and Trinh

T. Minh-ha *Woman/Native/Other* (Bloomington: Indiana University Press, 1989).

14 Okin, "Gender Inequality," 7.

15 McKay, "Acknowledging Differences," 273. See also Williams, *The Alchemy of Race and Rights*; and Toni Morrison, *Beloved* (New York: Signet, 1991).

16 Paul Gilroy, *The Black Atlantic: Modernity and Double Consciousness* (Cambridge, MA: Harvard University Press, 1993), 46.

17 McKay, "Acknowledging Differences," 276.

18 Toni Morrison, *Playing in the Dark: Whiteness and the Literary Imagination* (New York: Vintage), 10.

19 Ibid., 12.

20 McKay, "Acknowledging Differences," 276.

21 Ibid., 273.

22 On the meamng and uses of "raced," see Jane Flax, "Minerva's Owl," *Disputed Subjects* (New York: Routledge, 1993), 3–33. Contemporary American practices mark only some persons as "racialized," that is, as defined and determined by "race." All of us are, in fact, "raced"; no one exists outside socially constructed race/gender relations.

23 Gilroy, *Black Atlantic*, 2. See also Maria Lugones, "Purity, Impurity, and Separation," *Signs* 19, no. 3 (1994): 458–79; and Evelyn Brooks Higgenbotham, "African-American Women's History and the Metalanguage of Race," *Signs* 17, no. 2 (1992): 251–74.

24 Morrison, *Playing in the Dark*, 63; and Michael Omi and Howard Winat, *Racial Formations in the United States: From the 1960's to the 1980's* (New York: Routledge, 1986).

25 Wendy Brown, "Wounded Attachments," *Political Theory* 21, no. 3 (1993): 390–410.

26 Okin, "Gender Inequality," 19.

---

43   A Response to Jane Flax

Susan Moller Okin

It is difficult to respond to Jane Flax's critique. She finds me at fault, partly for not doing what I did not set out to do – that is, for not focusing on questions of race and gender in the United States. She also criticizes me for doing what I tried to do – that is, for pointing out that there appear to be many similarities between the oppression of poor women in poor countries and that of many women in well-off Western industrialized countries. Flax says that my argument "does nothing to reduce [her] suspicion of internally undifferentiated concepts of gender that define 'woman' in terms of shared oppression." This is not surprising, for two reasons. First, I am not claiming what she thinks I am. Second, she pays no attention to the specifics of my argument, either philosophical or empirical.

From *Political Theory*, vol. 23, no. 3 (August 1995), 511–16. Reprinted with permission.

In critiquing the anti-essentialist position, I do not say anything about what "defines 'woman.'" I do not claim that women in the First World "share" the oppression of Third World women (I do not know what this means); rather, I argue that in certain important respects their oppression is similar. Neither do I, as Flax claims, put forward "an internally undifferentiated and conflict-free concept of gender." I do not think that all aspects of gender oppression are similar in different contexts (see, e.g., my "Gender and Inequality and Cultural Difference," *Political Theory* 22, no. 1 [1994], 15–16), and I am clearly aware that race and class, as well as gender, are important factors in women's (and men's) lives (ibid., 7). I try to do two main things in the essay. I argue that those who charge "essentialism" at every turn should take on some of the burden of proof – should provide evidence that the differences among the situations of women are so much greater than the similarities that no meaningful generalizations can be made. And I provide at least some preliminary evidence that there are some important aspects of oppression that are cross-culturally experienced by many women. Thus Flax misrepresents the claims made in my essay.[1]

Second, it is unlikely that my argument will persuade Flax of anything unless she pays some attention to it. She does not address the two philosophical objections I raise regarding E. V. Spelman's critique of essentialism ("Gender Inequality," 7). Nor does she mention any of the points I make or evidence I refer to about similarities in forms of women's oppression, whether to reject them or to concede them. Her focus, rather, is on my presumptuousness in even attempting to address the subject of such similarities. This is interesting given that, as I explained ("Gender Inequality," 8–9), I was responding to the suggestion made by Spelman – a leading anti-essentialist – that "we have to investigate different women's lives and see what they have in common." However, Flax claims that my attention to Third World women amounts to my "enlisting," "appropriat[ing]," and "objectif[ying]" them [see p. 437]. Rather than evaluating what I say, she asserts that the very structure of my text undermines my claim about similarities, for I "split agency and determination so that the agency exercised by racialized and 'Third World women' and the determined aspects of First World women theorists are invisible" [see p. 437].

I would like to respond to this point, in so far as I can understand what it means. If the first part of it means that I have not listened directly to the speech of Third World women, but have relied on writings of others about them, I acknowledge this. Both my lack of the many relevant languages and the lack of opportunity of many such women to express themselves in writing made it difficult for me to gain more direct access. Nevertheless, I thought (and still think) it worthwhile to present some of what I had learned from a sampling of the development literature most focused on women to an audience of theorists probably unfamiliar with much of it, in an attempt to evaluate the claim of anti-essen-

tialists that differences among different groupings of women preclude the making of any generalizations about gender oppression.

As for the second part of Flax's assertion, I am not sure what I am supposed to do about my own "determined aspects" as a First World woman theorist, but I thought that trying to educate myself about the very different situations of some other women (even if only second-hand) might help. Should I instead reveal the aspects of my constituted self that Flax thinks are likely to have "determined" my beliefs? Not knowing me at all, she attempts to do this for me. But her attempt to psychoanalyze me *in absentia*, so as to derepress the unconscious guilt and other passions that apparently underlie the need of those like me to "project . . . the marks and burdens of race/gender . . . onto the other [see p. 439 above]," reveals some of the difficulties of such an enterprise. While she appears to think of me as a racially unmarked American, who must therefore harbor unconscious guilt about Black slavery, she neglects to mention the Maori wars, for which I am surely much more responsible, by her criteria, and which must presumably have played a larger determining role in the constitution of my psyche. While my racial and ethnic background may well be relevant to what I think about, as well as to what I think, I doubt that attempts to analyze me from a distance will help most readers to assess the merits of my argument.

While I am not only open to, but ready to, respond to criticism on the grounds that I am wrong, I am unsure of how to respond to criticism on the grounds that what I have done is offensive because of who I am. With the first kind of criticism, one can either try to argue against the points made, offering clarification or perhaps new evidence, or concede after reconsideration of them that the critic is right. But Flax's objection is not to any of the specific points that make up my argument, but that I have made it at all. "[E]vidently," she chides, I do not "hear how offensive" some of my statements might sound.[2] I could respond by apologizing. However, that would be hypocritical, for I knew even before I wrote the essay that it might offend some people. Angela Harris, for example, had already said that any finding by White women that the problems of women of other races were "similar to ours but more so" was insulting (quoted in "Gender Inequality," 8). I do not usually set out to risk insulting people, but in this case I thought it sufficiently important to try to further rational discussion among feminists about similarities and differences in women's lives that I was willing to take the chance of being considered offensive.

I am fundamentally at odds with Flax over two things. The first is her extreme subjectivism – her apparent underlying conviction that each person's situatedness renders her incapable of saying, and somehow reprehensible for trying to say, anything about anyone in a situation different from her own. Does this mean that what Alexis de Tocqueville had to say about democracy in the United States, what Gunnar Myrdal had to say about race relations, and what John Stuart Mill had to say about women are not only worthless but offensive pieces of argument that had been better not made? The far-reaching implications of this position undermine the possibility of any kind of social science or social theory – indeed, the possibility of any writing at all that is not autobiographical narrative (and maybe of that, too). According to Flax, my mistakes stem from my failure to grasp that "discourses of difference," which "represent attempts to theorize and undo relations of domination," "cannot be understood outside their specific historical contexts and purposes" [see p. 436 above]. And indeed, I *am* completely at a loss to understand how any discourse so socially situated that it cannot be understood outside its specific historical context and purposes could possibly have the critical force necessary for theorizing [about], much less undoing, any relations of domination. It would be helpful to have an example of one such discourse – even if no one but those from whose particular context it emanated would be able to understand it. Unfortunately, Flax is not apt to cite examples to clarify such general statements, nor evidence to back them up. Taken as a whole, the response reinforces one of the points I made in the paper – that there is a tendency on the part of postmodernist scholars to eschew the necessity of empirical evidence for their assertions.

This makes arguing with them similar to disputing the Trinity with a devout Catholic. Until there is some agreement about whether evidence is necessary, about whether it should be gathered and discussed even at the risk of offending people, and about who can presume to write about what, it will be difficult to carry on a dialogue.

The second major cause of Flax's and my disagreement is due to our different prioritizing of trust (in contexts of difference), the redistribution of power, and justice. I think that considerations of justice – which should recognize differences as well as similarities – need to undergird efforts to redistribute power, and that trust is likely to be achieved in the process. Flax thinks that trust, achieved through acts of linguistic contrition and self-revelation, must come first; every person must completely acknowledge her situatedness, her consequent potential for error, and her guilt for any privilege in which she might be implicated. Only then can just practices emerge. But it is not at all clear how justice is supposed to emerge. If justice is "undermined by domination," as Flax suggests [p. 441 above], then it cannot be used to overthrow the relations of domination. Will this be done by "the new, unplatonic loves" of difference, and if so, how?

While this debate continues, women are being beaten by their husbands and are dying needlessly from botched illegal abortions, girls go undernourished and uneducated, and development policy is decided and executed. This is a critical juncture for feminist issues in a global context. The past few years have brought about a renewed focus on women's basic rights – routinely violated in many societies – as an essential part of "human rights." There has also been widespread recognition, on the international stage, that women's and girls' welfare in many regions of the world lags seriously behind that of males, and that the well-being, the education, and the empowerment of women, important as they are to women themselves, are also crucial to the well-being of children and to the success of attempts to enable communities to become self-sustaining and to control population growth. This is a time when feminist scholars can contribute valuably to the efforts being made by international and non-governmental organizations to understand and to improve women's position in many parts of the world. It is important not to forget that many of women's concerns and needs vary from one social and cultural context to another and that the best ways of resisting oppression are also likely to be context-specific. But it is surely not the best of times to retreat into self-analysis or abstruse theorizing, on the grounds that differences among women make it impossible for us to speak about anyone but ourselves.

Notes

I would like to thank Brooke Ackerly and Elisabeth Hansot for their invaluable help in thinking about these issues. Neither, of course, should be considered responsible for anything I say.,

1 Flax also says that my "argument relies on the assumption that First World women *are* outside the social relations that produce poor ones" [see p. 438 above, emphasis in original]. However, nothing in my paper rests on this assumption. I do not directly address relations between First World women and poor Third World women, which are in many cases very complex, but this does not mean that I assume there are no such relations. I would venture to suggest that some of the most oppressive and constraining practices inflicted on poor women in Third World countries have a lot more to do with their fathers' or their husbands' perceived needs and desires than with mine or Flax's. I am, nevertheless, aware that many of the clothes, toys, and other goods that she and I both buy are probably produced by the extremely low-paid labor of Third World women. My recognition of the connections between First World consumerism and Third World exploitation, however, does not undermine the evidence that there are some important similarities in the sexism practiced in both places. Why, after all, do so many of our consumer goods depend on the poorly paid labor of Third World *women*, who probably, like many women in our own society, go home from their low-paid jobs to do virtually all of the unpaid family work?

2 The statement Flax finds so offensive is the following: "*committed* outsiders can often be better analysts and critics of social injustice than those who live within the relevant culture." Is the statement offensive because of its content, or because

of my status as an outsider? I raise the question because I have noticed, recently, statements similarly implying the presence of false consciousness in women made by feminists who have the benefit of being partly inside and partly outside of the cultural contexts they describe. Rosemary Ofeibea Ofei-Aboagye, a Ghanaian studying in Canada, was inspired by a Canadian court case to do something about wife beating in Ghana. Her study revealed that, although the abused wives perceived the beatings as "serious enough to warrant some outsider action," they had never thought about taking such action because "things could be worse. . . . They had little or no information as to what to do, or, indeed, whether they had the 'right' to do anything at all." Pointing out how the physical punishment of disobedient wives is imbibed as a norm by small Ghanaians in their bedtime stories, Ofei-Aboagye says, "Attempts to eliminate domestic violence must deal with the bigger problem of *how to free someone from bondage who does not necessarily experience herself as being in bondage*," "Altering the Strands of the Fabric: A Preliminary Look at Domestic Violence in Ghana" *Signs* 19, no. 4 (1994): 924–38; quotations from 929, 936 (emphasis added). Farida Shaheed, a Pakistani sociologist, explaining the work done by Women Living under Muslim Laws, writes that the organization believes

that the seeming helplessness of a majority of women in the Muslim world in effectively mobilizing against and overcoming adverse laws and customs stems not only from their being economically and politically less powerful but also from *their* erroneous belief that the only existence possible for a Muslim woman that allows her to maintain her identity – however that may be defined – is the one delineated for her in her own national context.

By contacts that inform these women of "the multiplicity of women's realities within the Muslim context . . . [and] the diversity of existing laws within the Muslim world," the group "gives material shape to alternatives . . . [and] encourage[s] women to dream of different realities – the first step in changing the present one." "Controlled or Autonomous: Identity and the Experience of the Network, Women Living under Muslim Laws," *Signs* 19, no. 4 (1994), 997–1019; quotations from 1006–7 (emphasis added). While both these women come from the cultures which they are now, in part, critiquing, they perceive their role as bringing information from outside the narrower cultural context, to help those within to envisage a different kind of life for themselves. I realize as I cite these articles that Flax may find me culpable of enlisting and exploiting their authors. Sorry, Drs Ofei-Aboagye and Shaheed; I hope you do not feel the same way.

SUGGESTED FURTHER READING

The Nature of Morality: What is Morality?

Blanshard, Brand, *Reason and Goodness*. London: George Allen & Unwin, 1961.

Brandt, Richard, *Ethical Theory*. Englewood Cliffs, NJ: Prentice-Hall, 1959.

Bruening, William, *The Is–Ought Problem*. Washington, DC: University Press of America, 1978.

Darwall, Stephen, *Philosophical Ethics*. Boulder, CO: Westview Press, 1998.

Foot, Philippa, *Virtues and Vices*. Berkeley, CA: University of California Press, 1978.

Frankena, William K., *Ethics*. Englewood Cliffs, NJ: Prentice Hall, 1973.

Hancock, Roger N., *Twentieth-Century Ethics*. New York: Columbia University Press, 1974.

Hare, R. M., *The Language of Morals*. Oxford: Clarendon Press, 1952.

Hudson, W. D., *The Is–Ought Question*. London: Macmillan, 1969.

Hudson, W. D., *A Century of Moral Philosophy*. New York: St. Martin's Press, 1980.

Hudson, W. D., *Modern Moral Philosophy*. New York: St. Martin's Press, 1983.

Kerner, George C., *The Revolution in Ethical Theory*. London: Oxford University Press, 1966.

MacIntyre, Alasdair, *Whose Justice? Which Rationality?* Notre Dame, IN: University of Notre Dame Press, 1988.

Moore, G. E., *Ethics*. London: Oxford University Press, 1912.

Ross, W. D., *The Right and the Good*. Oxford: Clarendon Press, 1930.

Stevenson, C. L., *Ethics and Language*. New Haven, CT: Yale University Press, 1944.

Wallace, G., and Walker, A. D. M., *The Definition of Morality*. London: Methuen, 1970.

Warnock, Mary, *Ethics since 1900*. London: Oxford University Press, 1966.

The Justification of Morality: Why be Moral?

Baier, Kurt, *The Moral Point of View*. Ithaca, NY: Cornell University Press, 1958.

Brandt, Richard, *A Theory of the Good and the Right*. Oxford: Oxford University Press, 1979.

Foot, Philippa, *Virtues and Vices*. Berkeley, CA: University of California Press, 1978.

Gert, Bernard, *Morality*. New York: Oxford University Press, 1998

Gewirth, Alan, *Reason and Morality*. Chicago, IL: University of Chicago Press, 1978.

Monro, D. H., *Empiricism & Ethics*. Cambridge: Cambridge University Press, 1967.

Nagel, Thomas, *The Possibility of Altruism*. Oxford: Clarendon Press, 1970.

Nagel, Thomas, *The View from Nowhere*. New York: Oxford University Press, 1986.

Olson, Robert G., *The Morality of Self-Interest*. New York: Harcourt Brace and World, 1965.

Rachels, James, *The Elements of Moral Philosophy*. New York: Random House, 1986.

Regis, Edward, Jr., *Gewirth's Ethical Rational-*

ism. Chicago, IL: University of Chicago Press, 1984.

Schmidtz, David, *Rational Choice and Moral Agency*. Princeton, NJ: Princeton University Press, 1995

Singer, Peter, *How Are We to Live?* New York: Prometheus Books, 1995.

Sterba, James P., *Justice for Here and Now*. New York: Cambridge University Press, 1998.

Thomas, Laurence, (ed.), *Kurt Baier Festschrift, Synthese*, vol. 72, nos 1 and 2 (1987).

Williams, Bernard, *Ethics and the Limits of Philosophy*. Cambridge, MA: Harvard University Press, 1985.

Alternative Moral Perspectives: What Does Morality Require?

Utility

Boralevi, Lea Campos, "Utilitarianism and Feminism," in Ellen Kennedy and Susan Mendus (eds.), *Women in Western Political Philosophy*. Brighton: Wheatsheaf Books, 1987.

Brink, David, "Mill's Deliberative Utilitarianism," *Philosophy and Public Affairs*, 21 (1992): 67–103.

Donner, Wendy, *The Liberal Self: John Stuart Mill's Moral and Political Philosophy*. Ithaca, NY: Cornell University Press, 1991.

Gorowitz, S. (ed.), *Utilitarianism and Critical Essays*. Indianapolis, IN: Bobbs-Merrill, 1971.

Hardin, Russell, *Morality within the Limits of Reason*. Chicago, IL: University of Chicago, 1988.

Hare, R. M., *Moral Thinking*. Oxford: Oxford University Press, 1981.

Lyons, David, *Rights, Welfare, and Mill's Moral Theory*. New York: Oxford University Press, 1994.

Miller, Harlan B., and Williams, William (eds.), *The Limits of Utilitarianism*. Minneapolis, MN: University of Minnesota Press, 1982.

Plamenatz, John, *The English Utilitarians*. Oxford: Basil Blackwell, 1949.

Quinton, Anthony, *Utilitarian Ethics*. New York: Macmillan, 1973.

Scheffler, Samuel (ed.), *Consequentialism and Its Critics*. Oxford: Oxford University Press, 1988.

Scheffler, Samuel, *The Rejection of Consequentialism*. Oxford: Clarendon Press, 1982.

Sen, Amartya, and Bernard Williams (ed.), *Utilitarianism and Beyond*. Cambridge: Cambridge University Press, 1982.

Smart, J. J. C., and Williams, Bernard, *Utilitarianism: For and Against*. Cambridge: Cambridge University Press, 1973.

Duty

Allison, Henry, *Kant's Theory of Freedom*. Cambridge: Cambridge University Press, 1991.

Baron, Marcia, *Kantian Ethics, Almost without Apology*. Ithaca, NY: Cornell University Press, 1995.

Blum, Lawrence A., "Kant's and Hegel's Moral Rationalism: A Feminist Perspective." *Canadian Journal of Philosophy*, vol. XII, 2 (1982): 287–302.

Cartwright, David, "Kant's View of the Moral Significance of Kindhearted Emotions and the Moral Insignificance of Kant's View." *The Journal of Value Inquiry*, vol. 21 (1987): 291–304.

Herman, Barbara, *The Practice of Moral Judgment*. Cambridge, MA: Harvard University Press, 1993.

Hill, Thomas E., Jr., *Dignity and Practical Reason in Kant's Moral Theory*. Ithaca, NY: Cornell University Press, 1992.

Hospers, John, *Libertarianism*. Los Angeles, CA: Nash Publishing, 1971.

Korsgaard, Christine M., *Creating the Kingdom of Ends*. Cambridge: Cambridge University Press, 1996.

Nozick, Robert, *Anarchy, State and Utopia*. New York: Basic Books, 1974.

O'Neill, Onora, *Acting on Principle: An Essay on Kantian Ethics*. New York: Columbia University Press, 1975.

Rawls, John, *A Theory of Justice*. Cambridge, MA: Harvard University Press, 1971.

Rawls, John, "Themes in Kant's Moral Philosophy," in *Kant's Transcendental Deductions*, ed. Eckart Förster. Stanford, CA: Stanford University Press, 1989.

Schneewind, J. B., "Autonomy, Obligation, and Virtue: An Overview of Kant's Moral Philosophy," in *The Cambridge Companion to Kant*, ed. Paul Guyer. Cambridge: Cambridge University Press, 1992.

Sterba, James P., *Justice for Here and Now*. New York: Cambridge University Press, 1998.

Virtue

Anscombe, Elizabeth, "Modern Moral Philosophy." *Philosophy*, 33 (1958).

Blum, Lawrence A., *Friendship, Altruism, and Morality*. New York: Routledge and Kegan Paul, 1980.

Broadie, Sarah, *Ethics with Aristotle*. Oxford: Oxford University Press, 1991.

Donagan, Alan, *The Theory of Morality*. Chicago, IL: University of Chicago Press, 1977.

Foot, Philippa, *Virtues and Vices*. Oxford: Blackwell, 1978.

Hardie, W. F. R., *Aristotle's Ethical Theory*. Oxford: Clarendon Press, 1968.

Irwin, T. H., *Aristotle's First Principles*. Oxford: Oxford University Press, 1988.

Kraut, Richard, *Aristotle on the Human Good*. Princeton, NJ: Princeton University Press, 1989.

Kruschwitz, Robert, and Roberts, Robert (eds.), *The Virtues*. Belmont, CA: Wadsworth, 1987.

Louden, Robert, *Morality and Moral Theory: A Reappraisal and Reaffirmation*. Oxford University Press, 1992.

MacIntyre, Alasdair, *After Virtue*. Notre Dame, IN: University of Notre Dame Press, 1981.

Matthews, Gareth B., "Gender and Essence in Aristotle," in *Women and Philosophy*, ed. Janna L. Thompson. Bundoora, Australia: Australian Association of Philosophy, 1986.

Mayo, Bernard, *Ethics and the Moral Life*. New York: Macmillan, 1958.

Murdoch, Iris, *The Sovereignty of Good*. New York: Schocken Books, 1971.

Pence, Gregory, "Recent Work on Virtues." *American Philosophical Quarterly*, 21 (1984).

Pincoffs, Edmund, *Quandries and Virtues*. Lawrence, KS: University of Kansas Press, 1986.

Trianosky, Gregory, "Supererogation, Wrongdoing, and Vice: On the Autonomy of the Ethics of Virtue." *Journal of Philosophy*, 83 (1986), 26–40.

Trianosky, Gregory, "Virtue, Action, and the Good Life: A Theory of the Virtues." *Pacific Journal of Philosophy* (1988).

Wallace, James, *Virtues and Vices*. Ithaca, NY: Cornell University Press, 1978.

Challenges to Morality

Feminism

Baier, Annette, *Moral Prejudices*. Cambridge, MA: Harvard University Press, 1995.

Card, Claudia, *Feminist Ethics*. Lawrence, KS: University of Kansas Press, 1991.

Cole, Eve Browning and Coultrap-McQuin (eds.), *Explorations in Feminist Ethics*. Bloomington, IN: Indiana University Press, 1992.

Digby, Tom (ed.), *Men Doing Feminism*. New York: Routledge, 1997.

Gilligan, Carol, *In a Different Voice*. Cambridge, MA: Harvard University Press, 1982.

Held, Virginia, *Feminist Morality*. Chicago, IL: University of Chicago, 1993.

Held, Virginia, *Justice and Care*. Boulder, CO: Westview, 1995.

Jaggar, Alison, *Feminist Politics and Human Nature*. Totowa, NJ: Rowman & Allanheld, 1983.

Kittay, Eva Feder, and Meyers, Diana T. (eds.), *Women and Moral Theory*. Totowa, NJ: Rowman and Littlefield, 1987.

Kourany, Janet, Sterba, James, and Tong, Rosemarie, *Feminist Philosophies*, 2nd edn. Englewood Cliffs, NJ: Prentice-Hall, 1998.

Okin, Susan, *Justice, Gender and the Family*. New York: Basic Books, 1989.

Sommer, Christina, *Who Stole Feminism?* New York: Simon and Schuster, 1994.

Sterba, James P., *Justice for Here and Now*. New

York: Cambridge University Press, 1998.

Tong, Rosemarie, *Feminist Thought*, 2nd edn. Boulder, CO: Westview Press, 1998.

Young, Iris, *Justice and the Politics of Difference*. Princeton, NJ: Princeton University Press, 1990.

Environmentalism

Armstrong, Susan, and Botzler, Richard, *Environmental Ethics*. New York: McGraw Hill, 1993.

Attfield, Robin, *Environmental Philosophy*. Aldershot: Avebury, 1994.

Carruthers, Peter, *The Animals Issue*. Cambridge: Cambridge University Press, 1992.

Dombrowski, D., *The Philosophy of Vegetarianism*. Amherst, MA: University of Massachusetts Press, 1984.

Frey, R. G., *Rights, Killing and Suffering*. Oxford: Basil Blackwell, 1983.

Gore, Al, *Earth in the Balance*. New York: Houghton Mifflin, 1992.

Hargrove, Eugene, *The Foundations of Environmental Ethics*. Englewood Cliffs, NJ: Prentice-Hall, 1988.

Marrietta, Don, *For People and the Planet*. Philadelphia, PA: Temple University Press, 1995.

Plumwood, Val, *Feminism and the Mastery of Nature*. London: Routledge, 1993.

Rachels, James, *Created from Animals*. Oxford: Oxford University Press, 1990.

Regan, T., *The Case for Animal Rights*. Berkeley, CA: University of California Press, 1984.

Regan, T., and Singer, P. (eds.), *Animal Rights and Human Obligation*. Englewood Cliffs, NJ: Prentice-Hall, 1976.

Singer, P., *Animal Liberation* (rev. edn). New York: New York Review, 1990.

Sterba, James P., *Earth Ethics*. New York: Macmillan, 1993.

Stone, C., *Earth and Other Ethics*. New York: Harper & Row, 1987.

Taylor, Paul W., *Respect for Nature: A Theory of Environmental Ethics*. Princeton, NJ: Princeton University Press, 1986.

Postmodernism

Best, Steven and Kellner, Douglas, *Postmodern Theory*. New York: The Guilford Press, 1991.

Cahoone, Lawrence, *From Modernism to Postmodernism*. Cambridge, MA: Blackwell, 1996.

Caputo, John, *Against Ethics*. Bloomington, IN: Indiana University Press, 1993.

Cornell, Drucilla, Rosenfeld, Michel, and Carlson, David Gray (eds.), *Deconstruction and the Possibility of Justice*. New York: Routledge, 1992.

Critchley, Simon, *The Ethics of Deconstruction: Derrida and Levinas*. Oxford: Blackwell, 1992.

Eagleton, Terry, *The Illusions of Postmodernism*. Oxford: Blackwell, 1996.

Foucault, Michel, *The Archaeology of Knowledge*. New York: Pantheon, 1972.

Lyotard, Jean-François, *The Postmodern Condition*. Minneapolis, MN: University of Minnesota Press, 1984.

Nicholson, Linda, *Feminism/Postmodernism*. New York: Routledge, 1990.

INDEX

Valuable Ethics Resources

CONTEMPORARY ETHICS:
Taking Account of Utilitarianism
William Shaw
0-631-20294-3 paperback
0-631-20293-5 hardcover

EXPLORING ETHICS:
A Traveller's Tale
Brenda Almond
0-631-19953-5 paperback

AN INTRODUCTION TO BUSINESS ETHICS
Jennifer Jackson
0-631-19533-5 paperback
0-631-19532-7 hardcover

ETHICS:
The Classic Readings
Edited by David E. Cooper
0-631-20633-7 paperback
0-631-20632-9 hardcover

THREE METHODS OF ETHICS:
A Debate
By Marcia Baron, Philip Pettit, and Michael Slote
0-631-19435-5 paperback
0-631-19434-7 hardcover

ETHICS AND INTERNATIONAL RELATIONS
Gordon Graham
0-631-19683-8 paperback
0-631-19682-X hardcover

SOCIAL ETHICS:
A Student's Guide
Jenny Teichman
0-631-19609-9 paperback
0-631-19608-0 hardcover

TRUTH IN ETHICS
Edited by Brad Hooker
0-631-19701-X paperback

THE BLACKWELL ENCYCLOPEDIC DICTIONARY OF BUSINESS ETHICS
Edited by Patricia Werhane and R. Edward Freeman
0-631-21080-6 paperback

THE MORAL PROBLEM
Michael Smith
0-631-19246-8 paperback

WESTERN ETHICS:
An Historical Introduction
Robert L. Arrington
0-631-19416-9 paperback
0-631-19415-0 hardcover

A COMPANION TO ETHICS
Edited by Peter Singer
0-631-18785-5 paperback

ETHICS AND HUMAN WELL-BEING
An Introduction to Moral Philosophy
E. J. Bond
0-631-19551-3 paperback
0-631-19549-1 hardcover

ETHICS IN PRACTICE:
An Anthology
Edited by Hugh LaFollette
1-55786-640-6 paperback
1-55786-639-2 hardcover

TO ORDER CALL :
1-800-216-2522 (N. America orders only) or
24-hour freephone on 0500 008205
(UK orders only)

BLACKWELL *Publishers*

VISIT US ON THE WEB : http://www.blackwellpublishers.co.uk